Programming Language Semantics: Imperative and Object-Oriented Languages

Programming Language Semantics: Imperative and Object-Oriented Languages

Bjørn Kirkerud

Department of Informatics
University of Oslo

INTERNATIONAL THOMSON COMPUTER PRESS
I(T)P™ An International Thomson Publishing Company

London • Bonn • Boston • Johannesburg • Madrid • Melbourne • Mexico City • New York • Paris
Singapore • Tokyo • Toronto • Albany, NY • Belmont, CA • Cincinnati, OH • Detroit, MI

Programming Language Semantics: Imperative and Object-Oriented Languages

I(T)P A division of International Thomson Publishing Inc.
The ITP logo is a trademark under licence.

For more information, contact:

International Thomson Computer Press
Berkshire House
168-173 High Holborn
London WC1V 7AA
UK

International Thomson Computer Press
20 Park Plaza
Suite 1001
Boston, MA 02116
USA

Imprints of International Thomson Publishing

International Thomson Publishing GmbH
Königswinterer Straße 418
53227 Bonn
Germany

International Thomson Publishing Asia
60 Albert Street #15-01
Albert Complex
Singapore 189969

Thomas Nelson Australia
102 Dodds Street
South Melbourne, 3205
Victoria
Australia

International Thomson Publishing Japan
Hirakawacho Kyowa Building, 3F
2-2-1 Hirakawacho
Chiyoda-ku, 102 Tokyo
Japan

Nelson Canada
1120 Birchmount Road
Scarborough, Ontario
Canada M1K 5G4

International Thomson Editores
Seneca, 53
Colonia Polanco
11560 Mexico D. F. Mexico

International Thomson Publishing South Africa
PO Box 2459
Halfway House
1685 South Africa

International Thomson Publishing France
Tours Maine-Montparnasse
33 avenue du Maine
75755 Paris Cedex 15
France

British Library Cataloguing-in-Publication Data
A catalogue record for this book is available from the British Library

Library of Congress Cataloging-in-Publication Data
A catalog record for this book is available from the Library of Congress

First Printed 1997

ISBN 1-85032-273-2

Typeset by Bjørn Kirkerud
Cover Designed by SPY Design, London
Printed in the UK by Cambridge University Press, Cambridge

To Inger

Contents

Chapter 1
Introduction

A *computer program* is a sequence of instructions intended to be executed by a computer. A *programming language* is a notational system for writing computer programs.

When studying a language, be it one of the ordinary human languages like English, Latin or Esperanto, or a programming language like Fortran or Cobol, Simula or ML, many find it advantageous to split the study into three parts: *syntax*, *semantics* and *pragmatics*:

Syntax deals with the *form* and *structure* of sentences and other constructs of a language, and gives rules for *grammatically correct* use of the language.

The syntax of an ordinary human language (such languages are often called *natural* languages in order to distinguish them from the artificial programming languages) is quite complex, with rules for inflection, declension and conjugation, for correct spelling, for hyphenation, for constructing new words, and for much more. Most of these rules are rather involved, with many special cases and many exceptions.

The syntax of any programming language is very much simpler than the syntax of any natural language, and may be completely specified by rules that are few and simple (at least compared to syntax rules for natural languages), and normally without exceptions. This made it possible for J. Backus and P. Naur, as early as 1960, to introduce a notation that makes it easy to give complete formal specifications of major parts of the syntax of most programming languages. This notation was first used in [Algol60] to give a formal specification of the syntax of the programming language Algol 60. Today almost all programming languages have their syntax specified in this way, and most programmers are familiar with how so-called *BNF productions* (*BNF* is short for *B*ackus *N*aur *F*orm) may be used to define the syntax of programming languages. In this book quite simple BNF productions will be used to specify the syntax of various small programming languages, and we assume that the reader is familiar with this method.

Semantics deals with the *meaning* of syntactically correct constructs of a language.

The semantics of a natural language is learned partly by reading and hearing definitions and explanations, partly by experience (sometimes frustrating or even painful).

The semantics of a programming language specifies what effects programs in the language have when they are executed by computers. It is frequently learned in a fashion similar to that in which the semantics of a natural language is learned: partly by reading and hearing descriptions which explain what will happen when programs that use various constructs of the language are executed by computers, partly by seeing (and sometimes experiencing dire consequences of poorly understood semantics) what happens when programs are executed.

Pragmatics deals with the usability of the language, and gives rules for its proper and profitable use. We will not treat the pragmatics of programming languages in this book.

Why formal specifications?

The existence of formal methods and notations for specifying the syntax of programming languages has had several beneficial effects. One is that the syntax of modern programming languages – which have been designed with BNF notation as a tool – is much cleaner than the syntax of older languages designed without such help. Another, possibly more important benefit, has been the development of better *parsing methods*, and even automatic or semi-automatic generation of parsers. So-called *parser generators* have been constructed that take formal syntax specifications as input and generate systems that may be used to parse programs in the specified language and to check such programs for syntactic correctness.

Making a formal specification of the semantics of a programming language will also have beneficial effects, some of which are achievable today, others may be achieved first when and if more advanced formal specification methods and notations have been developed. Some of the actual and potential benefits of formal semantic specifications are as follows:

- A formal specification of the semantics of a programming language may serve as a precise and unambiguous complete documentation of the meaning and effect of each construct of the language. A programmer may use this is a final resort if there is any doubt about the meaning of any part of the language.

- Designers of programming languages often find that any inconsistency, impreciseness, ambiguity or forgotten part in the specification of the semantics of a language is easier to avoid (and to discover, should such specification errors happen, as they are prone to do) if they use a formal method that forces them to proceed in a well-behaved manner, than if an informal and more forgiving method is used.

- A formal specification of not only the syntax but also the semantics of a programming language may be used as the basis for making complete implementations of the language. If and when sufficiently strong formal methods and notations are developed, it may be possible to let formal specifications of both syntax and semantics be input to automatic or at least semi-automatic generators of compilers and interpreters.

  As will be seen later in this book, methods that are available today, make it quite easy – almost semi-automatic – to use formal semantic specifications to construct interpreters that may serve at least as prototype implementations of programming languages with quite complex and realistic features.

- Formal specification methods make it possible to state and rigorously prove interesting properties of programs and programming languages. An example: To prove formally that a given program satisfies a given specification, that is that the meaning of the program is in agreement with the intended meaning as expressed by the specification, it is necessary to formalize both meanings.

  Another example: An implementation (be it a compiler or an interpreter) of a given language is specified by specifying the syntax and semantics of the language. To verify formally that an implementation is correct, a formal specification of both syntax and semantics of the language is needed.

- The semantics of many programming languages have parts that are often overly obscure and intricate. It may be hoped that if a designer of a new language from the start of his or her work uses a formal method to specify the semantics of the language, a much cleaner and comprehensible semantics will be the outcome.

Semantic specification

Simpler parts of many programming languages have rather simple semantics, not very difficult to describe and understand. But most programming languages have parts with intricate semantics, not easily understood at first or even second glance. It is therefore quite complex to give complete specifications of the semantics of realistic programming languages. Several methods and notations for writing formal specifications of the semantics of such languages have been developed (we will have much to say about this later in this book), but none has achieved a popularity and universal acceptance that is close to that achieved by the Backus-Naur method for formal specification of syntax. The semantics of most programming languages is therefore described only informally, using English or some other natural language as the main vehicle. An example: The report [Algol60], in which formal syntax specification was first employed, used English to explain the semantics of the various constructs of Algol 60. The resulting specification was by necessity informal, but also imprecise, ambiguous and incomplete in spite of much effort expended to avoid precisely these pitfalls.

One not very satisfying way of making a precise, unambiguous and complete specification of the semantics of a programming language, is by constructing a *standard implementation* of the language, i.e., by making an interpreter or a compiler for the language on some given computer, and then stating that the semantics of the language is defined by this implementation. The idea is then to use the standard implementation to resolve any question about the meaning or effect of any program or part of a program of the language: Simply execute the program on the given computer and see what happens.

Defining the semantics of a programming language by a standard implementation is, of course, not very satisfactory. One obvious drawback is that the definition of the language will depend completely on a certain program and that this program runs flawlessly on a certain computer. The definition will hence be quite vulnerable and very far from being portable and machine independent. But a much more important deficiency is that few, if any, of the benefits of formal specification described above will be attainable.

Several more abstract methods that may be used to give formal specifications of the semantics of programming languages have been developed. The three most well known are the following:

Operational semantics explains the meaning of programs in a given language by specifying how programs in the language are executed on an abstract and extremely simplified machine.

Denotational semantics specifies the meaning of every construct in a language as a mathematical object, usually a function, which is said to be the *denotation* of the construct. An example: The denotation of a program is a function that maps input to output.

Axiomatic semantics specifies the meaning of constructs in a programming language indirectly by defining rules for proving various properties about the constructs.

This book puts its main emphasis on denotational semantics, but will also explain the two other methods.

Imperative and functional languages

A large number (too large, according to many observers) of programming languages have been constructed during the short time man has needed to write computer programs. These languages vary greatly with respect to syntax, semantics and pragmatics, and are based on quite different ideas about what programs are and how they should be written. Some people feel the differences to be so substantial that it is justified to talk about different *paradigms*.

Two of the main classes of programming languages are *imperative* and *functional* languages:

Imperative languages: The fundamental feature of an imperative programming language is that a program in such a language may use *variables* that store values, and that the values stored in these variables may change as a result of executing certain parts of the program.

Functional languages: A program in a functional language uses no variables or other entities with values that may change when the program is executed, or rather *evaluated*, which is a much better term to use when we talk of programs in functional languages.

As the discerning reader probably has guessed from its title, this book deals with the semantics of imperative programming languages. Not much, if anything, will be said about how to specify the semantics of functional languages. We will, however, in a few places in the book, use the functional language ML to show how denotational semantic specifications of an imperative language may be transformed quite easily into a program in ML that may be used as an interpreter of the language.

Intended readership

The material in this book was originally developed for a course given to students in their final year at the Department of Informatics at the University of Oslo. These students normally have studied informatics (computer science) for two or three years, and have at least some background and training in formal methods and mathematics.

We assume that a reader of this book has a similar background.

Overview

This book contains 13 chapters in addition to this introductory chapter. Chapter 2 introduces and exemplifies a few of the concepts and techniques that may be used to give denotational specifications of the semantics of programming languages. The language used as an example in this chapter is so simple that no runtime errors or infinite computations can occur when programs in the language are executed. The reason for such simplicity is to make it possible to specify fully the semantics of the language using only methods that are very simple and require no nontrivial mathematics.

Chapter 3 shows how the formal specifications of the semantics of the language from chapter 2 may be implemented in the functional programming language ML. This chapter serves only as an example, and may be skipped by any reader who is not comfortable with ML. Neither reading chapter 3 nor understanding ML is a prerequisite to understanding the rest of this book.

Chapters 4 and 5 introduce, and explain in much detail, various mathematical tools that later will be used to specify the semantics of languages that are richer than the language treated in chapter 2. Chapter 4 describes *algebras*, which we will use in the rest of the book to modularize the many definitions given. Chapter 5 describes so-called *complete partial orders* and proves a mathematical theorem called the *Fixpoint Theorem*. The mathematics introduced in this chapter is essential to the rest of the book.

In chapter 6 we show how to give a denotational specification of the semantics of a language in which errors and infinite loops are possible. Chapter 7 shows how to give operational definitions of the semantics of the same language. We do this by defining an interpreter and a compiler for the language, and prove that these are correct relative to the denotational specification given in chapter 6.

Chapter 8 describes two different methods of defining what may be called *proof-theoretical semantics* for the language of chapter 6. The first method is called *natural semantics*, the second is *axiomatic semantics*.

Chapters 9 to 13 show how to give denotational specifications of the semantics of various constructs that are in common use in many imperative programming languages: Chapter 9 treats *declarations of data structures*, chapter 10 is about *procedures* and *functions*, chapter 11 about *objects* and *classes*, chapter 12 treats *jumps* and chapter 13 shows how to specify the semantics of *nondeterminism* and *concurrency*.

The final chapter of the book, 14, describes mathematics that may be used to solve so-called *domain equations*.

Chapter 2
A very simple language

Our main purpose in this chapter is to introduce and exemplify a few (but not all!) of the concepts and techniques that are available when we give what is called a *denotational* description of the semantics of a programming language.

Most realistic programming languages have features which necessarily entail that any definition of the semantics of the languages will have many details, some quite intricate and not easy to understand. To avoid getting bogged down in a morass of details, we have chosen a very simple and unproblematic programming language as our first language. This language, which we call Loop, is too simple to be of much practical use. Only integer calculations can be performed by Loop programs; and there are no declarations (all identifiers are assumed to be predeclared integer variables). The language is designed such that no runtime errors or infinite computations can occur when programs in the language are executed.

We start by defining the syntax of Loop. After a short informal description of the intuitive semantics of the language, we give a formal definition of the semantics. The chapter closes with an example and some exercises.

⟨*program*⟩	::=	**begin** ⟨*imp*⟩ **end**	
⟨*imp*⟩	::=	**skip**	(Do nothing)
	|	**put** ⟨*iexp*⟩	(Output)
	|	**get** ⟨*ident*⟩	(Input to variable)
	|	⟨*ident*⟩ := ⟨*iexp*⟩	(Assignment)
	|	⟨*imp*⟩; ⟨*imp*⟩	(Sequence)
	|	**if** ⟨*bexp*⟩ **then** ⟨*imp*⟩ **else** ⟨*imp*⟩ **fi**	(Condition)
	|	**loop** ⟨*iexp*⟩ **times** ⟨*imp*⟩ **endloop**	(Finite loop)
⟨*iexp*⟩	::=	⟨*literal*⟩	(Binary numeral)
	|	⟨*ident*⟩	(Variable)
	|	(⟨*iexp*⟩ + ⟨*iexp*⟩)	(Sum)
	|	(⟨*iexp*⟩ * ⟨*iexp*⟩)	(Product)
⟨*bexp*⟩	::=	(⟨*iexp*⟩ = ⟨*iexp*⟩)	(Equality)
	|	(⟨*iexp*⟩ < ⟨*iexp*⟩)	(Less than)
	|	(**not** ⟨*bexp*⟩)	(Negation)
	|	(⟨*bexp*⟩ **and** ⟨*bexp*⟩)	(Conjunction)
⟨*literal*⟩	::=	**0** | **1** | ⟨*literal*⟩**0** | ⟨*literal*⟩**1**	
⟨*ident*⟩	::=	⟨*letter*⟩ | ⟨*ident*⟩⟨*letter*⟩	
⟨*letter*⟩	::=	a | b | c | d | e | f | g | h | i	
	|	j | k | l | m | n | o | p | q | r	
	|	s | t | u | v | w | x | y | z	

Figure 2.1: BNF productions for Loop

2.1 Concrete syntax

Loop can be used to program only integer calculations. Its syntax is quite simple, with the following *syntactic categories* or *domains*:

Program:	Consists of all Loop *programs*
Imp:	Consists of *imperatives* (often called *statements*)
Iexp:	Consists of *integer expressions*
Bexp:	Consists of *Boolean expressions*
Literal:	Consists of *literals* (sometimes called *constants*)
Ident:	Consists of *identifiers*
Letter:	Consists of *letters*

These domains are defined by the BNF productions in figure 2.1. An example of a very simple Loop program is given in figure 2.2.

```
begin
  get xx;
  loop xx times get q; y := (y + q) endloop;
  put y
end
```

Figure 2.2: A very simple Loop program

2.2 Concrete and abstract syntax

When studying a formal language, it is sometimes advantageous to distinguish between *concrete* and *abstract* syntax. BNF productions like those used in figure 2.1 define the concrete syntax of a language. Such productions may be used to generate sequences of *terminal symbols*, i.e., keywords, operator symbols, semi-colons, etc. But in our context - where we are mainly interested in the *meaning* of programs, and not in their syntactic *appearance* - it is often sufficient to consider only the syntactic *structure* of the language we describe. We may disregard the precise details of its concrete syntax, for instance which keywords that have to be used to signify the start and end of various imperatives, or exactly where semi-colons have to be put, or which symbols should be used to signify various operations. In such cases it may be convenient to give a more abstract definition of the syntax of the language (to be *more abstract* means - at least here - that concrete details are left out: they are 'abstracted' away). In an abstract specification of the syntax of a language we will not, for instance, specify exactly which keywords or operators and other symbols should be used when writing programs in the language.

An abstract definition of the syntax of a language will usually describe the various constructs of the language as trees, called *syntax trees*. Such trees have nodes of various kinds, viz. one kind for each grammatical category of the language. An informal definition of the abstract syntax of Loop may for instance start as follows:

- A *program* consists of an imperative.
- An *imperative* may have one of the following forms:
  - A *skip* imperative, which is empty.
  - A *put* imperative, which consists of an integer expression.
  - A *seq* imperative, which consists of two imperatives.
  - etc.

Observe that this does not say anything about keywords or other symbols that are used in concrete programs. It does not, for instance, say that two imperatives in a sequence should be separated by a semicolon.

Section 4.5.1 on page 64 contains more about concrete and abstract syntax.

2.3 Informal, operational semantics

An informal and intuitive description of the semantics of Loop, may be given by describing what happens when Loop programs are executed on a computer. Such a description is said to be an *operational* semantics for a programming language.

A Loop program consists of one or more imperatives and is executed by executing its constituent imperatives in the order that they occur in the program.

The effect of executing a Loop imperative on a computer, is to change the *state* of the computer. Such a state consists of descriptions of everything that may change when imperatives are executed. For our present language, a state must contain:

- An *input sequence*: a sequence of integers, which are read (one at a time) by the computer whenever it executes a **get** imperative.
- A *store*: a set of *cells*, each capable of storing an integer. We assume that the number of cells in the store is sufficient to allow us to associate one cell to each variable that occurs in any given program. We say that the cell associated to a variable, is *bound* to the variable. The value stored in the cell bound to a variable var may be changed by executing an assignment, i.e., an imperative on the form var := expr, or an input imperative **get** var (this imperative inputs an integer and assigns it to the cell associated to var). We say that the value stored in the cell bound to an identifier has been *assigned* to the identifier.
- An *output sequence*: a sequence of integers, produced by executing **put** imperatives

The effect of executing a Loop program on a computer is to read an input sequence and produce an output sequence, see figure 2.3.

The details of what happens when Loop programs are executed on a computer should be obvious, at least to readers with some acquaintance to any programming language in the Fortran/Algol/Pascal families. If there are any uncertainties, a very complete and formal description of the semantics of Loop is given in section 2.4. A few details will, however, be described informally here:

- Binary notation is used in the literals. This means that the value of the literal **101** is the integer denoted by 5 in ordinary decimal notation.

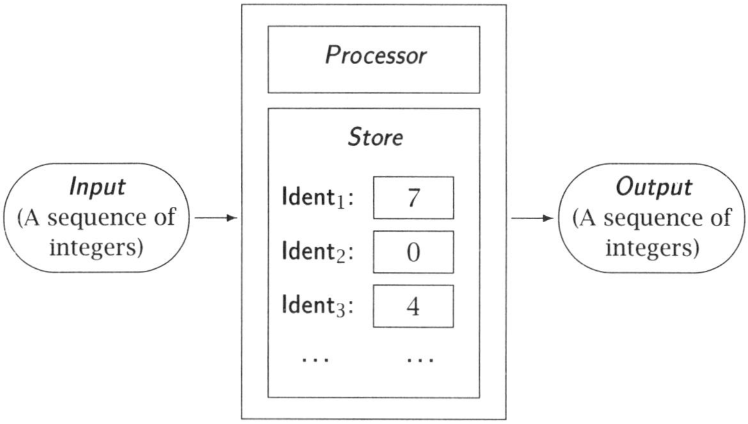

Figure 2.3: Model for a computer that executes Loop programs

- Given an initial state $\mathsf{st}_0 = \langle \mathrm{in}_0, \mathrm{h}_0, \mathrm{out}_0 \rangle$, where in_0 is an input sequence, h_0 is a store and out_0 is an output sequence, a **loop** imperative

  loop ie **times** imp **endloop**

  is executed as follows:

  (1) The value of the integer expression ie is found by 1) replacing every identifier var in ie by the integer last assigned to the h_0-cell bound to var, 2) replacing every literal in ie by its integer value, and 3) evaluating the resulting arithmetic expression. Let n denote the result. Should the result be negative, let $n = 0$.

  (2) The imperative imp is then executed n times, producing states $\mathsf{st}_1, \mathsf{st}_2, \ldots \mathsf{st}_n$, where st_i is the result of executing imp from the state st_{i-1} for $i = 1, 2, \ldots, n$.

  (3) The state after executing the **loop** imperative is st_n.

- The effect of a **get** imperative such as **get** var, is as follows: The first element of the input sequence is removed from the input sequence and its value is assigned to var (i.e., it is stored in the cell bound to var). Should the input sequence be empty, 0 is assigned to var.

An important distinction between the **loop** imperatives and the **while** imperatives found in many programming languages, is that in Loop, the number of times a *loop body* (i.e., the imperative between '**times**' and '**endloop**') will be executed, is determined *before* the loop is started. This guarantees that every loop must eventually terminate, which certainly is quite distinct from what may happen in languages that contain **while** imperatives (or similar constructs). Chapter 6 shows how to give a denotational definition of the semantics of imperatives that may enter infinite loops, e.g., **while** imperatives.

Another feature which ensures that Loop is an unproblematic and simple language, is that the language has been carefully designed to exclude all 'runtime errors': division by 0 cannot occur because the division operator is not allowed in integer expressions in Loop, arithmetic overflow will not happen (we assume that the cells in the store are able to store integers of any size), and a default value (viz. 0) is used whenever input is attempted from an empty input sequence.

2.4 Formal, denotational semantics

A *semantic interpretation* of a language - be it a programming language like Loop or a *natural* language like Latin - consists of *mappings* (functions) from language constructs to meaning. Every legal (i.e., syntactically correct) construct in the language is given a value by these mappings. This value is said to be the *denotation* of the construct.

Semantic values may be simple (for instance physical objects or numbers) or more complex (for instance mathematical functions). Some simple examples:

- The denotation (semantic value) of the term 'Venus' (used in an astronomical context) is a certain planet. The terms 'the morning star' and 'the evening star' (used in English and in an astronomical context) have the same denotation.

- The Loop term '**101**' has the same denotation as the terms 'five', 'fem' and '5' (the term 'five' is in English, 'fem' is in Norwegian, and '5' is in 'arithmetic').

Numerous examples of more complex denotations are given in the rest of this book.

The semantic interpretation of Loop given in this section is defined by five semantic mappings, each of which maps a syntactic domain into what is called a *semantic domain*. This is quite general: For each syntactic domain in the languages we treat, we shall define a semantic domain and a semantic mapping (see figure 2.4). For some syntactic domains in some languages, it may be appropriate to define more than one semantic mapping.

Before we continue, it is convenient to introduce some notation: Let *Syn* be a syntactic domain, $\mathcal{S}$ a semantic mapping that maps *Syn* to a semantic domain *Sem*, and s an element of *Syn*. We then use

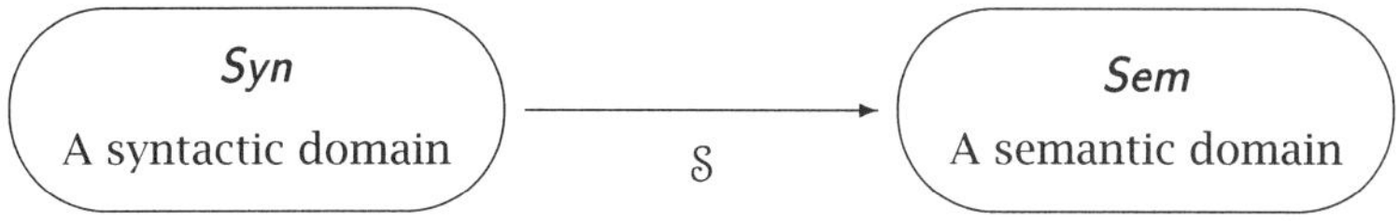

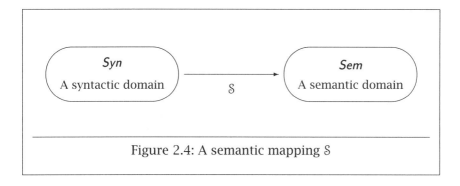

Figure 2.4: A semantic mapping $\mathcal{S}$

$$\mathcal{S}[\![\mathsf{s}]\!]$$

for the result of applying $\mathcal{S}$ to s, that is for the denotation of the syntactic object s as defined by the semantic mapping $\mathcal{S}$. Observe the special brackets '$[\![$' and '$]\!]$'. By convention within the field of denotational semantics these special brackets are used to bracket a syntactic argument to a semantic mapping.

The rest of this section contains definitions of semantic domains and semantic mappings for the syntactic domains of Loop (except for *Ident* and *Letter*, which are treated only indirectly):

$$\begin{array}{rcll} \mathcal{A} & \in & (\mathit{Literal} & \rightarrow \text{Semantic domain for } \mathit{Literal}) \\ \mathcal{V} & \in & (\mathit{Iexp} & \rightarrow \text{Semantic domain for } \mathit{Iexp}) \\ \mathcal{B} & \in & (\mathit{Bexp} & \rightarrow \text{Semantic domain for } \mathit{Bexp}) \\ \mathcal{M} & \in & (\mathit{Imp} & \rightarrow \text{Semantic domain for } \mathit{Imp}) \\ \mathcal{P} & \in & (\mathit{Prog} & \rightarrow \text{Semantic domain for } \mathit{Prog}) \end{array}$$

Explanation of the notation used above: When A and B are two sets, we use $(A \rightarrow B)$ to denote the set of all functions (mappings) that map A to B, and $\mathsf{f} \in (A \rightarrow B)$ to express that f is one of these functions.

2.4.1 Literals

It is obvious that the denotation of a literal like **101** must be an integer. This means that the semantic domain that consists of the denotations of literals must be the set of all integers, and that the semantic mapping $\mathcal{A}$ must have the following signature:

$$\mathcal{A} \in (\mathit{Literal} \rightarrow \mathit{Int})$$

where *Int* denotes the set of integers, i.e.,

$$\mathit{Int} \stackrel{d}{=} \{\ldots, -2, -1, 0, 1, 2, \ldots\}$$

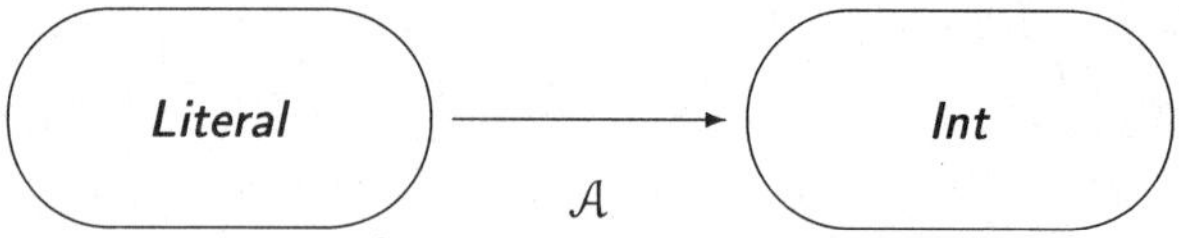

Equations that define $\mathcal{A}$:

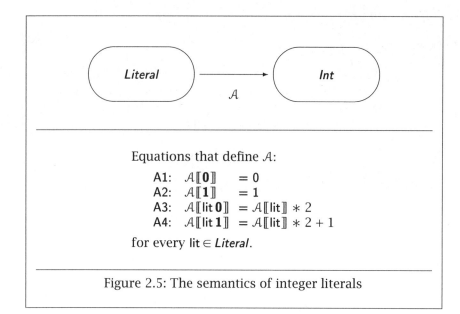

$$
\begin{aligned}
&\text{A1:} \quad \mathcal{A}[\![\mathbf{0}]\!] &&= 0 \\
&\text{A2:} \quad \mathcal{A}[\![\mathbf{1}]\!] &&= 1 \\
&\text{A3:} \quad \mathcal{A}[\![\mathsf{lit}\,\mathbf{0}]\!] &&= \mathcal{A}[\![\mathsf{lit}]\!] * 2 \\
&\text{A4:} \quad \mathcal{A}[\![\mathsf{lit}\,\mathbf{1}]\!] &&= \mathcal{A}[\![\mathsf{lit}]\!] * 2 + 1
\end{aligned}
$$

for every $\mathsf{lit} \in \mathit{Literal}$.

Figure 2.5: The semantics of integer literals

If we use our informal understanding of the meaning of literals (they are binary numerals), it is not difficult to define the semantic mapping $\mathcal{A}$ by induction on the syntactic complexity of literals. The definition is given in figure 2.5.

An example that shows how to use the definition of $\mathcal{A}$ to find the semantic value of a literal:

$$
\begin{aligned}
\mathcal{A}[\![\mathbf{101}]\!] &= \mathcal{A}[\![\mathbf{10}]\!] * 2 + 1 && \text{(by A4)} \\
&= (\mathcal{A}[\![\mathbf{1}]\!] * 2) * 2 + 1 && \text{(by A3)} \\
&= ((1) * 2) * 2 + 1 && \text{(by A2)} \\
&= 5 && \text{(by arithmetics)}
\end{aligned}
$$

2.4.2 Integer expressions

What is the denotation, or meaning, of an integer expression? An example: Let iexp be the integer expression (xx + **101**). The identifier xx is a variable, which may have been assigned a new value between one evaluation of iexp and another. The variable xx can therefore *not* denote a fixed integer. This entails that the meaning of iexp cannot be some specific integer. The meaning of an expression like iexp can, however, be determined by considering its operational use in a program, which is to specify how to compute an integer value given the values last assigned to the variables that occur in it.

An integer expression can in general be looked upon as a prescription for computing an integer given that the identifiers that occur in the expression have been assigned integer values. This means that the denotation, or meaning, of an integer expression can be considered to be a function which produces an integer value given an assignment of values (integers) to the variables that occur in the expression. Let us define the domain ***Store*** to consist of the functions that map identifiers to integers:

$$\mathit{Store} \stackrel{d}{=} (\mathit{Ident} \rightarrow \mathit{Int})$$

The meaning of an integer expression may then be considered to be a function that takes a function in ***Store*** as its argument and produces an integer as a result. Thus, we can let the denotational domain for ***Iexp*** be the set that consists of all functions that map ***Store*** to ***Int***, and let the semantic mapping $\mathcal{V}$ have the following signature:

$$\mathcal{V} \in (\mathit{Iexp} \rightarrow (\mathit{Store} \rightarrow \mathit{Int}))$$

An example: Assume that $\mathsf{h}_1 \in \mathit{Store}$ is a function which has value 7 for the argument xx, i.e., $\mathsf{h}_1(\mathsf{xx}) = 7$. Alternatively, we may say that the store h_1 assigns 7 to the identifier xx. The function

$$\mathcal{V}[\![(\mathsf{xx}+\mathbf{101})]\!] \in (\mathit{Store} \rightarrow \mathit{Int})$$

- which is the denotation of the expression $(\mathsf{xx}+\mathbf{101})$ - is a function that maps ***Store*** to ***Int*** and has value 12 for the argument h_1:

$$\mathcal{V}[\![(\mathsf{xx}+\mathbf{101})]\!](\mathsf{h}_1) = \mathsf{h}_1(\mathsf{xx}) + \mathcal{A}[\![\mathbf{101}]\!] = 7 + 5 = 12$$

The semantic function $\mathcal{V}$ can be defined by induction on the syntactic complexity of integer expressions. The definition is given in figure 2.6. An example which shows how to use the definition of $\mathcal{V}$: Assume that $\mathsf{h}_2 \in \mathit{Store}$ is such that $\mathsf{h}_2(\mathsf{xx}) = 7$ and $\mathsf{h}_2(\mathsf{yy}) = 9$. Then

$$\begin{array}{lll}
\mathcal{V}[\![((\mathsf{xx}+\mathbf{101})+\mathsf{yy})]\!](\mathsf{h}_2) & & \\
\quad = \mathcal{V}[\![(\mathsf{xx}+\mathbf{101})]\!](\mathsf{h}_2) + \mathcal{V}[\![\mathsf{yy}]\!](\mathsf{h}_2) & & \text{by V3} \\
\quad = (\mathcal{V}[\![\mathsf{xx}]\!](\mathsf{h}_2) + \mathcal{V}[\![\mathbf{101}]\!](\mathsf{h}_2)) + \mathcal{V}[\![\mathsf{yy}]\!](\mathsf{h}_2) & & \text{by V3} \\
\quad = (\mathsf{h}_2(\mathsf{xx}) + \mathcal{A}[\![\mathbf{101}]\!]) + \mathsf{h}_2(\mathsf{yy}) & & \text{by V1, V2} \\
\quad = (7 + \mathcal{A}[\![\mathbf{101}]\!]) + 9 & & \text{by def. of } \mathsf{h}_2 \\
\quad = (7 + 5) + 9 & & \text{by A1–A4} \\
\quad = 21 & & \text{by arithmetics}
\end{array}$$

Observe that the symbol '+' is used in two quite different ways here: 1) as a notational symbol used in Loop expressions (for instance in the Loop expression $(\mathsf{xx}+\mathbf{101})$), and 2) as a symbol for ordinary addition of integers (for instance in $(7 + 5) + 9$). The first occurrence is as part of the *object language*, i.e., Loop – the language we are defining the semantics of, and the second as part of the *meta-language*, i.e., the language which we use (and intuitively should understand) to define the semantics of the object language. In this book we use English extended with some quite simple mathematical notation as our meta-language.

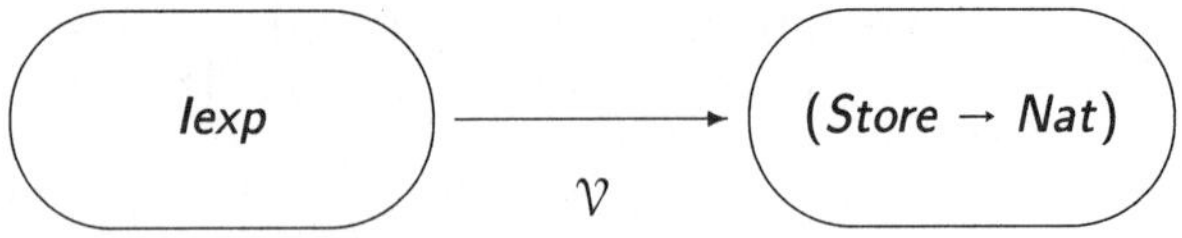

Defining equations for $\mathcal{V}$:

$$
\begin{aligned}
&\text{V1: } \mathcal{V}[\![\mathsf{id}]\!](\mathsf{h}) &&= \mathsf{h}(\mathsf{id})\\
&\text{V2: } \mathcal{V}[\![\mathsf{lit}]\!](\mathsf{h}) &&= \mathcal{A}[\![\mathsf{lit}]\!]\\
&\text{V3: } \mathcal{V}[\![(\mathsf{ie}_1 + \mathsf{ie}_2)]\!](\mathsf{h}) &&= (\mathcal{V}[\![\mathsf{ie}_1]\!](\mathsf{h}) + \mathcal{V}[\![\mathsf{ie}_2]\!](\mathsf{h}))\\
&\text{V4: } \mathcal{V}[\![(\mathsf{ie}_1 * \mathsf{ie}_2)]\!](\mathsf{h}) &&= (\mathcal{V}[\![\mathsf{ie}_1]\!](\mathsf{h}) * \mathcal{V}[\![\mathsf{ie}_2]\!](\mathsf{h}))
\end{aligned}
$$

for every $\mathsf{id} \in \mathit{Ident}$, $\mathsf{lit} \in \mathit{Literal}$, $\mathsf{ie}_1, \mathsf{ie}_2 \in \mathit{Iexp}$ and $\mathsf{h} \in \mathit{Store}$.

Figure 2.6: The semantics of integer expressions

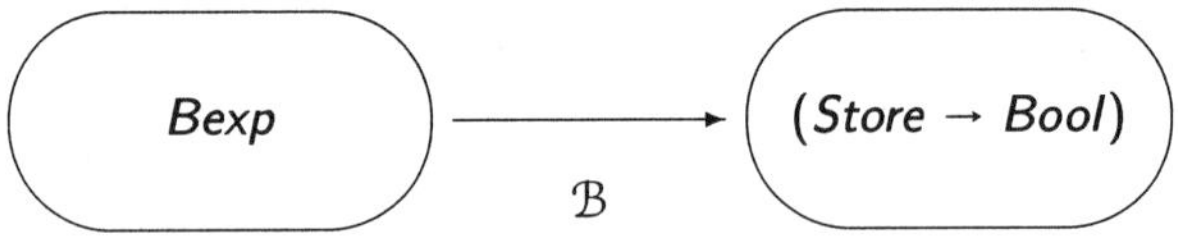

Defining equations for $\mathcal{B}$:

$$
\begin{aligned}
&\text{B1: } \mathcal{B}[\![(\mathsf{ie}_1 = \mathsf{ie}_2)]\!](\mathsf{h}) &&= \begin{cases} \mathbf{true} & \text{if } \mathcal{V}[\![\mathsf{ie}_1]\!](\mathsf{h}) = \mathcal{V}[\![\mathsf{ie}_2]\!](\mathsf{h}) \\ \mathbf{false} & \text{otherwise} \end{cases}\\
&\text{B2: } \mathcal{B}[\![(\mathsf{ie}_1 < \mathsf{ie}_2)]\!](\mathsf{h}) &&= \begin{cases} \mathbf{true} & \text{if } \mathcal{V}[\![\mathsf{ie}_1]\!](\mathsf{h}) < \mathcal{V}[\![\mathsf{ie}_2]\!](\mathsf{h}) \\ \mathbf{false} & \text{otherwise} \end{cases}\\
&\text{B3: } \mathcal{B}[\![(\mathsf{be}_1 \textbf{ and } \mathsf{be}_2)]\!](\mathsf{h}) &&= \begin{cases} \mathbf{false} & \text{if } \mathcal{B}[\![\mathsf{be}_1]\!](\mathsf{h}) = \mathbf{false} \\ \mathbf{false} & \text{if } \mathcal{B}[\![\mathsf{be}_2]\!](\mathsf{h}) = \mathbf{false} \\ \mathbf{true} & \text{otherwise} \end{cases}\\
&\text{B4: } \mathcal{B}[\![(\textbf{not } \mathsf{be})]\!](\mathsf{h}) &&= \begin{cases} \mathbf{true} & \text{if } \mathcal{B}[\![\mathsf{be}]\!](\mathsf{h}) = \mathbf{false} \\ \mathbf{false} & \text{if } \mathcal{B}[\![\mathsf{be}]\!](\mathsf{h}) = \mathbf{true} \end{cases}
\end{aligned}
$$

for every $\mathsf{ie}_1, \mathsf{ie}_2 \in \mathit{Iexp}$, $\mathsf{be}, \mathsf{be}_1, \mathsf{be}_2 \in \mathit{Bexp}$, and $\mathsf{h} \in \mathit{Store}$.

Figure 2.7: The semantics of Boolean expressions

2.4.3 Boolean expressions

Boolean expressions are treated quite similarly to integer expressions. The denotation of a Boolean expression is a function that produces a Boolean value (i.e., one of the two truth-values **true** and **false**) given an assignment of values (only integers in the present language) to identifiers. Thus, the signature of the semantic mapping $\mathcal{B}$ must be as follows:

$$\mathcal{B} \in (\mathit{Bexp} \to (\mathit{Store} \to \mathit{Bool}))$$

where

$$\mathit{Bool} \stackrel{d}{=} \{\textbf{true}, \textbf{false}\}$$

The semantic function $\mathcal{B}$ is defined by induction on the syntactic complexity of the argument. The definition is given in figure 2.7.

2.4.4 Imperatives

According to our informal and operational description of the semantics of Loop, the effect of executing an imperative on a computer is to change the state of the computer. This means that we consider an imperative to be a prescription that shows how to get one state from another. Thus, we can let the semantic domain for *Imp* consist of functions that produce one state given another.

More formally: We define the domain *State* to be the Cartesian product of the three domains *Input*, *Store* and *Output*, i.e.,

$$\mathit{State} \stackrel{d}{=} \mathit{Input} \times \mathit{Store} \times \mathit{Output}$$

where

$$\mathit{Input} \stackrel{d}{=} \mathit{Int}^* \stackrel{d}{=} \text{the set of all finite } \mathit{Int} \text{ sequences}$$
$$\mathit{Output} \stackrel{d}{=} \mathit{Int}^*$$

We then define the semantic mapping $\mathcal{M}$ to be a function with signature

$$\mathcal{M} \in (\mathit{Imp} \to (\mathit{State} \to \mathit{State}))$$

The semantic function $\mathcal{M}$ is defined by induction on the syntactic structure of its first argument (which is an imperative). The definition is given in figure 2.8.

Explanation of some notation used in figure 2.8 in the equations that define $\mathcal{M}$:

- If $\mathsf{q} = \langle \mathsf{q}_1, \mathsf{q}_2, \ldots, \mathsf{q}_n \rangle$, $n \geq 0$ is a finite sequence and a is an element, we use $\mathsf{q} \vdash \mathsf{a} = \langle \mathsf{q}_1, \mathsf{q}_2, \ldots, \mathsf{q}_n, \mathsf{a} \rangle$ to denote the sequence we get by appending a to the right end of q.

  Similarly, $\mathsf{a} \dashv \mathsf{q} = \langle \mathsf{a}, \mathsf{q}_1, \mathsf{q}_2, \ldots, \mathsf{q}_n \rangle$ denotes the sequence we get by appending a at the left end of q.

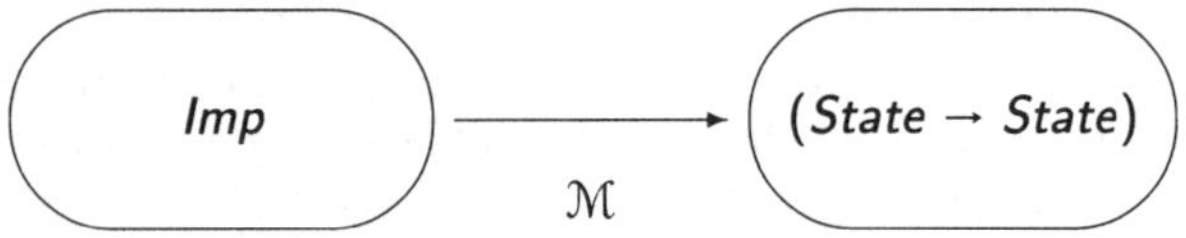

Defining equations for $\mathcal{M}$:

M1: $\mathcal{M}[\![\textbf{skip}]\!](s) = s$

M2: $\mathcal{M}[\![\textbf{put}\ ie]\!](\langle inp, h, outp\rangle)$
$= \langle inp, h, outp \vdash \mathcal{V}[\![ie]\!](h)\rangle$

M3.1: $\mathcal{M}[\![\textbf{get}\ id]\!](\langle \varepsilon, h, outp\rangle)$
$= \langle \varepsilon, h[id := 0], outp\rangle$

M3.2: $\mathcal{M}[\![\textbf{get}\ id]\!](\langle n \dashv inp, h, outp\rangle)$
$= \langle inp, h[id := n], outp\rangle$

M4: $\mathcal{M}[\![id := ie]\!](\langle inp, h, outp\rangle)$
$= \langle inp, h[id := \mathcal{V}[\![ie]\!](h)], outp\rangle$

M5: $\mathcal{M}[\![imp_1; imp_2]\!](s)$
$= \mathcal{M}[\![imp_2]\!](\mathcal{M}[\![imp_1]\!](s))$

M6: $\mathcal{M}[\![\textbf{if}\ be\ \textbf{then}\ imp_1\ \textbf{else}\ imp_2\ \textbf{fi}]\!](\langle inp, h, outp\rangle)$
$= \mathit{if}\ \mathcal{B}[\![be]\!](h) = \textbf{true}$
$\mathit{then}\ \mathcal{M}[\![imp_1]\!](\langle inp, h, outp\rangle)$
$\mathit{else}\ \mathcal{M}[\![imp_2]\!](\langle inp, h, outp\rangle)$

M7: $\mathcal{M}[\![\textbf{loop}\ ie\ \textbf{times}\ imp\ \textbf{endloop}]\!](\langle inp, h, outp\rangle)$
$= \textbf{let}\ n = \mathcal{V}[\![ie]\!](h)$
$\textbf{in}\ (\mathcal{M}[\![imp]\!])^n(\langle inp, h, outp\rangle)$

for every $ie \in \mathit{Iexp}$, $id \in \mathit{Ident}$, $be \in \mathit{Bexp}$, $imp, imp_1, imp_2 \in \mathit{Imp}$ and every $s = \langle inp, h, outp\rangle \in \mathit{State}$.

Figure 2.8: The semantics of imperatives

- If $q = \langle q_1, q_2, \ldots, q_n\rangle$, $n \geq 0$, and $r = \langle r_1, r_2, \ldots, r_m\rangle$, $m \geq 0$, are two finite sequences, we use $q \vdash\!\dashv r = \langle q_1, q_2, \ldots, q_n, r_1, r_2, \ldots, r_m\rangle$ to denote the concatenation of q and r.
- The symbol ε denotes an empty sequence.
- If f is a function that maps a set A to a set B, a an element in A and b is in B, $f[a := b]$ denotes the function which is identical to

f except for argument a for which $f[a := b]$ has value b. Thus, for every $x \in A$:

$$f[a := b](x) = \begin{cases} b & \textit{if } x = a \\ f(x) & \textit{otherwise} \end{cases}$$

- If e_1 and e_2 are two expressions and x is a variable, the value of the expression **let** $x = e_1$ **in** e_2 is found by evaluating e_2 but using the value of e_1 for every occurrence of x inside e_2. Thus, the value of **let** $t = 2 * 3$ **in** $(t + 1) * (t - 1)$ is 35.

- If f is a function that maps a set A to itself, and n is an integer, we use f^n to denote n-fold application of f. Thus, for every argument $x \in A$:

$$f^n(x) = \begin{cases} x & \textit{if } n \leq 0 \\ f(f^{n-1}(x)) & \textit{if } n > 0 \end{cases}$$

An example that shows how to use the $\mathcal{M}$ equations: What is the result of executing the imperatives

get x; x := (x + **101**); **put** x

if the input sequence is $\langle 3 \rangle$? To see if we get the expected result (i.e., the output sequence $\langle 8 \rangle$) when we use our formal definitions, let us define four imperatives S_1, S_2, S_3 and S_4 as follows:

S_1 = **get** x
S_2 = x := (x + **101**)
S_3 = **put** x
S_4 = S_1; S_2; S_3

Furthermore, let the state s_0 be defined by:

$$s_0 = \langle \langle 3 \rangle, h_0, \varepsilon \rangle$$

where

- $\langle 3 \rangle$ denotes the sequence that consists of the single integer 3,

- h_0 is a function in *Store* that assigns 0 to every identifier, i.e., $h_0(id) = 0$ for every $id \in \textit{Ident}$, and

- ε denotes the empty sequence.

We shall find the value of the denotation of S_4, i.e., the value of the function $\mathcal{M}[\![S_4]\!]$, when it is applied to the argument s_0. To do this, we start by using the definition of $\mathcal{M}$ for sequential composition of imperatives (equation M5) repeatedly:

$$\begin{aligned}
\mathcal{M}[\![S_4]\!](s_0) &= \mathcal{M}[\![S_1;\ S_2;\ S_3]\!](s_0) \\
&= \mathcal{M}[\![S_3]\!](\mathcal{M}[\![S_1;\ S_2]\!](s_0)) \\
&= \mathcal{M}[\![S_3]\!](\mathcal{M}[\![S_2]\!](\mathcal{M}[\![S_1]\!](s_0))) \\
&= \mathcal{M}[\![S_3]\!](\mathcal{M}[\![S_2]\!](s_1)) && \text{where } s_1 = \mathcal{M}[\![S_1]\!](s_0) \\
&= \mathcal{M}[\![S_3]\!](s_2) && \text{where } s_2 = \mathcal{M}[\![S_2]\!](s_1) \\
&= s_3 && \text{where } s_3 = \mathcal{M}[\![S_3]\!](s_2)
\end{aligned}$$

By the defining equation for **get** imperatives (i.e., M3), we see that

$$s_1 = \mathcal{M}[\![\textbf{get}\ x]\!](s_0) = \langle \varepsilon,\ h_1,\ \varepsilon \rangle$$

where the store h_1 is such that for every identifier id:

$$h_1(\mathrm{id}) = (\mathit{if}\ \mathrm{id} = x\ \mathit{then}\ 3\ \mathit{else}\ 0)$$

By the $\mathcal{M}$ equation for assignment imperatives (M4), we get that

$$s_2 = \mathcal{M}[\![x := (x + \mathbf{101})]\!](s_1) = \langle \varepsilon,\ h_2,\ \varepsilon \rangle$$

where for every id $\in$ *Ident*

$$h_2(\mathrm{id}) = (\mathit{if}\ \mathrm{id} = x\ \mathit{then}\ 8\ \mathit{else}\ 0)$$

By the $\mathcal{M}$ equation for **put** imperatives (M2), we get

$$s_3 = \mathcal{M}[\![\textbf{put}\ x]\!](s_2) = \langle \varepsilon,\ h_2,\ \langle 8 \rangle \rangle$$

Thus, the output component of the state that is the result of evaluating the denotation of the imperative $S_4 = S_1;\ S_2;\ S_3$ on the state s_0, is the sequence $\langle 8 \rangle$, as expected from our operational understanding of how the imperatives are executed.

2.4.5 Programs

The observable effect of a Loop program is to read integers from an input sequence and produce an output sequence. We may therefore consider the meaning of a program to be a function that produces an output sequence given an input sequence, and define the semantic function $\mathcal{P}$ to have the following signature:

$$\mathcal{P} \in (\mathit{Prog} \to (\mathit{Input} \to \mathit{Output}))$$

$\mathcal{P}$ is defined in figure 2.9. Some notation that is used in the defining equation for $\mathcal{P}$ is defined as follows:

- The function Store'default $\in$ *Store* = (*Ident* $\to$ *Int*) is an auxiliary function that assigns the integer 0 to every identifier:

  $$\text{Store'default}(\mathrm{id}) = 0 \quad \text{for every id} \in \mathit{Ident}$$

- If $s = \langle s_1, s_2, \ldots, s_n \rangle$ is an n-tuple or a sequence with n elements, and i is a positive integer not greater than n, we use $s{\downarrow}i$ to denote the ith element of s:

  $$\langle s_1,\ s_2,\ \ldots,\ s_n \rangle{\downarrow}i = s_i$$

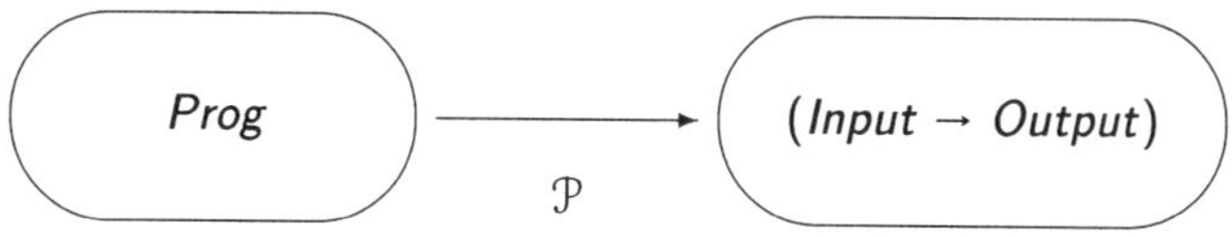

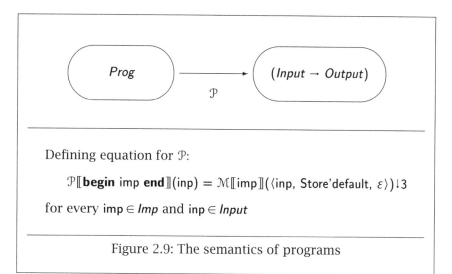

Defining equation for $\mathcal{P}$:

$$\mathcal{P}[\![\textbf{begin}\ \mathsf{imp}\ \textbf{end}]\!](\mathsf{inp}) = \mathcal{M}[\![\mathsf{imp}]\!](\langle \mathsf{inp},\ \mathsf{Store'default},\ \varepsilon\rangle)\downarrow 3$$

for every $\mathsf{imp} \in \mathit{Imp}$ and $\mathsf{inp} \in \mathit{Input}$

Figure 2.9: The semantics of programs

2.5 An example

Assume that PS is the Loop program in figure 2.2 on page 9, and that

$$\mathsf{inp}_0 = \langle 3,\ 4,\ 5,\ 2\rangle$$

is an input sequence that consists of the integers 3, 4, 5 and 2. What is the value of $\mathcal{P}[\![\mathsf{PS}]\!](\mathsf{inp}_0)$?

To see how our formal definition of the semantics of Loop work, and to see that they are in accordance with the intuitive, operational definition, we proceed as follows: First we define the imperatives

$$\begin{aligned}
\mathsf{S}_1 &= \textbf{get}\ \mathsf{xx}\\
\mathsf{S}_{2,1} &= \textbf{get}\ \mathsf{q}\\
\mathsf{S}_{2,2} &= \mathsf{y} := (\mathsf{y} + \mathsf{q})\\
\mathsf{Sb} &= \mathsf{S}_{2,1};\ \mathsf{S}_{2,2}\\
\mathsf{S}_2 &= \textbf{loop}\ \mathsf{xx}\ \textbf{times}\ \mathsf{Sb}\ \textbf{endloop}\\
\mathsf{S}_3 &= \textbf{put}\ \mathsf{y}\\
\mathsf{S}_4 &= \mathsf{S}_1;\ \mathsf{S}_2;\ \mathsf{S}_3
\end{aligned}$$

According to the definition of $\mathcal{P}$ and the definition of $\mathcal{M}$ (using the equation for ';', i.e., M5):

$$\begin{aligned}
\mathcal{P}[\![\mathsf{PS}]\!](\mathsf{inp}_0) &= \mathcal{M}[\![\mathsf{S}_4]\!](\mathsf{s}_0)\downarrow 3 && \text{where } \mathsf{s}_0 = \langle \mathsf{inp}_0,\ \mathsf{h}_0,\ \varepsilon\rangle\\
& && \text{and } \quad \mathsf{h}_0 = \mathsf{Store'default}\\
&= \mathcal{M}[\![\mathsf{S}_3]\!](\mathcal{M}[\![\mathsf{S}_2]\!](\mathcal{M}[\![\mathsf{S}_1]\!](\mathsf{s}_0)))\downarrow 3\\
&= \mathcal{M}[\![\mathsf{S}_3]\!](\mathcal{M}[\![\mathsf{S}_2]\!](\mathsf{s}_1))\downarrow 3 && \text{where } \mathsf{s}_1 = \mathcal{M}[\![\mathsf{S}_1]\!](\mathsf{s}_0)\\
&= \mathcal{M}[\![\mathsf{S}_3]\!](\mathsf{s}_2)\downarrow 3 && \text{where } \mathsf{s}_2 = \mathcal{M}[\![\mathsf{S}_2]\!](\mathsf{s}_1)\\
&= \mathsf{s}_3\downarrow 3 && \text{where } \mathsf{s}_3 = \mathcal{M}[\![\mathsf{S}_3]\!](\mathsf{s}_2)
\end{aligned}$$

By using equation M3.2 for **get** imperatives, we get that

$$s_1 = \langle\langle 4, 5, 2\rangle, h_1, \varepsilon\rangle, \quad \text{where } h_1(\mathsf{id}) = (\mathit{if}\ \mathsf{id} = \mathsf{xx}\ \mathit{then}\ 3\ \mathit{else}\ 0)$$

By the equation for **loop** imperatives (M7), and using that $\mathcal{V}[\![\mathsf{xx}]\!](h_1) = 3$, we get that

$$\begin{aligned} s_2 &= (\mathcal{M}[\![\mathsf{Sb}]\!])^3(s_1) \\ &= \mathcal{M}[\![\mathsf{Sb}]\!](\mathcal{M}[\![\mathsf{Sb}]\!](\mathcal{M}[\![\mathsf{Sb}]\!](s_1))) \\ &= \mathcal{M}[\![\mathsf{Sb}]\!](\mathcal{M}[\![\mathsf{Sb}]\!](s_{1,1})) && \text{where } s_{1,1} = \mathcal{M}[\![\mathsf{Sb}]\!](s_1) \\ &= \mathcal{M}[\![\mathsf{Sb}]\!](s_{1,2}) && \text{where } s_{1,2} = \mathcal{M}[\![\mathsf{Sb}]\!](s_{1,1}) \end{aligned}$$

Using M5, M3.2 and M4, we get that

$$\begin{aligned} s_{1,1} &= \mathcal{M}[\![S_{2,2}]\!](\mathcal{M}[\![S_{2,1}]\!](s_1)) \\ &= \langle\langle 5, 2\rangle, h_{1,1}, \varepsilon\rangle \end{aligned}$$

where

$$\begin{aligned} h_{1,1}(\mathsf{id}) = {} & \mathit{if}\ \mathsf{id} = \mathsf{xx}\ \mathit{then}\ 3\ \mathit{else} \\ & \mathit{if}\ \mathsf{id} = \mathsf{q}\ \ \mathit{then}\ 4\ \mathit{else} \\ & \mathit{if}\ \mathsf{id} = \mathsf{y}\ \ \mathit{then}\ 4 \\ & \mathit{else}\ 0 \end{aligned}$$

Similarly,

$$\begin{aligned} s_{1,2} &= \mathcal{M}[\![\mathsf{Sb}]\!](s_{1,1}) \\ &= \langle\langle 2\rangle, h_{1,2}, \varepsilon\rangle \\ h_{1,2}(\mathsf{id}) &= \mathit{if}\ \mathsf{id} = \mathsf{xx}\ \mathit{then}\ 3\ \mathit{else} \\ & \quad\ \mathit{if}\ \mathsf{id} = \mathsf{q}\ \ \mathit{then}\ 5\ \mathit{else} \\ & \quad\ \mathit{if}\ \mathsf{id} = \mathsf{y}\ \ \mathit{then}\ 9 \\ & \quad\ \mathit{else}\ 0 \\ s_2 &= \mathcal{M}[\![\mathsf{Sb}]\!](s_{1,2}) \\ &= \langle\varepsilon, h_2, \varepsilon\rangle \\ h_2(\mathsf{id}) &= \mathit{if}\ \mathsf{id} = \mathsf{xx}\ \mathit{then}\ 3\ \mathit{else} \\ & \quad\ \mathit{if}\ \mathsf{id} = \mathsf{q}\ \ \mathit{then}\ 2\ \mathit{else} \\ & \quad\ \mathit{if}\ \mathsf{id} = \mathsf{y}\ \ \mathit{then}\ 11 \\ & \quad\ \mathit{else}\ 0 \end{aligned}$$

Finally,

$$\begin{aligned} \mathcal{P}[\![\mathsf{PS}]\!](\mathsf{inp}_0) &= \mathcal{M}[\![S_3]\!](s_2){\downarrow}3 \\ &= \mathcal{M}[\![\textbf{put}\ \mathsf{y}]\!](s_2){\downarrow}3 \\ &= \langle\varepsilon, h_2, \langle\mathcal{V}[\![\mathsf{y}]\!](h_2)\rangle\rangle{\downarrow}3 \\ &= \langle\varepsilon, h_2, \langle 11\rangle\rangle{\downarrow}3 \\ &= \langle 11\rangle \end{aligned}$$

2.6 Exercises

2.6.1 Three small imperatives

Assume that s is some *State*, and find the value of

$$\mathcal{M}[\![\textbf{put } \mathbf{101}]\!](\mathsf{s})$$
$$\mathcal{M}[\![\mathsf{x} := \mathbf{101}]\!](\mathsf{s})$$
$$\mathcal{M}[\![\mathsf{x} := \mathbf{10};\ \mathsf{x} := (\mathsf{x} + \mathsf{x});\ \textbf{put}\ \mathsf{x}]\!](\mathsf{s})$$

2.6.2 Two small programs

Find the value of

$$\mathcal{P}[\![\textbf{begin put(10 + 10) end}]\!](\varepsilon)$$
$$\mathcal{P}[\![\textbf{begin get}\ \mathsf{x};\ \textbf{get}\ \mathsf{y};\ \textbf{put}\ (\mathsf{x} + \mathsf{y})\ \textbf{end}]\!](\langle 2, 3\rangle)$$

2.6.3 A program to compute the factorial

Use the definitions of the semantic mappings to find the value of

$$\begin{array}{l}\mathcal{P}[\![\textbf{begin}\\ \quad \textbf{get}\ \mathsf{n};\\ \quad \mathsf{f} := \mathbf{1};\ \mathsf{i} := \mathbf{0};\\ \quad \textbf{loop}\ \mathsf{n}\ \textbf{times}\ \mathsf{i} := (\mathsf{i} + \mathbf{1});\ \mathsf{f} := (\mathsf{f} * \mathsf{i})\ \textbf{endloop};\\ \quad \textbf{put}\ \mathsf{f}\\ \ \textbf{end}]\!](\langle 3\rangle)\end{array}$$

2.6.4 More operators

Introduce other operators and functions, like for instance subtraction (−), multiplication ($*$) and logical disjunction (**or**), and extend the semantic mappings $\mathcal{V}$ and $\mathcal{B}$ such that they are able to handle the new functions.

If you try to introduce division as a new operator, you will have to decide how to handle division by 0. One way is to extend *Int* with a special error element. Much more about how to do this may be found in chapter 6.

2.6.5 Equivalent imperatives

We say that two imperatives imp_1 and imp_2 are *semantically equivalent* - written $\mathsf{imp}_1 \cong \mathsf{imp}_2$ - if and only if they have the same denotations, i.e., if and only if $\mathcal{M}[\![\mathsf{imp}_1]\!] = \mathcal{M}[\![\mathsf{imp}_2]\!]$. Prove that

loop ex **times** imp **endloop** $\cong$ **if** ex $>$ **0 then**
imp;
loop (ex $-$ **1**) **times** imp **endloop**
else skip fi

under the assumption that the imperative imp does not assign new values to any variables that may occur in the expression ex. Assume that Loop has been extended with an operator for subtraction, viz. $-$, as asked for in exercise 2.6.4.

2.6.6 Conditional expressions

Extend the syntax of Loop by conditional integer expressions described by adding the following BNF production:

$$\langle iexp\rangle ::= \ldots \mid \textbf{if}\ \langle bexp\rangle\ \textbf{then}\ \langle iexp\rangle\ \textbf{else}\ \langle iexp\rangle\ \textbf{fi}$$

Give a formal, denotational definition of the semantics of such expressions.

2.6.7 Imperatives for adding to variables

Extend the syntax of Loop by the following new BNF productions:

$$\langle imp\rangle ::= \ldots \mid \langle ident\rangle\text{++} \mid \langle ident\rangle :=+ \langle ident\rangle$$

The operational effect of executing an imperative xx++ should be to increase the value assigned to xx by 1, i.e., equivalent to executing the imperative xx := xx + 1. The effect of executing xx :=+ y should be equivalent to executing xx := xx + y.

Give a formal, denotational definition of the semantics of the new imperatives.

2.6.8 Swap imperatives

Extend the syntax of Loop by the following new BNF production:

$$\langle imp\rangle ::= \ldots \mid \langle ident\rangle :=: \langle ident\rangle$$

The operational effect of executing an imperative xx :=: yy is to *swap* the values assigned to xx and yy, i.e., equivalent to executing the three imperatives aux := xx; xx := yy; yy := aux, where aux is an auxiliary variable that is not used elsewhere in the program.

Give a formal, denotational definition of the semantics of swap imperatives.

2.6.9 Input in expressions

Extend the syntax of **Loop** by the following new BNF production:

$$\langle iexp \rangle ::= \ldots \mid \textbf{getint}$$

The intuitive, operational semantics of **getint** is simple: Its value is equal to the value of the first element (the *head*) of the input sequence, 0 if the input sequence is empty. The head of the input sequence is removed from the sequence when **getint** is evaluated.

Show how to extend and change the denotational definition of the semantics of **Loop** to handle integer expressions of the form **getint**.

Note: It is not obvious how to do this correctly. The problem is that the evaluation of **getint** has a *side-effect*: the state is changed when the head of the input sequence is removed. To handle this, $\mathcal{V}$ must get a new signature:

$$\mathcal{V} \in (\mathit{Iexp} \rightarrow (\mathit{State} \rightarrow \mathit{State} \times \mathit{Int}))$$

This entails that all equations using $\mathcal{V}$ must be changed.

2.6.10 Unbounded loops

Extend the syntax of **Loop** by the following new BNF production:

$$\langle imp \rangle ::= \ldots \mid \textbf{while} \ \langle bexp \rangle \ \textbf{do} \ \langle imp \rangle \ \textbf{od}$$

with obvious operational semantics. What problems do you encounter in defining the semantics of such so-called **while** imperatives in a formal, denotational manner?

Note: It is quite difficult to give a correct and complete denotational definition of **while** imperatives. Chapter 6 shows one way of doing it.

Chapter 3
Implementing Loop in ML

ML is a programming language which is very well suited for writing executable specifications of the syntax and semantics of programming languages. In this chapter we show how this may be done for the Loop language. There are two reasons why we do this:

- The first is to demonstrate that it is straightforward to translate denotational definitions like those given in this book into ML, and hence not difficult to construct an interpreter for a programming language if we can base the construction on a denotational definition of the semantics of the language. Such an interpreter may serve as a prototype implementation of the language, and may for instance be used to test the usefulness of its various onstructs. It would, however, be too inefficient for other purposes than prototyping.

- An interpreter which is an almost direct translation of a proposed definition of the semantics of some programming language may be used to test the correctness and adequacy of the definition.

Executing such an interpreter on judiciously chosen sample programs will often make errors or lacking clauses in the proposed definition quite obvious.

Neither reading this chapter nor understanding ML is a prerequisite to understanding the rest of this book. Except in a few sections and exercises in some of the ensuing chapters, we will not asssume that the reader has read and understood the present chapter.

It is beyond the scope of this book to give an introduction to ML. We assume instead that the reader has a working knowledge of the language, which he or she may acquire by reading one of the many books that describe ML. An example, which we recommend even if it contains much more than that necessary for our purposes, is [Paulson; 91]. Much of the ML code used below for parsing is in fact borrowed from this book.

The ML programs in this chapter, and other ML programs described in the rest of this book, may be found at URL

`http://www.ifi.uio.no/~bjornk/semantics/`

3.1 Abstract syntax of Loop in ML

An abstract syntax (see section 2.2) of Loop may be defined in ML as an ML structure that contains one type for each of the six grammatical categories of the language:

```
structure LoopSyntax =
struct

  type Literal = int;
  type Ident   = string;

  datatype Prog = Program    of Imp

    and    Imp  = Skip
                | Put        of IExp
                | Get        of Ident
                | Asg        of Ident * IExp
                | Seq        of Imp * Imp
                | If         of BExp * Imp * Imp
                | Loop       of IExp * Imp

    and    IExp = Constant   of Literal
                | Variable   of Ident
                | Sum        of IExp * IExp
                | Prod       of IExp * IExp

    and    BExp = Eql        of IExp * IExp
                | Less       of IExp * IExp
```

```
                  | Not        of BExp
                  | And        of BExp * BExp;
end;
```

Observe that there are no rules here that describe the syntactic structure of literals, but that we instead postulate that any ML integer may be used as a literal. This means that we have changed the language slightly compared to what we did in figure 2.1. This is done in order to make the language a little easier to use (binary notation for integers is, of course, not very user-friendly).

3.2 Semantics of Loop in ML

The semantics of Loop may be specified by the following ML structure:

```
structure LoopSemantics =
struct
  open LoopSyntax;
  (* Definitions of types, see section 3.2.1 *)
  local
    (* Definitions of some auxiliary functions, see section 3.2.2 *)
  in
    (* Definitions of semantic mappings, see section 3.2.3 *)
end;
```

3.2.1 Types in LoopSemantics

The structure LoopSemantics contains one type for each of the semantic domains used in section 2.4 to define the semantics of Loop, i.e., for each of the domains Input, Output, Store and State. These types may be defined in ML as follows:

```
type Input  = int list;
type Output = int list;
type Store  = Ident -> int;
type State  = Input * Store * Output;
```

3.2.2 Auxiliary functions in LoopSemantics

In the definitions of semantic mappings in LoopSemantics, it is convenient to use a few few auxiliary functions to access and change states in various ways. These functions are defined as follows:

```
fun initstate(i)        = (i, (fn x => 0), []);
fun bind(h, id, v)      = (fn x => (if id = x then v else h x));
fun store(inp, h, out)  = h;
```

```
fun output(inp, h, out)   = out;
fun get(([], h, out), id)   = ([], bind(h, id, 0), out)
  | get((x::s, h, out), id) = (s, bind(h, id, x), out);
fun put((inp, h, out), v)   = (inp, h, out@[v]);
fun assign((inp, h, out), id, v)
                            = (inp, bind(h, id, v), out);
```

We also need the following auxiliary function in the definition of the semantics of **loop** imperatives:

```
fun rep(0, mv, s) = s
  | rep(n, mv, s) = rep(n - 1, mv, (mv s));
```

3.2.3 Semantic mappings in LoopSemantics

We are now ready to define functions in the structure LoopSemantics that correspond to the semantic mappings $\mathcal{V}$, $\mathcal{B}$. $\mathcal{M}$ and $\mathcal{B}$ defined in section 2.4:

```
fun VV (Variable id)       = (fn h => h(id))
  | VV (Constant lit)      = (fn h => lit)
  | VV (Sum(e1, e2))       = (fn h => ((VV e1 h) + (VV e2 h)))
  | VV (Prod(e1, e2))      = (fn h => ((VV e1 h) * (VV e2 h)))

fun BB (Equal(e1, e2))     = (fn h => ((VV e1 h) = (VV e2 h)))
  | BB (Less(e1, e2))      = (fn h => ((VV e1 h) < (VV e2 h)))
  | BB (And(b1, b2))       = (fn h => ((BB b1 h) andalso (BB b2 h)))
  | BB (Not(b))            = (fn h => (not (BB b h)))

fun MM(Skip)               = (fn s => s)
  | MM(Put e)              = (fn s => put(s, (VV e (store(s)))))
  | MM(Asg(id, e))         = (fn s => assign(s, id, (VV e (store(s)))))
  | MM(Get id)             = (fn s => get(s, id))
  | MM(Seq(im1, im2))      = (MM im2) o (MM im1)
  | MM(If(b, im1, im2))    = (fn s => if (BB b (store s))
                                      then (MM im1 s)
                                      else (MM im2 s))
  | MM(Loop(e, im))        = (fn s => rep((VV e (store s)), MM im, s))

fun PP (Program im)        = (fn i => output(MM im (initstate i)))
```

Observe that an ML version of the mapping $\mathcal{A}$ is not needed because we have assumed (in section 3.1 in the definition of abstract syntax for Loop) that any integer may be used as a literal.

3.3 An interpreter of abstract Loop programs

The two structures LoopSyntax and LoopSemantics as defined in sections 3.1 and 3.2 together give a complete specification in ML of the abstract syntax and the semantics of Loop. This specification is executable, but is only able to interpret what may be called *abstract programs*, i.e., values in the type Prog defined in the structure LoopSyntax. An example: The concrete Loop program

begin **get** xx; **put** (xx + 3) **end**

has an abstract form which is written as follows in ML (using the definitions in LoopSyntax):

Program(Seq(Get("xx"), Put(Sum(Variable("xx"), Constant(3)))))

If we would like to have this abstract program interpreted by the ML code in LoopSyntax and LoopSemantics, we may proceed as follows:

- Place the code in LoopSyntax and LoopSemantics in a file, named for instance `loop.sml`.

- Start an ML interpreter on your computer (on some computers this may be done by isssuing the command `sml` to the operating system).

- Give the following commands to the ML interpreter:

  ```
  use "loop.sml";
  open LoopSyntax;
  open LoopSemantics;
  PP(Program(Seq(Get("xx"),
    Put(Sum(Variable("xx"), Constant(3))))))[2];
  ```

  The ML interpreter will then respond as follows:

  ```
  val it = [5] : Output
  ```

  which of course is the correct result when the ML program

  begin **get** xx; **put** (xx + 3) **end**

  is executed from an input sequence consisting of the integer 2.

As can be seen from this example, it is very cumbersome to write abstract programs. If we want to use ML to interpret more than very few and very simple programs, it is advisable to construct a parser for our programming language. This method is shown in the next section. The reader should be warned that this section contains some ML code which may not be immediately understandable. It is, however, possible - and in our opinion not very difficult - to construct parsers for most programming languages even without having a complete understanding of the details in the code given below by simply changing some of it.

3.4 Parsing Loop

A *parser* for a programming language is a function that transforms a concrete program to an abstract version of the same program.

It is usual - and advantageous - to split a parser into two parts: the first is a function - called a *scanner* - that transforms a given string into a sequence of so-called *tokens*; the second part - the main part of the parser - is a function that transforms the sequence of tokens into a syntax tree, i.e., into an abstract representation of the program represented concretely by the initially given string.

3.4.1 A scanner

A *scanner* for a programming language like Loop is a function that takes a string (a concrete program in the language) as its argument, and produces a sequence of tokens as its value. A *token* is either a keyword, an identifier, a literal, an operator symbol or a separator symbol of the language. To define a scanner for a given language, we therefore first have to specify precisely what is allowed as keywords, literals, identifiers, operators and separators in the language. For the sake of simplicity, let us assume that the language we study is such that integers, and only integers, may be used as literals, and that an identifier is a sequence of letters (which, of course, is the case for Loop). Under this assumption, a specification of the keywords, operators and separators of a language should suffice to construct a scanner for the language. The following ML structure contains this information for Loop:

```
structure LoopSymbols =
 struct
  val keywords  = ["begin", "end",
                   "skip", "put", "get",
                   "loop", "times", "endloop",
                   "if", "then", "else", "fi",
                   "not", "and"]
  and operators  = ["+", "*", "=", "<", ":="]
  and separators = [";", "(", ")"]
 end;
```

Given this structure, we may get a scanner for Loop by using the functor ScanFun. A *functor* is in general a high-level ML function that may have structures as arguments and as value. The functor ScanFun is defined to take a structure (like LoopSymbols above) as an argument, and to produce a structure with the following signature as its value:

```
signature SCANNER =
 sig
  datatype token      =  Key of string | Symbol of string |
```

```
                           Literal of int  | Ident of string;
  val token_as_string :  token -> string
  val scan            :  string -> token list;
end;
```

This means that the result of applying the functor ScanFun to LoopSymbols is a structure that contains

- A datatype token which may have values of four kinds: either a Key (a keyword of the language), a Symbol (a separator or operator), a Literal (an integer) or an Ident (an identifier).
- A function token_as_string that produces a string when applied to a token.
- A function scan that produces a list of tokens when applied to a string.

The functor ScanFun may be defined as follows:

```
functor ScanFun(structure Symbols : SYMBOLS) : SCANNER =
struct

  datatype token = Key of string | Symbol of string |
                   Literal of int | Ident of string;

  fun token_as_string(Key(s))       = s
    | token_as_string(Symbol(s)) = s
    | token_as_string(Literal(i))   = "int"
    | token_as_string(Ident(s))     = s;

  fun scan cs = scanning([], explode cs)
    (* The functions scanning and explode are explained below *)

end;
```

The function explode transforms a string cs into a list containing the characters of cs. The function scanning takes two parameters, the first a list of tokens, the second a list of characters. The value of scanning(toks, cs) is a list of tokens which is equal to toks concatenated with the result of transforming the string cs into a list of tokens. The function scanning may be defined as follows:

```
fun scanning(toks, []) = <the list toks reversed>
  | scanning(toks, c::cs) =
      if<c is a digit> then
        let val (lit, cs2) = numeric(c, cs)
          in scanning(Literal(lit) :: toks, cs2) end else
      if <c is a letter> then
        let val (id, cs2) = alphanum(c, cs)
          in if elem(id, Symbols.keywords)
               then scanning(Key(id) :: toks, cs2)
```

```
            else  scanning(Ident(id) :: toks, cs2) end else
      if <c is a symbol that may occur in an operator
            or a separator> then
        let val (symb, cs2) = symbolic(c, cs)
          in scanning(Symbol(symb) :: toks, cs2) end
      else scanning(toks, cs)
```

The functions numeric, alphanum and symbolic used above in the definition of scanning are defined such that

```
numeric(c, cs)   = <a pair (i, cs2) where i is the integer found
                   by concatenating the digit c with as many
                   digits from the head of cs as possible,
                   and cs2 is cs with these digits removed>;
alphanum(c, cs) = <a pair (id, cs2) where id is found by
                   concatenating the letter c with as many
                   letters from the head of cs as possible,
                   and cs2 is cs with these letters removed>;
symbolic(c, cs)  = <a pair (os, cs2) where os is the operator or
                   separator found by concatenating c with
                   a character from the head of cs if this is
                   necessary to get an operator/separator,
                   cs2 is cs with such a character removed>;
```

We may apply the functor ScanFun to the structure LoopSymbols to get a structure Scanner that contains a scanner for Loop:

```
structure Scanner = ScanFun(structure Symbols = LoopSymbols);
```

3.4.2 Tools for parsing

A parser for a language must be written such that every grammatical rule of the language (as expressed for instance by BNF productions) is taken into account, and is much more complex to design than a scanner for the language. But it is possible to define tools (ML functions) that makes it relatively easy to transform BNF productions for the grammar of a language almost directly into ML code for a function that may be used as a parser for the language.

ParseFun is a functor that when applied to a structure Scanner that has SCANNER as signature will have as value a structure that contains the following ML functions that may be used to define a parser for a programming language:

- A number of functions, called
  - $, $$, >>, -- and ||
  - id, lit, repsep and empty

These functions may be used to mimic BNF productions that specify the concrete syntax of a language. Exactly how this is done, may best be seen by studying the code in section 3.4.4 below.

- A function called reader. This function takes as argument a function ph which should be such that it will parse a sequence of tokens. It is possible to write such functions such that they mimic the BNF productions that define various concrete grammatical categories. How this may be done by using the functions above is shown in section 3.4.4 below.

  The function reader is defined as follows:

  ```
  fun reader ph cs
       = (case ph (Scanner.scan cs) of
              (x, []) => x
            | (x, t)  => raise SynError("Unparsed code"))
  ```

  This means that the value of reader(ph) is a function that parses a string cs by first giving cs to the scanner found in the structure given as parameter to the functor ParseFun, and then applying the function ph to the resulting sequence of tokens. SynError is an exception (defined by ParseFun) which will be raised should strings with syntax errors be given to the parser.

A structure that contains these functions may be constructed by applying the functor ParseFun to a structure that contains a scanner for a language:

```
structure Parser = ParseFUN(Scanner);
```

3.4.3 A parser for Loop

The structure LoopParser is defined as follows:

```
structure LoopParser =
struct
 local
   <Definitions of an auxiliary function for each nonterminal
     phrase used in the BNF productions. Each of these has
     one or more tokens as arguments and an abstract syntactic
     object as value>;
   fun makeProgram((_,i),_) = Program(i);
   fun makeSkip(_)           = Skip;
   etc., see section 3.4.5 below.

   <Definitions of an auxiliary function for each grammatical
     category. Each of these takes a sequence of tokens as
     argument and has as value an abstract syntactic
```

```
    object which is the result of parsing the given tokens>;
  fun prog  toks = <abstract representation of the
                     program specified by the list toks>
  and imps  toks = <abstract representation of the
                     sequence of imperatives specified by toks>
  and imp   toks = <abstract representation of the
                     imperative specified by toks>
  and iexp  toks = <abstract representation of the
                     integer expresssion specified by toks>
  and bexp  toks = <abstract representation of the
                     Boolean expression specified by toks>
 in
  val parse = Parser.reader prog;
 end;
end;
```

If pp is a concrete program (a string), we get

```
parse pp = Parser.reader prog pp
         = case prog (Scanner.scan p) of
               (x, []) => x
             | (x, t)  => raise SynError("Unparsed code")
```

This means that if pp is without syntactic errors, the value of parse p will be a pair (x, []) where x is an abstract representation of pp. Should pp contain anything after the final **end**, the exception SynError is raised with parameter "Unparsed code". Should pp have any other syntax errors, the same exception will be raised, with a different parameter but by other parts of the code (how this may happen is explained below).

3.4.4 Functions that parse Loop

The function prog is defined as follows, using the auxiliary functions −−, >>, $, makeProgram and imps (the first three of these are defined by ParseFun, the last two in LoopParser):

```
fun prog toks =
    ($"begin" -- imps -- $"end"   >> makeProgram
    ) toks
```

The binary functions −− and >> are specified to be written infixed in their definitions in the functor ParseFun, and so is the function || (which will be used in many definitions in section 3.4.5 below). The reason for this is to make it possible to write the definitions of the functions prog, imp, imps, iexp and bexp in a manner that mimics as closely as possible the way we write BNF productions for the grammatical categories of a language. Had the functions −− and >> been written prefixed, the definition of prog could have been written as follows:

```
fun prog toks =
    >>(--(--($"begin", imps), $"end")), makeProgram) toks
```

To understand what the definition of prog means, we have to look at the definitions of -- and >> in the functor ParseFun:

```
fun (ph1 -- ph2) toks = let val (x, toks2) = ph1 toks
                            val (y, toks3) = ph2 toks2
                        in ((x,y), toks3) end;

fun (ph >> f) toks    = let val (x, toks2) = ph toks
                        in (f x, toks2) end;
```

To show how this works, let us see what happens if we apply prog to the following list of tokens (which is the result of scanning the concrete program "begin skip end"):

```
toks0 = ["begin", "skip", "end"]
```

In the computation of the value of prog toks0, it is convenient to use the following function names:

```
mp   = makeProgram
phb  = $"begin"
phs  = $"skip"
phe  = $"end"
phi  = phb -- imps
php  = phi -- phe
     = $"begin" -- imps -- $"end"
```

We then get:

```
prog toks0 = (php >> mp)(toks0)
           = let val (x, toks1) = php toks0
             in (mp x, toks1) end
```

The value of php toks0 may be found as follows:

```
= let val (x, toks3) = phi  toks0
      val (y, toks4) = phe toks3
  in ((x,y), toks4) end;
```

The value of phi toks0 may be found as follows:

```
= let val (x, toks1) = phb  toks0
      val (y, toks2) = imps toks1
  in ((x,y), toks2) end;
```

To find the value of phb toks0 = $"begin"(tok), we have to look at the definition of the function $:

```
fun $ a (b :: toks) =
  if a = b then (a, toks)
  else raise SynError("Expected " ^ a ^ ", found " ^ b)
```

We then get

```
phb toks0 = $"begin"(toks0)
          = ("begin", ["skip", "end"])
```

We leave it as an exercise to use the definition of the function imps (it is defined in LoopParser, the definition may be found in section 3.4.5 below) to prove that

```
imps ["skip", "end"] = (Skip, ["end"])
```

We then get

```
phi ["begin", "skip", "end"] = (("begin", Skip), ["end"])
```

We now have to find the value of phe ["end"], which we easily see is equal to the pair ("end", []). We are then able to find the value php toks0:

```
php toks0 = let val (x, toks1) = phi toks0
                               = (("begin", Skip) toks1)
                val (y, toks2) = phe toks1
                               = ("end", [])
             in ((x, y), toks2) end
          = ((("begin", Skip), "end"), [])
```

Finally, we find the value of prog toks0:

```
prog toks0 = (php >> mp)(toks0)
           = let val (x, toks1) = php toks0
                                  ((("begin", Skip), "end"), [])
              in (mp (("begin", Skip), "end"), []) end
           = (makeProgram(("begin", Skip), "end"), []
           = (Program(Skip), [])
```

3.4.5 The auxiliary functions in LoopParser

The first set of auxiliary functions in the structure LoopParser is defined as follows:

```
open LoopSyntax;
fun makeProgram((_,i),_)       = Program(i);
fun makeSkip(_)                = Skip;
fun makePut(_, e)              = Put(e);
fun makeGet(_, v)              = Get(v);
fun makeAssign((v, _), e)      = Asg(v, e);
```

```
fun makeImps([])                        = Skip
|   makeImps(i::[])                     = i
|   makeImps(i::s)                      = Seq(i, makeImps(s));
fun makeIf((((((_,e),_),i1),_),i2),_) = If(e, i1, i2);
fun makeLoop((((_,e),_),i),_)          = Loop(e, i);
fun makeVariable(v)                     = Variable(v);
fun makeConstant(i)                     = Constant(i);
fun makeSum((((_,e1),_),e2),_)         = Sum(e1, e2);
fun makeProd((((_,e1),_),e2),_)        = Prod(e1, e2);
fun makeEqual((((_,e1),_),e2),_)       = Equal(e1, e2);
fun makeLess((((_,e1),_),e2),_)        = Less(e1, e2);
fun makeAnd((((_,b1),_),b2),_)         = And(b1, b2);
fun makeNot((_,b),_)                    = Not(b);
```

The remaining auxiliary functions are defined as follows:

```
open Parser;

fun prog toks =
  ($"begin" -- imps -- $"end"   >> makeProgram
  ) toks

and imps toks =
  (repsep imp ";"               >> makeImps
  ) toks

and imp toks =
  ( $"skip"                     >> makeSkip
  || $"put" -- iexp             >> makePut
  || $"get" -- id               >> makeGet
  || id -- $$":=" -- iexp       >> makeAssign
  || $"if" -- bexp --
       $"then" -- imps --
       $"else" -- imps --
       $"fi"                    >> makeIf
  || $"loop" -- iexp --
       $"times" -- imps --
       $"endloop"               >> makeLoop
  ) toks
and iexp toks =
  ( id                         >> makeVariable
  || lit                       >> makeConstant
  || $$"(" -- iexp -- $$"+"
       -- iexp -- $$")"        >> makeSum
  || $$"(" -- iexp -- $$"*"
       -- iexp -- $$")"        >> makeProd
  ) toks
and bexp toks =
  ( $$"(" -- iexp -- $$"="
       -- iexp -- $$")"        >> makeEqual
```

```
|| $$"(" -- iexp -- $$"<"
   -- iexp -- $$")"              >> makeLess
|| $$"(" -- bexp -- $"and"
   -- bexp -- $$")"              >> makeAnd
|| $$"(" -- $"not"
   -- bexp -- $$")"              >> makeNot
) toks;
```

3.5 Exercises

3.5.1 Extensions

Extend the ML interpreter described in this chapter such that it is able to handle the various extensions to Loop defined in the exercises at the end of chapter 2, i.e.,

- Conditional expressions
- Imperatives for adding to variables
- Swap imperatives
- Input in expressions

Chapter 4
Algebras

Denotational definitions of the semantics of most programming languages consist of definitions of large numbers of domains and functions. In order to reduce the chances of getting lost among all the details, it may be advantageous to modularize the definitions. In this chapter, we describe tools for doing this.

4.1 Algebras

An *algebra* is a mathematical structure that consists of one or more sets, which we say are the *carriers*, *sorts* or *domains* of the algebra, and one or more *operations* or *functions*. An example is the algebra *Bool* of truth-values. It has a single carrier consisting of the two elements **true** and **false**, and obvious operations: $\neg$ (not), $\wedge$ (and), $\vee$ (or) etc. Another example is the algebra *Nat* of the so-called *natural numbers*, i.e., the non-negative integers. It has carrier $\{0, 1, 2, \dots\}$ and operations $+$, $*$, $-$, $=$ etc. A third example is the algebra *Nat** which has a carrier that consists of all finite sequences of *Nat* members and has operations append (which we often write $\vdash$ infixed, see section 4.3.3 below), length, head and tail.

4.1.1 Defining the carriers of an algebra

The carrier(s) of an algebra may be defined in two different ways: Either *explicitly*, usually by listing or describing the elements of the carriers, as we did above for the carriers of *Bool*, *Nat* and *Nat**; or *inductively* by showing how the elements of the carrier may be *generated by induction*. The carrier of the algebra *Nat* may for instance be defined inductively as follows:

> Nat_1: $0 \in Nat$
> Nat_2: For every $n \in Nat$: $\mathrm{suc}(n) \in Nat$
> Nat_3: *Nat* is the smallest set that satisfies Nat_1 and Nat_2

The function $\mathrm{suc} \in (Nat \to Nat)$ used in clause Nat_2 of this definition, is the *successor function*. This function is such that $\mathrm{suc}(n)$ is the integer that follows n, i.e., $\mathrm{suc}(n) = n + 1$ for every $n \in Nat$.

Observe that we use the same name (*Nat* in this case) for an algebra and its carrier (or one of its carriers, should the algebra have more than one). The reason for this slightly ambiguous language (which is quite innocent, there should not be any danger of serious confusion) is to reduce either the number of names we have to invent (and you have to remember) or the amount of decoration with which we have to embellish the names of algebras and carriers in order to make them different.

An inductive definition of a carrier is in general given by introducing one or more *generating functions*, which we say are the *generators* of the carrier. *Nat* has for instance two generators, namely the 0-ary function $0 \in (\cdot \to Nat)$ and the unary function $\mathrm{suc} \in (Nat \to Nat)$. Some notation: i) We use $(A \to B)$ to denote the set that contains every function from the set *A* to the set *B*, i.e., every f that has *A* as its domain and *B* as its range. ii) A *0-ary function* is a degenerate function that takes no (i.e., 0) arguments. We use $(\cdot \to A)$ to denote the set of all 0-ary functions that have values in *A*. Every element a of *A* has an obvious corresponding function in $(\cdot \to A)$, namely the 0-ary function that has a as value. We use a as a name of this function.

Another example of an inductively defined carrier, is the carrier of the algebra *Nat**, which we may specify to be generated by the following two functions:

$$\varepsilon \in (\cdot \to Nat^*)$$
$$\vdash \in (Nat^* \times Nat \to Nat^*)$$

where ε is a 0-ary function that has the empty sequence as its value, and $\vdash$ is a binary function which is such that for any sequence $ns \in Nat^*$ and integer $n \in Nat$, $ns \vdash n$ is the sequence we get when we append n to the right end of ns. Given these functions, the carrier of *Nat** may be defined inductively as follows:

> Nat_1^*: $\varepsilon \in Nat^*$
> Nat_2^*: For every $n \in Nat$, $ns \in Nat^*$: $(ns \vdash n) \in Nat^*$
> Nat_3^*: Nat^* is the smallest set that satisfies Nat_1^* and Nat_2^*

4.1.2 The observers and producers of an algebra

The nongenerating functions of an algebra are said to be either *observers* or *producers*, the former if they have values outside the algebra, the latter if their values are within the algebra. Thus, addition and multiplication are *Nat* producers, and integer equality (which is a function that takes two integers as arguments and produces a truth value) is a *Nat* observer.

The observers and producers of an inductively defined algebra are usually defined by so-called *generator induction*, i.e., by giving *axioms* (rules) which show how to compute the values of the functions for combinations of arguments systematically constructed by using the generators. An example: The *Nat* producers + and $*$ may be defined by generator induction as follows:

$$\begin{aligned} n + 0 &= n \\ n + suc(m) &= suc(n + m) \\ n * 0 &= 0 \\ n * suc(m) &= (n * m) + n \end{aligned}$$

When presenting a set of axioms like this, we implicitly assume each axiom to be valid for every free variable that occurs in it (in this case for every $n, m \in Nat$).

Many more examples which show how to define functions by generator induction are given in later sections and chapters.

4.1.3 Signatures of functions and algebras

The *signature of a function* is a specification of the name, domain and range of the function. Thus, the signature of integer addition is as follows:

$$+ \in (Nat \times Nat \rightarrow Nat)$$

This is a specification of a function that has name +, domain $Nat \times Nat$ (this is the set that consists of all pairs $\langle n, m \rangle$ where $n, m \in Nat$), and range *Nat*.

The *signature of an algebra* is a list that contains 1) the name(s) of the carrier(s) of the algebra, and 2) the signatures of the function(s) of the algebra. The signature of *Nat* is for instance as follows:

Carrier: *Nat*

Functions:
$$\begin{aligned} 0 &\in (\cdot \rightarrow Nat) \\ suc &\in (Nat \rightarrow Nat) \\ + &\in (Nat \times Nat \rightarrow Nat) \\ * &\in (Nat \times Nat \rightarrow Nat) \\ = &\in (Nat \times Nat \rightarrow Bool) \\ < &\in (Nat \times Nat \rightarrow Bool) \end{aligned}$$

4.1.4 Algebra specifications

To *specify* an algebra means to specify the carrier(s) and function(s) of the algebra. A specification may be more or less complete, but should minimally include the signature of the algebra, i.e., the name(s) of the carrier(s) and the signatures of the function(s) of the algebra. In addition, a specification of an algebra may contain information about the contents of the carrier(s) and the values of the function(s). The minimal part of a specification only gives information about the *syntax* of an algebra: it specifies the names of the carrier(s) and function(s) of the algebra, and specifies the types of the arguments and the values of the functions, but gives no information about the contents of the carrier(s) and the values of the function(s). Information of this latter kind is information about the *semantics* of the algebra that is being specified. The more semantic information is given, that is the more which is said about the contents of the carrier(s) and about the values of the functions, the more *complete* the specification is said to be.

An *algebra specification* may have the following three parts, only the first of which is obligatory:

Syntax: This part consists of an algebra signature which contains the name(s) of the carrier(s) and the signatures of the functions of an algebra.

An example is the signature of *Nat* given in section 4.1.3 above.

Semantics of carrier(s): This part specifies the contents of each carrier, either by enumeration, or by explicit set-theoretical definition, or by induction.

An example of specification by enumeration is given on page 41, where we said that the carrier of the algebra *Bool* should consist of the two elements **true** and **false**. Two examples of specification by induction are given in section 4.1.1 above where we specified the carriers of *Nat* and *Nat** by induction. Examples of specification by set-theoretical definition will be given later.

Semantics of function(s): This part specifies what values the functions should have for particular arguments, normally by a set of axioms for the functions. These axioms are usually (at least in our context) given as *identities*, i.e., equations that implicitly are assumed to be valid for all values of the variables that occur in them.

An example: the four identities given at the end of section 4.1.2 above constitute a set of axioms for the *Nat* functions $+$ and $*$.

It is important to distinguish between algebras and algebra specifications: Algebras are mathematical structures that consist of sets (carriers) and functions; algebra specifications are descriptions of algebras. The distinction is similar to the distinction between music and musical scores: music is something we listen to, a musical score is a specification of music.

An algebra *A* is said to *satisfy* an algebra specification *S* if 1) *A* contains one carrier for each carrier name of *S* and one function for each function name of *S*, and 2) each semantic specification given in *S* holds in *A*. The functions and the carriers of *A* are then said to be *interpretations* of the corresponding function and carrier names of *S*. We will sometimes say that an algebra that satisfies an algebra specification is an *implementation* or a *model* of the specification.

An incomplete algebra specification may of course be satisfied by more than one algebra. An example is the following algebra specification:

Carrier: *NN*
Functions: $\mathsf{e} \in (\cdot \to NN)$
$\mathsf{a} \in (NN \to NN)$
$\mathsf{b} \in (NN \times NN \to NN)$
Axioms: $\mathsf{b}(\mathsf{e}, \mathsf{x}) = \mathsf{x}$, $\mathsf{b}(\mathsf{x}, \mathsf{e}) = \mathsf{x}$

This specification is obviously incomplete (the contents of the carrier are not specified; for instance do the axioms not tell us how to evaluate the function b if e does not occur as one of the arguments), and many algebras will therefore satisfy it. We get one example of an algebra that is a model for this specification by interpreting *NN* as the set of integers and interpreting the functions e, a and b as 0, suc (the successor function) and + respectively. Another model may be found by interpreting *NN* as the set {**true**, **false**} and interpreting e, a and b as **true**, ¬ and ∧ respectively.

If we extend an incomplete algebra specification *S* by adding semantic information, the resulting specification *S'* contains more concrete details and may therefore be said to be *less abstract* than the original specification *S*. It is obvious that the less abstract (and more concrete) a specification is, the fewer algebras will satisfy it. But an algebra specification may never be fully concrete in the sense that there is only one concrete algebra that satisfies it. An example: Consider the following algebra specification *SN*:

Carrier: *NN*: *Inductively generated by* z, s
Functions: $\mathsf{z} \in (\cdot \to NN)$
$\mathsf{s} \in (NN \to NN)$
$\mathsf{a} \in (NN \times NN \to NN)$
$\mathsf{e} \in (NN \times NN \to Bool)$
Axioms: $\mathsf{a}(\mathsf{n}, \mathsf{z}) = \mathsf{n}$, $\mathsf{a}(\mathsf{n}, \mathsf{s}(\mathsf{m})) = \mathsf{s}(\mathsf{a}(\mathsf{n}, \mathsf{m}))$
$\mathsf{e}(\mathsf{z}, \mathsf{z}) = \mathbf{true}$,
$\mathsf{e}(\mathsf{z}, \mathsf{s}(\mathsf{n})) = \mathbf{false}$, $\mathsf{e}(\mathsf{s}(\mathsf{n}), \mathsf{z}) = \mathbf{false}$,
$\mathsf{e}(\mathsf{s}(\mathsf{n}), \mathsf{s}(\mathsf{m})) = \mathsf{e}(\mathsf{n}, \mathsf{m})$

This specification is as complete as we can get it: the contents of the carrier are fully specified, and so are the producer a and the observer e, which are the only nongenerating functions of the algebra. Nonetheless, many algebras will satisfy it. One should be obvious: interpret *NN* as *Nat*, z as 0, s as suc, a as + and e as equality. Another, which may be less obvious, is a so-called *term algebra.* The domains of such algebras consist of *terms*, i.e., of syntactical objects in some language. In our case we define the domain to be the so-called *generator universe* G for *SN* which is defined to be the set of all terms constructed from the generators z and s:

$$G \stackrel{d}{=} \{\mathsf{z}, \mathsf{s}(\mathsf{z}), \mathsf{s}(\mathsf{s}(\mathsf{z})), \mathsf{s}(\mathsf{s}(\mathsf{s}(\mathsf{z}))), \ldots\}$$

We may define this domain more precisely (avoiding the ellipsis '...') by induction as follows:

G_1: The term z is in G
G_2: If the term g is in G, then so is the term s(g)
G_3: G is the smallest set that satisfies G_1 and G_2

The interpretation of a is a function $\mathsf{a}_G \in (G \times G \to G)$ which is defined by induction on the size of the elements of G as follows:

a_1: $\mathsf{a}_G(\mathsf{g}, \mathsf{z}) = \mathsf{g}$ for every term $\mathsf{g} \in G$
a_2: $\mathsf{a}_G(\mathsf{g}_1, \mathsf{s}(\mathsf{g}_2)) = \mathsf{s}(\mathsf{a}_G(\mathsf{g}_1, \mathsf{g}_2))$ for all terms $\mathsf{g}_1, \mathsf{g}_2 \in G$

The interpretation of e is a function $\mathsf{e}_G \in (G \times G \to Bool)$ defined as follows (also by induction):

e_1: $\mathsf{e}_G(\mathsf{z}, \mathsf{z}) = \textbf{true}$,
e_2: $\mathsf{e}_G(\mathsf{z}, \mathsf{s}(\mathsf{g})) = \textbf{false}$, for every term $\mathsf{g} \in G$
e_3: $\mathsf{e}_G(\mathsf{s}(\mathsf{g}), \mathsf{z}) = \textbf{false}$, for every term $\mathsf{g} \in G$
e_4: $\mathsf{e}_G(\mathsf{s}(\mathsf{g}_1), \mathsf{s}(\mathsf{g}_2)) = \mathsf{e}_G(\mathsf{g}_1, \mathsf{g}_2)$ for every term $\mathsf{g}_1, \mathsf{g}_2 \in G$

Exercise: Check that the term algebra really is a model of *SN*.

But even if the algebra specification *SN* has more than one model, it is possible to prove that all its models have exactly the same structure. Given two models for *SN* it is in fact possible to define a so-called *isomorphism* between them (what an isomorphism is, is explained below). This means that two *SN* models only differ in what names their carriers and functions have. Remembering what Shakespeare wrote: *What's in a name? That which we call a rose by any other name would smell as sweet*, we identify isomorphic models and say that *SN* is a complete algebra specification.

In the rest of this chapter, and also in the following chapters, we will present many algebra specifications. The first of these may be found in figure 4.1 – which contains a specification for the algebra *Bool*, the second in figure 4.2 where a specification for *Nat* may be found.

4.1.5 Isomorphism between algebras

Two algebras *A* and *B* with the same signature are said to be isomorphic if they have exactly the same structure, i.e., if their structures

Bool *The truth-values*

Bool: *Generated by* **true**, **false**

Functions:

$$
\begin{array}{lll}
\mathbf{true} & \in (\cdot \to Bool) & \\
\mathbf{false} & \in (\cdot \to Bool) & \\
\neg & \in (Bool \to Bool) & \text{(not)} \\
\wedge & \in (Bool \times Bool \to Bool) & \text{(and)} \\
\vee & \in (Bool \times Bool \to Bool) & \text{(or)} \\
= & \in (Bool \times Bool \to Bool) & \text{(equality)}
\end{array}
$$

Axioms:

$$\neg\, \mathbf{false} = \mathbf{true}, \quad \neg\, \mathbf{true} = \mathbf{false}$$

$$\mathbf{false} \wedge b = \mathbf{false}, \quad b \wedge \mathbf{false} = \mathbf{false}$$
$$\mathbf{true} \wedge \mathbf{true} = \mathbf{true}$$

$$(b1 \vee b2) = \neg(\neg b1 \wedge \neg b2)$$

$$(b1 = b2) = (\neg b1 \wedge \neg b2) \vee (\neg b2 \wedge \neg b1)$$

Figure 4.1: Specification for the algebra *Bool*

Nat *The non-negative integers*

Carrier: *Nat*: *Generated by* 0, suc

Functions:

$$
\begin{array}{ll}
0 & \in (\cdot \to Nat) \\
\mathrm{suc} & \in (Nat \to Nat) \\
+ & \in (Nat \times Nat \to Nat) \\
* & \in (Nat \times Nat \to Nat) \\
< & \in (Nat \times Nat \to Bool) \\
= & \in (Nat \times Nat \to Bool)
\end{array}
$$

Axioms:

$$
\begin{array}{llll}
m + 0 = m, & m + \mathrm{suc}(n) = \mathrm{suc}(m + n) & & \\
m * 0 = 0, & m * \mathrm{suc}(n) = (m * n) + m & & \\
(0 < 0) & = \mathbf{false}, & (0 < \mathrm{suc}(n)) & = \mathbf{true} \\
(\mathrm{suc}(n) < 0) & = \mathbf{false}, & (\mathrm{suc}(n) < \mathrm{suc}(m)) & = (n < m) \\
(0 = 0) & = \mathbf{true}, & (0 = \mathrm{suc}(m)) & = \mathbf{false} \\
(\mathrm{suc}(n) = 0) & = \mathbf{false}, & (\mathrm{suc}(n) = \mathrm{suc}(m)) & = (n = m)
\end{array}
$$

Figure 4.2: Specification for the algebra *Nat*

are identical. But what does it mean for two algebras to have identical structures?

The first and obvious requirement to be satisfied before we may say that two algebras have identical structures, is that the carriers of the algebras should have an identical number of elements. Let us here for the sake of simplicity - but without any serious loss of generality (it is in fact quite easy to extend the definitions given below to the more general case) - assume that the common signature of the two algebras specifies that each model of the signature has only a single carrier. A precise way of formulating the requirement that the carriers of two algebras have an equal number of elements, is then to require that there exists a function that pairs every element in the carrier A of the first algebra with a unique element in the carrier B of the second algebra in such a way that every element in B is paired with an element in A (this is for instance a simple way of determining - without explicit counting - whether or not there are equally many people and chairs in a room). Such a function is said to be a *bijection* from A to B. We define this concept formally as follows:

Definition 4.1 Injection, surjection, bijection:

> *A function* $\mathsf{b} \in (A \rightarrow B)$ *is said to be an* injection *if* $\mathsf{a}_1 \neq \mathsf{a}_2$ *then* $\mathsf{b}(\mathsf{a}_1) \neq \mathsf{b}(\mathsf{a}_2)$ *for every* $\mathsf{a}_1, \mathsf{a}_2$ *in* A.
>
> *A function* $\mathsf{b} \in (A \rightarrow B)$ *is said to be a* surjection *if for every element* b *in* B *there exists an element* a *in* A *such that* $\mathsf{b}(\mathsf{a}) = \mathsf{b}$.
>
> *A function* $\mathsf{b} \in (A \rightarrow B)$ *is said to be a* bijection *if it is both surjective and injective.*

Two sets are said to be of the same *cardinality*, i.e., to have the same number of elements, if there exists a bijection between the two sets. Observe that what you really do when you count how many members a given set has, is to construct a bijection between the set and a sequence of natural numbers with standardized names.

A second requirement that must be satisfied before we may say that two algebras with a common signature have identical structures, is that the interpretations of the functions that are specified in the signature have identical behaviours in the algebras. Before we give a formal definition of what this means, let us consider the example given at the end of the previous section where we described a signature $SN = (NN; \mathsf{z}, \mathsf{s}, \mathsf{a}, \mathsf{e})$ with two models: the algebra of natural numbers $(Nat; 0, \mathsf{suc}, +, =)$ and the term algebra $(G; \mathsf{z}, \mathsf{s}, \mathsf{a}_G, \mathsf{e}_G)$. We define a function $\mathsf{b} \in (Nat \rightarrow G)$ by induction as follows:

$$\begin{aligned} \mathsf{b}(0) &= \mathsf{z} \\ \mathsf{b}(\mathsf{suc}(\mathsf{n})) &= \mathsf{s}(\mathsf{b}(\mathsf{n})) \end{aligned}$$

It is not very difficult to see that b - which is such that $\mathsf{b}(\mathsf{n})$ is a term consisting of n applications of the function symbol s to the symbol z - is a bijection from the algebra Nat to the term algebra G.

The function symbols a and e are interpreted as + and = in *Nat*, and as a_G and e_G in *G*. It is easy to prove (by induction on *m*) that

$$\begin{aligned} b(+(n, m)) &= a_G(b(n), b(m)) \\ =(n, m)) &= e_G(b(n), b(m)) \end{aligned}$$

for every *n*, *m* in *Nat* (we write + and = prefixed here to make the general structure of these identities more perspicuous), which means that the interpretations of the function symbols behave identically.

We are now ready to define what it means for two algebras to be isomorphic:

Definition 4.2 Isomorphic algebras:

Two algebras $A = (A;\ f_{A1},\ldots,f_{An})$ *and* $B = (B;\ f_{B1},\ldots,f_{Bn})$ *with a common signature* $(S;\ f_1,\ldots,f_n)$, *are said to be* isomorphic *if*

(1) *There exists a bijection* $b \in (A \to B)$.

(2) *For every function symbol* f *and* g *in the signature: Let us (also here without serious loss of generality) assume that these symbols in the signature are specified to have the following function signatures*

$$\begin{aligned} f &\in (S \times T \to S) \\ g &\in (S \times T \to R) \end{aligned}$$

where T and R are carriers distinct from S. We must then have that

$$\begin{aligned} b(f_A(a, t)) &= f_B(b(a), t) \\ g_A(a, t) &= g_B(b(a), t) \end{aligned}$$

for every a *in A and* t *in T.*

4.1.6 Naming conventions

In order to avoid confusion, the names of all carriers and functions (generators, producers and observers) that are defined in an algebra (or, to be very precise: in a specification for an algebra) must be unique within the algebra (or – to be very precise once more – within the specification of the algebra). But in order to reduce the number of names that must be invented (and remembered!), we do not demand that carriers and functions must be given names that are unique throughout a context that may contain many algebras. If we need to refer to a function or a carrier defined in an algebra outside the algebra (for instance inside another algebra), we achieve uniqueness in naming (assuming that all algebras are given names that are unique within the given context) by prefixing the name of the 'imported' function (or carrier) with the name of the owner algebra, separating the names with a single quote mark ('). Thus, if f is a function defined in an algebra *A*, we may use A'f to refer to f outside *A*.

We do not, however, adhere strictly to this naming convention when we refer to some of the most common functions. We will, for instance, use the symbols ∧, ¬ etc. as names of the usual logical operations of the algebra *Bool* (these operations are defined in figure 4.1, which contains a complete specification for *Bool*), and not *Bool*'∧, *Bool*'¬ etc., which are their 'full names' outside the specification of *Bool* according to our naming convention. We will similarly employ **true** and **false** everywhere - instead of Bool'**true** and Bool'**false** - as names of the members of the elements of the carrier of *Bool*.

Furthermore, we will not adhere to the naming convention when we use functions that are written *infixed*. An example is the binary function + which is in (*Nat* × *Nat* → *Nat*). Its full name outside the *Nat* algebra (which is specified in figure 4.2) is Nat'+, and if we adhered strictly to the naming convention, we would write for instance 'Nat'+(e, f)' outside *Nat*. Instead we may write simply 'e + f' when it is clear from the context that e and f denote elements in the *Nat* algebra.

Partly to reduce the number of parentheses that may be necessary in an expression in which many functions are used, and partly to make the meaning of many expressions more obvious, we will sometimes use *dot notation*, which was originally invented for the programming language Simula. When we use this method for referring to functions, we write a.f instead of f(a) or A'f(a), and a_1.f(a_2, ..., a_n) instead of f(a_1, a_2, ..., a_n). When dot notation is used, complex expressions often become shorter and easier to understand. We may for example write

Nat'0.suc.suc.suc.suc

instead of the more cumbersome and less perspicuous

Nat'suc(Nat'suc(Nat'suc(Nat'suc(Nat'0))))

Another example: Assume that f, g and h are functions that map an algebra *A* to itself, and that a is an element of the carrier of *A*. We may then write

a.f.g.h

instead of

h(g(f(a)))

The effect of this is not only to reduce the size of the expression, but - more significantly - to make the evaluation sequence more perspicuous: When we read the dotted expression from left to right (as is natural when one is used to languages like English or Norwegian), it is read as follows: *start with the element* a, *then apply* f, *then* g, *and finally* h, whereas the undotted expression is read as follows: *apply* h *to the result of applying* g *to the result of applying* f *to* a: the expression is hence read in the opposite direction of that in which its functions should be applied.

Unit	*Units*
Carrier:	*Unit*: *Generated by* ι
Functions:	$\iota \in (\cdot \to Unit)$ $= \in (Unit \times Unit \to Bool)$
Axioms:	$(\iota = \iota) =$ **true**

Figure 4.3: Specification for the algebra *Unit*

Letter	*Letters*
Carrier:	*Letter* = {a, b, ..., z, A, B, ..., Z}
Functions:	rank $\in$ (*Letter* → *Nat*) = $\in$ (*Letter* × *Letter* → *Bool*)
Axioms:	rank(a) = 1, rank(b) = 2, ..., rank(Z) = 52 (x = y) = (rank(x) = rank(y))

Figure 4.4: Specification for the algebra *Letter*

4.2 Basic algebras

We need many different algebras when we give modular definitions of the semantics of programming languages. Some of these algebras have quite simple structures, other algebras are more complex. In this section we specify four basic algebras: *Bool*, *Nat*, *Unit* and *Letter*. In the next section we show a few ways of constructing compound algebras from given simpler algebras.

Two commonly used algebras are the algebra *Bool* of Boolean values (truth-values) and the algebra *Nat* of non-negative integers. Figures 4.1 and 4.2 contain specifications for these algebras.

A very simple algebra, is the algebra *Unit*. This algebra - which is specified in figure 4.3 - has a carrier that consists of a single element denoted by 'ι'. *Unit* has no functions besides a 0-ary function $\iota \in (\cdot \to Unit)$ and equality, and may seem to be too simple to be useful. Nonetheless, we will frequently find good use for this algebra to construct quite complex algebras in a simple manner (numerous examples are given in later sections and chapters).

Figure 4.4 contains a specification for the algebra *Letter* whose carrier consists of all letters. Two observers are specified for *Letter*: a unary function rank $\in$ (*Letter* → *Nat*) that associates a unique integer with each element of the domain, and a binary equality function. The former of these functions is introduced mainly in order to reduce the number of axioms needed to specify equality among letters (without the rank function or something similar, $(26 + 26) * (26 + 26)$ axioms would be necessary to specify *Letter*'=). If we had introduced notation for *hiding* some of the functions or carriers of an algebra (thus making it impossible to access such functions and carriers outside the algebra specification), it would have been reasonable to hide the rank function.

In figure 4.4, the carrier of *Letter* is specified (by explicit enumeration) to consist of 52 elements {a, b, ..., z, A, B, ..., Z}. Equivalently, we could have introduced 52 0-ary functions a $\in$ ($\cdot \rightarrow$ *Letter*), ..., Z $\in$ ($\cdot \rightarrow$ *Letter*), and specified the carrier of *Letter* to be generated by these functions.

4.3 Compound algebras

In this section we describe some commonly used methods for specifying compound algebras from previously specified simpler algebras.

4.3.1 Product algebras

The *Cartesian product* of two single-carrier algebras A and B is an algebra that is denoted by $(A \times B)$, and that has a carrier equal to the set that consists of all pairs $\langle a, b \rangle$ where a is an element of the carrier of A, and b is an element of the carrier of B. More formally:

$$(A \times B) \stackrel{d}{=} \{\langle a, b \rangle \mid a \in A, b \in B\}$$

The following functions are defined in a product algebra $(A \times B)$:

- A *pairing function* $\langle \_, \_ \rangle$ which takes two arguments: an element a in A and an element b in B, and has the pair $\langle a, b \rangle \in (A \times B)$ as its value.
- Two *projections* named 'fst' and 'snd' that maps a Cartesian product $(A \times B)$ to its factors A and B respectively. We will sometimes (but not always) write these functions using dot notation, i.e., suffixed and separated by a dot from their arguments. Thus, $\langle a, b \rangle$. fst = fst(a, b) = a and $\langle a, b \rangle$. snd = snd(a, b) = b.

  If the two algebras A and B are distinct (and hence have distinct names), we may use A and B as alternative names - usually more understandable than fst and snd - of the projection functions. Thus, $\langle a, b \rangle$. A = fst(a, b) = a and $\langle a, b \rangle$. B = snd(1, b) = b.
- The equality function. Two elements in a Cartesian product are equal if their components are pairwise equal.

Figure 4.5 shows how to specify the Cartesian product of two given algebras.

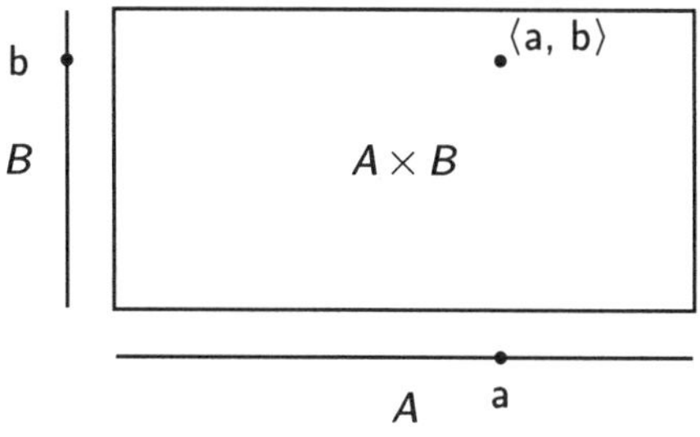

(A × B): *The Cartesian product of A and B*

Carrier: $A \times B = \{\langle a, b\rangle \mid a \in A, b \in B\}$

Functions:
$\langle\_,\_\rangle \in (A \times B \to (A \times B))$
$\mathsf{fst} \in ((A \times B) \to A)$ (Projection to A)
$\mathsf{snd} \in ((A \times B) \to B)$ (Projection to B)
$= \in ((A \times B) \times (A \times B) \to Bool)$ (Equality)

Axioms:
$\mathsf{fst}(\langle a, b\rangle) = a, \ \mathsf{sn}(\langle a, b\rangle) = b$
$(\langle a_1, b_1\rangle = \langle a_2, b_2\rangle) = ((a_1 = a_2) \wedge (b_1 = b_2))$

Figure 4.5: The Cartesian product of two algebras *A* and *B*

Int *The integers*

Carrier: $Int = \mathsf{sign}{:}\ Bool \times \mathsf{abs}{:}\ Nat$

Functions:
$+ \in (Int \times Int \to Int)$
$* \in (Int \times Int \to Int)$
$- \in (Int \to Int)$
$< \in (Int \times Int \to Bool)$
$= \in (Int \times Int \to Bool)$

Axioms:
$-\langle s, n\rangle = \langle \neg s, n\rangle$
$\langle s_1, n_1\rangle * \langle s_2, n_2\rangle = \langle s_1 = s_2, n_1 * n_2\rangle$
$\langle s_1, n_1\rangle = \langle s_2, n_2\rangle = (s_1 = s_2 \wedge n_1 = n_2) \vee (n_1 = n_2 = 0)$

Axioms for the other functions are left as exercises

Figure 4.6: Specification for the algebra *Int*

In the specification given in figure 4.5, the carrier of the Cartesian product of the algebras A and B, is specified to be equal to the set $\{\langle a, b\rangle \mid a \in A, b \in B\}$. Equivalently, we could have specified the carrier to be inductively generated by the pairing function.

It is frequently necessary to define Cartesian products of more than two algebras. Assume as an example that we would like to construct the Cartesian product of $A_1, A_2, \ldots, A_n$. This may of course be done by repeatedly constructing Cartesian products of two algebras, as follows:

$$(\ldots((A_1 \times A_2) \times A_3) \times \ldots \times A_n)$$

But it is simpler to define the Cartesian product of $A_1, A_2, \ldots, A_n$ directly as an algebra with the following carrier:

$$A_1 \times A_2 \times \ldots \times A_n \stackrel{d}{=} \{\langle a_1, a_2, \ldots, a_n\rangle \mid a_1 \in A_1, \ldots, a_n \in A_n\}$$

The elements of the carrier of a Cartesian product of n algebras are generated by a *tupling function* $\langle \_, \_, \ldots, \_\rangle$ that takes n arguments.

A *labelled Cartesian product* ($\mathsf{name\_A}: A \times \mathsf{name\_B}: B$) of two (or more) algebras is a Cartesian product where the factors are given names (for instance name_A and name_B, which must be distinct) that are used as more readable or understandable names of the projection functions. We may for example define an algebra of dates as follows:

$$Date \stackrel{d}{=} \mathsf{day}: Nat \times \mathsf{month}: Nat \times \mathsf{year}: Nat$$

Then for any $\mathsf{dt} = \langle \mathsf{d}, \mathsf{m}, \mathsf{y}\rangle \in Date$: $\mathsf{dt.month} = \mathsf{month(dt)} = \mathsf{m}$.

A specification for a labelled Cartesian product is of course very similar to a specification for an ordinary Cartesian product, the only difference being that the given labels name_A and name_B are used as names of the projection functions.

An example that shows the use of a labelled Cartesian product is given in figure 4.6 which shows how to specify the algebra *Int* that consists of *all* integers (negative as well as non-negative) as a labelled Cartesian product of *Bool* (sign) and *Nat* (absolute value). The negative integer -3 is for instance represented as $\langle Bool'\mathsf{false}, Nat'\mathsf{0.suc.suc.suc}\rangle$ in the algebra *Int*.

4.3.2 Sum algebras

The *disjoint sum* of two algebras A and B is an algebra $(A + B)$ that has a single carrier consisting of all elements of the carriers of both A and B. The elements in the carrier of the disjoint sum are marked in such a way that it is possible to determine the *origin* of any element in the sum. To mark the elements, any distinct values may be used, for instance 0 and 1. If these integers are used as marks, the carrier of the disjoint sum may be defined as follows:

$$A + B \stackrel{d}{=} \{\langle a, 0\rangle \mid a \in A\} \cup \{\langle b, 1\rangle \mid b \in B\}$$

The following functions are defined in a disjoint sum $A + B$:

- Two so-called *injection functions* which we denote by in_A and in_B. These functions 'lift' elements from the addends A and B to the sum, and have signatures in_A $\in (A \rightarrow A + B)$ and in_B $\in (B \rightarrow A + B)$. If a is an element of the addend A, a . in_A = ⟨a, 0⟩ is an element of the disjoint sum $A + B$.
- Two functions called is_A and is_B, both in $(A + B \rightarrow Bool)$, which may be used to determine whether or not a given element of the disjoint sum has the first or the second addend as origin. An example: (a . in_A) . is_B = ⟨a, 0⟩ . is_B = **false** and (a . in_A) . is_A = ⟨a, 0⟩ . is_A = **true**.
- Two functions qua_A $\in (A + B \rightarrow A)$ and qua_B $\in (A + B \rightarrow B)$, which may be used to find the original value of a given element of the disjoint sum, i.e., which *unmark* the elements of the disjoint sum. An example: (a . in_A) . qua_A = ⟨a, 0⟩ . qua_A = a. The value of (a . in_A) . qua_B = ⟨a, 0⟩ . qua_B is undefined, and so is (b . in_B) . qua_A.
- The equality function. Two elements of the disjoint sum are equal if they have the same origin and have equal values when unmarked.

Figure 4.7 contains a specification for the disjoint sum $(A + B)$ of two given algebras A and B.

In the specification given in figure 4.7, the carrier of the disjoint sum of the algebras A and B, is specified to be equal to the set $\{\langle a, 0\rangle \mid a \in A\} \cup \{\langle b, 1\rangle \mid b \in B\}$. Equivalently, we could have specified the carrier to be inductively generated by the functions in_A and in_B.

The *labelled disjoint sum* (name_A:A + name_B:B) of two algebras A and B is a disjoint sum where the elements are marked with specified labels name_A and name_B (which must be distinct). These labels may then be used to give more readable names to the functions of the disjoint sum. A specification of the labelled sum of two algebras is, of course, quite similar to the specification of the ordinary disjoint sum of the same algebras. The only difference is that 'name_A'and 'name_B' are substituted for 'A' and 'B' in the names of the producers and observers of the algebra.

Two of the functions - qua_A and qua_B - of a disjoint sum are only *partially defined*. It would of course be an error to apply, for instance, the first of these two functions to an element ⟨b, 1⟩ which originates from an element b not in A. In the definition of $A + B$ given in figure 4.7, we therefore specify (as one of the axioms) that the values of (b . in_B) . qua_A and (a . in_A) . qua_B are *undefined*. In chapter 5 below, we will introduce a more powerful way of handling functions that may be undefined for certain arguments. Instead of specifying that

$A + B$:	*The disjoint sum of two algebras A and B*
Carrier:	$A + B = \{\langle a, 0\rangle \mid a \in A\} \cup \{\langle b, 1\rangle \mid b \in B\}$
Functions:	$\text{in\_A} \in (A \to A + B)$ $\text{in\_B} \in (B \to A + B)$ $\text{qua\_A} \in (A + B \to A)$ $\text{qua\_B} \in (A + B \to B)$ $\text{is\_A} \in (A + B \to Bool)$ $\text{is\_B} \in (A + B \to Bool)$ $= \in ((A + B) \times (A + B) \to Bool)$
Axioms:	$\text{in\_A}(a) = \langle a, 0\rangle$, $\quad \text{in\_B}(b) = \langle b, 1\rangle$ $\text{in\_A}(a).\text{qua\_A} = a$, $\quad \text{in\_B}(b).\text{qua\_A}$: undefined $\text{in\_B}(b).\text{qua\_B} = b$, $\quad \text{in\_A}(a).\text{qua\_B}$: undefined $\text{in\_A}(a).\text{is\_A} = \mathbf{true}$, $\quad \text{in\_B}(b).\text{is\_A} = \mathbf{false}$ $\text{in\_A}(a).\text{is\_B} = \mathbf{false}$, $\quad \text{in\_B}(b).\text{is\_B} = \mathbf{true}$ $(\text{in\_A}(a_1) = \text{in\_A}(a_2)) = (a_1 = a_2)$ $(\text{in\_B}(b_1) = \text{in\_B}(b_2)) = (b_1 = b_2)$ $(\text{in\_A}(a) = \text{in\_B}(b)) = \mathbf{false}$, $(\text{in\_B}(b) = \text{in\_A}(a)) = \mathbf{false}$

Figure 4.7: The disjoint sum of two algebras A and B

such a function is undefined for some specified arguments, we introduce special error elements, and use these elements as values where we otherwise would have said that the function is undefined.

It is often necessary to define disjoint sums that consist of more than two algebras. Assume as an example that we would like to construct the disjoint sum of $A_1, A_2, A_3, \ldots, A_n$. This may of course be done by repeatedly constructing disjoint sums with two addends, as follows:

$$(\ldots((A_1 + A_2) + A_3) + \ldots + A_n)$$

But it is simpler to define the disjoint sum of $A_1, A_2, \ldots, A_n$ directly as an algebra with the following carrier:

$$A_1 + A_2 + \ldots + A_n \stackrel{d}{=} \{\langle a_1, 1\rangle \mid a_1 \in A_1\} \cup \ldots \cup \{\langle a_n, n\rangle \mid a_n \in A_n\}$$

If A is defined as the disjoint sum $(A_1 + A_2 + \ldots + A_n)$ (possibly with labelled addends) it is frequently convenient to use so-called *case notation* to define a function f from A to some range. Assume that we would like to define f such that its value for an argument $a \in A$ depends upon the origin of a in the following way: if $a = in\_A_i(a_i) = \langle a_i, i \rangle$ for some $i \in \{1, \ldots, n\}$ (this means that A_i is the origin of a), then $f(a) = f_i(a_i)$, where f_i is a previously defined function. An axiom which defines f may then be written as follows (we are not using case notation here):

$$
\begin{aligned}
f(a) = {} & \textbf{if } a.is\_A_1 \textbf{ then } f_1(a.qua\_A_1) \textbf{ else} \\
& \textbf{if } a.is\_A_2 \textbf{ then } f_2(a.qua\_A_2) \textbf{ else} \\
& \ldots \\
& \textbf{if } a.is\_A_n \textbf{ then } f_n(a.qua\_A_n)
\end{aligned}
$$

Using case notation this definition may equivalently be written as follows:

$$
\begin{aligned}
f(a) = {} & \textbf{case } a \textbf{ of} \\
& \quad a_1 \textbf{ in } A_1 \Rightarrow f_1(a_1) \\
& \quad a_2 \textbf{ in } A_2 \Rightarrow f_2(a_2) \\
& \quad \ldots \\
& \quad a_n \textbf{ in } A_n \Rightarrow f_n(a_n) \\
& \textbf{endcase}
\end{aligned}
$$

To reduce the amount of writing, we will sometimes (when no confusion should be possible) drop '**endcase**' from case-expressions.

Sometimes we would like to single out just a few of the cases for special treatment, and treat the remaining cases equally. In such cases we may write

$$
\begin{aligned}
f(a) = {} & \textbf{case } a \textbf{ of} \\
& \quad a_1 \textbf{ in } A_1 \Rightarrow f_1(a_1) \\
& \quad \textbf{otherwise} \Rightarrow g(a)
\end{aligned}
$$

as shorthand for

$$
\begin{aligned}
f(a) = {} & \textbf{case } a \textbf{ of} \\
& \quad a_1 \textbf{ in } A_1 \Rightarrow f_1(a_1) \\
& \quad a_2 \textbf{ in } A_2 \Rightarrow g(a) \\
& \quad \ldots \\
& \quad a_n \textbf{ in } A_n \Rightarrow g(a) \\
& \textbf{endcase}
\end{aligned}
$$

An example to show the use of labelled disjoint sums and case notation: Assuming that we had specified an algebra *Nat1* of the positive integers (the specification of *Nat1* would, of course, be very similar to the specification of *Nat*, the only difference being to replace the generator 0 by a generator 1), we could specify the algebra *Int* of all integers as a disjoint sum as follows:

$$Int = \text{Negative: } Nat1 \ + \ \text{Zero: } Unit \ + \ \text{Positive: } Nat1$$

If *Int* is specified like this, an axiom for the *Int* function $- \in (Int \to Int)$ (i.e., unary minus, which we write prefixed) may be written as follows:

$$
\begin{aligned}
-\mathrm{i} = \mathbf{case}\ \mathrm{i}\ \mathbf{of} \\
&\mathrm{n}\ \mathbf{in}\ \mathrm{Negative} \Rightarrow \mathrm{in\_Positive(n)} \\
&\iota\ \mathbf{in}\ \mathrm{Zero} \Rightarrow \mathrm{Nat'0} \\
&\mathrm{n}\ \mathbf{in}\ \mathrm{Positive} \Rightarrow \mathrm{in\_Negative(n)} \\
&\mathbf{endcase}
\end{aligned}
$$

If one or more of the addends of a disjoint sum is a labelled *Unit* algebra (as it is in *Int*), we may simplify a case expression by dropping 'ι **in**' (which, of course, does not convey any information). An axiom for the *Int* function abs $\in$ (*Int* $\rightarrow$ *Nat*) may therefore be written as follows:

$$
\begin{aligned}
\mathrm{i.abs} = \mathbf{case}\ \mathrm{i}\ \mathbf{of} \\
&\mathrm{n}\ \mathbf{in}\ \mathrm{Negative} \Rightarrow \mathrm{n} \\
&\mathrm{Zero} \Rightarrow \mathrm{Nat'0} \\
&\mathrm{n}\ \mathbf{in}\ \mathrm{Positive} \Rightarrow \mathrm{n} \\
&\mathbf{endcase}
\end{aligned}
$$

We leave as an exercise to write axioms for the other *Int* functions.

Another example to show the use of labelled disjoint sums: The algebra *Bool could* have been specified as a labelled disjoint sum with carrier

$$Bool = \mathrm{True}{:}\ Unit + \mathrm{False}{:}\ Unit$$

Had we specified *Bool* like this, we would have had to introduce **true** and **false** as two 0-ary functions in ($\cdot \rightarrow$ *Bool*) with the following axioms:

$$\mathbf{true} = \mathrm{in\_True}(\iota), \quad \mathbf{false} = \mathrm{in\_False}(\iota)$$

Axioms for the other functions of *Bool* could then have been written as follows, using case notation (dropping 'ι **in**' everywhere):

$$
\begin{aligned}
\neg\, \mathrm{b} = \mathbf{case}\ \mathrm{b}\ \mathbf{of} \\
&\mathrm{True} \Rightarrow \mathbf{false} \\
&\mathrm{False} \Rightarrow \mathbf{true} \\
&\mathbf{endcase}
\end{aligned}
$$

$$
\begin{aligned}
\mathrm{b}_1 \wedge \mathrm{b}_2 = \mathbf{case}\ \mathrm{b}_1\ \mathbf{of} \\
&\mathrm{True} \Rightarrow \mathrm{b}_2 \\
&\mathrm{False} \Rightarrow \mathbf{false} \\
&\mathbf{endcase}
\end{aligned}
$$

A final example: We could have specified the algebra *Letter* (the original specification of this algebra is given in figure 4.4 on page 51) to be a disjoint sum with one addend for each letter:

$$Letter = \mathrm{a}{:}\ Unit + \mathrm{b}{:}\ Unit + \ldots + \mathrm{Z}{:}\ Unit$$

Had we done this, we could have specified the rank function (using case notation) as follows:

A^*:	*Finite sequences of A elements*		
Carrier:	A^*: *Inductively generated by* ε, $\vdash$		
Functions:	ε	$\in (\cdot \to A^*)$	(The empty sequence)
	$\vdash$	$\in (A \times A^* \to A^*)$	(Append at right end)
	$\dashv$	$\in (A \times A^* \to A^*)$	(Append at left end)
	$\vdash\!\dashv$	$\in (A^* \times A^* \to A^*)$	(Concatenate)
	$=$	$\in (A^* \times A^* \to Bool)$	(Equality)
	$\#$	$\in (A^* \to Nat)$	(Length)
	head	$\in (A^* \to A)$	(First element)
	tail	$\in (A^* \to A^*)$	(Remove first element)
	$\downarrow$	$\in (A^* \times Nat \to A)$	(Element number)
Axioms:	$s_1 \vdash\!\dashv \varepsilon = s_1, \; s_1 \vdash\!\dashv (s_2 \vdash a) = (s_1 \vdash\!\dashv s_2) \vdash a$		
	$\#\varepsilon = 0, \; \#(s \vdash a) = \#s + 1$		

Axioms for the other functions are left as exercises

Figure 4.8: The algebra of finite A sequences

```
rank(x) = case x of
              a  ⇒  1
              b  ⇒  2
              ...
              Z  ⇒  52
          endcase
```

4.3.3 Sequence algebras

Given an algebra A, we define the *sequence algebra* A^* to be the algebra which has a carrier that consists of every finite A sequence (including the empty sequence), and which has the following functions that may be used to generate, produce and observe sequences:

- The carrier of A^* is generated by two functions $\varepsilon \in (\cdot \to A^*)$ and $\vdash \in (A^* \times A \to A^*)$. ε denotes the empty sequence (it is a 0-ary function), and $\vdash$ is the *right append* function: for any $a \in A$ and any sequence $s = \langle s_1, \ldots, s_n \rangle \in A^*$, $s \vdash a = \langle s_1, \ldots, s_n, a \rangle$ is the result of appending a to the right end of s.

  Some notation: we use $\langle a_1, a_2, \ldots, a_n \rangle$ as 'shorthand' for the sequence $(\varepsilon \vdash a_1 \vdash a_2 \vdash \ldots \vdash a_n)$.

- A *left append* function $\dashv$ that appends an element in A to the left end of a sequence. For any $a \in A$ and any sequence $s = \langle s_1, \ldots, s_n \rangle \in A^*$, $a \dashv s = \langle a, s_1, \ldots, s_n \rangle$.

- A function $\vdash\!\dashv \in (A^* \times A^* \rightarrow A^*)$ that *concatenates* two sequences. If $s = \langle s_1, s_2, \ldots, s_m \rangle$ and $t = \langle t_1, t_2, \ldots, t_n \rangle$ are two sequences, $s \vdash\!\dashv t$ denotes the sequence $\langle s_1, s_2, \ldots, s_m, t_1, t_2, \ldots, t_n \rangle$.

- Two functions head $\in (A^* \rightarrow A)$ and tail $\in (A^* \rightarrow A^*)$ that find the *head* and *tail* of a given sequence. If $s = \langle s_1, s_2, \ldots, s_n \rangle$ is a non-empty sequence (i.e., $n > 0$), $s.\mathsf{head} = s_1$ and $s.\mathsf{tail} = \langle s_2, \ldots, s_n \rangle$. If $n = 1$, $s.\mathsf{tail} = \varepsilon$.

  Applying head or tail to an empty sequence is an error and the result is undefined.

- A function $\# \in (A^* \rightarrow Nat)$ that may be used to find the length of a sequence. Thus, $\#\langle s_1, s_2, \ldots, s_n \rangle = n$.

- A function $\downarrow \in (A^* \times Nat \rightarrow A)$ that may be used to find an element with a specified position in a given sequence. Thus, $\langle s_1, s_2, \ldots, s_n \rangle \downarrow i = s_i$ if $1 \leq i \leq n$. Should $i < 1$ or $n < i$, the value of $\langle s_1, s_2, \ldots, s_n \rangle \downarrow i$ is undefined.

- Finally, equality, which of course is a function in $(A^* \times A^* \rightarrow Bool)$. Two sequences are equal if they have the same length and their elements are pairwise equal. Thus, $\langle s_1, \ldots, s_m \rangle = \langle t_1, \ldots, t_n \rangle$ if and only if $n = m$ and $s_i = t_i$ for $i = 1, \ldots, n$.

Figure 4.8 shows how to specify the sequence algebra A^* for any given algebra A.

Another algebra which we sometimes need is the algebra A^+ of all *non-empty* finite A sequences. This algebra is of course quite similar to A^*, and it is not difficult to specify it. Its domain is generated by two generators: 1) singleton $\in (A \rightarrow A^+)$ and 2) the right append function $\vdash \in (A \times A^+ \rightarrow A^+)$. The function singleton may be used to generate sequences that consist of a single element, which means that the value of singleton(a) is the sequence $\langle a \rangle$. The right append function $\vdash$ is as specified for A^*. It is left as an exercise to make a specification for A^+.

4.3.4 Function algebras

Given two sets A and B, the algebra $(A \rightarrow B)$ has a carrier that consists of every function that maps A to B:

$$(A \rightarrow B) \stackrel{d}{=} \{f \mid f \textit{ is a function with } A \textit{ as domain and range} \subseteq B\}$$

It is sometimes natural to consider a function $f \in (A \rightarrow B)$ to be a set of pairs $\langle a, b \rangle$ where $a \in A$, $b \in B$ that satisfy certain conditions:

$$\begin{aligned}(A \rightarrow B) \stackrel{d}{=} \{f \subseteq A \times B \mid\ & \forall a \in A: \exists b \in B: \langle a, b \rangle \in f \wedge \\ & \forall a \in A: \forall b_1, b_2 \in B: \langle a, b_1 \rangle \in f \wedge \langle a, b_2 \rangle \in f \\ & \Rightarrow b_1 = b_2\}\end{aligned}$$

The following functions are defined in the algebra $(A \to B)$:

- A function constantfunc $\in (B \to (A \to B))$.

  This function is such that for every b $\in B$, constantfunc(b) is the function in $(A \to B)$ which has constant value b for every a $\in A$.

- A function apply $\in ((A \to B) \times A \to B)$.

  If f is a function in $(A \to B)$ and a is an element in A, the value of apply(f, a) is equal to f(a), i.e., the result of applying f to a. We will normally not use the apply function explicitly, but write just f(a) instead of apply(f, a). In the cases where apply is used explicitly, we will often use dot notation and write f.apply(a) instead of apply(f, a).

- A function bind $\in ((A \to B) \times A \times B \to (A \to B))$.

  If f is a function in $(A \to B)$, a is an element in A, and b is an element in B, the value of bind(f, a, b), which we often write as f.bind(a, b) using dot notation, is a function f' in $(A \to B)$. This new function is such that it has value b for argument a, and gives the same result as the original function f for all arguments that are not equal to a. We often write f[a := b] (this notation is introduced on page 19) instead of f.bind(a, b).

Observe that the functions apply and bind take functions as arguments, and that the functions constantfunc and bind have functions as values. Such *higher-order functions* - sometimes called *functionals* - are quite common when we specify the denotational semantics of a programming language.

Figure 4.9 shows how to specify the algebra $(A \to B)$ for two given algebras A and B.

An algebra which is quite similar to the algebra $(A \to B)$, but which for good reasons may be considered conceptually simpler, is the algebra $\mathcal{F}(A \to B)$ whose carrier consists of all functions from A to B that has a finite range. Thus, for every f $\in \mathcal{F}(A \to B)$, the set $\{f(a) \mid a \in A\}$ (which is the range of f) has only a finite number of distinct elements, all of which are elements of B. A specification for $\mathcal{F}(A \to B)$ is given in figure 4.10.

There are two reasons we say that $\mathcal{F}(A \to B)$ is simpler than $(A \to B)$. The first is that $\mathcal{F}(A \to B)$ is inductively generated, whereas $(A \to B)$ is not - and cannot be - inductively generated. The second is that whereas $(A \to B)$ contains uncountably many elements when A has at least two elements and B is countably infinite (as often will be the case), $\mathcal{F}(A \to B)$ is only countable under the same assumptions.

4.4 Constructing algebras

With very few exceptions, it is possible to construct every algebra we need to give denotational definitions of the semantics of programming

$(A \to B)$	*Every function that maps A to B*
Carrier:	$(A \to B) = \{\mathsf{f} \mid \mathsf{f}$ *is a function that maps A to B*$\}$
Functions:	constantfunc $\in (B \to (A \to B))$ bind $\in ((A \to B) \times A \times B \to (A \to B))$ apply $\in ((A \to B) \times A \to B)$
Axioms:	constantfunc(b).apply(a) = b f.bind(a_1, b).apply(a_2) = **if** $a_1 = a_2$ **then** b **else** f.apply(a_2)

Figure 4.9: The algebra of all functions that map A to B

$\mathcal{F}(A \to B)$	*Every finite range function that maps A to B*
Carrier:	$\mathcal{F}(A \to B)$: *Inductively generated by* constantfunc *and* bind
Functions:	constantfunc $\in (B \to \mathcal{F}(A \to B))$ bind $\in ((\mathcal{F}(A \to B) \times A \times B) \to \mathcal{F}(A \to B))$ apply $\in ((\mathcal{F}(A \to B) \times A) \to B)$
Axioms:	constantfunc(b).apply(a) = b f.bind(a_1, b).apply(a_2) = **if** $a_1 = a_2$ **then** b **else** f.apply(a_2)

Figure 4.10: The algebra of finite range functions

languages by starting with the very simple *Unit* algebra as the only basis algebra, and constructing more complex algebras using the algebra producers $(\_ \times \_)$, $(\_ + \_)$ and $(\_ \to \_)$, and also letting algebras be defined recursively in a simple manner. We define a set - it may be called a *meta-algebra* - $\mathcal{A}$lg of algebras as follows:

- *Unit* $\in \mathcal{A}$lg
- $A, B \in \mathcal{A}\text{lg} \Rightarrow (A \times B) \in \mathcal{A}\text{lg}, (A + B) \in \mathcal{A}\text{lg}, (A \to B) \in \mathcal{A}\text{lg}$
- If A is an algebra in $\mathcal{A}$lg and $\mathsf{F}(X)$ is an expression constructed from members of $\mathcal{A}$lg and the algebra variable X using only the algebra operator $(\_ \times \_)$, then the equation

  $$X = A + \mathsf{F}(X)$$

  has a solution which is an algebra in $\mathcal{A}$lg.

That the simple algebra *Bool* is in $\mathcal{A}$lg is obvious:

$$Bool = \text{True}: Unit \ + \ \text{False}: Unit$$

Nat is in $\mathcal{A}$lg because it may be defined *recursively*, i.e., as a solution of an algebra equation:

$$Nat = 0: Unit \ + \ \text{suc}: Nat$$

If A is an algebra in $\mathcal{A}$lg, then so is A^* and A^+:

$$A^* = \text{Empty}: Unit \ + \ \text{Append}: (A^* \times A)$$
$$A^+ = \text{Singleton}: A \ + \ \text{Append}: (A^+ \times A)$$

If A and B are algebras in $\mathcal{A}$lg, then so is $\mathcal{F}(A \to B)$:

$$\mathcal{F}(A \to B) = \text{constantfunc}: B \ + \ \text{bind}: (\mathcal{F}(A \to B) \times \mathcal{F}(A \to B))$$

It is not obvious that algebra equations are always solvable. How can we construct an algebra that satisfies equations like those used above to define *Nat* and A^*? In chapter 14 we will have much more to say about solving algebra equations of a special type, namely equations in which every participating algebra is a so-called *complete partial order* (this concept is defined in chapter 5). The equations used above are also of a special and very simple type, namely

$$X = A \ + \ (A_1 \ \times \ \ldots \ \times \ A_n)$$

where each A_i is either a previously defined algebra or the unknown X. An algebra X that satisfies such an equation may be defined by generator induction using two generators: in_A $\in (A \to X)$ is one, the other generator has signature $((A_1 \ \times \ \ldots \ \times \ A_n) \to X)$. Two examples: The generator determined by the expression suc: X has signature suc $\in (X \to X)$, and the expression Append: $(X \times A)$ gives rise to the generator Append $\in ((X \times A) \to X)$.

4.5 Modular, algebraic semantics

A modular, algebraic definition of the semantics of a programming language consists of

(1) *Syntax algebras* - which contain definitions of the so-called *abstract syntax* of the language. In section 4.5.1 below, we explain what abstract syntax is, and as an example show how to define syntax algebras for the language Loop introduced in chapter 2.

(2) *Semantic algebras* - which contain definitions of semantic domains and of various *auxiliary functions* (functions that we use to define the semantic mappings of the language).

The semantic algebras that are needed to define the semantics of Loop are defined in section 4.5.2.

(3) *Semantic mappings* - which map syntax algebras to semantic algebras. These mappings may be considered to be observers of syntax, i.e., they may be considered to be defined as functions in the syntax algebras.

In section 4.5.3 we show how to define semantic mappings for Loop.

4.5.1 Abstract syntax and syntax algebras

The BNF productions given on page 9 in section 2.1 define the *concrete syntax* of Loop, and may be used to generate strings that consist of *terminal symbols* (i.e., keywords, letters, semi-colons, etc.). In our context - where we are mainly interested in the *meaning* of programs, and not in their syntactic *appearance* - it is convenient to consider only the syntactic *structure* of the languages we describe, and forget about the precise details (often quite arcane) of their concrete syntax. We will therefore in the following define the syntax of the language in a more *abstract* manner (to be more abstract means - at least in this context - not to consider some of the concrete details), and define the so-called *abstract syntax* of our language.

The boundary between *abstract* and *concrete* is in general often quite fluid. But in our case we may at least point to the following distinctions:

- Concrete syntax describes strings of symbols, abstract syntax describes trees (often called *syntax trees*).
- A concrete symbol string is often *ambiguous*, i.e., it may be *parsed* in several ways; an abstract syntax tree is never ambiguous. (To *parse* a symbol string means to determine its grammatical structure, i.e., to construct a syntax tree for the string.)

We define an abstract syntax for a language by specifying one or more algebras. Taken together, these algebras should contain one carrier for each grammatical category of the language. Each of these carriers may be specified either inductively with one generator for each of the BNF productions that define the grammatical category associated with the carrier, or as a disjoint sum with one addend for each production of the associated category.

Figure 4.11 contains a specification of a syntax algebra for Loop. This algebra has six carriers, one for each grammatical category of Loop. Each of these carriers is specified to be a disjoint sum with one addend for each production that defines the corresponding grammatical category. A conceptual problem with the specifications given in figure 4.11 is that three of the carriers (viz. *Imp*, *Iexp* and *Bexp*) are defined *recursively*. It is not at all obvious that it is meaningful to define carriers in this manner. In a later chapter we will study these matters, and describe if/when it is meaningful to define carriers of algebras

Abstract syntax for Loop

Carriers: Program, Imp, Iexp, Bexp, Literal, Ident

$$
\begin{array}{lll}
\textit{Program} & = & \textit{Imp} \\
\textit{Imp} & = & \textsf{Skip}: \textit{Unit} \\
 & + & \textsf{Put}: \textit{Iexp} \\
 & + & \textsf{Get}: \textit{Ident} \\
 & + & \textsf{Assign}: \textit{Ident} \times \textit{Iexp} \\
 & + & \textsf{Sequence}: \textit{Imp} \times \textit{Imp} \\
 & + & \textsf{If}: \textit{Bexp} \times \textit{Imp} \times \textit{Imp} \\
 & + & \textsf{Loop}: \textit{Iexp} \times \textit{Imp} \\
\textit{Iexp} & = & \textsf{Constant}: \textit{Literal} \\
 & + & \textsf{Variable}: \textit{Ident} \\
 & + & \textsf{Sum}: \textit{Iexp} \times \textit{Iexp} \\
 & + & \textsf{Product}: \textit{Iexp} \times \textit{Iexp} \\
\textit{Bexp} & = & \textsf{Eql}: \textit{Iexp} \times \textit{Iexp} \\
 & + & \textsf{Less}: \textit{Iexp} \times \textit{Iexp} \\
 & + & \textsf{Not}: \textit{Bexp} \\
 & + & \textsf{And}: \textit{Bexp} \times \textit{Bexp} \\
\textit{Literal} & = & \textsf{0}: \textit{Unit} + \textsf{1}: \textit{Unit} + \textsf{Suc0}: \textit{Literal} + \textsf{Suc1}: \textit{Literal} \\
\textit{Ident} & = & \textit{Letter}^{+}
\end{array}
$$

Figure 4.11: Abstract syntax algebra for Loop, using disjoint sums

recursively. In the meantime it may be prudent to use the alternative specification of the abstract syntax of Loop given in figure 4.12. In this specification, there is one single-carrier algebra for each grammatical category of Loop. Each carrier is specified to be inductively generated, with one generator for each production of the associated grammatical category.

The reason we present two versions of the abstract syntax of Loop is not that we need both versions, but rather that these versions illustrate two different methods for specifying abstract syntax algebras.

It is easy to see how either of the specifications in figures 4.11 and 4.12 may be produced (automatically, if so desired), given BNF productions for a language like Loop. We presume the reader is more familiar with BNF productions than abstract syntax algebras. Such productions are also more compact to write than specifications of equivalent syntax algebras. We will therefore, in the rest of the book, often define the syntax of various programming languages by BNF productions, and assume that these productions are processed into equivalent specifi-

Program	*Programs*	
Carrier:	*Program* = *Imp*	
Imp	*Imperatives*	
Carrier:	*Imp*: *Generated by* skip, put, get, assign, seq, if, loop	
Functions:	skip	$\in (\cdot \to \mathit{Imp})$
	put	$\in (\mathit{Iexp} \to \mathit{Imp})$
	get	$\in (\mathit{Ident} \to \mathit{Imp})$
	assign	$\in (\mathit{Ident} \times \mathit{Iexp} \to \mathit{Imp})$
	seq	$\in (\mathit{Imp} \times \mathit{Imp} \to \mathit{Imp})$
	if	$\in (\mathit{Bexp} \times \mathit{Imp} \times \mathit{Imp} \to \mathit{Imp})$
	loop	$\in (\mathit{Iexp} \times \mathit{Imp} \to \mathit{Imp})$
Iexp	*Integer expressions*	
Carrier:	*Iexp*: *Generated by* constant, variable, sum, product	
Functions:	constant	$\in (\mathit{Literal} \to \mathit{Iexp})$
	variable	$\in (\mathit{Ident} \to \mathit{Iexp})$
	sum, product	$\in (\mathit{Iexp} \times \mathit{Iexp} \to \mathit{Iexp})$
Bexp	*Boolean expressions*	
Carrier:	*Bexp*: *Generated by* eql, less, not, and	
Functions:	eql, less	$\in (\mathit{Iexp} \times \mathit{Iexp} \to \mathit{Bexp})$
	not	$\in (\mathit{Bexp} \to \mathit{Bexp})$
	and	$\in (\mathit{Bexp} \times \mathit{Bexp} \to \mathit{Bexp})$
Literal	*Literals*	
Carrier:	*Literal*: *Generated by* 0, 1, suc0, suc1	
Functions:	0, 1	$\in (\cdot \to \mathit{Literal})$
	suc0, suc1	$\in (\mathit{Literal} \to \mathit{Literal})$
Ident	*Identifiers*	
Carrier:	$\mathit{Ident} = \mathit{Letter}^{+}$	

Figure 4.12: Inductively generated abstract syntax algebras for Loop

cations of abstract syntax algebras.

4.5.2 Semantic algebras

In chapter 2 we used four semantic domains to define the semantics of the programming language Loop, namely *Store* (mappings from identifiers to integers), *Input* (sequences of integers), *Output* (sequences of integers) and *State* (the Cartesian product of *Input*, *Store* and *Output*). Figure 4.13 contains specifications of one semantic algebra for each of these domains.

Observe that the semantic algebra *Store* is not specified to be the algebra of *all* functions that map *Ident* to *Int*, but rather to be the algebra of those functions from *Ident* to *Int* that have finite range. There are several reasons why we have chosen *Store* to be the restricted algebra $\mathcal{F}(Ident \to Int)$, and not the full algebra $(Ident \to Int)$. One reason is that any store that may be implemented on a finite computer is only able to store a finite number of distinct values. A store which is the result of executing a finite program on a finite computer in finite time using discrete time steps, will contain only a finite number of distinct values. Another reason is that there are far too many (uncountably many, in fact) functions in the set of *all* functions to a range that is infinite in size (like *Int*). We only need very few of these functions. Finally, the algebra $\mathcal{F}(Ident \to Int)$ is inductively generated, $(Ident \to Int)$ is not and (more importantly) *cannot* be inductively generated. We will later explain why inductively generated algebras are preferable to algebras that cannot be inductively generated.

4.5.3 Semantic mappings

In section 4.5.1 we presented two different specifications for the syntax of Loop. The *form* of the definitions of the semantic mappings of Loop - but not their *values*, if we avoid mistakes - will, of course, depend heavily upon which of these specifications is used. In figure 4.14 we show how to define semantic mappings for Loop under the assumption that the syntax specification given in figure 4.11 is used (in this specification, the carriers of the syntax algebra are specified to be disjoint sums), and in figure 4.15 we show how to define the same mappings assuming the syntax specification given in figure 4.12 (where the syntax algebras are inductively generated).

The semantic mappings defined in this section have signatures that are almost identical to the signatures of the semantic mappings defined for Loop in chapter 2. We have made only two seemingly slight changes. On figure 2.6 on page 16 in chapter 2, we defined the semantic mapping $\mathcal{V}$ to be a function in $(Iexp \to (Store \to Int))$. In the definitions given in this section, we replace *Store* by *State*. Thus, for any integer expression iexp, $\mathcal{V}[\![\text{iexp}]\!]$ is a function that maps a state (and not a store) to an integer. The reason for this change (and a similar change in the

Store

Carrier: $\mathit{Store} = \mathcal{F}(\mathit{Ident} \to \mathit{Int})$

Functions:

$$\begin{aligned} &\mathsf{assign} \in (\mathit{Store} \times \mathit{Ident} \times \mathit{Int} \to \mathit{Store}) \\ &\mathsf{default} \in (\cdot \to \mathit{Store}) \\ &\mathsf{access} \in (\mathit{Store} \times \mathit{Ident} \to \mathit{Int}) \end{aligned}$$

Axioms:

$$\begin{aligned} \mathsf{h.assign(id,\ n)} &= \mathsf{h[id := n]} \\ \mathsf{default} &= \mathsf{constantfunc(Int'0)} \\ \mathsf{h.access(id)} &= \mathsf{h.apply(id)} \end{aligned}$$

Input

Carrier: $\mathit{Input} = \mathsf{Int}^*$

Output

Carrier: $\mathit{Output} = \mathsf{Int}^*$

State

Carrier: $\mathit{State} = \mathit{Input} \times \mathit{Store} \times \mathit{Output}$

Functions:

$$\begin{aligned} &\mathsf{init} \in (\mathit{Input} \to \mathit{State}) \\ &\mathsf{put} \in (\mathit{State} \times \mathit{Int} \to \mathit{State}) \\ &\mathsf{get0} \in (\mathit{State} \times \mathit{Ident} \to \mathit{State}) \\ &\mathsf{assign} \in (\mathit{State} \times \mathit{Ident} \times \mathit{Int} \to \mathit{State}) \\ &\mathsf{access} \in (\mathit{State} \times \mathit{Ident} \to \mathit{Int}) \\ &\mathsf{repeat} \in ((\mathit{State} \to \mathit{State}) \times \mathit{Nat} \times \mathit{State} \to \mathit{State}) \end{aligned}$$

Axioms:

$$\begin{aligned} \mathsf{init(in)} &= \langle \mathsf{in},\ \mathit{Store}\mathsf{'default},\ \varepsilon \rangle \\ \langle \mathsf{in,\ h,\ out} \rangle \mathsf{.put(n)} &= \langle \mathsf{in,\ h,\ out} \vdash \mathsf{n} \rangle \\ \langle \varepsilon,\ \mathsf{h,\ out} \rangle \mathsf{.get0(id)} &= \langle \varepsilon,\ \mathsf{h.assign(id,\ 0),\ out} \rangle \\ \langle \mathsf{n} \dashv \mathsf{in,\ h,\ out} \rangle \mathsf{.get0(id)} &= \langle \mathsf{in,\ h.assign(id,\ n),\ out} \rangle \\ \langle \mathsf{in,\ h,\ out} \rangle \mathsf{.assign(id,\ n)} &= \langle \mathsf{in,\ h.assign(id,\ n),\ out} \rangle \\ \langle \mathsf{in,\ h,\ out} \rangle \mathsf{.access(id)} &= \mathsf{h.access(id)} \\ \mathsf{f.repeat(Nat'0,\ s)} &= \mathsf{s} \\ \mathsf{f.repeat(n.suc,\ s)} &= \mathsf{f.repeat(n,\ f(s))} \end{aligned}$$

Figure 4.13: Semantic algebras for Loop

definition of the semantic mapping $\mathcal{B}$) from what we did in chapter 2, is to make the definitions somewhat more abstract and modular. In the definitions of $\mathcal{V}$ and $\mathcal{B}$ given in chapter 2, it is necessary to know concrete details about the carrier of the ***State*** algebra (namely that it is defined as a Cartesian product). In the definitions given in this section

$$\mathcal{A} \in (\textit{Literal} \to \textit{Int})$$

$$(\textit{Literal} = 0\text{: } \textit{Unit} + 1\text{: } \textit{Unit} + \text{Suc0: } \textit{Literal} + \text{Suc1: } \textit{Literal})$$

$$\begin{array}{lrll} \mathcal{A}[\![\text{lit}]\!] = \textbf{case}\ \text{lit}\ \textbf{of} & \iota & \textbf{in}\ 0 & \Rightarrow 0 \\ & \iota & \textbf{in}\ 1 & \Rightarrow 1 \\ & \text{lit}_1 & \textbf{in}\ \text{suc0} & \Rightarrow \mathcal{A}[\![\text{lit}_1]\!] * 2 \\ & \text{lit}_1 & \textbf{in}\ \text{suc1} & \Rightarrow (\mathcal{A}[\![\text{lit}_1]\!] * 2) + 1 \end{array}$$

$$\mathcal{V} \in (\textit{Iexp} \to (\textit{State} \to \textit{Int}))$$

$$\begin{array}{lll} (\textit{Iexp} = & \text{Constant: } \textit{Literal} & + \text{ Variable: } \textit{Ident} \\ & + \text{ Sum: } \textit{Iexp} \times \textit{Iexp} & + \text{ Product: } \textit{Iexp} \times \textit{Iexp}) \end{array}$$

$$\begin{array}{lll} \multicolumn{3}{l}{\mathcal{V}[\![\text{ie}]\!] = \lambda \text{s} \in \textit{State}\text{: } \textbf{case}\ \text{ie}\ \textbf{of}} \\ \text{lit} & \textbf{in}\ \text{Constant} & \Rightarrow \mathcal{A}[\![\text{lit}]\!] \\ \text{id} & \textbf{in}\ \text{Variable} & \Rightarrow \text{s.access(id)} \\ \langle \text{ie}_1, \text{ie}_2 \rangle & \textbf{in}\ \text{Sum} & \Rightarrow \mathcal{V}[\![\text{ie}_1]\!](\text{s}) + \mathcal{V}[\![\text{ie}_2]\!](\text{s}) \\ \langle \text{ie}_1, \text{ie}_2 \rangle & \textbf{in}\ \text{Product} & \Rightarrow \mathcal{V}[\![\text{ie}_1]\!](\text{s}) * \mathcal{V}[\![\text{ie}_2]\!](\text{s}) \end{array}$$

$$\mathcal{B} \in (\textit{Bexp} \to (\textit{State} \to \textit{Bool}))$$

$$\begin{array}{lll} (\textit{Bexp} = & \text{Eql: } \textit{Iexp} \times \textit{Iexp} & + \text{ Less: } \textit{Iexp} \times \textit{Iexp} \\ & + \text{ Not: } \textit{Bexp} & + \text{ And: } \textit{Bexp} \times \textit{Bexp}) \end{array}$$

$$\begin{array}{lll} \multicolumn{3}{l}{\mathcal{B}[\![\text{be}]\!] = \lambda \text{s} \in \textit{State}\text{: } \textbf{case}\ \text{be}\ \textbf{of}} \\ \langle \text{ie}_1, \text{ie}_2 \rangle & \textbf{in}\ \text{Eql} & \Rightarrow \mathcal{V}[\![\text{ie}_1]\!](\text{s}) = \mathcal{V}[\![\text{ie}_2]\!](\text{s}) \\ \langle \text{ie}_1, \text{ie}_2 \rangle & \textbf{in}\ \text{Less} & \Rightarrow \mathcal{V}[\![\text{ie}_1]\!](\text{s}) < \mathcal{V}[\![\text{ie}_2]\!](\text{s}) \\ \text{be}_1 & \textbf{in}\ \text{Not} & \Rightarrow \neg\ \mathcal{B}[\![\text{be}_1]\!](\text{s}) \\ \langle \text{be}_1, \text{be}_2 \rangle & \textbf{in}\ \text{And} & \Rightarrow \mathcal{B}[\![\text{be}_1]\!](\text{s}) \wedge \mathcal{B}[\![\text{be}_2]\!](\text{s}) \end{array}$$

$$\mathcal{M} \in (\textit{Imp} \to (\textit{State} \to \textit{State}))$$

$$\begin{array}{l} (\textit{Imp} = \text{Skip: } \textit{Unit} + \text{Put: } \textit{Iexp} + \text{Get: } \textit{Ident} + \text{Assign: } \textit{Ident} \times \textit{Iexp} \\ \quad + \text{ Seq: } \textit{Imp} \times \textit{Imp} + \text{If: } \textit{Iexp} \times \textit{Imp} \times \textit{Imp} + \text{Loop: } \textit{Iexp} \times \textit{Imp}) \end{array}$$

$$\begin{array}{lll} \multicolumn{3}{l}{\mathcal{M}[\![\text{imp}]\!] = \lambda \text{s} \in \textit{State}\text{: } \textbf{case}\ \text{imp}\ \textbf{of}} \\ \iota & \textbf{in}\ \text{Skip} & \Rightarrow \text{s} \\ \text{ie} & \textbf{in}\ \text{Put} & \Rightarrow \text{s.put}(\mathcal{V}[\![\text{ie}]\!](\text{s})) \\ \text{id} & \textbf{in}\ \text{Get} & \Rightarrow \text{s.get0(id)} \\ \langle \text{id}, \text{ie} \rangle & \textbf{in}\ \text{Assign} & \Rightarrow \text{s.assign(id, } \mathcal{V}[\![\text{ie}]\!](\text{s})) \\ \langle \text{i}_1, \text{i}_2 \rangle & \textbf{in}\ \text{Seq} & \Rightarrow \mathcal{M}[\![\text{i}_2]\!](\mathcal{M}[\![\text{i}_1]\!](\text{s})) \\ \langle \text{be}, \text{i}_1, \text{i}_2 \rangle & \textbf{in}\ \text{If} & \Rightarrow \textbf{if}\ \mathcal{B}[\![\text{be}]\!](\text{s})\ \textbf{then}\ \mathcal{M}[\![\text{i}_1]\!](\text{s})\ \textbf{else}\ \mathcal{M}[\![\text{i}_2]\!](\text{s}) \\ \langle \text{ie}, \text{i}_1 \rangle & \textbf{in}\ \text{Loop} & \Rightarrow \mathcal{M}[\![\text{i}_1]\!]\text{.repeat}(\mathcal{V}[\![\text{ie}]\!](\text{s})\text{.abs, s}) \end{array}$$

$$\mathcal{P} \in (\textit{Program} \to (\textit{Input} \to \textit{Output}))$$

$$(\textit{Program} = \text{Imp})$$

$$\mathcal{P}[\![\text{p}]\!] = \lambda \text{inp} \in \textit{Input}\text{: } \mathcal{M}[\![\text{p}]\!](\text{State'init(inp)})\text{.Output}$$

Figure 4.14: Semantic mappings for Loop

$\mathcal{A} \in (\mathit{Literal} \to \mathit{Int})$

($\mathit{Literal}$ is generated by 0, 1, suc0, suc1)

$$\begin{aligned}
\mathcal{A}[\![0]\!] &= \mathsf{Int'0}\\
\mathcal{A}[\![1]\!] &= \mathsf{Int'0.suc}\\
\mathcal{A}[\![\mathsf{lit.suc0}]\!] &= \mathcal{A}[\![\mathsf{lit}]\!] * 2\\
\mathcal{A}[\![\mathsf{lit.suc1}]\!] &= (\mathcal{A}[\![\mathsf{lit}]\!] * 2) + 1
\end{aligned}$$

$\mathcal{V} \in (\mathit{Iexp} \to (\mathit{State} \to \mathit{Int}))$

(Iexp is generated by constant, variable, sum, product)

$$\begin{aligned}
\mathcal{V}[\![\mathsf{constant(lit)}]\!] &= \lambda \mathsf{s} \in \mathit{State}\colon \mathcal{A}[\![\mathsf{lit}]\!]\\
\mathcal{V}[\![\mathsf{variable(id)}]\!] &= \lambda \mathsf{s} \in \mathit{State}\colon \mathsf{s.access(v)}\\
\mathcal{V}[\![\mathsf{sum(ie_1,\ ie_2)}]\!] &= \lambda \mathsf{s} \in \mathit{State}\colon \mathcal{V}[\![\mathsf{ie_1}]\!](\mathsf{s}) + \mathcal{V}[\![\mathsf{ie_2}]\!](\mathsf{s})\\
\mathcal{V}[\![\mathsf{product(ie_1,\ ie_2)}]\!] &= \lambda \mathsf{s} \in \mathit{State}\colon \mathcal{V}[\![\mathsf{ie_1}]\!](\mathsf{s}) * \mathcal{V}[\![\mathsf{ie_2}]\!](\mathsf{s})
\end{aligned}$$

$\mathcal{B} \in (\mathit{Bexp} \to (\mathit{State} \to \mathit{Bool}))$

(Bexp is generated by eql, less, not, and)

$$\begin{aligned}
\mathcal{B}[\![\mathsf{eql(ie_1,\ ie_2)}]\!] &= \lambda \mathsf{s} \in \mathit{State}\colon \mathcal{V}[\![\mathsf{ie_1}]\!](\mathsf{s}) = \mathcal{V}[\![\mathsf{ie_2}]\!](\mathsf{s})\\
\mathcal{B}[\![\mathsf{less(ie_1,\ ie_2)}]\!] &= \lambda \mathsf{s} \in \mathit{State}\colon \mathcal{V}[\![\mathsf{ie_1}]\!](\mathsf{s}) < \mathcal{V}[\![\mathsf{ie_2}]\!](\mathsf{s})\\
\mathcal{B}[\![\mathsf{not(be)}]\!] &= \lambda \mathsf{s} \in \mathit{State}\colon \neg\ \mathcal{B}[\![\mathsf{be}]\!](\mathsf{s})\\
\mathcal{B}[\![\mathsf{and(be_1,\ be_2)}]\!] &= \lambda \mathsf{s} \in \mathit{State}\colon \mathcal{B}[\![\mathsf{be_1}]\!](\mathsf{s}) < \mathcal{B}[\![\mathsf{be_2}]\!](\mathsf{s})
\end{aligned}$$

$\mathcal{M} \in (\mathit{Imp} \to (\mathit{State} \to \mathit{State}))$

(Imp is generated by skip, put, get, assign, seq, if, loop)

$$\begin{aligned}
\mathcal{M}[\![\mathsf{skip}]\!] &= \lambda \mathsf{s} \in \mathit{State}\colon \mathsf{s}\\
\mathcal{M}[\![\mathsf{put(ie)}]\!] &= \lambda \mathsf{s} \in \mathit{State}\colon \mathsf{s.put}(\mathcal{V}[\![\mathsf{ie}]\!](\mathsf{s}))\\
\mathcal{M}[\![\mathsf{get(id)}]\!] &= \lambda \mathsf{s} \in \mathit{State}\colon \mathsf{s.get0(id)}\\
\mathcal{M}[\![\mathsf{assign(id,\ ie)}]\!] &= \lambda \mathsf{s} \in \mathit{State}\colon \mathsf{s.assign}(\mathsf{id},\ \mathcal{V}[\![\mathsf{ie}]\!](\mathsf{s}))\\
\mathcal{M}[\![\mathsf{seq(i_1,\ i_2)}]\!] &= \lambda \mathsf{s} \in \mathit{State}\colon \mathcal{M}[\![\mathsf{i_2}]\!](\mathcal{M}[\![\mathsf{i_1}]\!](\mathsf{s}))\\
\mathcal{M}[\![\mathsf{if(be,\ i_1,\ i_2)}]\!] &= \lambda \mathsf{s} \in \mathit{State}\colon \mathbf{if}\ \mathcal{B}[\![\mathsf{be}]\!](\mathsf{s})\ \mathbf{then}\ \mathcal{M}[\![\mathsf{i_1}]\!](\mathsf{s})\\
&\qquad\qquad\qquad\qquad\qquad\quad \mathbf{else}\ \mathcal{M}[\![\mathsf{i_2}]\!](\mathsf{s})\\
\mathcal{M}[\![\mathsf{loop(ie,\ imp)}]\!] &= \lambda \mathsf{s} \in \mathit{State}\colon \mathcal{M}[\![\mathsf{imp}]\!]\mathsf{.repeat}(\mathcal{V}[\![\mathsf{ie}]\!](\mathsf{s})\mathsf{.abs},\ \mathsf{s})
\end{aligned}$$

$\mathcal{P} \in (\mathit{Program} \to (\mathit{Input} \to \mathit{Output}))$

$(\mathit{Program} = \mathit{Imp})$

$$\mathcal{P}[\![\mathsf{p}]\!] = \lambda \mathsf{inp} \in \mathit{Input}\colon \mathcal{M}[\![\mathsf{p}]\!](\mathsf{State'init(inp)})\mathsf{.Output}$$

Figure 4.15: Alternative definition of semantic mappings for Loop. The syntax algebras and their generators are specified in figure 4.12

it is only necessary to know signature of the ***State*** algebra, and nothing about its carrier.

4.6 Compositionality

The definitions of the semantical mappings as defined in figures 4.14 and 4.15 are such that the denotation of any composite syntactical object is given in terms of the denotations of its immediate constituents. Any definition which satisfies this demand is said to be *compositional.*

A denotational definition of the semantics of a programming language is such that any syntactically correct construct of the language is assigned a well-defined mathematical object, which we say is the denotation of the object. One way of ensuring that all denotations are well defined, is by letting all syntax algebras be inductively generated, and demanding that all semantical mappings are defined by generator induction, i.e, that the definitions are compositional.

4.7 Exercises

4.7.1 Integers

Specify the functions addition, multiplication and equality for the algebra ***Int*** of integers. Use first the specification for this algebra given in figure 4.6 at the end of section 4.3.1 (where ***Int*** is specified to be a Cartesian product), and then the specification for the same algebra given at the end of section 4.3.2 (here ***Int*** is specified to be a labelled disjoint sum).

4.7.2 The rational numbers

A *rational number* may be defined to be a quotient between two integers, a *nominator* and a *denominator*, the latter not equal to 0. Specify an algebra for the rational numbers.

4.7.3 Sequence functions

Signatures for the sequence functions tail, =, head and el_nr are given in figure 4.8. Make axioms that specify these functions.

4.7.4 Non-empty sequences

Specify the algebra A^+ which has a carrier that consists of all non-empty finite sequences of A elements.

4.7.5 Finite sets

Specify an algebra for finite sets of elements from some given algebra A. The algebra should be inductively generated (you should decide which functions to use as generators), and contain common set operations like $\in$, $\cup$, $\cap$ and equality.

4.7.6 Arrays

Specify an algebra for one-dimensional arrays of elements from some given algebra A. New arrays may be generated by new(hi, lo, def) where new is a function that generates arrays, hi, lo are integers, and def $\in A$ is a default element. An array arr may be updated by arr.update(ind, val), where ind is an integer and val $\in A$, and accessed by arr.access(ind).

Chapter 5
Fixpoint theory

5.1 Undefined operations and infinite loops

In the next chapter we define a new language, which we call While, by extending the language Loop with a few new constructs. These constructs introduce some problems not encountered in Loop (this latter language was, in fact, designed so as to avoid these problems):

Undefined operations and errors: We include division as an operator in While, and must then prepare for the possibility of division by 0. Furthermore, we abandon the unrealistic assumption that storage cells can store integers of any size, and must hence devise a method for handling arithmetic overflow.

Infinite loops: We include imperatives of the form

while bexp **do** imp **od**

with obvious informal operational semantics: execute the imperative imp as long as the Boolean expression bexp is true. Execution of such imperatives may obviously last forever (at least in theory), which entails that a method for handling infinite loops must be devised.

It is not obvious how, and even if, the techniques used in the previous chapter can be applied to define the semantics of these new constructs. We have to decide what to use as value of, for instance,

$$\mathcal{V}[\![(\mathsf{x} \mathbin{/} \mathsf{y})]\!](\mathsf{h})$$

if the store h is such that $\mathsf{h}(\mathsf{y}) = 0$, and also how to define

$$\mathcal{M}[\![\textbf{while 1 = 1 do skip od}]\!](\mathsf{s})$$

for any state s.

One way of treating such problems is to let the semantic mappings be *partial functions*, i.e., let them be *undefined* for certain arguments. But we do not consider this approach to be a very satisfactory solution. One disadvantage is that it introduces discrepancies with the intuitive, informal semantics of programming languages. When, for instance, a real computer executes a program that performs division by 0, the result is not undefined, but some error message.

We think it is a better solution to introduce special *error elements,* which stand for the result of performing illegal operations like division by 0. We may then define the denotations of expressions (integer and Boolean) to be *total* functions, i.e., functions that have defined values for every argument. It is perhaps tempting to introduce one error element for each kind of error that possibly may occur during execution of programs. But in order to reduce the number of details we have to consider, we will introduce only a single error element in each domain.

By letting the result of an infinite loop be an error element - a special *error state* - we may even define the denotations of **while** imperatives (and imperatives in general) to be total functions.

If we denote the error elements introduced in the domains *Int* and *State* by $\perp_{Int}$ and $\perp_{State}$ respectively (the symbol $\perp$ is pronounced *bottom,* for reasons to be made clear later in this chapter), we are going to define the semantic mappings $\mathcal{V}$ and $\mathcal{M}$ such that

$$\mathcal{V}[\![(\mathsf{x} \mathbin{/} \mathsf{y})]\!](\mathsf{h}) = \perp_{Int}$$

if the store h is such that $\mathsf{h}(\mathsf{y}) = 0$, and

$$\mathcal{M}[\![\textbf{while 1 = 1 do skip od}]\!](\mathsf{s}) = \perp_{State}$$

for any state s.

This technique for handling errors and infinite loops is - as can be seen in the following sections and chapters - quite general and flexible. But some care must be taken if it is to work. We must, for instance, extend the definitions of many functions (like ordinary addition of integers) such that they behave correctly should any of their arguments be error elements. We show how to do this later in this chapter.

Errors like division by 0 are, of course, very different from errors that consist in entering an infinite loop: Whereas so-called *runtime errors* may be discovered, and even compensated for, when a program is executed, this is not possible for infinite looping. The reason this is impossible, is that it has been proved - by Alan Turing, in a proof outside the scope of this book - to be impossible to construct a program that would determine whether a given program halts or enters an infinite loop for some given input. It may be argued that we should therefore distinguish between runtime errors and infinite loops by using two different error elements in the semantic algebras, at least in some of them. We choose, however, not to do that, mainly because it would clutter up many of the definitions of semantic mappings to be given in the following chapters.

5.2 Recursively defined mappings

Determining the denotations of errors and infinite loops is not the only problem we encounter when we try to employ the ideas from the previous chapters to define the semantics of the While language. According to these ideas, imperatives should have functions that map states to states as their denotations. Thus, the denotation of a given **while** imperative **while** be **do** imp **od** should be a function mw $\in$ (*State* $\rightarrow$ *State*). By our intuitive understanding of how **while** imperatives are executed, mw should satisfy the following equation for any state s:

$$(\alpha):\ \ \mathsf{mw(s)} = \textbf{if } \mathcal{B}[\![\mathsf{be}]\!](\mathsf{s}) \textbf{ then } \mathsf{mw}(\mathcal{M}[\![\mathsf{imp}]\!](\mathsf{s})) \textbf{ else } \mathsf{s} \textbf{ fi}$$

For anyone who is used to programming languages in which recursive procedures are allowed, it is tempting to take this equation to be a definition of mw and hence a definition of the semantics of the given **while** imperative. But doing this would leave us with the problem of defining the semantics of recursive procedures - and this problem does not seem to be any simpler than defining the semantics of **while** imperatives. It would therefore be like putting the cart in front of the horse to use equation (α) as a definition of the semantics of a **while** imperative. We may try to circumvent the problem by writing (α) as follows:

$$\begin{aligned}(\beta):\ \ &\mathcal{M}[\![\textbf{while}\ \mathsf{be}\ \textbf{do}\ \mathsf{imp}\ \textbf{od}]\!](\mathsf{s}) \\ &\quad = \textbf{if } \mathcal{B}[\![\mathsf{be}]\!](\mathsf{s}) \textbf{ then } \mathcal{M}[\![\textbf{while}\ \mathsf{be}\ \textbf{do}\ \mathsf{imp}\ \textbf{od}]\!](\mathcal{M}[\![\mathsf{imp}]\!](\mathsf{s})) \\ &\quad\qquad \textbf{else}\ \ \mathsf{s}\end{aligned}$$

May this equation be taken as a definition of $\mathcal{M}[\![$**while** be **do** imp **od**$]\!]$? It is obvious that (β) describes how to execute the **while** imperative for a given start state s: First, evaluate the Boolean expression be for s.Store. Should the value be **false**, stop the execution with s as the end state. Should the value of be for s be **true**, repeat the execution of the whole imperative, using the state as it is after having executed the imperative imp from s as new start state. Equation (β) may hence be used as an *operational* definition of the semantics of the **while** imperative. But such a definition presupposes that we have previously defined what it means to *evaluate*, *execute* and *repeat*. We may of course define these concepts in terms of a computer which follows some given algorithm, but then we are left with the problem of defining this computer and its algorithm - which seems to be a rather complex problem, certainly much more involved than our original problem.

What we would like to do, is to define the denotation of **while** imperatives to be a well-defined mathematical object, just as we do for any other syntactical object. In chapter 2 we defined semantical mappings by induction on syntactic complexity: The denotation of any composite syntactical object was defined in terms of the denotations of its immediate constituents. When we define a mapping in this way - which certainly is mathematically acceptable - the mapping is defined compositionally (this concept is defined in section 4.6). Equation (β) is not compositional: the denotation of the **while** imperative is not defined in terms of the denotations of its two immediate constituents (i.e., be and imp), but rather in terms of the denotations of its two constituents *and of itself*. Equation (β) may therefore not be used to define the semantics of **while** imperative by induction on syntactic complexity.

In order to give a mathematically acceptable definition of the semantics of **while** imperatives, we return to equation (α). It is obvious that if we are able to find a function mw $\in$ $(State \to State)$ that satisfies (α), we may define the denotation of the **while** imperative to be equal to mw. Given some experience with programming in a language that allows recursively defined functions, our intuition tells us that such a function does indeed exist. We know very well what happens when a **while** imperative is executed on a computer, and we know that the equation given in (α) for mw can be used as a recursive definition of mw. But not all equations like the one given for mw can be used as definitions of functions. Some examples of this will be given below, but before we do that, we introduce some notation that will be convenient to use here and later:

> When we define a function f $\in$ $(A \to B)$, we usually do it by explaining how the function may be evaluated for any argument a. This explanation is often given in the form
>
> $$\text{For every } a \in A\text{: } f(a) = \ldots a \ldots a \ldots$$
>
> where '...a...a...' is a formula in which a may occur. Often it is more convenient to define the same function using so-called *lambda notation*. We then write
>
> $$f \stackrel{d}{=} \lambda a \in A\!: \ldots a \ldots a \ldots$$
>
> The expression $\lambda a \in A\!: \ldots a \ldots a \ldots$ may be read as follows: *the function that maps an argument* a $\in$ *A to a value that may be found by evaluating ... a... a...*

> An example: Assume that the function pp is defined as follows
>
> $$\mathsf{pp} \stackrel{d}{=} \lambda n \in \mathit{Nat}: 2 * n + n * (n+1)$$
>
> We may then find the value of pp applied to, for instance, the integer 4 by evaluating the formula $2 * n + n * (n+1)$ after substituting 4 for n, i.e., $2 * 4 + 4 * (4+1)$.

After this brief detour to the outskirts of the 'lambda world', we return to the problems of recursive definitions and present three simple examples: Can the following equations be used as acceptable recursive definitions of functions f_1, f_2 and f_3 that map *Nat* to *Nat*?

$$(\gamma_1): \quad f_1 = \lambda x \in \mathit{Int}: f_1(x) + 1$$
$$(\gamma_2): \quad f_2 = \lambda x \in \mathit{Int}: f_2(x)$$
$$(\gamma_3): \quad f_3 = \lambda x \in \mathit{Int}: \textbf{if } x = 0 \textbf{ then } 1 \textbf{ else } f_3(x-1)*x$$

It is obvious that the equations γ_1, γ_2 and γ_3 given above are problematic if used as recursive definitions of functions f_1, f_2 and f_3: *No* function (except the totally undefined) satisfies the first equation, *every* function from *Nat* to *Nat* satisfies the second, and a single function (the factorial function) satisfies the last. It should be obvious that equations similar to these three and the one in (α), cannot always be used to define functions uniquely and completely. Can we then be quite certain that equation (α) submitted as a definition of mw (and hence of **while** imperatives) really defines mw completely and uniquely?

What (α) really says is that the denotation of a **while** imperative should be a function mw that satisfies the following equation:

$$\mathsf{mw} = \mathsf{QW}(\mathsf{mw})$$

where QW is a function defined as follows:

$$\lambda \mathsf{mw} \in \mathit{SS}: \lambda s \in \mathit{State}: \textbf{if } \mathcal{B}[\![\mathsf{be}]\!](s) \textbf{ then } \mathsf{mw}(\mathcal{M}[\![\mathsf{imp}]\!](s)) \textbf{ else } s \textbf{ fi}$$

where $\mathit{SS} \stackrel{d}{=} (\mathit{State} \to \mathit{State})$.

A solution x of an equation $x = f(x)$ is said to be a *fixpoint* of f. What we are looking for then is a fixpoint of the function QW. But can we be certain that this function really has a fixpoint? Which fixpoint should be used if QW should have more than one?

In the rest of this chapter we introduce some mathematical concepts and tools which may help us to determine which functions have fixpoints and to find fixpoints of those that do. In particular, we state and prove a theorem - the *Fixpoint Theorem* - which says that equations like α, γ_1, γ_2 and γ_3 may be used to define functions, and also shows which functions are defined by such equations.

The reader should be warned that the next few sections will present some material the way mathematics traditionally is presented, namely *bottom-up*: First some definitions, then some propositions, then more definitions, and more propositions, etc., etc., before we finally present something useful. It will not be clear until the next chapter that the terms defined and the propositions proved in this chapter have much to do with defining the semantics of programming languages. Should we, however, have tried to present the material of this chapter in a *top-down* manner, the chapter would have been much longer and probably more difficult to understand.

5.3 Complete partial orders

5.3.1 Partial orders

A *binary relation* over a set C may be looked upon in two equivalent ways: Either as a subset of the Cartesian product $C \times C$, or as a function with signature $(C \times C \rightarrow Bool)$. If $\sqsubseteq$ is a binary relation, we normally use $\sqsubseteq$ as an *infixed* symbol, and write '$c \sqsubseteq d$' to express that (c, d) is in the set $\sqsubseteq$, or (equivalently) that the value of the function application $\sqsubseteq(c, d)$ is equal to the element **true** $\in Bool$.

A binary relation $\sqsubseteq$ over a set C is said to be *reflexive* if and only if $x \sqsubseteq x$ for every $x \in C$, it is *transitive* if and only if $x \sqsubseteq y$ and $y \sqsubseteq z$ imply that $x \sqsubseteq z$ for every $x, y, z \in C$, and it is *anti-symmetric* if and only if $x \sqsubseteq y$ and $y \sqsubseteq x$ imply that $x = y$ for every $x, y \in C$. We write $c \sqsubset d$ to express that $c \sqsubseteq d$ but $c \neq d$.

A binary relation over a set C which is reflexive, transitive and anti-symmetric, is said to be a *partial ordering* of C. An algebra which contains among its operations a binary relation which partially orders the carrier of the algebra, is said to be a *partial order* under that relation.

We will often consider several partial orders at the same time. In order to distinguish between the different partial orderings, we will - if there is any serious chance of misunderstanding - suffix the name of the algebra to the name of the ordering, and use for instance $\sqsubseteq_C$ to denote a partial ordering of an algebra C.

Some examples:

(1) The set $Nat = \{0, 1, 2, \ldots\}$ of non-negative integers is partially ordered by the relation 'less than or equal' (i.e., $\leq$), but not by $<$.

(2) The relation '**divides**' (i.e., x **divides** y if and only if x is a divisor of y) is a partial ordering of the set of positive integers.

(3) The set $\{1, 2, \ldots n\}$ is partially ordered by both $\leq$ and **divides**.

(4) The set $Bool$ = {**false**, **true**} is partially ordered by the relations $\preceq_{f<t}$ and $\preceq_{t<f}$ defined by:

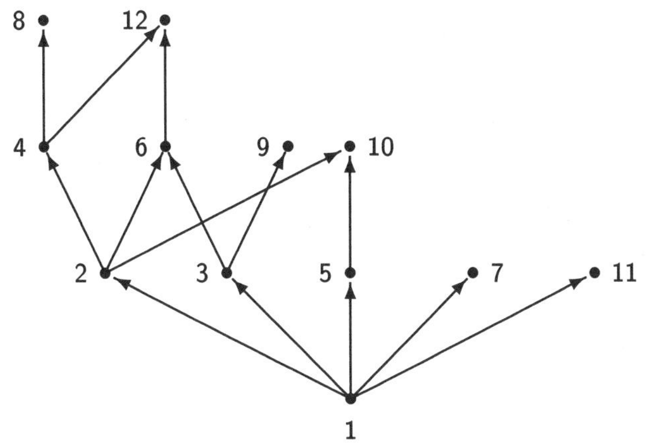

Figure 5.1: The integers {1, 2, ..., 12} ordered by divides

$$x \preceq_{\mathsf{f<t}} y \overset{d}{\iff} (x = \textbf{false} \vee x = y)$$
$$x \preceq_{\mathsf{t<f}} y \overset{d}{\iff} (x = \textbf{true} \vee x = y)$$

We use $Bool_{\mathsf{f<t}}$ to denote the algebra that has *Bool* as its carrier and which is ordered by $\preceq_{\mathsf{f<t}}$. The algebra $Bool_{\mathsf{t<f}}$ has the same carrier, but is ordered by $\preceq_{\mathsf{t<f}}$.

(5) The *powerset* $\mathcal{P}(A)$ ($\overset{d}{=}$ the set that consists of all subsets of the set A) of any set A is partially ordered by the subset relation (i.e., $\subseteq$).

It is often helpful to visualize a partial order by drawing the elements of the order as points, and connecting two points x and y with an arrow from x to y if $x \sqsubset y$ and there is no z such that $x \sqsubset z \sqsubset y$. An example is given in figure 5.1, which visualizes the partial order that consists of the integers {1, 2, ..., 12} ordered by divides.

5.3.2 Chains

An infinite sequence $\langle c_0, c_1, c_2, \ldots \rangle$ of elements c_i in a set C which is partially ordered by a relation $\sqsubseteq$, is said to be a $\sqsubseteq$ *chain in C* (or just *chain in C*, or even simply *chain*, when no reasonable misunderstanding should be possible), if and only if $c_i \sqsubseteq c_{i+1}$ for $i = 0, 1, 2, \ldots$ We will frequently use $\{c_i\}_{i=0}^{\infty}$ to denote the sequence $\langle c_0, c_1, c_2, \ldots \rangle$.

Some examples:

(1) The infinite sequence $\{2 * i + 1\}_{i=0}^{\infty} = \langle 1, 3, 5, 7, \ldots \rangle$ of odd positive integers is a $\leq$ chain in *Nat*, but not a **divides** chain.

(2) The infinite sequence $\{2^i\}_{i=0}^{\infty} = \langle 2, 4, 8, 16, 32, \ldots \rangle$ of powers of 2, is a $\leq$ chain and a **divides** chain in *Nat*.

(3) The chain $\{1\}_{i=0}^{\infty} = \langle 1, 1, 1, \ldots \rangle$ (i.e., an infinite sequence where every element is equal to 1) is a chain in *Nat* for any partial ordering of *Nat*.

(4) An infinite sequence $\langle$**false**, **false**, ..., **false**, **true**, **true**, ...$\rangle$ (a sequence which first has a finite number of **false**'s and then an infinite number of **true**'s), is a chain in the partial ordering $\preceq_{f<t}$ of $Bool_{f<t}$ defined in section 5.3.1 above.

(5) Let us for each $i \geq 0$ define the set X_i as follows:

$$X_i \stackrel{d}{=} \{1, 3, 5, \ldots, 2 * i + 1\}$$

Then $\{X_i\}_{i=0}^{\infty}$ is a $\subseteq$ chain in $\mathcal{P}(Nat)$.

(6) If we let the real number r_i be equal to $1 - 2^{-i}$ for each $i \geq 0$, then $\{r_i\}_{i=0}^{\infty}$ is a $\leq$ chain in $E = \{r \mid 0 \leq r \leq 1\}$.

5.3.3 Least upper bounds

An element c^* is said to be an *upper bound* of a chain $\{c_i\}_{i=0}^{\infty}$ if and only if $c_i \sqsubseteq c^*$ for $i = 0, 1, 2, \ldots$ It is said to be the *least upper bound* of the chain if $c^* \sqsubseteq c'$ for any other upper bound c' of the chain. Thus, c^* is the least upper bound of a chain $\{c_i\}_{i=0}^{\infty}$ if and only if

- $\forall i \in Nat: c_i \sqsubseteq c^*$
- $\forall c' \in C: (\forall i \in Nat: c_i \sqsubseteq c') \Rightarrow c^* \sqsubseteq c'$

Some examples:

(1) The $\leq$ chain $\langle 1, 3, 5, 7, \ldots \rangle$ in *Nat* does not have any upper bounds.

(2) The $\leq$ chain cc $\stackrel{d}{=} \langle 0, 0.9, 0.99, 0.999, \ldots \rangle$ of real numbers has 1 as its least upper bound. Observe that if we let $U \stackrel{d}{=} \{x \in Real \mid 0 \leq x < 1\}$, cc is a chain in U, but the least upper bound of cc is *not* a member of U.

(3) A chain $\{c_i\}_{i=0}^{\infty}$ is said to be *finite* if it is constant from some element (i.e., if there exists $n \geq 0$ such that $c_i = c_n$ for every $i \geq n$). Every finite chain has an obvious least upper bound. An example is the **divides** chain $\langle 2, 4, 8, 16, 16, 16, \ldots \rangle$ in *Nat*, which of course has many upper bounds, three of which are 16, 42 and 160; 16 is the least upper bound of this chain.

Some notation: If a chain $\{c_i\}_{i=0}^{\infty}$ has a least upper bound (not all chains do!), we use

$$\bigsqcup_{i=0}^{\infty}{}_{C}(c_i)$$

or just $\bigsqcup_C c_i$, or even simply $\bigsqcup c_i$ when the C can be inferred from context, to denote the least upper bound of the chain.

5.3.4 Cpo's

An algebra C with a partial ordering $\sqsubseteq_C$ is said to be a *complete partial order*, or just *cpo*, if and only if

- Every $\sqsubseteq_C$ chain of C elements has a least upper bound, and this least upper bound is an element of C.
- There exists an element in C which is $\sqsubseteq_C$ less than all other elements in C. We usually denote this $\sqsubseteq_C$ least element by $\perp_C$, or just $\perp$ when the C can be inferred from context. Hence, $\perp_C$ is an element in C which is such that $\perp_C \sqsubseteq_C c$ for any c in C. We often say that $\perp_C$ is the *bottom* element of C. Observe that because $\sqsubseteq_C$ is reflexive, the least element of a cpo C is unique.

Thus, a cpo is an algebra which among its operations has a binary relation which is a complete partial ordering of the carrier of the algebra and which is such that the carrier of the algebra has a member which is least in the ordering. Some examples:

(1) The set $\{1, 2, 3, \ldots, N\}$ ordered by divides is a cpo, with 1 as its least element, for any $N \geq 1$. But $\{2, 3, \ldots, N\}$ (where $N \geq 2$), ordered by the same relation, is *not* a cpo (there is no least divides element in this set).

(2) *Nat* ordered by $\leq$ is *not* a cpo (many chains, for instance $\{i\}_{i=0}^{\infty} = \langle 0, 1, 2, \ldots \rangle$, do not have an upper bound). But any finite subset of *Nat*, ordered by the same relation, *is* a cpo.

(3) The set $U = \{x \in \mathit{Real} \mid 0 \leq x < 1\}$ ordered by $\leq$ is a partial order, but not a complete partial order. The set $E = \{x \in \mathit{Real} \mid 0 \leq x \leq 1\}$ is, however, ordered to a cpo by $\leq$.

(4) The set *Fem* of human females, ordered by the binary relation 'is-mother-of', is a not cpo (the relation is neither reflexive nor transitive). But the *reflexive, transitive closure* m* of the relation is-mother-of, defined as follows:

$$f_1 \text{ m* } f_2 \overset{d}{\iff} \text{Either } f_1 = f_2$$
$$\text{or} \quad \exists f' \in \mathit{Fem}: (f_1 \text{ m* } f') \wedge (f' \text{ is-mother-of } f_2)$$

orders the set *Fem* to a cpo (assuming that there is a first human female, presumably Eve, who then is the least element in *Fem*, i.e., $\bot_{Fem}$).

(5) The partial order $Bool_{f<t}$, is ordered to a cpo by the relation $\preceq_{f<t}$ (defined on page 79 above).

(6) On page 79 we defined the powerset $\mathcal{P}(A)$ of a set A to consist of every subset of A, and stated that $\mathcal{P}(A)$ is partially ordered by the subset relation $\subseteq$. $\mathcal{P}(A)$ is a cpo. Its least element is the empty set, which we denote by $\emptyset$. If $\{X_i\}_{i=0}^{\infty}$ is a chain in $\mathcal{P}(A)$, then its least upper bound is

$$\bigsqcup_{i=0}^{\infty}{}_{\mathcal{P}(A)} X_i = \bigcup_{i=0}^{\infty} X_i = X_0 \cup X_1 \cup X_2 \cup \ldots$$

(7) For any set A we define its *finite powerset* $\mathcal{P}_f(A)$ to consist of every finite subset of A. $\mathcal{P}_f(A)$ is of course partially ordered by $\subseteq$, but is *not* a cpo for every set A. We leave it as an exercise to prove this.

Proposition 5.1 *Assume that C is a cpo, and that the C elements $c_{i,j}$ (where $i \geq 0, j \geq 0$) are such that $\{c_{i,j}\}_{i=0}^{\infty}$ is a chain for every $j \geq 0$ and $\{c_{i,j}\}_{j=0}^{\infty}$ is a chain for every $i \geq 0$. Then:*

$$\bigsqcup_{i=0}^{\infty}{}_{C} \bigsqcup_{j=0}^{\infty}{}_{C}\, c_{i,j} = \bigsqcup_{i=0}^{\infty}{}_{C}\, c_{i,i} = \bigsqcup_{i=0}^{\infty}{}_{C} \bigsqcup_{j=0}^{\infty}{}_{C}\, c_{j,i}$$

Proof: Exercise for the mathematically inclined.

5.3.5 Flat cpo's

Any single-carrier algebra A can be ordered into a *flat* cpo $A_\bot$ as follows: First, choose an element not in A, denote this element by $\bot_A$, and let

$$A_\bot \stackrel{d}{=} A \cup \{\bot_A\}$$

Then, define a binary relation $\sqsubseteq_A$ on $A_\bot \times A_\bot$ by

$$a_1 \sqsubseteq_A a_2 \stackrel{d}{\iff} (a_1 = \bot_A) \vee (a_1 = a_2)$$

for any a_1, a_2 in $A_\bot$.

Proposition 5.2 $A_\bot$ *ordered by* $\sqsubseteq_A$ *is a cpo with* $\bot_A$ *as its least element.*

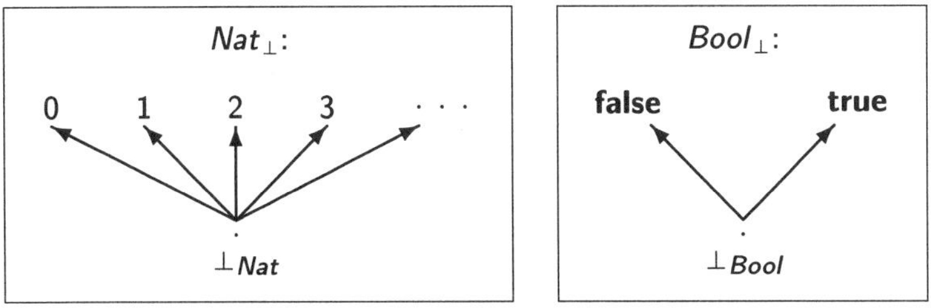

Figure 5.2: The flat cpo's $Nat_\perp$ and $Bool_\perp$

Proof: That $\perp_A \sqsubseteq_A$ a for any $a \in A$ and that $\sqsubseteq_A$ is a partial ordering of $A_\perp$, follow immediately from the definition of $\sqsubseteq_A$.

To prove that $\sqsubseteq_A$ is a complete ordering of $A_\perp$, assume that $\{a_i\}_{i=0}^{\infty}$ is a $\sqsubseteq_A$ chain. The way $\sqsubseteq_A$ has been defined, the elements of this chain must either be constantly equal to $\perp_A$ (and then $\perp_A$, of course, is its least upper bound), or consist of first 0 or more occurrences of $\perp_A$, and then be constant: $\{a_i\}_{i=0}^{\infty} = \langle \perp_A, \ldots, \perp_A, a, a, \ldots \rangle$. But then the chain must have a least upper bound, namely a, which is in A.

Three examples:

$Nat_\perp$ We extend the domain of the algebra *Nat* (defined in figure 4.2 on page 47) with an element $\perp_{Nat}$ (which we sometimes may interpret as an *undefined integer* or an *error integer*), and define $\sqsubseteq_{Nat}$ as indicated above. The resulting algebra $Nat_\perp$ is a cpo, which is illustrated in the left part of figure 5.2.

In the next chapter, we will define the denotation of an integer expression to be a function that maps a given state to an element of $Nat_\perp$. For instance, the denotation of the expression x/y will be a function that has value $\perp_{Nat}$ for any state with a store in which y has value 0.

$Bool_\perp$ The algebra *Bool* (defined in figure 4.1 on page 47) ordered into a flat cpo has three elements: **true**, **false** and $\perp_{Bool}$. Its structure is visualized in the right part of figure 5.2.

$State_\perp$ The result of extending the algebra *State* with a new object $\perp_{State}$, which we may think of either as an error state (for instance the state after an attempt at reading from an empty input sequence) or as an undefined state.

5.3.6 Function cpo's

Assume that A and C are two algebras and that C is ordered to a cpo by a partial order $\sqsubseteq_C$. The algebra $(A \rightarrow C)$ (defined in section 4.3.4 on page 60) consists of all functions that map A to C. This algebra may be made into a cpo by defining a relation $\sqsubseteq_{(A \rightarrow C)}$ - which we say is the *canonical* order of $(A \rightarrow C)$ *induced* by the order $\sqsubseteq_C$ - as follows:

$$\mathsf{f} \sqsubseteq_{(A \rightarrow C)} \mathsf{g} \overset{d}{\Longleftrightarrow} \forall \mathsf{a} \in A: \mathsf{f}(\mathsf{a}) \sqsubseteq_C \mathsf{g}(\mathsf{a})$$

for all f, g in $(A \rightarrow C)$. This means that a function is less than or equal to another function if the value of the first function for a given argument is never greater than the value of the second function for the same argument.

The least element $\perp_{(A \rightarrow C)}$ in $(A \rightarrow C)$ relative to the canonical order $\sqsubseteq_{(A \rightarrow C)}$ is a function that has value $\perp_C$ for every argument $\mathsf{a} \in A$, i.e.,

$$\perp_{(A \rightarrow C)} \overset{d}{=} \lambda \mathsf{a} \in A: \perp_C$$

Proposition 5.3 *If A is an algebra and C is a cpo, the algebra $(A \rightarrow C)$, ordered by the relation $\sqsubseteq_{(A \rightarrow C)}$ (defined above), is a cpo with least element $\perp_{(A \rightarrow C)}$ (also defined above). The least upper bound of a chain of functions $\{\mathsf{f}_i\}_{i=0}^{\infty}$ in $(A \rightarrow C)$ is a function f^* which for any $\mathsf{a} \in A$ has value equal to the least upper bound of the C chain $\{\mathsf{f}_i(\mathsf{a})\}_{i=0}^{\infty}$, i.e.,*

$$\bigsqcup(A \rightarrow C)_{i=0}^{\infty} \mathsf{f}_i = \mathsf{f}^* = \lambda \mathsf{a} \in A: \bigsqcup C_{i=0}^{\infty} \mathsf{f}_i(\mathsf{a})$$

Proof: That $\sqsubseteq_{(A \rightarrow C)}$ is a partial ordering of $(A \rightarrow C)$ follows from the fact that $\sqsubseteq_C$ is a partial ordering of C. That $\perp_{(A \rightarrow C)}$ is $\sqsubseteq_{(A \rightarrow C)}$ least in $(A \rightarrow C)$ follows from the fact that $\perp_C$ is $\sqsubseteq_C$-least in C.

As for completeness, assume that $\{\mathsf{f}_i\}_{i=0}^{\infty}$ is a $\sqsubseteq_{(A \rightarrow C)}$ chain. We have to show that this chain has a least upper bound which is a function in $(A \rightarrow C)$. Let a be an element in A. Using the definition of $\sqsubseteq_{(A \rightarrow C)}$ and our assumption $\mathsf{f}_i \sqsubseteq_{(A \rightarrow C)} \mathsf{f}_{i+1}$, we get that $\mathsf{f}_i(\mathsf{a}) \sqsubseteq_C \mathsf{f}_{i+1}(\mathsf{a})$ for every $i \geq 0$. This means that $\{\mathsf{f}_i(\mathsf{a})\}_{i=0}^{\infty}$ is a chain in C. By assumption, C is a cpo, which means that this chain has a least upper bound in C. We may therefore define a function $\mathsf{f}^* \in (A \rightarrow C)$ by letting $\mathsf{f}^*(\mathsf{a})$ be equal to the least upper bound of the C chain $\bigsqcup \mathsf{f}_i(\mathsf{a})$ for any $\mathsf{a} \in A$. It is not difficult to verify that f^* is a least upper bound of the chain $\bigsqcup \mathsf{f}_i$:

$\mathsf{f}_i \sqsubseteq \mathsf{f}^*$ ***for every*** $i \geq 0$: It is sufficient to prove that $\mathsf{f}_i(\mathsf{a}) \sqsubseteq \mathsf{f}^*(\mathsf{a})$ for every $\mathsf{a} \in A$. This holds because $\mathsf{f}^*(\mathsf{a})$ is defined to be the least upper bound of the chain $\{\mathsf{f}_i(\mathsf{a})\}_{i=0}^{\infty}$.

If $f_i \sqsubseteq f'$ ***for every*** $i \geq 0$ ***then*** $f^* \sqsubseteq f'$: It suffices to prove that $f^*(a) \sqsubseteq f'(a)$ for every $a \in A$. This holds because by assumption $f_i(a) \sqsubseteq f'(a)$ for every $i \geq 0$, and by definition $f^*(a)$ is the *least* upper bound of $\{f_i(a)\}_{i=0}^{\infty}$.

If we interpret $\perp_C$ as the undefined C element, we may interpret the 'bottom function' $\perp_{(A \to C)}$ as a function that maps A to C but which is undefined for every argument $a \in A$. If C is a flat cpo, we may also interpret $f \sqsubseteq_{(A \to C)} g$ to mean: *for every argument* $a \in A$, $f(a)$ *is either undefined or equal to* $g(a)$, or - less wordy - as f *is equal to or less defined than* g or g *is at least as well defined as* f. An example (in which we write just $\sqsubseteq$ instead of $\sqsubseteq_{(Nat \to Nat_\perp)}$):

$$\begin{aligned}\perp_{(Nat \to Nat_\perp)} &= \lambda x \in Nat: \perp_{Nat} \\ &\sqsubseteq \lambda x \in Nat: \textbf{if } x = 3 \textbf{ then } 5 \textbf{ else } \perp_{Nat} \textbf{ fi} \\ &\sqsubseteq \lambda x \in Nat: \textbf{if } x \leq 6 \textbf{ then } x + 2 \textbf{ else } \perp_{Nat} \textbf{ fi} \\ &\sqsubseteq \lambda x \in Nat: x + 2\end{aligned}$$

Another example: Define a function $g_i \in (Nat \to Nat_\perp)$ for every $i \geq 0$ as follows:

$$g_i = \lambda x \in Nat: \textbf{if } x < i \textbf{ then } x^2 \textbf{ else } \perp_{Nat}$$

We leave it as an exercise to prove that $\{g_i\}_{i=0}^{\infty}$ is a chain, and to find the least upper bound of this chain.

5.4 Continuous functions

The denotation of an imperative will in the next chapter be defined to be a function that maps the flat cpo $State_\perp$ to itself. Similarly, the denotation of every syntactically correct construct of a programming language will be defined to be a function mapping one cpo to another. All these functions will be seen (or rather proved) to satisfy certain conditions which make it possible to solve equations of the kind we found for the denotations of **while** imperatives. In this section we study these conditions.

Assume that C and D are two cpo's. A function $f \in (C \to D)$ is said to be *strict* if and only if

$$f(\perp_C) = \perp_D$$

A function $f \in (C \to D)$ is said to be *monotonic* if and only if

$$\forall\, c_1, c_2 \in C: c_1 \sqsubseteq_C c_2 \Rightarrow f(c_1) \sqsubseteq_D f(c_2)$$

Observe that if f is a monotonic function from C to D and $\{c_i\}_{i=0}^{\infty}$ is a chain in C, then $\{f(c_i)\}_{i=0}^{\infty}$ is a chain in D, which has a least upper bound in the cpo D.

A monotonic function $f \in (C \to D)$ is said to *preserve least upper bounds* if and only if f applied to the least upper bound of a chain is always equal to the least upper bound of f applied to each of the elements of the chain, i.e.,

$$f(\sqcup_C|_{i=0}^{\infty} c_i) = \sqcup_D|_{i=0}^{\infty} f(c_i)$$

for every C chain $\{c_i\}_{i=0}^{\infty}$. By the observation above, the right-hand side of this equation is well defined.

A function f that maps one cpo to another is said to be *continuous* if and only if it is monotonic and preserves least upper bounds.

Some examples:

(1) Let $Nat_N \stackrel{d}{=} \{1, 2, \ldots, N\}$, where N is some positive integer, be ordered to a cpo by the divides relation. Define a function is_prime that maps Nat_N to $Bool_{t<f}$ as follows for every $n \in Nat_N$:

$$\text{is\_prime}(n) \stackrel{d}{=} \textbf{if } \exists\, n_1, n_2 \in Nat_N\colon n_1, n_2 > 1 \wedge (n = n_1 * n_2) \textbf{ then false else true}$$

The function is_prime is strict, monotonic and continuous:

is_prime ***is strict***: The divides-least element in Nat_N is 1, which is mapped by is_prime to **true** which is $\sqsubseteq_{t<f}$-least in $Bool_{t<f}$.

is_prime ***is monotonic***: If n_1 divides n_2 then either $n_1 = 1$ or n_2 is not prime, i.e., is_prime(n_2) = **false**. In both cases is_prime(n_1) $\sqsubseteq_{t<f}$ is_prime(n_2).

is_prime ***is continuous***: Any chain $\{n_i\}_{i=0}^{\infty}$ in the finite cpo Nat_N is finite and hence with a least upper bound equal to its last element, which we may assume to be n_k. Then is_prime$(\bigsqcup n_i)$ = is_prime(n_k). Because is_prime is a monotonic function, $\{\text{is\_prime}(n_i)\}_{i=0}^{\infty}$ is a chain in $Bool_{t<f}$. Because this latter cpo is finite, the least upper bound of $\{\text{is\_prime}(n_i)\}_{i=0}^{\infty}$ is equal to is_prime(n_k) for some $k \geq 0$. But then is_prime$(\bigsqcup n_i)$ = is_prime(n_k) = $\bigsqcup$is_prime(n_i). Hence, the function is_prime preserves least upper bounds, and is therefore continuous.

(2) Ordinary multiplication $*$ is a function that maps the Cartesian product $Nat \times Nat$ to Nat. We extend this function to a function $*_\perp$ that maps $Nat_\perp \times Nat_\perp$ to $Nat_\perp$ as follows:

$$n *_\perp m = \textbf{if } n = \perp_{Nat} \vee m = \perp_{Nat} \textbf{ then } \perp_{Nat} \textbf{ else } n*m$$

Thus, $*_\perp$ is the *strict* extension of $*$. We leave it as an exercise to prove that $*_\perp$ is continuous in both its arguments.

In the sequel we will assume that other common functions, like for instance $+$ and $-$, are strictly extended. To reduce the amount of typographical clutter, we will not decorate the names of these extended functions with any suffixed $_\perp$. We will, for instance, simply write $*$ when it is obvious from the context that we mean the strict $*_\perp$.

(3) Let A be any algebra and C a cpo. Define a function is_total that maps $(A \to C)$ to $Bool_{f<t}$ as follows:

$$\text{is\_total}(f) = \textbf{if } \exists a \in A\text{: } f(a) = \perp_C \textbf{ then false else true}$$

The function is_total is strict and monotonic, but not always continuous:

is_total ***is strict***: The function $\perp_{(A \to C)}$ is mapped by is_total to **false**, which is least in $Bool_{f<t}$.

is_total ***is monotonic***: Assume that $f_1 \sqsubseteq_{(A \to C)} f_2$. It suffices to prove that it is then impossible that is_total(f_1) = **true** and is_total(f_2) = **false**. The assumption means that $f_1(a) \sqsubseteq_C f_2(a)$ for every $a \in A$. This entails that $f_2(a) \neq \perp_C$ whenever $f_1(a) \neq \perp_C$. But then it must be impossible that $f_2(a) = \perp_C$ for some a if $f_1(a) \neq \perp_C$ for every a.

is_total ***is not always continuous***: Assume that $A = Nat$ and $C = Nat_\perp$, and for each $i \geq 0$ define a function $f_i \in (Nat \to Nat_\perp)$ as follows:

$$f_i \stackrel{d}{=} \lambda x \in Nat\text{: }\textbf{if } x < i \textbf{ then } x \textbf{ else } \perp_{Nat}$$

Then it is easy to see that $f_i \sqsubseteq f_{i+1}$ for every $i \geq 0$, and that the chain $\{f_i\}_{i=0}^{\infty}$ has a least upper bound which is equal to $\lambda x \in Nat\text{: } x$. But then is_total($\bigsqcup f_i$) = **true**. On the other hand, $\bigsqcup$is_total(f_i) = $\bigsqcup$**false** = **false**, which entails that is_total does not always preserve upper bounds.

(4) Assume that A is an algebra and C a cpo, and that a is any element in A and c any element in C. Define a function $\text{Update}_{a,c}$ that maps the cpo $(A \to C)$ to itself as follows:

$$\text{Update}_{a,c} = \lambda f \in (A \to C)\text{: } \lambda x \in A\text{: } \textbf{if } x = a \textbf{ then } c \textbf{ else } f(x)$$

It is not difficult to see that if $c \neq \perp_C$, $\text{Update}_{a,c}$ is not strict but continuous. On the other hand, if $c = \perp_C$, $\text{Update}_{a,c}$ is strict but not monotonic (and therefore not continuous).

Proposition 5.4 *Any strict function that maps a flat cpo to a cpo is continuous.*

Proof: Assume that f is a strict mapping of the flat cpo $A_\perp$ to the cpo B. We must prove that f is monotonic and preserves least upper bounds:

f *is monotonic*: Assume that $a_1 \sqsubseteq_A a_2$. Because $A_\perp$ is flat, this means $a_1 = \perp_A$ or $a_1 = a_2$. In the former case, $f(a_1) = \perp_B$ because f is assumed to be strict, and then $f(a_1) \sqsubseteq_B f(a_2)$ by definition of $\perp_B$. In the latter case, $f(a_1) \sqsubseteq_B f(a_2)$ follows immediately because $\sqsubseteq_B$ is reflexive.

f *preserves least upper bounds*: By flatness of $A_\perp$, any chain $\{a_i\}_{i=0}^{\infty}$ in A is constant from some element, i.e., there must exist $n \geq 0$ such that $a_i = a_n$ for every $i \geq n$. But then $\bigsqcup a_i = a_n$, and also $f(\bigsqcup a_i) = f(a_n) = \bigsqcup f(a_i)$.

Proposition 5.5 *Any monotonic function that maps a finite cpo to a cpo is continuous.*

Proof: Any chain in a finite cpo is finite, and must hence have its last element as a least upper bound.

If A is any algebra and C is a cpo, we define $[A \to C]$ to be the algebra that consists of every continuous function that maps A to C.

Proposition 5.6 *If C is an algebra and D is a cpo, the algebra $[C \to D]$ ordered by the canonical order $\sqsubseteq_{(C \to D)}$ is a cpo with $\perp_{(C \to D)}$ as its least element.*

Proof: Proposition 5.3 entails that $[C \to D]$ is a partial order. It is therefore only necessary to prove that $\perp_{(C \to D)}$ is continuous, and that the least upper bound of a chain of continuous functions that map C to D is a continuous function. To prove the first of these claims is straightforward.

As for the second claim, assume that $f^* = \bigsqcup f_i$ the least upper bound of a chain $\{f_i\}_{i=0}^{\infty}$ of functions in $[C \to D]$. By proposition 5.3, $f^* \in (C \to D)$. It only remains to prove that f^* is monotonic and preserves least upper bounds. We leave this as an exercise.

5.5 Strict extensions of functions

If A and B are two algebras, and $f \in (A \to B)$ is a function that maps A to B, the *strict extension* of f is a function f^s that maps the flat cpo $A_\perp$ to the flat cpo $B_\perp$ which is defined as follows:

$$f^s \stackrel{d}{=} \lambda a \in A\text{: }\mathbf{if}\ a = \perp_A\ \mathbf{then}\ \perp_B\ \mathbf{else}\ f(a)$$

Similarly, the strict extension of an n-ary function that maps a Cartesian product $A_1 \times \ldots \times A_n$ of n sets to a set B, is defined to be the function that maps $A_{1,\perp} \times \ldots \times A_{n,\perp}$ to $B_\perp$ and which has value $\perp_B$ if any of its n arguments is equal to a $\perp$ element and is equal to the original function otherwise. By proposition 5.4 above, the strict extension of any function is continuous in every argument.

In particular, if $B_\perp$ is defined to be the Cartesian product of n algebras $A_1, \ldots, A_n$ extended to a flat cpo, i.e.,

$$B_\perp = A_{1\perp} \times \ldots \times A_{n\perp} \cup \{\perp_B\}$$

where $\perp_B$ is some new object not in any of the algebras A_i, we define the *strict tupling function* to be a function $\langle \_, \_, \ldots, \_ \rangle^s$ that maps $A_{1\perp} \times \ldots \times A_{n\perp}$ to $B_\perp$ defined as follows for any $a_1 \in A_{1\perp}, \ldots, a_n \in A_{n\perp}$:

$$\langle a_1, \ldots, a_n \rangle^s = \textbf{if } a_1 = \perp_{A_1} \vee \ldots \vee a_n = \perp_{A_n} \textbf{ then } \perp_B \\ \textbf{else } \langle a_1, \ldots, a_n \rangle$$

We will sometimes use the notation $\underline{\lambda} a \in A{:} \ldots a \ldots$ to denote the strict extension of a nameless function $\lambda a \in A{:} \ldots a \ldots$, i.e.,

$$\underline{\lambda} a \in A{:} \ldots a \ldots \stackrel{d}{=} \lambda a \in A{:} \textbf{ if } a = \perp_A \textbf{ then } \perp_B \textbf{ else } \ldots a \ldots$$

5.6 Fixpoints

Assume that f is a function in $(A \rightarrow A)$, where A is some set. An element $a^* \in A$ is said to be a *fixpoint of* f if and only if

$$a^* = f(a^*)$$

Not every function has a fixpoint, and some have many. Some examples:

(1) The function $suc = (\lambda x \in Nat{:}\, x + 1) \in (Nat \rightarrow Nat)$ does not have any fixpoints in $Nat = \{0, 1, 2, \ldots\}$. But if suc is extended strictly to be a function suc^s that maps the flat cpo $Nat_\perp$ to itself, i.e., such that $suc^s(\perp_{Nat}) = \perp_{Nat}$, then suc^s *does* have a fixpoint in $Nat_\perp$, namely $\perp_{Nat}$.

(2) Every $a \in A$ is a fixpoint of the function $id_A \stackrel{d}{=} \lambda x \in A{:}\, x$.

(3) The function $poly \stackrel{d}{=} \lambda x \in Int{:}\, (x^2 + 2 * x - 6) \in (Int \rightarrow Int)$ has two fixpoints in Int, namely -3 and 2. The strict extension of poly to a function $poly^s \in (Int_\perp \rightarrow Int_\perp)$ has *three* fixpoints ($\perp_{Int}$ is the third).

We are particularly interested in fixpoints of functions that map cpo's to themselves, and will in this section show how to find fixpoints of such functions. The reason for our interest is that many semantic functions can best be defined as fixpoints of functions that map functions to functions. An example is the function mw which was submitted earlier in this chapter as an attempt at defining the semantics of **while** imperatives. Equation (α) given for mw on page 75 is of the form

$$\text{mw} = \text{qw}(\text{mw})$$

where qw is a function that maps the algebra ($\mathit{State} \rightarrow \mathit{State}_{\perp}$) to itself. Thus, the function mw - if it exists - can be found as a fixpoint of qw.

5.6.1 The Fixpoint Theorem

In this section we prove that any continuous function f that maps a cpo C to itself, has at least one fixpoint, namely the least upper bound of the chain $\{\perp_C, \text{f}(\perp_C), \text{f}(\text{f}(\perp_C)), \text{f}(\text{f}(\text{f}(\perp_C))), \dots\}$. But first we prove that this infinite sequence really *is* a chain:

Proposition 5.7 *If C is a cpo and f is a continuous function that maps C to itself, the sequence $\{\text{f}^i(\perp_C)\}_{i=0}^{\infty} = \{\perp_C, \text{f}(\perp_C), \text{f}(\text{f}(\perp_C)), \text{f}(\text{f}(\text{f}(\perp_C))), \dots\}$ is a chain.*

Proof: It is sufficient to prove that $\text{f}^i(\perp_C) \sqsubseteq_C \text{f}^{i+1}(\perp_C)$ for every $i \geq 0$. This is proved by induction on i as follows:

$i = 0$: $\text{f}^0(\perp_C) = \perp_C \sqsubseteq_C \text{f}^1(\perp_C)$

$i + 1$: Assume as induction hypothesis that $\text{f}^i(\perp_C) \sqsubseteq_C \text{f}^{i+1}(\perp_C)$. The function f is assumed to be continuous, and hence monotonic. The induction hypothesis then entails that $\text{f}^{i+1}(\perp_C) \sqsubseteq_C \text{f}^{i+2}(\perp_C)$.

For any cpo C, we define the *fixpoint operator* for C to be a function $\text{Y}_C \in ([C \rightarrow C] \rightarrow C)$ that maps any continuous function $\text{f} \in [C \rightarrow C]$ to the least upper bound of the C chain $\{\text{f}^i(\perp_C)\}_{i=0}^{\infty}$. Y_C is defined as follows:

$$\text{Y}_C \stackrel{d}{=} \lambda \text{f} \in [C \rightarrow C] : \bigsqcup_C \text{f}^i(\perp_C)$$

Theorem 5.1 The Fixpoint Theorem:
Assume that C is a cpo. For any continuous function $\text{f} \in [C \rightarrow C]$, let $\text{c}_\text{f}^* \stackrel{d}{=} \text{Y}_C(\text{f})$. Then

$$(1): \text{c}_\text{f}^* = \text{f}(\text{c}_\text{f}^*)$$
$$(2): \forall \text{c}' \in C : (\text{c}' = \text{f}(\text{c}')) \Rightarrow \text{c}_\text{f}^* \sqsubseteq_C \text{c}'$$

(1) *says that* c_f^* *is a fixpoint of* f, *and* (2) *that* c_f^* *is the* least *fixpoint of* f.

Proof: It suffices to prove $\alpha : \text{c}_\text{f}^*$ is well defined, $\beta : \text{c}_\text{f}^*$ is a fixpoint for f and $\gamma : \text{c}_\text{f}^*$ is the least fixpoint of f:

α : c_f^* *is well defined:*
This follows directly from proposition 5.7, using our assumption that C is a cpo.

β : c_f^* *is a fixpoint for* f, *i.e.,* $\text{c}_\text{f}^* = \text{f}(\text{c}_\text{f}^*)$:

$$\begin{aligned}
f(c_f^*) &= f(\lfloor C \rfloor_{i=0}^{\infty} f^i(\bot_C)) && \textit{(By def. of } c_f^*\textit{)}\\
&= \lfloor C \rfloor_{i=0}^{\infty} f(f^i(\bot_C)) && \textit{(Because f is continuous)}\\
&= \lfloor C \rfloor_{i=0}^{\infty} f^{i+1}(\bot_C) && \textit{(By def. of } f^{i+1}\textit{)}\\
&= \lfloor C \rfloor_{i=1}^{\infty} f^i(\bot_C) &&\\
&= \lfloor C \rfloor_{i=0}^{\infty} f^i(\bot_C) &&\\
&= c_f^* && \textit{(By def. of } c_f^*\textit{)}
\end{aligned}$$

γ: c_f^* *is the* least *fixpoint of* f:

Assume that $c' \in C$ is a fixpoint of f. By induction on i, we prove that $f^i(\bot_C) \sqsubseteq_C c'$ for every $i \geq 0$:

$i = 0$: $f^0(\bot_C) = \bot_C \sqsubseteq_C c'$.

$i + 1$: Assume as induction hypothesis that $f^i(\bot_C) \sqsubseteq_C c'$. Because f is a monotonic function, the induction hypothesis immediately entails that $f^{i+1}(\bot_C) \sqsubseteq_C f(c')$. But $f(c') = c'$ because c' is assumed to be a fixpoint of f, and hence $f^{i+1}(\bot_C) \sqsubseteq_C c'$.

Thus: c' - which by assumption is a fixpoint for f - is an upper bound for the chain $\{f^i(\bot_C)\}_{i=0}^{\infty}$. By definition, c_f^* is the *least* upper bound of this chain, and therefore $c_f^* \sqsubseteq_C c'$.

This concludes the proof of the Fixpoint Theorem.

In the next chapter, we will use the Fixpoint Theorem to define the semantics of **while** imperatives.

5.6.2 An example

An example follows showing how the Fixpoint Theorem can be used: Define a function Fk_0 that maps the set $NN_0 = (Nat \to Nat)$ to itself as follows:

$$Fk_0 = \lambda f \in NN_0 : \lambda x \in Nat : \textbf{if } x = 0 \textbf{ then } 1 \textbf{ else } x * f(x-1)$$

Does Fk_0 have a fixpoint? A function $f' \in NN_0$ is by definition a fixpoint for Fk_0 if and only if $f' = Fk_0(f')$. Two functions are equal if and only if they have the same domain and the same value for every argument in their common domain. This means that the two functions f' and $Fk_0(f')$ are equal if and only if

$$\begin{aligned}
f'(x) &= Fk_0(f')(x)\\
&= \textbf{if } x = 0 \textbf{ then } 1 \textbf{ else } x * f'(x-1)
\end{aligned}$$

for every $x \in Nat$.

This means that the *factorial function*

$$\lambda x \in Nat : x! \stackrel{d}{=} \lambda x \in Nat : 1 * 2 * \ldots * (x-1) * x$$

is a fixpoint for Fk_0. But is this the fixpoint given by the Fixpoint Theorem? As stated above, the Fixpoint Theorem is only applicable to continuous functions that map a cpo to itself. NN_0 is, however, not ordered into a cpo, and it is therefore meaningless to consider Fk_0 to be a continuous function. The Fixpoint Theorem can therefore not be applied directly to find a fixpoint of Fk_0. But let us instead consider the set $NN \stackrel{d}{=} (Nat \rightarrow Nat_\perp)$, i.e., the set of all functions that map Nat to the flat cpo $Nat_\perp$. By proposition 5.3 on page 84, we know that NN is a cpo. Furthermore, let us extend Fk_0 to a function Fk that maps NN to itself as follows:

$$\mathsf{Fk} = \lambda \mathsf{f} \in NN: \lambda \mathsf{x} \in Nat: \textbf{if } \mathsf{x} = 0 \textbf{ then } 1 \textbf{ else } \mathsf{x} * \mathsf{f}(\mathsf{x}-1)$$

For any given $\mathsf{f} \in NN$, $\mathsf{f}(\mathsf{x}-1)$ may possibly be equal to $\perp_{Nat}$, for instance if $\mathsf{f} = \perp_{NN}$. This entails that we have to extend the multiplication function $*$ to be a function in $(Nat_\perp \times Nat_\perp \rightarrow Nat_\perp)$. The most natural way of doing this, is by extending $*$ strictly, such that $\mathsf{x} * \mathsf{y} = \perp_{Nat}$ if and only if $\mathsf{x} = \perp_{Nat}$ or $\mathsf{y} = \perp_{Nat}$. By proposition 5.4 we know that the strict extension of $*$ is continuous in both arguments.

To be able to use the Fixpoint Theorem, we must first prove that that Fk is a continuous function:

Lemma 5.1 Fk *is continuous.*

Proof: We must prove that Fk is monotonic and preserves least upper bounds:

Fk ***is monotonic***: Assume that $\mathsf{f} \sqsubseteq_{NN} \mathsf{g}$. We must prove that $\mathsf{Fk}(\mathsf{f}) \sqsubseteq_{NN} \mathsf{Fk}(\mathsf{g})$, which by definition of $\sqsubseteq_{NN} = \sqsubseteq_{(Nat \rightarrow Nat_\perp)}$ is equivalent to proving

$$\mathsf{Fk}(\mathsf{f})(\mathsf{x}) \sqsubseteq_{Nat} \mathsf{Fk}(\mathsf{g})(\mathsf{x})$$

for every $\mathsf{x} \in Nat$. There are two cases to consider:

$\mathsf{x} = 0$: By definition of Fk, $\mathsf{Fk}(\mathsf{f})(0) = 1 = \mathsf{Fk}(\mathsf{g})(0)$, and then $\mathsf{Fk}(\mathsf{f})(0) \sqsubseteq_{Nat} \mathsf{Fk}(\mathsf{g})(0)$ holds because $\sqsubseteq_{Nat}$ is reflexive.

$\mathsf{x} > 0$: Then $\mathsf{Fk}(\mathsf{f})(\mathsf{x}) = \mathsf{x} * \mathsf{f}(\mathsf{x}-1)$ and $\mathsf{Fk}(\mathsf{g})(\mathsf{x}) = \mathsf{x} * \mathsf{g}(\mathsf{x}-1)$. By assumption, $\mathsf{f}(\mathsf{x}-1) \sqsubseteq_{Nat} \mathsf{g}(\mathsf{x}-1)$. Because the strict extension of the multiplication function is continuous and hence monotonic, we get $\mathsf{x} * \mathsf{f}(\mathsf{x}-1) \sqsubseteq_{Nat} \mathsf{x} * \mathsf{g}(\mathsf{x}-1)$ - which is what is wanted.

Fk ***preserves least upper bounds***: Assume that $\{\mathsf{f}\}_{i=0}^{\infty}$ is a chain in NN. We must prove that

$$\mathsf{Fk}(\bigsqcup_{NN} \mathsf{f}_i) = \bigsqcup_{NN}{}_{i=0}^{\infty} \mathsf{Fk}(\mathsf{f}_i)$$

Two functions are equal if and only if they have the same value for every argument. To prove the equation above, it is therefore sufficient to prove

$$(\mathsf{Fk}(\underline{\lfloor NN \rfloor}\mathsf{f}_i))(\mathsf{x}) = (\underline{\lfloor NN \rfloor}_{i=0}^{\infty}\mathsf{Fk}(\mathsf{f}_i))(\mathsf{x})$$

for every $\mathsf{x} \in \mathit{Nat}$. Applying proposition 5.3 on page 84 to the right-hand side of this equation, we get that it suffices to prove

$$(\mathsf{Fk}(\underline{\lfloor NN \rfloor}\mathsf{f}_i))(\mathsf{x}) = \underline{\lfloor Nat \rfloor}_{i=0}^{\infty}(\mathsf{Fk}(\mathsf{f}_i)(\mathsf{x}))$$

for every $\mathsf{x} \in \mathit{Nat}$. There are two cases to consider:

$\mathsf{x} = 0$: Then

$$\begin{aligned}(\mathsf{Fk}(\underline{\lfloor NN \rfloor}\mathsf{f}_i))(\mathsf{x}) &= 1\\ &= \underline{\lfloor Nat \rfloor}_{i=0}^{\infty}1\\ &= \underline{\lfloor Nat \rfloor}_{i=0}^{\infty}(\mathsf{Fk}(\mathsf{f}_i)(\mathsf{x}))\end{aligned}$$

$\mathsf{x} > 0$: Then

$$\begin{aligned}(\mathsf{Fk}(\underline{\lfloor NN \rfloor}\mathsf{f}_i))(\mathsf{x}) &= \mathsf{x}*((\underline{\lfloor NN \rfloor}\mathsf{f}_i)(\mathsf{x}-1)) && \text{By definition of Fk}\\ &= \mathsf{x}*(\underline{\lfloor Nat \rfloor}_{i=0}^{\infty}(\mathsf{f}_i(\mathsf{x}-1))) && \text{By proposition 5.3}\\ &= \underline{\lfloor Nat \rfloor}_{i=0}^{\infty}(\mathsf{x}*\mathsf{f}_i(\mathsf{x}-1)) && * \text{ is continuous}\\ &= \underline{\lfloor Nat \rfloor}_{i=0}^{\infty}(\mathsf{Fk}(\mathsf{f}_i)(\mathsf{x})) && \text{By definition of Fk}\end{aligned}$$

This concludes the proof that Fk is continuous. The Fixpoint Theorem can now be applied, and we get that Fk does indeed have a fixpoint, and that its least fixpoint is

$$\mathsf{p} \stackrel{d}{=} \mathsf{Y}_{NN}(\mathsf{Fk}) = \underline{\lfloor NN \rfloor}_{i=0}^{\infty}\mathsf{Fk}^i(\bot_{NN})$$

Let us see if this p is equal to the factorial function: By proposition 5.3, the value of p for any $\mathsf{x} \in \mathit{Nat}$ can be found as follows:

$$\begin{aligned}\mathsf{p}(\mathsf{x}) &= (\underline{\lfloor NN \rfloor}_{i=0}^{\infty}\mathsf{Fk}^i(\bot_{NN}))(\mathsf{x})\\ &= \underline{\lfloor Nat \rfloor}_{i=0}^{\infty}(\mathsf{Fk}^i(\bot_{NN})(\mathsf{x}))\end{aligned}$$

To find the value of p(x), let us determine the first few elements in the *Nat* chain $\{\mathsf{Fk}^i(\bot_{NN})(\mathsf{x})\}_{i=0}^{\infty}$:

$$\begin{aligned}
\mathsf{Fk}^0(\bot_{NN})(\mathsf{x}) &= \bot_{NN}(\mathsf{x}) \\
&= \bot_{Nat} \\
\mathsf{Fk}^1(\bot_{NN})(\mathsf{x}) &= \mathsf{Fk}(\bot_{NN})(\mathsf{x}) \\
&= \textbf{if } \mathsf{x} = 0 \textbf{ then } 1 \textbf{ else } \mathsf{x}{*}\bot_{NN}(\mathsf{x}{-}1) \\
&= \textbf{if } \mathsf{x} = 0 \textbf{ then } 1 \textbf{ else } \mathsf{x}{*}\bot_{Nat} \\
&= \textbf{if } \mathsf{x} = 0 \textbf{ then } 1 \textbf{ else } \bot_{Nat} \\
\mathsf{Fk}^2(\bot_{NN})(\mathsf{x}) &= \mathsf{Fk}(\mathsf{Fk}^1(\bot_{NN}))(\mathsf{x}) \\
&= \textbf{if } \mathsf{x} = 0 \textbf{ then } 1 \\
&\qquad\qquad \textbf{else } \mathsf{x}{*}\mathsf{Fk}^1(\bot_{NN})(\mathsf{x}{-}1) \\
&= \textbf{if } \mathsf{x} = 0 \textbf{ then } 1 \\
&\qquad\qquad \textbf{else } \mathsf{x}{*}(\textbf{if } \mathsf{x} - 1 = 0 \textbf{ then } 1 \textbf{ else } \bot_{Nat}) \\
&= \textbf{if } \mathsf{x} < 2 \textbf{ then } 1 \textbf{ else } \bot_{Nat}
\end{aligned}$$

We generalize our computations, and conjecture that for any $i \geq 0$:

$$\mathsf{Fk}^i(\bot_{NN})(\mathsf{x}) = \textbf{if } \mathsf{x} < i \textbf{ then } \mathsf{x}! \textbf{ else } \bot_{Nat}$$

We prove this by induction on i: That our conjecture holds for $i = 0$, is obvious. The case $i + 1$:

$$\begin{aligned}
\mathsf{Fk}^{i+1}(\bot_{NN})(\mathsf{x}) &= \mathsf{Fk}(\mathsf{Fk}^i(\bot_{NN}))(\mathsf{x}) \\
&= \textbf{if } \mathsf{x} = 0 \textbf{ then } 1 \\
&\quad\ \textbf{else } \mathsf{x}{*}\mathsf{Fk}^i(\bot_{NN})(\mathsf{x}{-}1) \\
&= \textbf{if } \mathsf{x} = 0 \textbf{ then } 1 \\
&\quad\ \textbf{else } \mathsf{x}{*}(\textbf{if } \mathsf{x}{-}1 < i \textbf{ then } (\mathsf{x}{-}1)! \textbf{ else } \bot_{Nat}) \\
&= \textbf{if } \mathsf{x} = 0 \textbf{ then } 1 \\
&\quad\ \textbf{else } (\textbf{if } \mathsf{x} < i+1 \textbf{ then } \mathsf{x}{*}(\mathsf{x}{-}1)! \textbf{ else } \mathsf{x}{*}\bot_{Nat}) \\
&= \textbf{if } \mathsf{x} < i+1 \textbf{ then } \mathsf{x}! \textbf{ else } \bot_{Nat}
\end{aligned}$$

(The induction hypothesis is used to justify the third equation above.)

This result entails that the chain $\{\mathsf{Fk}^i(\bot_{NN})(\mathsf{x})\}_{i=0}^{\infty}$ consists of first $\mathsf{x}{+}1$ occurrences of $\bot_{Nat}$, and then the chain is constant with each element equal to x!:

$$\{\mathsf{Fk}^i(\bot_{NN})(\mathsf{x})\}_{i=0}^{\infty} = \{\bot_{Nat}, \bot_{Nat}, \ldots, \bot_{Nat}, \mathsf{x}!, \mathsf{x}!, \ldots\}$$

But p(x) is defined to be equal to the least upper bound of this chain, which of course is equal to x!. Thus, $\mathsf{p}(\mathsf{x}) = \mathsf{x}!$ for all $\mathsf{x} \in Nat$. The fixpoint given by the Fixpoint Theorem is indeed the factorial function.

It may be helpful to consider $\mathsf{Fk}^i(\bot_{NN})$ for $i = 0, 1, \ldots$ to be functions that *approximate* the function which is the fixpoint of Fk: Think (perhaps a little too anthropomorphically) of $\mathsf{Fk}^i(\bot_{NN})$ as a function 'who' is 'willing' to loop maximally i times. If a function value distinct from $\bot_{Nat}$ has not been found after i loops, it 'gives up' and produces the value $\bot_{Nat}$, i.e., the element in the extended domain ***Nat*** which can be thought of as the 'undefined integer'.

Furthermore, the function $\mathsf{Fk}^{i+1}(\bot_{NN})$ is a better approximation to the factorial function than the function $\mathsf{Fk}^i(\bot_{NN})$ in the sense that it succeeds over a larger domain:

$\mathsf{Fk}^0(\bot_{NN})$	gives up (with value $\bot_{Nat}$) for every argument,
$\mathsf{Fk}^1(\bot_{NN})$	manages to produce a value different from $\bot_{Nat}$ for at least one argument (viz. 0),
$\mathsf{Fk}^{i+1}(\bot_{NN})$	does in general produce values different from $\bot_{Nat}$ for more arguments than $\mathsf{Fk}^i(\bot_{NN})$ does. But $\mathsf{Fk}^{i+1}(\bot_{NN})$ agrees with $\mathsf{Fk}^i(\bot_{NN})$ for every argument for which this latter function produces a result not equal to $\bot_{Nat}$.

It is therefore natural to think of the intuitive meaning of the relation $\sqsubseteq_{NN}$ as *less than or equally defined*: $\mathsf{Fk}^i(\bot_{NN}) \sqsubseteq_{NN} \mathsf{Fk}^{i+1}(\bot_{NN})$ means that either the two functions are equal, or the last of the two functions is better defined than the first: It finds the same values as the first function does for all arguments for which the first function has a value not equal to $\bot_{Nat}$, but there are arguments for which the first function gives up, but the second does not.

5.7 Exercises

5.7.1 A chain of squares

For each $i \geq 0$ define the function $\mathsf{g}_i \in NN \stackrel{d}{=} (Nat \to Nat_\bot)$ as follows:

$$\mathsf{g}_i \stackrel{d}{=} \lambda n \in Nat: \textbf{if } n \leq i \textbf{ then } n^2 \textbf{ else } \bot_{Nat}$$

Prove that $\mathsf{g}_i \sqsubseteq_{NN} \mathsf{g}_{i+1}$ for each $i \geq 0$, i.e., that $\{\mathsf{g}_i\}_{i=0}^{\infty}$ is a chain. What is the least upper bound of this chain?

5.7.2 Strict multiplication

On page 86 we defined $*_\bot$ to be the strict extension of ordinary multiplication of integers. Prove that $*_\bot$ is continuous in both arguments.

5.7.3 The unit interval

The *unit interval* E consists of all reals between 0 and 1, i.e.,

$$E \stackrel{d}{=} \{x \in Real \mid 0 \leq x \leq 1\}$$

Prove that E is a cpo (this is stated without proof on page 81). Define the functions id, f, g, h and k (all mapping E to itself) as follows:

$$\begin{aligned}
\mathsf{id} &\stackrel{d}{=} \lambda x \in E{:}\, x \\
\mathsf{f} &\stackrel{d}{=} \lambda x \in E{:}\, \textbf{if } x < 0.5 \textbf{ then } x \textbf{ else } 1 \\
\mathsf{g} &\stackrel{d}{=} \lambda x \in E{:}\, 4x(1-x) \\
\mathsf{h} &\stackrel{d}{=} \lambda x \in E{:}\, 4x^2 - 4x + 1 \\
\mathsf{k} &\stackrel{d}{=} \lambda x \in E{:}\, (x+1)/3
\end{aligned}$$

Which of id, f, g, h and k are strict? monotonic? continuous? Use the Fixpoint Theorem to find a fixpoint for every continuous function among the five functions. Do these functions have other fixpoints? Can discontinuous functions have fixpoints?

5.7.4 Finite powersets

The finite powerset $\mathcal{P}_f(A)$ of a set A consists of every finite subset of A and is partially ordered by $\subseteq$. Find a set A such that $\mathcal{P}_f(A)$ *not* a cpo.

5.7.5 Two set functions

Let $P\omega$ be the cpo $\mathcal{P}(Nat)$ (which is ordered by $\subseteq$ and has the empty set $\varnothing$ as its least element), and let the cpo $Bool_{f<t}$ be as defined in section 5.3.1 (i.e., $Bool_{f<t}$ has domain {**false, true**} and an ordering $\preceq_{f<t}$ in which **false** $\preceq_{f<t}$ **true**).

Define two functions is-nonempty and is-infinite that map $P\omega$ to $Bool_{f<t}$ as follows for any x in $P\omega$:

$$\begin{aligned}
\mathsf{is_nonempty(x)} &\stackrel{d}{=} \textbf{if } \mathsf{x} = \varnothing \quad \textbf{then false else true} \\
\mathsf{is_infinite(x)} &\stackrel{d}{=} \textbf{if } \mathsf{x} \text{ is finite } \textbf{then false else true}
\end{aligned}$$

Which of these functions are strict? monotonic? continuous?

5.7.6 The FM function

Define the function FM $\in (A \to A)$ where $A \stackrel{d}{=} (Nat \times Nat \to Nat_\bot)$ as follows for every $\mathsf{m} \in A$:

$$\begin{aligned}
\mathsf{FM(m)} \stackrel{d}{=} \lambda\langle \mathsf{x,y}\rangle \in (Nat \times Nat){:}\, &\textbf{if } \mathsf{x} = 0 \textbf{ then } \mathsf{y} \\
&\textbf{else } \mathsf{m(m(pred(x), y), m(x, pred(y)))}
\end{aligned}$$

where $\mathsf{pred(x)} \stackrel{d}{=}$ **if** x>0 **then** x–1 **else** 0.

Prove that FM is continuous. What is the least fixpoint of FM? Is the max function a fixpoint of FM? Does FM have other fixpoints? If so, which?

5.7.7 The 91 function

Assume that we would like to define a function $\mathsf{g} \in NN \stackrel{d}{=} (Nat \to Nat_\perp)$ as follows:

$$\mathsf{g} \stackrel{d}{=} \lambda x \in Nat: \textbf{if } x > 100 \textbf{ then } x - 10 \textbf{ else } \mathsf{g}(\mathsf{g}(x+1))$$

Show how g can be found as the fixpoint of a function which is in the domain $[NN \to NN]$. Find a simple definition of g.

When you succeed in finding a simple definition of g, you may ponder upon the fact that whereas it is usually quite easy to check whether or not a given element (in this case the simply defined g) really is a fixpoint of some given function F (in this case the function that for any argument g is evaluated by the formula at the right-hand side of the equation above), it is frequently very much more difficult to construct a fixpoint of F.

5.7.8 The value_at_bottom function

Assume that C is a cpo and define the function $\mathsf{value\_at\_bottom}_C$ that maps $[C \to C]$ to C as follows:

$$\mathsf{value\_at\_bottom}_C \stackrel{d}{=} \lambda \mathsf{f} \in [C \to C]: \mathsf{f}(\perp_C)$$

Is $\mathsf{value\_at\_bottom}_C$ strict? monotonic? continuous?

Show that if C is a flat cpo, then the function $\mathsf{value\_at\_bottom}_C$ can be used to find fixpoints of continuous functions mapping C to itself, i.e., that for any $\mathsf{f} \in [C \to C]$, $\mathsf{value\_at\_bottom}_C(\mathsf{f})$ is a fixpoint for f. Is this fixpoint the least fixpoint of f?

May $\mathsf{value\_at\_bottom}_C$ be used to find fixpoints if C is nonflat?

5.7.9 Some meta-functions

Assume that C and D are two cpo's. Define three functions is_strict, is_monotone and is_continuous that maps $(C \to D)$ to *Bool* and that may be used to determine whether or not given functions are strict, monotonic and continuous. Are the three functions you have defined strict? monotonic? or continuous?

Chapter 6
A language with errors and infinite loops

6.1 A richer language

In this chapter we introduce a simple programming language which we call While, and give a denotational definition of its semantics.

The While language is at first glance not very unlike Loop, but there are a few differences, some of which are important:

(1) There are more operations and relations in While than in Loop. Of special interest is the inclusion of *division*, which entails that we must define the semantics of division by 0, and in general decide how to treat undefined operations.

(2) There is a limit to the size of integers that can be assigned to a variable. Should the value of an integer expression be greater than this limit ('arithmetic overflow'), an error occurs.

(3) If the input sequence is empty, an error will occur if a **get** imperative is executed.

(4) Possibly more important, at least conceptually, than the various error possibilities, is that we allow **while** imperatives in While programs. Such imperatives may lead to infinite loops, and their semantics must therefore be quite unlike the semantics of the **loop** imperatives of the Loop language.

(5) In order to reduce the number of details in our language, we do not include **loop** imperatives in While, and place integer and Boolean expressions in one syntactical category.

The While language is a little more realistic than Loop, but still a very simple language: Only integer calculations can be programmed, and there are, for instance, no declarations, no side-effects and no abstractions (i.e., no procedures, no classes and no functions). In later chapters we show how to define the semantics of richer and more powerful languages where such constructions are allowed.

We start our treatment of the While language by defining the syntax of the language. The intended, operational semantics of the While language should be obvious, and is not defined. A formal, denotational definition of the semantics of the While language is then given. After presenting a few worked examples of how the semantic definitions can be used to find the results of executing small programs, we prove a theorem (the *While Theorem*) which bridges the gap between the formal and rather mathematical definition of the semantics of **while** imperatives given in this chapter, and other and more operational definitions given in the ensuing chapters. The chapter closes with some exercises.

6.2 Syntax of While

The While language has the following syntactical categories:

Program:	Programs
Imp:	Imperatives
Exp:	Expressions
Literal:	Literals
Binop:	Binary operators (+, /, =, <, ∧ etc.)
Unop:	Unary operators (¬ and −)
Ident:	Identifiers

Abstract syntax algebras for these categories are defined implicitly by the BNF rules given in figure 6.1. The syntax algebras *Ident* and *Literal* are as defined for the Loop language in section 4.5.1 on page 64.

The informal semantics of the While language should be obvious, and is not given here. The only feature that may require explanation is how the expressions after **if** and **while** are used: Such an expression is

⟨*program*⟩	::=	**begin** ⟨*imp*⟩ **end**	
⟨*imp*⟩	::=	**skip**	(Do nothing)
	$\mid$	**put** ⟨*exp*⟩	(Output of integer value)
	$\mid$	**get** ⟨*ident*⟩	(Input to a variable)
	$\mid$	⟨*ident*⟩ := ⟨*exp*⟩	(Assignment to a variable)
	$\mid$	⟨*imp*⟩; ⟨*imp*⟩	(Sequential composition)
	$\mid$	**if** ⟨*exp*⟩ **then** ⟨*imp*⟩ **else** ⟨*imp*⟩ **fi**	(Conditional)
	$\mid$	**while** ⟨*exp*⟩ **do** ⟨*imp*⟩ **od**	(Unbounded loop)
⟨*exp*⟩	::=	⟨*literal*⟩	(Numeral)
	$\mid$	⟨*ident*⟩	(Variable)
	$\mid$	(⟨*exp*⟩ ⟨*binop*⟩ ⟨*exp*⟩)	(Compound binary expr.)
	$\mid$	(⟨*unop*⟩ ⟨*exp*⟩)	(Compound unary expr.)
⟨*binop*⟩	::=	$+ \mid - \mid * \mid /$	(Binary integer operators)
	$\mid$	$= \mid \neq \mid < \mid \leq \mid \geq \mid >$	(Integer relations)
	$\mid$	$\wedge \mid \vee \mid \Rightarrow \mid \Leftrightarrow$	(Binary logical operators)
⟨*unop*⟩	::=	$- \mid \neg$	(Unary operators)

Figure 6.1: BNF productions for While

considered to be true for a given state if its value (an integer) is greater than 0, and false otherwise.

6.3 Standard semantics of While

A formal, denotational definition of the semantics of a programming language like While, consists of mappings from syntax to semantics: For each syntax algebra we define a semantic observer that maps the syntax algebra to a semantic algebra. Every syntactically legal construction is mapped to its denotation - which we take to be the meaning of the construction - by these mappings. Semantic mappings for the While language are defined in section 6.3.2 below. But before defining these mappings, we define various semantic algebras: first some basic domains, and then domains that consists of the denotations of the constructions of the language.

6.3.1 Semantic algebras for While

Often when we give a denotational definition of the semantics of a programming language, we start by defining three algebras whose carriers contain what we say are the *expressible*, the *storable* and the *denotable* values of the language. The expressible values are those values that may occur as values of expressions (or rather, more precisely, values of denotations of expressions), the storable values are those values that may be assigned to variables, and the denotable values are those values that may be bound (by declarations) to identifiers.

In the While language, expressions may have integers and Booleans as values. The algebra of expressible values - which we denote by *E* - is therefore defined (in figure 4.2 on page 47) to be equal to the disjoint sum of the algebras *Int* and *Bool*, i.e., *Bool* + *Int*.

We have already said that While is somewhat more realistic than Loop in the sense that there is a limit to the size of integers that may be assigned to variables. We have also said that all variables are implicitly assumed to be integer variables. This means that the algebra of storable values - which we denote by *S* - may be defined to have a carrier that consists of all integers with an absolute value less than some given integer maxint:

$$S \stackrel{d}{=} \{\mathrm{i} \in Int \mid \mathrm{abs(i)} < \mathrm{maxint}\}$$

We could, of course, have limited the set of expressible values in the same manner, but have chosen not to do so in order to reduce the amount of details in the semantic equations below. Our main reason for limiting the size of *S* elements is to show how it may done.

There are no declarations in the While language, and an algebra of denotable values is therefore not necessary to define for this language.

Later in this chapter, we define the denotation of any imperative in the While language to be a function that maps states to states, just as we did for the Loop language described in chapter 2. We therefore introduce semantic algebras *Store*, *Input*, *Output* and *State*, quite similar to algebras introduced for Loop in figure 4.13 on page 68. But the algebras defined in this chapter are not identical to the same-named algebras defined in chapter 4. One difference is that a While-*Store* is a function that maps identifiers to integers of limited size (members of *S*), and not to *all* integers (as a Loop-*Store* does). Another, more important difference is that the main functions of the algebra *State* for While are defined differently from functions with the same names in the *State* algebra for Loop, they even have somewhat different signatures. The reason for these latter differences is that the new *State* functions may have ⊥ elements as values. Figure 6.2 contains definitions of the semantic algebras of the While language. The functions of the *State* algebra are defined in figure 6.3.

Expressible values:

$E \stackrel{d}{=} Bool + Int$

Storable values:

$S \stackrel{d}{=} \{\mathrm{i} \in Int \mid \mathrm{abs(i)} < \mathrm{maxint}\}$

States etc.:

$Store \stackrel{d}{=} (Ident \to S), \quad Input \stackrel{d}{=} \mathrm{Int}^*, \quad Output \stackrel{d}{=} \mathrm{Int}^*$

$State \stackrel{d}{=} Input \times Store \times Output$

Functions: Defined in figure 6.3

Denotations:

PV	$\stackrel{d}{=} (Input \to Output_\bot)$	*(Denotations of programs)*
MV	$\stackrel{d}{=} (State_\bot \to State_\bot)$	*(Denotations of imperatives)*
EV	$\stackrel{d}{=} (State_\bot \to E_\bot)$	*(Denotations of expressions)*
BOV	$\stackrel{d}{=} (E_\bot \times E_\bot \to E_\bot)$	*(Denotations of binary operators)*
UOV	$\stackrel{d}{=} (E_\bot \to E_\bot)$	*(Denotations of unary operators)*
LV	$\stackrel{d}{=} Int$	*(Denotations of literals)*

Figure 6.2: Semantic algebras for the While language

6.3.2 Semantic mappings for While

A formal, denotational definition of the semantics of a programming language like While consists of mappings from syntax to semantics: For each syntax algebra a semantic mapping (function) is defined which maps the syntax algebra to a semantic algebra. Every syntactically legal construction of the language is mapped to its denotation (which we take to be the meaning of the construction) by semantic mappings.

In this section we define semantic mappings for each of the syntax algebras of the While language:

State

Carrier: $State = Input \times Store \times Output$

Functions:

$$
\begin{array}{lll}
\text{init} & \in & (Input \to State) \\
\text{access} & \in & (State \times Ident \to S) \\
\text{get} & \in & (State \times Ident \to State_\perp) \\
\text{assign} & \in & (State \times Ident \times E_\perp \to State_\perp) \\
\text{put} & \in & (State \times E_\perp \to State_\perp)
\end{array}
$$

Axioms:

$$
\begin{array}{ll}
\text{init(inp)} & = \langle \text{inp}, \lambda \text{id} \in Ident\text{: } 0, \varepsilon \rangle \\
\text{access}(\langle \text{inp, h, out} \rangle, \text{id}) & = \text{h(id)} \\
\text{get}(\langle \text{inp, h, out} \rangle, \text{id}) & = \textbf{case} \text{ inp } \textbf{of } Int^* \\
& \quad \varepsilon \quad \Rightarrow \perp_{State} \\
& \quad (\text{n} \dashv \text{i'}) \quad \Rightarrow \langle \text{i', h.bind(id, n), out} \rangle \\
& \quad \textbf{endcase} \\
\text{assign}(\langle \text{inp, h, out} \rangle, \text{id, e}) & = \textbf{case} \text{ e } \textbf{of } E_\perp \\
& \quad \perp_E \quad \Rightarrow \perp_{State} \\
& \quad \text{n } \textbf{in } Int \quad \Rightarrow \langle \text{inp, h.bind(id, n), out} \rangle \\
& \quad \textbf{endcase} \\
\text{put}(\langle \text{inp, h, out} \rangle, \text{e}) & = \textbf{case} \text{ e } \textbf{of } E_\perp \\
& \quad \perp_E \quad \Rightarrow \perp_{State} \\
& \quad \text{n } \textbf{in } Int \quad \Rightarrow \langle \text{inp, h, out} \vdash \text{n} \rangle \\
& \quad \textbf{endcase}
\end{array}
$$

Figure 6.3: The *State* algebra for the While language

$\mathcal{P}$	$\in (Prog \to PV)$	*PV* is the semantic algebra for *Prog*
$\mathcal{M}$	$\in (Imp \to MV)$	*MV* is the semantic algebra for *Imp*
$\mathcal{E}$	$\in (Exp \to EV)$	*EV* is the semantic algebra for *Exp*
$\mathcal{BO}$	$\in (Binop \to BOV)$	*BOV* is the semantic algebra for *Binop*
$\mathcal{UO}$	$\in (Unop \to UOV)$	*UOV* is the semantic algebra for *Unop*
$\mathcal{A}$	$\in (Literal \to LV)$	*LV* is the semantic algebra for *Literal*

There are three important differences between the way we defined the semantics of Loop and how we define the semantics of the While language:

(1) We are more general in our treatment of operators.

(2) We treat various error possibilities, using $\perp$ elements as error values.

(3) The semantics of **while** imperatives are of course quite different from the semantics of **loop** imperatives because of the possibilities for infinite looping. We use the $\perp$ element of the algebra $State_\perp$ as the 'result' of infinite loops.

Observe that $\perp$ elements are used for two quite different purposes in the definition of the semantics of While as given in this chapter: 1) as error elements, and 2) as 'results' of infinite loops. It is certainly possible to distinguish these cases by including two (or more, should distinction between various kinds of errors be desirable) distinct 'undefined' elements in the various algebras. This is not done here. We deem the cost in added complexity to outweigh the possible benefits in the definition of the semantics of the rather simple While language. In later chapters we show how to define the semantics of languages with facilities for exception handling and error catching, and will then show how to distinguish between various kinds of errors.

Semantic mappings for the While language are defined in figure 6.4. The semantic mapping for *Literal*, viz. $\mathcal{A}$, is identical to the same mapping for Loop, and is defined in figure 4.14 on page 69.

Some of the equations in figure 6.4 and some of the notation used in these equations may need some explanation:

- If $\mathsf{f} \in (C \to D)$ is a function that maps a cpo C to a cpo D, the notation $\underline{\lambda}\mathsf{c} \in C\colon \mathsf{f}(\mathsf{c})$ was introduced in section 5.5 as shorthand for $\lambda\mathsf{c} \in C\colon \mathbf{if}\ \mathsf{c} = \perp_C\ \mathbf{then}\ \perp_D\ \mathbf{else}\ \mathsf{f}(\mathsf{c})$. Thus, $\underline{\lambda}\mathsf{c} \in C\colon \mathsf{f}(\mathsf{c})$ is always a strict function, called the strict extension of f.

- If A, B and C are three cpo's (not necessarily distinct), f is a function in $(A \to B)$ and g a function in $(B \to C)$, we define the *composition* $\mathsf{g} \circ \mathsf{f}$ of f and g to be a function in $(A \to C)$ which is defined as follows:

$$\mathsf{g} \circ \mathsf{f} \stackrel{d}{=} \lambda\mathsf{a} \in A\colon \mathsf{g}(\mathsf{f}(\mathsf{a}))$$

  Observe that if f and g are strict functions, then so is $\mathsf{g} \circ \mathsf{f}$.

- The function $\mathsf{cond} \in (EV \times MV \times MV \to MV)$ is defined as follows for any $\mathsf{ev} \in EV$ and $\mathsf{mv}_1, \mathsf{mv}_2 \in MV$:

$$\begin{aligned}\mathsf{cond}(\mathsf{ev}, \mathsf{mv}_1, \mathsf{mv}_2) = \underline{\lambda}\mathsf{s} \in State_\perp\colon\ & \mathbf{case}\ \mathsf{ev}(\mathsf{s})\ \mathbf{of}\ E_\perp \\ & \quad \mathbf{true} \Rightarrow \mathsf{mv}_1(\mathsf{s}) \\ & \quad \mathbf{false} \Rightarrow \mathsf{mv}_2(\mathsf{s}) \\ & \quad \mathbf{otherwise}\ \perp_{State}\end{aligned}$$

  Observe that we write **true** and **false** instead of the more cumbersome E'in_Bool(**true**) and E'in_Bool(**false**), which of course is what we should have written if we followed our naming conventions (described in section 4.1.6) to the letter.

$\mathcal{E} \in (Exp \to EV) = (Exp \to (State_\perp \to E_\perp))$

$$\begin{aligned}
&\mathcal{E}[\![\text{lit}]\!] &&= \underline{\lambda} s \in State_\perp{:}\ \mathcal{A}[\![\text{lit}]\!]\\
&\mathcal{E}[\![\text{id}]\!] &&= \underline{\lambda} s \in State_\perp{:}\ \text{s.access(id)}\\
&\mathcal{E}[\![\text{ex}_1 \text{ binop ex}_2]\!] &&= \underline{\lambda} s \in State_\perp{:}\ \mathcal{BO}[\![\text{binop}]\!](\mathcal{E}[\![\text{ex}_1]\!](s), \mathcal{E}[\![\text{ex}_2]\!](s))\\
&\mathcal{E}[\![\text{unop ex}]\!] &&= \underline{\lambda} s \in State_\perp{:}\ \mathcal{UO}[\![\text{unop}]\!](\mathcal{E}[\![\text{ex}]\!](s))
\end{aligned}$$

$\mathcal{UO} \in (Unop \to UOV) = (Unop \to (E_\perp \to E_\perp))$

$$\begin{aligned}
\mathcal{UO}[\![\neg]\!] = \underline{\lambda} e \in E_\perp{:}\ &\textbf{case } e \textbf{ of } E{:}\\
&\quad b \in Bool \Rightarrow \textbf{if then true else false}\\
&\quad \textbf{otherwise} \Rightarrow \perp_E
\end{aligned}$$

The denotation of – (minus) is defined similarly

$\mathcal{BO} \in (Binop \to BOV) = (Binop \to (E_\perp \times E_\perp \to E_\perp))$

$$\begin{aligned}
\mathcal{BO}[\![<]\!] = \underline{\lambda}\langle e_1, e_2\rangle \in (E_\perp \times E_\perp){:}\ &\textbf{case } \langle e_1, e_2\rangle{:}\\
&\langle i_1, i_2\rangle \in (Int \times Int) \Rightarrow (\textbf{if } i_1 < i_2 \textbf{ then true else false})\\
&\textbf{otherwise} \Rightarrow \perp_E\\
\mathcal{BO}[\![/]\!] = \underline{\lambda}\langle e_1, e_2\rangle \in (E_\perp \times E_\perp){:}\ &\textbf{case } \langle e_1, e_2\rangle{:}\\
&\langle i_1, i_2\rangle \in (Int \times Int) \Rightarrow (\textbf{if } i_2 = 0 \textbf{ then } \perp_E \textbf{ else } i_1 / i_2)\\
&\textbf{otherwise} \Rightarrow \perp_E
\end{aligned}$$

The denotations of the other operators are defined similarly

$\mathcal{M} \in (Imp \to MV) = (Imp \to (State_\perp \to State_\perp))$

$$\begin{aligned}
&\mathcal{M}[\![\textbf{skip}]\!] &&= id_{State_\perp} \stackrel{d}{=} \underline{\lambda} s \in State_\perp{:}\ s\\
&\mathcal{M}[\![\textbf{put } \text{ex}]\!] &&= \underline{\lambda} s \in State_\perp{:}\ \text{s.put}(\mathcal{E}[\![\text{ex}]\!](s))\\
&\mathcal{M}[\![\textbf{get } \text{id}]\!] &&= \underline{\lambda} s \in State_\perp{:}\ \text{s.get(id)}\\
&\mathcal{M}[\![\text{id} := \text{ex}]\!] &&= \underline{\lambda} s \in State_\perp{:}\ \text{s.assign}(\text{id}, \mathcal{E}[\![\text{ex}]\!](s))\\
&\mathcal{M}[\![\text{imp}_1;\ \text{imp}_2]\!] &&= \mathcal{M}[\![\text{imp}_2]\!] \circ \mathcal{M}[\![\text{imp}_1]\!]\\
&\mathcal{M}[\![\textbf{if } \text{ex } \textbf{then } \text{imp}_1 \textbf{ else } \text{imp}_2 \textbf{ fi}]\!] &&\\
& &&= \text{cond}(\mathcal{E}[\![\text{ex}]\!], \mathcal{M}[\![\text{imp}_1]\!], \mathcal{M}[\![\text{imp}_2]\!])\\
&\mathcal{M}[\![\textbf{while } \text{ex } \textbf{do } \text{imp } \textbf{od}]\!] &&\\
& &&= Y_{MV}(\lambda w \in MV{:} \text{cond}(\mathcal{E}[\![\text{ex}]\!],\\
& &&\qquad w \circ \mathcal{M}[\![\text{imp}]\!], id_{State_\perp}))
\end{aligned}$$

$\mathcal{P} \in (Program \to PV) = (Program \to (Input \to Output_\perp))$

$$\begin{aligned}
\mathcal{P}[\![\textbf{begin } \text{imp } \textbf{end}]\!] = \lambda ip \in Input{:}\ &\textbf{case } \mathcal{M}[\![\text{imp}]\!](State\text{'init}(ip)) \textbf{ of}\\
&\quad \perp_{State} \Rightarrow \perp_{Output}\\
&\quad s \textbf{ in } State \Rightarrow \text{s.Output}
\end{aligned}$$

Figure 6.4: Standard semantic mappings for the While language

In accordance with our discussion in section 5.2, we have in figure 6.4 defined the denotation of a **while** imperative **while** ex **do** imp **od** to be a fixpoint of the function $\mathsf{qw} = \lambda \mathsf{w} \in MV\colon \mathsf{cond}(\mathcal{E}[\![\mathsf{ex}]\!],\ \mathsf{w} \circ \mathcal{M}[\![\mathsf{imp}]\!],\ \mathsf{id}_{State_\perp})$. The Fixpoint Theorem (page 90) only guarantees that continuous functions have fixpoints. In order to use this theorem to find a fixpoint of qw, we must therefore prove that qw is continuous:

Proposition 6.1 *The function*

$$\mathsf{qw} \stackrel{d}{=} \lambda \mathsf{w} \in MV\colon \mathsf{cond}(\mathcal{E}[\![\mathsf{ex}]\!],\ \mathsf{w} \circ \mathcal{M}[\![\mathsf{imp}]\!],\ \mathsf{id}_{State_\perp})$$

is a continuous function.

Proof: We must prove that qw is monotonic and preserves least upper bounds. To do that, let us first consider the value of qw for any $\mathsf{w'} \in MV$ and any $\mathsf{s'} \in State$:

$$\begin{aligned}\mathsf{qw}(\mathsf{w'})(\mathsf{s'}) &= \mathsf{cond}(\mathcal{E}[\![\mathsf{ex}]\!],\ \mathsf{w'} \circ \mathcal{M}[\![\mathsf{imp}]\!],\ \mathsf{id}_{State_\perp})(\mathsf{s'})\\ &= \textbf{if } \mathcal{E}[\![\mathsf{ex}]\!](\mathsf{s'}) = \textbf{true then } (\mathsf{w'} \circ \mathcal{M}[\![\mathsf{imp}]\!])(\mathsf{s'}) \textbf{ else}\\ &\quad\ \textbf{if } \mathcal{E}[\![\mathsf{ex}]\!](\mathsf{s'}) = \textbf{false then } \mathsf{id}_{State_\perp}(\mathsf{s'})\\ &\quad\ \textbf{else } \perp_{State}\\ &= \textbf{if } \mathcal{E}[\![\mathsf{ex}]\!](\mathsf{s'}) = \textbf{true then } \mathsf{w'}(\mathcal{M}[\![\mathsf{imp}]\!](\mathsf{s'})) \textbf{ else}\\ &\quad\ \textbf{if } \mathcal{E}[\![\mathsf{ex}]\!](\mathsf{s'}) = \textbf{false then } \mathsf{s'}\\ &\quad\ \textbf{else } \perp_{State}\end{aligned}$$

qw ***is monotonic***: Assume that $\mathsf{w}_1 \sqsubseteq_{MV} \mathsf{w}_2$. We must prove that $\mathsf{qw}(\mathsf{w}_1) \sqsubseteq_{MV} \mathsf{qw}(\mathsf{w}_2)$. By definition of qw and the definition of $\sqsubseteq_{MV}$, this is equivalent to proving

$$\mathsf{qw}(\mathsf{w}_1)(\mathsf{s}) \sqsubseteq_{State_\perp} \mathsf{qw}(\mathsf{w}_2)(\mathsf{s})$$

for every $\mathsf{s} \in State$.

If $\mathcal{E}[\![\mathsf{ex}]\!](\mathsf{s}) \neq$ **true**, $\mathsf{qw}(\mathsf{w}_1)(\mathsf{s}) = \mathsf{qw}(\mathsf{w}_2)(\mathsf{s})$, and the desired conclusion follows because $\sqsubseteq_{State_\perp}$ is reflexive.

If $\mathcal{E}[\![\mathsf{ex}]\!](\mathsf{s}) =$ **true**, $\mathsf{qw}(\mathsf{w}_i)(\mathsf{s}) = \mathsf{w}_i(\mathcal{M}[\![\mathsf{imp}]\!](\mathsf{s}))$ for $i = 1, 2$, and we must prove that

$$\mathsf{w}_1(\mathcal{M}[\![\mathsf{imp}]\!](\mathsf{s})) \sqsubseteq_{State_\perp} \mathsf{w}_2(\mathcal{M}[\![\mathsf{imp}]\!](\mathsf{s}))$$

This holds because by assumption $\mathsf{w}_1 \sqsubseteq_{MV} \mathsf{w}_2$, which means that $\mathsf{w}_1(\mathsf{s'}) \sqsubseteq_{State_\perp} \mathsf{w}_2(\mathsf{s'})$ for every state s', in particular for the state $\mathsf{s'} = \mathcal{M}[\![\mathsf{imp}]\!](\mathsf{s})$.

qw ***preserves least upper bounds***: Assume that $\{\mathsf{w}_i\}_{i=0}^{\infty}$ is a chain in MV. We have just proved that qw is monotonic. Applying this to the assumption, we get that $\{\mathsf{qw}(\mathsf{w}_i)\}_{i=0}^{\infty}$ is a chain. We must prove that

$$\mathsf{qw}(\lfloor MV \rfloor_{i=0}^{\infty} \mathsf{w}_i) = \lfloor MV \rfloor_{i=0}^{\infty} (\mathsf{qw}(\mathsf{w}_i))$$

Two functions are equal if and only if they have equal values for all arguments. Our conclusion therefore follows if we can prove

$$\mathsf{qw}(\lfloor MV \rfloor_{i=0}^{\infty} \mathsf{w}_i)(\mathsf{s}) = (\lfloor MV \rfloor_{i=0}^{\infty} \mathsf{qw}(\mathsf{w}_i))(\mathsf{s})$$

for every state s. By proposition 5.3 on page 84 applied to the right-hand side of this equation, it suffices to prove that

$$\mathsf{qw}(\lfloor MV \rfloor_{i=0}^{\infty} \mathsf{w}_i)(\mathsf{s}) = \lfloor State_\perp \rfloor_{i=0}^{\infty} (\mathsf{qw}(\mathsf{w}_i)(\mathsf{s}))$$

for every state s. Therefore, let s be any given state, and consider the value of $\mathcal{E}[\![\mathsf{ex}]\!]$ for s:

If s is such that $\mathcal{E}[\![\mathsf{ex}]\!](\mathsf{s}) = \textbf{false}$:

$$\begin{aligned}
\mathsf{qw}(\lfloor MV \rfloor_{i=0}^{\infty} \mathsf{w}_i)(\mathsf{s}) &= \mathsf{s} \\
&= \lfloor State_\perp \rfloor_{i=0}^{\infty} \mathsf{s} \\
&= \lfloor State_\perp \rfloor_{i=0}^{\infty} (\mathsf{qw}(\mathsf{w}_i)(\mathsf{s}))
\end{aligned}$$

If s is such that $\mathcal{E}[\![\mathsf{ex}]\!](\mathsf{s}) = \textbf{true}$:

$$\begin{aligned}
\mathsf{qw}(\lfloor MV \rfloor_{i=0}^{\infty} \mathsf{w}_i)(\mathsf{s}) &= (\lfloor MV \rfloor_{i=0}^{\infty} \mathsf{w}_i) \circ (\mathcal{M}[\![\mathsf{imp}]\!])(\mathsf{s}) \\
&= (\lfloor MV \rfloor_{i=0}^{\infty} \mathsf{w}_i)(\mathcal{M}[\![\mathsf{imp}]\!](\mathsf{s})) \\
&= \lfloor State_\perp \rfloor_{i=0}^{\infty} \mathsf{w}_i(\mathcal{M}[\![\mathsf{imp}]\!](\mathsf{s})) \\
&= \lfloor State_\perp \rfloor_{i=0}^{\infty} (\mathsf{qw}(\mathsf{w}_i)(\mathsf{s}))
\end{aligned}$$

Finally, the case that s is such that $\mathcal{E}[\![\mathsf{ex}]\!](\mathsf{s}) \notin \{\textbf{true}, \textbf{false}\}$:

$$\begin{aligned}
\mathsf{qw}(\lfloor MV \rfloor_{i=0}^{\infty} \mathsf{w}_i)(\mathsf{s}) &= \perp_{State} \\
&= \lfloor State_\perp \rfloor_{i=0}^{\infty} \perp_{State} \\
&= \lfloor State_\perp \rfloor_{i=0}^{\infty} (\mathsf{qw}(\mathsf{w}_i)(\mathsf{s}))
\end{aligned}$$

End of proof of proposition 6.1.

6.4 Examples

6.4.1 A very simple program

Let PS be the following program:

begin get x; **put** (x + **10**) **end**

The value of the denotation of this program applied to the input sequence $\langle 2\rangle$ should of course be the output sequence $\langle 4\rangle$. Let us see if this is the case:

$$\begin{aligned}
\mathcal{P}[\![\mathsf{PS}]\!](\langle 2\rangle) &= \mathcal{M}[\![\mathbf{get}\ \mathsf{x};\ \mathbf{put}\ (\mathsf{x}+\mathbf{10})]\!](\mathsf{s}_0)\,.\,\mathsf{Output} \\
&\quad \text{where } \mathsf{s}_0 = \mathsf{State'init}(\langle 2\rangle) = \langle\langle 2\rangle,\ \mathsf{h}_0,\ \varepsilon\rangle \\
&\qquad\qquad \mathsf{h}_0 = \lambda \mathsf{id}{:}\,0 \\
&= \mathcal{M}[\![\mathbf{put}\ (\mathsf{x}+\mathbf{10})]\!](\mathcal{M}[\![\mathbf{get}\ \mathsf{x}]\!](\mathsf{s}_0))\,.\,\mathsf{Output} \\
&= \mathcal{M}[\![\mathbf{put}\ (\mathsf{x}+\mathbf{10})]\!](\mathsf{s}_0\,.\,\mathsf{get}(\mathsf{x}))\,.\,\mathsf{Output} \\
&= \mathcal{M}[\![\mathbf{put}\ (\mathsf{x}+\mathbf{10})]\!](\mathsf{s}_1)\,.\,\mathsf{Output} \\
&\quad \text{where } \mathsf{s}_1 = \langle\varepsilon,\ \mathsf{h}_1,\ \varepsilon\rangle \\
&\qquad\qquad \mathsf{h}_1 = \lambda \mathsf{id}{:}\,(\mathbf{if}\ \mathsf{id}=\mathsf{x}\ \mathbf{then}\ 2\ \mathbf{else}\ 0) \\
&= \mathsf{s}_1\,.\,\mathsf{put}(\mathcal{E}[\![(\mathsf{x}+\mathbf{10})]\!](\mathsf{s}_1))\,.\,\mathsf{Output} \\
&= \mathsf{s}_1\,.\,\mathsf{put}(\mathcal{BO}[\![+]\!](\mathcal{E}[\![\mathsf{x}]\!](\mathsf{s}_1), \\
&\qquad\qquad \mathcal{E}[\![\mathbf{10}]\!](\mathsf{s}_1)))\,.\,\mathsf{Output} \\
&= \mathsf{s}_1\,.\,\mathsf{put}(\mathcal{BO}[\![+]\!](\mathsf{s}_1\,.\,\mathsf{access}(\mathsf{x}), \\
&\qquad\qquad \mathcal{A}[\![\mathbf{10}]\!]))\,.\,\mathsf{Output} \\
&= \mathsf{s}_1\,.\,\mathsf{put}(\mathcal{BO}[\![+]\!](2,\ 2))\,.\,\mathsf{Output} \\
&= \mathsf{s}_1\,.\,\mathsf{put}(2+2)\,.\,\mathsf{Output} \\
&= \langle\varepsilon,\ \mathsf{h}_1,\ \varepsilon \vdash 4\rangle\,.\,\mathsf{Output} \\
&= \langle\varepsilon,\ \mathsf{h}_1,\ \langle 4\rangle\rangle\,.\,\mathsf{Output} \\
&= \langle 4\rangle
\end{aligned}$$

- as expected.

6.4.2 A finite loop

Let Imp_2 be the following imperative:

$$\mathbf{while}\ (\mathsf{x} > \mathbf{0})\ \mathbf{do}\ \mathsf{x} := (\mathsf{x} - \mathbf{1})\ \mathbf{od}$$

and let s_0 be a state which is such that

$$\mathsf{s}_0\,.\,\mathsf{access}(\mathsf{x}) = 2$$

According to the intended, operational semantics of **while** imperatives, it is obvious what happens when Imp_2 is executed from s_0: A state s' for which $\mathsf{s'}\,.\,\mathsf{access}(\mathsf{x}) = 0$ is produced. Let us see if our formal definitions give the same result. We must apply the denotation of Imp_2 (which by definition is a fixpoint) to the state s_0:

$$\mathcal{M}[\![\mathsf{Imp}_2]\!](\mathsf{s}_0) = \mathsf{Y}_{MV}(\mathsf{qw})(\mathsf{s}_0)$$

where

$$\begin{aligned}
\mathsf{qw} &= \lambda \mathsf{w} \in MV{:}\,(\mathsf{cond}(\mathsf{bv},\ \mathsf{w}\circ\mathsf{mv},\ \mathsf{id}_{State_\perp})) \\
\mathsf{bv} &= \mathcal{E}[\![\mathsf{x} > \mathbf{0}]\!] \\
\mathsf{mv} &= \mathcal{M}[\![\mathsf{x} := (\mathsf{x}-\mathbf{1})]\!]
\end{aligned}$$

By the Fixpoint Theorem

$$\begin{aligned}
Y_{MV}(\mathsf{qw})(\mathsf{s}_0) &= (\lfloor MV \rfloor_{i=0}^{\infty} \mathsf{qw}^i(\bot_{MV}))(\mathsf{s}_0) \\
&= \lfloor State_\bot \rfloor_{i=0}^{\infty}(\mathsf{m}_i(\mathsf{s}_0)) \qquad \text{where } \mathsf{m}_i = \mathsf{qw}^i(\bot_{MV})
\end{aligned}$$

Proposition 5.3 on page 84 justifies the latter of these equations.

Let us study the states in the $State_\bot$ chain $\{\mathsf{m}_i(\mathsf{s}_0)\}_{i=0}^{\infty}$ to see if we can determine their least upper bound:

$$\begin{aligned}
\mathsf{m}_0(\mathsf{s}_0) &= \mathsf{qw}^0(\bot_{MV})(\mathsf{s}_0) \\
&= \bot_{MV}(\mathsf{s}_0) \\
&= \bot_{State}
\end{aligned}$$

In general, for any $i \geq 0$ and any s' which is such that s' . access(x) > 0:

$$\begin{aligned}
\mathsf{m}_{i+1}(\mathsf{s'}) &= \mathsf{qw}^{i+1}(\bot_{MV})(\mathsf{s'}) \\
&= \mathsf{qw}(\mathsf{qw}^i(\bot_{MV}))(\mathsf{s'}) \\
&= \mathsf{qw}(\mathsf{m}_i)(\mathsf{s'}) \\
&= \mathsf{cond}(\mathsf{bv}, (\mathsf{m}_i \circ \mathsf{mv}), \mathsf{id}_{State_\bot})(\mathsf{s'}) \\
&= \textbf{if } \mathsf{bv}(\mathsf{s'}) = \textbf{true then } (\mathsf{m}_i \circ \mathsf{mv})(\mathsf{s'}) \textbf{ else} \\
&\quad\ \textbf{if } \mathsf{bv}(\mathsf{s'}) = \textbf{false then } \mathsf{id}_{State_\bot}(\mathsf{s'}) \\
&\quad\ \textbf{else } \bot_{State} \\
&= (\mathsf{m}_i \circ \mathsf{mv})(\mathsf{s'}) \\
&\qquad \text{Because } \mathsf{bv}(\mathsf{s'}) = \mathcal{E}[\![\mathsf{x} > \mathbf{0}]\!](\mathsf{s'}) \\
&\qquad\qquad = \mathcal{BO}[\![>]\!](\mathcal{E}[\![\mathsf{x}]\!](\mathsf{s'}), \mathcal{E}[\![\mathbf{0}]\!](\mathsf{s'})) \\
&\qquad\qquad = \mathcal{BO}[\![>]\!](\mathsf{t}\,.\,\mathsf{access}(\mathsf{x}), 0) \\
&\qquad\qquad = \textbf{true} \\
&= \mathsf{m}_i(\mathsf{mv}(\mathsf{s'})) \\
&= \mathsf{m}_i(\mathsf{s''}) \\
&\qquad \text{where } \mathsf{s''} = \mathsf{mv}(\mathsf{s'}) \\
&\qquad\qquad = \mathcal{M}[\![\mathsf{x} := (\mathsf{x} - \mathbf{1})]\!](\mathsf{s'}) \\
&\qquad\qquad = \mathsf{s'}\,.\,\mathsf{assign}(\mathsf{x}, \mathcal{E}[\![\mathsf{x} - \mathbf{1}]\!](\mathsf{s'})) \\
&\qquad\qquad = \mathsf{s'}\,.\,\mathsf{assign}(\mathsf{x}, \mathsf{s'}\,.\,\mathsf{access}(\mathsf{x}) - 1) \\
&\qquad \text{Hence: } \mathsf{s''}\,.\,\mathsf{access}(\mathsf{x}) = \mathsf{s'}\,.\,\mathsf{access}(\mathsf{x}) - 1
\end{aligned}$$

But then

$$\begin{aligned}
\mathsf{m}_1(\mathsf{s}_0) &= \mathsf{m}_0(\mathsf{s}_1) \\
&\qquad \text{where } \mathsf{s}_1 = \mathsf{mv}(\mathsf{s}_0) \\
&\qquad\qquad = \mathsf{s}_0\,.\,\mathsf{assign}(\mathsf{x}, \mathsf{s}_0\,.\,\mathsf{access}(\mathsf{x}) - 1) \\
&\qquad\qquad = \mathsf{s}_0\,.\,\mathsf{assign}(\mathsf{x}, 1) \\
&\qquad \text{Hence: } \mathsf{s}_1\,.\,\mathsf{access}(\mathsf{x}) = 1 \\
&= \mathsf{qw}^0(\bot_{MV})(\mathsf{s}_1) \\
&= \bot_{MV}(\mathsf{s}_1) \\
&= \bot_{State}
\end{aligned}$$

$$\begin{aligned}
\mathsf{m}_2(\mathsf{s}_0) &= \mathsf{m}_1(\mathsf{s}_1) \\
&= \mathsf{m}_0(\mathsf{s}_2) \\
&\qquad \text{where } \mathsf{s}_2 = \mathsf{mv}(\mathsf{s}_1) \\
&\qquad\qquad = \mathsf{s}_1\,.\,\mathsf{assign}(\mathsf{x}, \mathsf{s}_1\,.\,\mathsf{access}(\mathsf{x}) - 1) \\
&\qquad\qquad = \mathsf{s}_1\,.\,\mathsf{assign}(\mathsf{x}, 0) \\
&\qquad \text{Hence: } \mathsf{s}_2\,.\,\mathsf{access}(\mathsf{x}) = 0
\end{aligned}$$

$$
\begin{aligned}
&= \mathsf{qw}^0(\bot_{MV})(\mathsf{s}_2)\\
&= \bot_{MV}(\mathsf{s}_2)\\
&= \bot_{State}
\end{aligned}
$$

$$
\begin{aligned}
\mathsf{m}_3(\mathsf{s}_0) &= \mathsf{m}_2(\mathsf{s}_1)\\
&= \mathsf{m}_1(\mathsf{s}_2)\\
&= \mathsf{qw}(\mathsf{m}_0)(\mathsf{s}_2)\\
&= \mathsf{cond}(\mathsf{bv}, (\mathsf{m}_0 \circ \mathsf{mv}), \mathsf{id}_{State_\bot})(\mathsf{s}_2)\\
&= \mathsf{id}_{State_\bot}(\mathsf{s}_2)\\
&\quad \text{Because } \mathsf{bv}(\mathsf{s}_2) = \mathcal{BO}[\![>]\!](\mathsf{s}_2\,.\,\mathsf{access}(\mathsf{x}), 0)\\
&\quad \phantom{\text{Because } \mathsf{bv}(\mathsf{s}_2)} = \mathcal{BO}[\![>]\!](0, 0)\\
&\quad \phantom{\text{Because } \mathsf{bv}(\mathsf{s}_2)} = \mathbf{false}\\
&= \mathsf{s}_2
\end{aligned}
$$

It is easy to prove by induction that for every $i \geq 0$:

$$
\begin{aligned}
\mathsf{m}_i(\mathsf{s}_0) &= \bot_{State} && \text{if } i \leq 2\\
&= \mathsf{s}_2 && \text{if } i > 2
\end{aligned}
$$

The least upper bound of the chain

$$\{\mathsf{m}_i(\mathsf{s}_0)\}_{i=0}^{\infty} = \langle \bot_{State}, \bot_{State}, \bot_{State}, \mathsf{s}_2, \mathsf{s}_2, \mathsf{s}_2, \ldots \rangle$$

is hence equal to s_2, as expected.

Observe the distinction between the states in the set $\{\mathsf{m}_0(\mathsf{s}_0), \mathsf{m}_1(\mathsf{s}_0), \mathsf{m}_2(\mathsf{s}_0), \ldots\}$ and the states in the set $\{\mathsf{s}_0, \mathsf{s}_1, \mathsf{s}_2, \ldots\}$, where s_{i+1} is the result of applying the denotation of $\mathsf{x} := (\mathsf{x} - \mathbf{1})$ to s_i. We have seen above that the states in the former set constitute a chain (which is constant from a certain point, i.e., it is a finite chain). It is, however, *not* true that $\mathsf{s}_i \sqsubseteq \mathsf{s}_{i+1}$, and the states in the set $\{\mathsf{s}_0, \mathsf{s}_1, \mathsf{s}_2, \ldots\}$ do therefore *not* constitute a chain.

It may perhaps be helpful to think of $\mathsf{m}_i(\mathsf{s}_0)$ as a state which is the result of applying a computer which is only able to loop at most i times when executing a **while** imperative to the state s_0. If i iterations are insufficient to reach a state for which the guard of the **while** imperative is false, the computer 'gives up' with an undefined state.

6.4.3 An infinite loop

Let Imp_3 be the following imperative:

$$\mathbf{while}\ (\mathbf{0} = \mathbf{0})\ \mathbf{do\ skip\ od}$$

It is intuitively obvious that an infinite loop will occur if this imperative is executed. Let us see what the denotation of Imp_3 is:

$$
\begin{aligned}
\mathcal{M}[\![\mathsf{Imp}_3]\!] &= \mathcal{M}[\![\mathbf{while}\ (\mathbf{0} = \mathbf{0})\ \mathbf{do}\ \mathsf{imp}\ \mathbf{od}]\!]\\
&= \mathsf{Y}_{MV}(\mathsf{qw})\\
&\quad \text{where } \mathsf{qw} = \lambda \mathsf{w} \in MV\colon (\mathsf{cond}(\mathsf{bv}, \mathsf{w} \circ \mathsf{mv}, \mathsf{id}_{State_\bot}))\\
&\quad \phantom{\text{where }} \mathsf{bv} = \mathcal{E}[\![\mathbf{0} = \mathbf{0}]\!]\\
&\quad \phantom{\text{where }} \mathsf{mv} = \mathcal{M}[\![\mathbf{skip}]\!]\\
&= \bigsqcup_{MV}{}_{i=0}^{\infty} \mathsf{qw}^i(\bot_{MV})
\end{aligned}
$$

Let us study the elements in the MV chain $\{\mathsf{qw}^i(\bot_{MV})\}_{i=0}^{\infty}$:

$$
\begin{aligned}
\mathsf{qw}^0(\bot_{MV}) &= \bot_{MV} \\
\mathsf{qw}^1(\bot_{MV}) &= \mathsf{qw}(\bot_{MV}) \\
&= \mathsf{cond}(\mathsf{bv},\ \bot_{MV} \circ \mathsf{mv},\ \mathsf{id}_{State_\bot}) \\
&= \underline{\lambda}\mathsf{s} \in State_\bot\colon \textbf{if } \mathsf{bv(s)} = \textbf{true then } (\bot_{MV} \circ \mathsf{mv})(\mathsf{s}) \textbf{ else} \\
&\qquad\qquad \textbf{if } \mathsf{bv(s)} = \textbf{false then } \mathsf{id}_{State_\bot}(\mathsf{s}) \\
&\qquad\qquad \textbf{else } \bot_{State} \\
&= \underline{\lambda}\mathsf{s} \in State_\bot\colon (\bot_{MV} \circ \mathsf{mv})(\mathsf{s}) \\
&\qquad \text{Because } \mathsf{bv(s)} = \mathcal{E}[\![\mathbf{0} = \mathbf{0}]\!](\mathsf{s}) \\
&\qquad\qquad\qquad = \textbf{true} \\
&= \underline{\lambda}\mathsf{s} \in State_\bot\colon \bot_{MV}(\mathsf{mv(s)}) \\
&= \underline{\lambda}\mathsf{s} \in State_\bot\colon \bot_{State} \\
&= \bot_{MV}
\end{aligned}
$$

Let us now as an induction hypothesis assume that $\mathsf{qw}^i(\bot_{Mv}) = \bot_{MV}$. We then get:

$$
\begin{aligned}
\mathsf{qw}^{i+1}(\bot_{MV}) &= \mathsf{qw}(\mathsf{qw}^i(\bot_{MV})) \\
&= \mathsf{cond}(\mathsf{bv},\ (\mathsf{qw}^i(\bot_{MV})) \circ \mathsf{mv},\ \mathsf{id}_{State_\bot}) \\
&= \underline{\lambda}\mathsf{s} \in State_\bot\colon (\mathsf{qw}^i(\bot_{MV}) \circ \mathsf{mv})(\mathsf{s}) && \text{(As above)} \\
&= \underline{\lambda}\mathsf{s} \in State_\bot\colon (\bot_{MV} \circ \mathsf{mv})(\mathsf{s}) && \text{(Ind. hyp.)} \\
&= \underline{\lambda}\mathsf{s} \in State_\bot\colon \bot_{MV}(\mathsf{mv(s)}) \\
&= \underline{\lambda}\mathsf{s} \in State_\bot\colon \bot_{State} \\
&= \bot_{MV}
\end{aligned}
$$

This means that $\mathsf{qw}^i(\bot_{MV}) = \bot_{MV}$ for every $i \geq 0$, and therefore

$$
\begin{aligned}
\mathcal{M}[\![\mathsf{Imp}_3]\!] &= \lfloor MV \rfloor_{i=0}^{\infty} \mathsf{qw}^i(\bot_{MV}) \\
&= \lfloor MV \rfloor_{i=0}^{\infty} \bot_{MV} \\
&= \bot_{MV} \\
&= \underline{\lambda}\mathsf{s} \in State_\bot\colon \bot_{State}
\end{aligned}
$$

Hence, $\bot_{State}$ is always the result when we apply the denotation of the imperative **while (0 = 0) do imp od** to any state.

6.5 Semantic equivalence

Two programs P_1 and P_2 are said to be *semantically equivalent*, written

$$\mathsf{P}_1 \cong \mathsf{P}_2$$

if and only if they have identical denotations, i.e., $\mathcal{P}[\![\mathsf{P}_1]\!] = \mathcal{P}[\![\mathsf{P}_2]\!]$. Equivalence of imperatives are defined similarly: Two imperatives imp_1, imp_2 are semantically equivalent - written $\mathsf{imp}_1 \cong \mathsf{imp}_2$ - if and only if $\mathcal{M}[\![\mathsf{imp}_1]\!] = \mathcal{M}[\![\mathsf{imp}_2]\!]$.

An example of two semantically equivalent imperatives:

Proposition 6.2 *For any Boolean expression* b *and any imperative* imp:

$$\textbf{while}\ \mathsf{b}\ \textbf{do}\ \mathsf{imp}\ \textbf{od} \cong \textbf{if}\ \mathsf{b}\ \textbf{then}\ \mathsf{imp};\ \textbf{while}\ \mathsf{b}\ \textbf{do}\ \mathsf{imp}\ \textbf{od}\ \textbf{else}\ \textbf{skip}\ \textbf{fi}$$

Proof: Define

$$\mathsf{mw} \stackrel{d}{=} \mathcal{M}[\![\textbf{while}\ \mathsf{be}\ \textbf{do}\ \mathsf{imp}\ \textbf{od}]\!]$$
$$\mathsf{qw} \stackrel{d}{=} \lambda \mathsf{w} \in MV\!: \mathsf{cond}(\mathcal{E}[\![\mathsf{be}]\!],\ \mathsf{w} \circ \mathcal{M}[\![\mathsf{imp}]\!],\ \mathsf{id}_{State_\perp})$$

Then

$$\begin{aligned}
\mathsf{mw} &= \mathsf{Y}_M(\mathsf{qw}) \\
&= \mathsf{qw}(\mathsf{Y}_M(\mathsf{qw})) \qquad \text{(because } \mathsf{Y}_M(\mathsf{qw}) \text{ is a fixpoint of } \mathsf{qw}\text{)} \\
&= \mathsf{qw}(\mathsf{mw}) \\
&= \mathsf{cond}(\mathcal{E}[\![\mathsf{be}]\!],\ \mathsf{mw} \circ \mathcal{M}[\![\mathsf{imp}]\!],\ \mathsf{id}_{State_\perp}) \\
&= \mathsf{cond}(\mathcal{E}[\![\mathsf{be}]\!],\ (\mathcal{M}[\![\textbf{while}\ \mathsf{be}\ \textbf{do}\ \mathsf{imp}\ \textbf{od}]\!]) \circ \mathcal{M}[\![\mathsf{imp}]\!],\ \mathsf{id}_{State_\perp}) \\
&= \mathsf{cond}(\mathcal{E}[\![\mathsf{be}]\!],\ \mathcal{M}[\![\mathsf{imp};\ \textbf{while}\ \mathsf{be}\ \textbf{do}\ \mathsf{imp}\ \textbf{od}]\!],\ \mathcal{M}[\![\textbf{skip}]\!]) \\
&= \mathcal{M}[\![\textbf{if}\ \mathsf{be}\ \textbf{then}\ \mathsf{imp};\ \textbf{while}\ \mathsf{be}\ \textbf{do}\ \mathsf{imp}\ \textbf{od}\ \textbf{else}\ \textbf{skip}\ \textbf{fi}]\!]
\end{aligned}$$

Observe that to prove this proposition, it suffices to use just one fact about the denotation of the **while** imperative, namely that it is a fixpoint of the function qw. For other results, viz. the While theorem presented in the next section, more 'power' is needed: We must use the fact that the denotation is the *least* fixpoint and that it is defined as the least upper bound of a certain chain of state transformers.

6.6 The While theorem

The denotation of a **while** imperative is defined to be the least fixpoint of a certain function qw. This definition is of course not very useful if you wish to see what will be the result of executing a given **while** imperative on a computer.

The Fixpoint Theorem (page 90) may, however, be used to get a somewhat more applicable description of the denotation of a **while** imperative. According to this theorem, the least fixpoint of the function qw can be found as a least upper bound of a chain of simpler functions m_i. Each function m_i can be thought of as embodying the effect of a computer which is able to perform at most i iterations when executing **while** imperatives. If i iterations are insufficient to reach a state for which the guard of the imperative is false, the m_i computer 'gives up', with the result undefined ($\perp_{State}$). This may be used to determine the result of executing a given **while** imperative from a given start state s_0: Compute $\mathsf{m}_0(\mathsf{s}_0)$, $\mathsf{m}_1(\mathsf{s}_0)$, $\mathsf{m}_2(\mathsf{s}_0)$, etc., until you find the first k such that $\mathsf{s}' = \mathsf{m}_k(\mathsf{s}_0)$ not is undefined. The result of executing the given **while** imperative from s_0 is then equal to s'. This method for finding the result of executing a **while** imperative is of course extremely inefficient (because each attempt at computing $\mathsf{m}_k(\mathsf{s}_0)$ for another k starts from scratch, and does not utilize computations for $i < k$), and is hence quite unlike what happens when a **while** imperative is executed by a real computer.

In this section we prove a theorem which shows that the denotational definition of the effect of **while** imperatives is in agreement with how we usually think that such imperatives are executed. The theorem also serves to bridge the gap from the rather mathematical definition given in this chapter to more operational definitions given in ensuing chapters.

Theorem 6.1 The While theorem:
Let be *be an expression and* imp *an imperative. Let* s_0 *be a state. Define:*

$$\begin{array}{lll} s^* & \stackrel{d}{=} \mathcal{M}[\![\textbf{while}\ \mathsf{be}\ \textbf{do}\ \mathsf{imp}\ \textbf{od}]\!](s_0) & \\ s_{i+1} & \stackrel{d}{=} \mathcal{M}[\![\mathsf{imp}]\!](s_i) & \textit{for every } i \geq 0 \\ b_i & \stackrel{d}{=} \mathcal{E}[\![\mathsf{be}]\!](s_i).\mathsf{qua\_Bool} & \textit{for every } i \geq 0 \end{array}$$

Then one, and only one, of the following three cases will hold:

$$\alpha\text{: } s^* = \bot_{State} \wedge \forall\, n \geq 0\text{: } b_n = \textbf{true}$$

$$\beta\text{: } s^* \neq \bot_{State} \wedge \exists\, n \geq 0\text{: } (\forall\, i < n\text{: } b_i = \textbf{true} \wedge s^* = s_n \wedge b_n = \textbf{false})$$

$$\gamma\text{: } s^* = \bot_{State} \wedge \exists\, n \geq 0\text{: } (\forall\, i < n\text{: } b_i = \textbf{true} \wedge (s_n = \bot_{State} \vee b_n = \bot_{Bool}))$$

Case α corresponds to an infinite loop, β is normal termination, γ will be the case if either 1) an error occurs in the evaluation of be *or during execution of* imp *or 2) an infinite loop occurs inside* imp.

Proof: Define

$$\begin{array}{ll} \mathsf{qw} & \stackrel{d}{=} \lambda \mathsf{w} \in MV\text{: } (\mathsf{cond}(\mathcal{E}[\![\mathsf{be}]\!],\ (\mathsf{w} \circ \mathcal{M}[\![\mathsf{imp}]\!]),\ \mathsf{id}_{State_\bot})) \\ m^* & \stackrel{d}{=} \mathcal{M}[\![\textbf{while}\ \mathsf{be}\ \textbf{do}\ \mathsf{imp}\ \textbf{od}]\!] \\ m_i & \stackrel{d}{=} \mathsf{qw}^i(\bot_{MV}) \qquad \text{for each } i \geq 0 \end{array}$$

We know that m^* is a fixpoint for qw, i.e., $m^* = \mathsf{qw}(m^*)$. This fact implies a simple lemma:

Lemma 6.1 *Assume n is such that* $b_i = \textbf{true}$ *for all* $i < n$.
Then: $s^* = m^*(s_n)$

This lemma is proved by induction on n:

$n = 0$: The claim is true by definition of s^* and m^*.

$$\begin{array}{lll} n > 0\text{: } s^* & = m^*(s_{n-1}) & \text{By the induction hypothesis} \\ & = \mathsf{qw}(m^*)(s_{n-1}) & \text{Because } m^* \text{ is a fixpoint for qw} \\ & = \textbf{if}\ \mathcal{E}[\![\mathsf{be}]\!](s_{n-1}) = \textbf{true}\ \textbf{then}\ m^*(\mathcal{M}[\![\mathsf{imp}]\!](s_{n-1}))\ \textbf{else} & \end{array}$$

$$
\begin{aligned}
&\textbf{if } \mathcal{E}[\![\mathsf{be}]\!](\mathsf{s}_{n-1}) = \textbf{false then } \mathsf{s}_{n-1} \textbf{ else } \bot_{State} \\
&= \mathsf{m}^*(\mathcal{M}[\![\mathsf{imp}]\!](\mathsf{s}_{n-1})) \quad \text{By assumption } \mathsf{b}_{n-1} = \textbf{true} \\
&= \mathsf{m}^*(\mathsf{s}_n) \quad \text{By definition of } \mathsf{s}_n
\end{aligned}
$$

End of proof of lemma 6.1.

Lemma 6.2 *Assume* b_n *is true for every* $n \geq 0$.
Then: $\forall\, i \geq 0{:}\ \forall\, n \geq 0{:}\ \mathsf{m}_i(\mathsf{s}_n) = \bot_{State}$

Proof of this lemma is by induction on i:

$i = 0$: For every $n \geq 0$:

$$
\begin{aligned}
\mathsf{m}_0(\mathsf{s}_n) &= \bot_{MV}(\mathsf{s}_n) \\
&= \bot_{State}
\end{aligned}
$$

$i > 0$: Assume as induction hypothesis that $\mathsf{m}_{i-1}(\mathsf{s}_n) = \bot_{State}$ for every $n \geq 0$. Then for every $n \geq 0$:

$$
\begin{aligned}
\mathsf{m}_i(\mathsf{s}_n) &= \mathsf{qw}(\mathsf{m}_{i-1})(\mathsf{s}_n) && \text{By definition of } \mathsf{m}_i \\
&= \mathsf{m}_{i-1}(\mathcal{M}[\![\mathsf{imp}]\!](\mathsf{s}_n)) && \text{By definition of } \mathsf{qw},\ \mathsf{b}_n = \textbf{true} \\
&= \mathsf{m}_{i-1}(\mathsf{s}_{n+1}) && \text{By definition of } \mathsf{s}_{n+1} \\
&= \bot_{State} && \text{By induction hypothesis}
\end{aligned}
$$

End of proof of lemma 6.2.

Now consider the sequence $\{\mathsf{b}_i\}_{i=0}^{\infty}$. If not all b_n are true, there must exist a least n for which $\mathsf{b}_n \neq \textbf{true}$. For such an n - which may well be equal to 0 - either $\mathsf{b}_n = \textbf{false}$ or $\mathsf{b}_n \notin \{\textbf{true}, \textbf{false}\}$. This means that one of the following three cases must hold:

(1) $\forall\, n \geq 0{:}\ \mathsf{b}_n = \textbf{true}$

(2) $\exists\, n \geq 0{:}\ \mathsf{b}_n = \textbf{false} \wedge \forall\, i < n{:}\ \mathsf{b}_i = \textbf{true}$

(3) $\exists\, n \geq 0{:}\ \mathsf{b}_n \notin \{\textbf{true}, \textbf{false}\} \wedge \forall\, i < n{:}\ \mathsf{b}_i = \textbf{true}$

We consider these three cases separately:

(1) When $\mathsf{b}_n = \textbf{true}$ for every $n \geq 0$, we get that

$$
\begin{aligned}
\mathsf{s}^* &= \mathsf{m}^*(\mathsf{s}_0) \\
&= \mathsf{Y}_{MV}(\mathsf{qw})(\mathsf{s}_0) && \text{By definition of } \mathsf{m}^* \\
&= (\lfloor MV \rfloor_{i=0}^{\infty} \mathsf{qw}^i(\bot_{MV}))(\mathsf{s}_0) && \text{By the Fixpoint Theorem} \\
&= \lfloor State \rfloor_{i=0}^{\infty} (\mathsf{qw}^i(\bot_{MV})(\mathsf{s}_0)) && \text{By proposition 5.3} \\
&= \lfloor State \rfloor_{i=0}^{\infty} (\mathsf{m}_i(\mathsf{s}_0)) && \text{By definition of } \mathsf{m}_i \\
&= \lfloor State \rfloor_{i=0}^{\infty} \bot_{State} && \text{By lemma 6.2} \\
&= \bot_{State}
\end{aligned}
$$

Hence, case α in the theorem holds when case (1) holds.

(2) We assume that n is such that b_n = **false** and b_i = **true** for every $i < n$. Then:

$s^* = m^*(s_n)$	By lemma 6.1
$= qw(m^*)(s_n)$	m^* is a fixpoint for qw
$= s_n$	By definition of qw, using b_n = **false**

Case β in the theorem thus holds.

(3) We assume that n is such that $b_n \notin$ {**true**, **false**} and b_i = **true** for every $i < n$. We then get:

$s^* = m^*(s_n)$	By lemma 6.1
$= qw(m^*)(s_n)$	m^* is a fixpoint for qw
$= \bot_{State}$	By definition of qw and assumption

Case γ in the theorem holds.

End of proof of the While theorem.

6.7 While in ML

It is neither difficult nor very laborious to write an interpreter for the While language in ML if we base the construction on the denotational definitions given in this chapter and take ideas from the Loop interpreter written in ML and described in chapter 3. In this section we show how this may be done.

6.7.1 Abstract syntax of While in ML

The abstract syntax of the While language may be defined in ML by the structure given in figure 6.5. To reduce the amount of code, we have not included every binary operator.

6.7.2 Semantics of While in ML

The semantics of the While language may be defined in ML by three structures. The first of these contains definitions of semantic domains, the second contains definitions of functions that may be used to access a state, and the final structure contains definitions of semantic mappings.

An ML structure containing definitions of semantic domains for the While language may be found in figure 6.6. These definitions closely parallel the definitions given in figure 6.2. There are only two significant differences: The first is that the domain ***S*** of storable values is defined to be equal to ***Int***, and thus not restricted to consist only of integers with absolute values below a specified limit. But the function

```
structure WhileSyntax =
struct
  type Literal = int;
  type Ident   = string;

  datatype Prog  = Program   of Imp

      and  Imp   = Skip
                 | Put       of Exp
                 | Get       of Ident
                 | Asg       of Ident * Exp
                 | Seq       of Imp * Imp
                 | If        of Exp * Imp * Imp
                 | While     of Exp * Imp

      and  Exp   = Constant  of Literal
                 | Variable  of Ident
                 | BOP       of Binop * Exp * Exp
                 | UOP       of Unop * Exp

      and  Binop = Plus | Sub | Mult | Div | Eql | Less | And

      and  Unop  = Not | Minus
end
```

Figure 6.5: Abstract syntax of While in ML

bind that 'binds' integers to identifiers in the store is defined in figure 6.7 in such a manner that only integers with limited absolute values are 'stored'. The second significant difference is that we do not introduce special $\perp$ elements in the domains. Errors are instead handled by raising exceptions, as shown in figures 6.7 and 6.8.

A structure that contains definitions of functions that may be used to access and change a given state may be found in figure 6.7.

6.7.3 A parser for While in ML

An ML structure with definitions of semantic mappings for While may be found in figure 6.8. The fixpoint function is defined by recursion in the ML code given in this figure. It could alternatively have been defined as follows, in a manner that - even if it does use recursion - is closer to the mathematical definition:

```
exception BottomState;
fun BottomMV(s) = raise BottomState;
fun Rep(q, qr)   = (fn s => qr(s)
```

```
structure WhileDomains =
struct
  type E        = int;
  type S        = int;
  type Ident    = string;
  type Input    = int list;
  type Output   = S list;
  type Store    = Ident -> S;
  type State    = Input * Store * Output;

  type PV       = (Input -> Output);
  type MV       = (State -> State);
  type EV       = (State -> E);
  type BOV      = (E * E -> E);
  type UOV      = (E -> E);
end;
```

Figure 6.6: Semantic domains for While in ML

```
structure StateFunctions =
struct
  exception InputEmpty;
  exception OverFlow;
  val maxint = 1000000;

  fun bind(h, id, v) = if abs(v) > maxint then raise OverFlow
                       else (fn x => (if id = x then v else h x))
  fun initstate(i)                = (i, (fn x => 0), []);
  fun assign((inp, h, out), id, v) = (inp, bind(h, id, v), out);
  fun get(([], h, out), id)       = raise InputEmpty
    | get((x::in, h, out), id)    = (in, bind(h, id, x), out);
  fun put((inp, h, out), v)       = (inp, h, out@[v]);
  fun access((inp, h, out), id)   = h(id);
  fun output(inp, h, out)         = out;
end;
```

Figure 6.7: State functions

```
structure WhileSemantics =
struct
  open WhileSyntax;
  open WhileDomains;
  open StateFunctions;

  exception ZeroDiv;

  fun cond(ev, mv1, mv2)
            = (fn s => if (ev(s) > 0) then mv1(s) else mv2(s))

  fun fix(q) = (fn s => q(fix(q))(s))

  fun BO (Plus)  = (fn (i1, i2) => i1 + i2)
    | BO (Sub)   = (fn (i1, i2) => i1 - i2)
    | BO (Mult)  = (fn (i1, i2) => i1 * i2)
    | BO (Div)   = (fn (i1, i2) => (if i2 = 0  then raise ZeroDiv
                                                else  i1 div i2))
    | BO (Eql)   = (fn (i1, i2) => (if i1 = i2 then 1 else 0))
    | BO (Less)  = (fn (i1, i2) => (if i1 < i2 then 1 else 0))
    | BO (And)   = (fn (i1, i2) => i1 * i2)

  fun UO (Not)    = (fn i => if i > 0 then 0 else 1)
    | UO (Minus)  = (fn i => -i)

  fun EE (Variable id)     = (fn s => access(s, id))
    | EE (Constant lit)    = (fn s => lit)
    | EE (BOP(b, e1, e2))  = (fn s => (BO(b)((EE e1 s), (EE e2 s))))
    | EE (UOP(u, e))       = (fn s => (UO(u)(EE e s)))

  fun MM (Skip)                = (fn s => s)
    | MM (Put e)               = (fn s => put(s, (EE e s)))
    | MM (Asg(id, e))          = (fn s => assign(s, id, (EE e s)))
    | MM (Get id)              = (fn s => get(s, id))
    | MM (Seq(imp1, imp2))     = (MM imp2) o (MM imp1)
    | MM (If(b, imp1, imp2))   = cond(EE b, MM imp1, MM imp2)
    | MM (While(e, imp))       = fix(fn w =>
                       cond(EE e, w o (MM imp), fn s => s))

  fun PP (Program imp) = (fn i => output(MM imp (initstate i)))

end;
```

Figure 6.8: Semantic mappings for While in ML

```
structure WhileSymbols =
 struct
  val keywords  = ["begin", "end", "skip", "put", "get",
                   "while", "do", "od",
                   "if", "then", "else", "fi",
                   "not", "and", "minus"]
  and operators  = ["+", "*", "/", "=", "<", ":="]
  and separators = [";", "(", ")"]
end;
```

Figure 6.9: Keywords, operators and separators of While

```
structure WhileParser =
struct
 open WhileSyntax;
 fun makeProgram((_,i),_)          = Program(i);
 fun makeSkip(_)                   = Skip;
 fun makePut(_, e)                 = Put(e);
 fun makeGet(_, v)                 = Get(v);
 fun makeAssign((v, _), e)         = Asg(v, e);
 fun makeImps([])                  = Skip
   | makeImps(i::[])               = i
   | makeImps(i::s)                = Seq(i, makeImps(s));
 fun makeIf((((((_,b),_),i1),_),i2),_) = If(b, i1, i2);
 fun makeWhile((((_,e),_),i),_)    = While(e, i);
 fun makeVariable(v)               = Variable(v);
 fun makeConstant(i)               = Constant(i);
 fun makeBOP((((_,e1),b),e2),_)    = BOP(b, e1, e2);
 fun makeUOP(((_,u), e),_)         = UOP(u, e);
 fun makePlus(_)                   = Plus;
 fun makeSub(_)                    = Sub;
 fun makeMult(_)                   = Mult;
 fun makeDiv(_)                    = Div;
 fun makeEql(_)                    = Eql;
 fun makeLess(_)                   = Less;
 fun makeAnd(_)                    = And;
 fun makeNot(_)                    = Not;
 fun makeMinus(_)                  = Minus;
```

Figure 6.10: A parser for the concrete syntax of the While language, first part

```
open Parser;

fun prog toks =
  ( $"begin" -- imps -- $"end"          >> makeProgram
  ) toks
and imps toks =
  ( repsep imp ";"                       >> makeImps
  ) toks
and imp toks =
  ( $"skip"                              >> makeSkip
  || $"put" -- exp                       >> makePut
  || $"get" -- id                        >> makeGet
  || id -- $$":=" -- exp                 >> makeAssign
  || $"if" -- exp -- $"then" -- imps
       -- $"else" -- imps -- $"fi"       >> makeIf
  || $"while" -- exp -- $"do"
       -- imps -- $"od"                  >> makeWhile
  ) toks
and exp toks =
  ( id                                   >> makeVariable
  || lit                                 >> makeConstant
  || $$"(" -- exp -- binop
       -- exp -- $$")"                   >> makeBOP
  || $$"(" -- unop -- exp -- $$")"       >> makeUOP
  ) toks
and binop toks =
  ( $$"+"                                >> makePlus
  || $$"-"                               >> makeSub
  || $$"*"                               >> makeMult
  || $$"/"                               >> makeDiv
  || $$"="                               >> makeEql
  || $$"<"                               >> makeLess
  || $"and"                              >> makeAnd
  ) toks
and unop toks =
  ( $"not"                               >> makeNot
  || $$"-"                               >> makeMinus
  ) toks;

end;
```

Figure 6.11: A parser for the concrete syntax of the While language, second part

```
                     handle BottomState => Rep(q, q(qr))(s));
fun fix(q)           = Rep(q, BottomMV)
```

6.7.4 A scanner for While in ML

To define a scanner for the While language, we may use the functor ScanFun described in section 3.4.1 on page 32. To produce a scanner for a language, this functor must be given, as a parameter, a structure that contains definitions of the keywords, operators and separators of the language. Such a structure may be found in figure 6.9.

A parser for While in ML is given in figures 6.10 and 6.11.

6.8 Exercises

6.8.1 A program to compute factorials

Construct a While program that computes and outputs the factorial of an integer that is read from input.

Evaluate, in as much detail as possible, the result of applying the denotation of your program to the input sequence $\langle 3 \rangle$.

6.8.2 Conditional expressions

Define the semantics of conditional expressions of the form

$$\langle iexp \rangle ::= \textbf{if } \langle bexp \rangle \textbf{ then } \langle iexp \rangle \textbf{ else } \langle iexp \rangle \textbf{ fi}$$

6.8.3 Simple conditional imperatives

Define the semantics of conditional imperatives of the form

$$\langle imp \rangle ::= \textbf{if } \langle bexp \rangle \textbf{ then } \langle imp \rangle \textbf{ fi}$$

6.8.4 Multiple assignments

Give a formal definition of the semantics of *multiple assignments* of the form

$$\langle imp \rangle ::= (\langle ident \rangle, \langle ident \rangle) := (\langle iexp \rangle, \langle iexp \rangle)$$

The informal semantics of such imperatives is simple: First, the two integer expressions on the right-hand side of := are evaluated. Then the value of the first expression is assigned to the first identifier and the value of the second expression is assigned to the second identifier. An example: The effect of executing the two imperatives

$$\mathsf{x} := \mathbf{10};$$
$$(\mathsf{x}, \mathsf{y}) := (\mathbf{1}, (\mathsf{x} + \mathbf{1}))$$

is to assign 1 to x and 3 to y.

6.8.5 Swap imperatives

Give a formal definition of the semantics of *swaps*, which are imperatives of the form

$$\langle imp \rangle ::= \langle ident \rangle :=: \langle ident \rangle$$

The effect of a swap is that the two identifiers swap values.

6.8.6 Repeat imperatives

Define the semantics of **repeat** imperatives of the form

$$\langle imp \rangle ::= \textbf{repeat } \langle imp \rangle \textbf{ until } \langle bexp \rangle \textbf{ endrep}$$

Prove that

$$\textbf{repeat}\ \mathsf{imp}\ \textbf{until}\ \mathsf{be}\ \textbf{endrep} \quad \cong \quad \mathsf{imp};\ \textbf{while not}\ \mathsf{be}\ \textbf{do}\ \mathsf{imp}\ \textbf{od}$$

for every imperative imp and every expression be.

6.8.7 Looping 'n plus half' times

Define the semantics of imperatives of the form

$$\langle imp \rangle ::= \textbf{loop } \langle imp \rangle \textbf{ while } \langle bexp \rangle\text{: } \langle imp \rangle \textbf{ endrep}$$

The intuitive semantics is as follows: 1) Perform the first imperative, 2) Evaluate the expression, 3) If it is false, terminate the imperative, and 4) If it is true, perform the second imperative and repeat from the start.

6.8.8 Input in expressions

Change the denotational definition of the semantics of While to handle integer expressions of the form **getint**. The intuitive, operational semantics of **getint** is simple: If the input sequence is empty, an error occurs. Otherwise, remove the top element and use it as the value of the expression **getint**.

6.8.9 Better error handling

Change the semantics of While such that any 'runtime error' will stop the program and output a suitable error message.

6.8.10 An interpreter

Construct a While interpreter in one of the common programming languages. Use the denotational definition of the semantics of the While language as a basis for the interpreter. Try to be as faithful as possible to the denotational definitions.

Chapter 7
Operational semantics

7.1 Introduction

There is a great - and obvious - difference between the denotational definition of the meaning of a program as presented in the previous chapters, and the meaning a program implicitly acquires by being executable on a real computer. In this chapter we study this difference.

When we use the techniques of denotational semantics, we define the meaning of various constructs in programming languages to be mathematical objects, usually functions. But when we design a program, the aim is hardly ever to define mathematical objects, but rather to construct something which can be executed by a computer and which will steer the computer to perform some desirable actions. The *operational semantics* of a program is defined in terms of what happens when the program is executed by a computer.

In this chapter we bridge the gap between the denotational meaning of programs and meaning in terms of execution on computers. We use the While language described in chapter 6 as a sample language and give two rather different operational definitions of its meaning: First we define an *interpreter* for the language and then a *compiler*.

We also prove that the interpreter and the compiler are correct for the programming language.

7.2 Computers

The computers we consider are such that at any moment of time it is possible - at least in principle - to give a complete description of everything that may be changed by actions performed by the computer and that may affect the ensuing behaviour of the computer. Such a complete description is called a *state* for the computer. The computers we consider are furthermore such that they work in *discrete time-steps*. This means that the state is not changed gradually (as states of analogue computers do), but is constant and unchanging between each step. Finally, we assume that the computers considered in this chapter are *deterministic*indexdeterministic. This means that the state of a computer at any given moment uniquely and completely determines the state of the computer after the next step, i.e., in the next moment of time.

A specification of a computer M consists of three parts:

- A specification of the states of M: which components these states have and how the states may be changed and observed. Such a specification may be given by defining an algebra - which we usually call *M-State* (sometimes $_{M}State$) - with a carrier that consists of all legal M-states, and with functions that may be used to generate, change and observe M-states.

- A specification of how the state of the computer is changed at each time-step. We have assumed that our computers are deterministic and hence that a given state uniquely determines the next state. This entails that we may specify how the state changes by defining a function

  $$\mathbf{step}_M \in (\textit{M-State} \to \textit{M-State})$$

  Then $\mathbf{s.step}_M$ denotes the M-state that follows immediately after the M-state $\mathbf{s}$.

  Normally, every step is small: it changes the state only a little, no more than that which realistic hardware components may do.

- A specification of how it is determined that the computer stops (if it *does* stop; not all computers do, except due to power failure or physical degradation). This may be done by defining a function

  $$\mathbf{terminal}_M \in (\textit{M-State} \to \textit{Bool})$$

Then the computer will stop if the state s is such that $\mathsf{s.terminal}_M$ = **true**.

Given a specification of a computer M, the computer operates as follows (we use parts of the While language as a meta-language):

$$\begin{array}{l} \mathsf{s} := \langle \textit{Initial state} \rangle \\ \textbf{while not } \mathsf{s.terminal}_M \textbf{ do } \mathsf{s} := \mathsf{s.step}_M; \end{array}$$

This may be stated more informally as follows: *As long as the state is not terminal, the computer performs another step.*

Some notation: We write

$$\mathsf{s} \underset{M}{\rightarrow} \mathsf{s'}$$

(or simply $\mathsf{s} \rightarrow \mathsf{s'}$ when no misunderstanding should be possible) to express that the computer M goes from state s to state s' in a single step, i.e., that $\mathsf{s'} = \mathsf{s.step}_M$. We furthermore write $\mathsf{s} \xrightarrow{*} \mathsf{s}^*$ to express that the computer goes from s to s^* in 0 or more steps. This means that $\xrightarrow{*}$ is the reflexive and transitive closure of $\rightarrow$, which may be defined as follows:

$$\mathsf{s} \underset{M}{\xrightarrow{*}} \mathsf{s}^* \overset{d}{\iff} \exists\, n \geq 0, \mathsf{s}_0, \mathsf{s}_1, \ldots, \mathsf{s}_n\colon \begin{array}[t]{l} \mathsf{s}_0 = \mathsf{s} \wedge \\ \forall i < n\colon \mathsf{s}_i \underset{M}{\rightarrow} \mathsf{s}_{i+1} \wedge \\ \mathsf{s}_n = \mathsf{s}^* \end{array}$$

Finally, we write $\mathsf{s} \xrightarrow{!} \mathsf{s}^*$ to express that the computer goes from s to s^* in 0 or more steps and that s^* is terminal:

$$\mathsf{s} \underset{M}{\xrightarrow{!}} \mathsf{s}^* \overset{d}{\iff} \mathsf{s} \underset{M}{\xrightarrow{*}} \mathsf{s}^* \wedge \mathsf{s}^*\mathsf{.terminal}_M$$

If a state s is such that there exists a state s^* such that $\mathsf{s} \xrightarrow{!} \mathsf{s}^*$, we say that the computer *converges* from s to s^*. If the state s is such that the computer does not converge to any state from s, we say that the computer *diverges* from s. Observe that the computer diverges from s if and only if for every s' such that $\mathsf{s} \xrightarrow{*} \mathsf{s'}$ there exists a state s'' such that $\mathsf{s'} \rightarrow \mathsf{s''}$. Thus, divergence means that the computer enters an infinite loop. We will sometimes write $\mathsf{s} \xrightarrow{*} \bot_{\textit{M-State}}$ to express that M diverges from s.

Given a computer M - with state algebra *M-State*, step function step_M and termination function $\mathsf{terminal}_M$ - we define a function named $\mathcal{M}\mathsf{achine}_M$ that may be used to find the state towards which M converges (if it *does* converge) from any given initial state. This function has signature

$$\mathcal{M}\mathsf{achine}_M \in (\textit{M-State} \rightarrow \textit{M-State}_\bot)$$

and is defined as follows:

$$\mathcal{M}\mathsf{achine}_M \overset{d}{=} \lambda \mathsf{s} \in \textit{M-State}: \begin{cases} \mathsf{s}^* & \text{if } \mathsf{s} \xrightarrow[M]{!} \mathsf{s}^* \\ \bot_{\textit{M-State}} & \text{if } M \text{ diverges from } \mathsf{s} \end{cases}$$

We have assumed above that the computers we consider in this chapter are deterministic. This entails that if a computer converges to a state s^* from some initial state s, then the final state s^* is uniquely determined by the initial state s. This means that the value of $\mathcal{M}\mathsf{achine}(\mathsf{s})$ is well defined for every state s.

Observe that the function $\mathcal{M}\mathsf{achine}_M$ satisfies the following equation

$$\mathcal{M}\mathsf{achine}_M = \underline{\lambda} \mathsf{s} \in \textit{M-State}_\bot: \textbf{if } \mathsf{s}.\mathsf{terminal}_M \textbf{ then } \mathsf{s} \\ \textbf{else } \mathcal{M}\mathsf{achine}_M(\mathsf{s}.\mathsf{step}_M)$$

This means that if we order *M-State* to be a cpo and prove that a certain function is continuous, we may define $\mathcal{M}\mathsf{achine}_M$ using the fixpoint operator and hence give a denotational definition of the effects of computers. We are, however, only interested in the operational effects of computers (at least in this chapter where we study the transition from denotational to operational semantics), and will therefore not do this here.

7.3 An interpreter

An *interpreter* is a computer that is able to execute programs directly. In this section we describe a simple interpreter for the While language, and use it to define an operational semantics for this language.

7.3.1 Interpreter states

The states of our interpreter have five components:

(1) An input sequence $\in \textit{Input} = \textit{Int}^*$.

(2) A store $\in \textit{Store} = \mathcal{F}(\textit{Ident} \to S)$, where S consists of all storable values (integers of bounded size).

(3) An output sequence $\in \textit{Output} = \textit{Int}^*$.

These first three components of an interpreter state constitute a state for the standard semantics of the While language (defined in section 6.3.1 on page 102), and are of course used similarly to the corresponding components of a standard state. In addition to these three standard components, an interpreter state has two additional components that are special for the interpreter:

$_I$*State*	*Interpreter states*
Carrier:	$_I\mathsf{State} = \mathit{Input} \times \mathit{Store} \times \mathit{Output} \times \mathit{Stack} \times \mathit{Control}$ $= {}_S\mathit{State} \times \mathit{Stack} \times \mathit{Control}$
Functions:	$\langle \ldots \rangle^S \in ({}_S\mathit{State}_\perp \times \mathit{Stack}_\perp \times \mathit{Control} \to {}_I\mathit{State})$ $\mathsf{Output} \in ({}_I\mathit{State}_\perp \to \mathit{Output}_\perp)$ $_S\mathsf{State} \in ({}_I\mathit{State}_\perp \to {}_S\mathit{State}_\perp)$ $\mathsf{Stacktop} \in ({}_I\mathit{State}_\perp \to E_\perp)$
Axioms:	$\langle \mathsf{s, st, c} \rangle^S = \textbf{if } \mathsf{s} = \perp_{{}_S\mathit{State}} \vee \mathsf{st} = \perp_{\mathit{Stack}} \textbf{ then } \perp_{{}_I\mathit{State}}$ $\textbf{else } \langle \mathsf{s, st, c} \rangle$ $\langle \mathsf{s, st, c} \rangle . \mathsf{Output} = \mathsf{s.Output}$ $\langle \mathsf{s, st, c} \rangle . {}_S\mathsf{State} = \mathsf{s}$ $\langle \mathsf{s, st, c} \rangle . \mathsf{Stacktop} = \mathsf{st.top}$ $\perp_{{}_I\mathit{State}} . \mathsf{Output} = \perp_{\mathit{Output}}$ $\perp_{{}_I\mathit{State}} . {}_S\mathsf{State} = \perp_{{}_S\mathit{State}}$ $\perp_{{}_I\mathit{State}} . \mathsf{Stacktop} = \perp_E$

Figure 7.1: The $_I$*State* algebra

(4) A *value stack*, which will be used to keep the values found during evaluation of expressions. A value stack is an element of an algebra called *Stack* (which is defined below) and may contain expressible values (values that occur as values of expressions).

(5) A *control stack*, which will be used to keep programs, imperatives, expressions and other syntactic objects that are to be executed or evaluated by the interpreter. A control stack is an element of an algebra called *Control*, which is defined below.

In order to distinguish between the name of the algebra of standard states and the name of the algebra of interpreter states, we will - whenever necessary to avoid confusion - 'decorate' the names of these algebras (and the names of other semantic algebras and of semantic mappings) with prefixed, lowered symbols. We will use '$_S$' to signify standard, denotational, semantics as defined in the previous chapter, and '$_I$' to signify interpreter semantics. Thus, $_S$*State* is the algebra of standard states, and $_I$*State* is the algebra of interpreter states. This latter algebra is defined in figure 7.1, and has the following carrier:

$$
\begin{aligned}
{}_I\mathit{State} &\stackrel{d}{=} \mathit{Input} \times \mathit{Store} \times \mathit{Output} \times \mathit{Stack} \times \mathit{Control} \\
&= {}_S\mathit{State} \times \mathit{Stack} \times \mathit{Control}
\end{aligned}
$$

The semantic algebra *Stack* has a carrier that is equal to E^*, where $E = \mathit{Bool} + \mathit{Int}$ is the algebra of expressible values for the While language

(*E* is defined in figure 6.2 on page 103). The stack of an interpreter will be used to keep temporary results found during evaluation of compound expressions. An expression like (ex_1 + ex_2) will, for instance, be evaluated as follows: 1) ex_1 is evaluated and its value is placed on top of the stack, 2) ex_2 is evaluated and its value is placed on top of the stack (above the value of ex_1), 3) the two top elements of the stack are removed and their sum is placed on top of the stack. Thus, the total effect is to place the value of (ex_1 + ex_2) on top of the stack. To be able to use stacks in this fashion, we need the following functions to produce and observe stacks:

- A function **push** $\in (Stack_\perp \times E_\perp \rightarrow Stack_\perp)$ that places an *E* value on top of a stack.
- A function **top** $\in (Stack_\perp \rightarrow E_\perp)$ that finds the top element of a stack.
- A function **pop** $\in (Stack_\perp \rightarrow Stack_\perp)$ that removes the top element from a stack.
- A function **apply1** $\in (Stack_\perp \times (E_\perp \rightarrow E_\perp) \rightarrow Stack_\perp)$ that may be used to replace the top element of a stack with the result of applying a given unary function (in $(E_\perp \rightarrow E_\perp)$) to this element.
- A function **apply2** $\in (Stack_\perp \times (E_\perp \times E_\perp \rightarrow E_\perp) \rightarrow Stack_\perp)$ that replaces the top two elements of a stack with the result of applying a given binary function to these elements.

A specification of the *Stack* algebra - with signatures and axioms for these functions - is given in figure 7.2.

The algebra *Control* has a carrier that consists of stacks of certain syntactic elements: programs, imperatives, expressions, operators and so-called *interpreter commands*. It is defined as follows:

$$Control \stackrel{d}{=} (Program + Imperative + Expression + Binop + Unop + Command)^*$$

The domains *Program*, *Imperative*, *Expression*, *Binop* and *Unop* are syntactic domains for the While language, and are defined in section 6.2. The domain *Command* of interpreter commands is defined to consist of the following syntactic objects: {**put**, **asg**, **if**}

7.3.2 How the interpreter steps and stops

To define a computer, it is necessary - as stated in section 7.2 - to define the state algebra of the computer and to describe how the computer steps and stops. The state algebra $_IState$ of the interpreter is defined above. We now specify how the interpreter steps and stops:

Stack	*Stacks of expressible values*
Carrier:	E^*, *i.e., generated by* ε *and* $\vdash$
Functions:	$\varepsilon \in (\cdot \to \mathit{Stack})$
	$\vdash \in (\mathit{Stack} \times E \to \mathit{Stack})$
	$\mathsf{push} \in (\mathit{Stack}_\bot \times E_\bot \to \mathit{Stack}_\bot)$
	$\mathsf{pop} \in (\mathit{Stack}_\bot \to \mathit{Stack}_\bot)$
	$\mathsf{top} \in (\mathit{Stack}_\bot \to E_\bot)$
	$\mathsf{apply1} \in (\mathit{Stack}_\bot \times (E_\bot \to E_\bot) \to \mathit{Stack}_\bot)$
	$\mathsf{apply2} \in (\mathit{Stack}_\bot \times (E_\bot \times E_\bot \to E_\bot) \to \mathit{Stack}_\bot)$
Axioms:	$\mathsf{st.push(e)} = \mathbf{if}\ \mathsf{st} = \bot_{\mathit{Stack}} \vee \mathsf{e} = \bot_E\ \mathbf{then}\ \bot_{\mathit{Stack}}\ \mathbf{else}\ (\mathsf{st} \vdash \mathsf{e})$
	$(\mathsf{st} \vdash \mathsf{e}).\mathsf{pop} = \mathsf{st},\ \varepsilon.\mathsf{pop} = \bot_{\mathit{Stack}},\ \bot_{\mathit{Stack}}.\mathsf{pop} = \bot_{\mathit{Stack}}$
	$(\mathsf{st} \vdash \mathsf{e}).\mathsf{top} = \mathsf{e},\ \varepsilon.\mathsf{top} = \bot_E,\ \bot_{\mathit{Stack}}.\mathsf{top} = \bot_E$
	$\mathsf{st.push(e).apply1(uv)} = \mathsf{st.push(uv(e))}$
	$\mathsf{st.push(e_1).push(e_2).apply2(bv)} = \mathsf{st.push(bv(e_1, e_2))}$

Figure 7.2: The *Stack* algebra

- The interpreter stops as soon as the control stack is empty. The terminal function for the interpreter is therefore quite simple to define:

$$\mathsf{terminal}_I \stackrel{d}{=} \underline{\lambda}_I \mathsf{s} \in {}_I\mathit{State}\colon \mathbf{if}\ {}_I\mathsf{s.Control} = \varepsilon\ \mathbf{then\ true\ else\ false}$$

- The interpreter performs a step as follows: First, the top element of the control stack is removed. Then, an action that depends on this top element is performed: If the top element is a compound imperative or compound expression, its immediate components are pushed on the control stack, usually together with a special syntactic object (from the domain *Command*) that will steer the interpreter to behave in a specific manner when its turn comes. If the top element is atomic (a literal, an identifier or one of the command objects), either the value stack or the standard part of the state is changed in a manner that depends upon the element. All of this is precisely defined in figure 7.3 which contains a definition of the step function for the interpreter. Observe that we write $\langle \mathsf{s, st, c} \rangle \to \langle \mathsf{s', st', c'} \rangle$ instead of $\mathsf{step}(\langle \mathsf{s, st, c} \rangle) = \langle \mathsf{s', st', c'} \rangle$.

An example to show how the interpreter executes a program: Assume that s_0 is the standard state $\mathsf{State'init}(\langle 2 \rangle) = \langle \langle 2 \rangle, \lambda \mathsf{id}{:}\,0, \varepsilon \rangle$, and that wimp is the imperative

$$\mathbf{while}\ \mathsf{xx} > \mathbf{0}\ \mathbf{do\ put}\ \mathsf{xx};\ \mathsf{x} := \mathsf{x} - \mathbf{1}\ \mathbf{od}$$

Program

$$\langle \mathsf{s}, \mathsf{st}, (\mathbf{begin}\ \mathsf{imp}\ \mathbf{end}) \dashv \mathsf{c}\rangle \rightarrow \langle \mathsf{s}, \mathsf{st}, \mathsf{imp} \dashv \mathsf{c}\rangle$$

Imperative

$$\langle \mathsf{s}, \mathsf{st}, \mathbf{skip} \dashv \mathsf{c}\rangle \rightarrow \langle \mathsf{s}, \mathsf{st}, \mathsf{c}\rangle$$
$$\langle \mathsf{s}, \mathsf{st}, (\mathbf{get}\ \mathsf{id}) \dashv \mathsf{c}\rangle \rightarrow \langle \mathsf{s}.\mathsf{get}(\mathsf{id}), \mathsf{st}, \mathsf{c}\rangle^{s}$$
$$\langle \mathsf{s}, \mathsf{st}, (\mathbf{put}\ \mathsf{exp}) \dashv \mathsf{c}\rangle \rightarrow \langle \mathsf{s}, \mathsf{st}, \mathsf{exp} \dashv \mathbf{put} \dashv \mathsf{c}\rangle$$
$$\langle \mathsf{s}, \mathsf{st}, (\mathsf{id} := \mathsf{exp}) \dashv \mathsf{c}\rangle \rightarrow \langle \mathsf{s}, \mathsf{st}, \mathsf{exp} \dashv \mathbf{asg} \dashv \mathsf{id} \dashv \mathsf{c}\rangle$$
$$\langle \mathsf{s}, \mathsf{st}, (\mathsf{imp}_1;\ \mathsf{imp}_2) \dashv \mathsf{c}\rangle \rightarrow \langle \mathsf{s}, \mathsf{st}, \mathsf{imp}_1 \dashv \mathsf{imp}_2 \dashv \mathsf{c}\rangle$$
$$\langle \mathsf{s}, \mathsf{st}, (\mathbf{if}\ \mathsf{exp}\ \mathbf{then}\ \mathsf{imp}_1\ \mathbf{else}\ \mathsf{imp}_2\ \mathbf{fi}) \dashv \mathsf{c}\rangle$$
$$\quad \rightarrow \langle \mathsf{s}, \mathsf{st}, \mathsf{exp} \dashv \mathbf{if} \dashv \mathsf{imp}_1 \dashv \mathsf{imp}_2 \dashv \mathsf{c}\rangle$$
$$\langle \mathsf{s}, \mathsf{st}, (\mathbf{while}\ \mathsf{exp}\ \mathbf{do}\ \mathsf{imp}\ \mathbf{od}) \dashv \mathsf{c}\rangle$$
$$\quad \rightarrow \langle \mathsf{s}, \mathsf{st}, \mathsf{exp} \dashv \mathbf{if} \dashv (\mathsf{imp};\ \mathbf{while}\ \mathsf{exp}\ \mathbf{do}\ \mathsf{imp}\ \mathbf{od}) \dashv \mathbf{skip} \dashv \mathsf{c}\rangle$$

Expression

$$\langle \mathsf{s}, \mathsf{st}, \mathsf{lit} \dashv \mathsf{c}\rangle \rightarrow \langle \mathsf{s}, \mathsf{st}.\mathsf{push}(\mathsf{E'in\_Int}(\mathcal{A}[\![\mathsf{lit}]\!])), \mathsf{c}\rangle$$
$$\langle \mathsf{s}, \mathsf{st}, \mathsf{id} \dashv \mathsf{c}\rangle \rightarrow \langle \mathsf{s}, \mathsf{st}.\mathsf{push}(\mathsf{E'in\_Int}(\mathsf{s}.\mathsf{access}(\mathsf{id}))), \mathsf{c}\rangle$$
$$\langle \mathsf{s}, \mathsf{st}, (\mathsf{uop}\ \mathsf{exp}) \dashv \mathsf{c}\rangle \rightarrow \langle \mathsf{s}, \mathsf{st}, \mathsf{exp} \dashv \mathsf{uop} \dashv \mathsf{c}\rangle$$
$$\langle \mathsf{s}, \mathsf{st}, (\mathsf{exp}_1\ \mathsf{bop}\ \mathsf{exp}_2) \dashv \mathsf{c}\rangle \rightarrow \langle \mathsf{s}, \mathsf{st}, \mathsf{exp}_1 \dashv \mathsf{exp}_2 \dashv \mathsf{bop} \dashv \mathsf{c}\rangle$$

Binop + Unop

$$\langle \mathsf{s}, \mathsf{st}, \mathsf{uop} \dashv \mathsf{c}\rangle \rightarrow \langle \mathsf{s}, \mathsf{st}.\mathsf{apply1}(\mathcal{U}[\![\mathsf{uop}]\!]), \mathsf{c}\rangle^{s}$$
$$\langle \mathsf{s}, \mathsf{st}, \mathsf{bop} \dashv \mathsf{c}\rangle \rightarrow \langle \mathsf{s}, \mathsf{st}.\mathsf{apply2}(\mathcal{B}[\![\mathsf{bop}]\!]), \mathsf{c}\rangle^{s}$$

Control

$$\langle \mathsf{s}, \mathsf{st}, \mathbf{put} \dashv \mathsf{c}\rangle \rightarrow \langle \mathsf{s}.\mathsf{put}(\mathsf{st}.\mathsf{top}), \mathsf{st}.\mathsf{pop}, \mathsf{c}\rangle^{s}$$
$$\langle \mathsf{s}, \mathsf{st}, \mathbf{asg} \dashv \mathsf{id} \dashv \mathsf{c}\rangle \rightarrow \langle \mathsf{s}.\mathsf{assign}(\mathsf{id}, \mathsf{st}.\mathsf{top}), \mathsf{st}.\mathsf{pop}, \mathsf{c}\rangle^{s}$$
$$\langle \mathsf{s}, \mathsf{st}, \mathbf{if} \dashv \mathsf{imp}_1 \dashv \mathsf{imp}_2 \dashv \mathsf{c}\rangle$$
$$\rightarrow \langle \mathsf{s}, \mathsf{st}.\mathsf{pop}, \mathbf{if}\ \mathsf{s}.\mathsf{top} = \mathbf{true}\ \mathbf{then}\ \mathsf{imp}_1 \dashv \mathsf{c}\ \mathbf{else}\ \mathbf{if}\ \mathsf{s}.\mathsf{top} = \mathbf{false}\ \mathbf{then}\ \mathsf{imp}_2 \dashv \mathsf{c}\ \mathbf{else}\ \bot\rangle^{s}$$

Figure 7.3: The step function of the interpreter

Then for any st $\in$ *Stack* and any c $\in$ *Control*:

$$
\begin{aligned}
&\langle s_0,\ st,\ (\mathbf{begin\ get}\ xx;\ wimp\ \mathbf{end})\dashv c\rangle\\
&\to \langle s_0,\ st,\ (\mathbf{get}\ xx;\ wimp)\dashv c\rangle\\
&\to \langle s_0,\ st,\ (\mathbf{get}\ xx)\dashv wimp\dashv c\rangle\\
&\to \langle s_1,\ st,\ wimp\dashv c\rangle\\
&\qquad\qquad \text{where } s_1 = s_0 . get(xx) = \langle \varepsilon,\ h_1,\ \varepsilon\rangle\\
&\qquad\qquad \text{where } h_1 = (\lambda id{:}\,0) . bind(xx,\ 2)\\
&\to \langle s_1,\ st,\ (xx > \mathbf{0})\dashv \mathbf{if}\dashv(\mathbf{put}\ xx;\ xx := xx - \mathbf{1};\ wimp)\dashv \mathbf{skip}\dashv c\rangle\\
&\to \langle s_1,\ st,\ xx\dashv \mathbf{0}\dashv >\dashv \mathbf{if}\dashv \ldots \dashv \mathbf{skip}\dashv c\rangle\\
&\to \langle s_1,\ st . push(2),\ \mathbf{0}\dashv >\dashv \mathbf{if}\dashv \ldots \dashv \mathbf{skip}\dashv c\rangle\\
&\to \langle s_1,\ st . push(2) . push(0),\ >\dashv \mathbf{if}\dashv \ldots \dashv \mathbf{skip}\dashv c\rangle\\
&\to \langle s_1,\ st . push(>(2,\ 0)),\ \mathbf{if}\dashv \ldots \dashv \mathbf{skip}\dashv c\rangle\\
&= \langle s_1,\ st . push(\mathbf{true}),\ \mathbf{if}\dashv(\mathbf{put}\ xx;\ xx := xx - \mathbf{1};\ wimp)\dashv \mathbf{skip}\dashv c\rangle\\
&\to \langle s_1,\ st,\ (\mathbf{put}\ xx;\ xx := xx - \mathbf{1};\ wimp)\dashv c\rangle\\
&\to \langle s_1,\ st,\ (\mathbf{put}\ xx)\dashv(xx := xx - \mathbf{1};\ wimp)\dashv c\rangle\\
&\to \langle s_1,\ st,\ xx\dashv \mathbf{put}\dashv(xx := xx - \mathbf{1};\ wimp)\dashv c\rangle\\
&\to \langle s_1,\ st . push(2),\ \mathbf{put}\dashv(xx := xx - \mathbf{1};\ wimp)\dashv c\rangle\\
&\to \langle s_2,\ st,\ (xx := xx - \mathbf{1};\ wimp)\dashv c\rangle\\
&\qquad\qquad \text{where } s_2 = s_1 . put(2) = \langle \varepsilon,\ h_1,\ \langle 2\rangle\rangle\\
&\to \langle s_2,\ st,\ (xx := xx - \mathbf{1})\dashv wimp\dashv c\rangle\\
&\to \langle s_2,\ st,\ (xx - \mathbf{1})\dashv \mathbf{asg}\dashv xx\dashv wimp\dashv c\rangle\\
&\overset{*}{\to} \langle s_2,\ st . push(1),\ \mathbf{asg}\dashv xx\dashv wimp\dashv c\rangle\\
&\to \langle s_3,\ st,\ wimp\dashv c\rangle\\
&\qquad\qquad \text{where } s_3 = s_2 . assign(xx,\ 1)\\
&\qquad\qquad\qquad\quad = \langle \varepsilon,\ (\lambda id{:}\,0) . bind(xx,\ 1),\ \langle 2\rangle\rangle\\
&\overset{*}{\to} \langle s_4,\ st,\ wimp\dashv c\rangle\\
&\qquad\qquad \text{where } s_4 = s_3 . put(1) . assign(xx,\ 0)\\
&\qquad\qquad\qquad\quad = \langle \varepsilon,\ (\lambda id{:}\,0) . bind(xx,\ 0),\ \langle 2,\ 1\rangle\rangle\\
&\to \langle s_4,\ st,\ (xx > \mathbf{0})\dashv \mathbf{if}\dashv(\mathbf{put}\ xx;\ xx := xx - \mathbf{1};\ wimp)\dashv \mathbf{skip}\dashv c\rangle\\
&\overset{*}{\to} \langle s_4,\ st . push(\mathbf{false}),\ \mathbf{if}\dashv(\mathbf{put}\ xx;\ xx := xx - \mathbf{1};\ wimp)\dashv \mathbf{skip}\dashv c\rangle\\
&\to \langle s_4,\ st,\ \mathbf{skip}\dashv c\rangle\\
&\to \langle s_4,\ st,\ c\rangle\\
&\qquad\qquad \text{where } s_4 = \langle \varepsilon,\ \lambda id{:}\,0,\ \langle 2,\ 1\rangle\rangle
\end{aligned}
$$

- as expected.

7.3.3 Interpreter semantics

The interpreter we have defined may be used to execute programs and imperatives of the While language and to evaluate expressions of the same language, and hence to give operational meaning to the constructs of the While language. In this section we study the meaning thus implicitly given to the While language by the interpreter, and prove that this operationally defined semantics is congruent with the standard, denotationally defined, semantics of the language.

To execute a given While program prog from a given input sequence inp, we use the interpreter as follows: Start the interpreter from an initial state that has an input sequence equal to inp, a default store, an empty output sequence, an empty value stack and a control stack that consists of the program prog, and see what happens. If the interpreter terminates, extract the output sequence from the terminal state and let that be the result of the computation. If the interpreter diverges, let $\perp_{Output}$ be the result.

Used in this manner, the interpreter implicitly defines a semantic mapping for While programs which we denote by ${}_I\mathcal{P}$. This mapping has the same signature as the standard semantic mapping for While programs:

$${}_I\mathcal{P} \in (\mathit{Program} \to (\mathit{Input} \to \mathit{Output}_\perp))$$

and is defined as follows:

$${}_I\mathcal{P}[\![\mathsf{prog}]\!] = \lambda \mathsf{inp} \in \mathit{Input}\colon \mathcal{M}\mathsf{achine}_I(\langle {}_S\mathsf{State'Init(inp)},\ \varepsilon,\ \langle \mathsf{prog}\rangle\rangle)\,.\,\mathsf{Output}$$

The interpreter may be used to execute a given imperative imp from a given standard state s as follows: If the interpreter terminates from the initial state $\langle \mathsf{s},\ \varepsilon,\ \langle \mathsf{imp}\rangle\rangle$, take the standard state part of the terminal interpreter state to be the result of the execution. If the interpreter does not terminate, let $\perp_{State}$ be the result. The semantic mapping implicitly defined by using the interpreter like this, is called ${}_I\mathcal{M}$. It has signature

$${}_I\mathcal{M} \in (\mathit{Imperative} \to ({}_S\mathit{State}_\perp \to {}_S\mathit{State}_\perp))$$

and is defined as follows:

$${}_I\mathcal{M}[\![\mathsf{imp}]\!] = \underline{\lambda} \mathsf{s} \in {}_S\mathit{State}_\perp\colon \mathcal{M}\mathsf{achine}_I(\langle \mathsf{s},\ \varepsilon,\ \langle \mathsf{imp}\rangle\rangle)\,.\,{}_S\mathsf{State}$$

Finally, we may use the interpreter to evaluate a given expression exp for a given standard state s by starting it from initial state $\langle \mathsf{s},\ \varepsilon,\ \langle \mathsf{exp}\rangle\rangle$. If it terminates in an interpreter state $\langle \mathsf{s'},\ \mathsf{st},\ \varepsilon\rangle$, we take st.top to be the value of the expression. The semantic mapping ${}_I\mathcal{E}$ implicitly defined by such use of the interpreter, has signature

$${}_I\mathcal{E} \in (\mathit{Expression} \to ({}_S\mathit{State}_\perp \to E_\perp))$$

and is defined as follows:

$${}_I\mathcal{E}[\![\mathsf{exp}]\!] = \underline{\lambda} \mathsf{s} \in {}_S\mathit{State}_\perp\colon \mathcal{M}\mathsf{achine}_I(\langle \mathsf{s},\ \varepsilon,\ \langle \mathsf{exp}\rangle\rangle)\,.\,\mathsf{Stacktop}$$

The three semantic mappings ${}_I\mathcal{P}$, ${}_I\mathcal{M}$ and ${}_I\mathcal{E}$ defined here, constitute an alternative semantics for the While language. This alternative semantics is said to be an *operational* semantics because the definitions of the three semantic mappings are based on the operationally defined $\mathcal{M}$achine function, that is on how the interpreter (which is a computer) works.

It is, of course, not very satisfying simply to give an alternative definition of the semantics of a language, and then just claim that this really *is* an alternative semantics for the language. We should also justify our claim, and *prove* that the alternative definition is equivalent to the original definition. This is done in the following theorem.

Theorem 7.1 The interpreter is correct:
The interpreter versions of the three semantic mappings are equal to their corresponding standard mappings for every argument:

$$_I\mathcal{E} = {}_S\mathcal{E}, \quad _I\mathcal{M} = {}_S\mathcal{M}, \quad _I\mathcal{P} = {}_S\mathcal{P}$$

Proof: We must prove three claims:

1): $_I\mathcal{E}[\![\mathsf{exp}]\!] = {}_S\mathcal{E}[\![\mathsf{exp}]\!]$ for every expression exp,
2): $_I\mathcal{M}[\![\mathsf{imp}]\!] = {}_S\mathcal{M}[\![\mathsf{imp}]\!]$ for every imperative imp,
3): $_I\mathcal{P}[\![\mathsf{prog}]\!] = {}_S\mathcal{P}[\![\mathsf{prog}]\!]$ for every While program prog.

These claims are proved below:

Claim 1): To prove that $_I\mathcal{E}[\![\mathsf{exp}]\!] = {}_S\mathcal{E}[\![\mathsf{exp}]\!]$ holds for every expression exp, it suffices to prove that

$$_S\mathcal{E}[\![\mathsf{exp}]\!](\mathsf{s}) = \mathcal{M}\mathsf{achine}_I(\langle \mathsf{s},\ \varepsilon,\ \langle \mathsf{exp}\rangle\rangle).\mathsf{Stacktop}$$

holds for every standard state s. To prove this, it is - by the definition of $\mathcal{M}\mathrm{achine}_I$ (on page 128) - sufficient to prove that

$$\langle \mathsf{s},\ \varepsilon,\ \mathsf{exp}\rangle \overset{!}{\underset{I}{\rightarrow}} \langle \mathsf{s},\ \varepsilon\,.\,\mathsf{push}({}_S\mathcal{E}[\![\mathsf{exp}]\!](\mathsf{s})),\ \varepsilon\rangle$$

This follows from the following proposition:

Proposition 7.1 *For every* exp ∈ *Expression*, s ∈ $_S$*State*, st ∈ *Stack and* c ∈ *Control:*

$$\langle \mathsf{s},\ \mathsf{st},\ \mathsf{exp}\dashv\mathsf{c}\rangle \overset{*}{\underset{I}{\rightarrow}} \langle \mathsf{s},\ \mathsf{st}\,.\,\mathsf{push}({}_S\mathcal{E}[\![\mathsf{exp}]\!](\mathsf{s})),\ \mathsf{c}\rangle^S$$

Proof of this proposition is by induction on the syntactic complexity of the expression exp. We consider only the most complex case, viz. exp = (exp_1 bop exp_2), and leave the other cases as exercises. Let s be any standard state, st any value stack and c any control stack. Define $\mathsf{e}_i = \mathcal{E}[\![\mathsf{exp}_i]\!](\mathsf{s})$ for $i = 1, 2$, and assume as induction hypothesis that the proposition holds for exp_1 and exp_2. Then

$$
\begin{array}{lll}
\multicolumn{2}{l}{\langle \mathsf{s},\ \mathsf{st},\ (\mathsf{exp}_1\ \mathsf{bop}\ \mathsf{exp}_2)\dashv\mathsf{c}\rangle} & \\
\rightarrow & \langle \mathsf{s},\ \mathsf{st},\ \mathsf{exp}_1\dashv\mathsf{exp}_2\dashv\mathsf{bop}\dashv\mathsf{c}\rangle & \text{(By definition of } \rightarrow)\\
\overset{*}{\rightarrow} & \langle \mathsf{s},\ \mathsf{st}\,.\,\mathsf{push}(\mathsf{e}_1),\ \mathsf{exp}_2\dashv\mathsf{bop}\dashv\mathsf{c}\rangle^S & \text{(By ind. hyp. for } \mathsf{exp}_1)\\
\overset{*}{\rightarrow} & \langle \mathsf{s},\ \mathsf{st}\,.\,\mathsf{push}(\mathsf{e}_1)\,.\,\mathsf{push}(\mathsf{e}_2),\ \mathsf{bop}\dashv\mathsf{c}\rangle^S & \text{(By ind. hyp. for } \mathsf{exp}_2)\\
\rightarrow & \langle \mathsf{s},\ \mathsf{st}\,.\,\mathsf{push}(\mathsf{e}_1)\,.\,\mathsf{push}(\mathsf{e}_2)\,.\,\mathsf{apply2}(\mathcal{B}[\![\mathsf{bop}]\!]),\ \mathsf{c}\rangle^S & \text{(By def. of } \rightarrow)\\
= & \langle \mathsf{s},\ \mathsf{st}\,.\,\mathsf{push}(\mathcal{B}[\![\mathsf{bop}]\!](\mathsf{e}_1,\ \mathsf{e}_2)),\ \mathsf{c}\rangle^S & \text{(By axiom for apply2)}\\
= & \langle \mathsf{s},\ \mathsf{st}\,.\,\mathsf{push}({}_S\mathcal{E}[\![\mathsf{e}_1\ \mathsf{bop}\ \mathsf{e}_2]\!](\mathsf{s})),\ \mathsf{c}\rangle^S & \text{(By definition of } {}_S\mathcal{E})
\end{array}
$$

Thus, the claim in the proposition holds for (exp_1 bop exp_2).

Claim 2): That $_I\mathcal{M}[\![\mathsf{imp}]\!] = {}_S\mathcal{M}[\![\mathsf{imp}]\!]$ holds for every imperative imp, follows from the definition of $_I\mathcal{M}$ (and the definition of $\mathcal{M}\mathsf{achine}_I$) and the following proposition:

Proposition 7.2 *For every* imp ∈ *Imperative*, s ∈ $_S$*State*, st ∈ *Stack and* c ∈ *Control:*

$$\langle \mathsf{s, st, imp} \dashv \mathsf{c} \rangle \xrightarrow[I]{*} \langle {}_S\mathcal{M}[\![\mathsf{imp}]\!](\mathsf{s}), \mathsf{st}, \mathsf{c} \rangle^S$$

Proof of this proposition is by induction on the syntactic complexity of the imperative imp. We consider only **put** and **while** imperatives here, and leave the other cases as exercises. First, the case imp = **put** exp. Let s be any standard state, st any value stack and c any control stack. Define e = $\mathcal{E}[\![\mathsf{exp}]\!](\mathsf{s})$. Then

$$
\begin{array}{lll}
\langle \mathsf{s, st, (\textbf{put}\ exp)} \dashv \mathsf{c} \rangle & & \\
\quad \to \langle \mathsf{s, st, exp} \dashv \textbf{put} \dashv \mathsf{c} \rangle & & (\textit{By definition of} \to) \\
\quad \xrightarrow{*} \langle \mathsf{s, st.push(e)}, \textbf{put} \dashv \mathsf{c} \rangle^S & & (\textit{By proposition 7.1}) \\
\quad \to \langle \mathsf{s.put(e), st, c} \rangle^S & & (\textit{By definition of} \to) \\
\quad = \langle {}_S\mathcal{M}[\![\textbf{put}\ \mathsf{exp}]\!](\mathsf{s}), \mathsf{st, c} \rangle^S & & (\textit{By definition of } {}_S\mathcal{M})
\end{array}
$$

Then, the case imp = **while** exp **do** impb **od**. Assume as induction hypothesis that the proposition holds for the component imperative impb. Let s be any standard state, st any value stack and c any control stack. Define a standard state s* and standard states s_i and *E*-values e_i for every $i \geq 0$:

$$
\begin{array}{ll}
\mathsf{s}^* & = {}_S\mathcal{M}[\![\mathsf{imp}]\!](\mathsf{s}) \\
\mathsf{s}_0 & = \mathsf{s} \\
\mathsf{s}_{i+1} & = {}_S\mathcal{M}[\![\mathsf{impb}]\!](\mathsf{s}_i) \\
\mathsf{e}_i & = {}_S\mathcal{E}[\![\mathsf{exp}]\!](\mathsf{s}_i)
\end{array}
$$

Assume first that case β (normal termination) of the While theorem (page 114) holds. Then there exists $n \geq 0$ such that 1) $\mathsf{s}^* = \mathsf{s}_n \neq \bot_{S\,State}$, 2) for every $i < n$: e_i = **true**, 3) e_n = **false**. Under these assumptions the following claim holds for every $i \leq n$:

$$\langle \mathsf{s, st, imp} \dashv \mathsf{c} \rangle \xrightarrow{*} \langle \mathsf{s}_i, \mathsf{st, imp} \dashv \mathsf{c} \rangle$$

where imp is the whole **while** imperative. This claim may be proved by induction on i. That the claim holds for $i = 0$ is obvious ($\xrightarrow{*}$ is a reflexive relation). Assume then that $(i + 1) \leq n$ and, as induction hypothesis, that the claim holds for i. Then

$$
\begin{array}{lll}
\langle \mathsf{s, st, imp} \dashv \mathsf{c} \rangle & & \\
\quad = \langle \mathsf{s}_0, \mathsf{st}, (\textbf{while}\ \mathsf{exp}\ \textbf{do}\ \mathsf{impb}\ \textbf{od}) \dashv \mathsf{c} \rangle & & \\
\quad \xrightarrow{*} \langle \mathsf{s}_i, \mathsf{st}, (\textbf{while}\ \mathsf{exp}\ \textbf{do}\ \mathsf{impb}\ \textbf{od}) \dashv \mathsf{c} \rangle & & (\textit{By ind. hyp. for } i) \\
\quad \to \langle \mathsf{s}_i, \mathsf{st, exp} \dashv \textbf{if} \dashv (\mathsf{impb; imp}) \dashv \textbf{skip} \dashv \mathsf{c} \rangle & & \\
\quad \xrightarrow{*} \langle \mathsf{s}_i, \mathsf{st.push(e}_i), \textbf{if} \dashv (\mathsf{impb; imp}) \dashv \textbf{skip} \dashv \mathsf{c} \rangle & & (\textit{By proposition 7.1}) \\
\quad \to \langle \mathsf{s}_i, \mathsf{st, (impb; imp)} \dashv \mathsf{c} \rangle & & (\mathsf{s}_i = \textbf{true}) \\
\quad \to \langle \mathsf{s}_i, \mathsf{st, impb} \dashv \mathsf{imp} \dashv \mathsf{c} \rangle & & (\textit{By definition of} \to) \\
\quad \xrightarrow{*} \langle \mathsf{s}_{i+1}, \mathsf{st, imp} \dashv \mathsf{c} \rangle & & (\textit{By ind. hyp. for } \mathsf{impb})
\end{array}
$$

The claim is proved, and we may use it for $i = n$:

$\langle$s, st, imp$\dashv$c$\rangle$
$\overset{*}{\rightarrow}$ $\langle s_n$, st, imp$\dashv$c$\rangle$
= $\langle s_n$, st, (**while** exp **do** impb **od**)$\dashv$c$\rangle$ (*By definition of* imp)
$\rightarrow$ $\langle s_n$, st, exp$\dashv$**if**$\dashv$(impb; imp)$\dashv$**skip**$\dashv$c$\rangle$
$\overset{*}{\rightarrow}$ $\langle s_n$, st.push(e_n), **if**$\dashv$(impb; imp)$\dashv$**skip**$\dashv$c$\rangle$
$\rightarrow$ $\langle s_n$, st, **skip**$\dashv$c$\rangle$ (e_n = **false**)
$\rightarrow$ $\langle s_n$, st, c$\rangle$ (*By definition of* $\rightarrow$)
= $\langle$s*, st, c$\rangle$ (s* = s_n)
= $\langle {}_S\mathcal{M}[\![imp]\!]$(s), st, c$\rangle$ (*By definition of* s*)

If case α (infinite loop) of the While theorem holds, e_n = **true** for every $n \geq 0$ and s* = $\perp_{SState}$. It is easy to see (similarly to the evaluations for case β above) that the interpreter diverges from $\langle$s, st, (**while** exp **do** impb **od**)$\dashv$c$\rangle$, i.e., that $\langle$s, st, (**while** exp **do** impb **od**)$\dashv$c$\rangle$ $\overset{*}{\rightarrow}$ $\perp_{IState}$. But then:

$\langle$s, st, imp$\dashv$c$\rangle$
$\overset{*}{\rightarrow}$ $\perp_{IState}$
= $\langle \perp_{SState}$, st, c$\rangle^S$ (*By definition of the function* $\langle \ldots \rangle^S$)
= $\langle$s*, st, c$\rangle^S$
= $\langle {}_S\mathcal{M}[\![imp]\!]$(s), st, c$\rangle^S$ (*By definition of* s*)

Case γ of the While theorem is left as an exercise.

Claim 3): To prove that ${}_I\mathcal{P}[\![$prog$]\!]$ = ${}_S\mathcal{P}[\![$prog$]\!]$ holds for every While program prog = **begin** imp **end**, let inp be any input sequence. Define s_0 = ${}_S$State'init(inp). Then:

${}_I\mathcal{P}[\![$**begin** imp **end**$]\!]$(inp)
= $\mathcal{M}$achine$_I$($\langle s_0$, ε, $\langle$**begin** imp **end**$\rangle\rangle$).Output
= $\mathcal{M}$achine$_I$($\langle s_0$, ε, $\langle$imp$\rangle\rangle$).Output
= $\mathcal{M}$achine$_I$($\langle s_0$, ε, $\langle$imp$\rangle\rangle$).${}_S$State.Output
= ${}_I\mathcal{M}[\![$imp$]\!]$(s_0).Output
= ${}_S\mathcal{M}[\![$imp$]\!]$(s_0).Output
= ${}_S\mathcal{P}[\![$**begin** imp **end**$]\!]$(inp)

End of proof of theorem 7.1.

7.4 A compiler

A *compiler* is a function that maps one programming language - called the *source language* - to another programming language - the *target language*. The reason for compiling is usually that the target language is either directly executable on a computer, or at least closer to executability than the source language.

In this section we describe a compiler that compiles the While language to a language that is close to being directly executable on real computers, namely a language that is a simplified version of the *machine languages* of certain real computers.

We start by describing an idealized computer and its rather simple machine language. We then show how to compile from the While language to this machine language, and prove that the compiler is correct in the sense that the effect of executing a compiled While program on the idealized computer, is as specified by the standard (denotational) semantics for the While language.

7.4.1 A computer and its machine language

We give our computer the name C. Its state algebra ${}_C\mathit{State}$ is an algebra with a carrier defined as follows:

$$\begin{aligned} {}_C\mathit{State} &\stackrel{d}{=} \mathit{Input} \times \mathit{Store} \times \mathit{Output} \times \mathit{Stack} \times \mathit{C\text{-}Program} \times \mathit{Counter{:}\ Int} \\ &= {}_S\mathit{State} \times \mathit{Stack} \times \mathit{C\text{-}Program} \times \mathit{Counter{:}\ Int} \end{aligned}$$

The algebras $\mathit{Input} = \mathit{Int}^*$, $\mathit{Store} = (\mathit{Ident} \to S)$ and $\mathit{Output} = \mathit{Int}^*$ are the same as those used to define the standard semantics of the While language (they are defined in section 6.3.1), and $\mathit{Stack} = E^*$ is the stack algebra used in our interpreter (it is defined in figure 7.2). A precise definition of ${}_C\mathit{State}$ is quite similar to the definition of the algebra ${}_I\mathit{State}$ of interpreter states given in figure 7.1 on page 129, with projection functions ${}_S$State, Output and Stacktop, and a strict tupling function $\langle \ldots \rangle^s$.

The algebra *C-Program* is a syntax algebra that is implicitly defined by BNF productions given in figure 7.4. It has a carrier that consists of all programs in a language said to be the *machine language* of C. Such programs consist of finite sequences of C *instructions*. Each of these instructions will – when executed by C – change the state of the computer 'a little'. The C instructions that may be used in C programs are described informally in figure 7.5. An operational definition of the semantics of the C language is given below, where we describe how C programs are executed by a C computer.

The last component of a ${}_C\mathit{State}$ is a so-called *program counter*: an integer that indicates which instruction in the program is to be executed by the computer.

In section 7.2 we said that a computer may be defined by defining its state algebra and how it steps and stops. The algebra ${}_C\mathit{State}$ of C states has already been defined. The functions step_C and $\mathsf{terminal}_C$ – which specify how C steps and stops – are defined as follows for every $\mathsf{s} \in {}_S\mathit{State}$, $\mathsf{st} \in \mathit{Stack}$, $\mathsf{p} \in \mathit{C\text{-}Program}$ and $\mathsf{pc} \in \mathit{Counter}$:

$$\begin{aligned} \langle \mathsf{s, st, p, pc} \rangle . \mathsf{terminal}_C &= (\mathsf{pc} < 1) \vee (\mathsf{pc} > \#(\mathsf{p})) \\ \langle \mathsf{s, st, p, pc} \rangle . \mathsf{step}_C &= \langle \mathsf{s, st, p, pc} \rangle . \mathsf{exec}(\mathsf{p} \downarrow \mathsf{pc}) \end{aligned}$$

The auxiliary function exec embodies the effect of executing a single C instruction. It has signature

$\langle$*C-program*$\rangle$ ::= $\langle$*C-instruction*$\rangle$*

$\langle$*C-instruction*$\rangle$ ::= **cload** $\langle$*literal*$\rangle$
| **vload** $\langle$*ident*$\rangle$
| **store** $\langle$*ident*$\rangle$
| **put**
| **get** $\langle$*ident*$\rangle$
| $\langle$*unop*$\rangle$
| $\langle$*binop*$\rangle$
| **jump** $\langle$*rel*$\rangle$
| **cjump** $\langle$*rel*$\rangle$

$\langle$*rel*$\rangle$ ::= ... -2 | -1 | 0 | 1 | 2 | ...

$\langle$*ident*$\rangle$, $\langle$*literal*$\rangle$, $\langle$*unop*$\rangle$ and $\langle$*binop*$\rangle$ are as in the While language

Figure 7.4: The C language (machine language of the C computer)

$$\text{exec} \in ({}_C\textit{State} \times \textit{C-Instruction} \rightarrow {}_C\textit{State}_\perp)$$

and is defined by cases (one for each kind of *C* instruction) in figure 7.6.

Informally, we may describe *C*'s behaviour as follows. Assume that the state of *C* is ⟨s, st, p, pc⟩, where s is a standard state, st a stack, p a *C* program and pc an integer. If the program counter pc has a value less than 1 or greater than #(p) (which is equal to the number of instructions in the program p), *C* stops. Otherwise, instruction p↓pc (this is the instruction found at position number pc in p) is executed. When an instruction is executed, the effect is 1) to change either a standard component or the stack or both (what will change and how it changes, depends upon the instruction - one of the instructions (**jump**) changes none of these state components), and 2) for all instructions except the jump instructions to increment the program counter with 1.

It is not very difficult to prove the following proposition, which will be useful when we study the behaviour of *C* programs (as we will do below when we prove that the compiler to be defined is correct).

Proposition 7.3 *Assume that* p_1, p_2 *are two C programs, and that* $p = p_1 \mathbin{\text{⧺}} p_2$ *is their concatenation. Then for every* s, s', s'' $\in {}_S\textit{State}$ *and* st, st', st'' $\in$ *Stack:*

$$\begin{array}{ll} \textit{If} & \langle s,\ st,\ p_1,\ 1\rangle \xrightarrow{*} \langle s',\ st',\ p_1,\ \#(p_1)+1\rangle \\ \textit{and} & \langle s',\ st',\ p_2,\ 1\rangle \xrightarrow{*} \langle s'',\ st'',\ p_2,\ \#(p_2)+1\rangle \\ \textit{then} & \langle s,\ st,\ p,\ 1\rangle \xrightarrow{*} \langle s'',\ st'',\ p,\ \#(p)+1\rangle \end{array}$$

cload lit	where lit is a literal (a binary numeral, as in the **While** language). The effect of this instruction is to push the value of the literal onto the stack.
vload id	where id is an identifier. Pushes store(id) onto the stack.
store id	Pops the stack and assigns its top to store(id).
put	Pops the stack and moves its top to the output sequence.
get id	Removes the head of the input sequence and assigns it to store(id).
uop	where uop is a unary operator. The effect is to replace the top of the stack with the result of applying the unary operator uop to it.
bop	where bop is a binary operator. Replaces the two top elements of the stack with the result of applying the operator to them.
jump rel	where rel is an integer. The effect of executing this so-called *relative jump instruction* is to add rel (which may be positive or negative) to the program counter.
cjump rel	where rel is an integer. This is a *conditional jump instruction*, which first pops the stack and then adds rel to the program counter if the top of the stack is the Boolean value **false**.

Figure 7.5: Informal descriptions of the C instructions

For every $\mathsf{s} \in {}_{S}\mathit{State}$, $\mathsf{st} \in \mathit{Stack}$, $\mathsf{p} \in \mathit{C\text{-}Program}$, $\mathsf{pc} \in \mathit{Int}$:

$$
\begin{aligned}
\langle s, st, p, pc\rangle.\mathrm{exec}(\mathbf{cload}\ lit) &= \langle s, st.\mathrm{push}(\mathcal{A}[\![lit]\!]), p, pc+1\rangle \\
\langle s, st, p, pc\rangle.\mathrm{exec}(\mathbf{vload}\ id) &= \langle s, st.\mathrm{push}(s.\mathrm{access}(id)), p, pc+1\rangle \\
\langle s, st, p, pc\rangle.\mathrm{exec}(\mathbf{store}\ id) &= \langle s.\mathrm{assign}(id, st.\mathrm{top}), st.\mathrm{pop}, p, pc+1\rangle^{s} \\
\langle s, st, p, pc\rangle.\mathrm{exec}(\mathbf{get}\ id) &= \langle s.\mathrm{get}(id), st, p, pc+1\rangle^{s} \\
\langle s, st, p, pc\rangle.\mathrm{exec}(\mathbf{put}) &= \langle s.\mathrm{put}(st.\mathrm{top}), st.\mathrm{pop}, p, pc+1\rangle^{s} \\
\langle s, st, p, pc\rangle.\mathrm{exec}(uop) &= \langle s, st.\mathrm{apply1}(\mathcal{U}[\![uop]\!]), p, pc+1\rangle^{s} \\
\langle s, st, p, pc\rangle.\mathrm{exec}(bop) &= \langle s, st.\mathrm{apply2}(\mathcal{B}[\![bop]\!]), p, pc+1\rangle^{s} \\
\langle s, st, p, pc\rangle.\mathrm{exec}(\mathbf{jump}\ r) &= \langle s, st, p, pc+r\rangle \\
\langle s, st, p, pc\rangle.\mathrm{exec}(\mathbf{cjump}\ r) &= \langle s, st.\mathrm{pop}, p, \\
&\qquad pc+(\mathbf{if}\ st.\mathrm{top} = \mathbf{false\ then}\ r\ \mathbf{else}\ 1)\rangle^{s}
\end{aligned}
$$

Figure 7.6: The exec function of the *C* computer

Program:

$\mathcal{C}$ompile(**begin** imp **end**) = $\mathcal{C}$ompile(imp)

Imperative:

$\mathcal{C}$ompile(**put** exp) = $\mathcal{C}$ompile(exp) ⊢⊣ ⟨**put**⟩
$\mathcal{C}$ompile(**get** id) = ⟨**get** id⟩
$\mathcal{C}$ompile(id := exp) = $\mathcal{C}$ompile(exp) ⊢⊣ ⟨**store** id⟩
$\mathcal{C}$ompile(imp_1; imp_2) = $\mathcal{C}$ompile(imp_1) ⊢⊣ $\mathcal{C}$ompile(imp_2)

$\mathcal{C}$ompile(**if** exp **then** imp_1 **else** imp_2 **fi**)
  = **let** $pimp_1$ = $\mathcal{C}$ompile(imp_1), $pimp_2$ = $\mathcal{C}$ompile(imp_2) **in**
    $\mathcal{C}$ompile(exp) ⊢⊣ ⟨**cjump** #($pimp_1$) + 2⟩ ⊢⊣
    $pimp_1$ ⊢⊣ ⟨**jump** #($pimp_2$) + 1⟩ ⊢⊣ $pimp_2$

$\mathcal{C}$ompile(**while** exp **do** imp **od**)
  = **let** pexp = $\mathcal{C}$ompile(exp), pimp = $\mathcal{C}$ompile(imp) **in**
    pexp ⊢⊣ ⟨**cjump** #(pimp) + 2⟩ ⊢⊣ pimp ⊢⊣
    ⟨**jump** − (#(pexp) + #(pimp) + 1)⟩

Expression:

$\mathcal{C}$ompile(lit) = ⟨**cload** lit⟩
$\mathcal{C}$ompile(id) = ⟨**vload** id⟩
$\mathcal{C}$ompile(uop exp) = $\mathcal{C}$ompile(exp) ⊢⊣ ⟨uop⟩
$\mathcal{C}$ompile(exp_1 bop exp_2) = $\mathcal{C}$ompile(exp_1) ⊢⊣ $\mathcal{C}$ompile(exp_2) ⊢⊣ ⟨bop⟩

Figure 7.7: The compiler

7.4.2 The compiler

The compiler we define in this section is a function that maps programs, imperatives and expressions of the While language to *C* programs. It has signature

$\mathcal{C}$ompile ∈ ((*Program* + *Imperative* + *Expression*) → *C-program*)

and is defined, by induction on syntactic complexity, in figure 7.7. An example that shows how the compiler works:

$\mathcal{C}$ompile(**begin**
  get xx;
  fac := **1**;
  while xx > **0** **do** fac := fac ∗ xx; xx := xx − **1** **od**;

```
       put fac;
      end)
  = Compile(get xx) ʜ
    Compile(fac := 1) ʜ
    Compile(while xx > 0 do fac := fac * xx; xx := xx - 1 od) ʜ
    Compile(put fac)
  = ⟨get xx⟩ ʜ
    Compile(1) ʜ ⟨store fac⟩ ʜ
    (let pexp = Compile(xx > 0),
         pimp = Compile(fac := fac * xx; xx := xx - 1)
     in  pexp ʜ ⟨cjump #(pimp) + 2⟩ ʜ pimp ʜ
         ⟨jump - (#(pexp) + #(pimp) + 1)⟩) ʜ
    Compile(fac) ʜ ⟨put⟩
  = ⟨get xx⟩ ʜ
    ⟨cload 1⟩ ʜ ⟨store fac⟩ ʜ
    (let pexp = ⟨vload xx⟩ ʜ ⟨cload 0⟩ ʜ ⟨>⟩
         pimp = ⟨vload fac⟩ ʜ ⟨vload xx⟩ ʜ ⟨*⟩ ʜ ⟨store fac⟩ ʜ
                ⟨vload xx⟩ ʜ ⟨cload 1⟩ ʜ ⟨-⟩ ʜ ⟨store xx⟩
     in  pexp ʜ ⟨cjump #(pimp) + 2⟩ ʜ pimp ʜ
         ⟨jump - (#(pexp) + #(pimp) + 1)⟩
    ) ʜ
    ⟨vload fac⟩ ʜ ⟨put⟩
  = ⟨get xx⟩ ʜ
    ⟨cload 1⟩ ʜ ⟨store fac⟩ ʜ
    ⟨vload xx⟩ ʜ ⟨cload 0⟩ ʜ ⟨>⟩ ʜ
    ⟨cjump 10⟩ ʜ
    ⟨vload fac⟩ ʜ ⟨vload xx⟩ ʜ ⟨*⟩ ʜ ⟨store fac⟩ ʜ
    ⟨vload xx⟩ ʜ ⟨cload 1⟩ ʜ ⟨-⟩ ʜ ⟨store xx⟩ ʜ
    ⟨jump -12⟩ ʜ
    ⟨vload fac⟩ ʜ ⟨put⟩
  = ⟨get xx, cload 1, store fac, vload xx, cload 0, >,
     cjump 10, vload fac, vload xx, *, store fac,
     vload xx, cload 1, -, store xx,
     jump -12, vload fac, put⟩
```

7.4.3 Compiler semantics

Having access to a compiler that compiles from the While language to the machine language of the *C* computer, we may use the computer to execute While programs and imperatives and to evaluate While expressions. If we, for instance, would like to execute a given While program wp from a given input sequence inp we may proceed as follows: First, compile wp. Assume that pimp is the result. Then start the computer with an initial state that has an input sequence equal to inp, a default store, an empty output sequence, a program equal to pimp and a program counter equal to 1, that is the state ⟨$_S$State'init(inp), ε, pimp, 1⟩.

If the computer terminates from this initial state, extract the output sequence from the terminal state and let that be the result of the computation. If the computation does not terminate, let $\bot_{Output}$ be the result.

Used together like this, the computer and the compiler define a semantic mapping which we call ${}_C\mathcal{P}$ and which is a function with signature

$${}_C\mathcal{P} \in (\mathit{Program} \rightarrow (\mathit{Input} \rightarrow \mathit{Output}_\bot))$$

This mapping is such that for every While program prog:

$${}_C\mathcal{P}[\![\mathsf{prog}]\!] \stackrel{d}{=} \lambda \mathsf{inp} \in \mathit{Input}\colon \mathcal{M}\mathsf{achine}_C(\langle {}_S\mathsf{State'init(inp)},\ \varepsilon,\ \mathcal{C}\mathsf{ompile(prog)},\ 1\rangle).\mathsf{Output}$$

If we want to use the computer and the compiler to evaluate a given While expression exp from a given standard state s, we start C from an initial state ⟨s, ε, cexp, 1⟩, where cexp is the result of compiling the expression. If the computer terminates from this state, let the top element of the stack in the terminal state be the result. If it does not terminate, let $\bot_E$ be the result. The semantic mapping

$${}_C\mathcal{E} \in (\mathit{Expression} \rightarrow ({}_S\mathit{State} \rightarrow E_\bot))$$

implicitly defined by such use of the computer and the compiler, is such that for every While expression exp:

$${}_C\mathcal{E}[\![\mathsf{exp}]\!] \stackrel{d}{=} \lambda \mathsf{s} \in {}_S\mathit{State}\colon \mathcal{M}\mathsf{achine}_C(\langle \mathsf{s},\ \varepsilon,\ \mathcal{C}\mathsf{ompile(exp)},\ 1\rangle).\mathsf{Stacktop}$$

Quite similarly, we may use the compiler and the computer to define a semantic mapping ${}_C\mathcal{M} \in (\mathit{Imperative} \rightarrow ({}_S\mathit{State} \rightarrow {}_S\mathit{State}_\bot))$ which for every While imperative imp satisfies the following equation:

$${}_C\mathcal{M}[\![\mathsf{imp}]\!] \stackrel{d}{=} \lambda \mathsf{s} \in {}_S\mathit{State}\colon \mathcal{M}\mathsf{achine}_C(\langle \mathsf{s},\ \varepsilon,\ \mathcal{C}\mathsf{ompile(imp)},\ 1\rangle).{}_S\mathsf{State}$$

The definitions of the semantic mappings ${}_C\mathcal{P}$, ${}_C\mathcal{E}$ and ${}_C\mathcal{M}$ are operational definitions because they are based on the operationally defined $\mathcal{M}\mathsf{achine}_C$ function, that is on how the C computer works.

It only remains to prove that the compiler and the computer taken together constitute a *correct implementation* of the While language in the sense that the semantic mappings defined operationally using the compiler and the computer, are equal to their corresponding standard semantic mappings as defined in chapter 6:

Theorem 7.2 The compiler is correct:
The compiler versions of the three semantic mappings are equal to their corresponding standard mappings:

$${}_C\mathcal{E} = {}_S\mathcal{E}, \quad {}_C\mathcal{M} = {}_S\mathcal{M}, \quad {}_C\mathcal{P} = {}_S\mathcal{P}$$

Proof: We prove

1): ${}_C\mathcal{E}[\![\mathsf{exp}]\!] = {}_S\mathcal{E}[\![\mathsf{exp}]\!]$ for every expression exp,
2): ${}_C\mathcal{P}[\![\mathsf{prog}]\!] = {}_S\mathcal{P}[\![\mathsf{prog}]\!]$ for every While program prog.
3): ${}_C\mathcal{M}[\![\mathsf{imp}]\!] = {}_S\mathcal{M}[\![\mathsf{imp}]\!]$ for every imperative imp,

That 1): ${}_C\mathcal{E}[\![\mathsf{exp}]\!] = {}_S\mathcal{E}[\![\mathsf{exp}]\!]$ holds for every expression exp follows easily from the following proposition:

Proposition 7.4 *For every* $\mathsf{exp} \in \mathit{Expression}$*, let* $\mathsf{pexp} = \mathcal{C}\mathsf{ompile}(\mathsf{exp})$. *Then for every* $\mathsf{s} \in {}_S\mathit{State}$, $\mathsf{st} \in \mathit{Stack}$*:*

$$\langle \mathsf{s},\ \mathsf{st},\ \mathsf{pexp},\ 1\rangle \xrightarrow{*} \langle \mathsf{s},\ \mathsf{st}\,.\,\mathsf{push}({}_S\mathcal{E}[\![\mathsf{exp}]\!](\mathsf{s})),\ \mathsf{pexp},\ \#(\mathsf{pexp}) + 1\rangle^{s}$$

Proof of this proposition is by induction on the syntactic complexity of the expression exp. We only treat the case $\mathsf{exp} = (\mathsf{exp}_1\ \mathsf{bop}\ \mathsf{exp}_2)$ here (the other cases are simpler). Let s be a standard state, st a stack. Define $\mathsf{e}_i = \mathcal{E}[\![\mathsf{exp}_i]\!](\mathsf{s})$, $\mathsf{pexp}_i = \mathcal{C}\mathsf{ompile}(\mathsf{exp}_i)$ for $i = 1, 2$, and

$$\mathsf{pexp} = \mathcal{C}\mathsf{ompile}(\mathsf{exp}) = \mathcal{C}\mathsf{ompile}(\mathsf{exp}_1) \mathbin{\vdash\!\dashv} \mathcal{C}\mathsf{ompile}(\mathsf{exp}_2) \mathbin{\vdash\!\dashv} \langle \mathsf{bop}\rangle$$

Then by the induction hypothesis for exp_1:

$$\begin{aligned} &\langle \mathsf{s},\ \mathsf{st},\ \mathsf{pexp}_1,\ 1\rangle \\ &\quad\xrightarrow{*} \langle \mathsf{s},\ \mathsf{st}\,.\,\mathsf{push}(\mathsf{e}_1),\ \mathsf{pexp}_1,\ \#(\mathsf{pexp}_1 + 1)\rangle^{s} \end{aligned}$$

By the induction hypothesis for exp_2 applied to the state s and the stack $\mathsf{st}\,.\,\mathsf{push}(\mathsf{e}_1)$:

$$\begin{aligned} &\langle \mathsf{s},\ \mathsf{st}\,.\,\mathsf{push}(\mathsf{e}_1),\ \mathsf{pexp}_2,\ 1\rangle \\ &\quad\xrightarrow{*} \langle \mathsf{s},\ \mathsf{st}\,.\,\mathsf{push}(\mathsf{e}_1)\,.\,\mathsf{push}(\mathsf{e}_2),\ \mathsf{pexp}_2,\ \#(\mathsf{pexp}_2 + 1)\rangle^{s} \end{aligned}$$

By the definition of the exec function,

$$\begin{aligned} &\langle \mathsf{s},\ \mathsf{st}\,.\,\mathsf{push}(\mathsf{e}_1)\,.\,\mathsf{push}(\mathsf{e}_2),\ \langle\mathsf{bop}\rangle,\ 1\rangle \\ &\quad\to \langle \mathsf{s},\ \mathsf{st}\,.\,\mathsf{push}(\mathsf{e}_1)\,.\,\mathsf{push}(\mathsf{e}_2)\,.\,\mathsf{apply2}(\mathcal{B}[\![\mathsf{bop}]\!]),\ \langle\mathsf{bop}\rangle,\ 2\rangle^{s} \end{aligned}$$

Proposition 7.3 used twice then gives

$$\begin{aligned} &\langle \mathsf{s},\ \mathsf{st},\ \mathsf{pexp},\ 1\rangle \\ &\quad= \langle \mathsf{s},\ \mathsf{st},\ \mathsf{pexp}_1 \mathbin{\vdash\!\dashv} \mathsf{pexp}_2 \mathbin{\vdash\!\dashv} \langle\mathsf{bop}\rangle,\ 1\rangle \\ &\quad\xrightarrow{*} \langle \mathsf{s},\ \mathsf{st}\,.\,\mathsf{push}(\mathsf{e}_1)\,.\,\mathsf{push}(\mathsf{e}_2)\,.\,\mathsf{apply2}(\mathcal{B}[\![\mathsf{bop}]\!]),\ \mathsf{pexp},\ \#(\mathsf{pexp} + 1)\rangle^{s} \end{aligned}$$

Using the axiom for apply2 and the definition of ${}_S\mathcal{E}$, we then get

$$\begin{aligned} &\langle \mathsf{s},\ \mathsf{st},\ \mathsf{pexp},\ 1\rangle \\ &\quad\xrightarrow{*} \langle \mathsf{s},\ \mathsf{st}\,.\,\mathsf{push}(\mathsf{e}_1)\,.\,\mathsf{push}(\mathsf{e}_2)\,.\,\mathsf{apply2}(\mathcal{B}[\![\mathsf{bop}]\!]),\ \mathsf{pexp},\ \#(\mathsf{pexp} + 1)\rangle^{s} \\ &\quad= \langle \mathsf{s},\ \mathsf{st}\,.\,\mathsf{push}(\mathcal{B}[\![\mathsf{bop}]\!](\mathsf{e}_1,\ \mathsf{e}_2)),\ \mathsf{pexp},\ \#(\mathsf{pexp} + 1)\rangle^{s} \\ &\quad= \langle \mathsf{s},\ \mathsf{st}\,.\,\mathsf{push}({}_S\mathcal{E}[\![\mathsf{exp}_1\ \mathsf{bop}\ \mathsf{exp}_2]\!](\mathsf{s})),\ \mathsf{pexp},\ \#(\mathsf{pexp} + 1)\rangle^{s} \end{aligned}$$

Hence, the claim in the proposition holds for $\mathsf{exp}_1\ \mathsf{bop}\ \mathsf{exp}_2$.

That 2): ${}_C\mathcal{M}[\![\mathsf{imp}]\!] = {}_S\mathcal{M}[\![\mathsf{imp}]\!]$ holds for every imperative imp follows from this proposition:

Proposition 7.5 *For every* imp $\in$ *Imperative, let* pimp = $\mathcal{C}$ompile(imp). *Then for every* s $\in$ $_S$*State*, st $\in$ *Stack:*

$$\langle \mathsf{s, st, pimp, 1} \rangle \xrightarrow{*} \langle {_S}\mathcal{M}[\![\mathsf{imp}]\!](\mathsf{s}), \mathsf{st, pimp}, \#(\mathsf{pimp}) + 1 \rangle^S$$

Proof is by induction on the syntactic complexity of the imperative imp. We consider two of the cases here (the other may be treated quite similarly). First, the case imp = **put** exp. Let s be a state and st a stack, and define e = $\mathcal{E}[\![\mathsf{exp}]\!](\mathsf{s})$, and pimp = $\mathcal{C}$ompile(imp) = pexp ⊢ ⟨**put**⟩ where pexp = $\mathcal{C}$ompile(exp). Then by proposition 7.4

$$\langle \mathsf{s, st, pexp, 1} \rangle \xrightarrow{*} \langle \mathsf{s, st.push(e), pexp}, \#(\mathsf{pexp}) + 1 \rangle^S$$

By definition of exec

$$\langle \mathsf{s, st.push(e), pexp}, \langle \mathbf{put} \rangle, 1 \rangle \rightarrow \langle \mathsf{s.put(e), st, pexp}, \langle \mathbf{put} \rangle, 2 \rangle^S$$

By proposition 7.3 we then get

$$\begin{aligned} &\langle \mathsf{s, st, pimp, 1} \rangle \\ &\quad = \langle \mathsf{s, st, pexp} \vdash \langle \mathbf{put} \rangle, 1 \rangle \\ &\quad \xrightarrow{*} \langle \mathsf{s.put(e), st, pimp}, \#(\mathsf{pimp}) + 1 \rangle^S \\ &\quad = \langle {_S}\mathcal{M}[\![\mathbf{put}\ \mathsf{exp}]\!](\mathsf{s}), \mathsf{st, pimp}, \#(\mathsf{pimp}) + 1 \rangle^S \end{aligned}$$

The latter of these equations holds by the definition of $_S\mathcal{M}$.

Then, the case imp = **while** exp **do** impb **od**: Define

$$\begin{aligned} \mathsf{pexp} &= \mathcal{C}\mathsf{ompile(exp)} \\ \mathsf{pimpb} &= \mathcal{C}\mathsf{ompile(impb)} \\ \mathsf{pimp} &= \mathcal{C}\mathsf{ompile(imp)} \\ &= \mathsf{pexp} \vdash \langle \mathbf{cjump}\ \#(\mathsf{pimpb}) + 2 \rangle \vdash \mathsf{pimpb} \vdash \\ &\quad \langle \mathbf{jump} - (\#(\mathsf{pexp}) + \#(\mathsf{pimpb}) + 1) \rangle \end{aligned}$$

Let s be any standard state and st any stack. Define s* = $_S\mathcal{M}[\![\mathsf{imp}]\!](\mathsf{s})$, and let the standard states s_i and *E*-values e_i be defined as follows for $i \geq 0$:

$$\begin{aligned} \mathsf{s}_0 &= \mathsf{s} \\ \mathsf{s}_{i+1} &= {_S}\mathcal{M}[\![\mathsf{impb}]\!](\mathsf{s}_i) \\ \mathsf{e}_i &= {_S}\mathcal{E}[\![\mathsf{exp}]\!](\mathsf{s}_i) \end{aligned}$$

The induction hypothesis for the proposition applied to the imperative impb gives that

$$\langle \mathsf{s, st, pimpb, 1} \rangle \xrightarrow{*} \langle {_S}\mathcal{M}[\![\mathsf{impb}]\!](\mathsf{s}), \mathsf{st, pimpb}, \#(\mathsf{pimpb}) + 1 \rangle^S$$

Assume first that case β (normal termination) of the While theorem holds. Then there exists $n \geq 0$ such that 1) s* = $\mathsf{s}_n \neq \perp_{S\,State}$, 2) for every $i < n$: e_i = **true**, 3) e_n = **false**. We first prove that the following claim holds for every $i \leq n$:

$$\langle \mathsf{s}_0,\ \mathsf{st},\ \mathsf{pimp},\ 1\rangle \xrightarrow{*} \langle \mathsf{s}_i,\ \mathsf{st},\ \mathsf{pimp},\ 1\rangle^s$$

This claim is proved by induction on i. That the claim holds for $i = 0$ is obvious ($\xrightarrow{*}$ is reflexive).

Assume that $i + 1 \leq n$, and - as an induction hypothesis - that the claim holds for i. Then

$$\begin{aligned}
&\langle \mathsf{s}_0,\ \mathsf{st},\ \mathsf{pimp},\ 1\rangle\\
&\quad \xrightarrow{*} \langle \mathsf{s}_i,\ \mathsf{st},\ \mathsf{pimp},\ 1\rangle^s\\
&\quad \xrightarrow{*} \langle \mathsf{s}_i,\ \mathsf{st.push(e}_i\mathsf{)},\ \mathsf{pimp},\ \#(\mathsf{pexp}) + 1\rangle^s\\
&\quad \rightarrow \langle \mathsf{s}_i,\ \mathsf{st},\ \mathsf{pimp},\ \#(\mathsf{pexp}) + 2\rangle^s\\
&\quad \xrightarrow{*} \langle \mathsf{s}_i,\ \mathsf{st},\ \mathsf{pimp},\ \#(\mathsf{pexp}) + 2\rangle^s\\
&\quad \xrightarrow{*} \langle \mathsf{s}_{i+1},\ \mathsf{st},\ \mathsf{pimp},\ \#(\mathsf{pexp}) + 1 + \#(\mathsf{pimpb}) + 1\rangle^s\\
&\quad \xrightarrow{*} \langle \mathsf{s}_{i+1},\ \mathsf{st},\ \mathsf{pimp},\ 1\rangle^s
\end{aligned}$$

Our claim is then proved. We apply it to the case $i = n$, and get

$$\begin{aligned}
&\langle \mathsf{s}_0,\ \mathsf{st},\ \mathsf{pimp},\ 1\rangle\\
&\quad \xrightarrow{*} \langle \mathsf{s}_n,\ \mathsf{st},\ \mathsf{pimp},\ 1\rangle^s\\
&\quad \xrightarrow{*} \langle \mathsf{s}_n,\ \mathsf{st.push(e}_n\mathsf{)},\ \mathsf{pimp},\ \#(\mathsf{pexp}) + 1\rangle^s\\
&\quad \rightarrow \langle \mathsf{s}_n,\ \mathsf{st},\ \mathsf{pimp},\ \#(\mathsf{pexp}) + 1 + \#(\mathsf{pimpb}) + 2\rangle^s\\
&\quad = \langle \mathsf{s}_n,\ \mathsf{st},\ \mathsf{pimp},\ \#(\mathsf{pimp}) + 1\rangle^s\\
&\quad = \langle \mathsf{s}^*,\ \mathsf{st},\ \mathsf{pimp},\ \#(\mathsf{pimp}) + 1\rangle^s\\
&\quad = \langle {}_S\mathcal{M}[\![\mathsf{imp}]\!](\mathsf{s}),\ \mathsf{st},\ \mathsf{pimp},\ \#(\mathsf{pimp}) + 1\rangle^s
\end{aligned}$$

If case α ('infinite loop') of the While theorem holds, $\mathsf{e}_n = \mathbf{true}$ for every $n \geq 0$ and $\mathsf{s}^* = \bot_{S\,State}$. It is easy to see (similarly to our evaluations for case β above) that the C computer will diverge from $\langle \mathsf{s},\ \mathsf{st},\ \langle\mathsf{imp}\rangle,\ 1\rangle$. This means that $\langle \mathsf{s},\ \mathsf{st},\ \langle\mathsf{imp}\rangle,\ 1\rangle \xrightarrow{*} \bot_{C\,State}$. But then:

$$\begin{aligned}
&\langle {}_S\mathcal{M}[\![\mathsf{imp}]\!](\mathsf{s}),\ \mathsf{st},\ \mathsf{pimp},\ 1\rangle^s\\
&\quad = \langle \mathsf{s}^*,\ \mathsf{st},\ \mathsf{c}\rangle^s\\
&\quad = \langle \bot_{S\,State},\ \mathsf{st},\ \mathsf{c}\rangle^s\\
&\quad = \bot_{C\,State} && \textit{By definition of the function } \langle\ldots\rangle^s
\end{aligned}$$

- which entails that the claim in the proposition holds also in this case.

Case γ of the While theorem is left as an exercise.

To prove that 3): ${}_C\mathcal{P}[\![\mathsf{prog}]\!] = {}_S\mathcal{P}[\![\mathsf{prog}]\!]$ holds for every While program prog = **begin** imp **end**, let inp be any input sequence and define $\mathsf{s}_0 = {}_S\mathsf{State'Init(inp)}$. Then:

$$\begin{aligned}
&{}_C\mathcal{P}[\![\mathbf{begin}\ \mathsf{imp}\ \mathbf{end}]\!](\mathsf{inp})\\
&\quad = \mathcal{M}\mathsf{achine}_C(\langle \mathsf{s}_0,\ \varepsilon,\ \mathcal{C}\mathsf{ompile}(\mathbf{begin}\ \mathsf{imp}\ \mathbf{end}),\ 1\rangle).\mathsf{Output}\\
&\quad = \mathcal{M}\mathsf{achine}_C(\langle \mathsf{s}_0,\ \varepsilon,\ \mathcal{C}\mathsf{ompile}(\mathsf{imp}),\ 1\rangle).\mathsf{Output}\\
&\quad = \mathcal{M}\mathsf{achine}_C(\langle \mathsf{s}_0,\ \varepsilon,\ \mathcal{C}\mathsf{ompile}(\mathsf{imp}),\ 1\rangle).{}_S\mathsf{State.Output}\\
&\quad = {}_C\mathcal{M}[\![\mathsf{imp}]\!](\mathsf{s}_0).\mathsf{Output}\\
&\quad = {}_S\mathcal{M}[\![\mathsf{imp}]\!](\mathsf{s}_0).\mathsf{Output}\\
&\quad = {}_S\mathcal{P}[\![\mathbf{begin}\ \mathsf{imp}\ \mathbf{end}]\!](\mathsf{inp})
\end{aligned}$$

End of proof of theorem 7.2.

7.5 Exercises

7.5.1 An example for the interpreter

Study - in as much detail as possible - how the interpreter executes the imperative

```
sum := 0;
get num;
while num > 0 do sum := sum + num; get num od;
put sum
```

Use ⟨2, 3, 0⟩ as input sequence for the interpreter.

7.5.2 An example for the compiler

Study how the compiler translates the program in the previous exercise, and how the compiled program is executed.

7.5.3 An extended interpreter

Include **getint** as an expression in the language (this is, of course, an expression that changes the state when it is executed), and extend the interpreter such that it is able to evaluate such expressions.

Give standard, denotational semantics for the state-changing expressions, and prove that the extended interpreter is correct.

7.5.4 Error handling

Change the *C* computer and the compiler such that errors (for instance division by 0, or an attempt to **get** from empty input) are handled in a better fashion. One way is to set the program counter to 0 whenever an error is discovered after outputting a suitable text. Change the standard semantics similarly, and prove the compiler correct.

Chapter 8
Proof-theoretical semantics

8.1 Introduction

In *proof-theoretical semantics* we specify the semantics of a programming language indirectly by specifying what can be *proved* about the effects and values of programs, imperatives, expressions and other constructs of the language.

In this chapter we study two different kinds of proof-theoretical semantics, and show how they may be used to specify the semantics of the While language. In the first kind - called *natural semantics* - the semantics of imperatives are specified by defining how to prove statements that have the following form:

$$s \rightarrow (\mathit{Imp}\text{: imp}) \rightarrow s'$$

The intuitive meaning of this statement is that if the state is as specified in s, then the result of executing the imperative imp is a state which is as specified in s' - assuming that the imperative terminates normally. The semantics of programs and expressions are specified similarly.

In the second kind of proof-theoretical semantics - called *axiomatic semantics* - the semantics of imperatives are specified by showing how we may prove statements of the form:

$$\{P\}\ \text{imp}\ \{Q\}$$

where P and Q are assertions that say something about the state (less informally: P and Q specify conditions on the state). The intuitive meaning of {P} imp {Q} is that if the state is such that P is true before the imperative imp is executed, then Q is true after imp has been executed, provided that imp terminates normally.

Before we describe these two proof-theoretical methods for defining the semantics of programming languages, we give a general description of what it means to give a *formal* proof of a statement.

8.2 Formal deductive calculi

To *prove* a statement means to demonstrate that it is true. A *formal proof* of a statement is a proof that considers only the form of the statement, or - in other words - a proof that may be checked (but not necessarily constructed) by a computer.

A *formal deductive calculus*, or *axiomatic system*, is a calculus or system that may be used to prove statements formally. Such a calculus is defined by two set of rules:

- Rules that define the language of the calculus, in particular the set of sentences of the calculus. We usually call these sentences *well-formed formulae*, or just *wff*'s.

  The rules must be such that the set of wff's is *recursive* (*computable*), which means that it must be possible to write a program that may be used to decide whether or not a given string of characters is a well-formed formula.

- Rules that define the set of *theorems* in the calculus. This set is usually defined inductively, and the defining rules are of two kinds: *Axioms* and *deduction rules* . The axioms constitute the basis for the inductive definition of the set of theorems, and say that all wff's that have certain specified forms are theorems. The deduction rules constitute the inductive steps of the definition of the set of theorems, and say that if a specified number of wff's, each having a specified form, are theorems, then certain other wff's are theorems as well. Examples are given below.

  We often employ a graphical notation for deduction rules and write

$$\frac{P_1, \ldots, P_n}{Q}$$

  to express a deduction rule that says that the wff Q is deducible from the wff's $P_1, \ldots, P_n$.

The axioms and deduction rules of a formal calculus must be such that the set of theorems is *recursively enumerable*, which means that it must be possible to write a program that generates the set of theorems. But the set of theorems does not have to be *recursive*. For many interesting formal systems, the theorem set is, in fact, not recursive, which means that it is not possible to construct a program that may be used to determine whether or not a given wff is a theorem.

For most formal calculi the sets of axioms and deduction rules are recursive (in some cases even finite), and then it is easy to see that the set of theorems is recursively enumerable.

A *proof* in a formal calculus *D* is a finite sequence of *D* wff's P_1, P_2, ..., P_n such that for each $i = 1, \ldots, n$ either 1) P_i is an axiom of *D* or 2) one of the deduction rules of *D* applied to wff's earlier in the sequence gives P_i. A *D* wff P is said to be a *theorem* of *D* if and only if there exists a proof in *D* with P as its last wff.

Alternatively we may define a *D*-proof to be a tree with axioms at its leaves and deduction rules at its branch nodes:

- If P is an axiom of *D* then P is a proof in *D*.
- If $T_1, \ldots, T_n$ are proofs in *D* with $P_1, \ldots, P_n$ as their roots, and *D* has a deduction rule which says that the wff Q is deducible from the wff's $P_1, \ldots, P_n$, then the tree

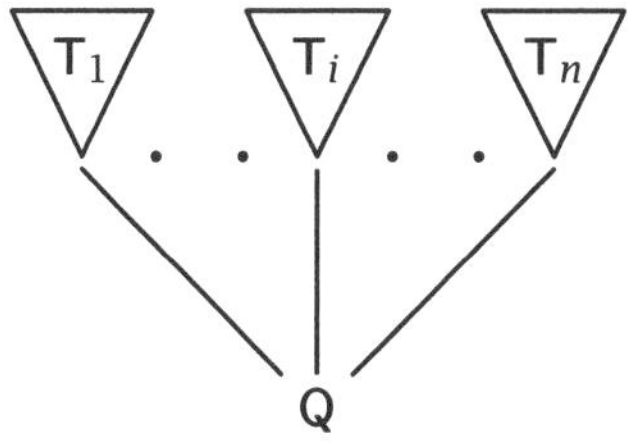

  - which has Q as its root - is a proof in *D*.

If we define proofs to be trees, we say that a wff P is a theorem if and only if there exists a proof with P as its root. It is not difficult to verify that a wff is a theorem in the tree sense if and only if it is a theorem in the sequence sense.

We often write

$$\vdash_D P$$

to express that P is a theorem in the formal calculus *D*. When no misunderstanding should be possible, we may drop the *D* decoration, and write just $\vdash P$

A formal deductive calculus is usually defined in order to formalize intuitive notions of what it means to prove a sentence and of which sentences are true. In such cases we have an interpretation (a semantic mapping) $\mathfrak{I}$ of the sentences of the formal calculus, and write

$$\models_{\mathfrak{I}} \mathsf{P}$$

to express that the sentence P is *true* under $\mathfrak{I}$, i.e., that the interpretation $\mathfrak{I}[\![\mathsf{P}]\!]$ of P is intuitively provable and hence true. For a formal deductive calculus *D* to be a correct formalization of the intuitive provability notion, it is necessary that it is *sound* for the interpretation $\mathfrak{I}$ in the sense that only sentences that are true under $\mathfrak{I}$ are provable in *D*:

$$D \text{ is } \textit{sound} \text{ for } \mathfrak{I} \quad \overset{d}{\Longleftrightarrow} \quad \text{for every sentence } \mathsf{P}\text{: } (\vdash_D \mathsf{P} \;\Rightarrow\; \models_{\mathfrak{I}} \mathsf{P})$$

It is very easy to construct calculi that are sound for some given interpretation but nonetheless of little interest or value: simply define a calculus with no axioms and no deduction rules. To be useful relative to an interpretation, a formal calculus must be sufficiently strong to enable as many as possible - preferably all - of the sentences that are true under the interpretation to be provable. If *every* sentence that is true under an interpretation $\mathfrak{I}$ is formally provable in a calculus *D*, we say that the calculus is *complete* for the interpretation:

$$D \text{ is } \textit{complete} \text{ for } \mathfrak{I} \quad \overset{d}{\Longleftrightarrow} \quad \text{for every sentence } \mathsf{P}\text{: } (\models_{\mathfrak{I}} \mathsf{P} \;\Rightarrow\; \vdash_D \mathsf{P})$$

But a formal calculus may be of value even if it is not complete for its intended interpretation. As long as a sufficiently large portion of the true sentences are provable, we may consider the calculus to be adequate for a given purpose. We will have more to say about this later in this chapter.

One may ask: Why construct formal deductive calculi? Why not be content with intuitive notions that usually are easier to understand - being more intuitive - than the corresponding formal notions? There are two important reasons for constructing formal calculi:

- The first is that we sometimes wish to study the limits of what can be proved, in particular to characterize that which cannot be proved. It is usually much easier to perform such studies in formal calculi than if we employ the informal notions.

- Another reason is to enable computers to be used to check or even construct proofs. For a proof to be amenable for handling by computers, it is necessary that they are written in a formal language and that they adhere to rules that may be recognized by computers.

Before we introduce and describe proof-theoretical semantics of programming language, we present three examples of formal deductive calculi. We do this partly to illustrate the concepts introduced above, partly because we need some of the material presented in these examples when we define one of the two kinds of proof-theoretical semantics.

8.2.1 Example 1: The propositional calculus

A *proposition* is a statement that is either true or false. Two examples:

$$2 + 2 = 4$$

The moon is made of green cheese

Propositions like these - which are not constructed from simpler propositions - are said to be *atomic* propositions. *Compound* propositions may be constructed by using the *propositional connectives*

$\neg$	$\wedge$	$\vee$	$\Rightarrow$	$\Leftrightarrow$
(*not*)	(*and*)	(*or*)	(*implies*)	(*if and only if*)

Thus, the following are examples of compound propositions:

$$(2 + 3 = 4) \Leftrightarrow \neg(\textit{Santa Claus is 2 feet tall})$$

$$\neg(\textit{The moon is made of green cheese}) \wedge (\textit{John loves Marsha})$$

To determine the truth of most propositions - including the ones used as examples here - it is necessary 1) to know the meaning of the words that occur in the propositions and 2) to know sufficiently about the subject matter that is treated to determine the truth-value of each atomic part of the propositions. (Exercise: Determine the truth-value of the propositions used as examples above.) For some compound propositions it is possible to determine whether or not they are true solely on the basis of their *form*, using only knowledge of the meaning of the propositional connectives that occur in the proposition, and without any knowledge about the truth-value of its constituent subpropositions. Some examples: Assume that P and Q are two given propositions, and that we do not know anything about the meaning of the words that occur in them nor about the subject matter that they treat. The only assumptions we make on P and Q are that they are propositions, and hence either true or false. The compound propositions

$$\mathsf{P} \vee \neg \mathsf{P}$$

$$(\mathsf{P} \wedge \mathsf{Q}) \Leftrightarrow (\mathsf{Q} \wedge \mathsf{P})$$

$$\neg(\mathsf{P} \wedge \mathsf{Q}) \Leftrightarrow (\neg \mathsf{P} \vee \neg \mathsf{Q})$$

will then be true, regardless of what P and Q mean and what truth-values they may have.

A proposition that is always true, regardless of the truth-values of its constituent atomic subpropositions, is said to be a *tautology*. Thus, the three propositions above are tautologies. We write

$$\models \mathsf{P}$$

to express that the wff P is a tautology. Observe that a tautology is a proposition that is valid for every interpretation of its atomic subpropositions, as long as each of them is interpreted as something that is either true or false.

The *propositional calculus* is a formal deductive calculus - which we will call *PC* - that may be used to give formal proofs of tautologies. *PC* may be defined as follows:

- **Wff's:** Assume that $PVar = \{pv_1, pv_2, \ldots\}$ is a set of so-called *propositional variables* (think of them as variables that may have any atomic proposition as value and hence be either true or false). The set of well-formed formulae for the propositional calculus is defined inductively as follows:

  (1) Every propositional variable is a wff, which is said to be an *atomic* wff.

  (2) If P and Q are wff's, so are $\neg P$ and $(P \Rightarrow Q)$.

  In addition we allow the following abbreviations:

  $$\begin{array}{lll} P \vee Q & \text{abbreviates} & \neg P \Rightarrow Q \\ P \wedge Q & \text{abbreviates} & \neg(P \Rightarrow \neg Q) \\ P \Leftrightarrow Q & \text{abbreviates} & (P \Rightarrow Q) \wedge (Q \Rightarrow P) \end{array}$$

- **Axioms:** If P, Q and R are any wff's, then the following wff's are axioms:

  $$\begin{array}{l} \text{A1: } (P \Rightarrow (Q \Rightarrow P)) \\ \text{A2: } ((P \Rightarrow (Q \Rightarrow R)) \Rightarrow ((P \Rightarrow Q) \Rightarrow (P \Rightarrow R))) \\ \text{A3: } ((\neg P \Rightarrow \neg Q) \Rightarrow (Q \Rightarrow P)) \end{array}$$

- **Deduction rule:** If P and $P \Rightarrow Q$ are theorems, then so is Q. In a more graphic notation, this rule - which is called *modus ponens* - may be expressed as follows:

  $$\text{MP:} \quad \frac{P; \quad P \Rightarrow Q}{Q}$$

We will write

$$\vdash_{\overline{PC}} P$$

to express that P is a theorem in the propositional calculus *PC*, and

$$\Gamma \vdash_{\overline{PC}} P$$

where Γ is a list of wff's, to express that P may be *deduced* in *PC* from Γ, i.e., that P is a theorem in the formal deductive calculus we get from *PC* by adding all wff's in Γ as new axioms. Two examples:

$$P \vdash_{\overline{PC}} (Q \Rightarrow P)$$

$$\neg\neg P \vdash_{\overline{PC}} P$$

So far we have only studied the *syntax* of the formal deductive calculus *PC*. The *semantics* of the sentences (wff's) of the calculus may be defined similarly to how we define the semantics of expressions of programming languages. Intuitively it is obvious that the meaning of a *PC* wff P may be considered to be a function that takes as its argument an assignment of truth-values to the propositional variables that occur in P, and produces a truth-value as result (this is, of course, very similar to the semantics of Boolean expressions). We therefore define the domain *Valuation* to consist of every mapping from the set *PVar* of propositional variables to the domain *Bool*:

$$\mathit{Valuation} \stackrel{d}{=} (\mathit{PVar} \rightarrow \mathit{Bool})$$

The semantic domain *PV* that consists of all denotations of *PC* wff's may then be defined as follows:

$$\mathit{PV} \stackrel{d}{=} (\mathit{Valuation} \rightarrow \mathit{Bool})$$

The semantic mapping for *PC* wff's is a function $\mathcal{W}_{PC}$ with signature

$$\mathcal{W}_{PC} \in (\mathit{PC\text{-}Wff} \rightarrow \mathit{PV})$$

where *PC-Wff* is the syntactic domain consisting of all *PC* wff's. (We use $\mathcal{W}$ as name of this mapping because it finds the denotations of Wff's.)

The mapping $\mathcal{W}_{PC}$ is defined as follows by induction on the syntactic complexity of *PC* wff's:

$$\begin{aligned}
\mathcal{W}_{PC}[\![\mathsf{pv}]\!] &= \lambda \mathsf{v} \in \mathit{Valuation}{:}\ \mathsf{v}(\mathsf{pv}) \\
\mathcal{W}_{PC}[\![\neg \mathsf{P}]\!] &= \lambda \mathsf{v} \in \mathit{Valuation}{:}\ \textbf{if } \mathcal{W}_{PC}[\![\mathsf{P}]\!](\mathsf{v}) = \textbf{true then false} \\
&\qquad\qquad\qquad\qquad\quad \textbf{else true} \\
\mathcal{W}_{PC}[\![\mathsf{P}_1 \Rightarrow \mathsf{P}_2]\!] &= \lambda \mathsf{v} \in \mathit{Valuation}{:}\ \textbf{if } \mathcal{W}_{PC}[\![\mathsf{P}_1]\!](\mathsf{v}) = \textbf{false then true} \\
&\qquad\qquad\qquad\qquad\quad \textbf{else } \mathcal{W}_{PC}[\![\mathsf{P}_2]\!](\mathsf{v})
\end{aligned}$$

Having defined the semantic mapping $\mathcal{W}_{PC}$, we may give a precise definition of when a *PC* wff P is a tautology:

$$\models \mathsf{P} \quad \stackrel{d}{\Longleftrightarrow} \quad \forall\, \mathsf{v} \in \mathit{Valuation}{:}\ \mathcal{W}_{PC}[\![\mathsf{P}]\!](\mathsf{v}) = \textbf{true}$$

The formal deductive calculus *PC* is intended to be a calculus in which it is possible to give formal proofs of tautologies. But if we are to trust the results we get by using *PC* instead of the more intuitive notions, it is necessary to prove that *PC* is adequate for the task for which it is intended. This is done in the following two propositions which say that *PC* is a sound and complete formalization of what it means to be a tautology:

Proposition 8.1 Soundness of the propositional calculus:
Every PC theorem is a tautology:

$$\vdash_{\overline{PC}} \mathsf{P} \;\Rightarrow\; \models \mathsf{P}$$

for every PC wff P.

Proposition 8.2 Completeness of the propositional calculus:
Every tautology is a PC theorem:

$$\models \mathsf{P} \;\Rightarrow\; \vdash_{PC} \mathsf{P}$$

for every PC wff P.

We do not prove these propositions here. Proofs may be found in any textbook on mathematical logic, for instance [Shoenfield; 67].

8.2.2 Example 2: First-order predicate calculi

The language of the propositional calculus is, of course, too simple to be of much use. To be able to express anything but the simplest statements, we need more linguistic power than that which is available when we are only allowed to use atomic propositions compounded by propositional connectives.

A *first-order predicate calculus* is a formal deductive calculus with a language that allows the use of *individual variables, predicates, functions* and *quantifiers* (i.e., $\forall$ and $\exists$). (A *second-order* predicate calculus would in addition allow variables for functions and predicates and quantifiers over such variables. We will not treat such calculi here.)

Assume that *Rel*, *Func*, *Const* and *Xvar* are disjoint sets, and that arity is a function that maps $Rel \cup Func$ to *Nat*. We say that the members of *Rel* are *relation symbols*, that the members of *Func* are *function symbols*, that the members of *Const* are *constant names*, and that the members of *Xvar* are *individual variables* .

The *first-order language with equality* based on $\langle$*Rel*, *Func*, *Const*, arity$\rangle$ (observe that *Xvar* is *not* included in this list; this is because the set of individual variables is assumed to be the same in every first-order language) is defined as follows:

- **Terms:** The set of *terms* based on $\langle$*Func*, *Const*, arity$\rangle$ is defined inductively as follows:
  - Every constant name $\mathsf{c} \in Const$ is a term.
  - Every individual variable $\mathsf{x} \in Xvar$ is a term.
  - If $\mathsf{f} \in Func$ is a function symbol with arity $n \geq 0$ and $\mathsf{t}_1,\ldots,\mathsf{t}_n$ are terms, then $\mathsf{f}(\mathsf{t}_1,\ldots,\mathsf{t}_n)$ is a term.
- **Predicates:** The set of *predicates* based on $\langle$*Rel*, *Func*, *Const*, arity$\rangle$ is defined inductively as follows:
  - If $\mathsf{r} \in Rel$ is a relation symbol with arity $n \geq 0$ and $\mathsf{t}_1,\ldots,\mathsf{t}_n$ are terms, then $\mathsf{r}(\mathsf{t}_1,\ldots,\mathsf{t}_n)$ is a predicate, which is said to be an *atomic* predicate.
  - If t_1 and t_2 are two terms, then $\mathsf{t}_1 = \mathsf{t}_2$ is a predicate, which is also considered to be an atomic predicate.

- If P and Q are predicates, then so are $\neg$P, (P$\Rightarrow$Q), (P$\vee$Q) and (P$\wedge$Q).
- If P is a predicate and x $\in$ *Xvar* is an individual variable, then ($\exists$ x: P) and ($\forall$ x: P) are predicates.

We will sometimes use *Pred*($\langle$*Rel*, *Func*, *Const*, arity$\rangle$) (or simply *Pred*) to denote the set of predicates based on $\langle$*Rel*, *Func*, *Const*, arity$\rangle$.

An example of a first-order predicate language is the first-order predicate language for arithmetics, which we will call *Arith* . This language is based on

$$
\begin{aligned}
&Rel_N \overset{d}{=} \{<\} \\
&Func_N \overset{d}{=} \{+, *, \mathsf{suc}\} \\
&Const_N \overset{d}{=} \{0\} \\
&\mathsf{arity}_N(<) \overset{d}{=} 2,\ \mathsf{arity}_N(+) \overset{d}{=} 2,\ \mathsf{arity}_N(*) \overset{d}{=} 2,\ \mathsf{arity}_N(\mathsf{suc}) \overset{d}{=} 1
\end{aligned}
$$

Some concepts that we will need later:

- An individual variable x is said to be *bound* in the quantified predicates $\exists$ x: P and $\forall$ x: P. An unbound occurrence of an individual variable in a predicate, is said to be a *free* occurrence.
- If P is a predicate in which the variable x may have a free occurrence, we say that a term t is *free for* x *in* P if t does not contain a variable y such that x occurs in a subpredicate ($\forall$ y: Q) or ($\exists$ y: Q) of P. If t is not free for x in P, it is in a certain sense unsafe to substitute t for x in P.
- A predicate in which there are no free occurrences of individual variables, is said to be a *sentence*.

An *interpretation* of a first-order predicate language based on $\langle$*Rel*, *Func*, *Const*, arity$\rangle$ is defined by a single-carrier algebra *A* - which we say is an *interpreting algebra* for the language - that satisfies the following conditions:

- For each relation symbol r $\in$ *Rel* of arity *n*, *A* contains an observer $r_A \in (A^n \to Bool)$.
- For each function symbol f $\in$ *Func* of arity *n*, *A* contains a producer $f_A \in (A^n \to A)$.
- For each constant name c $\in$ *Const*, the carrier of *A* contains an element $c_A \in A$.

An example: The algebra *Nat* is an interpreting algebra for the first-order predicate language *Arith*.

Given a first-order predicate language with an interpreting algebra *A*, we define two semantic mappings $\mathcal{E}_A$ and $\mathcal{T}_A$ that map the terms and predicates of the language to their denotations. It should be obvious that if we let A provide interpretations of the relation symbols, function symbols and constant names that occur in terms and predicates, the denotation of a term must be a function that takes as its argument an assignment of values (which should be elements of the carrier of A) to the individual variables that occur in the term, and produces a member of the carrier of A as its value. Similarly, the denotation of a predicate should be a function that takes the same kind of argument as the denotations of terms, and produces a truth-value as result. The semantic mappings $\mathcal{E}_A$ and $\mathcal{T}_A$ should hence have signatures

$$\begin{array}{ll} \mathcal{E}_A & \in (\mathit{Term} \to (\mathit{Varval}_A \to A)) \\ \mathcal{T}_A & \in (\mathit{Predicate} \to (\mathit{Varval}_A \to \mathit{Bool})) \end{array}$$

where the semantic domain Varval_A is defined as follows:

$$\mathit{Varval}_A \stackrel{d}{=} (\mathit{Xvar} \to A)$$

$\mathcal{E}_A$ and $\mathcal{T}_A$ are defined by induction on syntactic complexity in figure 8.1.

Assume that A is an interpreting algebra for a first-order predicate language. A predicate P is said to be *true in A* if $\mathcal{T}_A[\![\mathsf{P}]\!](\mathsf{vv}) = \mathbf{true}$ for every $\mathsf{vv} \in \mathit{Varval}_A$. We express that P is true in A by writing

$$\models_A \mathsf{P}$$

A predicate in a first-order predicate language is said to be *valid* if it is true in every algebra that interprets the language. We express this by writing

$$\models \mathsf{P}$$

Some examples: The *Arith* predicates

$$\begin{array}{c} \mathsf{suc(suc(0)) + suc(suc(0)) = suc(suc(suc(suc(0))))} \\ \mathsf{x + y = y + x} \\ \forall\, \mathsf{x}\colon (0 = \mathsf{x} \vee 0 < \mathsf{x}) \end{array}$$

are true in the algebra *Nat*, but they are not valid. (Exercise: construct an algebra that provides interpretations of the symbols of the *Arith* language, but is such that the predicates above are not true.) The predicates

$$\begin{array}{c} (\mathsf{x} = 0) \vee \neg(\mathsf{x} = 0) \\ (\forall\, \mathsf{x}\colon 0 < \mathsf{t}_1) \Rightarrow (0 < \mathsf{t}_1[\mathsf{x} := \mathsf{t}_2]) \end{array}$$

where t_1, t_2 are any two *Arith* terms and $\mathsf{t}[\mathsf{x} := \mathsf{s}]$ is the term we get by replacing every occurrence of the variable x in the term t by the term s, are valid predicates.

The definition of validity given above is not easy to use as a basis for proving that a given predicate is valid (assuming that it really *is* valid). Neither is it suitable for use in a specification for a computer

$\mathcal{E}_A \in (\mathit{Term} \to (\mathit{Varval}_A \to A))$

$\mathcal{E}_A[\![c]\!] = \lambda vv \in \mathit{Varval}_A: c_A$

$\mathcal{E}_A[\![x]\!] = \lambda vv \in \mathit{Varval}_A: vv(x)$

$\mathcal{E}_A[\![f(t_1,\ldots,t_n)]\!] = \lambda vv \in \mathit{Varval}_A: f_A(\mathcal{E}_A[\![t_1]\!](vv),\ldots,\mathcal{E}_A[\![t_n]\!](vv))$

$\mathcal{T}_A \in (\mathit{Predicate} \to (\mathit{Varval}_A \to \mathit{Bool}))$

$\mathcal{T}_A[\![t_1 = t_2]\!] = \lambda vv \in \mathit{Varval}_A:$ **if** $\mathcal{E}_A[\![t_1]\!](vv) = \mathcal{E}_A[\![t_2]\!](vv)$ **then true else false**

$\mathcal{T}_A[\![P(t_1,\ldots,t_n)]\!] = \lambda vv \in \mathit{Varval}_A: P_A(\mathcal{E}_A[\![t_1]\!](vv),\ldots,\mathcal{E}_A[\![t_n]\!](vv))$

$\mathcal{T}_A[\![P_1 \Rightarrow P_2]\!] = \lambda vv \in \mathit{Varval}_A:$ **if** $\mathcal{T}_A[\![P_1]\!](vv) =$ **false then true else** $\mathcal{T}_A[\![P_2]\!](vv)$

$\mathcal{T}_A[\![P_1 \wedge P_2]\!] = \lambda vv \in \mathit{Varval}_A:$ **if** $\mathcal{T}_A[\![P_1]\!](vv) =$ **false then false else** $\mathcal{T}_A[\![P_2]\!](vv)$

$\mathcal{T}_A[\![P_1 \vee P_2]\!] = \lambda vv \in \mathit{Varval}_A:$ **if** $\mathcal{T}_A[\![P_1]\!](vv) =$ **true then true else** $\mathcal{T}_A[\![P_2]\!](vv)$

$\mathcal{T}_A[\![\forall x: P]\!] = \lambda vv \in \mathit{Varval}_A:$ **if** $\forall a \in A: \mathcal{T}_A[\![P]\!](vv[x := a]) =$ **true then true else false**

$\mathcal{T}_A[\![\exists x: P]\!] = \lambda vv \in \mathit{Varval}_A:$ **if** $\exists a \in A: \mathcal{T}_A[\![P]\!](vv[x := a]) =$ **true then true else false**

$\mathcal{T}_A[\![\neg P]\!] = \lambda vv \in \mathit{Varval}_A:$ **if** $\mathcal{T}_A[\![P]\!](vv) =$ **false then true else false**

Figure 8.1: Semantic mappings for terms and predicates of a first-order predicate calculus

program that is to be employed to construct or check proofs of assertions that say that given predicates are valid. Partly to get tools that are more suitable for these and similar purposes, we define formal deductive calculi that may be used to give formal proofs of validity of predicates in first-order predicate languages.

There are many different ways of defining such formal calculi. One is by extending the formal propositional calculus given in section 8.2.1 by some axioms and deduction rules. Figure 8.2 shows one way of doing this. In order to reduce the number of details, we do not include rules for some of the connectives and for the existential quantifier, which we instead treat as abbreviations. $\exists x: P$ may, for instance, be considered to be an abbreviation of $\neg\forall x: \neg P$.

Another kind of predicate calculi are the so-called *natural deduction calculi*. In these calculi, axioms and deductions rules are expressed

Axioms:

For every predicate P, Q, R, *every individual variable* x, y *and every term* t, *the following predicates are axioms:*

P1: $(P \Rightarrow (Q \Rightarrow P))$

P2: $((P \Rightarrow (Q \Rightarrow R)) \Rightarrow ((P \Rightarrow Q) \Rightarrow (P \Rightarrow R)))$

P3: $((\neg P \Rightarrow \neg Q) \Rightarrow (Q \Rightarrow P))$

P4: $((\forall x{:}\, P) \Rightarrow P)$ *Restriction:* x *is not free in* P

P5: $((\forall x{:}\, P) \Rightarrow P[x{:=}t])$ *Restriction:* t *is free for* x *in* P

E1: $x = x$

E2: $(x = y) \Rightarrow (P \Rightarrow P[x{:=}y]^*)$
where $P[x{:=}y]^*$ *is the result of replacing zero or more (but not necessarily all) occurrences of* x *in* P *by* y

Deduction rules:

For every predicate P, Q, *and every individual variable* x:

MP: $\dfrac{P;\ (P \Rightarrow Q)}{Q}$ Gen: $\dfrac{P}{\forall x{:}\, P}$

Figure 8.2: Axioms and deduction rules for first-order predicate calculi

using *sequents*, which are statements of the form

$$P_1, P_2, \ldots, P_n \vdash Q$$

The meaning of the sequent above is that the predicate Q is deducible from the predicates $P_1, P_2, \ldots, P_n$. Axioms and deduction rules for a natural deduction calculus for first-order predicates are given in figure 8.3. In this figure, we use Γ to denote any list of predicates.

The following proposition (which we refrain from proving) says that the two kinds of first-order predicate calculi are equivalent:

$$\text{Assumption: } \frac{\varepsilon}{P \vdash P}$$

$$\text{Thinning: } \frac{\Gamma \vdash P}{\Gamma, Q \vdash P}$$

Introduction rules:

$$\wedge\text{I: } \frac{\Gamma \vdash P; \quad \Gamma \vdash Q}{\Gamma \vdash (P \wedge Q)}$$

$$\vee\text{I: } \frac{\Gamma \vdash P}{\Gamma \vdash (P \vee Q)} \quad \frac{\Gamma \vdash Q}{\Gamma \vdash (P \vee Q)}$$

$$\Rightarrow\text{I: } \frac{\Gamma, P \vdash Q}{\Gamma \vdash (P \Rightarrow Q)}$$

$$\neg\text{I: } \frac{\Gamma, Q \vdash P; \quad \Gamma, Q \vdash \neg P}{\Gamma \vdash \neg Q}$$

$$\forall\text{I: } \frac{\Gamma \vdash P}{\Gamma \vdash \forall x{:}\, P} \ (*)$$

$$\exists\text{I: } \frac{\Gamma \vdash P[x := t]}{\Gamma \vdash \exists x{:}\, P}$$

Elimination rules:

$$\wedge\text{E: } \frac{\Gamma \vdash (P \wedge Q)}{\Gamma \vdash P} \quad \frac{\Gamma \vdash (P \wedge Q)}{\Gamma \vdash P}$$

$$\vee\text{E: } \frac{\Gamma \vdash (P \vee Q); \quad \Gamma, P \vdash R; \quad \Gamma, Q \vdash R}{\Gamma \vdash R}$$

$$\Rightarrow\text{E: } \frac{\Gamma \vdash (P \Rightarrow Q)}{\Gamma, P \vdash Q}$$

$$\neg\text{E: } \frac{\Gamma, \neg Q \vdash P; \quad \Gamma, \neg Q \vdash \neg P}{\Gamma \vdash Q}$$

$$\forall\text{E: } \frac{\Gamma \vdash \forall x{:}\, P}{\Gamma \vdash P[x := t]}$$

$$\exists\text{E: } \frac{\Gamma \vdash \exists x{:}\, P; \ \Gamma, P \vdash Q}{\Gamma \vdash Q} \ (*)$$

$$\text{Reflexivity: } \frac{\varepsilon}{\vdash x = x}$$

$$\text{Substitutivity: } \frac{\Gamma \vdash x = y; \ \Gamma \vdash P}{\Gamma \vdash P[x := y]^*}$$

Restrictions on the rules marked with $*$:

In rule $\forall$I: x must not be free in Γ
In rule $\exists$E: x must not be free in Γ, Q

Figure 8.3: Axioms and deduction rules for first-order natural deduction

Proposition 8.3 *For every first-order predicate* P *and every list* Γ *of predicates:* P *is deducible from* Γ *by the axioms and rules given in figure 8.2 if and only if* $\Gamma \vdash$ P *is deducible by the natural deduction rules given in figure 8.3.*

If we are to trust the results we get by using a formal deductive calculus instead of more intuitive notions, it is necessary to prove that the formal calculus is adequate for the tasks for which it shall be used. This is done in the following two propositions which say that the axioms and deduction rules given in figure 8.2 constitute a sound and complete formalization of what it means to be a valid first-order predicate:

Proposition 8.4 Soundness of the axioms and deduction rules for predicate calculi:

$$\vdash \mathsf{P} \;\Rightarrow\; \models \mathsf{P}$$

for every first-order predicate P.

Proposition 8.5 Gödel's Completeness Theorem:

$$\models \mathsf{P} \;\Rightarrow\; \vdash \mathsf{P}$$

for every first-order predicate P.

Proofs of these propositions may be found in most textbooks on mathematical logic, for instance [Shoenfield; 67], and are not given here.

8.2.3 Example 3: A formal calculus for arithmetics

The axioms and deduction rules for predicate calculi presented in section 8.2.2 (in figure 8.2 or in figure 8.3), can only be used to prove predicates that are necessarily true in *every* interpretation of a calculus, and are therefore said to be *logical* axioms and rules (logics is concerned with that which is necessarily true). A predicate calculus which contains only logical axioms and rules, is said to a *pure* predicate calculus, and is of limited usefulness.

An *applied predicate calculus* contains what are said to be *proper* or *mathematical* axioms and rules in addition to the logical axioms and rules. These additional axioms and rules may be used to prove theorems that are not necessarily valid, i.e., they may not necessarily be true in every algebra that interprets the language of the calculus. An algebra in which every theorem of the calculus is true is said to be a *model* for the calculus.

Predicate calculi are often defined in order to formalize truth in some specific given algebra (for instance the algebra *Nat*). To achieve this aim fully, three requirements should be satisfied:

(1) The given algebra must be an interpretation of the calculus.

This requirement is easy to satisfy: Simply introduce one function symbol or relation symbol of proper arity for each function of the algebra (relation symbols should be used, for every function that has *Bool* has its range).

For most algebras of interest, it is necessary to enrich the language of the calculus such that it has individual variables of various types. This is not difficult to do, but we will not treat these matters here.

(2) Every predicate that is provable in the calculus should be true in the model, i.e., the given algebra should be a model of the calculus.

To satisfy this requirement, the mathematical axioms and deduction rules of the calculus should not be too strong. It is not difficult to achieve this, for instance by letting the calculus have only very weak mathematical axioms and rules. But a calculus in which it is only possible to prove a few of the sentences that are true in the given algebra, is of course of rather limited usefulness: it is too weak. On the other hand, if we let the set of axioms and rules be very strong, we run the risk of making the calculus *inconsistent* , which means that for some sentence P both P and ¬P are provable in the calculus. It is of course impossible for a sentence and its negation to be simultaneously true in an algebra, which means that an inconsistent calculus cannot have *any* model.

If we manage to construct a set of axioms and deduction rules that is just short of inconsistency, it may sometimes be difficult to *prove* that the requirement that the given algebra is a model of the calculus is satisfied (assuming that it really is satisfied).

(3) Every predicate that is true in the model should be provable in the calculus. If this demand is satisfied, we say that the calculus is *complete* for the model.

This last requirement is not easy to satisfy for many algebras of interest, at least not without breaking the requirement that the algebra should be a model of the calculus. For many interesting algebras it is, in fact, *impossible* to construct a first-order deductive calculus that has the algebra as a model and at the same time is complete for the algebra. More will be said about this below.

The formal calculus *Arith* for arithmetics contains mathematical axioms and deduction rules for the ordinary arithmetical operations and relations, and is intended to constitute a formal characterization of truth in the algebra *Nat*. Its language (which is defined on page 157 in the previous section) contains three functions symbols (suc, $+$ and $*$), one relation symbol ($<$) and one constant name (0). Proper (mathematical) axioms and a proper deduction rule (the so-called *induction rule*) for *Arith* are given in figure 8.4.

Mathematical axioms:

A1:	$x = y \Rightarrow (x = z \Rightarrow y = z)$
A2:	$x = y \Rightarrow suc(x) = suc(y)$
A3:	$suc(x) = suc(y) \Rightarrow x = y$
A4:	$\neg(0 = suc(x))$
A5:	$x + 0 = x$
A6:	$x + suc(y) = suc(x + y)$
A7:	$x * 0 = 0$
A8:	$x * suc(y) = (x * y) + x$
A9:	$\neg(0 < 0)$
A10:	$0 < suc(x)$
A11:	$x < y \Rightarrow suc(x) < suc(y)$

Induction rule:

$$\frac{P[x{:=}0];\ \forall x{:}\,(P \Rightarrow P[x{:=}suc(x)])}{\forall x{:}\,P} \quad \text{for every predicate P}$$

Figure 8.4: Proper axioms and deduction rules of the applied first-order predicate calculus *Arith* (a formal deductive calculus for arithmetics)

It is not very difficult to see that the algebra *Nat* (as defined in figure 4.2 on page 47) is a model for the predicate calculus *Arith*. *Arith* does therefore satisfy the first two requirements for constituting a formalization of truth in *Nat*. But what about the last requirement? Is every arithmetical truth provable in *Arith*, thus making *Arith* complete for *Nat*), or do predicates exist that are true in *Nat* but not provable in *Arith*?

In 1931 the German logician and mathematician Kurt Gödel surprised the mathematical world by proving the following theorem (in a somewhat different form):

Theorem 8.1 Gödel's Incompleteness Theorem: [Gödel; 31]
Any consistent first-order predicate calculus is incomplete for arithmetics.

In more detail: If A is any first-order predicate calculus that has the algebra Nat as an interpretation then

Either: *A is inconsistent. This means that for some sentence (i.e., a predicate without free variables)* P *both* P *and* ¬P *are provable in A, which implies that A cannot have* any *model. In particular, Nat is not a model for A if A is inconsistent.*

Or: *A is incomplete: A sentence* W_A *can be found (it may in fact be explicitly constructed given the axioms and rules of A) such that* W_A *is arithmetically true (i.e., true in the algebra Nat) but not provable in A.*

We will not prove this theorem here. The proof is quite long, but interesting: it fully repays the effort to study one of the proofs, preferably (in the author's opinion) the original proof given by Gödel in [Gödel; 31] (an English translation is given in [Gödel; 62]). The proof is based on an old and simple idea, namely the so-called *liar paradox*. The sentence *This sentence is false* is a paradoxical sentence: it is true if and only if it is false! The sentence W_A is cleverly constructed in the proof of the Incompleteness Theorem in such a way that its interpretation in the algebra *Nat* is 'W_A *is not formally provable in the deductive calculus A*'. But then W_A cannot be provable in *A*: if it were provable, it would not be true (we assume here that *A* is sound, i.e., that every sentence that is provable in *A* is true in *Nat*). Hence W_A is a sentence which is true but not provable: it is a witness to the incompleteness of *A*.

It may possibly be tempting to try to circumvent the Incompleteness Theorem by adding new axioms or rules to an incomplete calculus. Would we not get a complete calculus if we for instance extended *Arith* by adding W_{Arith} as a new axiom? No, we would not: The Incompleteness Theorem may be applied to the extended calculus *Arith'*, and we could construct a new sentence $W_{Arith'}$ that witnessed the incompleteness of *Arith'*. There is no escape from the Incompleteness Theorem!

Even if the calculus *Arith* by the Incompleteness Theorem is incomplete for *Nat*, it is in a sense close to being complete. The unprovable sentence W_{Arith} is a very peculiar sentence, which we would not risk encountering in ordinary arithmetics. For practical purposes, *Arith* may be considered to constitute an adequate formalization of arithmetical truth.

8.3 Natural semantics

8.3.1 Introduction

In the kind of semantics for programming languages that is called *natural semantics*, the semantics of programs, imperatives, expressions and other constructs of a language are specified by defining formal deductive calculi that allow us to prove statements about the values, effects and other aspects of the constructs. The techniques of natural semantics may even be used to construct interpreters, compilers and so-called *type checkers* for a language. In this section we only show how natural semantics may be used to define the semantics of the simple While language. For further descriptions of natural semantics, in particular how it may be used for purposes other than those we describe and how it may be implemented quite easily, the reader is referred to [Plotkin; 81] and [Kahn; 87] where the ideas were originally introduced.

To specify the semantics of While programs using the methods of natural semantics, we define (in section 8.3.7 below) a formal deductive calculus *Prog* that contains axioms and deduction rules that allow us to prove statements of the form

$$\mathsf{inp} \rightarrow (\mathit{Prog}\colon \mathsf{prog}) \rightarrow \mathsf{out}$$

The meaning of this statement is that if the program prog is executed from the input sequence inp, then out will be the resulting output sequence, provided that the program terminates normally.

The semantics of imperatives is specified (in section 8.3.6) by defining a formal deductive calculus *Imp* in which we may prove statements of the form

$$\mathsf{s} \rightarrow (\mathit{Imp}\colon \mathsf{imp}) \rightarrow \mathsf{s'}$$

The meaning of this statement is that if the imperative imp is executed from the state s, then the result will be the state s', assuming that the imp terminates normally from s.

To specify the semantics of expressions, we define a formal deductive calculus *Exp* (in section 8.3.5) that contains axioms and deduction rules for proving statements that have the form

$$\mathsf{s} \rightarrow (\mathit{Exp}\colon \mathsf{exp}) \rightarrow \mathsf{e}$$

The meaning of this statement is that in state s, the value of the expression exp will be e, assuming that the value of exp is not undefined for s.

But before we define calculi for programs, imperatives and expressions, we define some auxiliary calculi.

8.3.2 A calculus for expressible values

In the calculus for expressions, we need an auxiliary calculus *EC* for the algebra *E* = *Int*. This calculus must contain axioms and deductive rules that allow us to prove theorems of the form

$$\vdash_{EC} (e_1 \text{ bop } e_2) = e_3$$

$$\vdash_{EC} (\text{uop } e_1) = e_2$$

where e_1, e_2 and e_3 are expressible values (i.e., integers), and bop and uop are any of the operators that are allowed in the programming language.

Before defining the *EC* calculus, we have to determine how to handle undefined operations, for instance division by 0. There are two alternatives: The first is to let there be no axioms or rules in *EC* that allow us to prove any theorems about undefined values. The second is to introduce one or more special error terms (for instance **err**) in the *EC* language. Using the second approach, we would include rules in *EC* that allowed us to prove $(e/0) = \textbf{err}$ for every *EC* term e. We will, however, stick to the first approach, mainly because it reduces the number of details that have to be described. This means that for no *EC* terms e, e' should the predicate $(e/0) = e'$ be provable in *EC*.

We leave it as an exercise to define *EC*. It is not difficult to do this such that the calculus *EC* becomes sound and complete for the algebra *E*. This means that for all expressible values e_1, e_2 and e_3 and all operators uop, bop, the following should hold:

$$(\vdash_{EC} (\text{uop } e_1) = e_2) \iff (\mathcal{U}[\![\text{uop}]\!](e_1) = e_2)$$

$$(\vdash_{EC} (e_1 \text{ bop } e_2) = e_3) \iff (\mathcal{B}[\![\text{bop}]\!](e_1, e_2) = e_3)$$

The reader may perhaps be a little surprised at being asked to construct a complete calculus for the algebra *E*. Does not *E* include *Nat*, and therefore does not Gödel's Incompleteness Theorem apply to *E*? The answer is - of course - that the Incompleteness Theorem *does* apply to *E*, and that it therefore is impossible to construct a complete first-order predicate calculus for *E*. The catch is in the term *first-order predicate calculus*: A first-order predicate calculus is a calculus for proving sentences that are built from atomic sentences using propositional connectives and first-order quantifiers. Gödel's Incompleteness Theorem says that it is impossible to construct a sound calculus in which every first-order sentence that is true in *Nat* is provable, and does not say anything about calculi with weaker languages. The task here is to construct a calculus in which every *atomic* proposition that is true in the algebra *E* is provable, and such a simple calculus is not at all precluded by the Incompleteness Theorem.

8.3.3 Calculi for stores and states

In the calculi for imperatives and expressions, we need an auxiliary calculus ***State*** that may be used to prove the following types of statements:

$$\begin{array}{l} \mathsf{s} \rightarrow (\textit{State}\text{: } \mathbf{assign}(\mathsf{id},\ \mathsf{n})) \rightarrow \mathsf{s'} \\ \mathsf{s} \rightarrow (\textit{State}\text{: } \mathbf{access}(\mathsf{id})) \rightarrow \mathsf{n} \\ \mathsf{s} \rightarrow (\textit{State}\text{: } \mathbf{put}(\mathsf{n})) \rightarrow \mathsf{s'} \\ \mathsf{s} \rightarrow (\textit{State}\text{: } \mathbf{get}(\mathsf{id})) \rightarrow \mathsf{s'} \end{array}$$

The interpretation of the first of these statements is that if s is a state, id an identifier and n a storable integer, then s' is the state as it is after n has been assigned to id. The interpretations of the other statements are similarly simple to define.

Deduction rules for the first two of these types of statements are quite easy to give if we first define an auxiliary calculus *Store* in which the following kinds of statements may be proved:

$$\begin{array}{l} \mathsf{h} \rightarrow (\textit{Store}\text{: } \mathbf{assign}(\mathsf{id},\ \mathsf{n})) \rightarrow \mathsf{h'} \\ \mathsf{h} \rightarrow (\textit{Store}\text{: } \mathbf{access}(\mathsf{id})) \rightarrow \mathsf{n} \end{array}$$

where h and h' are stores (i.e., in the algebra $\textit{Store} = (\textit{Ident} \rightarrow S)$ which is defined in figure 4.10 on page 62), id an identifier and n an integer. The interpretations of these statements should be obvious.

Axioms and deduction rules for the *Store* and *State* calculi are given in figures 8.5 and 8.6. The very simple auxiliary calculus *Ident* that is used in one of the deduction rules of *Store* contains axioms and rules that allow us to prove statements of the form $\mathsf{id} = \mathsf{id'}$ and $\mathsf{id} \neq \mathsf{id'}$ where id and id' are identifiers. We leave it as an exercise to define *Ident*.

The following proposition - which is not very difficult to prove - says that the *State* calculus is a correct formalization of truth in the *State* algebra:

Proposition 8.6 *The State calculus is sound and complete for the State algebra. In details: For any state* s, s'*, identifier* id *and integer* n*:*

$$\begin{array}{lcl} (\mathsf{s.assign(id,\ n)} = \mathsf{s'} \neq \bot_{\textit{State}}) & \Longleftrightarrow & (\mathsf{s} \rightarrow (\textit{State}\text{: } \mathbf{assign}(\mathsf{id},\ \mathsf{n})) \rightarrow \mathsf{s'}) \\ (\mathsf{s.access(id)} = \mathsf{n} \neq \bot_{\textit{Int}}) & \Longleftrightarrow & (\mathsf{s} \rightarrow (\textit{State}\text{: } \mathbf{access}(\mathsf{id})) \rightarrow \mathsf{n}) \\ (\mathsf{s.get(id)} = \mathsf{s'} \neq \bot_{\textit{State}}) & \Longleftrightarrow & (\mathsf{s} \rightarrow (\textit{State}\text{: } \mathbf{get}(\mathsf{id})) \rightarrow \mathsf{s'}) \\ (\mathsf{s.put(n)} = \mathsf{s'} \neq \bot_{\textit{State}}) & \Longleftrightarrow & (\mathsf{s} \rightarrow (\textit{State}\text{: } \mathbf{put}(\mathsf{n})) \rightarrow \mathsf{s'}) \end{array}$$

8.3.4 A calculus for literals

The first semantic calculus we define is a simple calculus *Lit* in which we may prove statements about the values of literals. These statements are of the form

$$\varepsilon \rightarrow (\textit{Lit}\text{: } \mathsf{lit}) \rightarrow \mathsf{n}$$

The interpretation of this statement is that the literal lit has value n. Axioms and deduction rules for the *Lit* calculus are given in figure 8.7.

The following two propositions say that *Lit* is a correct formalization of the standard semantics for literals:

$$\frac{\vdash_{EC} \text{abs(n)} < \text{maxint}}{\text{h} \rightarrow (\textit{Store}\text{: } \textbf{assign}\text{(id, n))} \rightarrow \text{h . assign(id, n)}}$$

$$\frac{}{\text{default(n)} \rightarrow (\textit{Store}\text{: } \textbf{access}\text{(id))} \rightarrow \text{n}}$$

$$\frac{}{\text{h . assign(id, n)} \rightarrow (\textit{Store}\text{: } \textbf{access}\text{(id))} \rightarrow \text{n}}$$

$$\frac{\text{h} \rightarrow (\textit{Store}\text{: } \textbf{access}\text{(id))} \rightarrow \text{n}; \quad \vdash_{\textit{Ident}} \text{id} \neq \text{id'}}{\text{h . assign(id', n')} \rightarrow (\textit{Store}\text{: } \textbf{access}\text{(id))} \rightarrow \text{n}}$$

Figure 8.5: Axioms and deduction rules of the *Store* calculus

$$\frac{\text{h} \rightarrow (\textit{Store}\text{: } \textbf{assign}\text{(id, n))} \rightarrow \text{h'}}{\langle \text{inp, h, out} \rangle \rightarrow (\textit{State}\text{: } \textbf{assign}\text{(id,n))} \rightarrow \langle \text{inp, h', out} \rangle}$$

$$\frac{\text{h} \rightarrow (\textit{Store}\text{: } \textbf{access}\text{(id))} \rightarrow \text{n}}{\langle \text{inp, h, out} \rangle \rightarrow (\textit{State}\text{: } \textbf{access}\text{(id))} \rightarrow \text{n}}$$

$$\frac{\text{h} \rightarrow (\textit{Store}\text{: } \textbf{assign}\text{(id, n))} \rightarrow \text{h'}}{\langle \text{n} \dashv \text{inp, h, out} \rangle \rightarrow (\textit{State}\text{: } \textbf{get}\text{(id))} \rightarrow \langle \text{inp, h', out} \rangle}$$

$$\frac{}{\langle \text{inp, h, out} \rangle \rightarrow (\textit{State}\text{: } \textbf{put}\text{(n))} \rightarrow \langle \text{inp, h, out} \vdash \text{n} \rangle}$$

Figure 8.6: Axioms and deduction rules of the *State* calculus

Proposition 8.7 Soundness:
For every literal lit: $(\varepsilon \rightarrow (\textit{Lit}\text{: lit}) \rightarrow \text{n}) \implies (\mathcal{A}[\![\text{lit}]\!] = \text{n})$

Proposition 8.8 Completeness:
For every literal lit: $(\mathcal{A}[\![\text{lit}]\!] = \text{n}) \implies (\varepsilon \rightarrow (\textit{Lit}\text{: lit}) \rightarrow \text{n})$

Proof ***of proposition 8.7 (soundness):***
Assume that $\varepsilon \rightarrow (\textit{Lit}\text{: lit}) \rightarrow \text{n}$ is provable in *Lit*. Let us consider proofs to be trees of predicates (and not sequences, see the discussion on page 151). Our assumption then means that there exists a proof tree in *Lit* with $\varepsilon \rightarrow (\textit{Lit}\text{: lit}) \rightarrow \text{n}$ as its root. We prove

$$\mathbf{L}_1: \frac{\varepsilon}{\varepsilon \rightarrow (\mathit{Lit}\text{: } \mathbf{0}) \rightarrow 0} \qquad \mathbf{L}_2: \frac{\varepsilon}{\varepsilon \rightarrow (\mathit{Lit}\text{: } \mathbf{1}) \rightarrow 1}$$

$$\mathbf{L}_3: \frac{\varepsilon \rightarrow (\mathit{Lit}\text{: lit}) \rightarrow \mathsf{n}}{\varepsilon \rightarrow (\mathit{Lit}\text{: lit}\mathbf{0}) \rightarrow 2 * \mathsf{n}} \qquad \mathbf{L}_4: \frac{\varepsilon \rightarrow (\mathit{Lit}\text{: lit}) \rightarrow \mathsf{n}}{\varepsilon \rightarrow (\mathit{Lit}\text{: lit}\mathbf{1}) \rightarrow (2 * \mathsf{n} + 1)}$$

Figure 8.7: Axioms and rules for the *Lit* calculus

that $\mathcal{A}[\![\text{lit}]\!] = \mathsf{n}$ holds by induction on the structure of the proof tree (the proof would be by induction on the length of proofs should we consider formal proofs to be sequences (and not trees) of predicates). The induction proof has four cases to consider, one for each of the four ***Lit*** rules that may have been used to justify the root of the proof tree:

(1) Rule $\mathbf{L}_1$ has been used to deduce $\varepsilon \rightarrow (\mathit{Lit}\text{: } \mathbf{0}) \rightarrow 0$. It then suffices to prove that $\mathcal{A}[\![\mathbf{0}]\!] = 0$, which of course is an immediate consequence of the definition of the semantic mapping $\mathcal{A}$.

(2) Rule $\mathbf{L}_2$: Similar to the previous case.

(3) Rule $\mathbf{L}_3$ has been applied to deduce $\varepsilon \rightarrow (\mathit{Lit}\text{: lit}\mathbf{0}) \rightarrow \mathsf{m}$, and we must prove that $\mathcal{A}[\![\text{lit}\mathbf{0}]\!] = \mathsf{m}$. That $\mathbf{L}_3$ has been used implies that for some integer n

(1): $\varepsilon \rightarrow (\mathit{Lit}\text{: lit}) \rightarrow \mathsf{n}$
(2): $\mathsf{m} = 2 * \mathsf{n}$

The proof in ***Lit*** for $\varepsilon \rightarrow (\mathit{Lit}\text{: lit}) \rightarrow \mathsf{n}$ is part of - and therefore simpler than - the proof for $\varepsilon \rightarrow (\mathit{Lit}\text{: lit}\mathbf{0}) \rightarrow \mathsf{m}$, and we may therefore apply the induction hypothesis to (1), which gives

(3): $\mathcal{A}[\![\text{lit}]\!] = \mathsf{n}$

We then get

$$\begin{aligned} \mathcal{A}[\![\text{lit}\mathbf{0}]\!] &= 2 * \mathcal{A}[\![\text{lit}]\!] && \textit{(By definition of } \mathcal{A}\textit{)} \\ &= 2 * \mathsf{n} && \textit{(By (3))} \\ &= \mathsf{m} && \textit{(By (2))} \end{aligned}$$

- as claimed.

(4) Rule $\mathbf{L}_4$: Similar to the previous case.

End of proof of proposition 8.7.

$$\mathbf{E}_1: \frac{\varepsilon \to (\mathit{Lit}\text{: lit}) \to \mathsf{n}}{\mathsf{s} \to (\mathit{Exp}\text{: lit}) \to \mathsf{n}} \qquad \mathbf{E}_2: \frac{\mathsf{s} \to (\mathit{State}\text{: } \mathbf{access}(\mathsf{id})) \to \mathsf{n}}{\mathsf{s} \to (\mathit{Exp}\text{: id}) \to \mathsf{n}}$$

$$\mathbf{E}_3: \frac{\mathsf{s} \to (\mathit{Exp}\text{: } \mathsf{exp}_1) \to \mathsf{e}_1; \quad \vdash_{EC} \mathsf{uop}\ \mathsf{e}_1 = \mathsf{e}_2}{\mathsf{s} \to (\mathit{Exp}\text{: } (\mathsf{uop}\ \mathsf{exp}_1)) \to \mathsf{e}_2}$$

$$\mathbf{E}_4: \frac{\mathsf{s} \to (\mathit{Exp}\text{: } \mathsf{exp}_1) \to \mathsf{e}_1;\ \mathsf{s} \to (\mathit{Exp}\text{: } \mathsf{exp}_2) \to \mathsf{e}_2;\ \vdash_{EC} \mathsf{e}_1\ \mathsf{bop}\ \mathsf{e}_2 = \mathsf{e}_3}{\mathsf{s} \to (\mathit{Exp}\text{: } (\mathsf{exp}_1\ \mathsf{bop}\ \mathsf{exp}_2)) \to \mathsf{e}_3}$$

Figure 8.8: Rules for the *Exp* calculus

Proof ***of proposition 8.8 (completeness):***

Assume that $\mathcal{A}[\![\mathsf{lit}]\!] = \mathsf{n}$. We prove that $\varepsilon \to (\mathit{Lit}\text{: lit}) \to \mathsf{n}$ is a theorem in *Lit* by induction on the syntactic complexity of lit:

(1) $\mathsf{lit} = \mathbf{0}$: Then $\mathcal{A}[\![\mathsf{lit}]\!] = 0$, and it suffices to prove that $\varepsilon \to (\mathit{Lit}\text{: lit}) \to 0$ is a theorem in *Lit*. This follows by axiom $\mathbf{L}_1$.

(2) $\mathsf{lit} = \mathbf{1}$: Similar to the previous case.

(3) $\mathsf{lit} = \mathsf{lit}_1\mathbf{0}$: Then $\mathcal{A}[\![\mathsf{lit}]\!] = 2 * \mathsf{n}$ where $\mathsf{n} = \mathcal{A}[\![\mathsf{lit}_1]\!]$. We must prove that $\varepsilon \to (\mathit{Lit}\text{: } \mathsf{lit}\mathbf{0}) \to \mathsf{m}$, where $\mathsf{m} = 2 * \mathsf{n}$. By the induction hypothesis, $\varepsilon \to (\mathit{Lit}\text{: } \mathsf{lit}_1) \to \mathsf{n}$. Applying *Lit* rule $\mathbf{L}_3$ gives the desired conclusion.

(4) $\mathsf{lit} = \mathsf{lit}_1\mathbf{1}$: Similar to the previous case.

End of proof of proposition 8.8.

8.3.5 A calculus for expressions

The formal calculus *Exp* contains rules that allow us to prove statements that have the form

$$\mathsf{s} \to (\mathit{Exp}\text{: exp}) \to \mathsf{e}$$

The interpretation of this statement is that the expression exp has value e in state s.

Rules for the *Exp* calculus are given in figure 8.8.

The following two propositions say that *Exp* is a correct formalization of the standard semantics for expressions:

Proposition 8.9 Soundness:
For every expression exp, *state* s *and expressible value* e*:*

$$(\mathsf{s} \rightarrow (\mathit{Exp}\text{: exp}) \rightarrow \mathsf{e}) \quad \Rightarrow \quad (\mathcal{E}[\![\text{exp}]\!](\mathsf{s}) = \mathsf{e})$$

Proof: Exercise. Use induction on proof structure. The proof is quite similar to the proof for proposition 8.7 above.

Proposition 8.10 Completeness:
For every expression exp, *state* s *and expressible value* e*:*

$$(\mathcal{E}[\![\text{exp}]\!](\mathsf{s}) = \mathsf{e} \neq \bot_E) \quad \Rightarrow \quad (\mathsf{s} \rightarrow (\mathit{Exp}\text{: exp}) \rightarrow \mathsf{e})$$

Proof: Exercise. Use induction on syntactic complexity of exp.

The *Exp* calculus implicitly defines the following alternative semantical mapping ${}_N\mathcal{E} \in (\mathit{Exp} \rightarrow (\mathit{State} \rightarrow E_\bot))$:

$${}_N\mathcal{E}[\![\text{exp}]\!] \stackrel{d}{=} \underline{\lambda}\mathsf{s} \in \mathit{State}\text{: } \mathbf{if}\ \exists\ \mathsf{e}\text{: } (\mathsf{s} \rightarrow (\mathit{Exp}\text{: exp}) \rightarrow \mathsf{e})\ \mathbf{then}\ \mathsf{e}\ \mathbf{else}\ \bot_E$$

Propositions 8.9 and 8.10 entail that ${}_N\mathcal{E} = {}_S\mathcal{E}$.

8.3.6 A calculus for imperatives

The formal calculus *Imp* contains rules that allow us to prove statements of the form

$$\mathsf{s} \rightarrow (\mathit{Imp}\text{: imp}) \rightarrow \mathsf{s}'$$

The interpretation of this statement is that if the imperative imp terminates normally when executed from s, then s' is the state after imp has terminated.

Axioms and deduction rules for the *Imp* calculus are given in figure 8.9. In order to make it easier to understand the ideas behind some of the rules in this figure, we use **true** as shorthand for a positive integer and let **false** stand for an integer less than or equal to 0. The premiss of the first **while** rule, i.e., $\mathbf{Wh}_1$, would for instance have been as follows without use of this shorthand notation:

$$\mathsf{s} \rightarrow (\mathit{Exp}\text{: exp}) \rightarrow \mathsf{n}; \quad \mathsf{n} \leq 0$$

We will use this shorthand notation for the rest of this section.

The following propositions say that *Imp* is a correct formalization of the standard semantic mapping for imperatives:

Proposition 8.11 Soundness:
For every imperative imp *and states* s, s'*:*

$$(\mathsf{s} \rightarrow (\mathit{Imp}\text{: imp}) \rightarrow \mathsf{s}') \quad \Rightarrow \quad (\mathcal{M}[\![\text{imp}]\!](\mathsf{s}) = \mathsf{s}')$$

$$\textbf{Skip:}\quad \frac{\varepsilon}{\mathsf{s} \rightarrow (\mathit{Imp}\text{: }\mathbf{skip}) \rightarrow \mathsf{s}}$$

$$\textbf{Put:}\quad \frac{\mathsf{s} \rightarrow (\mathit{Exp}\text{: exp}) \rightarrow \mathsf{n};\quad \mathsf{s} \rightarrow (\mathit{State}\text{: }\mathbf{put}(\mathsf{n})) \rightarrow \mathsf{s}'}{\mathsf{s} \rightarrow (\mathit{Imp}\text{: }\mathbf{put}\text{ exp}) \rightarrow \mathsf{s}'}$$

$$\textbf{Get:}\quad \frac{\mathsf{s} \rightarrow (\mathit{State}\text{: }\mathbf{get}(\mathsf{id})) \rightarrow \mathsf{s}'}{\mathsf{s} \rightarrow (\mathit{Imp}\text{: }\mathbf{get}\text{ id}) \rightarrow \mathsf{s}'}$$

$$\textbf{Asg:}\quad \frac{\mathsf{s} \rightarrow (\mathit{Exp}\text{: exp}) \rightarrow \mathsf{n};\quad \mathsf{s} \rightarrow (\mathit{State}\text{: }\mathbf{assign}(\mathsf{id, n})) \rightarrow \mathsf{s}'}{\mathsf{s} \rightarrow (\mathit{Imp}\text{: id := exp}) \rightarrow \mathsf{s}'}$$

$$\textbf{Seq:}\quad \frac{\mathsf{s} \rightarrow (\mathit{Imp}\text{: imp}_1) \rightarrow \mathsf{s}';\ \mathsf{s}' \rightarrow (\mathit{Imp}\text{: imp}_2) \rightarrow \mathsf{s}''}{\mathsf{s} \rightarrow (\mathit{Imp}\text{: imp}_1\text{; imp}_2) \rightarrow \mathsf{s}''}$$

$$\textbf{If}_1\textbf{:}\quad \frac{\mathsf{s} \rightarrow (\mathit{Exp}\text{: exp}) \rightarrow \mathbf{true};\quad \mathsf{s} \rightarrow (\mathit{Imp}\text{: imp}_1) \rightarrow \mathsf{s}'}{\mathsf{s} \rightarrow (\mathit{Imp}\text{: }\mathbf{if}\text{ exp }\mathbf{then}\text{ imp}_1\ \mathbf{else}\text{ imp}_2\ \mathbf{fi}) \rightarrow \mathsf{s}'}$$

$$\textbf{If}_2\textbf{:}\quad \frac{\mathsf{s} \rightarrow (\mathit{Exp}\text{: exp}) \rightarrow \mathbf{false};\quad \mathsf{s} \rightarrow (\mathit{Imp}\text{: imp}_2) \rightarrow \mathsf{s}'}{\mathsf{s} \rightarrow (\mathit{Imp}\text{: }\mathbf{if}\text{ exp }\mathbf{then}\text{ imp}_1\ \mathbf{else}\text{ imp}_2\ \mathbf{fi}) \rightarrow \mathsf{s}'}$$

$$\textbf{Wh}_1\textbf{:}\quad \frac{\mathsf{s} \rightarrow (\mathit{Exp}\text{: exp}) \rightarrow \mathbf{false}}{\mathsf{s} \rightarrow (\mathit{Imp}\text{: }\mathbf{while}\text{ exp }\mathbf{do}\text{ imp }\mathbf{od}) \rightarrow \mathsf{s}}$$

$$\textbf{Wh}_2\textbf{:}\quad \frac{\mathsf{s} \rightarrow (\mathit{Exp}\text{: exp}) \rightarrow \mathbf{true};\quad \mathsf{s} \rightarrow (\mathit{Imp}\text{: (imp; }\mathbf{while}\text{ exp }\mathbf{do}\text{ imp }\mathbf{od})) \rightarrow \mathsf{s}'}{\mathsf{s} \rightarrow (\mathit{Imp}\text{: }\mathbf{while}\text{ exp }\mathbf{do}\text{ imp }\mathbf{od}) \rightarrow \mathsf{s}'}$$

Figure 8.9: Axioms and deduction rules for the *Imp* calculus

Proposition 8.12 Completeness:
For every imperative imp *and states* s, s':

$$(\mathcal{M}[\![\mathsf{imp}]\!](\mathsf{s}) = \mathsf{s}' \neq \bot_{\mathit{State}}) \quad \Longrightarrow \quad (\mathsf{s} \rightarrow (\mathit{Imp}\text{: imp}) \rightarrow \mathsf{s}')$$

Before we prove these propositions, let us note that there are no rules in the *Imp* calculus that allow us to prove that a program does not terminate normally for a given state. Assuming that we extend the *Exp* calculus with rules that allow us to prove statements about undefined operations (as discussed on page 167 above), it is not difficult to extend *Imp* with axioms and rules that may be used to prove theorems of the form

s →(*Imp*: imp)→ **error-in-expression**

We can, however, *not* extend *Imp* with a complete set of rules that allow us to prove all statements that say that an imperative enters an infinite loop. Such statements could for instance be as follows:

s →(*Imp*: imp)→ **infinite-loop**

The meaning of such a statement is that imp would enter an infinite loop if executed from s. It is not difficult to make axioms and rules that allowed us to deduce some true statements of this form. But it can be proved that it is impossible to construct a set of axioms and rules that is complete for nontermination. It is, however, outside the scope of this book to prove this result, which is closely related to the so-called *halting problem*. The reader is referred to any book on automata theory or computability theory where this problem is shown to be undecidable.

Proof ***of proposition 8.11 (soundness):***

By induction on the structure of proofs in the *Imp* calculus. We treat only the case where the root of the proof tree is justified by *Imp* rule $\mathbf{Wh}_2$, and leave the other (simpler) cases as exercises.

Assume then that rule $\mathbf{Wh}_2$ has been applied to deduce

(1): s →(*Imp*: **while** exp **do** impb **od**)→ s'

Application of rule $\mathbf{Wh}_2$ with this conclusion is only possible if the proof tree above the root contains proof trees with the following roots:

(2): s →(*Exp*: exp)→ **true**
(3): s →(*Imp*: (impb; **while** exp **do** impb **od**))→ s'

By proposition 8.9, (2) gives

(4): $\mathcal{E}[\![\text{exp}]\!](\text{s}) = \textbf{true}$

The induction hypothesis applied to (3) gives

(5): $\mathcal{M}[\![\text{impb; } \textbf{while} \text{ exp } \textbf{do} \text{ impb } \textbf{od}]\!](\text{s}) = \text{s'}$

By proposition 6.2 on page 113, (4) entails that

(6): $\mathcal{M}[\![\text{impb; } \textbf{while} \text{ exp } \textbf{do} \text{ impb } \textbf{od}]\!](\text{s})$
$= \mathcal{M}[\![\textbf{while} \text{ exp } \textbf{do} \text{ impb } \textbf{od}]\!](\text{s})$

(5) and (6) together give the desired conclusion:

(7): $\mathcal{M}[\![$**while** exp **do** impb **od**$]\!](s) = s'$

End of proof of proposition 8.11.

Proof ***of proposition 8.12 (completeness):***

By induction on the syntactic complexity of imp. We only treat the case where imp = **while** exp **do** impb **od**, and leave the other cases as exercises.

Assume then that

(1): $\mathcal{M}[\![$**while** exp **do** impb **od**$]\!](s_0) = s^* \neq \bot_{State}$

We have to prove that

s_0 →(*Imp*: **while** exp **do** impb **od**)→ s^*

For each $i \geq 0$ define s_i and b_i as follows:

(2): $s_{i+1} = \mathcal{M}[\![\text{impb}]\!](s_i)$
(3): $b_i \quad = \mathcal{E}[\![\text{exp}]\!](s_i)$

We now use the While theorem (page 114). Case β must hold because $s^* \neq \bot_{State}$. There must therefore exist $n \geq 0$ such that

(4): $s_i \neq \bot_{State}$ for $i \leq n$
(5): b_i = **true** for $i < n$
(6): b_n = **false**
(7): $s^* = s_n$

By the induction hypothesis (for the proposition we are proving, i.e., proposition 8.12) applied to (2), using (4), we get that

(8): s_i →(*Imp*: impb)→ s_{i+1} for $i < n$

By completeness of the *Exp* calculus (proposition 8.10) applied to (3), (5) and (6) give

(9): s_i →(*Exp*: exp)→ **true** for $i < n$
(10): s_n →(*Exp*: exp)→ **false**

If $n = 0$, (10) gives that rule $\mathbf{Wh}_1$ may be applied, giving

(11): s_0 →(*M*: **while** exp **do** impb **od**)→ s_0

By (7) $s^* = s_0 = s_n$, and the desired conclusion follows.

If $n > 0$, the desired conclusion is entailed by the following lemma:

Lemma: *For* $j = 1, \ldots, n$: s_{n-j} →(*Imp*: **while** exp **do** impb **od**)→ s_n

Proof: By induction on j:

$j = 1$: Rule $\mathbf{Wh}_1$ applied to (10) gives that

(12): $s_n \rightarrow$(M: **while** exp **do** impb **od**)$\rightarrow s_n$

Rule **Seq** applied to (8) (for $i = n - 1$) and (12) gives

(13): $s_{n-1} \rightarrow$(M: impb; **while** exp **do** impb **od**)$\rightarrow s_n$

Rule **Wh**$_2$ applied to (9) (for $i = n - 1$) and (13) then gives

(14): $s_{n-1} \rightarrow$(M: **while** exp **do** impb **od**)$\rightarrow s_n$

- as claimed in the lemma.

$j > 1, j \leq n$: The induction hypothesis for $j - 1$ says that

(15): $s_{n-(j-1)} \rightarrow$(Imp: **while** exp **do** impb **od**)$\rightarrow s_n$

Rule **Seq** applied to (8) (for $i = n - j$) and (15) gives

(16): $s_{n-j} \rightarrow$(M: impb; **while** exp **do** impb **od**)$\rightarrow s_n$

Rule **Wh**$_2$ applied to (9) (for $i = n - j$) and (16) then gives

(17): $s_{n-j} \rightarrow$(M: **while** exp **do** impb **od**)$\rightarrow s_n$

- as claimed in the lemma.

Applying the lemma for $j = n$ gives

(18): $s_0 \rightarrow$(M: **while** exp **do** impb **od**)$\rightarrow s_n$

- as claimed in the proposition.

End of proof of proposition 8.12.

The rules of the *Imp* calculus may be used to define an alternative semantical mapping ${}_N\mathcal{M} \in$ (*Imp* $\rightarrow$ (*State* $\rightarrow$ *State*$_\perp$)) as follows:

$$_N\mathcal{M}[\![\text{imp}]\!] \stackrel{d}{=} \underline{\lambda} s \in \textit{State}\text{: } \textbf{if } \exists\, s'\text{: } (s \rightarrow (\textit{Imp}\text{: imp}) \rightarrow s') \textbf{ then } s' \textbf{ else } \perp_{\textit{State}}$$

Propositions 8.12 and 8.11 entail that ${}_N\mathcal{M} = {}_S\mathcal{M}$.

8.3.7 A calculus for programs

The formal calculus *Prog* contains rules that allow us to prove statements of the form

inp $\rightarrow$(*Prog*: prog)$\rightarrow$ out

The interpretation of this statement is that if the program prog is executed from the input sequence inp then the result will output the sequence out, provided prog terminates normally from inp.

The *Prog* calculus contains a single deduction rule, which is given in figure 8.10.

The following proposition says that *Prog* is a correct formalization of the standard semantic mapping for programs.

$$\frac{{}_S\mathsf{State'Initial(inp)} \rightarrow (\mathit{Imp}\colon \mathsf{imp}) \rightarrow \mathsf{s}}{\mathsf{inp} \rightarrow (\mathit{Prog}\colon \mathbf{begin}\ \mathsf{imp}\ \mathbf{end}) \rightarrow \mathsf{s.Output}}$$

Figure 8.10: The deduction rule of the *Prog* calculus

Proposition 8.13 *For every program* prog, *input sequence* inp *and output sequence* out:

$$(\mathcal{P}[\![\mathsf{prog}]\!](\mathsf{inp}) = \mathsf{out} \neq \bot_{\mathit{Output}}) \iff (\mathsf{inp} \rightarrow (\mathit{Prog}\colon \mathsf{prog}) \rightarrow \mathsf{out})$$

Proof: Directly from the soundness and completeness of the *Imp* calculus.

We may define an alternative semantic mapping

$${}_N\mathcal{P} \in (\mathit{Imp} \rightarrow (\mathit{Input} \rightarrow \mathit{Output}_\bot))$$

as follows:

$$\begin{aligned} {}_N\mathcal{P}[\![\mathsf{prog}]\!] \stackrel{d}{=} \ & \underline{\lambda}\mathsf{inp} \in \mathit{Input}\colon \\ & \quad \mathbf{if}\ \exists\ \mathsf{out} \in \mathit{Output}\colon (\mathsf{inp} \rightarrow (\mathit{Prog}\colon \mathsf{prog}) \rightarrow \mathsf{out})\ \mathbf{then}\ \mathsf{out} \\ & \quad \mathbf{else}\ \bot_{\mathit{Output}} \end{aligned}$$

By proposition 8.13, it follows that ${}_N\mathcal{P} = {}_S\mathcal{P}$.

8.4 Axiomatic semantics

8.4.1 Introduction

In his seminal paper *An Axiomatic Basis for Computer Programming* [Hoare; 69], C.A.R. Hoare gives an indirect and partial definition of the semantics of a simple programming language, using a proof-theoretical method. In his paper Hoare writes:

> *One of the most important properties of a program is whether or not it carries out its intended function. The intended function of a program, or part of a program, can be specified by making general assertions about the values which the relevant variables will take* after *execution of the program. ...*
>
> *In many cases, the validity of the results of a program (or part of a program) will depend on the values taken by the*

> *the variables before that program is initiated. These initial preconditions of successful use can be specified by the same type of general assertion as is used to describe the results on termination. To state the required connection between a precondition (P), a program (Q) and a description of the results of its execution (R), we introduce a new notation:*
>
> P{Q}R

Hoare's interpretation of P{Q}R, which it is now customary to write as {P} Q {R}, is

> *If the assertion P is true before initiation of the program Q, then the assertion R will be true on its completion, provided that the program successfully terminates.*

It is obvious that if we are able to determine whether or not {P} imp {R} holds for any given imperative imp and assertions P and R, then we must have a rather good understanding of the semantics of imp (and, of course, of P and R). We may therefore consider a precise definition that enables us to determine whether or not {P} imp {R} holds for imperatives in a programming language, to constitute an indirect, but possibly only partial, definition of the semantics of the imperatives of the programming language. When we say that the definition may only be partial, it is because we may know how to determine whether or not {P} imp {R} holds without knowing anything about the conditions for the termination of imp.

In [Hoare; 69], Hoare gives axioms and deduction rules that allow us to prove true assertions of the form {P} imp {R} for imperatives in a simple programming language (quite similar to our While language, but without imperatives for input and output). He states that *the specification of proof techniques provides an adequate formal definition of a programming language*, hence taking the axioms and rules to constitute a definition of the semantics of the language.

In a certain sense, axiomatic semantics may be considered even more abstract than denotational semantics.

The paper [Hoare; 69] (which is partly based on ideas from Floyd, Naur and von Neumann) gave rise to enormous amounts of research, and tools have now been developed that make it possible to define the semantics of very rich and complex programming languages axiomatically. It is, however, outside the scope of this book to describe most of this. The reader is referred to [Dahl; 92] or [Cousot; 90] for more complete descriptions of the axiomatic method.

In this section we show how Hoare's axiomatic semantics may be used to specify the semantics of a simplified version of the While language. We will study the connection between axiomatic semantics and denotational semantics, and show that the axioms and rules used are sound and, in a certain sense, complete.

8.4.2 A somewhat simplified While language

In order to reduce the number of details (some of them nontrivial and involved, others quite simple but lengthy to depict) to be described, we will not give an axiomatic semantics for the full While language of chapter 6. Instead we will use a simplified version which we call While_H. The differences between the full and the simplified While languages are as follows:

- While_H programs perform no input and no output.
- We distinguish between integer expressions and Boolean expressions in While_H.
- No undefined operations will occur when While_H expressions are evaluated and While_H imperatives are executed. This is achieved by 1) not including division and other error-prone operations among the operations of While_H, and 2) assuming that integers of any size may be assigned to variables. But While_H imperatives *may* enter infinite loops.

It *is* possible to define the semantics of the full While language axiomatically, but in order to reduce the size of this section, we will not do that here.

BNF productions that define the syntax of the While_H language are given in figure 8.11.

8.4.3 Hoare assertions: Syntax and semantics

A *Hoare assertion* {P} imp {Q} consists of two predicates P and Q in some first-order predicate language and one imperative imp in a given programming language.

The two languages that are used in Hoare assertions must be related, both syntactically and semantically. The syntactic relation must be such that every integer (Boolean) expression of the programming language is a term (predicate) of the predicate language (or at least that for every integer (Boolean) expression, an equivalent term (predicate) may be written in the predicate language). Such a relationship may be achieved by 1) letting the set *Xvar* of variables of the predicate language be equal to *Ident*, thus letting every variable of the programming language be a variable of the predicate language, and 2) basing the predicate language on sets ⟨*Rel*, *Func*, *Const*⟩ that include all operators and literals of the programming language. The predicate language to be used in conjunction with the language While_H defined in figure 8.11 is the first-order predicate language that is based on $Rel = \{=, <\}$, $Func = \{+, -, *\}$ and $Const = Literal$.

A Hoare assertion is either true or false. We may therefore define the semantics of Hoare assertions by defining which Hoare assertions are true and which are not. This may be done either 1) proof-theoretically by introducing a formal deductive system that allows us

$$
\begin{array}{rcl}
\langle imp \rangle & ::= & \textbf{skip} \\
& | & \langle variable \rangle := \langle exp \rangle \\
& | & \langle imp \rangle ;\ \langle imp \rangle \\
& | & \textbf{if}\ \langle bexp \rangle\ \textbf{then}\ \langle imp \rangle\ \textbf{else}\ \langle imp \rangle\ \textbf{fi} \\
& | & \textbf{while}\ \langle bexp \rangle\ \textbf{do}\ \langle imp \rangle\ \textbf{od} \\
\langle exp \rangle & ::= & \langle constant \rangle \\
& | & \langle variable \rangle \\
& | & (\langle exp \rangle\ \langle func \rangle\ \langle exp \rangle) \\
\langle bexp \rangle & ::= & (\langle exp \rangle\ \langle rel \rangle\ \langle exp \rangle) \\
& | & (\langle bexp \rangle \wedge \langle bexp \rangle) \\
& | & (\langle bexp \rangle \vee \langle bexp \rangle) \\
& | & (\neg \langle bexp \rangle) \\
\langle func \rangle & ::= & + \mid - \mid * \\
\langle rel \rangle & ::= & = \mid < \\
\langle constant \rangle & ::= & \langle literal \rangle \\
\langle variable \rangle & ::= & \langle ident \rangle
\end{array}
$$

Figure 8.11: BNF productions for the language While_H

to prove certain Hoare assertions (which we then take to constitute the true Hoare assertions), or 2) model-theoretically by interpreting Hoare assertions in a model. In this section we will define the semantics of Hoare assertions model-theoretically. In section 8.4.4 below, we will do the same proof-theoretically. We will also prove that the two definitions are equivalent.

A model-theoretical definition of the semantics of Hoare assertions is based on model-theoretical interpretations of the predicate language and the programming language used in the Hoare assertions. Let us therefore assume that an interpreting algebra is given for the predicate language. For the predicate language used in conjunction with the programming language While_H, we assume that *Int* - which is an algebra with carrier equal to the set of integers and with functions for each of the operators of the language - is used as an interpreting algebra. In section 8.2.2 we showed how an interpreting algebra for a predicate language may be used to define semantic mappings for the terms and predicates of the predicate language. We need two semantic mappings for our predicate language: $\mathcal{E}_{Int}$ that maps terms to $(Varval_{Int} \rightarrow Int)$, and $\mathcal{T}_{Int}$ that maps predicates to $(Varval_{Int} \rightarrow Bool)$, where $Varval_{Int} = (Ident \rightarrow Int)$. These mappings are defined as shown in section 8.2.2, and constitute a model-theoretical definition of the semantics of the predicate language.

We assume furthermore that semantic mappings are defined for the expressions and imperatives of the programming language. It is reasonable to assume that operators and variables that occur both in the predicates and the imperatives of Hoare assertions should be interpreted in the same way, and that therefore the semantic mappings for the programming language and for the predicate language should be defined relative to the same algebra, which is *Int* for While_H (this is the semantic relation between the predicate language and the programming language mentioned above). The semantics of the language While_H is defined as follows:

- The state algebra for While_H - which we call ${}_0State$ - is simpler than the state algebra for the full While language because there is no input and no output in While_H, and may be defined as follows:

$$\begin{aligned} {}_0State &\stackrel{d}{=} (Ident \to Int) \\ &= Varval_{Int} \end{aligned}$$

- By the syntactic relation between the predicate language and the programming language, we may assume that every integer expression of While_H is a term of the predicate language and every Boolean expression is a predicate. By the semantic relation between the languages, we may use the semantic mappings $\mathcal{E}_{Int}$ and $\mathcal{T}_{Int}$ for terms and predicates of the predicate language as semantic mappings for integer and Boolean expressions of the While_H language.

  The fact that no undefined operations may occur when While_H expressions are evaluated, makes these mappings somewhat easier to define than the semantic mapping for expressions of the full While language.

- The semantic mapping $\mathcal{M}$ for imperatives of While_H maps Imp_H to ${}_0MV$, where ${}_0MV$ consists of all functions that map ${}_0State_\perp$ to itself, and may be defined quite similarly to the corresponding function for the full While language.

Before we give a model-theoretic definition of the semantics of Hoare assertions, it is advantageous to define an alternative semantic mapping for predicates and an auxiliary function wlp:

The semantic mapping $\mathcal{T}_{Int}$ maps predicates and Boolean expressions to the semantic domain

$$PV \stackrel{d}{=} ({}_0State \to Bool)$$

It is sometimes convenient to use an alternative semantic mapping $\mathcal{P}$ that maps predicates and Boolean expressions to *PS* where

$$PS \stackrel{d}{=} \mathcal{P}({}_0State)$$

The set *PS* - which consists of all subsets of ${}_0State$ - may in a certain sense be considered to be congruent to the set *PV*: to every $ps \in PS$ may be found a unique corresponding function in *PV*, namely

$$\lambda s \in {}_0State\text{: } \mathbf{if}\ s \in pv\ \mathbf{then\ true\ else\ false}$$

Vice versa, to every $pv \in PV$ corresponds the set $\{s \mid pv(s) = \mathbf{true}\} \in PS$.

The alternative semantic mapping $\mathcal{P}$ maps predicates to *PS*, and is defined as follows for any predicate P:

$$\mathcal{P}[\![P]\!] = \{s \in {}_0State \mid \mathcal{T}[\![P]\!](s) = \mathbf{true}\}$$

Thus, $\mathcal{P}[\![P]\!]$ is the set that consists of all states that make the predicate P true. It is obvious that the two mappings $\mathcal{T}$ and $\mathcal{P}$ in a sense may be considered equivalent: either can be trivially defined in terms of the other. The reason we introduce both, is that in some circumstances it is more convenient to use $\mathcal{T}$, in other circumstances $\mathcal{P}$ is easier to use.

Observe that $\perp_{State} \notin \mathcal{P}[\![P]\!]$ for every predicate P, even if $\mathcal{T}[\![P]\!](s)$ should be equal to $\perp_{State}$ for some state s. This is because $\perp_{State}$ is chosen to be an element *not* in *State*, therefore $\perp_{State} \notin ps$ for every $ps \in PS$.

The function wlp (the name is an abbreviation for *weakest liberal precondition*, it was originally defined in [Dijkstra; 76]) is a function with signature

$$wlp \in (MV \times PS \to PS)$$

It is defined as follows for every $mv \in MV$, $ps \in PS$:

$$wlp(mv, ps) \overset{d}{=} \{s \in {}_0State \mid mv(s) \neq \perp_{State} \Rightarrow mv(s) \in ps\}$$

Thus, for every imperative imp and every predicate Q, $wlp(\mathcal{M}[\![imp]\!], \mathcal{P}[\![Q]\!])$ is the set that consists of *all* states s that are such that if imp terminates when started from s, it terminates in a state that makes Q true. Observe that $s \in wlp(\mathcal{M}[\![imp]\!], \mathcal{P}[\![Q]\!])$ if s is such that imp does not terminate when started from s.

We are now ready to give a model-theoretic definition of the semantics of Hoare assertions. According to the informal explanation given above - which is based on [Hoare; 69] - we say that a Hoare assertion $\{P\}\ imp\ \{Q\}$ is *true relative to interpretations* $\mathcal{T}$ and $\mathcal{M}$ if and only if for every state s:

$$\begin{aligned}\mathcal{T}[\![P]\!](s) = \mathbf{true}\ \wedge\ \mathcal{M}[\![imp]\!](s) \neq \perp_{State} \\ \Longrightarrow\ \mathcal{T}[\![Q]\!](\mathcal{M}[\![imp]\!](s)) = \mathbf{true}\end{aligned}$$

We write

$$\models_{T,M} \{P\}\ imp\ \{Q\}$$

(or simply $\models \{P\}\ \mathsf{imp}\ \{Q\}$) to express that $\{P\}\ \mathsf{imp}\ \{Q\}$ is true relative to $\mathcal{T}$ and $\mathcal{M}$.

Using the semantic mapping $\mathcal{P}$ and the function wlp, the model-theoretic definition of when a Hoare assertion is true may more succinctly be expressed as follows:

$$\models \{P\}\ \mathsf{imp}\ \{Q\} \quad \overset{d}{\Longleftrightarrow} \quad \mathcal{P}[\![P]\!] \subseteq \mathsf{wlp}(\mathcal{M}[\![\mathsf{imp}]\!], \mathcal{P}[\![Q]\!])$$

for every predicate P, Q and imperative imp.

8.4.4 The Hoare calculus

To define a calculus for Hoare assertions, we need an auxiliary calculus - which we will call *AC* (the *A* stands for *Arithmetic*) - that may be used to prove predicates that are true when interpreted in *Int*. The algebra *Int* contains everything that is included in the algebra *Nat*. This entails - by Gödel's Incompleteness Theorem - that *AC* necessarily is incomplete: a predicate may be constructed that is true in *Int* but unprovable in *AC*. But, as stated in section 8.2.3, it is not difficult to define *AC* in such a way that it is sound and for all practical purposes complete for *Int*.

The formal deductive calculus *H* contains rules and deduction rules that may be used to prove Hoare assertions $\{P\}\ \mathsf{imp}\ \{R\}$ for imperatives imp in the programming language While_H, and predicates P and Q in a first-order predicate language based on the set of operators of While_H. The axioms and rules of *H* are given in figure 8.12.

8.4.5 Soundness of the Hoare calculus

Proposition 8.14 Soundness of the Hoare calculus: *For every predicate* P, Q *and imperative* imp*:*

$$\vdash_H \{P\}\ \mathsf{imp}\ \{Q\} \quad \Rightarrow \quad \models \{P\}\ \mathsf{imp}\ \{Q\}$$

Proof: By induction on the structure of proofs in the Hoare calculus.

8.4.6 Completeness

A set *Pred* of predicates in some predicate language with a given interpretation $\mathcal{P} \in (Pred \rightarrow PS)$ is said to be *expressive* for a set *Imp* of imperatives with a given interpretation $\mathcal{M} \in (Imp \rightarrow MV)$ if and only if

$$\forall\ \mathsf{imp} \in Imp\colon \forall\ Q \in Pred\colon \exists\ P \in Pred\colon \mathcal{P}[\![P]\!] = \mathsf{wlp}(\mathcal{M}[\![\mathsf{imp}]\!], \mathcal{P}[\![Q]\!])$$

Proposition 8.15 *The first-order predicate language based on* $\langle Rel\colon\{=, <\}, Func\colon\{+, -, *\}, Const\colon Literal\rangle$ *with interpretation* $\mathcal{P}_{Int}$ *is expressive for the imperatives of the programming language* While_H *with semantic mapping* $\mathcal{M}$.

Axioms:

$$\vdash_H \{P\}\ \mathbf{skip}\ \{P\}$$

$$\vdash_H \{P[e{:=}x]\}\ x := e\ \{P\}$$

(*For every predicate* P, *variable* x, *and integer expression* e)

Deduction rules:

Seq rule:
$$\frac{\vdash_H \{P\}\ imp_1\ \{Q\};\quad \vdash_H \{Q\}\ imp_2\ \{R\}}{\vdash_H \{P\}\ imp_1;\ imp_2\ \{R\}}$$

If rule:
$$\frac{\vdash_H \{P \wedge be\}\ imp_1\ \{Q\};\quad \vdash_H \{P \wedge \neg be\}\ imp_2\ \{Q\}}{\vdash_H \{P\}\ \mathbf{if}\ be\ \mathbf{then}\ imp_1\ \mathbf{else}\ imp_2\ \mathbf{fi}\ \{Q\}}$$

While rule:
$$\frac{\vdash_H \{P \wedge be\}\ imp\ \{P\}}{\vdash_H \{P\}\ \mathbf{while}\ be\ \mathbf{do}\ imp\ \mathbf{od}\ \{P \wedge \neg be\}}$$

Cons rule:
$$\frac{\vdash_H \{P\}\ imp\ \{Q\};\quad \vdash_{AC} P' \Rightarrow P;\quad \vdash_{AC} Q \Rightarrow Q'}{\vdash_H \{P'\}\ imp\ \{Q'\}}$$

(*For every predicate* P, Q, R, P', Q', *variable* x, *imperative* imp, imp_1, imp_2, *and Boolean expression* be)

Figure 8.12: Axioms and deduction rules for the Hoare calculus *H*

Proof: By induction on the syntactic complexity of imp.

Proposition 8.16 *A first-order predicate language based on* ⟨*Rel:* {=, <}, *Func:* {+, −}, *Const: Literal*⟩ *with interpreting algebra* Int *is not expressive for the imperatives of the programming language we get by removing the multiplication operator from the language* While_H *with a semantic mapping* $\mathcal{M}$.

Proof: A complete proof may be found in [Cousot; 90].

Proposition 8.17 Relative completeness of the Hoare calculus: *Assuming that the auxiliary calculus AC is complete for* Int, *every true Hoare assertion is provable in H:*

$$\models \{P\}\ \mathsf{imp}\ \{Q\} \quad \Longrightarrow \quad \vdash_H \{P\}\ \mathsf{imp}\ \{Q\}$$

for every predicate P, Q *and imperative* imp.

Proof: By induction on the syntactic complexity of imp.

Chapter 9
Declarations of data structures

Declarations serve two purposes:

- To specify the meaning of identifiers that occur in programs.
- To enable checking of programs, in particular to discover misuse of identifiers and incorrect types of expressions.

The languages described in previous chapters have no declarations: Any identifier used in a program is implicitly assumed to be an integer variable. In this chapter we show how to define the semantics of declarations of variables, constants and arrays. In the next chapter we show how to define the semantics of declarations - and use - of procedures and functions. Chapter 11 is about the semantics of classes and objects, in particular about the semantics of declarations of classes.

The programming language we use as the main example in this chapter is a rather simple language which we call Decl_0. In this language we restrict ourselves to declarations of integer constants and variables of just two types, viz. **int** and **Bool**. But there are no conceptual difficulties in applying the ideas and methods used to specify the semantics of Decl_0 to more elaborate languages with other simple types, for instance **real** or **character**. In the last section of this chapter, we show how to treat declarations of arrays.

9.1 Decl_0: A language with variables and constants

Decl_0 is a programming language that differs from the While language of chapter 6 in the following respects:

- Every identifier that occurs in Decl_0 programs must be declared.
- All identifiers that occur in While programs are implicitly assumed to be integer variables (which may be repeatedly assigned new values), whereas identifiers in Decl_0 programs may be declared to be either *integer constants* (which are permanently bound to integer values), *integer variables* or *Boolean variables*.
- A new grammatical category - called *Var* - that contains everything that may be used as variables (i.e., on the left-hand side of assignments and in input imperatives), is introduced in Decl_0. In the simple language Decl_0, only identifiers are allowed to be members of *Var*, but richer languages may allow more complex members of this category, for instance arr[exp] where arr is an array and exp is an integer expression.
- We distinguish between integer and Boolean values in Decl_0, and let the domains *E* and *S* of expressible and storable values for the language both be equal to the disjoint sum of *Int* and *Bool*.

9.1.1 Syntax

Decl_0 has the following syntactic categories:

Prog	Programs
Imp	Imperatives
Decl	Declarations
Exp	Expressions
Var	Variables
Vartype	Types of variables
Binop	Binary operators
Unop	Unary operators
Literal	Literals

These domains are defined by the BNF productions in figure 9.1.

```
⟨program⟩  ::= ⟨imp⟩
⟨imp⟩      ::= skip                              (Do nothing)
             | put ⟨exp⟩                         (Output)
             | get ⟨var⟩                         (Input)
             | ⟨var⟩ := ⟨exp⟩                    (Assignment)
             | ⟨imp⟩; ⟨imp⟩                      (Sequential comp.)
             | begin ⟨decl⟩; ⟨imp⟩ end           (Block)
             | if ⟨exp⟩ then ⟨imp⟩
                    else ⟨imp⟩ fi                (Conditional)
             | while ⟨exp⟩ do ⟨imp⟩ od           (Unbounded loop)
⟨decl⟩     ::= const ⟨ident⟩ = ⟨literal⟩         (Decl. of constant)
             | var ⟨ident⟩: ⟨vartype⟩            (Decl. of variable)
             | ⟨decl⟩; ⟨decl⟩                    (Sequential comp.)
⟨vartype⟩  ::= int
             | Bool
⟨exp⟩      ::= ⟨literal⟩                         (Binary numeral)
             | ⟨ident⟩                           (Variable or constant)
             | (⟨exp⟩ ⟨binop⟩ ⟨exp⟩)             (Compound expr.)
             | (⟨unop⟩ ⟨exp⟩)
⟨var⟩      ::= ⟨ident⟩                           (Simple variable)
⟨binop⟩    ::= + | − | ∗ | / | = | <             (Binary operators)
⟨unop⟩     ::= − | ¬                             (Unary operators)
```

Figure 9.1: BNF productions for Decl$_0$

9.1.2 Informal semantics

The effect of a declaration is to *bind* one or more identifiers to some specified meanings and to make it legal to use the identifiers in parts of a program. The part of the program in which the declaration is valid is said to be the *scope* of the identifiers declared. Decl$_0$ is a *block-structured* language, which means 1) that we consider the scope of an identifier to be the block in which the declaration of the identifier occurs, and 2) that blocks may be nested (to any depth).

As can be seen from the syntactic productions, there are two different kinds of declarations:

(1) Declarations of *variables*: An example:

```
begin
   var num: int; var status: Bool;
   imps
end
```

The intended effect is, of course, to declare num to be an integer variable and status to be a Boolean variable, both of which may be used in the imperative *imps*.

(2) Declarations of *constants*: An example:

```
begin
  const three = 11;
  imps
end
```

The effect of the constant declaration in this example, is to bind the identifier three to the integer 3 (which is the value of the literal **11**). That three is a *constant* means that any attempt at assigning a new value to three would be an error.

A *block* is an imperative that contains first declarations of one or more identifiers, and then a sequence of imperatives. The declarations in a block are only valid in the imperatives of the block; and the identifiers declared in a block are said to be *local* to the block.

Decl_0 is a *block-structured* language (like, for instance, Algol and Simula, but unlike Pascal, C++ and Java), which means that *blocks* may be nested to any depth. A declaration in an inner block may *redeclare* an identifier declared further out in the block hierarchy, and give the identifier a new meaning which is only valid in the inner block.

9.2 Untyped semantics of Decl_0

The differences between the While language and Decl_0 mean that the methods used in defining the semantics of While are insufficient to define the semantics of Decl_0, and that some new techniques are needed:

- The fact that a declaration of an identifier is only valid for a limited part of the program, means that we must keep track of which identifiers are declared at any point in the program and to what these identifiers are bound. We do this by using *environments*, which are functions that map identifiers to those to which they are bound.

- The semantics of the While language is defined in such a way that variables (identifiers) are bound directly (by functions called *stores*) to storable values (integers or Booleans), and the effect of an assignment imperative is to change a store such that it binds a specified new value to a specified identifier. It is *possible* to use this scheme for Decl_0, but slightly awkward because it would be necessary to rename every variable that is declared in a block which is inner to a block in which a variable with the same name

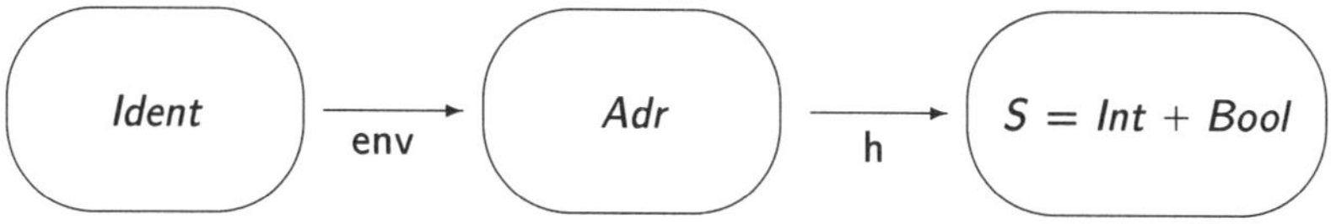

Figure 9.2: Environments and stores. The environment env maps identifiers to addresses, the store h maps addresses to storable values. Thus, h(env(id)) is the value last assigned to the variable id

is declared. But the scheme is insufficient for languages that allow arrays or other constructs that are such that an assignment of a new value to one variable at the same time may change the value of another variable (so-called *aliasing*, which is allowed in many languages, sometimes disguised for instance as certain kinds of parameters to procedures).

A simple way of handling such languages is to split the mapping from variables to values into *two* mappings: The first - an environment - maps the identifiers that are declared to be variables to so called *addresses*; the second - a store - binds addresses to storable values. Denotationally, we define a store to be a mapping from addresses to storable values. Operationally, we may consider a store to be something that consists of *locations* (storage cells), each of which 1) is identified by an address and 2) contains a storable value (integers or Booleans for $Decl_0$, possibly additional data types in other languages).

In order to prepare for the richer and more realistic languages to be described in later sections and chapters, we will employ a two-stage mapping from identifiers (declared to be variables) to values via addresses for $Decl_0$, even if it is not strictly necessary for this rather simple language.

Using these ideas, we define the standard denotational semantics of $Decl_0$ in the rest of this section. We start by defining some semantic algebras, then we define semantic mappings for $Decl_0$.

9.2.1 Semantic algebras

9.2.1.1 Denotable values and addresses

A declaration serves to bind an identifier to something. When we define the semantics of a programming language that allows declarations, we must of course decide what this 'something' is: We must decide what kinds of entities may be bound to identifiers.

An entity which can be bound by a declaration to an identifier is said to be *denotable* (it may be *denoted* by an identifier). It is fruitful to introduce a semantic algebra D that consists of all denotable entities. In the Decl_0 language, an identifier that is declared to be a constant is bound to an integer, and an identifier declared to be a variable is bound to an address. To enable some simple checking of programs, in particular to discover whether a given identifier is declared or not, we assume that any undeclared identifier is bound to a special value Unbound. We therefore define the domain D as follows:

$$D \stackrel{d}{=} \mathsf{Const}{:}\ Int + \mathsf{Var}{:}\ Adr + \mathsf{Unbound}{:}\ Unit$$

The algebra Adr of addresses used in this definition needs only to be partially specified. It suffices to assume that this algebra contains the following three functions (the first two may be generators of the algebra):

$$\begin{array}{ll} \mathsf{init} & \in (\cdot \to Adr) \\ \mathsf{next} & \in (Adr \to Adr) \\ = & \in (Adr \times Adr \to Bool) \end{array}$$

The algebra Adr and its three functions must be defined such that init, init . next, init . next . next, ... are always distinct, i.e. such that $\mathsf{init}\,.\,\mathsf{next}^n = \mathsf{init}\,.\,\mathsf{next}^m$ (where $\mathsf{init}\,.\,\mathsf{next}^n$ stands for the result of applying next n times to init) if and only if $n = m$.

To keep matters simple, we assume that an unlimited number of distinct addresses are available, such that init, init . next, init . next . next, ... are distinct no matter how many times next is applied. It is, however, not very difficult to change this assumption and instead postulate that the value of init . next . ... . next is equal to $\perp_{Adr}$ (or some other special value) as soon as the number of applications of next exceeds a certain fixed value (which may be thought of as the size of the store). If we did this, a few of the ensuing definitions would be marginally more complex.

9.2.1.2 Environments

An *environment* is a function that maps identifiers to denotable values.

The semantic algebra $Envir$ – which is specified in figure 9.3 – consists of all environments, and is specified to be generated by two functions:

$Envir = \mathcal{F}(Ident \to D)$

Environments: Mappings of identifiers to denotable values

Carrier: *Inductively generated by* Void *and* bind

Functions:

$$
\begin{array}{lll}
\text{Void} & \in & (\cdot \to Envir) \\
\text{bind} & \in & ((Envir \times Ident \times D) \to Envir) \\
\text{bound} & \in & ((Envir \times Ident) \to D) \\
\text{free\_adr} & \in & (Envir \to Adr) \\
\text{is\_free} & \in & ((Envir \times Adr) \to Bool)
\end{array}
$$

Axioms:

Void . bound(id)
    = D'Unbound
env . bind(id$_1$, d).bound(id$_2$)
    = **if** id$_1$ = id$_2$ **then** d **else** env . bound(id$_2$)

Void . free_adr
    = Adr'init
env . bind(id, d) . free_adr
    = **case** d **of** *D*
        int **in** Const ⇒ env . free_adr
        adr **in** Var ⇒ adr . next
        Unbound ⇒ env . free_adr

Void . is_free(adr)
    = **true**
env . bind(id, D'Const(int)) . is_free(adr)
    = env . is_free(adr)
env . bind(id, D'Var(adr')) . is_free(adr)
    = env . is_free(adr) ∧ ¬(adr = adr')

AF: env . is_free(env . free_adr) = **true**

Figure 9.3: The algebra *Envir* of environments

$$
\begin{array}{lll}
\text{Void} & \in & (\cdot \to Envir) \\
\text{bind} & \in & ((Envir \times Ident \times D) \to Envir)
\end{array}
$$

Envir'Void is an environment in which every identifier is unbound (i.e., Envir'Void binds D'Unbound to every identifier id), and env . bind(id, d) is an environment which is equal to the environment env except for the identifier id: the value bound by env . bind(id, d) to id is of course d.

The algebra *Envir* contains an observer bound that has the following signature:

$$\text{bound} \in (Envir \times Ident \to D)$$

This function is specified by axioms in figure 9.3 to be such that the value of env.bound(id) is equal to the *D* element last bound to id in env. If no *D* element is bound to id in env, then env.bound(id) = D'Unbound. Thinking of an environment env as a function that maps identifiers to elements in *D*, we will usually simply write env(id) as shorthand for the more cumbersome env.bound(id).

In a language that allows declarations of only simple variables and arrays we may use the environment to determine which addresses are in use (i.e., bound to an identifier) and also to find free and unused addresses to bind to new identifiers declared to be variables. The observer free_adr, which may be used for this purpose, has the following signature:

$$\text{free\_adr} \in (\mathit{Envir} \rightarrow \mathit{Adr})$$

The function free_adr is such that env.free_adr is an address that is *free* in env, i.e., it is not bound by env to any identifier. The axiom

$$\text{AF:} \qquad \text{env.is\_free(env.free\_adr)} = \textbf{true}$$

ensures that this is the case (the auxiliary *Envir* observer is_free has been introduced solely to be used in this axiom, and could be specified to be invisible outside *Envir*). The axioms for free_adr given in figure 9.3 are such that axiom AF will hold only if a certain discipline is adhered to in the use of environments. We may for instance ensure that AF always holds if, whenever an environment env is extended by binding an address adr to an identifier id, then this address is always equal to the free address of env, i.e, env.bind(id, D'Var(adr)) is only evaluated for adr = env.free_adr.

Observe that there is no function in *Envir* that may be used to *unbind* or *de-allocate* an address. Physical stores are not of infinite size, and such a function is therefore needed in any realistic implementation of a programming language like Decl_0. But in an abstract specification of the semantics of a language, we do not need to describe de-allocation.

9.2.1.3 Expressible and storable values

The algebra of *expressible* values consists of all values that may occur as values of expressions in the language, i.e., integers and Booleans for Decl_0:

$$E \stackrel{d}{=} \mathit{Int} + \mathit{Bool}$$

The algebra *S* of *storable* values consists of every value that may be assigned as a value to a variable. Decl_0 allows integer and Boolean variables, and hence *S* is defined as follows:

$$S \stackrel{d}{=} \mathit{Int} + \mathit{Bool}$$

We could, of course, have specified these algebras to consist only of integers with an absolute value less than some specified maximum value, but have chosen not to do so in order to reduce the number of details that have to be described.

9.2.1.4 Stores and states

The algebra *Store* has a carrier that consists of mappings from addresses to storable values. The following functions are defined to observe and produce stores:

$$\begin{array}{lll}
\text{init} & \in & (\cdot \to \mathit{Store}) \\
\text{bind} & \in & (\mathit{Store}_\perp \times \mathit{Adr} \times S_\perp \to \mathit{Store}_\perp) \\
\text{apply_to} & \in & (\mathit{Store}_\perp \times \mathit{Adr} \to S_\perp) \\
\text{assign} & \in & (\mathit{Store}_\perp \times \mathit{Adr} \times E_\perp \to \mathit{Store}_\perp) \\
\text{access} & \in & (\mathit{Store}_\perp \times \mathit{Adr} \to E_\perp)
\end{array}$$

Store is specified in figure 9.4.

The algebra *State* is defined to be the Cartesian product of *Input*, *Store* and *Output*, where $\mathit{Input} = \mathit{Output} = \mathit{Int}^*$. The following functions are defined in *State* to observe and produce states:

$$\begin{array}{lll}
\text{init} & \in & (\mathit{Input} \to \mathit{State}) \\
\text{assign} & \in & (\mathit{State}_\perp \times \mathit{Adr}_\perp \times E_\perp \to \mathit{State}_\perp) \\
\text{access} & \in & (\mathit{State}_\perp \times \mathit{Adr}_\perp \to E_\perp) \\
\text{put} & \in & (\mathit{State}_\perp \times E_\perp \to \mathit{State}_\perp) \\
\text{get} & \in & (\mathit{State}_\perp \times \mathit{Adr}_\perp \to \mathit{State}_\perp) \\
\text{output} & \in & (\mathit{State}_\perp \to \mathit{Output}_\perp)
\end{array}$$

These functions may be defined quite similarly to corresponding functions defined in figure 6.3 on page 104, and we leave the precise definitions to the reader.

9.2.2 Semantic mappings

We need a semantic mapping for each of the syntactic domains of Decl$_0$. These mappings should have the following signatures:

$$\begin{array}{llllll}
\mathcal{P} & \in \mathit{Prog} & \to & \mathit{PV}, & \text{where } \mathit{PV} & = (\mathit{Input} \to \mathit{Output}_\perp) \\
\mathcal{M} & \in \mathit{Imp} & \to & (\mathit{Envir} \to \mathit{MV}), & \text{where } \mathit{MV} & = (\mathit{State}_\perp \to \mathit{State}_\perp) \\
\mathcal{E} & \in \mathit{Exp} & \to & (\mathit{Envir} \to \mathit{EV}), & \text{where } \mathit{EV} & = (\mathit{State}_\perp \to E_\perp) \\
\mathcal{V} & \in \mathit{Var} & \to & (\mathit{Envir} \to \mathit{VV}), & \text{where } \mathit{VV} & = (\mathit{State}_\perp \to \mathit{Adr}_\perp) \\
\mathcal{D} & \in \mathit{Decl} & \to & (\mathit{Envir} \to \mathit{Envir}) & & \\
\mathcal{UO} & \in \mathit{Unop} & \to & \mathit{UOV}, & \text{where } \mathit{UOV} & = (E_\perp \to E_\perp) \\
\mathcal{BO} & \in \mathit{Binop} & \to & \mathit{BOV}, & \text{where } \mathit{BOV} & = (E_\perp \times E_\perp \to E_\perp) \\
\mathcal{A} & \in \mathit{Literal} & \to & \mathit{Int} & &
\end{array}$$

$Store = \mathcal{F}(Adr \to S_\perp)$

Stores: Mappings of addresses to storable values

Carrier: *Inductively generated by* init *and* bind

Functions:

$$\begin{array}{lll} \text{init} & \in & (\cdot \to Store_\perp) \\ \text{bind} & \in & (Store_\perp \times Adr \times S_\perp \to Store_\perp) \\ \text{apply\_to} & \in & (Store_\perp \times Adr \to S_\perp) \\ \text{assign} & \in & (Store_\perp \times Adr \times E_\perp \to Store_\perp) \\ \text{access} & \in & (Store_\perp \times Adr \to E_\perp) \end{array}$$

Axioms:

$$\begin{array}{l} \text{h.assign(adr, e)} \\ \quad = \textbf{case } \text{e } \textbf{of } E: \\ \qquad \text{int } \textbf{in } Int \Rightarrow \text{h.bind(adr, S'Int(int))} \\ \qquad \text{b } \textbf{in } Bool \Rightarrow \text{h.bind(adr, S'Bool(b))} \\ \qquad \perp_E \Rightarrow \perp_{Store} \end{array}$$

$$\begin{array}{l} \text{init.apply\_to(adr)} \\ \quad = \perp_S \\ \text{h.bind(adr}_1\text{, s).apply\_to(adr}_2\text{)} \\ \quad = \textbf{if } \text{adr}_1 = \text{adr}_2 \Rightarrow \text{s } \textbf{else } \text{h.apply\_to(adr}_2\text{)} \end{array}$$

$$\begin{array}{l} \text{h.access(adr)} \\ \quad = \textbf{case } \text{h.apply\_to(adr) } \textbf{of } S: \\ \qquad \text{int } \textbf{in } Int \Rightarrow \text{E'Int(int)} \\ \qquad \text{b } \textbf{in } Bool \Rightarrow \text{E'Bool(b)} \\ \qquad \perp_S \Rightarrow \perp_E \end{array}$$

Figure 9.4: The algebra ***Store*** of mappings from addresses to storable values

$State = Input \times Store \times Output$

$$\begin{array}{lll} \text{init} & \in & (Input \to State) \\ \text{assign} & \in & (State_\perp \times Adr_\perp \times E_\perp \to State_\perp) \\ \text{access} & \in & (State_\perp \times Adr_\perp \to E_\perp) \\ \text{put} & \in & (State_\perp \times E_\perp \to State_\perp) \\ \text{get} & \in & (State_\perp \times Adr_\perp \to State_\perp) \\ \text{output} & \in & (State_\perp \to Output_\perp) \end{array}$$

Axioms: *Similar to the axioms given in figure 6.3 on page 104*

Figure 9.5: The algebra ***State***

$$\mathcal{P}[\![\mathrm{imp}]\!] = \lambda \mathrm{inp} \in \mathit{Input}\colon \mathcal{M}[\![\mathrm{imp}]\!](\mathrm{Envir'Void})(\mathrm{State'init(inp)}) \,.\, \mathrm{Output}$$

$$\begin{aligned}
\mathcal{M}[\![\mathrm{var} := \mathrm{exp}]\!](\mathrm{env}) &= \underline{\lambda} \mathrm{s} \in \mathit{State}_\perp\colon \mathrm{s} \,.\, \mathrm{assign}(\mathcal{V}[\![\mathrm{var}]\!](\mathrm{env})(\mathrm{s}), \\
&\qquad\qquad \mathcal{E}[\![\mathrm{exp}]\!](\mathrm{env})(\mathrm{s})) \\
\mathcal{M}[\![\mathbf{skip}]\!](\mathrm{env}) &= \underline{\lambda} \mathrm{s} \in \mathit{State}_\perp\colon \mathrm{s} \\
\mathcal{M}[\![\mathbf{get}\ \mathrm{var}]\!](\mathrm{env}) &= \underline{\lambda} \mathrm{s} \in \mathit{State}_\perp\colon \mathrm{s} \,.\, \mathrm{get}(\mathcal{V}[\![\mathrm{var}]\!](\mathrm{env})(\mathrm{s})) \\
\mathcal{M}[\![\mathbf{put}\ \mathrm{exp}]\!](\mathrm{env}) &= \underline{\lambda} \mathrm{s} \in \mathit{State}_\perp\colon \mathrm{s} \,.\, \mathrm{put}(\mathcal{E}[\![\mathrm{exp}]\!](\mathrm{env})(\mathrm{s})) \\
\mathcal{M}[\![\mathrm{imp}_1;\ \mathrm{imp}_2]\!](\mathrm{env}) &= \mathcal{M}[\![\mathrm{imp}_2]\!](\mathrm{env}) \circ \mathcal{M}[\![\mathrm{imp}_1]\!](\mathrm{env}) \\
\mathcal{M}[\![\mathbf{begin}\ \mathrm{decl};\ \mathrm{imp}\ \mathbf{end}]\!](\mathrm{env}) &= \mathcal{M}[\![\mathrm{imp}]\!](\mathcal{D}[\![\mathrm{decl}]\!](\mathrm{env}))
\end{aligned}$$

$$\begin{aligned}
&\mathcal{M}[\![\mathbf{if}\ \mathrm{exp}\ \mathbf{then}\ \mathrm{imp}_1\ \mathbf{else}\ \mathrm{imp}_2]\!](\mathrm{env}) \\
&\qquad = \mathrm{cond}(\mathcal{E}[\![\mathrm{ex}]\!](\mathrm{env}), \mathcal{M}[\![\mathrm{imp}_1]\!](\mathrm{env}), \mathcal{M}[\![\mathrm{imp}_2]\!](\mathrm{env})) \\
&\mathcal{M}[\![\mathbf{while}\ \mathrm{ex}\ \mathbf{do}\ \mathrm{imp}\ \mathbf{od}]\!](\mathrm{env}) \\
&\qquad = \mathrm{Y}_{\mathit{MV}}(\lambda \mathrm{w} \in \mathit{MV}\colon\ \mathrm{cond}(\mathcal{E}[\![\mathrm{ex}]\!](\mathrm{env}),\ \mathrm{w} \circ \mathcal{M}[\![\mathrm{imp}]\!](\mathrm{env}), \\
&\qquad\qquad \underline{\lambda} \mathrm{s} \in \mathit{State}_\perp\colon \mathrm{s}))
\end{aligned}$$

$$\begin{aligned}
\mathcal{V}[\![\mathrm{id}]\!](\mathrm{env}) = \underline{\lambda} \mathrm{s} \in \mathit{State}_\perp\colon\ & \mathbf{case}\ \mathrm{env} \,.\, \mathrm{bound}(\mathrm{id})\ \mathbf{of}\ \mathit{D}\colon \\
& \quad \mathrm{adr}\ \mathbf{in}\ \mathit{Var} \Rightarrow \mathrm{adr} \\
& \quad \mathbf{otherwise} \Rightarrow \perp_{\mathit{Adr}}
\end{aligned}$$

$$\begin{aligned}
\mathcal{E}[\![\mathrm{lit}]\!](\mathrm{env}) &= \underline{\lambda} \mathrm{s} \in \mathit{State}_\perp\colon \mathrm{E'Int}(\mathcal{A}[\![\mathrm{lit}]\!]) \\
\mathcal{E}[\![\mathrm{id}]\!](\mathrm{env}) &= \underline{\lambda} \mathrm{s} \in \mathit{State}_\perp\colon \mathbf{case}\ \mathrm{env} \,.\, \mathrm{bound}(\mathrm{id})\ \mathbf{of}\ \mathit{D}\colon \\
&\qquad \mathrm{int}\ \mathbf{in}\ \mathit{Const} \Rightarrow \mathrm{E'Int(int)} \\
&\qquad \mathrm{adr}\ \mathbf{in}\ \mathit{Var} \Rightarrow \mathrm{s} \,.\, \mathrm{access(adr)} \\
&\qquad \mathrm{Unbound} \Rightarrow \perp_{\mathit{E}} \\
\mathcal{E}[\![\mathrm{ex}_1\ \mathrm{bop}\ \mathrm{ex}_2]\!](\mathrm{env}) &= \underline{\lambda} \mathrm{s} \in \mathit{State}_\perp\colon \mathcal{BO}[\![\mathrm{bop}]\!](\mathcal{E}[\![\mathrm{ex}_1]\!](\mathrm{env})(\mathrm{s}), \\
&\qquad \mathcal{E}[\![\mathrm{ex}_2]\!](\mathrm{env})(\mathrm{s})) \\
\mathcal{E}[\![\mathrm{uop}\ \mathrm{ex}]\!](\mathrm{env}) &= \underline{\lambda} \mathrm{s} \in \mathit{State}_\perp\colon \mathcal{UO}[\![\mathrm{uop}]\!](\mathcal{E}[\![\mathrm{ex}]\!](\mathrm{env})(\mathrm{s}))
\end{aligned}$$

$$\begin{aligned}
\mathcal{D}[\![\mathbf{const}\ \mathrm{id} = \mathrm{lit}]\!](\mathrm{env}) &= \mathrm{env.bind}(\mathrm{id}, \mathrm{D'Const}(\mathcal{A}[\![\mathrm{lit}]\!])) \\
\mathcal{D}[\![\mathbf{var}\ \mathrm{id}\colon \mathrm{vtype}]\!](\mathrm{env}) &= \mathrm{env.bind}(\mathrm{id}, \mathrm{D'Var}(\mathrm{env} \,.\, \mathrm{free_adr})) \\
\mathcal{D}[\![\mathrm{decl}_1;\ \mathrm{decl}_2]\!](\mathrm{env}) &= \mathcal{D}[\![\mathrm{decl}_2]\!](\mathcal{D}[\![\mathrm{decl}_1]\!](\mathrm{env}))
\end{aligned}$$

Figure 9.6: Untyped semantic mappings for Decl$_0$

The semantic mappings $\mathcal{P}$, $\mathcal{M}$, $\mathcal{D}$, $\mathcal{E}$ and $\mathcal{V}$ are defined in figure 9.6. The mappings $\mathcal{UO}$ and $\mathcal{BO}$ are as defined in section 6.3.2.

Observe that we do not define a semantic mapping for the syntactic domain *VarType* in this section. The reason is that vartypes are not used in the simple and untyped semantics for Decl_0 defined here. In section 9.5, we describe a *typed* semantics for Decl_0, and then we need - and define - a semantic mapping $\mathcal{T}$ for vartypes.

The names *PV*, *MV* etc. will be used repeatedly in the sequel. The following table may serve as an aid in remembering what these names denote:

PV:	**P**rogram **V**alues
MV:	i**M**perative **V**alues
EV:	**E**xpression **V**alues
VV:	**V**ariable **V**alues
UOV:	**U**nary **O**perator **V**alues
BOV:	**B**inary **O**perator **V**alues

9.2.3 An example

Let PS be the following Decl_0 program:

```
begin
  var x: int;
  const c = 1;
  get x;
  put x + c
end
```

By the informal semantics of Decl_0, this program should produce $\langle 3\rangle$ as output if it is executed with $\langle 2\rangle$ as input. Let us see if the formal semantics defined in this section gives the same result:

$$\begin{aligned}\mathcal{P}[\![\mathsf{PS}]\!](\langle 2\rangle) &= \mathcal{M}[\![\mathbf{get}\ \mathsf{x};\ \mathbf{put}\ (\mathsf{x}+\mathsf{c})]\!](\mathsf{env}_2)(\mathsf{s}_0)\,.\,\mathsf{Output}\\ &= \mathcal{M}[\![\mathbf{put}\ (\mathsf{x}+\mathsf{c})]\!](\mathsf{env}_2)(\mathcal{M}[\![\mathbf{get}\ \mathsf{x}]\!](\mathsf{env}_2)(\mathsf{s}_0))\,.\,\mathsf{Output}\\ &= \mathcal{M}[\![\mathbf{put}\ (\mathsf{x}+\mathsf{c})]\!](\mathsf{env}_2)(\mathsf{s}_1)\,.\,\mathsf{Output}\end{aligned}$$

where

$$\begin{aligned}\mathsf{s}_0 &= \mathsf{State'initstate}(\langle 2\rangle) = \langle\langle 2\rangle,\ \mathsf{h}_0,\ \varepsilon\rangle\\ &\qquad \text{where } \mathsf{h}_0 = \lambda\mathsf{id}\!:\!0\\ \mathsf{s}_1 &= \mathcal{M}[\![\mathbf{get}\ \mathsf{x}]\!](\mathsf{env}_2)(\mathsf{s}_0)\end{aligned}$$

and

$$\begin{aligned}\mathsf{env}_2 &= \mathcal{D}[\![\mathbf{var}\ \mathsf{x}\!:\ \mathbf{int};\ \mathbf{const}\ \mathsf{c} = \mathbf{1}]\!](\mathsf{Envir'Void})\\ &= \mathcal{D}[\![\mathbf{const}\ \mathsf{c} = \mathbf{1}]\!](\mathcal{D}[\![\mathbf{var}\ \mathsf{x}\!:\ \mathbf{int}]\!](\mathsf{Envir'Void}))\\ &= \mathcal{D}[\![\mathbf{const}\ \mathsf{c} = \mathbf{1}]\!](\mathsf{Envir'Void}\,.\,\mathsf{bind}(\mathsf{x},\ \mathsf{D'Var}(\mathsf{adr}_1)))\\ &\qquad \text{where } \mathsf{adr}_1 = \mathsf{Adr'init}\\ &= \mathsf{Envir'Void}\,.\,\mathsf{bind}(\mathsf{x},\ \mathsf{D'Var}(\mathsf{adr}_1))\\ &\qquad\qquad .\,\mathsf{bind}(\mathsf{c},\ \mathsf{D'Const}(1))\end{aligned}$$

But then

$$\begin{aligned}
s_1 &= \mathcal{M}[\![\textbf{get}\ x]\!](env_2)(s_0)\\
&= s_0\,.\,get(\mathcal{V}[\![x]\!](env_2)(s_0))\\
&= s_0\,.\,get(adr_1)\\
&= \langle \varepsilon,\ h_1,\ \varepsilon\rangle\\
&\qquad \text{where } h_1 = h_0\,.\,bind(adr_1,\ 2)
\end{aligned}$$

and

$$\begin{aligned}
\mathcal{P}[\![PS]\!](\langle 2\rangle) &= \mathcal{M}[\![\textbf{put}\ (x + c)]\!](env_2)(s_1)\,.\,Output\\
&= s_1\,.\,put(\mathcal{E}[\![(x + c)]\!](env_2)(s_1))\,.\,Output\\
&= s_1\,.\,put(\mathcal{BO}[\![+]\!](\mathcal{E}[\![x]\!](env_2)(s_1),\\
&\qquad\qquad \mathcal{E}[\![c]\!](env_2)(s_1)))\,.\,Output\\
&= s_1\,.\,put(\mathcal{BO}[\![+]\!](s_1\,.\,access(adr_1),\\
&\qquad\qquad E'Int(1)))\,.\,Output\\
&= s_1\,.\,put(\mathcal{BO}[\![+]\!](E'Int(2),\ E'Int(1)))\,.\,Output\\
&= s_1\,.\,put(E'Int(3))\,.\,Output\\
&= \langle \varepsilon,\ h_1,\ \langle 3\rangle\rangle\,.\,Output\\
&= \langle 3\rangle
\end{aligned}$$

- as expected.

9.3 Layered semantics of Decl_0

The denotation of an imperative may be considered to have two parts, a *dynamic denotation* and *static denotation*:

- The *dynamic denotation* is a member of the semantic algebra *MV*, i.e., a function that maps states to states (a *state transformer*).

- The *static denotation* is a member of (*Envir* → *MV*), i.e., a function that maps an environment (which is used to give meaning to the identifiers that occur in the imperative) to a state transformer.

Similarly, expressions have dynamic denotations in *EV* and static denotations in (*Envir* → *EV*). We say that *MV* and *EV*, and also *PV* and *VV*, are *dynamic semantic algebras.*

It is not very difficult to see that the static denotations of imperatives, expressions and other syntactic constructs of a language may be defined without complete specifications of the dynamic semantic algebras of the language. It is, as we will show in this section, only necessary to have partial and rather abstract specifications of these algebras to define what may be called the *static semantics* of a language.

This fact suggests that it may be advantageous to split the definition of the semantics of programming languages into *layers* or *levels*. A standard denotational definition of a programming language similar to Decl_0 may for instance be split into the following three layers:

Micro-semantics: This layer is at the bottom of a standard denotational definition of the semantics of any imperative programming language, and the layer that is most concrete and hence in a sense closest to an implementation of the language. At this layer we define which entities are storable - the algebra ***S*** is hence a micro-algebra - and give complete specifications of algebras for stores, states and similar objects.

The specifications given in section 9.2.1.4 for the algebras ***State***, ***Input***, ***Output***, ***Store*** and ***S*** constitute a micro-semantic layer for the Decl_0 language.

Intermediate semantics: This layer contains specifications of dynamic semantic algebras for the language, i.e., algebras that contain the dynamic denotations of the various constructs of the language. Thus, an intermediate semantics for the Decl_0 language should contain specifications of the algebras ***PV***, ***MV***, ***EV*** and ***VV***.

At the intermediate layer we also define which entities are expressible (the algebra ***E*** is therefore an intermediate-level algebra) and specify the meaning of the operators of the language. The intermediate semantics for Decl_0 should therefore contain specifications of the algebra ***E*** (which consists of all expressible values), and of the algebras ***BOV*** and ***UOV*** (which contain denotations of operators).

In order to achieve a good modular structure, it is advantageous to assume as little as possible about the the micro-semantic algebras when we define the intermediate semantics of a language. This means that we should base the intermediate layer on only a partial and abstract specification of the micro-semantic algebras.

Intermediate-level semantics for Decl_0 is defined in section 9.3.5 below.

Macro-semantics: At the macro-level, we define semantic mappings that map syntactic objects to their static semantic denotations. A macro-level semantics for the Decl_0 language should hence contain definitions of the semantic mappings $\mathcal{P}$, $\mathcal{M}$, $\mathcal{D}$, $\mathcal{E}$, $\mathcal{V}$, $\mathcal{A}$, $\mathcal{BO}$ and $\mathcal{UO}$.

For the sake of modularity, these definitions should be based only on partial and abstract specifications of the algebras of the intermediate layer, and should not assume anything about the micro-layer.

The macro-level contains definitions of what kind of elements may be bound to identifiers, i.e., what entities are denotable (the algebra ***D*** is therefore an algebra at the macro-level), and the domain of environments.

Macro-level definitions - in two versions - of the semantic mappings of Decl_0 are given in sections 9.3.2 and 9.5 below.

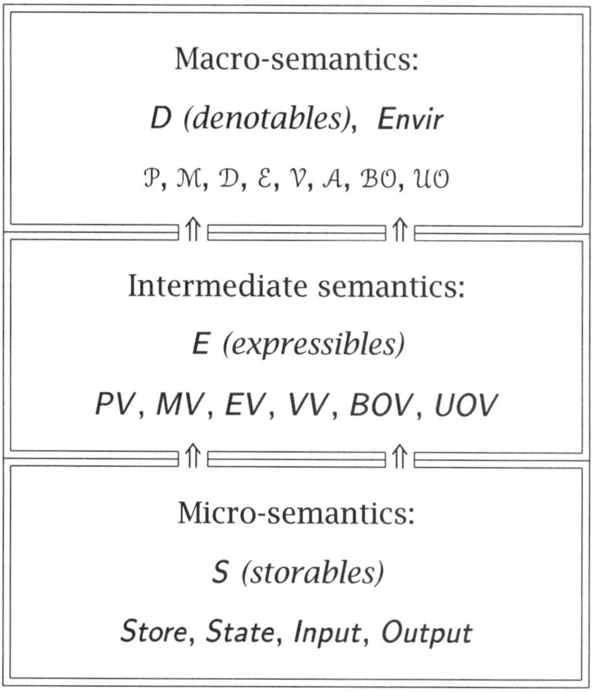

Figure 9.7: Layered semantics for Decl$_0$. The upward arrows in the openings from a lower to a higher layer indicate the abstract (partial) specification of the lower layer that may be used in the upper layer

The macro-semantic layer corresponds closely to that which is often called the *static semantics* of a programming language, i.e, that part of the semantics which can be handled before execution of the program, for instance by a compiler. The part of the semantics which is described in the intermediate layer and the micro-semantic layer is, on the other hand, often called the *dynamic semantics* of a language.

There are several good reasons for splitting the definition of the semantics of a programming language into layers, but also one or two reasons that advocate against layering. One reason that speaks for layering, is that layering may partition semantic definitions - which for most realistic programming languages are large, complex and not easy to comprehend - into more manageable and perspicuous modules.

Another reason for layering is that modularization in general and layering in particular, normally increases the possibilities for reuse of some parts of the definition of the semantics of one programming language in the definition of the semantics of another. A third reason is to make it much easier to give alternative definitions of the semantics of a programming language. A compiler for a language may for instance be defined by specifying a new intermediate layer for the language (and letting the macro-layer be as in a layered denotational definition of the semantics).

There are, however, reasons against layered semantics. One is that the number of algebras and functions needed for a complete definition of the semantics of a programming language, is normally larger in a layered than in a 'monolithic' definition. Another is that for some constructs that occur in some programming languages, it may be difficult or unnatural to factor the semantics into several layers (examples of this will be given in later chapters).

We do, however, deem the reasons against layering to be less compelling than the reasons for, and in the following we will therefore frequently layer our semantic definitions.

In the rest of this section, we specify macro-, intermediate- and micro-level semantics for the Decl_0 language.

9.3.1 Abstract intermediate algebras

Before we can specify the macro-semantics of Decl_0, we need partial, and hence abstract, specifications of the intermediate-level algebras *PV*, *MV*, *EV*, *VV*, *BOV* and *UOV*. Such specifications are given in figure 9.8. Observe that only names and signatures of certain functions of the intermediate algebras are given in the abstract specifications of figure 9.8 and that nothing is said about the carriers of the intermediate algebras nor about how the functions may be implemented. No axioms are given in these partial specifications, which only specify what is necessary to define the macro-semantics of our language.

9.3.2 Macro-semantics

A language is said to be *typed* if every expression and variable of the language may be assigned a *type*, i.e., an algebra which is such that the expression (variable) always has a value in that algebra when it is evaluated. The language Decl_0 is a typed language: 1) Every atomic expression and variable of Decl_0 may be assigned a type: the literals and the integer constants and variables have type *Int*, the Boolean variables have type *Bool*. 2) Every compound expression of Decl_0 may also be assigned a type. An expression (exp_1 bop exp_2) may, for instance, be assigned a type because the denotation of every binary operator bop of Decl_0 is a function with signature ($C \times C \to D$), where C and D are either *Int* or *Bool*. The denotation of $<$ is, for instance, a function

PV *Dynamic denotations of programs*

PV'Imp $\in (MV \to PV)$

MV *Dynamic denotations of imperatives*

MV'Assign $\in (VV \times EV \to MV)$
MV'Skip $\in$ MV
MV'Get $\in (VV \to MV)$
MV'Put $\in (EV \to MV)$
MV'Seq $\in (MV \times MV \to MV)$
MV'Cond $\in (EV \times MV \times MV \to MV)$
MV'While $\in (EV \times MV \to MV)$

VV *Dynamic denotations of variables*

VV'Adr $\in (Adr \to VV)$
VV'Error $\in$ VV

EV *Dynamic denotations of expressions*

EV'Int $\in (Int \to EV)$
EV'Bool $\in (Bool \to EV)$
EV'Adr $\in (Adr \to EV)$
EV'Binop $\in (BOV \times EV \times EV \to EV)$
EV'Unop $\in (UOV \times EV \to EV)$
EV'Error $\in$ EV

BOV *Denotations of binary operators*

BOV'Plus $\in$ BOV, BOV'Div $\in$ BOV,
BOV'Eql $\in$ BOV, BOV'Less $\in$ BOV,
etc.

UOV *Denotations of unary operators*

UOV'Not $\in$ UOV,
etc.

Figure 9.8: Abstract specifications of the intermediate-level semantics for Decl$_0$. When we specify the macro-level semantics of the language, we do not assume any knowledge about the intermediate layer other than that which is given in these specifications

that maps *Int* × *Int* to *Bool*. Thus the type of (exp_1 bop exp_2) is equal to the value type in the signature of bop. Similarly for unary compound expressions.

The determination of types belong to the static semantics of a language, and may be specified in the macro-layer.

An important use of types is to enable a compiler - or some other system that may be applied before program execution - to catch some of the errors that programmers are liable to make when they write their programs. An example: the expression (exp_1 < exp_2) contains a type error if the expressions exp_1 and exp_2 do not both have type *Int*. Another example: for an imperative var := exp to be type-correct, it is necessary that var and exp have the same types. Errors like these may be discovered before program execution for programs in a typed language.

Observe that the more specific the typing is, the more errors may be caught by a type-checker. Thus, if we only specify that the type of an expression is *E*, no type errors will be discovered.

In section 9.3.3 below we give a *untyped* macro-semantic specification of $Decl_0$. This means that the specifications will not show how to determine the types of expressions, nor will they say anything about how to treat programs that contain type errors.

In section 9.5 we give an alternative macro-semantic specification of $Decl_0$. This specification - which is based on the same abstract intermediate semantics as the specification given in the current section - is typed, which means 1) that it shows how to determine the types of expressions and variables, 2) that it gives special denotations for expressions and variables with type errors, and 3) that error messages are specified as part of the denotations of programs, imperatives, expressions and variables that may contain type errors.

9.3.3 Untyped macro-semantics

Two algebras are needed at the macro-level, namely the algebra *D* of denotable values and the algebra *Envir* of environments. These algebras have been defined previously in this chapter (*D* is defined on page 192, *Envir* is defined in figure 9.3 on page 193).

Macro-semantic versions of the semantic mappings $\mathcal{P}$, $\mathcal{M}$, $\mathcal{E}$, $\mathcal{V}$, $\mathcal{D}$, $\mathcal{BO}$ and $\mathcal{UO}$ (the semantic mapping $\mathcal{A}$ is as before) are defined in figure 9.9.

9.3.4 Abstract specification of the micro-level

To give a complete specification of the intermediate semantics of $Decl_0$, we need abstract specifications of the micro-level algebras *State*, *Input* and *Output*, i.e., specifications of the signatures of certain functions that are needed at the intermediate-level. Such specifications may be found in figure 9.5 on page 196.

$$\mathcal{P}[\![\text{imp}]\!] = \text{PV'Imp}(\mathcal{M}[\![\text{imp}]\!](\text{Envir'void}))$$

$$\begin{aligned}
&\mathcal{M}[\![\text{var} := \text{exp}]\!](\text{env}) &&= \text{MV'Assign}(\mathcal{V}[\![\text{var}]\!](\text{env}),\ \mathcal{E}[\![\text{exp}]\!](\text{env}))\\
&\mathcal{M}[\![\textbf{skip}]\!](\text{env}) &&= \text{MV'Skip}\\
&\mathcal{M}[\![\textbf{get}\ \text{var}]\!](\text{env}) &&= \text{MV'Get}(\mathcal{V}[\![\text{var}]\!](\text{env}))\\
&\mathcal{M}[\![\textbf{put}\ \text{exp}]\!](\text{env}) &&= \text{MV'Put}(\mathcal{E}[\![\text{exp}]\!](\text{env}))\\
&\mathcal{M}[\![\text{imp}_1;\ \text{imp}_2]\!](\text{env}) &&= \text{MV'Seq}(\mathcal{M}[\![\text{imp}_1]\!](\text{env}),\ \mathcal{M}[\![\text{imp}_2]\!](\text{env}))\\
&\mathcal{M}[\![\textbf{begin}\ \text{decl};\ \text{imp}\ \textbf{end}]\!](\text{env}) &&= \mathcal{M}[\![\text{imp}]\!](\mathcal{D}[\![\text{decl}]\!](\text{env}))\\
&\mathcal{M}[\![\textbf{if}\ \text{exp}\ \textbf{then}\ \text{imp}_1\ \textbf{else}\ \text{imp}_2]\!](\text{env}) &&\\
& &&= \text{MV'Cond}(\mathcal{E}[\![\text{ex}]\!](\text{env}),\\
& &&\qquad \mathcal{M}[\![\text{imp}_1]\!](\text{env}),\\
& &&\qquad \mathcal{M}[\![\text{imp}_2]\!](\text{env}))\\
&\mathcal{M}[\![\textbf{while}\ \text{ex}\ \textbf{do}\ \text{imp}\ \textbf{od}]\!](\text{env}) &&= \text{MV'While}(\mathcal{E}[\![\text{ex}]\!](\text{env}),\ \mathcal{M}[\![\text{imp}]\!](\text{env}))
\end{aligned}$$

$$\begin{aligned}
\mathcal{V}[\![\text{id}]\!](\text{env}) = \underline{\lambda} s \in \textit{State}_\perp:\ &\textbf{case}\ \text{env}.\text{bound}(\text{id})\ \textbf{of}\ D:\\
&\quad \text{adr}\ \textbf{in}\ \textit{Var}\ \Rightarrow \text{VV'Adr(adr)}\\
&\quad \textbf{otherwise}\ \Rightarrow \text{VV'Error}
\end{aligned}$$

$$\begin{aligned}
&\mathcal{E}[\![\text{lit}]\!](\text{env}) &&= \text{EV'Int}(\mathcal{A}[\![\text{lit}]\!])\\
&\mathcal{E}[\![\text{id}]\!](\text{env}) &&= \textbf{case}\ \text{env}.\text{bound}(\text{id})\ \textbf{of}\ D:\\
& &&\qquad \text{int}\ \textbf{in}\ \textit{Const} \Rightarrow \text{EV'Int(int)}\\
& &&\qquad \text{adr}\ \textbf{in}\ \textit{Var} \Rightarrow \text{EV'Adr(adr)}\\
& &&\qquad \text{Unbound} \Rightarrow \text{EV'Error}\\
&\mathcal{E}[\![\text{ex}_1\ \text{bop}\ \text{ex}_2]\!](\text{env}) &&= \text{EV'Binop}(\mathcal{BO}[\![\text{bop}]\!],\ \mathcal{E}[\![\text{ex}_1]\!](\text{env}),\ \mathcal{E}[\![\text{ex}_2]\!](\text{env}))\\
&\mathcal{E}[\![\text{uop ex}]\!](\text{env}) &&= \text{EV'Unop}(\mathcal{U}[\![\text{uop}]\!],\ \mathcal{E}[\![\text{ex}]\!](\text{env}))
\end{aligned}$$

$$\begin{aligned}
&\mathcal{D}[\![\textbf{const}\ \text{id} = \text{lit}]\!](\text{env}) &&= \text{env.bind(id, D'Const}(\mathcal{A}[\![\text{lit}]\!]))\\
&\mathcal{D}[\![\textbf{var}\ \text{id: vtype}]\!](\text{env}) &&= \text{env.bind(id, D'Var(env.free_adr))}\\
&\mathcal{D}[\![\text{decl}_1;\ \text{decl}_2]\!](\text{env}) &&= \mathcal{D}[\![\text{decl}_2]\!](\mathcal{D}[\![\text{decl}_1]\!](\text{env}))
\end{aligned}$$

$$\begin{aligned}
&\mathcal{BO}[\![+]\!] = \text{BOV'Plus}, && \mathcal{BO}[\![/]\!] = \text{BOV'Div}, && \textit{etc.}\\
&\mathcal{BO}[\![=]\!] = \text{BOV'Eql}, && \mathcal{BO}[\![<]\!] = \text{BOV'Less}, && \textit{etc.}\\
&\mathcal{UO}[\![\neg]\!] = \text{UOV'Not} && &&
\end{aligned}$$

Figure 9.9: Untyped macro-semantic mappings for Decl$_0$

$\boxed{PV} = (Input \to Output_\perp)$

$\mathsf{PV'Imp(mv)} = \lambda \mathsf{inp} \in Input\colon \mathsf{mv(State'init(inp)).Output}$

$\boxed{MV} = (State_\perp \to State_\perp)$

$\mathsf{MV'Skip} = \underline{\lambda} \mathsf{s} \in State_\perp\colon \mathsf{s}$
$\mathsf{MV'Get(vv)} = \underline{\lambda} \mathsf{s} \in State_\perp\colon \mathsf{s.get(vv(s))}$
$\mathsf{MV'Put(ev)} = \underline{\lambda} \mathsf{s} \in State_\perp\colon \mathsf{s.put(ev(s))}$
$\mathsf{MV'Assign(vv, ev)} = \underline{\lambda} \mathsf{s} \in State_\perp\colon \mathsf{s.assign(vv(s), ev(s))}$
$\mathsf{MV'Error} = \underline{\lambda} \mathsf{s} \in State_\perp\colon \perp_{State}$
$\mathsf{MV'Seq(mv_1, mv_2)} = \mathsf{mv_2} \circ \mathsf{mv_1}$
$\mathsf{MV'Cond(ev, mv_1, mv_2)}$
$\quad = \underline{\lambda} \mathsf{s} \in State_\perp\colon$ **case** $\mathsf{ev(s).qua\_Bool}$ **of** *Bool*:
$\qquad$ **true** $\Rightarrow \mathsf{mv_1(s)}$, **false** $\Rightarrow \mathsf{mv_2(s)}$
$\mathsf{MV'While(ev, mv)}$
$\quad = Y_{MV}(\lambda \mathsf{w} \in MV\colon \mathsf{MV'Cond(ev, MV'Seq(mv, w), MV'Skip)})$

$\boxed{VV} = (State_\perp \to Adr_\perp)$

$\mathsf{VV'Adr(adr)} = \underline{\lambda} \mathsf{s} \in State_\perp\colon \mathsf{adr}$
$\mathsf{VV'Error} = \underline{\lambda} \mathsf{s} \in State_\perp\colon \perp_{Adr}$

$\boxed{EV} = (State_\perp \to E_\perp)$

$\mathsf{EV'Int(int)} = \underline{\lambda} \mathsf{s} \in State_\perp\colon \mathsf{E'Int(int)}$
$\mathsf{EV'Bool(b)} = \underline{\lambda} \mathsf{s} \in State_\perp\colon \mathsf{E'Bool(b)}$
$\mathsf{EV'Adr(adr)} = \underline{\lambda} \mathsf{s} \in State_\perp\colon \mathsf{s.access(adr)}$
$\mathsf{EV'Binop(bov, ev_1, ev_2)} = \underline{\lambda} \mathsf{s} \in State_\perp\colon \mathsf{bov(ev_1(s), ev_2(s))}$
$\mathsf{EV'Unop(uov, ev)} = \underline{\lambda} \mathsf{s} \in State_\perp\colon \mathsf{uov(ev(s))}$
$\mathsf{EV'Error} = \underline{\lambda} \mathsf{s} \in State_\perp\colon \perp_E$

$\boxed{BOV} = (E_\perp \times E_\perp \to E_\perp)$

$\mathsf{BOV'Plus(e_1, e_2)} = \mathsf{E'Int(e_1.qua\_Int + e_2.qua\_Int)}$
$\mathsf{BOV'Eql(e_1, e_2)} = \mathsf{E'Bool(e_1.qua\_Int = e_2.qua\_Int)}$
$\mathsf{BOV'And(e_1, e_2)} = \mathsf{E'Bool(e_1.qua\_Bool \wedge e_2.qua\_Bool)}$
etc.

$\boxed{UOV} = (E_\perp \to E_\perp)$

$\mathsf{UOV'Not(e)} = \mathsf{E'Bool(\neg\, e.qua\_Bool)}$

Figure 9.10: Complete specifications of the intermediate-level semantics for $\mathsf{Decl_0}$

9.3.5 Complete specification of intermediate semantics

Complete specifications of the intermediate-level algebras are given in figure 9.10. Observe that these specifications only assume a partial specification of the three micro-level semantic algebras ***State***, ***Input*** and ***Output*** (see section 9.3.4 above).

9.3.6 An example

Consider once again the program PS used as an example in section 9.2.3:

begin var x: **int**; **const** c = **1**; **get** x; **put** (x + c) **end**

Using the definitions of the untyped macro-semantic mappings given in figure 9.9 we may find the macro-semantic denotation of this program as follows:

$$\begin{aligned}\mathcal{P}[\![\mathsf{PS}]\!] &= \mathsf{PV'Imp}(\mathcal{M}[\![\mathsf{PS}]\!](\mathsf{env}_0))\\ &\qquad\qquad \text{where } \mathsf{env}_0 = \mathsf{Envir'Void}\\ &= \mathsf{PV'Imp}(\mathcal{M}[\![\textbf{get}\ \mathsf{x};\ \textbf{put}\ (\mathsf{x}+\mathsf{c})]\!](\mathsf{env}_1))\end{aligned}$$

where

$$\begin{aligned}\mathsf{env}_1 &= \mathcal{D}[\![\textbf{var}\ \mathsf{x}\text{:}\ \textbf{int};\ \textbf{const}\ \mathsf{c} = \mathbf{1}]\!](\mathsf{env}_0)\\ &= \mathcal{D}[\![\textbf{const}\ \mathsf{c} = \mathbf{1}]\!](\mathcal{D}[\![\textbf{var}\ \mathsf{x}\text{:}\ \textbf{int}]\!](\mathsf{env}_0))\\ &= \mathcal{D}[\![\textbf{const}\ \mathsf{c} = \mathbf{1}]\!](\mathsf{env}_0\,.\,\mathsf{bind}(\mathsf{x},\ \mathsf{D'Var}(\mathsf{adr}_0)))\\ &\qquad\qquad \text{where } \mathsf{adr}_0 = \mathsf{Adr'init}\\ &= \mathsf{env}_0\,.\,\mathsf{bind}(\mathsf{x},\ \mathsf{D'Var}(\mathsf{Adr'init}))\\ &\qquad .\,\mathsf{bind}(\mathsf{c},\ \mathsf{D'Const}(\mathsf{E'Int}(1)))\end{aligned}$$

We then get

$$\begin{aligned}\mathcal{P}[\![\mathsf{PS}]\!] &= \mathsf{PV'Imp}(\mathsf{MV'Seq}(\mathcal{M}[\![\textbf{get}\ \mathsf{x}]\!](\mathsf{env}_1),\\ &\qquad\qquad \mathcal{M}[\![\textbf{put}\ (\mathsf{x}+\mathsf{c})]\!](\mathsf{env}_1)))\\ &= \mathsf{PV'Imp}(\mathsf{MV'Seq}(\mathsf{MV'Get}(\mathcal{V}[\![\mathsf{x}]\!](\mathsf{env}_1)),\\ &\qquad\qquad \mathsf{MV'Put}(\mathcal{E}[\![\mathsf{x}+\mathbf{1}]\!](\mathsf{env}_1))))\\ &= \mathsf{PV'Imp}(\mathsf{MV'Seq}(\mathsf{MV'Get}(\mathsf{VV'Adr}(\mathsf{adr}_0)),\\ &\qquad\qquad \mathsf{MV'Put}(\mathsf{EV'Binop}(\mathsf{BOV'Plus},\\ &\qquad\qquad\qquad\qquad \mathsf{EV'Adr}(\mathsf{adr}_0),\\ &\qquad\qquad\qquad\qquad \mathsf{EV'Int}(\mathsf{E'Int}(1))))))\end{aligned}$$

To see how this intermediate-level function above may be applied to an input sequence inp, we use the definitions of the intermediate-level semantics given in figure 9.10. But before doing this, it is convenient to give names to some functions and states:

$$\begin{aligned}\mathsf{ev}_1 &= \mathsf{EV'Binop}(\mathsf{BOV'Plus},\ \mathsf{EV'Adr}(\mathsf{adr}_0),\ \mathsf{EV'Int}(\mathsf{E'Int}(1)))\\ \mathsf{vv}_1 &= \mathsf{VV'Adr}(\mathsf{adr}_0)\\ \mathsf{s}_0 &= \mathsf{State'init}(\mathsf{inp})\end{aligned}$$

Using these definitions and the definitions in figure 9.10 we get:

$$\begin{aligned}
\mathcal{P}[\![\mathsf{PS}]\!](\mathsf{inp}) &= \mathsf{MV'Seq(MV'Get(vv_1),\ MV'Put(ev_1))(s_0)\,.\,Output}\\
&= \mathsf{MV'Put(ev_1)(MV'Get(vv_1)(s_0))\,.\,Output}\\
&= \mathsf{MV'Put(ev_1)(s_0\,.\,get(vv_1(s_0)))\,.\,Output}\\
&= \mathsf{MV'Put(ev_1)(s_0\,.\,get(adr_0))\,.\,Output}\\
&= \mathsf{s_1\,.\,put(ev_1(s_1))\,.\,Output}\\
&\qquad \text{where } \mathsf{s_1 = s_0\,.\,get(adr_0)}\\
&= \mathsf{s_1\,.\,put(BOV'Plus(EV'Adr(adr_0)(s_1),}\\
&\qquad\qquad\qquad\qquad \mathsf{EV'Int(E'Int(1))(s_1)))\,.\,Output}\\
&= \mathsf{s_1\,.\,put(BOV'Plus(s_1\,.\,access(adr_0),\ E'Int(1)))\,.\,Output}\\
&= \mathsf{s_1\,.\,put(E'Int(s_1\,.\,access(adr_0)\,.\,qua_int + 1))\,.\,Output}
\end{aligned}$$

The result of applying this function to, for instance, the input sequence $\langle 2\rangle$, may be found by using the definitions of micro-level functions given in figures 9.4 and 9.5 on page 196. In doing this, it is convenient to give names to the following states:

$$\begin{aligned}
\mathsf{s_0} &= \mathsf{State'init(\langle 2\rangle)}\\
&= \langle\langle 2\rangle,\ \lambda \mathsf{id}{:}\,0,\ \varepsilon\rangle\\
\mathsf{s_1} &= \mathsf{s_0\,.\,get(adr_0)}\\
&= \langle\varepsilon,\ (\lambda \mathsf{id}{:}\,0)\,.\,\mathsf{bind(adr_0,\ S'Int(2))},\ \varepsilon\rangle
\end{aligned}$$

We then get

$$\begin{aligned}
\mathcal{P}[\![\mathsf{PS}]\!](\langle 2\rangle) &= \mathsf{s_1\,.\,put(E'Int(s_1\,.\,access(adr_0)\,.\,qua_int + 1))\,.\,Output}\\
&= \mathsf{s_1\,.\,put(E'Int(2 + 1))\,.\,Output}\\
&= \langle\varepsilon,\ (\lambda \mathsf{id}{:}\,0)\,.\,\mathsf{bind(adr_0,\ S'Int(2))},\ \langle 3\rangle\rangle\,.\,\mathsf{Output}\\
&= \langle 3\rangle
\end{aligned}$$

- as before.

9.4 $\mathsf{Decl_0}$ in ML

In this section we show how $\mathsf{Decl_0}$ may be implemented in ML by translating the layered specifications given in section 9.3.

9.4.1 Abstract syntax of $\mathsf{Decl_0}$ in ML

The ML structure DeclSyntax given below is an implementation of the abstract syntax of $\mathsf{Decl_0}$, and is an almost direct translation of the BNF productions given in figure 9.1.

```
structure DeclSyntax =
struct

  type Literal = int;
```

```
type Ident = string;
datatype Prog    = Program of Imp
   and   Imp     = Skip
                 | Put      of Exp
                 | Get      of Var
                 | Asg      of Var * Exp
                 | Imps     of Imp * Imp
                 | Block    of Decl * Imp
                 | If       of Exp * Imp * Imp
                 | While    of Exp * Imp
   and   Decl    = EmptyDecl
                 | Const    of Ident * Literal
                 | Var      of Ident * Vartype
                 | Decls    of Decl * Decl
   and   Exp     = LitExp   of Literal
                 | IdExp    of Ident
                 | BOP      of Binop * Exp * Exp
                 | UOP      of Unop * Exp
   and   Var     = Variable of Ident
   and   Vartype = IntVar
                 | BoolVar
   and   Binop   = Plus | Sub | Mult | Div | Eql | Less | And
   and   Unop    = Not | Minus
end
```

9.4.2 Micro-semantics

The structure MicroSemantics contains definitions of the micro-semantic types and functions used to define the intermediate-level semantics of Decl$_0$.

```
structure MicroSemantics =
struct
   datatype S      = SInt of int | SBool of bool;
       type Adr    = int;
       type Input  = int list;
       type Output = int list;
       type Store  = Adr -> S;
       type State  = Input * Store * Output;

   exception TypeError;
   exception InputEmpty;

local
   fun bind(h, adr, v) = (fn x => (if adr = x then v else h x))
```

```
        fun StoInt(SInt(i))   = i
          | StoInt(SBool(b))= raise TypeError;
    in
        fun StateInit(inp)              = (inp, (fn x => SInt(0)), []);
        fun assign((inp, h, out), ad, v) = (inp, bind(h, ad, v), out);
        fun get(([], h, out), ad)       = raise InputEmpty
          | get((x::in, h, out), ad)    = (in, bind(h, ad, SInt(x)), out);
        fun put((inp, h, out), v)       = (inp, h, out@[StoInt(v)]);
        fun access((inp, h, out), ad)   = h(ad);
        fun output(inp, h, out)         = out;
    end; end;
```

9.4.3 Intermediate semantics

The ML structure InterSemantics contains definitions of the intermediate-level types and functions used to define the macro-semantics of $Decl_0$.

```
structure InterSemantics =
struct
    open MicroSemantics
    datatype E = EInt of int | EBool of bool;
        type PV  = (Input -> Output);
        type MV  = (State -> State);
        type EV  = (State -> E);
        type VV  = (State -> Adr);
        type BOV = (E * E -> E);
        type UOV = (E -> E);
    exception ZeroDiv;
local
    fun EquaInt(EInt(i))      = i
      | EquaInt(EBool(b))     = raise TypeError;
    fun EquaBool(EInt(i))     = raise TypeError
      | EquaBool(EBool(b))    = b;
    fun EtoS(EInt(i))         = SInt(i)
      | EtoS(EBool(b))        = SBool(b);
    fun StoE(SInt(i))         = EInt(i)
      | StoE(SBool(b))        = EBool(b);
    fun fix(q) = (fn s => q(fix(q))(s))
in
    fun BOVPlus(e1, e2)       = EInt(EquaInt(e1) + EquaInt(e2))
    fun BOVSub(e1, e2)        = EInt(EquaInt(e1) - EquaInt(e2))
    fun BOVMult(e1, e2)       = EInt(EquaInt(e1) * EquaInt(e2))
```

```
    fun BOVDiv(e1, e2)          = EInt(if EquaInt(e2) = 0
                                       then raise ZeroDiv
                                       else  (EquaInt(e1) div EquaInt(e2)))
    fun BOVEql(e1, e2)          = EBool(if e1 = e2 then true else false)
    fun BOVLess(e1, e2)         = EBool(if EquaInt(e1) < (EquaInt(e2))
                                        then true else false)
    fun BOVAnd(e1, e2)          = EBool(EquaBool(e1));

    fun UOVNot(e)               = EBool(not(EquaBool(e)))
    fun UOVMinus(e)             = EInt(0 - EquaInt(e))

    fun EVInt(i)                = (fn s => EInt(i))
    fun EVAdr(adr)              = (fn s => StoE(access(s, adr)))
    fun EVBinop(bov, ev1, ev2) = (fn s => bov(ev1(s), ev2(s)))
    fun EVUnop(uov, ev)         = (fn s => uov(ev(s)))

    fun VVAdr(adr)              = (fn s => adr)

    val MVSkip                  = (fn s => s)
    fun MVPut(ev)               = (fn s => put(s, EtoS(ev(s))))
    fun MVGet(vv)               = (fn s => get(s, vv(s)))
    fun MVAssign(vv, ev)        = (fn s => assign(s, vv(s), EtoS(ev(s))))
    fun MVSeq(mv1, mv2)         = mv2 o mv1
    fun MVCond(ev, mv1, mv2) = (fn s => if EquaBool(ev(s))
                                    then mv1(s) else mv2(s))
    fun MVWhile(ev, mv)         = fix(fn w => MVCond(ev, w o mv,
                                                     MVSkip))

    fun PVImp(mv)               = (fn inp => output(mv(StateInit(inp))));
end; end;
```

9.4.4 Macro-semantics

The ML structure MacroSemantics contains translations into ML of the macro-semantic types and functions used in section 9.3 to specify a layered semantics of Decl$_0$.

```
structure MacroSemantics =
struct
  open DeclSyntax;
  open InterSemantics;

  type      Ident = string;
  type      Adr   = int;
  datatype D      = DConst of int | DVar of Adr | Unbound;
  datatype Envir = Void | Bind of Envir * Ident * D;

  exception UnboundIdent;
  exception LitUsedasVar;

local
```

```
   fun bound(Void, id)                 = Unbound
     | bound(Bind(env, bid, d), id)    = (if bid = id then d
                                           else bound(env, id))
   fun freeadr(Void)                   = 0
     | freeadr(Bind(env, bid, DVar a)) = a + 1
     | freeadr(Bind(env, bid, _))      = freeadr(env)
in
   fun BO (Plus) = BOVPlus    | BO (Sub)   = BOVSub
     | BO (Mult) = BOVMult    | BO (Div)   = BOVDiv
     | BO (Eql)  = BOVEql     | BO (Less)  = BOVLess
     | BO (And)  = BOVAnd
   fun UO (Not)  = UOVNot     | UO (Minus) = UOVMinus
   fun EE (IdExp id)(env)          = (case bound(env, id) of
                                        DConst lit => EVInt(lit)
                                      | DVar adr   => EVAdr(adr)
                                      | Unbound    => raise UnboundIdent)
     | EE (LitExp lit)(env)        = EVInt(lit)
     | EE (BOP(b, e1, e2))(env)    = EVBinop(BO b, EE e1 env,
                                                     EE e2 env)
     | EE (UOP(u, e))(env)         = EVUnop(UO u, EE e env)
   fun VV (Variable id)(env)       = (case bound(env, id) of
                                        DConst lit => raise LitUsedasVar
                                      | DVar adr   => VVAdr(adr)
                                      | Unbound    => raise UnboundIdent)
   fun DD (EmptyDecl)(env)         = env
     | DD (Const(id, lit))(env)    = Bind(env, id, DConst(lit))
     | DD (Var(id, vt))(env)       = Bind(env, id, DVar(freeadr(env)))
     | DD (Decls(d1, d2))(env)     = DD(d2)(DD(d1)(env))
   fun MM (Skip)(env)                 = MVSkip
     | MM (Put e)(env)                = MVPut(EE e env)
     | MM (Asg(var, e))(env)          = MVAssign(VV var env, EE e env)
     | MM (Get var)(env)              = MVGet(VV var env)
     | MM (Block(decl, imp))(env)     = MM imp (DD(decl)(env))
     | MM (Imps(imp1, imp2))(env)     = MVSeq(MM imp1 env,
                                              MM imp2 env)
     | MM (If(b, imp1, imp2))(env)    = MVCond(EE b env, MM imp1 env,
                                                         MM imp2 env)
     | MM (While(e, imp))(env)        = MVWhile(EE e env, MM imp env)
   fun PP (Program imp)               = PVImp(MM imp Void)
end; end;
```

9.5 Typed semantics of Decl$_0$

To define a typed semantics for a language like Decl$_0$, we need to bind something which indicates the type to each identifier that is declared to be a variable. (Had Decl$_0$ allowed Boolean - and not only integer - constants, we would also have bound a type to every identifier declared to be a constant.) The simplest way to achieve this, is by introducing a new algebra *Type* of what may be called *type labels*. This algebra would consist of three unit elements, the first to indicate *Int*, the second to indicate *Bool*, and the last to indicate an error:

$$Type \stackrel{d}{=} \text{Int: } Unit + \text{Bool: } Unit + \text{Error: } Unit$$

The only function we need for the algebra *Type*, is equality (with an obvious definition).

In addition to an address, we will bind a type label (i.e., an element of the *Type* algebra) to each variable, and we therefore define the domain *D* as follows, somewhat enriched compared to the same-named domain used to define untyped macro-semantics:

$$D \stackrel{d}{=} \text{Const: } Int + \text{Var: } Type \times Adr + \text{Unbound: } Unit$$

A typed semantics for Decl$_0$ only differs from the untyped layered semantics defined in section 9.3 in the macro-part (the typing does not influence the intermediate and micro-levels). Semantic mappings for typed macro-semantics may be defined as follows for each of the syntactic algebras of Decl$_0$:

9.5.1 Vartypes

The denotation of a vartype vtp may be taken to be a pair ⟨tp, ev⟩, where tp is the type of vtp and ev is an element in $EV = (State_\perp \rightarrow E_\perp)$ that may be evaluated to find the initial value of a variable of the type. A semantic mapping $\mathcal{T}$ for the syntactic algebra *Vartype* should hence have the following signature:

$$\mathcal{T} \in (Vartype \rightarrow (Envir \rightarrow Type \times EV))$$

$\mathcal{T}$ is defined as follows:

$$\begin{aligned}
\mathcal{T}[\![\textbf{Bool}]\!](\text{env}) &= \langle \text{Type'Bool, EV'Bool}(\textbf{false})\rangle \\
\mathcal{T}[\![\textbf{int}]\!](\text{env}) &= \langle \text{Type'Int, EV'Int}(0)\rangle
\end{aligned}$$

The environment parameter to $\mathcal{T}$ is not needed for languages that only allow vartypes as simple as those allowed in Decl$_0$. But vartypes of richer languages may contain expressions (this will for instance be the case if declarations of arrays with variable bounds are allowed in the language), and then the mapping $\mathcal{T}$ needs an environment to determine the denotation of identifiers that occur in vartypes.

9.5.2 Declarations

Given an environment env, the denotation of a declaration decl is a tuple ⟨env', mv⟩, where env' is the result of extending env by binding each identifier declared in decl, and mv is a member of *MV* that specifies how to initialize the variables declared in decl. The semantic mapping $\mathcal{D}$ for declarations should therefore have the following signature:

$$\mathcal{D} \in (\mathit{Decl} \to (\mathit{Envir} \to \mathit{Envir} \times \mathit{MV}))$$

$\mathcal{D}$ may be defined as follows:

$$\begin{aligned}
&\mathcal{D}[\![\textbf{const}\ \mathsf{id} = \mathsf{lit}]\!](\mathsf{env}) = \langle \mathsf{env.bind(id,\ D'Const(}\mathcal{A}[\![\mathsf{lit}]\!])),\ \mathsf{MV'Skip}\rangle \\
&\mathcal{D}[\![\textbf{var}\ \mathsf{id\!: vtp}]\!](\mathsf{env}) = \textbf{let}\ \langle \mathsf{tp,\ ev}\rangle = \mathcal{T}[\![\mathsf{vtp}]\!](\mathsf{env}) \\
&\qquad \textbf{let}\ \mathsf{adr} = \mathsf{env.free_adr} \\
&\qquad \textbf{in}\ \langle \mathsf{env.bind(id,\ D'Var(tp,\ adr))}, \\
&\qquad\quad \mathsf{MV'Assign(VV'Adr(adr),\ ev)}\rangle \\
&\mathcal{D}[\![\mathsf{decl_1;\ decl_2}]\!](\mathsf{env}) = \textbf{let}\ \langle \mathsf{env_1,\ mv_1}\rangle = \mathcal{D}[\![\mathsf{decl_1}]\!](\mathsf{env}) \\
&\qquad \textbf{let}\ \langle \mathsf{env_2,\ mv_2}\rangle = \mathcal{D}[\![\mathsf{decl_2}]\!](\mathsf{env_1}) \\
&\qquad \textbf{in}\ \langle \mathsf{env_2,\ MV'Seq(mv_1,\ mv_2)}\rangle
\end{aligned}$$

Observe that according to this definition, an identifier may legally be defined more than once in a compound declaration (in such cases, the last declaration prevails). If it is desired to disallow such multiple declarations, we have to define the semantics of declarations somewhat differently.

9.5.3 Operators

The typed denotation of a binary operator bop is a tuple ⟨$\mathsf{atp_1}$, $\mathsf{atp_2}$, vtp, bov⟩ where $\mathsf{atp_1}$, $\mathsf{atp_2}$ are the argument types of bop, vtp is the value type of bop and bov is a member of $\mathit{BOV} = (E_\perp \times E_\perp \to E_\perp)$. The typed semantic mapping $\mathcal{BO}$ should therefore have the following signature:

$$\mathcal{BO} \in (\mathit{Binop} \to \mathit{Type} \times \mathit{Type} \times \mathit{Type} \times \mathit{BOV})$$

$\mathcal{BO}$ may be defined as follows:

$$\begin{aligned}
&\mathcal{BO}[\![+]\!] = \langle \mathsf{Type'Int,\ Type'Int,\ Type'Int,\ BOV'Plus}\rangle \\
&\mathcal{BO}[\![<]\!] = \langle \mathsf{Type'Int,\ Type'Int,\ Type'Bool,\ BOV'Less}\rangle
\end{aligned}$$

etc.

The typed semantic mapping $\mathcal{UO} \in (\mathit{Unop} \to \mathit{Type} \times \mathit{Type} \times \mathit{UOV})$ may be defined quite similarly.

9.5.4 Expressions

The typed macro-denotation of an expression exp is a pair ⟨tp, ev⟩ where tp is the type of exp and ev is a member of *EV* that specifies how to evaluate exp. The typed semantic mapping $\mathcal{E}$ should therefore have the following signature:

$$\mathcal{E} \in (\mathit{Expr} \to (\mathit{Envir} \to \mathit{Type} \times \mathit{EV}))$$

$\mathcal{E}$ may be defined as follows:

$$\mathcal{E}[\![\text{lit}]\!](\text{env}) = \langle \text{Type'Int},\ \text{EV'Int}(\mathcal{A}[\![\text{lit}]\!])\rangle$$

$$\begin{array}{lll} \mathcal{E}[\![\text{id}]\!](\text{env}) = \textbf{case}\ \text{env.bound(id) of } D: & & \\ \quad \text{int } \textbf{in} \text{ Int} & \Rightarrow \langle \text{Type'Int}, & \text{EV'Int(int)}\rangle \\ \quad \langle \text{tp, adr}\rangle\ \textbf{in} \text{ Var} & \Rightarrow \langle \text{tp}, & \text{EV'Adr(adr)}\rangle \\ \quad \text{Unbound} & \Rightarrow \langle \text{Type'Error}, & \text{EV'Error}\rangle \end{array}$$

$$\begin{array}{l} \mathcal{E}[\![\text{exp}_1 \text{ bop exp}_2]\!](\text{env}) \\ \quad = \textbf{let}\ \langle \text{tp}_1, \text{ev}_1\rangle = \mathcal{E}[\![\text{exp}_1]\!](\text{env}) \\ \quad\ \ \ \textbf{let}\ \langle \text{tp}_2, \text{ev}_2\rangle = \mathcal{E}[\![\text{exp}_2]\!](\text{env}) \\ \quad\ \ \ \textbf{let}\ \langle \text{atp}_1, \text{atp}_2, \text{vtp, bov}\rangle = \mathcal{BO}[\![\text{bop}]\!] \\ \quad\ \ \ \ \textbf{in if}\ \text{tp}_1 = \text{atp}_1 \wedge \text{tp}_2 = \text{atp}_2 \\ \qquad\quad \textbf{then}\ \langle \text{vtp}, \quad \text{EV'Binop}(\text{ev}_1, \text{ev}_2, \text{bov})\rangle \\ \qquad\quad \textbf{else}\ \langle \text{Type'Error}, \quad \text{EV'Error}\rangle \end{array}$$

$\mathcal{E}[\![\text{uop exp}]\!](\text{env})$: Similarly.

9.5.5 Variables

The typed denotation of a variable var is a pair ⟨tp, vv⟩ where tp is the type of var, vv is a member of *VV* that specifies how to evaluate the address of var. The semantic mapping $\mathcal{V}$ has the following signature:

$$\mathcal{V} \in (\mathit{Var} \to (\mathit{Envir} \to \mathit{Type} \times \mathit{VV}))$$

$\mathcal{V}$ may be defined as follows:

$$\begin{array}{lll} \mathcal{V}[\![\text{id}]\!](\text{env}) = \textbf{case}\ \text{env.bound(id) of } D: & & \\ \quad \langle \text{tp, adr}\rangle\ \textbf{in} \text{ Var} & \Rightarrow \langle \text{tp}, & \text{VV'Adr(adr)}\rangle \\ \quad \textbf{otherwise} & \Rightarrow \langle \text{Type'Error}, & \text{VV'Error}\rangle \end{array}$$

9.5.6 Imperatives

The denotation of an imperative imp is a member of *MV* that specifies how to execute imp. The semantic mapping $\mathcal{M}$ should therefore have the following signature:

$$\mathcal{M} \in (\mathit{Imp} \to (\mathit{Envir} \to \mathit{MV}))$$

$\mathcal{M}$ is defined in figure 9.11.

$$
\begin{array}{ll}
\mathcal{M}[\![\mathsf{var} := \mathsf{exp}]\!](\mathsf{env}) & = \textbf{let } \langle \mathsf{tpv}, \mathsf{vv}\rangle = \mathcal{V}[\![\mathsf{var}]\!](\mathsf{env}) \\
 & \quad \textbf{let } \langle \mathsf{tpe}, \mathsf{ev}\rangle = \mathcal{E}[\![\mathsf{exp}]\!](\mathsf{env}) \\
 & \quad \textbf{in if } \mathsf{tpv} = \mathsf{tpe} \textbf{ then } \mathsf{MV'Assign(vv, ev)} \\
 & \quad\quad\quad\quad\quad\quad\quad\quad \textbf{else } \mathsf{MV'Error} \\
\mathcal{M}[\![\textbf{skip}]\!](\mathsf{env}) & = \mathsf{MV'Skip} \\
\mathcal{M}[\![\textbf{get } \mathsf{var}]\!](\mathsf{env}) & = \textbf{let } \langle \mathsf{tp}, \mathsf{vv}\rangle = \mathcal{V}[\![\mathsf{var}]\!](\mathsf{env}) \\
 & \quad \textbf{in if } \mathsf{tp} = \mathsf{Type'Int} \textbf{ then } \mathsf{MV'Get(vv)} \\
 & \quad\quad\quad\quad\quad\quad\quad\quad\quad\quad \textbf{else } \mathsf{MV'Error} \\
\mathcal{M}[\![\textbf{put } \mathsf{exp}]\!](\mathsf{env}) & = \textbf{let } \langle \mathsf{tp}, \mathsf{ev}\rangle = \mathcal{E}[\![\mathsf{exp}]\!](\mathsf{env}) \\
 & \quad \textbf{in if } \mathsf{tp} = \mathsf{Type'Int} \textbf{ then } \mathsf{MV'Put(ev)} \\
 & \quad\quad\quad\quad\quad\quad\quad\quad\quad\quad \textbf{else } \mathsf{MV'Error} \\
\mathcal{M}[\![\mathsf{imp}_1;\ \mathsf{imp}_2]\!](\mathsf{env}) & = \mathsf{MV'Seq}(\mathcal{M}[\![\mathsf{imp}_1]\!](\mathsf{env}), \mathcal{M}[\![\mathsf{imp}_2]\!](\mathsf{env})) \\
\multicolumn{2}{l}{\mathcal{M}[\![\textbf{begin } \mathsf{decl};\ \mathsf{imp}\ \textbf{end}]\!](\mathsf{env})} \\
 & = \textbf{let } \langle \mathsf{env'}, \mathsf{mv'}\rangle = \mathcal{D}[\![\mathsf{decl}]\!](\mathsf{env}) \\
 & \quad \textbf{let } \mathsf{mv''} = \mathcal{M}[\![\mathsf{imp}]\!](\mathsf{env'}) \\
 & \quad \textbf{in } \mathsf{MV'Seq(mv', mv'')} \\
\multicolumn{2}{l}{\mathcal{M}[\![\textbf{while } \mathsf{exp}\ \textbf{do } \mathsf{imp}\ \textbf{od}]\!](\mathsf{env})} \\
 & = \textbf{let } \langle \mathsf{tp}, \mathsf{ev}\rangle = \mathcal{E}[\![\mathsf{exp}]\!](\mathsf{env}) \\
 & \quad \textbf{let } \mathsf{mv} = \mathcal{M}[\![\mathsf{imp}]\!](\mathsf{env}) \\
 & \quad \textbf{in if } \mathsf{tp} = \mathsf{Type'Bool} \textbf{ then } \mathsf{MV'While(ev, mv)} \\
 & \quad\quad\quad\quad\quad\quad\quad\quad\quad\quad\quad \textbf{else } \mathsf{MV'Error} \\
\multicolumn{2}{l}{\mathcal{M}[\![\textbf{if } \mathsf{exp}\ \textbf{then } \mathsf{imp}_1\ \textbf{else } \mathsf{imp}_2]\!](\mathsf{env}):\ \textit{Similarly}}
\end{array}
$$

Figure 9.11: Typed macro-semantics for the imperatives of Decl_0

9.5.7 Programs

The denotation of a program is a member of *PV* that specifies how to execute the program. The semantic mapping $\mathcal{P}$ has the following signature:

$$\mathcal{P} \in (\mathit{Prog} \to \mathit{PV})$$

$\mathcal{P}$ may be defined as follows:

$$\mathcal{P}[\![\mathsf{imp}]\!] = \mathsf{PV'Imp}(\mathcal{M}[\![\mathsf{imp}]\!](\mathsf{Envir'void}))$$

9.6 Decl$_1$: A language with arrays

9.6.1 Syntax and informal semantics

Let Decl$_1$ be the result of extending the language Decl$_0$ with the following BNF productions:

$$\begin{array}{lll} \langle vartype \rangle & ::= \ldots & \mid \textbf{array}\ [1 : \langle expr \rangle]\ \textbf{of}\ \langle vartype \rangle \\ \langle expr \rangle & ::= \ldots & \mid \langle var \rangle [\langle expr \rangle] \\ \langle var \rangle & ::= \ldots & \mid \langle var \rangle [\langle expr \rangle] \end{array}$$

Examples: The effect of the declarations

var aa: **array** [1 : **11**] **of int**;
var bb: **array** [1 : k] **of int**;
var cc: **array** [1 : p] **of array** [1 : m] **of int**

is to declare three arrays of variables, the first two are one-dimensional, the last is two-dimensional. The array aa will for instance consist of the variables aa[1], aa[2] and aa[3] (remember that the value of the literal **11** is 3). If p has value 2 and m has value 3, the array cc will consist of the following variables: cc[1][1], cc[1][2], cc[1][3], cc[2][1], cc[2][2] and cc[2][3].

If aa is declared to be an array and x an integer variable, the expression aa[x + 1] is said to be an *indexed expression* with x + 1 as *index*.

The construct '1 :' is not used for anything in an array declaration in Decl$_1$ (it is only superfluous 'syntactic sugar'), and is included partly for historical reasons, partly to indicate the possibility of array declarations that specify both lower and upper bounds for array indexes (see exercise 9.7.6).

Arrays in Decl$_1$ may be either *static* or *dynamic*. A static array is an array that has a size which may be computed before program execution. The array aa is therefore a static array, and the arrays bb and cc are static if k, p and m are either literals or declared (either previously in the block containing the array declarations or in an outer block) to be constants. Should, however, k be a variable (declared in an outer block) or an expression containing a variable, the size of the array bb cannot be known before the program is executed and k may be evaluated. In this case, the array bb is said to be dynamic. Observe that the size of any array - be it static or dynamic - is determined once and for all by its declaration, and that it will not change later. But the size of a dynamic array that is declared in an inner block may depend upon the value of variables that are declared further out, and may hence be different each time the block is executed.

We specify that it is legal in Decl$_1$ to assign new values not only to single variables and to *indexed variables* (i.e., variables of the form var[exp]), but also to arrays, and also that it is legal to output arrays. Thus, the following are syntactically correct - and hence semantically meaningful - imperatives in Decl$_1$:

cc[1][2] := aa[3];	*A new value is assigned to the indexed variable* cc[1][2].
aa := bb;	*Every variable in the array* aa *is assigned a new value. This will be erroneous should the arrays* aa *and* bb *differ in their lengths.*
cc[k] := aa;	*Every variable in column* k *of* cc *is assigned a new value.*
put aa;	*The values of all variables in* aa *are output.*
put cc[ind]	*The values of all variables in column* ind *of the array* cc *are output.*

9.6.2 Macro-semantics

In this section we define a typed macro-semantics for Decl_1.

9.6.2.1 Types

We start by considering what kind of types Decl_1 expressions may have. In Decl_0, every expression has a type that is either Int or Bool. But this is clearly insufficient for Decl_1. For instance, if we assume that aa is declared to be a one-dimensional integer array (as in the example in the previous section), and that bb is a two-dimensional array, then aa and bb[2] are legal Decl_0 expressions, which for instance may be used in **put** imperatives. What types should these expressions have? They may clearly be neither of type Int nor of type Bool, but rather of something like Array(Int). Similarly, the expression bb should have type Array(Array(Int)). To be able to use what may be said to be *array types* in this manner, we extend the algebra *Type* as follows:

$$Type \stackrel{d}{=} \mathsf{Int}\colon Unit + \mathsf{Bool}\colon Unit + \mathsf{Array}\colon Type + \mathsf{Error}\colon Unit$$

Observe that the size of an array is *not* part of its type. An array type contains information about the type of the variables of the arrays of the type, and implicitly about the number of dimensions of the arrays, but sets no limitation on the number of elements of arrays in the type. An example: assume that the three arrays aa, bb and cc are declared as follows:

```
var aa: array [1 : 1] of int;
var bb: array [1 : 11] of int;
var cc: array [1 : 111] of Bool
```

Then aa and bb are of the same type, which is different from the type of cc. An assignment aa := bb would be syntactically legal (i.e., no type error), but would lead to an error state if executed (because the two arrays have a different number of elements).

9.6.2.2 Recursively defined algebras

Observe that *Type* is defined recursively. It may not be obvious that an algebra defined in this manner is well-defined: remember the trouble we took to circumvent the intuitively obvious and seemingly innocent recursive definition of the semantics of **while** imperatives in chapter 6.

Some recursive definitions of algebras are, however, quite innocent and mathematically unproblematic. An example: In figure 4.2 on page 47 we defined the algebra *Nat* of non-negative integers by generator induction, using two generators $0 \in (\cdot \to Nat)$ and $\mathsf{suc} \in (Nat \to Nat)$. We *could*, however, have defined *Nat* equivalently as a disjoint sum as follows:

$$Nat \stackrel{d}{=} 0\colon Unit + \mathsf{suc}\colon Nat$$

This is a recursive definition that structurally is quite similar to the definition given of *Type*.

In section 4.3.2 we observed (on page 55) that a disjoint sum in general may be considered to be inductively generated by its injection functions. Thus, the definition given of *Type* may be taken to be a definition of an algebra that is inductively generated by the following four generators:

$$\begin{array}{lll}
\mathsf{Int} & \in & (\cdot \to Type) \\
\mathsf{Bool} & \in & (\cdot \to Type) \\
\mathsf{Array} & \in & (Type \to Type) \\
\mathsf{Error} & \in & (\cdot \to Type)
\end{array}$$

We may in general - without encountering any mathematical problems - similarly allow recursive algebra definitions that have the form

$$B \stackrel{d}{=} A_1 + A_2 + \ldots + A_n$$

if we restrict each addend A_i to be an algebra expression that is constructed from 1) names of previously defined algebras and 2) the name of the algebra that is being defined (i.e., B here), using only Cartesian products and sequence constructors to build compound algebra expressions. Such definitions may be considered to be inductive definitions in disguise, and hence quite unproblematic.

But not all recursive definitions of algebras are as unproblematic as the one used to define *Type*. For instance, if we would like to define an algebra P by the following equation

$$P \stackrel{d}{=} A + (P \to P)$$

it is not at all obvious that such P exists. In chapter 14 we will have more to say about such definitions, in particular about when they may be used to give proper definitions of algebras.

9.6.2.3 Semantic mappings

Macro-semantic mappings for Decl_1 may be defined to be extensions of the macro-semantic mappings defined for Decl_0. The extensions consist in specifications of denotations for the syntactic constructs that are in Decl_1 but not Decl_0:

Array vartypes The denotation of a vartype

$$\textbf{array}\ (1 : \mathsf{size\_exp})\ \textbf{of}\ \mathsf{vtp}$$

is a pair ⟨tp_arr, ev_arr⟩ where tp_arr is the type of the array and ev_arr is a member of *EV* that may be used to find initial values for the array. The type tp_arr must be equal to Type'Array(tp_elem), where tp_elem is the type of vtp.

Each type has a certain initial value. In section 9.5 (in the specification of the semantic mapping $\mathcal{T}$ on page 213), we specified 0 to be the initial value for the type *Int*, and **false** to be the initial value for *Bool*. The initial value for type Type'Array(tp_elem) should be an array of elements of type tp_elem, each with value equal to the initial value for type tp_elem. The number of elements in the array may be found by evaluating the expression size_exp. This means that the *EV* element ev_arr that will be used to find an initial value of type Type'Array(tp_elem), must have access to information about 1) how to evaluate the expression size_exp, and 2) how to find an initial value of type tp_elem. Let us assume that the intermediate-level exports an *EV* producer

$$\mathsf{EV'Array} \in (\mathit{EV} \times \mathit{EV} \to \mathit{EV})$$

which is such that EV'Array(ev_size, ev_elem) may be used to construct an array that consists of size elements (size is found by evaluating ev_size), each with the same value, namely the value that is found when ev_elem is evaluated. This value is said to be the *default value* for the type in question.

The function EV'Array may then be used to find initial values for arrays.

We are now able to give the following precise specification of the denotation of a vartype '**array** (1 : size_exp) **of** vtp':

$$
\begin{array}{l}
\mathcal{T}[\![\textbf{array}\ (1 : \mathsf{exp})\ \textbf{of}\ \mathsf{vtp}]\!](\mathsf{env}) \\
\quad = \textbf{let}\ \langle \mathsf{tp\_size}, \mathsf{ev\_size}\rangle = \mathcal{E}[\![\mathsf{exp}]\!](\mathsf{env})\ \textbf{in} \\
\qquad \textbf{case}\ \mathsf{tp\_size}\ \textbf{of}\ \mathit{Type}: \\
\qquad\quad \mathsf{Type'Int} \quad \Rightarrow \textbf{let}\ \langle \mathsf{tp\_elem}, \mathsf{ev\_elem}\rangle = \mathcal{T}[\![\mathsf{vtp}]\!](\mathsf{env}) \\
\qquad\qquad\qquad\qquad \textbf{in}\ \langle \mathsf{Type'Array(tp\_elem)}, \\
\qquad\qquad\qquad\qquad\quad \mathsf{EV'Array(ev\_size, ev\_elem)}\rangle \\
\qquad\quad \textbf{otherwise} \Rightarrow \langle \mathsf{Type'Error}, \mathsf{EV'Error}\rangle
\end{array}
$$

Indexed expressions For an indexed expression arr[ind] to be type-correct, arr must have type Type'Array(tp_elem), where tp_elem is a type, and ind must have type Int. If this is the case, arr[ind] has type tp_elem.

To evaluate arr[ind], we must know 1) how to find the address bound to arr, and 2) how to evaluate ind. Let us assume that the intermediate layer exports an *EV* producer

$$\text{EV'Indexed} \in (VV \times EV \to EV)$$

which is such that if vv is a member of *VV* that specifies how to evaluate the address of an array and ev is a member of *EV* that may be used to evaluate the value of an index, then EV'Indexed(vv, ev) may be used to find the value of the array at the position indicated by the index. Using this function, we specify the denotation of an indexed expression arr[ind] as follows:

```
ℰ⟦arr[ind]⟧(env)
   = let ⟨tp_arr, vv_arr⟩ = 𝒱⟦arr⟧(env)
     let ⟨tp_ind, ev_ind⟩ = ℰ⟦ind⟧(env)
     in if tp_arr.is_Array ∧ tp_ind.is_Int
        then ⟨tp_arr.qua_Array.Type,
              EV'Indexed(vv_arr, ev_ind)⟩
        else  ⟨Type'Error, EV'Error⟩
```

Indexed variables The denotation of an indexed variable arr[ind] may be specified quite similarly to how we specify the denotation of an indexed expression:

```
𝒱⟦arr[ind]⟧(env)
   = let ⟨tp_arr, vv_arr⟩ = 𝒱⟦arr⟧(env)
     let ⟨tp_ind, ev_ind⟩ = ℰ⟦ind⟧(env)
     in if tp_arr.is_Array ∧ tp_ind.is_Int
        then ⟨tp_arr.qua_Array.Type,
              VV'Indexed(vv_arr, ev_ind)⟩
        else  ⟨Type'Error, VV'Error⟩
```

The intermediate function VV'Indexed $\in (VV \times EV \to VV)$ used above is such that if vv is a member of *VV* that specifies how to evaluate the address of an array and ev is a member of *EV* that may be used to evaluate the value of an index, then VV'Indexed(vv, ev) may be used to find the address of the array and the sequence of indexes necessary to assign something to the variable specified by vv and ev.

9.6.3 Intermediate semantics

Let us assume that a is declared to be a one-dimensional integer array. The expressible value of the expression a (which may occur, for instance, in a **put** imperative) is then neither an integer nor a Boolean, but rather a sequence of integers. Generally, an expression **arr**, where **arr** is any array, has a value that is either 1) a sequence of basic values (i.e., integers or Booleans), 2) a sequence of sequences of basic values (this will be the case for two-dimensional arrays), or 3) a sequence of sequences of sequences of basic values (for three-dimensional arrays), etc. We may specify compound expressible values like these if we define the algebra E of expressible values to consist of basic values (integers and Booleans) and of sequences of expressible values:

$$E \stackrel{d}{=} Int + Bool + \mathsf{Array}\colon E^*$$

We need another algebra to specify the intermediate semantics of variables that possibly may be indexed, namely an algebra V that consists of pairs ⟨**adr**, **inds**⟩, where **adr** is an address and **inds** is a sequence of index values. The sequence **inds** will be empty for simple, un-indexed variables; it will contain a single integer for arrays of dimension one, etc. V is defined as follows:

$$V \stackrel{d}{=} Adr \times Int^*$$

The domains EV and VV that consist of the dynamic denotations of expressions and variables, are defined as follows:

$$EV \stackrel{d}{=} (State_\perp \to E_\perp)$$
$$VV \stackrel{d}{=} (State_\perp \to V_\perp)$$

The following intermediate functions were used in section 9.6.2.3 above to specify the macro-semantics of arrays and indexed variables:

$$\begin{array}{lll} \mathsf{VV'Indexed} & \in & (VV \times EV \to VV) \\ \mathsf{EV'Indexed} & \in & (VV \times EV \to EV) \\ \mathsf{EV'Array} & \in & (EV \times EV \to EV) \end{array}$$

These functions may be defined as follows:

VV'Indexed(vv_arr, ev_ind)
    = $\underline{\lambda}$s ∈ $State_\perp$: **let** ⟨adr, inds⟩ = vv_arr(s)
                in ⟨adr, inds ⊢ (ev_ind(s) . qua_Int)⟩

EV'Indexed(vv_arr, ev_ind)
    = $\underline{\lambda}$s ∈ $State_\perp$: **let** ⟨adr, inds⟩ = vv_arr(s)
                in s . access(⟨adr, inds ⊢ (ev_ind(s) . qua_Int)⟩)

EV'Array(ev_size, ev_elem)
    = $\underline{\lambda}$s ∈ $State_\perp$: E'Array(ev_elem(s)↑(ev_size(s) . qua_Int))

The *right append* operator ⊢ used above is such that if **inds** is a sequence of integers and **i** and integer, then **inds ⊢ i** is the index that is found by appending **i** to the right end of **inds**. It is defined in figure 4.8 on page 59.

The auxiliary function ↑ ∈ $(E \times Int \to E^*)$, also used above, is defined as follows for any e ∈ E and n ∈ Int:

$$\mathsf{e}\!\uparrow\!(\mathsf{n}) = \textbf{if } \mathsf{n} \le 0 \textbf{ then } \varepsilon \textbf{ else } (\mathsf{e}\!\uparrow\!(\mathsf{n}-1)) \vdash \mathsf{e}$$

Thus, for $\mathsf{n} \ge 0$, the value of $\mathsf{e}\!\uparrow\!(\mathsf{n})$ is a sequence $\langle \mathsf{e}, \mathsf{e}, \ldots, \mathsf{e} \rangle$ that consists of n occurrences of the element e.

9.6.4 Micro-semantics

Micro-semantics in general, and storage management in particular, will necessarily be more complex for a language that allows dynamic arrays or other constructs that entail that the amount of storage may change dynamically during program execution, than for languages in which every variable may be bound to a fixed address at the macro-level (as is possible for Decl$_0$ and for many commonly used programming languages, for instance Pascal and Fortran).

An easy way to manage the store for a language that allows dynamic arrays, is to let not only basic values be storable, but also arrays of storable values. We may achieve this by defining the algebra S of storable values quite similarly to how we defined E:

$$S = \mathit{Int} + \mathit{Bool} + \mathsf{Array}\colon S^*$$

But in order to be a little closer to an actual operational implementation, we choose to define S as follows:
S

$$S \overset{d}{=} \mathit{Int} + \mathit{Bool} + \mathsf{Array}\colon (\mathsf{Max}\colon \mathit{Int} \times \mathsf{Table}\colon \mathcal{F}(\mathit{Int} \to S))$$

The algebra S is defined in figure 9.12.

The algebra *Store* consists of functions that map addresses to storable values. A version that handles dynamic arrays is defined in figure 9.13.

To define the micro-level function assign we need an auxiliary function E_as_S that may be used to transform expressibles to storables. This function, which should have signature $(E \to S)$, may be defined as follows:

$$\begin{array}{llll} \mathsf{e.E\_to\_S} \overset{d}{=} \textbf{case } \mathsf{e}\colon & \mathsf{i} & \textbf{in } \mathit{Int} & \Rightarrow \mathsf{S'in\_Int(i)} \\ & \mathsf{b} & \textbf{in } \mathit{Bool} & \Rightarrow \mathsf{S'in\_Bool(b)} \\ & \mathsf{es} & \textbf{in } \mathsf{Array} & \Rightarrow \mathsf{S'in\_Array(es.EE\_to\_Array)} \end{array}$$

We leave it as exercises 1) to define an auxiliary function

$$\mathsf{EE\_to\_Array} \in (E^* \to \mathit{Array})$$

that transforms a sequence of E's to a corresponding Array (Array is a summand of S, see the definition of S above); and 2) to define an auxiliary function S_to_E $\in (S \to E)$ that is opposite to E_to_S and hence transforms storables to their corresponding expressibles.

$S = Int + Bool + \text{Array}: (\text{Max}: Int \times \text{Table}: \mathcal{F}(Int \to S))$

Functions: indexed $\in (S_\perp \times Int^* \to S_\perp)$
update $\in (S_\perp \times Int^* \times S_\perp \to S_\perp)$

Axioms: s . indexed(ε) = s
s . indexed(ind ⊣ inds)
= **let** ⟨max, tab⟩ = s . qua_Array **in**
if $\neg(1 \le \text{ind} \le \text{max})$ **then** $\perp_S$
else tab . apply_to(ind) . indexed(inds)

s . update(ε, s') = s'
s . update(ind ⊣ inds, s')
= **let** ⟨max, tab⟩ = s . qua_Array **in**
if $\neg(1 \le \text{ind} \le \text{max})$ **then** $\perp_S$
else let s" = tab . apply_to(ind)
. update(inds, s')
in S'Array(max, tab . bind(ind, s"))

Figure 9.12: The algebra *S* of storable entities, to be used in a standard micro-level semantics for Decl_1

$Store = \mathcal{F}(Adr \to S_\perp)$ *Inductively generated by* init *and* bind

Functions: init $\in (\cdot \to Store_\perp)$
bind $\in (Store_\perp \times Adr \times S_\perp \to Store_\perp)$
apply_to $\in (Store_\perp \times Adr \to S_\perp)$
assign $\in (Store_\perp \times Adr \times Int^* \times E_\perp \to Store_\perp)$
access $\in (Store_\perp \times Adr \times Int^* \to E_\perp)$

Axioms: h . assign(⟨adr, inds⟩, e)
= h . bind(adr, h . apply_to(adr)
. update(inds, e . E_as_S))

h . access(⟨adr, inds⟩)
= h . apply_to(adr) . indexed(inds) . S_as_E

apply_to: *As in figure 9.4*

Figure 9.13: *Store* with storage management for integers, Booleans and arrays of storables

9.7 Exercises

9.7.1 A very simple program

Use the formal specifications of the semantics of Decl_0 to find the output produced by the following simple program if it is executed with 2 as input.

```
begin var x: int;  var y: int;  get x; y := x + 1; put y end
```

Use first the unlayered definitions in section 9.2, then the layered semantics given in section 9.3, and finally the typed semantics of section 9.5.

9.7.2 Another simple program

Repeat the assignment in the previous exercise on the following program:

```
begin
  var x: int;
  get x;
  begin
    var a: array[1 : x] of int;
    get a[x - 1];
    put a[x]
  end
end
```

Assume first that the input sequence contains only the two integers 3 and 5. Then see what the formal semantic specifications say should happen if $\langle 1, 2\rangle$ or $\langle 0, 2\rangle$ is used as input.

9.7.3 Output of arrays

Define the micro-level function

$$\mathsf{put} \in (State_{\perp} \times EV \to MV)$$

such that s.put(ev) is evaluated correctly even when ev is the denotation of an array.

9.7.4 Input of arrays

Define the micro-level function

$$\mathsf{get} \in (\mathit{State}_\perp \times \mathit{VV} \to \mathit{MV})$$

such that s.get($\mathcal{V}$[[arr]]) is evaluated correctly when arr is declared to be an array.

9.7.5 Static arrays

A *static array* is an array that has a size which may be computed before program execution. If a language allows only static arrays (and does not allow other dynamic data structures), every indexed variable may be assigned an address already at the macro-level. The micro-semantics for languages like Decl_0, Pascal and Fortran that only allow static arrays, is of course much simpler than for languages that allow dynamic data structures. In this exercise you are asked to define the semantics of a language that only allows static data structures.

Define the semantics of the language that is the result of restricting Decl_1 such that only integer literals are allowed as array bounds. Thus, we restrict the production for array vartypes to be as follows:

$$\langle \mathit{vartype} \rangle ::= \ldots \mid \textbf{array}\ (1 : \langle \mathit{literal} \rangle)\ \textbf{of}\ \langle \mathit{vartype} \rangle$$

It is, of course, also possible to use the semantics defined in section 9.6 for Decl_1 for this restricted language, but in this exercise you are asked to give a simpler definition in which every indexed variable is bound to an address at the macro-level. You may do this by first defining a macro-semantic algebra *A* that consists of 1) all addresses, 2) all sequences of addresses, 3) all sequences of sequences of addresses, etc. You should then redefine the semantic mapping $\mathcal{T}$ to map a vartype vtp to a tuple ⟨tp, ev, a⟩ where tp is a type, ev is a member of *EV* that evaluates to the initial value of a single element, and a is a member of *A* that consists of all addresses assigned to vtp. The value of

$$\mathcal{T}[\![\textbf{array}\ (1:2)\ \textbf{of array}\ (1:3)\ \textbf{of int}]\!](\mathsf{env})$$

should for instance be a tuple

$$\begin{aligned}\langle\ & \mathsf{Type'Array(Type'Array(Type'Int))},\\ & \mathsf{EV'Int(0)},\\ & \langle\langle \mathsf{adr}_1, \mathsf{adr}_2, \mathsf{adr}_3\rangle, \langle \mathsf{adr}_4, \mathsf{adr}_5, \mathsf{adr}_6\rangle\rangle\\ \rangle\ & \end{aligned}$$

where $\mathsf{adr}_1 = \mathsf{env.free\_adr}$ and $\mathsf{adr}_{i+1} = \mathsf{adr}_i\mathsf{.next}$. You should determine and specify suitable intermediate and micro-level functions.

9.7.6 Arrays with lower and upper bounds

Assume that array declarations specify not only upper bounds for indexes, but also lower bounds, i.e., that the BNF production for ⟨*vartype*⟩ is as follows:

$$\langle \mathit{vartype} \rangle ::= \ldots \mid \textbf{array}\ [\langle \mathit{expr} \rangle : \langle \mathit{expr} \rangle]\ \textbf{of}\ \langle \mathit{vartype} \rangle$$

Change the semantic specifications given in section 9.6 to cater for arrays with both lower and upper index bounds.

9.7.7 Typed semantics in ML

Implement a typed semantics of Decl_0 in ML.

9.7.8 Arrays in ML

Implement Decl_1 in ML.

Chapter 10 Procedures and functions

A *procedure* may be considered to be a parametrized imperative. Similarly, a *function* may be considered to be a parametrized expression. In this chapter we show how to specify the semantics of procedures and functions. After describing various kinds of parameter transmissions, we first specify the semantics of a programming language that allows procedures and functions with simple parameters. We then show how to specify the semantics of some variants of the language, in particular variants that allow various kinds of parameter transmission.

10.1 A taxonomy of parameter transmissions

Parameter transmissions may be classified according to three independent dimensions: *when*, *where* and *how* actual parameters are evaluated and their values are bound to formal parameters.

When: At which time (or times) is the actual parameter evaluated? There are several possibilities, of which the following three are the most realistic:

(1) *Once*, before the procedure body is evaluated. This is the method which is most often used, and in the sequel we will talk of it as *normal transmission*. In many languages (for instance Pascal) no other parameter transmission is available.

(2) *Every time* the formal parameter is accessed. Transmission by **name** - available, for example, in Algol and Simula - is of this kind.

(3) *At most once*, namely when the formal parameter is accessed for the first time during execution of the procedure body. If it should happen that the formal parameter not is accessed during an execution of the body, the actual parameter will not be evaluated at all.

This mode for parameter transmission is often called *lazy* evaluation, and is presently available in only a few programming languages.

In this chapter we mainly describe normal transmission of parameters, but in section 10.3 we show how to specify the semantics of **name** parameters and **lazy** parameters.

Where: In which environment is the actual parameter evaluated? There are three possibilities that are meaningful:

(1) The environment valid at the invocation. Used in most programming languages.

(2) The environment valid at the place where the procedure is declared (*floating* parameters).

(3) The environment valid at the place where the formal parameter is accessed (*fluid* parameters). Some interpreted languages, for instance $\TeX$ (which is not only a program that is used for document production, for instance to typeset this book, but also a complete programming language with many interesting and some unusual, even strange, features) evaluate parameters fluidly.

We will specify the semantics of only the first of these, and leave the specification of the last as an exercise.

How: What *coercion* is applied to the value of the actual parameter before it (or something else that depends upon the value of the actual parameter) is bound to the formal parameter? Various such functions - with numerous variants - are in use in common programming languages. Three of these:

(1) By **val**: The value of the actual parameter is bound to the formal parameter, which only may be used as a constant inside the body of the procedure.

(2) By **var**: A *reference* or *address* to the actual parameter - which must be a variable - is bound to the formal parameter. A **var**-transmitted formal parameter may be used as a variable - and hence assigned new values - inside the procedure body.

(3) By **value**: The value of the actual parameter is assigned as initial value to the formal parameter, which is treated as if it had been declared as a variable in an implicit block surrounding the procedure body.

In section 10.2 we specify the syntax and semantics of a simple language Proc_0 that allows **val**, **var** and **value** parameters. In the remaining sections we show how to specify the semantics of some variants of this language: Section 10.3 shows how to specify the semantics of **name** parameters, section 10.4 treats **lazy** parameters and section 10.5 shows how to specify the semantics of floating procedures.

10.2 Var, val and value parameters

In this section we show how to give a denotational definition of the semantics of a simple programming language that allows procedures with parameters transmitted by **var**, **val** or **value**.

10.2.1 Syntax

Let Proc_0 be a programming language with a syntax defined by the BNF productions in figure 10.1. The following is an example of a Proc_0 program:

```
begin
   var x: int := 0;
   rec
      val Fact = func(val p: int) if p < 2 then 1 else p*Fact(p-1);
      val Rep = proc(val n: int)
                    if 0 < n then put Fact(n); Rep(n-1) else skip fi;
                endproc;
      val Q = proc(val f: func(int): int)
                  put f(x); x := x - 1;
                  if 0 < x then Q(f) else skip fi;
              endproc
   endrec;
   get x;
   Rep(x);
   Q(Fact)
end
```

⟨*program*⟩	::=	⟨*imp*⟩	
⟨*imp*⟩	::=	**skip**	
	|	**put** ⟨*exp*⟩	
	|	**get** ⟨*exp*⟩	
	|	⟨*exp*⟩ := ⟨*exp*⟩	
	|	⟨*imp*⟩; ⟨*imp*⟩	
	|	**while** ⟨*exp*⟩ **do** ⟨*imp*⟩ **od**	
	|	**if** ⟨*exp*⟩ **then** ⟨*imp*⟩ **else** ⟨*imp*⟩ **fi**	
	|	**begin** ⟨*vardecl*⟩; ⟨*constdecl*⟩; ⟨*imp*⟩ **end**	(Block)
	|	⟨*exp*⟩(⟨*exp*⟩)	(Procedure invocation)
⟨*exp*⟩	::=	⟨*constant*⟩	
	|	⟨*ident*⟩	
	|	⟨*exp*⟩ ⟨*binop*⟩ ⟨*exp*⟩	
	|	⟨*unop*⟩ ⟨*exp*⟩	
	|	**if** ⟨*exp*⟩ **then** ⟨*exp*⟩ **else** ⟨*exp*⟩	
	|	⟨*exp*⟩(⟨*exp*⟩)	(Invocation of function)
⟨*constant*⟩	::=	⟨*literal*⟩	
	|	⟨*proc*⟩	
	|	⟨*func*⟩	
⟨*proc*⟩	::=	**proc** (⟨*parspec*⟩) ⟨*imp*⟩ **endproc**	(Procedure)
⟨*func*⟩	::=	**func** (⟨*parspec*⟩) ⟨*exp*⟩	(Function)
⟨*vardecl*⟩	::=	**var** ⟨*ident*⟩: ⟨*vartype*⟩ := ⟨*exp*⟩	(Decl. of variable)
	|	⟨*vardecl*⟩; ⟨*vardecl*⟩	
⟨*constdecl*⟩	::=	**val** ⟨*ident*⟩ = ⟨*constant*⟩	(Decl. of constant)
	|	**rec** ⟨*constdecl*⟩ **endrec**	(Recursive decl.)
	|	⟨*constdecl*⟩; ⟨*constdecl*⟩	
⟨*parspec*⟩	::=	⟨*parmod*⟩ ⟨*ident*⟩: ⟨*partype*⟩	(Param. spec.)
⟨*parmod*⟩	::=	**var**	(Parameter modes)
	|	**val**	
	|	**value**	
⟨*partype*⟩	::=	**int**	(Parameter type)
	|	**Bool**	
	|	**proc**(⟨*partype*⟩)	
	|	**func**(⟨*partype*⟩): ⟨*vartype*⟩	
⟨*vartype*⟩	::=	**int**	
	|	**Bool**	

Figure 10.1: BNF productions for Proc$_0$. Productions for the syntactic categories ⟨*literal*⟩, ⟨*unop*⟩, ⟨*binop*⟩ and ⟨*ident*⟩ are as for the While language

As shown by this example, Proc_0 is such that procedures and functions may be used as parameters to procedures and functions. Procedures and functions are, however, not so-called *first-class citizens*, which means that they may not be assigned to variables - and hence not stored - and that they may not be used as values of Proc_0 functions. The language is, furthermore, such that it allows the use of *nameless* procedures and functions. The following is, for instance, an invocation of a nameless procedure:

$$(\textbf{proc}(\textbf{var}\ \mathsf{n}\colon \textbf{int})\mathsf{n} := \mathsf{n} * 2\ \textbf{endproc})(\mathsf{x})$$

The effect of this imperative is equivalent to executing the imperative $\mathsf{x} := \mathsf{x} * 2$ (assuming that the invocation occurs in the scope of a variable x declared to be of type **int**).

The keywords **rec** and **endrec** are used to signify the start and end of declarations of recursive procedures and functions. It is possible to treat all procedures and functions as if they were recursive, and hence to avoid the use of **rec** and **endrec** (this is the case for instance in Algol). We have chosen not to do this here in order to show how declarations of nonrecursive procedures and functions may be treated in a simpler manner than how we specify the semantics of declarations of recursive abstractions (see page 239).

Observe that in Proc_0 only procedures and functions that have exactly one parameter are allowed. It is not difficult to extend the language such that procedures and functions with more than one parameter, or with no parameter at all, are allowed. This would, however, increase the number of concepts and the amount of typographical decorations that are needed to specify the syntax and semantics of the language - and hence increase the possibilities that a reader may get lost in a conceptual and typographical jungle - without a corresponding increase of the chances for comprehension of the main ideas used in the specification of the semantics of procedures and functions. We will therefore only specify the semantics of procedures and functions with single parameters, and leave it as an exercise to extend the specifications of the syntax and semantics of the language such that procedures and functions with more than (or less than) one parameter are allowed.

To reduce the number of details we have to describe, and to keep matters in correspondence with common practice, we allow the functions in Proc_0 to take only **val** parameters (but Proc_0 procedures may in addition take **var** and **value** parameters).

Observe that a declaration of a variable in Proc_0 contains an expression, which of course will be used to initialize the variable when the declaration is executed. This differs from Decl_0, where variables are initialized to a default value that depends solely on the type of the variable.

Another difference between Decl_0 and Proc_0 is that Decl_0 had a special syntactic category ***Var*** that contained everything that could be used on the left-hand side of assignment imperatives and as argument to

get imperatives. No such special syntax exists in Proc_0. Instead any expression may be used where Decl_0 demanded something in *Var*. But a runtime error would of course be the result of attempting to execute imperatives like **11** := x or **get** 10.

10.2.2 Some semantic ideas

The intuitive semantics of an invocation of a procedure is simple to describe: Execute the imperative that constitutes the body of the procedure in an environment in which the formal parameter has been bound (in a manner that depends upon which mode of transmission has been specified for the parameter) to the actual parameter. This description is, however, lacking in one important respect: it does not say which environment to use to determine the meaning of identifiers (other than the formal parameter) that may occur in the procedure body. Consider as an example a procedure that is declared inside the scope of a variable named xx and that has a body that assigns a new value to xx, and assume that an invocation of the procedure is inside the scope of another variable with the same name. The question is now: which of the two variables shall be assigned a new value as a result of the invocation?

The informal semantics of most programming languages, in particular those that belong to the Algol family, is such that the meaning of any identifier that occurs in the body of a procedure (function) is determined by the environment which is valid where the procedure (function) is declared, and not the environment that is valid where it is invoked. For most versions of Lisp, it is the opposite: the denotations of identifiers that occur in a body of a Lisp function are determined by the environment that is valid at the invocation of the function. This means that whereas the meanings of Algol procedures and functions are fixed once and for all by their declarations, the meaning of a Lisp function may vary from one invocation to another, and are hence sometimes said to be 'floating' or dynamic.

In this section we show how to specify the *statically scoped semantics* (i.e., 'Algol semantics') of procedures, and in section 10.5 below we specify the *dynamically scoped semantics* ('Lisp semantics') of procedures.

The main idea we use in the ensuing formal specification of the semantics of Proc_0, is to consider the denotation of a procedure to be a mapping that takes a parameter value as an argument and produces a state transformer – namely the static denotation (this concept is explained in section 9.3 on page 199) of the body of the procedure – as a result. Similarly, the denotation of a function is considered to be a mapping from a parameter value to the static denotation of the expression specified in the declaration of the function.

Partly in order to reduce the number of concepts and the length of the specification, and partly to concentrate on the semantics of pro-

Basic values:	B	$\stackrel{d}{=}$ *Int* + *Bool*
Storable values:	S	$\stackrel{d}{=} B$
Locations:	L	$\stackrel{d}{=}$ *Adr* $\stackrel{d}{=}$ *Int*
Denotations of constants:	C	$\stackrel{d}{=} B + PP + FF$
Expressible values:	E	$\stackrel{d}{=} C + L$
Denotable values:	D	$\stackrel{d}{=} E$ + Unbound: *Unit*
Function values:	F	$\stackrel{d}{=} B$
Parameter values:	P	$\stackrel{d}{=} B + L + PP + FF$
Parameter modes:	PM	$\stackrel{d}{=}$ Var: *Unit* + Val: *Unit* + Value: *Unit*
Denotations of procedures:	PP	$\stackrel{d}{=} [P_\perp \to MV]$
Denotations of functions:	FF	$\stackrel{d}{=} [P_\perp \to (State_\perp \to F_\perp)]$
Denotations of imperatives:	MV	$\stackrel{d}{=} (State_\perp \to State_\perp)$
Denotations of expressions:	EV	$\stackrel{d}{=} (State_\perp \to E_\perp)$
Denotations of declarations of variables:		
	VV	$\stackrel{d}{=} (State_\perp \to (Envir \times State_\perp))$
Denotations of operators:	UOV	$\stackrel{d}{=} (B_\perp \to B_\perp)$
	BOV	$\stackrel{d}{=} (B_\perp \times B_\perp \to B_\perp)$

Figure 10.2: Semantic algebras for the language Proc_0

cedures and functions, we give only an untyped specification of the semantics of Proc_0, and leave it as an exercise to define a typed specification of the semantics of the language.

10.2.3 Semantic algebras

The possibly most important part of the specification of the semantics of any programming language consists in the specification of algebras for each of the various kinds of values that may be manipulated by programs of the language. For most languages, we need one algebra for the values that may be bound to identifiers by declarations (by convention this algebra is given the name D), another for values that expressions may have (E), a third for values that may be stored (S), etc. These algebras - which may be said to be *characteristic* for the language - are defined in figure 10.2 for Proc_0.

It should be easy to see why we say that the algebras defined in figure 10.2 are characteristic for the language. An example: by defining P (parameter values) to consist not only of basic values B and locations L, but also of denotations of procedures PP and functions FF, we allow procedures and functions to be used as parameters to procedures and functions. Another example: By *not* letting L, PP and FF be addends of the algebra S, we specify that locations, procedures and functions are not storable, i.e., that they may not be assigned to variables. A third example: The algebra F of function values is defined to consist only of basic values, which means that functions may have neither locations, procedures nor functions as values. Many languages that allow the use of *pointers* have L as addend of both S and F. Some languages even have PP and FF as addends of S and F, thereby letting procedures and functions be first-class citizens (which means that they – or rather their denotations – may be assigned to variables and be used as values of functions).

Why the domain VV of denotations of variable declarations is defined the way we do in figure 10.2, is explained on page 240 below.

Observe that we define the algebra PP of denotations of procedures to consist of only the *continuous* functions mapping Ident to $MV = (\mathit{State}_\perp \to \mathit{State}_\perp)$. Similarly, FF is defined to consist of only the continuous functions that map P to $(\mathit{State}_\perp \to F_\perp)$. Had we not restricted membership in PP and FF in some manner, the equations given above could not have served as definitions of any algebras: no set of algebras would satisfy equations like those given above if we did not in some meaningful way restrict membership in the algebras PP and FF. To see why this is so, let us assume that we had defined PP to consist of *all* functions mapping P to MV. The algebra P would then satisfy the following equation:

$$P = AA + (P \to MV)$$

– where AA stands for $B + L + FF$. We may prove that *no* algebra P satisfies this equation. The first step in the proof consists in defining a certain function $\mathsf{f}^* \in (P \to MV)$. This function is defined by showing how to find $\mathsf{f}^*(\mathsf{p})$ for any $\mathsf{p} \in P = AA + (P \to MV)$:

- If $\mathsf{p} \in AA$, let $\mathsf{f}^*(\mathsf{p}) = \mathsf{mv}_0$, where mv_0 is some fixed element of MV.

- If p is in the $(P \to MV)$ addend of P, find first $\mathsf{mv}_p = \mathsf{p}(\mathsf{p})$, i.e., mv_p is the result of applying the function p to itself. Then choose an element mv_p' which is distinct from mv_p (this is always possible under the assumption that MV has at least two elements, which MV of course does), and let $\mathsf{f}^*(\mathsf{p}) = \mathsf{mv}_p'$.

It is easy to see that the function f^* we have defined is different from every function in the $(P \to MV)$ addend of P: Assume that f is any element of $(P \to MV)$. Then $\mathsf{f}^*(\mathsf{f}) = \mathsf{mv}_f' \neq \mathsf{mv}_f = \mathsf{f}(\mathsf{f})$. Thus, f^* differs from f for at least one argument, namely f, and f^* and f must hence be distinct functions. This means that f* cannot be a member of the $(P \rightarrow MV)$ addend of P: if it were, it would be different from itself. But by its definition f* *is* a function that maps P to MV. We must therefore conclude that P cannot possibly have as an addend the algebra of *all* functions that maps P to MV.

The arguments given here show that we must restrict membership in PP - and FF - in some way if we allow procedures and functions to be used indiscriminately as parameters to procedures and functions. In the definitions of PP and FF given in figure 10.2, we restrict PP and FF to consist only of continuous functions (the function f* constructed above is a discontinuous function). But even if we restrict membership in this way, it is not at all obvious that the equations claimed to be definitions of the characteristic algebras of Proc_0 really are solvable (think of them as a set of equations to be solved for D, E, P, etc.). In chapter 14 we will go more deeply into these matters, and apply some nontrivial mathematics to show that equations like those given here *are* solvable in a certain sense, and even show how solutions may be constructed.

Instead of restricting *membership* in PP and FF, we could have avoided mathematical problems in the definitions of the characteristic algebras of our language (and thus escaped the need for the mathematics of chapter 14) by restricting the *use* of PP and FF. The most brutal way of doing this would be simply to disallow the use of procedures and functions as parameters. This is, however, much too restrictive: very many programming languages do - for good reasons - allow procedures and functions to be used as parameters, and we would like to be able to specify the semantics of every programming language feature that is in common use. A much weaker restriction would be to disallow that procedures were allowed to take themselves as parameters. Disallowing this possibility, which is legal in many languages in the Algol family but of questionable use (the author of this book cannot remember having seen any program in any of the languages of the Algol family that used procedures that received themselves as parameters except in clever examples designed either to illustrate this peculiar feature or to test that given compilers handle such procedures correctly; but the feature is of greater interest in Lisp), would make it possible to consider the equations for the characteristic algebras to be inductive definitions, similar to how we treated recursive algebra definitions in section 9.6.2.2 on page 219.

10.2.4 Semantic mappings

To specify the semantic of Proc_0, we need a semantic mapping for each of the syntactic categories of the language. Names and signatures for these mappings may be found in figure 10.3.

Observe that in the list of semantic mappings given in figure 10.3, there are no mappings for the syntactic categories *Partype* and *Vartype*. The reason for this is that in order to reduce the number of details

$$
\begin{array}{llll}
\mathcal{P} & \in (\mathit{Prog} & \rightarrow & (\mathit{Input} \rightarrow \mathit{Output}_{\perp})) \\
\mathcal{M} & \in (\mathit{Imp} & \rightarrow & (\mathit{Envir} \rightarrow \mathit{MV})) \\
\mathcal{E} & \in (\mathit{Exp} & \rightarrow & (\mathit{Envir} \rightarrow \mathit{EV})) \\
\mathcal{C} & \in (\mathit{Constant} & \rightarrow & (\mathit{Envir} \rightarrow \mathit{C})) \\
\mathcal{PP} & \in (\mathit{Proc} & \rightarrow & (\mathit{Envir} \rightarrow \mathit{PP})) \\
\mathcal{FF} & \in (\mathit{Func} & \rightarrow & (\mathit{Envir} \rightarrow \mathit{FF})) \\
\mathcal{VD} & \in (\mathit{Vardecl} & \rightarrow & (\mathit{Envir} \rightarrow \mathit{VV})) \\
\mathcal{CD} & \in (\mathit{Constdecl} & \rightarrow & (\mathit{Envir} \rightarrow \mathit{Envir})) \\
\mathcal{PM} & \in (\mathit{Parmod} & \rightarrow & (\mathit{Envir} \rightarrow \mathit{PM})) \\
\mathcal{UO} & \in (\mathit{Unop} & \rightarrow & (B \rightarrow B)) \\
\mathcal{BO} & \in (\mathit{Binop} & \rightarrow & ((B \times B) \rightarrow B))
\end{array}
$$

Figure 10.3: Signatures of the semantic mappings for Proc_0. The algebra $\mathit{Envir} = \mathcal{F}(\mathit{Ident} \rightarrow D)$ of environments is as for Decl_0

to be described, we specify only an untyped semantics of Proc_0 in this chapter. Should we desire to give a typed semantics, and specify which constructs are correctly typed and which are not, we would introduce an algebra of type labels, for instance as follows:

$$\mathit{Type} \stackrel{d}{=} \mathsf{Int}{:}\ \mathit{Unit} \ + \ \mathsf{Bool}{:}\ \mathit{Unit} \ + \ \mathsf{Proc}{:}\ \mathit{Type} \ + \ \mathsf{Func}{:}\ \mathit{Type} \times \mathit{Type}$$

and define semantic mappings $\mathcal{VT}$ and $\mathcal{PT}$ for the syntactic categories *Vartype* and *Partype*. These mappings could be given the following signatures:

$$
\begin{array}{l}
\mathcal{VT} \in (\mathit{Vartype} \rightarrow \mathit{Type}) \\
\mathcal{PT} \in (\mathit{Partype} \rightarrow \mathit{Type})
\end{array}
$$

We leave it as an exercise to specify a typed semantics for Proc_0.

In the rest of this section we define semantic mappings for Proc_0. The semantic mappings for programs ($\mathcal{P}$) and for unary and binary operators ($\mathcal{UO}$ and $\mathcal{BO}$, respectively) are similar to semantic mappings defined for Decl_0, and we do not repeat their definitions here.

Semantics of constants A constant in Proc_0 is either a literal, a procedure or a function. Its denotation, which is an element of the semantic domain C, may be found by the semantic mapping $\mathcal{C}$ which is defined as follows:

$$
\begin{array}{lll}
\mathcal{C}[\![\mathsf{lit}]\!](\mathsf{env}) = \mathcal{A}[\![\mathsf{lit}]\!] & & \textit{for any literal } \mathsf{lit} \\
\mathcal{C}[\![\mathsf{proc}]\!](\mathsf{env}) = \mathcal{PP}[\![\mathsf{proc}]\!](\mathsf{env}) & & \textit{for any procedure } \mathsf{proc} \\
\mathcal{C}[\![\mathsf{func}]\!](\mathsf{env}) = \mathcal{FF}[\![\mathsf{func}]\!](\mathsf{env}) & & \textit{for any function } \mathsf{func}
\end{array}
$$

The semantic mapping $\mathcal{A}$ is as defined in previous chapters, the two semantic mappings $\mathcal{P}$ and $\mathcal{F}$ are defined on page 241 below.

Semantics of declarations of constants It is most convenient to let the denotation of a sequence of one or more constant declarations be a function that maps an environment env (the environment valid before the declarations) to a new environment env' that binds the identifiers of the declarations, but that binds no other identifiers. Observe that this differs from the treatment of declarations in chapter 9, where we defined the denotation of a constant declaration to be a function that maps an initial environment to an environment which is an *extension* of the initial environment. The reason for the difference is to make it easier to define the semantics of recursive declarations.

We specify the denotation of a single *nonrecursive* constant declaration '**val** id = con' to be a function that maps an initial environment env to an environment env' that binds the identifier id to $\mathcal{C}[\![\text{con}]\!](\text{env})$, i.e., to the denotation of the constant con in the original environment env, and that binds no other identifiers.

The semantic mapping $\mathcal{CD}$ may be used to find the denotations of constant declarations. Adhering to the remarks above, we define $\mathcal{CD}$ as follows for nonrecursive constant declarations:

$$\begin{aligned}
\mathcal{CD}[\![\textbf{val}\ \text{id} = \text{con}]\!](\text{env}) &= \text{Envir'Void}\,.\,\text{bind}(\text{id},\ \mathcal{C}[\![\text{con}]\!](\text{env}))\\
\mathcal{CD}[\![\text{cd}_1;\ \text{cd}_2]\!](\text{env}) &= \mathcal{CD}[\![\text{cd}_1]\!](\text{env}) + \mathcal{CD}[\![\text{cd}_2]\!](\text{env})
\end{aligned}$$

Envir'Void is the empty environment (defined in section 9.2.1.2 on page 192) in which every identifier is unbound. The *sum* $\text{env}_1 + \text{env}_2$ of two environments env_1 and env_2 is an environment defined as follows:

$$\begin{aligned}
\text{env}_1 + \text{env}_2 \overset{d}{=} \lambda \text{id} \in \mathit{Ident}\colon \textbf{case}\ &\text{env}_2(\text{id})\ \textbf{of}\ D\colon\\
&\text{Unbound} \Rightarrow \text{env}_1(\text{id})\\
&\textbf{otherwise} \Rightarrow \text{d}
\end{aligned}$$

The denotation of a *recursive* constant declaration '**rec** cd **endrec**', where cd is a sequence containing one or more constant declarations, is a little more complex to define. We would like the definition to be such that the value of $\mathcal{CD}[\![\textbf{rec}\ \text{cd}\ \textbf{endrec}]\!](\text{env})$ should be an environment env* that satisfies the following equation:

$$\text{env}^* = \mathcal{CD}[\![\textbf{rec}\ \text{cd}\ \textbf{endrec}]\!](\text{env} + \text{env}^*)$$

This means that env* should be a fixpoint of the function $\lambda\text{env}'\colon \mathcal{CD}[\![\text{cd}]\!](\text{env} + \text{env}')$, which means that we may use the fixpoint operator to define the denotation of a recursive constant declaration:

$$\mathcal{CD}[\![\textbf{rec}\ \text{cd}\ \textbf{endrec}]\!](\text{env}) = Y_{\mathit{Envir}}(\lambda\text{env}'\colon \mathcal{CD}[\![\text{cd}]\!](\text{env} + \text{env}'))$$

In order to reduce the amount of details, we refrain from proving that the function $\lambda\text{env}'\colon \mathcal{CD}[\![\text{cd}]\!](\text{env} + \text{env}')$ is continuous.

Semantics of declarations of variables In a programming language that only allows declarations of simple variables, like for instance Decl_0, it is possible to let the environment keep track of which addresses are in use. In such languages, a declaration of a variable may then be most easily handled by first asking the environment for a free (i.e., new and unused) address, and then binding the variable to this address.

This simple scheme is, however, not sufficient for languages that allow recursive procedures (like Proc_0 does) or other constructs that may be used to create an unlimited number of simultaneously existing block instances or other objects having local variables. In such cases, where the number of variables that are in use by a program may vary unpredictably and unboundedly during program execution, the storage allocation cannot be performed before the program is executed, but must be done dynamically, at 'runtime'. This means that we have to use the state to keep track of which addresses are in use at any time. In order to do this, we extend the algebra ***State*** to include two new functions. The first of these may be used to ask a state for a free address, the second to *allocate* a previously unused address in a state such that it no longer may be given as a free address for the state. In concrete and realistic implementations of languages with dynamic storage allocation, we would of course also need functions for *de-allocation*, i.e., freeing, of addresses. But in an abstract specification of the semantics of a programming language, we are free to assume that the store is unbounded in size and that an unlimited set of addresses is available, and that we therefore never have to de-allocate any storage location.

A simple way of defining the two new functions is by first redefining the algebra ***State*** such that a state is a tuple that consists not only of input and output sequences in and out and a store h, but also of an integer max_adr, which is the maximum address in use at any time. The two new functions may then be defined as follows:

$$\langle \mathsf{in},\ \mathsf{out},\ \mathsf{h},\ \mathsf{max\_adr} \rangle\,.\,\mathsf{free\_address} \stackrel{d}{=} \mathsf{max\_adr} + 1$$
$$\langle \mathsf{in},\ \mathsf{out},\ \mathsf{h},\ \mathsf{max\_adr} \rangle\,.\,\mathsf{allocate(adr)} \stackrel{d}{=} \langle \mathsf{in},\ \mathsf{out},\ \mathsf{h},\ \mathsf{max(adr,\ max\_adr)} \rangle$$

After these deliberations, we specify the denotation of a variable declaration to be a function that maps an environment (the environment as it is before the declaration) to an element of the semantic domain *VV*, i.e., to a function that maps a state (the state before the execution of the declaration) to a new environment and a new state. The new environment binds the names of the variables that are declared (each will be bound to an address that is free in the initial state); the new state is the result of allocating the new addresses and assigning initial values to these addresses.

The semantic mapping $\mathcal{VD}$ that specifies the semantics of variable declarations may hence be defined as follows:

$$\mathcal{VD}[\![\textbf{var}\ \mathsf{id: vtp := exp}]\!](\mathsf{env}) = \mathsf{VV'Var}(\mathsf{id}, \mathcal{E}[\![\mathsf{exp}]\!](\mathsf{env}))$$
$$\mathcal{VD}[\![\mathsf{vd_1; vd_2}]\!](\mathsf{env}) = \mathsf{VV'Seq}(\mathcal{VD}[\![\mathsf{vd_1}]\!](\mathsf{env}), \mathcal{VD}[\![\mathsf{vd_2}]\!](\mathsf{env}))$$

The two intermediate-level functions VV'Var $\in$ $(\mathit{Ident} \times \mathit{EV} \to \mathit{VV})$ and VV'Seq $\in$ $(\mathit{VV} \times \mathit{VV} \to \mathit{VV})$ used above may be defined as follows:

$$\begin{aligned}
\mathsf{VV'Var(id, ev)} &\stackrel{d}{=} \underline{\lambda} \mathsf{s} \in \mathit{State}_\perp\!: \textbf{let}\ \mathsf{a = s.free.address}\ \textbf{in} \\
&\qquad \langle \mathsf{Envir'Void.bind(id, a)}, \\
&\qquad\ \mathsf{s.allocate(a)} \\
&\qquad\quad \mathsf{.assign(a, deref(s, ev(s)))} \rangle \\
\mathsf{VV'Seq(vd_1, vd_2)} &\stackrel{d}{=} \underline{\lambda} \mathsf{s} \in \mathit{State}_\perp\!: \textbf{let}\ \langle \mathsf{env_1, s_1} \rangle = \mathsf{vd_1(s)}\ \textbf{in} \\
&\qquad \textbf{let}\ \langle \mathsf{env_2, s_2} \rangle = \mathsf{vd_2(s_1)}\ \textbf{in} \\
&\qquad\quad \langle \mathsf{env_1 + env_2, s_2} \rangle
\end{aligned}$$

The auxiliary function deref $\in$ $((\mathit{State}_\perp \times E_\perp) \to B_\perp)$ used in the definition of VV'Var is defined as follows for any s $\in$ *State* and e $\in$ E:

$$\begin{aligned}
\mathsf{deref(s, e)} \stackrel{d}{=} &\ \textbf{if}\ \mathsf{e} \in L\ \textbf{then}\ \mathsf{s.access(e)}\ \textbf{else} \\
&\ \textbf{if}\ \mathsf{e} \in B\ \textbf{then}\ \mathsf{e} \\
&\ \textbf{else}\ \perp_B
\end{aligned}$$

Semantics of procedures and functions The denotations of procedures and functions may be found by the two semantic mappings $\mathcal{PP}$ and $\mathcal{FF}$:

$$\begin{aligned}
&\mathcal{PP}[\![\textbf{proc}(\mathsf{pmod\ pid: ptyp})\ \mathsf{imp}\ \textbf{endproc}]\!](\mathsf{env}) \\
&\qquad = \underline{\lambda} \mathsf{p} \in P_\perp\!:\ \mathsf{MV'Proc}(\mathcal{M}[\![\mathsf{imp}]\!], \mathsf{env}, \mathcal{PM}[\![\mathsf{pmod}]\!], \mathsf{pid, p}) \\
&\mathcal{FF}[\![\textbf{func}(\mathsf{pmod\ pid: ptyp})\ \mathsf{exp}]\!](\mathsf{env}) \\
&\qquad = \underline{\lambda} \mathsf{p} \in P_\perp\!:\ \mathsf{EV'Func}(\mathcal{E}[\![\mathsf{exp}]\!], \mathsf{env, pid, p})
\end{aligned}$$

The semantic mapping $\mathcal{PM}$ $\in$ $(\mathit{Parmod} \to (\mathit{Envir} \to \mathit{PM}))$ used here is very simple to define for each element in *Parmod*. The value of $\mathcal{PM}[\![\textbf{var}]\!]$ is, for instance, equal to Var. The other cases are equally trivial.

The intermediate-level functions MV'Proc and EV'Func used in the definitions of $\mathcal{PP}$ and $\mathcal{FF}$ have signatures:

$$\begin{aligned}
\mathsf{MV'Proc} &\in ((\mathit{Envir} \to \mathit{MV}) \times \mathit{Envir} \times \mathit{PM} \times \mathit{Ident} \times P \to \mathit{MV}) \\
\mathsf{EV'Func} &\in ((\mathit{Envir} \to \mathit{EV}) \times \mathit{Envir} \times \mathit{Ident} \times P \to \mathit{EV})
\end{aligned}$$

and are defined as follows:

$$\begin{aligned}
&\mathsf{MV'Proc(me, env, pm, pid, p)} \\
&\ \stackrel{d}{=} \underline{\lambda} \mathsf{s} \in \mathit{State}_\perp\!: \textbf{case}\ \mathsf{pm}\ \textbf{of}\ \mathit{PM} \\
&\qquad\qquad \mathsf{Val} \quad \Rightarrow \mathsf{me(env.bind(pid, deref(s, p)))(s)} \\
&\qquad\qquad \mathsf{Var} \quad \Rightarrow \textbf{if}\ \mathsf{p} \in \mathsf{L}\ \textbf{then}\ \mathsf{me(env.bind(pid, p))(s)}
\end{aligned}$$

$$
\begin{array}{ll}
 & \textbf{else} \ \perp_{State} \\
\text{Value} \Rightarrow & \textbf{let } a = s.\text{free\_adr } \textbf{in} \\
 & \textbf{let } s' = s.\text{allocate}(a).\text{assign}(a, \text{deref}(s, p)) \\
 & \textbf{in } \text{me}(\text{env}.\text{bind}(\text{pid}, a))(s')
\end{array}
$$

$$
\begin{array}{l}
\text{EV'Func}(\text{ee}, \text{env}, \text{pid}, p) \\
\quad \stackrel{d}{=} \underline{\lambda} s \in State_{\perp}\text{: } \text{ee}(\text{env}.\text{bind}(\text{pid}, \text{deref}(s, p)))(s)
\end{array}
$$

Observe that the function **EV'Func** does not take a parameter mode as one of its arguments. The reason for this is that at the end of section 10.2.1, we stipulated that functions in the language Proc_0 are allowed to take only **val** parameters.

Semantics of expressions The semantic mapping $\mathcal{E}$ may be defined by induction on the syntactic complexity of expressions as follows:

$$
\begin{array}{ll}
\mathcal{E}[\![\text{con}]\!](\text{env}) & = \text{EV'In}(\mathcal{C}[\![\text{con}]\!](\text{env})) \\
\mathcal{E}[\![\text{id}]\!](\text{env}) & = \textbf{case } \text{env}(\text{id}) \textbf{ of } D\text{: e } \textbf{in } E \quad \Rightarrow \text{EV'In}(e) \\
 & \qquad\qquad\qquad\qquad\quad \text{Unbound} \Rightarrow \text{EV'Error} \\
\mathcal{E}[\![\text{uop ex}]\!](\text{env}) & = \text{EV'Unop}(\mathcal{UO}[\![\text{uop}]\!], \mathcal{E}[\![\text{ex}]\!](\text{env})) \\
\mathcal{E}[\![\text{ex}_1 \text{ bop ex}_2]\!](\text{env}) & = \text{EV'Binop}(\mathcal{BO}[\![\text{bop}]\!], \mathcal{E}[\![\text{ex}_1]\!](\text{env}), \\
 & \qquad\qquad\qquad\qquad\qquad\quad \mathcal{E}[\![\text{ex}_2]\!](\text{env})) \\
\mathcal{E}[\![\text{fx}(\text{px})]\!](\text{env}) & = \text{EV'Call}(\mathcal{E}[\![\text{fx}]\!](\text{env}), \mathcal{E}[\![\text{px}]\!](\text{env}))
\end{array}
$$

Several intermediate-level functions are used here. They have the following signatures:

$$
\begin{array}{ll}
\text{EV'In} & \in (E \to EV) \\
\text{EV'Error} & \in EV \\
\text{EV'Unop} & \in ((UOV \times EV) \to EV) \\
\text{EV'Binop} & \in ((BOV \times (EV \times EV)) \to EV) \\
\text{EV'Call} & \in ((EV \times EV) \to EV)
\end{array}
$$

and may be defined as follows:

$$
\begin{array}{lll}
\text{EV'In}(e) & \stackrel{d}{=} & \underline{\lambda} s \in State_{\perp}\text{: e} \\
\text{EV'Error} & \stackrel{d}{=} & \underline{\lambda} s \in State_{\perp}\text{: } \perp_E \\
\text{EV'Unop}(\text{uov}, \text{ev}) & \stackrel{d}{=} & \underline{\lambda} s \in State_{\perp}\text{: uov}(\text{deref}(s, \text{ev}(s))) \\
\text{EV'Binop}(\text{bov}, \text{ev}_1, \text{ev}_2) & \stackrel{d}{=} & \underline{\lambda} s \in State_{\perp}\text{: bov}(\text{deref}(s, \text{ev}_1(s)), \\
 & & \qquad\qquad\qquad \text{deref}(s, \text{ev}_2(s))) \\
\text{EV'Call}(\text{fv}, \text{av}) & \stackrel{d}{=} & \underline{\lambda} s \in State_{\perp}\text{: } \textbf{case } \text{fv}(s) \textbf{ of } E\text{:} \\
 & & \qquad\qquad\qquad \text{ff} \in FF\text{: } \text{ff}(\text{av}(s))(s) \\
 & & \qquad\qquad\qquad \textbf{otherwise}\text{: } \perp_E
\end{array}
$$

Semantics of imperatives The semantic mapping $\mathcal{M}$ may be defined as follows by induction on the syntactic complexity of imperatives:

$$
\begin{aligned}
&\mathcal{M}[\![\textbf{skip}]\!](\mathsf{env}) && = \mathsf{MV'Skip}\\
&\mathcal{M}[\![\textbf{put}\ \mathsf{exp}]\!](\mathsf{env}) && = \mathsf{MV'Put}(\mathcal{E}[\![\mathsf{exp}]\!](\mathsf{env}))\\
&\mathcal{M}[\![\textbf{get}\ \mathsf{exp}]\!](\mathsf{env}) && = \mathsf{MV'Get}(\mathcal{E}[\![\mathsf{exp}]\!](\mathsf{env}))\\
&\mathcal{M}[\![\mathsf{lex} := \mathsf{rex}]\!](\mathsf{env}) && = \mathsf{MV'Assign}(\mathcal{E}[\![\mathsf{lex}]\!](\mathsf{env}),\ \mathcal{E}[\![\mathsf{rex}]\!](\mathsf{env}))\\
&\mathcal{M}[\![\mathsf{imp}_1;\ \mathsf{imp}_2]\!](\mathsf{env}) && = \mathsf{MV'Seq}(\mathcal{M}[\![\mathsf{imp}_1]\!](\mathsf{env}),\ \mathcal{M}[\![\mathsf{imp}_2]\!](\mathsf{env}))\\
&\mathcal{M}[\![\textbf{if}\ \mathsf{bx}\ \textbf{then}\ \mathsf{imp}_1\ \textbf{else}\ \mathsf{imp}_2\ \textbf{fi}]\!](\mathsf{env})\\
& && = \mathsf{MV'Cond}(\mathcal{E}[\![\mathsf{bx}]\!](\mathsf{env}),\ \mathcal{M}[\![\mathsf{imp}_1]\!](\mathsf{env}),\\
& && \qquad\qquad \mathcal{M}[\![\mathsf{imp}_2]\!](\mathsf{env}))\\
&\mathcal{M}[\![\textbf{while}\ \mathsf{bx}\ \textbf{do}\ \mathsf{imp}\ \textbf{od}]\!](\mathsf{env})\\
& && = \mathsf{MV'While}(\mathcal{E}[\![\mathsf{bx}]\!](\mathsf{env}),\ \mathcal{M}[\![\mathsf{imp}]\!](\mathsf{env}))\\
&\mathcal{M}[\![\textbf{begin}\ \mathsf{vardecl};\ \mathsf{constdecl};\ \mathsf{imp}\ \textbf{end}]\!](\mathsf{env})\\
& && = \mathsf{MV'Block}(\mathsf{env},\ \mathcal{VD}[\![\mathsf{vardecl}]\!](\mathsf{env}),\\
& && \qquad \mathcal{CD}[\![\mathsf{constdecl}]\!],\ \mathcal{M}[\![\mathsf{imp}]\!])\\
&\mathcal{M}[\![\mathsf{rx}(\mathsf{px})]\!](\mathsf{env}) && = \mathsf{MV'Call}(\mathcal{E}[\![\mathsf{rx}]\!](\mathsf{env}),\ \mathcal{E}[\![\mathsf{px}]\!](\mathsf{env}))
\end{aligned}
$$

The intermediate-level functions used in these definitions may be defined as follows:

$$
\begin{aligned}
&\mathsf{MV'Skip} && \stackrel{d}{=} \underline{\lambda}\mathsf{s} \in \mathit{State}_\perp:\ \mathsf{s}\\
&\mathsf{MV'Put}(\mathsf{ev}) && \stackrel{d}{=} \underline{\lambda}\mathsf{s} \in \mathit{State}_\perp:\ \mathsf{s.put}(\mathsf{deref}(\mathsf{s},\ \mathsf{ev}(\mathsf{s})))\\
&\mathsf{MV'Get}(\mathsf{ev}) && \stackrel{d}{=} \underline{\lambda}\mathsf{s} \in \mathit{State}_\perp:\ \mathsf{s.get}(\mathsf{ref}(\mathsf{ev}(\mathsf{s})))\\
&\mathsf{MV'Assign}(\mathsf{lv},\ \mathsf{rv}) && \stackrel{d}{=} \underline{\lambda}\mathsf{s} \in \mathit{State}_\perp:\ \mathsf{s.assign}(\mathsf{ref}(\mathsf{lv}(\mathsf{s})),\ \mathsf{deref}(\mathsf{s},\ \mathsf{rv}(\mathsf{s})))\\
&\mathsf{MV'Seq}(\mathsf{mv}_1,\ \mathsf{mv}_2) && \stackrel{d}{=} \underline{\lambda}\mathsf{s} \in \mathit{State}_\perp:\ \mathsf{mv}_2(\mathsf{mv}_1(\mathsf{s}))\\
&\mathsf{MV'Cond}(\mathsf{ev},\ \mathsf{mv}_1,\ \mathsf{mv}_2)\\
& && \stackrel{d}{=} \underline{\lambda}\mathsf{s} \in \mathit{State}_\perp:\ \textbf{case}\ \mathsf{deref}(\mathsf{s},\ \mathsf{ev}(\mathsf{s}))\ \textbf{of}\ E:\\
& && \quad \mathsf{b} \in \mathit{Bool} \Rightarrow \textbf{if}\ \mathsf{b}\ \textbf{then}\ \mathsf{mv}_1(\mathsf{s})\ \textbf{else}\ \mathsf{mv}_2(\mathsf{s})\\
& && \quad \textbf{otherwise} \Rightarrow \perp_{\mathit{State}}\\
&\mathsf{MV'While}(\mathsf{ev},\ \mathsf{mv}) && \stackrel{d}{=} Y_{MV}(\lambda \mathsf{w} \in MV\!: \mathsf{MV'Cond}(\mathsf{ev},\ \mathsf{MV'Seq}(\mathsf{mv},\ \mathsf{w}),\\
& && \qquad\qquad \mathsf{MV'Skip}))\\
&\mathsf{MV'Call}(\mathsf{pv},\ \mathsf{av}) && \stackrel{d}{=} \underline{\lambda}\mathsf{s} \in \mathit{State}_\perp:\ \textbf{case}\ \mathsf{pv}(\mathsf{s})\ \textbf{of}\ E:\\
& && \quad \mathsf{pp} \in PP\!:\ \mathsf{pp}(\mathsf{av}(\mathsf{s}))(\mathsf{s})\\
& && \quad \textbf{otherwise}\!:\ \perp_{\mathit{State}}
\end{aligned}
$$

The function MV'Block, which is used to specify the denotation of a block, has the following signature:

$$\mathsf{MV'Block} \in (\mathit{Envir} \times VV \times (\mathit{Envir} \to \mathit{Envir}) \times (\mathit{Envir} \to MV) \to MV)$$

and is defined as follows:

$$
\begin{aligned}
&\mathsf{MV'Block}(\mathsf{env},\ \mathsf{vv},\ \mathsf{edc},\ \mathsf{mve})\\
&\quad \stackrel{d}{=} \underline{\lambda}\mathsf{s} \in \mathit{State}_\perp\!:\ \textbf{let}\ \langle \mathsf{env}_v,\ \mathsf{s}_1\rangle = \mathsf{vv}(\mathsf{s})\ \textbf{in}\\
&\qquad\qquad\qquad\qquad \textbf{let}\ \mathsf{env}_c = \mathsf{edc}(\mathsf{env} + \mathsf{env}_v)\ \textbf{in}\\
&\qquad\qquad\qquad\qquad \mathsf{mve}(\mathsf{env} + \mathsf{env}_v + \mathsf{env}_c)(\mathsf{s}_1)
\end{aligned}
$$

The auxiliary function ref $\in (E_\perp \to L_\perp)$ used in the definitions of MV'Get and MV'Assign is defined as follows for any $\mathsf{e} \in E$:

$$\mathsf{ref}(\mathsf{e}) \stackrel{d}{=} \textbf{if}\ \mathsf{e} \in L\ \textbf{then}\ \mathsf{e}\ \textbf{else}\ \perp_L$$

10.2.5 Two simple examples

A variable and a constant The following very simple example illustrates how declarations of variables and integer constants may be handled in Proc_0.

$$\textbf{begin var } \mathsf{m}\text{: } \textbf{int} := 2;\ \textbf{val } \mathsf{c} = 1;\ \mathsf{put}(\mathsf{m} + \mathsf{c})\ \textbf{end}$$

The effect of executing this imperative should of course be that the integer 3 is appended to the output sequence. Let us see if this will be the result if we follow the definitions in the previous section to the letter. If env_0 is any environment and s_0 any state, we get:

$$\begin{aligned}&\mathcal{M}[\![\textbf{begin var } \mathsf{m}\text{: } \textbf{int} := 2;\ \textbf{val } \mathsf{c} = 1;\ \mathsf{put(m + c)}\ \textbf{end}]\!](\mathsf{env}_0)(\mathsf{s}_0)\\ &\quad = \mathsf{MV'Block}(\mathsf{env}_0, \mathsf{vv}_m, \mathsf{edc}_c, \mathsf{mve}_p)(\mathsf{s}_0)\end{aligned}$$

where

$$\begin{aligned}\mathsf{vv}_m &\stackrel{d}{=} \mathcal{VD}[\![\textbf{var } \mathsf{m}\text{: } \textbf{int} := 2]\!](\mathsf{env}_0)\\ &= \mathsf{VV'Var}(\mathsf{m}, \mathcal{E}[\![2]\!](\mathsf{env}_0))\\ &= \mathsf{VV'Var}(\mathsf{m}, \mathsf{EV'In}(2))\end{aligned}$$

$$\begin{aligned}\mathsf{edc}_c &\stackrel{d}{=} \mathcal{CD}[\![\textbf{val } \mathsf{c} = 1]\!]\\ &= \lambda \mathsf{env'}\text{: } \mathsf{Envir'Void.bind(c, 1)}\end{aligned}$$

$$\begin{aligned}\mathsf{mve}_p &\stackrel{d}{=} \mathcal{M}[\![\mathsf{put(m + c)}]\!]\\ &= \lambda \mathsf{env'}\text{: } \mathsf{MV'Put}(\mathcal{E}[\![\mathsf{m + c}]\!](\mathsf{env'}))\\ &= \lambda \mathsf{env'}\text{: } \mathsf{MV'Put(EV'Binop(BOV'Plus,}\\ &\qquad\qquad \mathsf{EV'In(env'(m)), EV'In(env'(c))))}\end{aligned}$$

Using the definition of MV'Block on page 243 we then get

$$\begin{aligned}&\mathcal{M}[\![\textbf{begin var } \mathsf{m}\text{: } \textbf{int} := 2;\ \textbf{val } \mathsf{c} = 1;\ \mathsf{put(m + c)}\ \textbf{end}]\!](\mathsf{env}_0)(\mathsf{s}_0)\\ &\quad = \mathsf{MV'Block}(\mathsf{env}_0, \mathsf{vv}_m, \mathsf{edc}_c, \mathsf{mve}_p)(\mathsf{s}_0)\\ &\quad = \textbf{let } \langle \mathsf{env}_m, \mathsf{s}_1\rangle = \mathsf{vv}_m(\mathsf{s}_0)\\ &\qquad\qquad\qquad\quad = \mathsf{VV'Var(m, EV'In(2))}(\mathsf{s}_0)\\ &\qquad\qquad\qquad\quad = \langle \mathsf{Envir'Void.bind}(\mathsf{m}, \mathsf{a}_m),\\ &\qquad\qquad\qquad\qquad \mathsf{s}_0\mathsf{.allocate}(\mathsf{a}_m)\mathsf{.assign}(\mathsf{a}_m, 2)\rangle\\ &\qquad\qquad\qquad\qquad \text{where } \mathsf{a}_m = \mathsf{s}_0\mathsf{.free\_address}\\ &\qquad \textbf{let } \mathsf{env}_c = \mathsf{edc}_c(\mathsf{env}_0 + \mathsf{env}_m)\\ &\qquad\qquad\quad = \mathsf{Envir'Void.bind(c, 1)}\\ &\qquad \textbf{in } \mathsf{mve}_p(\mathsf{env}_b)(\mathsf{s}_1)\\ &\qquad\quad \text{where } \mathsf{env}_b \stackrel{d}{=} \mathsf{env}_0 + \mathsf{env}_m + \mathsf{env}_c\\ &\quad = \mathsf{MV'Put(EV'Binop(BOV'Plus, EV'In}(\mathsf{env}_b(\mathsf{m})),\\ &\qquad\qquad\qquad\qquad\qquad \mathsf{EV'In}(\mathsf{env}_b(\mathsf{c}))))(\mathsf{s}_1)\\ &\quad = \mathsf{s}_1\mathsf{.put(deref}(\mathsf{s}_1, \mathsf{EV'Binop(BOV'Plus, EV'In}(\mathsf{a}_m),\\ &\qquad\qquad\qquad\qquad\qquad \mathsf{EV'In}(2))(\mathsf{s}_1)))\\ &\quad = \mathsf{s}_1\mathsf{.put(deref}(\mathsf{s}_1, \mathsf{BOV'Plus(EV'In}(\mathsf{a}_m)(\mathsf{s}_1), \mathsf{EV'In}(1)(\mathsf{s}_1))))\\ &\quad = \mathsf{s}_1\mathsf{.put(deref}(\mathsf{s}_1, \mathsf{BOV'Plus}(\mathsf{s}_1\mathsf{.access}(\mathsf{a}_m), 2)))\end{aligned}$$

$$
\begin{aligned}
&= \mathsf{s}_1\,.\,\mathsf{put}(\mathsf{deref}(\mathsf{s}_1,\ \mathsf{BOV'Plus}(2,\ 1)))\\
&= \mathsf{s}_1\,.\,\mathsf{put}(\mathsf{deref}(\mathsf{s}_1,\ 3))\\
&= \mathsf{s}_1\,.\,\mathsf{put}(3)
\end{aligned}
$$

- as expected.

A very simple procedure The following example shows how declarations and invocations of nonrecursive procedures are handled.

```
begin
  var m: int := 2;
  val q = proc(val x: int) put x endproc;
  q(m)
end
```

The effect of executing this imperative should of course be that the integer 2 is appended to the output sequence of the state. Let us see if the equations given in the previous section to specify the formal, denotational semantics of Proc_0 give the same result. We start by applying the equation for the denotation of a block to the imperative given above and some initial, global environment env_0:

$$
\begin{aligned}
&\mathcal{M}[\![\mathbf{begin}\ \textit{as above}\ \mathbf{end}]\!](\mathsf{env}_0)\\
&\qquad = \mathsf{MV'Block}(\mathsf{env}_0,\ \mathsf{vv},\ \mathsf{cde},\ \mathsf{mve})
\end{aligned}
$$

where

$$
\begin{aligned}
\mathsf{vv}\ &= \mathcal{VD}[\![\mathbf{var}\ \mathsf{m}\colon \mathbf{int} := 2]\!](\mathsf{env}_0)\\
&= \mathsf{VV'Var}(\mathsf{m},\ \mathsf{EV'In}(2))\\
\mathsf{mve} &= \mathcal{M}[\![\mathsf{q}(\mathsf{m})]\!]\\
&= \lambda\mathsf{env'}\colon \mathsf{MV'Call}(\mathcal{E}[\![\mathsf{q}]\!](\mathsf{env'}),\ \mathcal{E}[\![\mathsf{m}]\!](\mathsf{env'}))\\
&= \lambda\mathsf{env'}\colon \mathsf{MV'Call}(\mathsf{EV'In}(\mathsf{env'}(\mathsf{q})),\ \mathsf{EV'In}(\mathsf{env'}(\mathsf{m})))\\
\mathsf{cde}\ &= \mathcal{CD}[\![\mathbf{val}\ \mathsf{q} = \mathbf{proc}(\mathbf{val}\ \mathsf{x}\colon \mathbf{int})\ \mathbf{put}\ \mathsf{x}\ \mathbf{endproc}]\!]\\
&= \lambda\mathsf{env'}\colon \mathsf{Envir'Void}\,.\,\mathsf{bind}(\mathsf{q},\ \mathsf{pe}_q(\mathsf{env'}))
\end{aligned}
$$

where

$$
\begin{aligned}
\mathsf{pe}_q(\mathsf{env'}) &= \mathcal{P}[\![\mathbf{val}\ \mathsf{q} = \mathbf{proc}(\mathbf{val}\ \mathsf{x}\colon \mathbf{int})\ \mathbf{put}\ \mathsf{x}\ \mathbf{endproc}]\!](\mathsf{env'})\\
&= \underline{\lambda}\mathsf{p} \in P_\perp\colon \mathsf{MV'Proc}(\mathcal{M}[\![\mathbf{put}\ \mathsf{x}]\!],\ \mathsf{env'},\ \mathcal{PM}[\![\mathbf{val}]\!],\ \mathsf{x},\ \mathsf{p})\\
&= \underline{\lambda}\mathsf{p} \in P_\perp\colon \mathsf{MV'Proc}(\lambda\mathsf{env''}\colon \mathsf{MV'Put}(\mathsf{EV'In}(\mathsf{env''}(\mathsf{x})))\\
&\qquad\qquad\qquad \mathsf{env'},\ \mathsf{Val},\ \mathsf{x},\ \mathsf{p})
\end{aligned}
$$

The definition of MV'Block then gives that for any state s_0

$$
\begin{aligned}
&\mathsf{MV'Block}(\mathsf{env}_0,\ \mathsf{vv},\ \mathsf{cde},\ \mathsf{mve})(\mathsf{s}_0)\\
&\quad = \mathbf{let}\ \langle \mathsf{env}_v,\ \mathsf{s}_1\rangle = \mathsf{vv}(\mathsf{s}_0)\ \mathbf{in}\\
&\qquad\qquad = \mathsf{VV'Var}(\mathsf{m},\ \mathsf{EV'In}(2))(\mathsf{s}_0)\\
&\qquad\qquad = \langle \mathsf{Envir'Void}\,.\,\mathsf{bind}(\mathsf{m},\ \mathsf{a}_m),\\
&\qquad\qquad\qquad \mathsf{s}_0\,.\,\mathsf{allocate}\,.\,\mathsf{assign}(\mathsf{a}_m,\ 2)\rangle
\end{aligned}
$$

$$
\begin{aligned}
&\qquad \text{where } \mathsf{a}_m = \mathsf{s}_0\,.\,\mathsf{free\_address} \\
&\quad \textbf{let } \mathsf{env}_c = \mathsf{cde}(\mathsf{env}_0 + \mathsf{env}_v) \\
&\quad \textbf{in } \mathsf{mve}(\mathsf{env}_0 + \mathsf{env}_v + \mathsf{env}_c)(\mathsf{s}_1) \\
&= \mathsf{MV'Call}(\mathsf{EV'In}(\mathsf{p}_q, \mathsf{EV'In}(\mathsf{a}_m)))(\mathsf{s}_1) \\
&\quad \text{where } \mathsf{p}_q = \mathsf{pe}_q(\mathsf{env}_0 + \mathsf{env}_v) \\
&= \mathsf{p}_q(\mathsf{a}_m)(\mathsf{s}_1) \\
&= \mathsf{MV'Proc}(\lambda \mathsf{env''}: \mathsf{MV'Put}(\mathsf{EV'In}(\mathsf{env''}(\mathsf{x}))), \\
&\qquad\qquad \mathsf{env}_0 + \mathsf{env}_v, \mathsf{Val}, \mathsf{x}, \mathsf{a}_m)(\mathsf{s}_1) \\
&= \mathsf{MV'Put}(\mathsf{EV'In}(\mathsf{env''}(\mathsf{x})))(\mathsf{s}_1) \\
&\qquad \text{where } \mathsf{env''} = (\mathsf{env}_0 + \mathsf{env}_v)\,.\,\mathsf{bind}(\mathsf{x}, \mathsf{a}_m) \\
&= \mathsf{MV'Put}(\mathsf{EV'In}(\mathsf{deref}(\mathsf{s}_1, \mathsf{a}_m)))(\mathsf{s}_1) \\
&= \mathsf{MV'Put}(\mathsf{EV'In}(\mathsf{s}_1\,.\,\mathsf{access}(\mathsf{a}_m)))(\mathsf{s}_1) \\
&= \mathsf{MV'Put}(\mathsf{EV'In}(2))(\mathsf{s}_1) \\
&= \mathsf{s}_1\,.\,\mathsf{put}(2)
\end{aligned}
$$

10.3 Name parameters

Name parameters are allowed in some programming languages in the Algol family. In this section we show how to give a denotational specification of the semantics of such parameters.

Let us extend the syntax of Proc_0 by allowing the use of the parameter mode specifier **name** in addition to **var**, **val** or **value**:

$$\langle parmod \rangle ::= \textbf{var} \mid \textbf{val} \mid \textbf{value} \mid \textbf{name}$$

To reduce the number of details we have to describe, and to keep matters in correspondence with much actual practice, we allow only procedures to have name parameters.

The main idea we use to specify the semantics of name parameters is to bind a formal name parameter to the dynamic denotation (defined in section 9.3 on page 199) of the actual parameter, i.e., to a function that specifies how to evaluate the actual parameter (instead of binding the formal parameter to the value of actual parameter as we do for normal parameters).

To use this idea, we first extend the semantic algebras D and P as follows:

$$
\begin{aligned}
D &\stackrel{d}{=} B + L + PP + FF + \mathsf{Namepara}{:}\, EV \;+\; \mathsf{Unbound}{:}\, \mathit{Unit} \\
P &\stackrel{d}{=} B + L + PP + FF + \mathsf{Namepara}{:}\, EV
\end{aligned}
$$

We also redefine the algebra that contains the denotations of procedures such that a procedure value is now a pair where the first component signifies the parameter mode and the second is a function mapping a parameter value to a state transformer:

$$PP \stackrel{d}{=} PM \times [P \to MV]$$

PM is the previously defined domain of parameter mode extended with a Name component:

$$PM \stackrel{d}{=} \mathsf{Var}{:}\ \mathit{Unit} + \mathsf{Val}{:}\ \mathit{Unit} + \mathsf{Value}{:}\ \mathit{Unit} + \mathsf{Name}{:}\ \mathit{Unit}$$

The semantic mapping $\mathcal{PP}$ that defines the semantics of procedures may now be defined as follows:

$$\begin{aligned}&\mathcal{PP}[\![\mathbf{proc}(\mathsf{pmod\ pid{:}\ ptyp})\ \mathsf{imp}\ \mathbf{endproc}]\!]\\ &\quad = \langle \mathcal{PM}[\![\mathsf{pmod}]\!],\\ &\qquad \underline{\lambda}\mathsf{p} \in P_\perp{:}\ \ \mathsf{MV'Proc}(\mathcal{M}[\![\mathsf{imp}]\!],\ \mathsf{env},\ \mathcal{PM}[\![\mathsf{pmod}]\!],\ \mathsf{pid},\ \mathsf{p})\rangle\end{aligned}$$

The intermediate function MV'Call must be redefined to handle parameters transmitted by name:

$$\begin{aligned}&\mathsf{MV'Call(pv,\ av)} \stackrel{d}{=} \underline{\lambda}\mathsf{s} \in \mathit{State}_\perp{:}\ \ \mathbf{case}\ \mathsf{pv(s)}\ \mathbf{of}\ E{:}\\ &\qquad \langle \mathsf{pmd,\ pp}\rangle \in PP{:}\ \mathbf{if}\ \mathsf{pmd} = \mathsf{Name}\ \mathbf{then}\ \mathsf{pp(av)(s)}\\ &\qquad\qquad\qquad\qquad\qquad\qquad\qquad\quad \mathbf{else}\ \ \mathsf{pp(av(s))(s)}\\ &\qquad \mathbf{otherwise}{:}\qquad \perp_{\mathit{State}}\end{aligned}$$

Because environments now may bind an identifier (a formal parameter specified to be transmitted by name) to an element in *EV*, we have to extend the definition of $\mathcal{E}$ when applied to identifiers:

$$\begin{aligned}\mathcal{E}[\![\mathsf{id}]\!](\mathsf{env},\ \mathsf{s}) = \mathbf{case}\ &\mathsf{env.bound(id)}\ \mathbf{of}\ D{:}\\ &\mathsf{n}\ \ \ \mathbf{in}\ B + L + PP + FF \ \Rightarrow \mathsf{E'In(n)}\\ &\mathsf{ev}\ \ \mathbf{in}\ \mathsf{Namepara} \qquad\quad \Rightarrow \mathsf{ev(s)}\\ &\mathsf{Unbound} \qquad\qquad\qquad\ \ \Rightarrow \perp_E\end{aligned}$$

10.4 Lazy parameters

The semantics of lazy parameters may be specified in a manner which in many ways is quite similar to how we specify the semantics of name parameters. The only semantic difference between name parameters and lazy parameters is in how many times formal parameters are evaluated: As long as a lazy parameter fp has not been accessed inside the procedure (function) body, it is bound to an element $\mathsf{ev}_{\mathsf{fp}}$ of *EV* which specifies how to evaluate the value of the parameter (this is as for name parameters). If and when the formal parameter is accessed for the first time, $\mathsf{ev}_{\mathsf{fp}}$ is evaluated for the current state s, and the environment is changed such that the newly found value of $\mathsf{ev}_{\mathsf{fp}}(\mathsf{s})$ is bound to fp. This means that evaluating an expression that contains a lazy formal parameter as a side-effect will change the environment. The semantic mapping $\mathcal{E}$ must hence be redefined such that it has the following signature:

$$\mathcal{E} \in (\mathit{Exp} \to (\mathit{Envir} \to (\mathit{State} \to (\mathit{Envir} \times E_\perp))))$$

Every use of $\mathcal{E}$ in the various equations that define the semantic mappings must be redefined correspondingly in a manner which should be obvious for every equation except the following, which specifies the denotation of identifiers in general and formal parameters in particular:

$$\begin{aligned}
\mathcal{E}[\![\mathsf{id}]\!](\mathsf{env}, \mathsf{s}) = \textbf{case}\ & \mathsf{env.bound(id)}\ \textbf{of}\ D\text{:} \\
& \mathsf{n}\ \ \textbf{in}\ B + L + PP + FF \Rightarrow \langle \mathsf{env}, \mathsf{E'In(n)} \rangle \\
& \mathsf{ev}\ \ \textbf{in}\ \mathsf{Namepara} \Rightarrow \langle \mathsf{env}, \mathsf{ev(s)} \rangle \\
& \mathsf{ev}\ \ \textbf{in}\ \mathsf{Lazypara} \Rightarrow \textbf{let}\ \mathsf{e} = \mathsf{ev(s)}\ \textbf{in} \\
& \qquad \langle \mathsf{env.bind(id, e.E_to_D)}, \mathsf{e} \rangle \\
& \mathsf{Unbound} \Rightarrow \langle \mathsf{env}, \perp_E \rangle
\end{aligned}$$

10.5 Floating procedures and functions

In the previous sections we have assumed that the environment to be used when the body of a procedure (or function) is executed as a result of an invocation of the procedure (function), is the environment that is valid at the declaration of the procedure (function). But this is not the only possibility. In some programming languages, for instance TEX and many dialects of Lisp, it is the environment which is valid at the invocation of a procedure (function) which is used to determine the meanings of identifiers that occur in the body of the declaration of the procedure (function). The effect of an invocation of such a procedure (function) therefore depends upon the environment in which the invocation occurs, and we say that the procedure (function) is *floating*. In this section we show how to give formal specifications of the semantics of floating procedures and functions.

Let us extend the syntax of Proc_0 by allowing the use of the specifier **float** before **proc** or **func** to specify that a procedure or function is floating:

$$\begin{aligned}
\langle exp \rangle ::= \ \ldots \mid & \ \{\textbf{float}\}^? \ \textbf{proc}\ (\langle paraspec \rangle)\ \langle imp \rangle\ \textbf{endproc} \\
\mid & \ \{\textbf{float}\}^? \ \textbf{func}\ (\langle paraspec \rangle)\ \langle exp \rangle
\end{aligned}$$

A simple way of defining the semantics of a floating procedure is by binding the static denotation – and not the dynamic denotation as done for normal, nonfloating, procedures – of the body of the procedure declaration to the name of the procedure (the concepts *static denotation* and *dynamic denotation* are defined in section 9.3). Thus, if bimp is the body of a procedure named pf, we bind $\mathcal{M}[\![\mathsf{bimp}]\!]$ to pf, and not $\mathcal{M}[\![\mathsf{bimp}]\!](\mathsf{env})$ (where env is the environment valid at the declaration of pf). The environment env' valid at an invocation of the procedure may then be used to get a state transformer $\mathcal{M}[\![\mathsf{bimp}]\!](\mathsf{env'})$ which performs the effect of the procedure invocation.

To use this idea in the specification of the semantics of floating procedures and functions, we extend the algebras D, E and P such that they contain static denotations of imperatives and expressions:

$$D \stackrel{d}{=} \ldots + PP + FF + FPP + FFF$$
$$E \stackrel{d}{=} \ldots + PP + FF + FPP + FFF$$
$$P \stackrel{d}{=} \ldots + PP + FF + FPP + FFF$$

where

$$FPP \stackrel{d}{=} (Envir \rightarrow PP)$$
$$FFF \stackrel{d}{=} (Envir \rightarrow FF)$$

The definition of the semantic mapping $\mathcal{PP}$ must be extended to cater for floating procedures:

$$\mathcal{PP}[\![\textbf{float proc}(\text{pmod pid: ptyp) imp } \textbf{endproc}]\!](\text{env}) = \lambda\text{env}'\colon \underline{\lambda}\text{p} \in P_\perp\colon\ \text{MV'Proc}(\mathcal{M}[\![\text{imp}]\!], \text{env}', \mathcal{PM}[\![\text{pmod}]\!], \text{pid}, \text{p})$$

Observe that the environment env - which is the environment valid at the point of declaration - is *not* given to the function MV'Proc.

The denotation of a procedure invocation must be changed such that the environment valid at the invocation is given to the function MV'Call:

$$\mathcal{M}[\![\text{rx(px)}]\!](\text{env}) = \text{MV'Call}(\text{env}, \mathcal{E}[\![\text{rx}]\!](\text{env}), \mathcal{E}[\![\text{px}]\!](\text{env}))$$

The function MV'Call must be changed such that it passes the environment it receives as its first argument on to a floating procedure:

$$\text{MV'Call(env, pv, av)} \stackrel{d}{=} \underline{\lambda}\text{s} \in State_\perp\colon\ \begin{array}{l} \textbf{case}\ \text{pv(s)}\ \textbf{of}\ E\text{:} \\ \text{pp} \in PP\text{:}\quad \text{pp(av(s))(s)} \\ \text{ppp} \in PPP\text{: ppp(env, av(s))(s)} \\ \textbf{otherwise}\text{:}\quad \perp_{State} \end{array}$$

We leave it as an exercise to specify the semantics of floating functions.

10.6 Exercises

10.6.1 A simple program

Use the definitions in section 10.2 to find the denotation of the following program:

```
begin
  var m: int := 2;
  val q = proc(var x: int) get x endproc;
  q(m); put(m)
end
```

Observe that this program differs from the example given in section 10.2.5 in only three small places.

10.6.2 Name parameters and lazy parameters

Do the previous exercise again, but let the parameter x to procedure q be first a **name** parameter and then a **lazy** parameter.

10.6.3 Function procedures

Some languages (for instance Algol, Simula and Pascal) contain so-called *function procedures*. In this exercise you are asked to specify the semantics of such procedures.

Assume that the syntax of Proc_0 is extended with the following BNF production:

$$\langle \mathit{funcproc} \rangle ::= \mathbf{funcproc}(\langle \mathit{paraspec} \rangle)\ \langle \mathit{imp} \rangle\ \mathbf{result}\ \langle \mathit{exp} \rangle$$

and that the BNF production for $\langle \mathit{constant} \rangle$ is extended such a $\langle \mathit{funcproc} \rangle$ may be used as a $\langle \mathit{constant} \rangle$.

An invocation fp(exp) of a function procedure fp may be used as an expression. The operational effect of executing this invocation is first to execute the imperative given in the declaration of the function procedure (after a suitable parameter transmission), and then (assuming that the imperative terminates) to evaluate the result expression given in the declaration. The value of this expression is used as a value of the expression fp(exp).

Extend the specification of the semantics of Proc_0 such that the semantics of function procedures are specified. Do not forget that an invocation of a function procedure in general may have side-effects, i.e., the state may be changed.

10.6.4 Characteristic algebras for other languages

What are the characteristic algebras D, E, P, F and S of programming languages like Pascal, Algol, Simula, Fortran, Lisp, ML, Basic, Ada, Java, TeX and Cobol? Do different 'dialects' of these languages differ in their characteristic algebras?

Can you discover any general rules about the characteristic algebras of languages? One is $F \subseteq E$. Are there other such rules that the languages obey (or should obey)?

10.6.5 Floating parameters

Change the semantics of Proc_0 such that parameters to a procedure (function) are evaluated in the environment that is valid where the procedure is declared.

10.6.6 Frozen parameters

Change the semantics of Proc_0 such that a parameter to a procedure (function) is evaluated in the environment that is valid where the parameter is first (dynamically) accessed inside the body of the procedure (function).

10.6.7 A typed semantics for Proc_0

Give a typed semantics for Proc_0.

10.6.8 Several parameters

Extend the specification of the semantics of Proc_0 such that procedures and functions with more than one parameter, or no parameters at all, are allowed.

10.6.9 Proc_0 in ML

Implement Proc_0 in ML.

Chapter 11
Objects and classes

An *object* is a structure with data (variables and constants) and operations (procedures and functions). Often the data of an object is hidden, and may only be changed and accessed indirectly by using the operations of the object. A *class* is a description of objects, and is used as a pattern when objects are created.

Objects and classes were first introduced in 1967 in Simula. Today, many programming languages, for instance Smalltalk, C++ and Java, have adopted at least some of the ideas from Simula, and are then said to be *object oriented*.

In this chapter we show how to specify the semantics of simple classes and objects. We describe a language Class_0 which contains constructs that may be used to define classes and to create and access objects.

11.1 Syntax and informal semantics

11.1.1 Classes

The language Class_0 is an extension of Proc_0 described in chapter 10. It contains a single new syntactic category *Class*, which is defined by the following BNF production:

$$\langle \textit{class} \rangle ::= \textbf{class}\ \langle \textit{vardecl} \rangle;\ \langle \textit{constdecl} \rangle\ \textbf{endclass}$$

Here ⟨*vardecl*⟩ is a sequence of variable declarations and ⟨*constdecl*⟩ a sequence of constant declarations, i.e., declarations of procedures, functions and other constants, even new classes.

A *Class* may be used as a constant expression in some Class_0 constructs. The syntactic category *Constant* is therefore extended by the following production:

$$\langle \textit{constant} \rangle ::= \ldots \mid \langle \textit{class} \rangle$$

In particular, it is possible to use a constant declaration to give a name to a class, for instance as follows:

```
val V = class
          var x: int := 0;
          val asg = proc(val n: int) x := n endproc;
          val acc = func() x;
          val eql  = func(val q: obj) x = q.acc()
        endclass
```

The effect of this constant declaration is that the identifier V is bound to be the name of a class that contains declarations of a single variable x, a procedure asg and two functions acc and eql. Observe that the function acc is specified to have no parameters. Neither syntax nor semantics for parameterless procedures and functions have been formally specified in chapter 10, where we dealt with procedures and functions. It is, of course, simple to do this, and we leave the work to the reader as an exercise.

How a class like the one declared above may be used to create objects, is explained below.

11.1.2 Expressions

Class_0 allows two types of expressions that do not occur in Proc_0. These types are defined by the following BNF productions:

$$\langle \textit{exp} \rangle ::= \ldots \mid \textbf{new}\ \langle \textit{exp} \rangle \mid \langle \textit{exp} \rangle . \langle \textit{ident} \rangle(\langle \textit{exp} \rangle) \mid \textbf{none}$$

The value of an expression **new** cls, where the expression cls should be either a constant in the syntactic category *Class* or an identifier that has been declared to be the name of a class, is an object that contains variables and operations (procedures and functions) as specified by the declarations in the class. When the expression **new** cls is evaluated in some given state, a new object is created by allocating and initializing a new location in the state for each of the variables that are declared in the class. An example: The value of the expression **new** V, where V is as declared in the example above, is an object obv that contains a variable x, which is allocated a new location (initialized to 0) in the state, and three operations asg, acc and eql. The first of these operations may be used to assign a value to the variable x of obv, the second to access the value of the variable, and the third to determine whether or not the variables of two V objects have equal values.

An object that adheres to the description in a given class cls, i.e., an object created by evaluating the expression **new** cls and hence contains variables and operations declared in the class, is said to be an object *in* the class.

The value of an expression obx.f(argx) is found by first evaluating the expression obx. If the value of obx is an object ob that among its operations has a function named f, i.e., ob is in a class that contains a declaration of a function f, then this function is invoked with argx as parameter. The value found by the invocation is used as a value of the expression obx.f(argx). An error occurs in case the value of obx is not an object that contains a function named f.

The value of the expression **none** is an empty object, i.e., an object with no data structure and no operations.

11.1.3 Assigning an object to a variable

Assume that cls is either in the syntactic category *Class* or an identifier that has been declared to be the name of a class, and that vv is a variable. The effect of executing the imperative

vv := **new** cls

is then that an object in the class cls is created and assigned to the variable vv. For such an imperative to be syntactically correct, vv must in its declaration have been specified to be of type **obj**, where **obj** is a new element in the syntactic category *Vartype*:

$$\langle vartype \rangle ::= \ldots \mid \textbf{obj}$$

Assume, as an example, that the variable vv has been declared as by the following declaration:

var vv: **obj** := **none**

The effect of executing the imperative vv := **new** V is then that vv is assigned a new object in the class V.

11.1.4 New imperatives

The following BNF production defines a new type of imperatives for use in Class_0 programs (this is the only kind of Class_0 imperative that is new compared to Proc_0):

$$\langle imp \rangle ::= \ldots \mid \langle exp \rangle . \langle ident \rangle (\langle exp \rangle)$$

An imperative of this form, for instance obx.p(argx), is executed by first evaluating the expression obx. If the value is an object that contains a procedure named p, then this procedure is invoked with argx as the parameter. If the value of obx is not an object, or an object that does not contain a function named p, an error occurs.

11.1.5 Objects as parameters

Objects may be used as parameters to procedures and functions. An example of the latter may be found in the function eql in the class V declared in the example above. The syntactic category *Partype* is therefore extended as follows in Decl_0:

$$\langle partype \rangle ::= \ldots \mid \mathbf{obj}$$

11.1.6 Hidden data structures

Class_0 contains no expressions or imperatives that may be used to give direct access to the variables of an object. This is a consequence of our resolution to let the data structure of an object be local to the object and hidden from the rest of the program. The variables of an object may hence only be changed or accessed indirectly by using procedures or functions in the object, i.e., by using operations that are declared in the class of the object.

11.2 Semantic domains

The main new semantic domain needed to give a formal specification of the semantics of Class_0 is a domain which we call *CV* (for *C*lass *V*alues) and which consists of denotations of classes. In order to determine what kind of elements this domain should have, it is prudent to consider that classes are used solely to generate new objects and to remember that each such object consists of a data structure and set of operations. The data structure of an object consists of variables, each of which is allocated a new location in the state when the object is created.

The denotation of a class **class** vdecl; cdecl **endclass** may therefore be defined to be a function that maps a given state to a new state and a new environment oenv: The new state is the result of extending the original state by allocating and initializing the variables declared in the variable declarations vdecl; the environment oenv contains bindings for each of the identifiers that are declared in the constant declarations cdecl. The names of the variables declared in vdecl need only be known to the operations declared in cdecl, and therefore need not be included in the environment oenv which then contains only the part of the object which is visible to the rest of the program.

After these deliberations, we may define the semantic domain *CV* that contains denotations of classes as follows:

$$CV \stackrel{d}{=} (State_{\perp} \rightarrow (OE_{\perp} \times State_{\perp}))$$

where the semantic domain *OE* (for *O*bject *E*nvironment) is defined as follows:

$$OE \stackrel{d}{=} Envir$$

A class may be used as a constant, in particular in constant declarations, and the semantic domain *C* that contains denotations of all constants is therefore extended with a new addend:

$$C \stackrel{d}{=} \ldots + CV$$

A class may be bound to an identifier by a constant declaration, and the semantic domain *D* that contains everything that may be bound to identifiers is hence extended with a new addend:

$$D \stackrel{d}{=} \ldots + CV$$

We have previously said that the effect of executing an imperative vv := **new** cls is that an object in the class cls is generated and assigned to the variable vv. For this to work, we have to extend the semantic domains *E* and *S* such that something which represents the object becomes both expressible (i.e., an element of *E*) and storable (an element of *S*). As will be seen below, when we define the semantic mappings for Class_0 it suffices to let the visible part of an object represent the whole object. We therefore extend the definitions of *E* and *S* such that the domain *OE* becomes an addend of both. Because the value of the expression cls (which is a subexpression of the compound expression **new** cls) is an element in *CV*, we also let *CV* be an addend of *E*:

$$E \stackrel{d}{=} \ldots + CV + OE$$
$$S \stackrel{d}{=} \ldots + OE$$

The evaluation of an expression **new** cls changes the state by allocating and initializing the variables of the object which is created. Thus, the evaluation of Class_0 expressions may in general change the state, and we have to change the semantic domains that contain denotations of expressions and of functions accordingly:

$$EV \stackrel{d}{=} (State_{\perp} \rightarrow (E_{\perp} \times State_{\perp}))$$
$$FF \stackrel{d}{=} (P \rightarrow (State_{\perp} \rightarrow (E_{\perp} \times State_{\perp})))$$

11.3 Semantic mappings

In this section we give an unlayered specification of semantic mappings for Class_0. Most mappings are either identical to or simple transformations of mappings defined for Proc_0, and their definitions are not repeated here.

11.3.1 Classes

The language Class_0 contains a single new syntactic category *Class*, and we define a new semantic mapping $\mathcal{CC}$ that may be used to find the denotation of any class. According to our discussion in the previous section where we discussed semantic domains, this mapping should have the following signature:

$$\begin{aligned}\mathcal{CC} &\in (\mathit{Class} \to (\mathit{Envir} \to \mathit{CV})) \\ &= (\mathit{Class} \to (\mathit{Envir} \to (\mathit{State}_\perp \to (\mathit{OE}_\perp \times \mathit{State}_\perp))))\end{aligned}$$

The following equation defines $\mathcal{CC}$ for any class:

$$\begin{aligned}&\mathcal{CC}[\![\textbf{class}\ \mathsf{vardcl};\ \mathsf{constdcl}\ \textbf{endclass}]\!](\mathsf{env}) \\ &\quad = \underline{\lambda} \mathsf{s} \in \mathit{State}_\perp\text{: } \textbf{let}\ \langle \mathsf{env}_1, \mathsf{s}_1\rangle = \mathcal{VD}[\![\mathsf{vardcl}]\!](\mathsf{env}, \mathsf{s}) \\ &\qquad\qquad\qquad\quad \textbf{let}\ \mathsf{oenv} \quad\ = \mathcal{CD}[\![\mathsf{constdcl}]\!](\mathsf{env} + \mathsf{env}_1) \\ &\qquad\qquad\qquad\quad \textbf{in}\ \langle \mathsf{oenv}, \mathsf{s}_1\rangle\end{aligned}$$

11.3.2 Expressions

Evaluating a Class_0 expression may in general change the state. This means that the semantic mapping for expressions, i.e., $\mathcal{E}$, should have the following signature, which is different from the signature of the corresponding mapping for Proc_0:

$$\begin{aligned}\mathcal{E} &\in (\mathit{Exp} \to (\mathit{Envir} \to \mathit{EV})) \\ &= (\mathit{Exp} \to (\mathit{Envir} \to (\mathit{State}_\perp \to (\mathit{E}_\perp \times \mathit{State}_\perp))))\end{aligned}$$

The evaluation of many expressions will, however, not change the state, and for such expressions we may simply let the value of $\mathcal{E}$ for some given environment and state be a pair where the first component is the value found should we have used the $\mathcal{E}$ mapping defined for Proc_0, and the second is the given (unchanged) state. Thus the following equations define $\mathcal{E}$ for identifiers and constants:

$$\begin{aligned}\mathcal{E}[\![\mathsf{id}]\!](\mathsf{env}) &= \underline{\lambda} \mathsf{s} \in \mathit{State}_\perp\text{: } \langle \mathsf{env}(\mathsf{id}), \mathsf{s}\rangle \\ \mathcal{E}[\![\mathsf{con}]\!](\mathsf{env}) &= \underline{\lambda} \mathsf{s} \in \mathit{State}_\perp\text{: } \langle \mathcal{C}[\![\mathsf{con}]\!](\mathsf{env}), \mathsf{s}\rangle\end{aligned}$$

The semantic mapping $\mathcal{C}$ used here, finds the denotation of constants. The language Class_0 contains constants of a kind that are new compared to Proc_0, namely classes, and the definition of $\mathcal{C}$ is therefore extended by the following equation, where cls is in the syntactic category *Class*:

$$\mathcal{C}[\![\mathsf{cls}]\!](\mathsf{env}) = \mathcal{CC}[\![\mathsf{cls}]\!](\mathsf{env})$$

The equations that specify the value of $\mathcal{E}$ for various compound expressions have to cater for the possibility that the evaluation of any of the subexpressions may change the state. An example is the following equation, which specifies the $\mathcal{E}$ value of an expression with a binary operator:

$$\begin{aligned}\mathcal{E}[\![\mathsf{ex}_1\ \mathsf{bop}\ \mathsf{ex}_2]\!](\mathsf{env}) = \underline{\lambda}\mathsf{s} \in \mathit{State}_\perp\text{: } & \textbf{let}\ \langle \mathsf{e}_1, \mathsf{s}_1\rangle = \mathcal{E}[\![\mathsf{ex}_1]\!](\mathsf{env}, \mathsf{s})\\ & \textbf{let}\ \langle \mathsf{e}_2, \mathsf{s}_2\rangle = \mathcal{E}[\![\mathsf{ex}_2]\!](\mathsf{env}, \mathsf{s}_1)\\ & \textbf{in}\ \langle \mathcal{BO}[\![\mathsf{bop}]\!](\mathsf{e}_1, \mathsf{e}_2), \mathsf{s}_2\rangle\end{aligned}$$

We leave the specifications of the semantics of the remaining Proc_0 expressions as simple exercises.

The following equations specify the semantics of the expressions that are new to Class_0:

$$\begin{aligned}\mathcal{E}[\![\textbf{new}\ \mathsf{cls}]\!](\mathsf{env}) &= \underline{\lambda}\mathsf{s} \in \mathit{State}_\perp\text{: } \textbf{case}\ \mathcal{E}[\![\mathsf{cls}]\!](\mathsf{env}, \mathsf{s})\ \textbf{of}\ (E_\perp \times \mathit{State}_\perp)\\ &\qquad \langle \mathsf{cv}, \mathsf{s'}\rangle \in (CV \times \mathit{State}) \Rightarrow \mathsf{cv}(\mathsf{s'})\\ &\qquad \textbf{otherwise} \Rightarrow \langle \perp_E, \perp_{\mathit{State}}\rangle\\ \mathcal{E}[\![\textbf{none}]\!](\mathsf{env}) &= \underline{\lambda}\mathsf{s} \in \mathit{State}_\perp\text{: } \langle \mathsf{Envir'Void}, \mathsf{s}\rangle\end{aligned}$$

$$\begin{aligned}&\mathcal{E}[\![\mathsf{ex}_1 \,.\, \mathsf{m}(\mathsf{ex}_2)]\!](\mathsf{env})\\ &\quad = \underline{\lambda}\mathsf{s} \in \mathit{State}_\perp\text{: } \textbf{let}\ \langle \mathsf{e}_1, \mathsf{s}_1\rangle = \mathcal{E}[\![\mathsf{ex}_1]\!](\mathsf{env}, \mathsf{s})\\ &\qquad\qquad \textbf{let}\ \langle \mathsf{e}_2, \mathsf{s}_2\rangle = \mathcal{E}[\![\mathsf{ex}_2]\!](\mathsf{env}, \mathsf{s}_1)\\ &\qquad\qquad \textbf{in case}\ \mathsf{e}_1\ \textbf{of}\ E\\ &\qquad\qquad\quad \mathsf{oenv} \in OE \Rightarrow \textbf{case}\ \mathsf{oenv}(\mathsf{m})\ \textbf{of}\ D\\ &\qquad\qquad\qquad\qquad \mathsf{ff} \in FF \Rightarrow \mathsf{ff}(\mathsf{e}_2, \mathsf{s}_2)\\ &\qquad\qquad\qquad\qquad \textbf{otherwise} \Rightarrow \langle \perp_E, \perp_{\mathit{State}}\rangle\\ &\qquad\qquad\quad \textbf{otherwise} \Rightarrow \langle \perp_E, \perp_{\mathit{State}}\rangle\end{aligned}$$

11.3.3 Imperatives

The evaluation of Class_0 expressions may in general change the state, and we must therefore change the definition of the mapping $\mathcal{M}$ for every imperative that contains one or more expressions. We do this only for assignment imperatives, and leave the other as simple exercises.

$$\begin{aligned}&\mathcal{M}[\![\mathsf{ex}_1 := \mathsf{ex}_2]\!](\mathsf{env})\\ &\quad = \underline{\lambda}\mathsf{s} \in \mathit{State}_\perp\text{: } \textbf{let}\ \langle \mathsf{e}_1, \mathsf{s}_1\rangle = \mathcal{E}[\![\mathsf{ex}_1]\!](\mathsf{env}, \mathsf{s})\\ &\qquad\qquad \textbf{let}\ \langle \mathsf{e}_2, \mathsf{s}_2\rangle = \mathcal{E}[\![\mathsf{ex}_2]\!](\mathsf{env}, \mathsf{s}_1)\\ &\qquad\qquad \textbf{in}\ \mathsf{s}_2 \,.\, \mathsf{assign}(\mathsf{ref}(\mathsf{e}_1), \mathsf{deref}(\mathsf{s}_2, \mathsf{e}_2))\end{aligned}$$

The semantics of the imperatives of the kind that are new in Class_0, i.e., imperatives that invoke a procedure in an object, is specified by the following equation:

$$\begin{aligned}
&\mathcal{M}[\![\mathsf{ex}_1 \,.\, \mathsf{m}(\mathsf{ex}_2)]\!](\mathsf{env}) \\
&\quad = \underline{\lambda}\mathsf{s} \in \mathit{State}_\perp : \mathbf{let}\ \langle \mathsf{e}_1, \mathsf{s}_1 \rangle = \mathcal{E}[\![\mathsf{ex}_1]\!](\mathsf{env}, \mathsf{s}) \\
&\qquad\qquad\qquad\quad \mathbf{let}\ \langle \mathsf{e}_2, \mathsf{s}_2 \rangle = \mathcal{E}[\![\mathsf{ex}_2]\!](\mathsf{env}, \mathsf{s}) \\
&\qquad\qquad\qquad\quad \mathbf{in\ case}\ \mathsf{e}_1\ \mathbf{of}\ E \\
&\qquad\qquad\qquad\qquad \mathsf{oenv} \in OE \Rightarrow \mathbf{case}\ \mathsf{oenv}(\mathsf{m})\ \mathbf{of}\ D \\
&\qquad\qquad\qquad\qquad\qquad\qquad\qquad \mathsf{pp} \in PP \Rightarrow \mathsf{pp}(\mathsf{e}_2, \mathsf{s}_2) \\
&\qquad\qquad\qquad\qquad\qquad\qquad\qquad \mathbf{otherwise} \Rightarrow \perp_{\mathit{State}} \\
&\qquad\qquad\qquad\qquad \mathbf{otherwise} \quad \Rightarrow \perp_{\mathit{State}}
\end{aligned}$$

11.4 Subclasses and inheritance

A class may be a *superclass* to another class, which is then said to be a *subclass* of the superclass. The subclass *inherits* the declarations of the superclass, but may have its own additional declarations. Objects in the subclass will hence contain every variable and operation that belong to objects in the superclass, and have additional variables and operations as specified in the declaration of the subclass. In this section we show how to formally specify the semantics of subclasses.

11.4.1 Syntax and informal semantics

Let Class_1 be the result of extending Class_0 with the following BNF production:

⟨*class*⟩ ::= ... | **super** ⟨*ident*⟩ **class** ⟨*vardecl*⟩; ⟨*constdecl*⟩ **endclass**

An example: The following is a declaration of a subclass VSub of the class V declared on page 254:

```
val VSub = super V class
                      var y: int := 0;
                      asgy = proc(val n: int) y := n endproc;
                      val acc = func() x + y;
                    endclass;
```

The value of the expression **new** VSub will then be an object obvs that contains a datastructure with two variables x and y, the first of which is an inheritance from the superclass V. The object obvs contains four operations, of which two (asg and eql) are inherited unchanged from V, one (asgy) is a new operation, and the last (acc) is a redeclaration of an operation already declared in the superclass.

11.4.2 Static inheritance

The following equation is a first attempt at specifying the semantics of a declaration of a subclass:

$$
\begin{aligned}
&\mathcal{CC}[\![\textbf{super}\ \mathsf{sup}\ \textbf{class}\ \mathsf{vd};\ \mathsf{cd}\ \textbf{endclass}]\!]\\
&\quad = \textbf{case}\ \mathsf{env}(\mathsf{sup})\ \textbf{of}\ D\\
&\qquad \mathsf{cv} \in CV \ \Rightarrow\ \underline{\lambda}\mathsf{s} \in State_{\perp}:\\
&\qquad\qquad \textbf{let}\ \langle \mathsf{oenv}, \mathsf{s}_1\rangle = \mathsf{cv}(\mathsf{s})\\
&\qquad\qquad \textbf{let}\ \langle \mathsf{env}_1, \mathsf{s}_2\rangle = \mathcal{VD}[\![\mathsf{vd}]\!](\mathsf{env} + \mathsf{oenv}, \mathsf{s}_1)\\
&\qquad\qquad \textbf{let}\ \mathsf{env}_2 = \mathcal{CD}[\![\mathsf{cd}]\!](\mathsf{env} + \mathsf{oenv} + \mathsf{env}_1)\\
&\qquad\qquad \textbf{in}\ \langle \mathsf{oenv} + \mathsf{env}_2, \mathsf{s}_2\rangle\\
&\qquad \textbf{otherwise} \ \Rightarrow\ \langle \perp_{Envir}, \perp_{State}\rangle
\end{aligned}
$$

This way of specifying the semantics of subclasses is, however, too simple compared to how subclasses are used in languages like Simula and C++ (if so-called *virtual* operations are employed) and Smalltalk (always). The shortcomings may be seen by the following example: Assume that ovs_1 and ovs_2 are two objects in the class VSub declared in the example above, that the variables of both these objects have been assigned values (by executing $\mathsf{ovs}_i.\mathsf{asg}(\mathsf{v}_{x,i})$ and $\mathsf{ovs}_i.\mathsf{asgy}(\mathsf{v}_{y,i})$ for $i = 1, 2$), and that we would like to find the value of $\mathsf{ovs}_1 . \mathsf{eql}(\mathsf{ovs}_2)$. The value of this expression is found by invocation of the eql function, which is declared in the superclass V. According to this declaration, the value of the eql function is found by comparing the acc values of ovs_1 and ovs_2. But because eql is declared in the superclass, these values are found by using the acc function declared in the superclass when the relationship between a superclass and its subclasses is determined by the equation above. This is probably not what was intended, which was that the acc function of the Vsub objects, i.e., the version of acc declared in VSub, should have been used. The problem is that an operation like acc has a fixed and static meaning inside the superclass, and that any new version of the operation found in an object that belongs to a subclass is not seen by the superclass. Thus, the version of acc declared in the superclass is used by eql, even if this occurs in an object which is in the subclass.

The kind of relationship between a superclass and a subclass specified by the equation above, is usually called *static inheritance.*

11.4.3 Dynamic inheritance

In this section we show how to specify the relationship between a superclass and its subclasses to be such that the meaning in the superclass of an operation that is declared and used in the superclass but redeclared in the subclasses, will vary dynamically from object to object dependent upon which subclass the object belongs to. We call this kind of relationship between a superclass and its subclasses *dynamic inheritance.*

We start by defining a new version – called *DCV* (for *D*ynamic *C*lass *V*alues) – of the semantic domain that contains denotations of classes:

$$DCV \stackrel{d}{=} (State_{\perp} \rightarrow Envir \times (Envir \rightarrow Envir) \times State_{\perp})$$

The idea is that the value of dcv(s), where dcv is a *DCV* denotation of a class and s a state, is a triple ⟨oenv, oeoe, s'⟩ where oenv is an environment that describes the datastructure of a new object in the class, oeoe is a function that maps environments to environments and that is such that the result of applying oeoe to an environment env' of an object in a subclass gives an environment oeoe(env') which may be used inside the superclass to find the dynamic meaning of the operations of the class.

We re-specify the semantics of classes as follows:

$$
\begin{aligned}
&\mathcal{CC}[\![\textbf{class}\ \text{vardcl; constdcl}\ \textbf{endclass}]\!](\text{env}) = \underline{\lambda}\text{s} \in \textit{State}_\perp:\\
&\quad \textbf{let}\ \langle \text{env}_1, \text{s}_1\rangle = \mathcal{VD}[\![\text{vardcl}]\!](\text{env, s})\\
&\quad \textbf{let}\ \text{oeoe} \qquad = \lambda\text{env}' \in \textit{Envir}: \mathcal{CD}[\![\text{constdcl}]\!](\text{env} + \text{env}_1 + \text{env}')\\
&\quad \textbf{in}\ \langle \text{env}_1, \text{oeoe}, \text{s}_1\rangle
\end{aligned}
$$

The semantics of subclasses may then be specified as follows in order to achieve dynamic inheritance::

$$
\begin{aligned}
&\mathcal{CC}[\![\textbf{super}\ \text{sup}\ \textbf{class}\ \text{vd; cd}\ \textbf{endclass}]\!]\\
&\quad = \textbf{case}\ \text{env(sup)}\ \textbf{of}\ D\\
&\qquad \text{dcv} \in \textit{DCV} \Rightarrow\\
&\qquad\quad \underline{\lambda}\text{s} \in \textit{State}_\perp:\\
&\qquad\qquad \textbf{let}\ \langle \text{oenv}_s, \text{oeoe}, \text{s}_0\rangle = \text{dcv(s)}\\
&\qquad\qquad \textbf{let}\ \langle \text{env}_1, \text{s}_1\rangle = \mathcal{VD}[\![\text{vd}]\!](\text{env} + \text{oenv}_s, \text{s}_0)\\
&\qquad\qquad \textbf{let}\ \text{oeoe} = \lambda\text{env}' \in \textit{Envir}: \text{oeoe}(\mathcal{CD}[\![\text{cd}]\!](\text{env} + \text{oenv}_s +\\
&\qquad\qquad\qquad\qquad\qquad\qquad\qquad\qquad \text{env}_1 + \text{env}'))\\
&\qquad\qquad \textbf{in}\ \langle \text{env}_1, \text{oeoe}, \text{s}_1\rangle\\
&\qquad \textbf{otherwise} \Rightarrow \langle \perp_{\textit{Envir}}, \perp, \perp_{\textit{State}}\rangle
\end{aligned}
$$

The denotation of a class is different from what it is in section 11.3.2, and we re-specify the denotation of the expression **new** cls:

$$
\begin{aligned}
&\mathcal{E}[\![\textbf{new}\ \text{cls}]\!](\text{env}) = \underline{\lambda}\text{s} \in \textit{State}_\perp:\\
&\quad \textbf{case}\ \mathcal{E}[\![\text{cls}]\!](\text{env, s})\\
&\quad \langle \text{dcv, s}'\rangle \in \textit{DCV} \times \textit{State} \Rightarrow \textbf{let}\ \langle \text{env}', \text{oeoe}, \text{s}''\rangle = \text{dcv(s}')\\
&\qquad\qquad\qquad\qquad\qquad\qquad \textbf{in}\ \langle \text{Y}_{\textit{Envir}}(\text{oeoe}), \text{s}''\rangle\\
&\quad \textbf{otherwise} \Rightarrow \langle \perp_{\textit{Envir}}, \perp_{\textit{State}}\rangle
\end{aligned}
$$

Observe that the fixpoint operator Y is applied in this equation. The effect of this is that the environment used in the object which is the value of **new** cls, is a fixpoint of the environment-changing function oeoe.

11.5 Exercises

11.5.1 Visible data structures

Change the semantic mappings given in section 11.3 such that the variables of an object will be visible outside the object.

To access and change the variables of objects directly, introduce the following new syntax Class_0:

$$\langle exp \rangle ::= \ldots \mid \langle exp \rangle \,.\, \langle ident \rangle$$

Give an equation that specifies the formal semantics of this new construct.

11.5.2 Imperatives in classes

Some programming languages, in particular Simula, are such that a class may contain not only declarations of variables and operations, but also imperatives. The BNF production for classes is then as follows:

$$\langle class \rangle ::= \textbf{class}\ \langle vardecl \rangle;\ \langle constdecl \rangle;\ \langle imp \rangle\ \textbf{endclass}$$

The intended semantics of having imperatives in a class is that the imperatives is executed whenever an object in the class is generated.

Make changes in the specifications given in this chapter such that classes with imperatives are allowed.

11.5.3 References

Introduce a new imperative in Decl_0 with syntax specified by the following BNF production:

$$\langle imp \rangle ::= \ldots \mid \langle exp \rangle :- \langle exp \rangle$$

The intended effect of executing an imperative vx :− rx is as follows: If the value of rx is an address, assign this address to the location specified by vx. Should, however, the value of rx not be an address, but for instance an object (this would be the case if rx has the form **new** cls), proceed as follows: Allocate a new address, initialize this address with the value of rx, and assign the new address to the location specified by vx.

A variable that may contain an address should in its declaration be specified to have type **ref** (for *reference*). The syntactic category *Vartype* must therefore be extended to allow **ref** as a specifier.

Make changes in the specifications given in this chapter such that this new kind of imperative is allowed. Observe that the domain S has to be extended such that addresses become storable.

Observe that two different reference variables may very well reference the same object, so-called *aliasing*.

11.5.4 Layered semantics

Give a layered specification of the semantics of Class_0.

11.5.5 Typed semantics

Give a typed specification of the semantics of Class_0.

11.5.6 Class_0 in ML

Implement Class_0 in ML.

Chapter 12
Continuations and jumps

In previous chapters, we have defined the algebra of dynamic denotations of imperatives to be equal to $(\mathit{State}_\perp \to \mathit{State}_\perp)$. This means that we have considered the meaning of an imperative to be a state transformer, i.e., a function that produces a new state given an old state. We have furthermore defined the semantic function $\mathcal{M}$ such that the value of $\mathcal{M}[\![\mathsf{imp}_1;\ \mathsf{imp}_2]\!](\mathsf{env},\ \mathsf{s})$ for some environment env and state s may be found by first evaluating $\mathcal{M}[\![\mathsf{imp}_1]\!](\mathsf{env},\ \mathsf{s})$ and then applying $\mathcal{M}[\![\mathsf{imp}_2]\!](\mathsf{env})$ to the resulting state. This definition reflects the operational view that the effect of executing a sequence of two imperatives may be found by first executing the first imperative and then executing the second imperative.

This way of looking at imperatives and sequential composition of imperatives is adequate for many simple (and some not so simple) programming languages. But it seems difficult to try to use this perspective when we specify the semantics of goto's, exits, exceptions and other constructs that are allowed in many programming languages to denote *jumps* – which are breaks in the normal sequential execution of imperatives. It should be clear that the effect of executing a sequence of two imperatives of which the first is a jump, can *not* be found by first evaluating the jump and then evaluating the second imperative for the state as it is after the jump has terminated (unless, of course, the jump should be to the second of the two imperatives).

In this chapter we describe a method for giving formal specifications of the semantics of jumps, and show how this method may be used to specify the semantics of various kinds of jumps that are allowed in many programming languages.

> *A warning and some advice:* Many newcomers to the field of denotational semantics experience some confusion, and may even feel that they are confronted by a truly Copernican revolution where concepts are turned literally inside-out, when first presented with some of the concepts used in this chapter. One way of overcoming such confusion and getting an intuitive understanding of how the new concepts work, is to *use* the definitions given below: You should work through some examples, in as much detail as possible, even if it entails that you use a lot of paper and get some 'dirt' (ink?) on your hands.

We start our 'Copernican revolution' by defining some new ideas and concepts and showing how they may be used to specify the semantics of a language which is the result of extending Proc_0 with constructs that allow us to exit from compound imperatives and to stop a program. After giving a few examples, we prove that the semantics defined for Proc_0 in chapter 10 and the semantics defined in this chapter are congruent. The new concepts and ideas are then used to define the semantics of exception-handling and so-called goto's.

12.1 Exits and stops

12.1.1 Syntax and informal semantics

Let Jump_0 be the result of extending the programming language Proc_0 with the following new BNF productions:

$$\langle imp \rangle ::= \ldots \mid \mathbf{ex}\ \langle imp \rangle\ \mathbf{it}\ \langle ident \rangle \mid \mathbf{exit}\ \langle ident \rangle \mid \mathbf{stop}$$

The effect of executing an *exit block* '**ex** imp **it** label' is to execute its body (i.e., the imperative between **ex** and **it**) in an environment which is such that the effect of executing the imperative **exit** label is to leave the exit block immediately and then to continue with the imperative that succeeds the block. The effect of executing a **stop** imperative is, of course, to stop the program execution completely.

As a very simple example, consider the following program:

begin ex put 1; **exit** AA; **put** 2 **it** AA; **put** 3; **stop**; **put** 4 **end**

When executed, this program will first output 1, then exit the exit block and continue after AA where it outputs 3 and stops. The total effect of the program is therefore to produce the output sequence ⟨1, 3⟩.

Another example (where we use **true** as shorthand for some expression of type **bool** that is always true, for instance the expression 0 = 0):

```
begin
  var x: int
  get x;
  ex
    while true do
      if x > 0 then put x; x := x - 1
      else exit BB
    od
  it BB
end
```

In section 12.1.4 below, we prove that the exit block **ex** ... **it** BB in this program is equivalent to the imperative

while x > 0 **do** **put** x; x := x − 1 **od**

12.1.2 Semantics

To give a formal specification of the semantics of Jump_0 – and other programming languages that allow jumps of various kinds – it is expedient to consider the meaning of an imperative to be a function that produces the final state of the program to which the imperative belongs when the function is given arguments that specify

(1) the environment in which the imperative is to be executed;

(2) the rest of the program, i.e., the continuation of the program after the imperative has terminated – assuming that the imperative terminates normally and that it does not jump, enter an infinite loop or perform an error;

(3) the state as it is before the imperative is executed.

Thus, the denotation of an imperative imp is a function $\mathcal{M}[\![\text{imp}]\!]$ that takes three arguments env, c and s, where env is an environment; c is a function that represents what may be called the *no-jump continuation* of imp, which is the rest of the program to be executed if imp does not jump; and s is the state as it is before imp is executed. These arguments are used as follows: First env is used to determine the meaning of identifiers that occur in imp. Then imp is executed from s, producing a new state s'. If imp does not jump, s' is given to c, which is a function that produces the final state of the program. What will happen if imp *does* jump – in Jump_0 this will be the case if **exit** id or **stop** is executed – must be specified in some other way, either in the environment or in the state. One way of specifying this is described below.

In the rest of this section we shall describe how the function c may be constructed such that it *'represents the rest of the program execution'* and show how to specify the semantics of jumps.

Continuations Let us define a *continuation* to be a function that maps states to states, and define the semantic domain *Cont* to consist of all strict and continuous continuations:

$$Cont \stackrel{d}{=} [State_{\perp} \rightarrow State_{\perp}]^{s}$$

(We restrict continuations to be strict and continuous functions in order to be able to prove the continuity of certain functions to which the fixpoint operator is applied.)

According to what we have said above about how to view the denotations of imperatives, the semantic mapping $\mathcal{M}$ shall have the following signature:

$$\begin{aligned}\mathcal{M} \in (Imp \rightarrow (Envir \rightarrow (Cont \rightarrow [State_{\perp} \rightarrow State_{\perp}]^{s}))) = \\ (Imp \rightarrow (Envir \rightarrow (Cont \rightarrow Cont)))\end{aligned}$$

Thus, an imperative may henceforth be considered to be a *continuation transformer*, and not a *state transformer.*

We redefine the domain *MV* of denotations of imperatives as follows:

$$MV \stackrel{d}{=} (Cont \rightarrow Cont)$$

Whenever necessary to avoid confusion, we prefix *MV* with either a lowered *s* (for standard) or a lowered *c* (for continuation) to distinguish between *MV* as previously defined and as defined here. Thus,

$$\begin{aligned}{}_{s}MV &= (State \rightarrow State) \\ {}_{c}MV &= (Cont \rightarrow Cont)\end{aligned}$$

Nonjumping imperatives It is not difficult to specify a continuation semantics of the imperatives inherited from Proc_0. The semantics of **put** imperatives may for instance be specified as follows:

$$\mathcal{M}[\![\textbf{put}\ \mathsf{exp}]\!](\mathsf{env, c, s}) = \mathsf{c(s.put(deref(s,}\ \mathcal{E}[\![\mathsf{exp}]\!](\mathsf{env, s}))))$$

The idea is: 1) evaluate exp in env for s, 2) let s' = s.put(deref(s, e)), where e = $\mathcal{E}[\![\mathsf{exp}]\!]$(env, s), be the state after outputting the value of exp, and 3) give s' to the continuation c which produces the final state of the program.

Continuation semantics for the other primitive imperatives may be defined similarly:

$$\mathcal{M}[\![\textbf{skip}]\!](\text{env}) = \lambda\text{c}: \underline{\lambda}\text{s}: \text{c(s)}$$
$$\mathcal{M}[\![\textbf{get}\ \text{exp}]\!](\text{env}) = \lambda\text{c}: \underline{\lambda}\text{s}: \text{c(s.get(ref(}\mathcal{E}[\![\text{exp}]\!](\text{env, s}))))$$
$$\mathcal{M}[\![\text{exp}_1 := \text{exp}_2]\!](\text{env}) = \lambda\text{c}: \underline{\lambda}\text{s}: \text{c(s.assign(deref(s, }\mathcal{E}[\![\text{exp}_1]\!](\text{env, s})), \text{ref(}\mathcal{E}[\![\text{exp}_2]\!](\text{env, s}))))$$

The effect of executing an imperative sequence $\text{imp}_1;\ \text{imp}_2$ for given env, c and s_0 is as follows: First execute imp_1 in environment env from state s_0. If imp_1 does not jump and terminates normally in a state s_1, continue to execute imp_2 in env from s_1. If this execution terminates normally, give the resulting state s_2 to the continuation c, which produces the final result $c(s_2)$. Thus, the no-jump continuation of imp_1 is $\underline{\lambda}\text{s}': \mathcal{M}[\![\text{imp}_2]\!](\text{env, c, s}')$, and we may specify the denotation of $\text{imp}_1;\ \text{imp}_2$ as follows:

$$\begin{aligned}\mathcal{M}[\![\text{imp}_1;\ \text{imp}_2]\!](\text{env, c, s})\\ &= \mathcal{M}[\![\text{imp}_1]\!](\text{env}, \underline{\lambda}\text{s}': \mathcal{M}[\![\text{imp}_2]\!](\text{env, c, s}'), \text{s})\\ &= \mathcal{M}[\![\text{imp}_1]\!](\text{env}, \mathcal{M}[\![\text{imp}_2]\!](\text{env, c}), \text{s})\end{aligned}$$

which means that

$$\begin{aligned}\mathcal{M}[\![\text{imp}_1;\ \text{imp}_2]\!](\text{env}) &= \lambda\text{c}: \underline{\lambda}\text{s}: \mathcal{M}[\![\text{imp}_1]\!](\text{env}, \mathcal{M}[\![\text{imp}_2]\!](\text{env, c}), \text{s})\\ &= \lambda\text{c}: \mathcal{M}[\![\text{imp}_1]\!](\text{env}, \mathcal{M}[\![\text{imp}_2]\!](\text{env, c}))\\ &= \mathcal{M}[\![\text{imp}_1]\!](\text{env}) \circ \mathcal{M}[\![\text{imp}_2]\!](\text{env})\end{aligned}$$

This may seem strange, but remember that we now consider the denotation mv of an imperative imp to be a transformer of continuations: It transforms a given continuation c to a new continuation mv(c). The given c is the state transformation performed by the rest of the program *after* imp has terminated, the transformed mv(c) is the state transformation performed by first doing imp and then the rest of the program. We work backwards compared to what we have previously done (that is why we call this a Copernican revolution): Start with the continuation c *after* the imperative, apply mv and get the continuation *before* the imperative. A sequence of two imperatives then transforms a given continuation as follows: First apply the denotation of the last of the imperatives to get the continuation *between* the imperatives, and then apply the denotation of the first imperative to get the continuation before the sequence.

Continuation semantics of conditional imperatives may be defined as follows:

$$\begin{aligned}&\mathcal{M}[\![\textbf{if}\ \text{exp}\ \textbf{then}\ \text{imp}_1\ \textbf{else}\ \text{imp}_2\ \textbf{fi}]\!](\text{env})\\ &\quad = \lambda\text{c}: \text{Cont'Cond}(\mathcal{E}[\![\text{exp}]\!](\text{env}), \mathcal{M}[\![\text{imp}_1]\!](\text{env, c}), \mathcal{M}[\![\text{imp}_2]\!](\text{env, c}))\end{aligned}$$

where

$$\begin{aligned}\text{Cont'Cond(ev, c}_1, \text{c}_2) \stackrel{d}{=} \underline{\lambda}\text{s}: &\ \textbf{case}\ \text{deref(s, ev(s))}\ \textbf{of}\\ &\quad \text{b} \in \mathit{Bool} \Rightarrow \textbf{if}\ \text{b}\ \textbf{then}\ \text{c}_1\text{(s)}\ \textbf{else}\ \text{c}_2\text{(s)}\\ &\quad \textbf{otherwise} \Rightarrow \bot_{\mathit{State}}\end{aligned}$$

For a given environment env and continuation c, the denotation of an imperative **while** bx **do** imp **od** should be a new continuation c*:

$$\mathcal{M}[\![\textbf{while}\ \mathsf{bx}\ \textbf{do}\ \mathsf{imp}\ \textbf{od}]\!](\mathsf{env},\ \mathsf{c}) = \mathsf{c}^*$$

This continuation c* should be such that it satisfies the following equation for any state s:

$$\begin{aligned}\mathsf{c}^*(\mathsf{s}) = \textbf{case}\ &\mathsf{deref}(\mathsf{s},\ \mathcal{E}[\![\mathsf{bx}]\!](\mathsf{env})(\mathsf{s}))\ \textbf{of}\\ &\mathsf{b} \in \mathit{Bool} \Rightarrow \textbf{if}\ \mathsf{b}\ \textbf{then}\ \mathcal{M}[\![\mathsf{imp}]\!](\mathsf{env},\ \mathsf{c}^*,\ \mathsf{s})\ \textbf{else}\ \mathsf{c}(\mathsf{s})\\ &\textbf{otherwise} \Rightarrow \bot_{\mathit{State}}\end{aligned}$$

But this means that the continuation semantics of a **while** imperative may be specified to be a fixpoint of a function that transforms continuations:

$$\begin{aligned}&\mathcal{M}[\![\textbf{while}\ \mathsf{bx}\ \textbf{do}\ \mathsf{imp}\ \textbf{od}]\!](\mathsf{env},\ \mathsf{c})\\ &\quad = \mathsf{Y}_{\mathit{Cont}}(\lambda \mathsf{c}^* \in \mathit{Cont}\colon \mathsf{Cont'Cond}(\mathcal{E}[\![\mathsf{bx}]\!](\mathsf{env}),\ \mathcal{M}[\![\mathsf{imp}]\!](\mathsf{env},\ \mathsf{c}^*),\ \mathsf{c}))\end{aligned}$$

The new imperatives Now to the semantics of the imperatives that are new to Jump_0. For the **stop** imperative, it is quite easy to give a formal specification which is in accordance with the informal semantics of the imperative:

$$\mathcal{M}[\![\textbf{stop}]\!](\mathsf{env},\ \mathsf{c},\ \mathsf{s}) = \mathsf{s}$$

Thus, the effect of **stop** is that the program does nothing more to the state: the final state produced by the program is the state as it is when **stop** is executed. The no-jump continuation c is not taken when **stop** is executed, and is not used in the specification of the semantics of **stop**.

It is somewhat more complex to specify the semantics of **exit** imperatives. A simple method is to bind an exit label, i.e., an identifier that occurs at the end of an exit block, to the continuation to be taken when the exit block terminates normally by executing its last imperative (if this is not a jump). To be able to do this, we first extend the algebra of denotable values such that continuations are included among the denotables and therefore may be bound to identifiers:

$$D \overset{d}{=} \ldots + \mathit{Cont}$$

The effect of executing an exit block '**ex** imp **it** label' may then be specified to be equal to executing the body imp in an environment where the identifier label is bound to the continuation to be taken after the exit block:

$$\begin{aligned}&\mathcal{M}[\![\textbf{ex}\ \mathsf{imp}\ \textbf{it}\ \mathsf{label}]\!](\mathsf{env},\ \mathsf{c},\ \mathsf{s})\\ &\qquad = \mathcal{M}[\![\mathsf{imp}]\!](\mathsf{env}.\mathsf{bind}(\mathsf{label},\ \mathsf{D'Cont}(\mathsf{c})),\ \mathsf{c},\ \mathsf{s})\end{aligned}$$

The effect of executing an exit imperative **exit** label in an environment env is to continue with the continuation bound to label by env:

$$\mathcal{M}[\![\textbf{exit}\ \mathsf{label}]\!](\mathsf{env, c, s}) = \textbf{case}\ \mathsf{env(label)}\ \textbf{of}\ D\text{:}\quad \mathsf{c}\ \textbf{in}\ \mathsf{Cont} \Rightarrow \mathsf{c(s)}\quad \textbf{otherwise}\ \bot_{State}$$
$$= \mathsf{env(label).qua\_Cont(s)}$$

In a typed and layered specification of the semantics of Jump_0, any attempt at **exit**ing to an identifier that is not implicitly declared to be a label (by occurring at the end of an exit block), would be discovered at the macro-level.

Programs The effect of executing a program from some given input sequence is to execute the imperatives of the program in an initially empty environment from an initial state containing the given input sequence, and with a continuation that does nothing:

$$\mathcal{P}[\![\mathsf{imp}]\!](\mathsf{inp}) = \mathcal{M}[\![\mathsf{imp}]\!](\mathsf{Envir'Void, Cont'Stop, State'Init(inp)}).\mathsf{Output}$$

where Cont'Stop is a continuation defined as follows:

$$\mathsf{Cont'Stop} \stackrel{d}{=} \underline{\lambda}\mathsf{s} \in State_\bot\text{: } \mathsf{s}$$

12.1.3 Two simple examples

Exit and stop The following example, which is the same as the first example given in section 12.1.1, illustrates the use of the formal specifications of the semantics of exit blocks, exits and stops:

$$\mathcal{P}[\![\textbf{ex put}\ 1;\ \textbf{exit}\ \mathsf{AA};\ \textbf{put}\ 2\ \textbf{it}\ \mathsf{AA};\ \textbf{put}\ 3;\ \textbf{stop};\ \textbf{put}\ 4]\!](\varepsilon)$$
$$= \mathcal{M}[\![\textbf{ex} \ldots \textbf{it}\ \mathsf{AA};\ \textbf{put}\ 3;\ \textbf{stop};\ \textbf{put}\ 4]\!](\mathsf{env}_0, \mathsf{c}_0, \mathsf{s}_0).\mathsf{Output}$$
where $\mathsf{env}_0 = \mathsf{Envir'Void}$, $\mathsf{c}_0 = \mathsf{Cont'Stop}$, $\mathsf{s}_0 = \mathsf{State'Init}(\varepsilon) = \langle \varepsilon, \mathsf{Store'Init}, \varepsilon, 0\rangle$

$$= \mathcal{M}[\![\textbf{ex put}\ 1;\ \textbf{exit}\ \mathsf{AA};\ \textbf{put}\ 2\ \textbf{it}\ \mathsf{AA}]\!](\mathsf{env}_0, \mathsf{c}_1, \mathsf{s}_0).\mathsf{Output}$$
where $\mathsf{c}_1 = \mathcal{M}[\![\textbf{put}\ 3;\ \textbf{stop};\ \textbf{put}\ 4]\!](\mathsf{env}_0, \mathsf{c}_0)$

$$= \mathcal{M}[\![\textbf{put}\ 1;\ \textbf{exit}\ \mathsf{AA};\ \textbf{put}\ 2]\!](\mathsf{env}_1, \mathsf{c}_1, \mathsf{s}_0).\mathsf{Output}$$
where $\mathsf{env}_1 = \mathsf{env}_0.\mathsf{bind}(\mathsf{AA}, \mathsf{c}_1)$

$$= \mathcal{M}[\![\textbf{put}\ 1]\!](\mathsf{env}_1, \mathcal{M}[\![\textbf{exit}\ \mathsf{AA};\ \textbf{put}\ 2]\!](\mathsf{env}_1, \mathsf{c}_1), \mathsf{s}_0).\mathsf{Output}$$
$$= \mathcal{M}[\![\textbf{exit}\ \mathsf{AA};\ \textbf{put}\ 2]\!](\mathsf{env}_1, \mathsf{c}_1, \mathsf{s}_1).\mathsf{Output}$$
where $\mathsf{s}_1 = \mathsf{s}_0.\mathsf{put}(1)$

$$= \mathcal{M}[\![\textbf{exit}\ \mathsf{AA}]\!](\mathsf{env}_1, \mathcal{M}[\![\textbf{put}\ 2]\!](\mathsf{env}_1, \mathsf{c}_1), \mathsf{s}_1).\mathsf{Output}$$
$$= (\mathsf{env}_1(\mathsf{AA}).\mathsf{qua\_Cont})(\mathsf{s}_1).\mathsf{Output}$$
$$= \mathsf{c}_1(\mathsf{s}_1).\mathsf{Output}$$
$$= \mathcal{M}[\![\textbf{put}\ 3;\ \textbf{stop};\ \textbf{put}\ 4]\!](\mathsf{env}_0, \mathsf{c}_0, \mathsf{s}_1).\mathsf{Output}$$

$$= \mathcal{M}[\![\textbf{put } 3]\!](\mathsf{env}_0, \mathcal{M}[\![\textbf{stop}; \textbf{put } 4]\!](\mathsf{env}_0, \mathsf{c}_0), \mathsf{s}_1)\,.\,\mathsf{Output}$$
$$= \mathcal{M}[\![\textbf{stop}; \textbf{put } 4]\!](\mathsf{env}_0, \mathsf{c}_0, \mathsf{s}_2)\,.\,\mathsf{Output} \quad \text{where } \mathsf{s}_2 = \mathsf{s}_1\,.\,\mathsf{put}(3)$$
$$= \mathcal{M}[\![\textbf{stop}]\!](\mathsf{env}_0, \mathcal{M}[\![\textbf{put } 4]\!](\mathsf{env}_0, \mathsf{c}_0), \mathsf{s}_2)\,.\,\mathsf{Output}$$
$$= \mathsf{s}_2\,.\,\mathsf{Output}$$
$$= \langle 1, 3\rangle$$

A nonterminating imperative The following example (where **true** is shorthand for some Boolean expression that is always true, for instance $0 = 0$) shows how a nonterminating **while** imperative is treated when we use continuation semantics:

$$\mathcal{M}[\![\textbf{while true do put } 1 \textbf{ od}]\!](\mathsf{env}, \mathsf{c})$$
$$= \mathsf{Y}_{Cont}(\lambda \mathsf{c'}\colon \mathsf{Cont'Cond}(\mathcal{E}[\![\textbf{true}]\!](\mathsf{env}), \mathcal{M}[\![\textbf{put } 1]\!](\mathsf{env}, \mathsf{c'}), \mathsf{c}))$$
$$= \underline{|Cont|}\mathsf{c}_i \quad \text{where } \mathsf{c}_0 = \bot_{Cont} = \lambda \mathsf{s}\colon \bot_{State}$$
$$\mathsf{c}_{i+1} = \mathsf{Cont'Cond}(\mathcal{E}[\![\textbf{true}]\!](\mathsf{env}), \mathcal{M}[\![\textbf{put } 1]\!](\mathsf{env}, \mathsf{c}_i), \mathsf{c}) = \underline{\lambda}\mathsf{s}\colon \mathsf{c}_i(\mathsf{s}\,.\,\mathsf{put}(1))$$
$$= \underline{|Cont|}\bot_{Cont} \quad \text{By induction on } i \text{ it is easy to prove that } \forall i \ge 0\colon \mathsf{c}_i = \bot_{Cont}$$
$$= \bot_{Cont}$$

12.1.4 Two equivalent imperatives

Consider the following exit block:

ex while true do if bx **then** imp **else exit** W **fi od it** W

where W is an identifier that we assume occurs in neither bx nor imp.

According to the intuitive, informal semantics of Jump_0, the exit block above should be equivalent to the following **while** imperative:

while bx **do** imp **od**

That the formal specifications given in section 12.1.2 entail that the two imperatives really are equivalent may be proved as follows:

$$\mathcal{M}[\![\textbf{ex while true do if } \mathsf{bx} \textbf{ then } \mathsf{imp} \textbf{ else exit } \mathsf{W} \textbf{ fi od it } \mathsf{W}]\!](\mathsf{env}, \mathsf{c}_0)$$
$$= \mathcal{M}[\![\textbf{while true do if } \mathsf{bx} \textbf{ then } \mathsf{imp} \textbf{ else exit } \mathsf{W} \textbf{ fi od}]\!](\mathsf{env'}, \mathsf{c}_0) \quad \text{where } \mathsf{env'} = \mathsf{env}\,.\,\mathsf{bind}(\mathsf{W}, \mathsf{c}_0)$$
$$= \mathsf{Y}_{Cont}(\lambda \mathsf{c'}\colon \mathsf{Cont'Cond}(\mathcal{E}[\![\textbf{true}]\!](\mathsf{env'}), \mathcal{M}[\![\textbf{if}\ldots\textbf{fi}]\!](\mathsf{env'}, \mathsf{c'}), \mathsf{c}))$$
$$= \mathsf{Y}_{Cont}(\lambda \mathsf{c'}\colon \mathcal{M}[\![\textbf{if}\ldots\textbf{fi}]\!](\mathsf{env'}, \mathsf{c'}))$$
$$= \mathsf{Y}_{Cont}(\lambda \mathsf{c'}\colon \mathsf{Cont'Cond}(\mathcal{E}[\![\mathsf{bx}]\!](\mathsf{env'}), \mathcal{M}[\![\mathsf{imp}]\!](\mathsf{env'}, \mathsf{c'}),$$

$$\mathcal{M}[\![\textbf{exit } \mathsf{W}]\!](\mathsf{env}', \mathsf{c}')))$$
$$= Y_{Cont}(\lambda \mathsf{c}'\colon \mathsf{Cont'Cond}(\mathcal{E}[\![\mathsf{bx}]\!](\mathsf{env}'), \mathcal{M}[\![\mathsf{imp}]\!](\mathsf{env}', \mathsf{c}'), \mathsf{c}_0))$$
$$= Y_{Cont}(\lambda \mathsf{c}'\colon \mathsf{Cont'Cond}(\mathcal{E}[\![\mathsf{bx}]\!](\mathsf{env}), \mathcal{M}[\![\mathsf{imp}]\!](\mathsf{env}, \mathsf{c}'), \mathsf{c}_0))$$
$$= \mathcal{M}[\![\textbf{while } \mathsf{bx} \textbf{ do } \mathsf{imp} \textbf{ od}]\!](\mathsf{env}, \mathsf{c}_0)$$

The second but last of the equalities above is justified by our assumption that the identifier W occurs in neither imp nor bx.

12.1.5 Welldefinedness

Section 12.1.2 contains a number of equations that we claim constitute a definition of the semantic mapping $\mathcal{M}$. The following proposition says that the equations are mathematically sound in the sense that they do define a function. The only reason we need to prove such a proposition, is the fact that the fixpoint operator is used in one of the equations, and this may be done only if the function to which the fixpoint operator is applied is a continuous function. It is not at all obvious that this is the case.

Proposition 12.1 *The function* $\mathcal{M}[\![\mathsf{imp}]\!]$ *is well-defined for every* Jump_0 *imperative* imp.

This proposition may be proved by induction on the syntactic complexity of the imperative imp. Often when we prove something by induction, it is advantageous to use an induction hypothesis which is stronger than that which we strictly need, i.e., to prove more than actually claimed. In the current case, it is convenient to prove the following proposition, from which proposition 12.1 follows as an immediate corollary:

Proposition 12.2 *For every* Jump_0 *imperative* imp, *every environment* env *and every continuation* c:

- **i**: $\mathcal{M}[\![\mathsf{imp}]\!]$ *is well-defined,*
- **ii**: *If* $\mathsf{c} \in Cont$ *then* $\mathcal{M}[\![\mathsf{imp}]\!](\mathsf{env}, \mathsf{c}) \in Cont$,
- **iii**: $\mathcal{M}[\![\mathsf{imp}]\!](\mathsf{env})$ *is continuous,*

Proof: By induction on the syntactic complexity of the imperative imp. We only treat the case imp = **while** exp **do** imp' **od** here (the other cases are much simpler). The induction hypothesis says that claims **i, ii** and **iii** hold for imp' and every env and c.

In section 12.1.2 $\mathcal{M}[\![\mathsf{imp}]\!](\mathsf{env}, \mathsf{c})$ is specified to be the least fixpoint of the function

$$\mathsf{qc} = \lambda \mathsf{c}' \in Cont\colon \mathsf{Cont'Cond}(\mathcal{E}[\![\mathsf{exp}]\!](\mathsf{env}), \mathcal{M}[\![\mathsf{imp}']\!](\mathsf{env}, \mathsf{c}'), \mathsf{c})$$

The Fixpoint Theorem (page 90) gives that **i** and **ii** hold if we can prove

iv: qc is continuous,

v: If $\mathsf{c'} \in \mathit{Cont}$ then $\mathsf{qc(c')} \in \mathit{Cont}$.

For any continuation $\mathsf{c'} \in \mathit{Cont}$ and any state $\mathsf{s'} \in \mathit{State}$ we have:

$$\begin{aligned}
\mathsf{qc(c')(s')} &= \mathsf{Cont'Cond}(\mathcal{E}[\![\mathsf{exp}]\!](\mathsf{env}), \mathcal{M}[\![\mathsf{imp'}]\!](\mathsf{env, c'}), \mathsf{c, s'}) \\
&= \textbf{case } \mathsf{deref}(\mathsf{s}, \mathcal{E}[\![\mathsf{exp}]\!](\mathsf{env})(\mathsf{s})) \textbf{ of} \\
&\quad \mathsf{b} \in \mathit{Bool} \Rightarrow \textbf{if } \mathsf{b} \textbf{ then } \mathcal{M}[\![\mathsf{imp'}]\!](\mathsf{env, c', s}) \\
&\qquad\qquad\qquad\qquad \textbf{else } \mathsf{c(s)} \\
&\quad \textbf{otherwise} \Rightarrow \bot_{\mathit{State}}
\end{aligned}$$

Because the function $\mathcal{E}[\![\mathsf{exp}]\!](\mathsf{env})$ is strict, we then get that $\mathsf{qc(c')}(\bot_{\mathit{State}}) = \bot_{\mathit{State}}$, i.e., $\mathsf{qc(c')}$ is strict. Proposition 5.3 on page 84 then gives that $\mathsf{qc(c')}$ is continuous. Claim **v** therefore holds.

To prove claim **iv**, it suffices to prove that qc is monotonic and preserves least upper bounds:

qc **is monotonic:** Assume that $\mathsf{c_1} \sqsubseteq_{\mathit{Cont}} \mathsf{c_2}$. We must prove that $\mathsf{qc(c_1)} \sqsubseteq_{\mathit{Cont}} \mathsf{qc(c_1)}$. By definition of $\sqsubseteq_{\mathit{Cont}}$ it suffices to prove that

$$\mathsf{qc(c_1, s')} \sqsubseteq_{\mathit{State}_\bot} \mathsf{qc(c_2, s')}$$

holds for every $\mathsf{s'} \in \mathit{State}$. By the definition of qc and of $\mathsf{Cont'Cond}$, it is easy to see that it suffices to show that

$$\mathcal{M}[\![\mathsf{imp'}]\!](\mathsf{env, c_1, s'}) \sqsubseteq_{\mathit{State}_\bot} \mathcal{M}[\![\mathsf{imp'}]\!](\mathsf{env, c_2, s'})$$

i.e., that

$$\mathcal{M}[\![\mathsf{imp'}]\!](\mathsf{env, c_1}) \sqsubseteq_{\mathit{Cont}} \mathcal{M}[\![\mathsf{imp'}]\!](\mathsf{env, c_2})$$

i.e, that $\mathcal{M}[\![\mathsf{imp'}]\!](\mathsf{env})$ is monotonic. But this follows directly from the induction hypothesis for proposition 12.2, which says that $\mathcal{M}[\![\mathsf{imp'}]\!](\mathsf{env})$ is continuous.

qc **preserves least upper bounds:** Assume that $\{\mathsf{c}_i\}_{i=0}^{\infty}$ is a chain in *Cont*. We have just proved that qc is monotonic. Applying this to the assumption, we get that $\{\mathsf{qc(c}_i\mathsf{)}\}_{i=0}^{\infty}$ is a chain, which is in *Cont* according to claim **v** (which we have established to hold for qc). It suffices to prove that

$$\mathsf{qc}(\underline{|\mathit{Cont}|}_{i=0}^{\infty}\mathsf{c}_i) = \underline{|\mathit{Cont}|}_{i=0}^{\infty}(\mathsf{qc(c}_i))$$

Two functions are equal if and only if they have equal values for all arguments. Our conclusion therefore follows if we can prove

$$\mathsf{qc}(\underline{|\mathit{Cont}|}_{i=0}^{\infty}\mathsf{c}_i)(\mathsf{s'}) = (\underline{|\mathit{Cont}|}_{i=0}^{\infty}\mathsf{qc(c}_i))(\mathsf{s'})$$

for every state $\mathsf{s'}$. If $\mathsf{s'}$ is such that $\mathcal{E}[\![\mathsf{exp}]\!](\mathsf{env, s'}) = \textbf{true}$:

$$\mathsf{qc}(\lfloor \mathit{Cont} \rfloor_{i=0}^{\infty} \mathsf{c}_i)(\mathsf{s'}) = \mathcal{M}[\![\mathsf{imp'}]\!](\mathsf{env}, \lfloor \mathit{Cont} \rfloor_{i=0}^{\infty} \mathsf{c}_i)(\mathsf{s'})$$

By definition of qc and Cont'Cond

$$= (\lfloor \mathit{Cont} \rfloor_{i=0}^{\infty} \mathcal{M}[\![\mathsf{imp'}]\!](\mathsf{env}, \mathsf{c}_i))(\mathsf{s'})$$

By the induction hypothesis for imp'

$$= \lfloor \mathit{State}_{\perp} \rfloor_{i=0}^{\infty} \mathcal{M}[\![\mathsf{imp'}]\!](\mathsf{env}, \mathsf{c}_i)(\mathsf{s'})$$

By proposition 5.3 on page 84

$$= \lfloor \mathit{State}_{\perp} \rfloor_{i=0}^{\infty} (\mathsf{qc}(\mathsf{c}_i)(\mathsf{s'}))$$

By definition of qc and Cont'Cond

$$= \lfloor \mathit{Cont} \rfloor_{i=0}^{\infty} \mathsf{qc}(\mathsf{c}_i)(\mathsf{s'})$$

By proposition 5.3

If s' is such that $\mathcal{E}[\![\mathsf{exp}]\!](\mathsf{env}, \mathsf{s'}) \neq$ **true**, the desired equality is easy to prove.

To prove claim **iii** is left as an exercise.

12.1.6 Congruence

We have defined two sets of semantic mappings for programs and imperatives of Jump_0: standard semantics in chapter 10 and continuation semantics in this chapter. We now prove that semantic mappings in these two sets are pairwise congruent. To distinguish the two sets of mappings, we decorate the standard mappings with prefixed $_s$'s, and the continuation mappings with prefixed $_c$'s.

Proposition 12.3 *For every* Jump_0 *imperative* imp, *every environment* env, *every* c ∈ *Cont and every state* s*:*

$$_c\mathcal{M}[\![\mathsf{imp}]\!](\mathsf{env}, \mathsf{c}, \mathsf{s}) = \mathsf{c}(_s\mathcal{M}[\![\mathsf{imp}]\!](\mathsf{env}, \mathsf{s}))$$

Proof: By induction on the syntactic complexity of imp. We treat only a few of the cases here, and leave the remaining cases to the diligent reader.

put imperatives:

$$\begin{aligned} &_c\mathcal{M}[\![\mathbf{put}\ \mathsf{exp}]\!](\mathsf{env}, \mathsf{c}, \mathsf{s}) \\ &\quad = \mathsf{c}(\mathsf{s}.\mathsf{put}(\mathsf{deref}(\mathsf{s}, \mathcal{E}[\![\mathsf{exp}]\!](\mathsf{env}, \mathsf{s})))) \\ &\quad = \mathsf{c}(_s\mathcal{M}[\![\mathbf{put}\ \mathsf{exp}]\!](\mathsf{env}, \mathsf{s})) \end{aligned}$$

Sequentially composed imperatives:

$$
\begin{aligned}
&{}_c\mathcal{M}[\![\mathsf{imp_1;\ imp_2}]\!](\mathsf{env, c, s})\\
&\quad = {}_c\mathcal{M}[\![\mathsf{imp_1}]\!](\mathsf{env}, {}_c\mathcal{M}[\![\mathsf{imp_2}]\!](\mathsf{env, c}), \mathsf{s})\\
&\quad = {}_c\mathcal{M}[\![\mathsf{imp_2}]\!](\mathsf{env, c})({}_s\mathcal{M}[\![\mathsf{imp_1}]\!](\mathsf{env, s})) \quad \text{(By ind. hyp. for imp}_1\text{)}\\
&\quad = {}_c\mathcal{M}[\![\mathsf{imp_2}]\!](\mathsf{env, c}, {}_s\mathcal{M}[\![\mathsf{imp_1}]\!](\mathsf{env, s}))\\
&\quad = \mathsf{c}({}_s\mathcal{M}[\![\mathsf{imp_2}]\!](\mathsf{env}, {}_s\mathcal{M}[\![\mathsf{imp_1}]\!](\mathsf{env, s}))) \quad \text{(By ind. hyp. for imp}_2\text{)}\\
&\quad = \mathsf{c}({}_s\mathcal{M}[\![\mathsf{imp_1;\ imp_2}]\!](\mathsf{env, s}))
\end{aligned}
$$

while imperatives:

$$
\begin{aligned}
&{}_c\mathcal{M}[\![\textbf{while}\ \mathsf{exp}\ \textbf{do}\ \mathsf{imp}\ \textbf{od}]\!](\mathsf{env, c, s})\\
&\quad = Y_{\mathit{Cont}}(\lambda \mathsf{c'}\!: \mathsf{Cont'Cond}(\mathcal{E}[\![\mathsf{exp}]\!](\mathsf{env}), \mathcal{M}[\![\mathsf{imp}]\!](\mathsf{env, c'}), \mathsf{c}))(\mathsf{s})\\
&\quad = (\underline{|\mathit{Cont}}|_{i=0}^{\infty} \mathsf{c}_i)(\mathsf{s})\\
&\qquad\qquad \text{where } \mathsf{c}_0 = \bot_{\mathit{Cont}}\\
&\qquad\qquad\qquad\quad\ = \lambda \mathsf{s}\!: \bot_{\mathit{State}}\\
&\qquad\qquad\quad \mathsf{c}_{i+1} = \mathsf{Cont'Cond}(\mathcal{E}[\![\mathsf{exp}]\!](\mathsf{env}),\\
&\qquad\qquad\qquad\qquad\qquad \mathcal{M}[\![\mathsf{imp}]\!](\mathsf{env}, \mathsf{c}_i), \mathsf{c})\\
&\quad = \underline{|\mathit{State}}|_{i=0}^{\infty} \mathsf{c}_i(\mathsf{s})
\end{aligned}
$$

$$
\begin{aligned}
&\mathsf{c}({}_s\mathcal{M}[\![\textbf{while}\ \mathsf{exp}\ \textbf{do}\ \mathsf{imp}\ \textbf{od}]\!](\mathsf{env, s}))\\
&\quad = \mathsf{c}(\underline{|\mathit{State}}|_{i=0}^{\infty} \mathsf{mv}_i(\mathsf{s}))\\
&\qquad\qquad \text{where } \mathsf{mv}_0 = \bot_{\mathit{MV}}\\
&\qquad\qquad\qquad\quad\ = \lambda \mathsf{s}\!: \bot_{\mathit{State}}\\
&\qquad\qquad\quad \mathsf{mv}_{i+1} = {}_s\mathsf{MV'Cond}(\mathcal{E}[\![\mathsf{exp}]\!](\mathsf{env}),\\
&\qquad\qquad\qquad\qquad\qquad {}_s\mathsf{MV'Seq}(\mathcal{M}[\![\mathsf{imp}]\!](\mathsf{env}), \mathsf{mv}_i),\\
&\qquad\qquad\qquad\qquad\qquad {}_s\mathsf{MV'Skip})
\end{aligned}
$$

That the claim in the proposition holds for the **while** imperative then follows from this lemma:

Lemma 12.1 $\forall i \geq 0, \forall\ \mathsf{s} \in \mathit{State}\!: \mathsf{c}_i(\mathsf{s}) = \mathsf{c}(\mathsf{mv}_i(\mathsf{s}))$

Proof: By induction on i:

$$
\begin{aligned}
i = 0\!: \mathsf{c}(\mathsf{mv}_0(\mathsf{s})) &= \mathsf{c}(\bot_{\mathit{State}}) && \text{(By definition of mv}_0\text{)}\\
&= \bot_{\mathit{State}} && \text{(c is strict by assumption)}\\
&= \mathsf{c}_0(\mathsf{s}) && \text{(By definition of c}_0\text{)}
\end{aligned}
$$

$i + 1$: Assume first that $\mathcal{E}[\![\mathsf{exp}]\!](\mathsf{env, s}) = \textbf{true}$. Then

$$
\begin{aligned}
\mathsf{c}(\mathsf{mv}_{i+1}(\mathsf{s})) &= \mathsf{c}(\mathsf{mv}_i({}_s\mathcal{M}[\![\mathsf{imp}]\!](\mathsf{env, s}))) && \text{(By definition of mv}_{i+1}\text{)}\\
&= \mathsf{c}_i({}_s\mathcal{M}[\![\mathsf{imp}]\!](\mathsf{env, s})) && \text{(By ind. hyp. for } i\text{)}\\
&= {}_c\mathcal{M}[\![\mathsf{imp}]\!](\mathsf{env}, \mathsf{c}_i, \mathsf{s}) && \text{(By ind. hyp. for imp)}\\
&= \mathsf{c}_{i+1}(\mathsf{s}) && \text{(By definition of c}_{i+1}\text{)}
\end{aligned}
$$

The remaining case $\mathcal{E}[\![\mathsf{exp}]\!](\mathsf{env, s}) \neq \textbf{true}$ is simpler.

End of proof of lemma 12.1
End of proof of proposition 12.3

Theorem 12.1 *The standard semantics and the continuation semantics for* Jump$_0$ *are congruent: For every* Jump$_0$ *imperative* imp

$$_c\mathcal{P}[\![\mathsf{imp}]\!] = {}_s\mathcal{P}[\![\mathsf{imp}]\!]$$

Proof: $_c\mathcal{P}[\![\mathsf{imp}]\!](\mathsf{inp})$

$= {}_c\mathcal{M}[\![\mathsf{imp}]\!](\mathsf{Envir'Void, Cont'Stop, State'Init(inp)}).\mathsf{Output}$
By definition of $_c\mathcal{P}$

$= \mathsf{Cont'Stop}({}_s\mathcal{M}[\![\mathsf{imp}]\!](\mathsf{Envir'Void, State'Init(inp)})).\mathsf{Output}$
By proposition 12.3

$= {}_s\mathcal{M}[\![\mathsf{imp}]\!](\mathsf{Envir'Void, State'Init(inp)}).\mathsf{Output}$
By definition of Cont'Stop

$= {}_s\mathcal{P}[\![\mathsf{imp}]\!](\mathsf{inp})$
By definition of $_s\mathcal{P}$

12.2 Layered continuation semantics

Figure 12.1 contains a layered specification of the continuation semantics of the imperatives of Jump$_0$. Observe that standard semantics (i.e., noncontinuation) and continuation semantics of the nonjumping imperatives of Jump$_0$ are equal at macro- and micro-level. Only at the intermediate level is there any difference between the two ways of defining the semantics. We may say that continuations only are 'visible' at the intermediate layer.

For some of the imperatives it may not be obvious that the layered semantic specifications given in figure 12.1 are equivalent to the unlayered and more direct specifications given in section 12.1.2 above. An example: On page 270, we defined the denotation of a **while** imperative as follows:

$$\mathcal{M}[\![\textbf{while}\ \mathsf{bx}\ \textbf{do}\ \mathsf{imp}\ \textbf{od}]\!](\mathsf{env, c})$$
$$= \mathsf{Y}_{\mathit{Cont}}(\lambda \mathsf{c}^* \in \mathit{Cont}\colon \mathsf{Cont'Cond(bv, mv(c^*), c)})$$
$$\text{where } \mathsf{bv} = \mathcal{E}[\![\mathsf{bx}]\!](\mathsf{env}) \text{ and } \mathsf{mv} = \mathcal{M}[\![\mathsf{imp}]\!](\mathsf{env})$$

This definition is quite different from the definition given in figure 12.1, where the denotation of a **while** imperative is defined as follows:

$$\mathcal{M}[\![\textbf{while}\ \mathsf{bx}\ \textbf{do}\ \mathsf{imp}\ \textbf{od}]\!](\mathsf{env})$$
$$= \mathsf{Y}_{\mathit{MV}}(\lambda \mathsf{mv}^* \in \mathit{MV}\colon \mathsf{MV'Cond(bv, MV'Seq(mv, mv^*), MV'Skip)})$$

In order to prove that these definitions are equivalent, we use the Fixpoint Theorem, which says that the fixpoints may be found as least upper bounds of certain chains. Thus, for fixpoint used in the definition in section 12.1.2 we have

$$
\begin{aligned}
&\mathcal{M}[\![\textbf{skip}]\!](\mathrm{env}) &&= {}_c\mathrm{MV'Skip}\\
&\mathcal{M}[\![\textbf{put}\ \mathrm{exp}]\!](\mathrm{env}) &&= {}_c\mathrm{MV'Put}(\mathcal{E}[\![\mathrm{exp}]\!](\mathrm{env}))\\
&\mathcal{M}[\![\textbf{get}\ \mathrm{exp}]\!](\mathrm{env}) &&= {}_c\mathrm{MV'Get}(\mathcal{E}[\![\mathrm{exp}]\!](\mathrm{env}))\\
&\mathcal{M}[\![\mathrm{lex} := \mathrm{rex}]\!](\mathrm{env}) &&= {}_c\mathrm{MV'Assign}(\mathcal{E}[\![\mathrm{lex}]\!](\mathrm{env}),\ \mathcal{E}[\![\mathrm{rex}]\!](\mathrm{env}))\\
&\mathcal{M}[\![\mathrm{rx}(\mathrm{px})]\!](\mathrm{env}) &&= {}_c\mathrm{MV'Call}(\mathcal{E}[\![\mathrm{rx}]\!](\mathrm{env}),\ \mathcal{E}[\![\mathrm{px}]\!](\mathrm{env}))
\end{aligned}
$$

$$
\begin{aligned}
&\mathcal{M}[\![\mathrm{imp}_1;\ \mathrm{imp}_1]\!](\mathrm{env}) = {}_c\mathrm{MV'Seq}(\mathcal{M}[\![\mathrm{imp}_1]\!](\mathrm{env}),\ \mathcal{M}[\![\mathrm{imp}_1]\!](\mathrm{env}))\\
&\mathcal{M}[\![\textbf{if}\ \mathrm{b}\ \textbf{then}\ \mathrm{imp}_1\ \textbf{else}\ \mathrm{imp}_2\ \textbf{fi}]\!](\mathrm{env})\\
&\qquad = {}_c\mathrm{MV'Cond}(\mathcal{E}[\![\mathrm{b}]\!](\mathrm{env}),\ \mathcal{M}[\![\mathrm{imp}_1]\!](\mathrm{env}),\ \mathcal{M}[\![\mathrm{imp}_1]\!](\mathrm{env}))\\
&\mathcal{M}[\![\textbf{while}\ \mathrm{b}\ \textbf{do}\ \mathrm{imp}\ \textbf{od}]\!](\mathrm{env})\\
&\qquad = {}_c\mathrm{MV'While}(\mathcal{E}[\![\mathrm{b}]\!](\mathrm{env}),\ \mathcal{M}[\![\mathrm{imp}]\!](\mathrm{env}))\\
&\mathcal{M}[\![\textbf{begin}\ \mathrm{vd};\ \mathrm{cd};\ \mathrm{imp}\ \textbf{end}]\!](\mathrm{env})\\
&\qquad = {}_c\mathrm{MV'Block}(\mathrm{env},\ \mathcal{VD}[\![\mathrm{vd}]\!](\mathrm{env}),\ \mathcal{CD}[\![\mathrm{cd}]\!],\ \mathcal{M}[\![\mathrm{imp}]\!])
\end{aligned}
$$

$$
\begin{aligned}
&\mathcal{M}[\![\textbf{stop}]\!](\mathrm{env}) &&= {}_c\mathrm{MV'Stop}\\
&\mathcal{M}[\![\textbf{ex}\ \mathrm{imp}\ \textbf{it}\ \mathrm{x}]\!](\mathrm{env}) &&= {}_c\mathrm{MV'ExitBlock}(\mathcal{M}[\![\mathrm{imp}]\!],\ \mathrm{env},\ \mathrm{x})\\
&\mathcal{M}[\![\textbf{exit}\ \mathrm{id}]\!](\mathrm{env}) &&= {}_c\mathrm{MV'Exit}(\mathrm{env}(\mathrm{id}).\mathrm{qua\_Cont})
\end{aligned}
$$

$$
\begin{aligned}
&{}_c\mathrm{MV'Skip} &&\stackrel{d}{=} \lambda \mathrm{c}:\ \mathrm{c}\\
&{}_c\mathrm{MV'Put}(\mathrm{ev}) &&\stackrel{d}{=} \lambda \mathrm{c}: \underline{\lambda} \mathrm{s}:\ \mathrm{c}(\mathrm{s}.\mathrm{put}(\mathrm{deref}(\mathrm{s},\ \mathrm{ev}(\mathrm{s}))))\\
&{}_c\mathrm{MV'Get}(\mathrm{ev}) &&\stackrel{d}{=} \lambda \mathrm{c}: \underline{\lambda} \mathrm{s}:\ \mathrm{c}(\mathrm{s}.\mathrm{get}(\mathrm{ref}(\mathrm{ev}(\mathrm{s}))))\\
&{}_c\mathrm{MV'Assign}(\mathrm{lv},\ \mathrm{rv}) &&\stackrel{d}{=} \lambda \mathrm{c}: \underline{\lambda} \mathrm{s}:\ \mathrm{c}(\mathrm{s}.\mathrm{assign}(\mathrm{ref}(\mathrm{lv}(\mathrm{s})),\ \mathrm{deref}(\mathrm{s},\ \mathrm{rv}(\mathrm{s}))))\\
&{}_c\mathrm{MV'Seq}(\mathrm{mv}_1,\ \mathrm{mv}_2) &&\stackrel{d}{=} \mathrm{mv}_1 \circ \mathrm{mv}_2\\
&{}_c\mathrm{MV'While}(\mathrm{ev},\ \mathrm{mv}) &&\stackrel{d}{=} \mathrm{Y}_{MV}(\lambda \mathrm{mv}^* \in MV:\ {}_c\mathrm{MV'Cond}(\mathrm{ev},\\
& &&\qquad\qquad {}_c\mathrm{MV'Seq}(\mathrm{mv},\ \mathrm{mv}^*),\ {}_c\mathrm{MV'Skip}))\\
&{}_c\mathrm{MV'Call}(\mathrm{pv},\ \mathrm{av}) &&\stackrel{d}{=} \lambda \mathrm{c}: \underline{\lambda} \mathrm{s}:\ \textbf{case}\ \mathrm{pv}(\mathrm{s})\ \textbf{of}\ E\text{: } \mathrm{pp} \in PP\text{: } \mathrm{pp}(\mathrm{av}(\mathrm{s}),\ \mathrm{c},\ \mathrm{s})\\
& &&\qquad\qquad\qquad\qquad \textbf{otherwise}\text{: } \bot_{State}\\
&{}_c\mathrm{MV'Block}(\mathrm{env},\ \mathrm{vv},\ \mathrm{edc},\ \mathrm{mve}) &&\stackrel{d}{=} \lambda \mathrm{c}: \underline{\lambda} \mathrm{s}:\ \textbf{let}\ \langle \mathrm{env}_v,\ \mathrm{s}_1\rangle = \mathrm{vv}(\mathrm{s})\ \textbf{in}\\
& &&\qquad \textbf{let}\ \mathrm{env}_c = \mathrm{edc}(\mathrm{env} + \mathrm{env}_v)\ \textbf{in}\\
& &&\qquad \mathrm{mve}(\mathrm{env} + \mathrm{env}_v + \mathrm{env}_c)(\mathrm{c},\ \mathrm{s}_1)\\
&{}_c\mathrm{MV'Cond}(\mathrm{ev},\ \mathrm{mv}_1,\ \mathrm{mv}_2) &&\stackrel{d}{=} \lambda \mathrm{c}: \underline{\lambda} \mathrm{s}:\ \textbf{case}\ \mathrm{ev}(\mathrm{s})\ \textbf{of}\ E\text{:}\\
& &&\qquad \mathrm{b} \in Bool \Rightarrow \textbf{if}\ \mathrm{b}\ \textbf{then}\ \mathrm{mv}_1(\mathrm{c},\ \mathrm{s})\\
& &&\qquad\qquad\qquad\qquad\quad \textbf{else}\ \mathrm{mv}_2(\mathrm{c},\ \mathrm{s})\\
& &&\qquad \textbf{otherwise} \Rightarrow \bot_{State}\\
&{}_c\mathrm{MV'ExitBlock}(\mathrm{me},\ \mathrm{env},\ \mathrm{x}) &&\stackrel{d}{=} \lambda \mathrm{c}:\ \mathrm{me}(\mathrm{env}.\mathrm{bind}(\mathrm{x},\ \mathrm{D'Cont}(\mathrm{c})),\ \mathrm{c})\\
&{}_c\mathrm{MV'Exit}(\mathrm{xc}) &&\stackrel{d}{=} \lambda \mathrm{c}:\ \mathrm{xc}\\
&{}_c\mathrm{MV'Stop} &&\stackrel{d}{=} \lambda \mathrm{c}: \mathrm{Cont'Stop}\\
& &&\quad \text{where } \mathrm{Cont'Stop} = \underline{\lambda} \mathrm{s}:\ \mathrm{s}
\end{aligned}
$$

Figure 12.1: Layered continuation semantics for Jump_0 imperatives

$$
\begin{aligned}
&\mathsf{Y}_{Cont}(\lambda \mathsf{c}^* \in Cont\colon \mathsf{Cont'Cond(ev,\ mv(c^*),\ c)})\\
&\quad = \lfloor\underline{Cont}\rfloor \mathsf{c}_i \qquad \text{where } \mathsf{c}_0 = \bot_{Cont} = \lambda \mathsf{s} \in State_\bot\colon \bot_{State}\\
&\qquad\qquad\qquad\qquad\quad\ \mathsf{c}_{i+1} = \mathsf{Cont'Cond(bv,\ mv(c}_i\mathsf{),\ c)}
\end{aligned}
$$

whereas for the fixpoint in figure 12.1 we get:

$$
\begin{aligned}
&\mathsf{Y}_{MV}(\lambda \mathsf{mv}^* \in {}_cMV\colon {}_c\mathsf{MV'Cond(bv,\ }{}_c\mathsf{MV'Seq(mv,\ mv^*),\ }{}_c\mathsf{MV'Skip))}\\
&\quad = \lfloor\underline{{}_cMV}\rfloor \mathsf{mv}_i \qquad \text{where } \mathsf{mv}_0 = \bot_{MV} = \lambda \mathsf{c} \in Cont_\bot\colon \bot_{Cont}\\
&\qquad\qquad\qquad\qquad\quad\ \mathsf{mv}_{i+1} = {}_c\mathsf{MV'Cond(bv,\ }{}_c\mathsf{MV'Seq(mv,\ mv}_i\mathsf{),}\\
&\qquad\qquad\qquad\qquad\qquad\qquad\qquad\qquad {}_c\mathsf{MV'Skip)}\\
&\quad = \lambda \mathsf{c}\colon (\lfloor\underline{{}_cMV}\rfloor \mathsf{mv}_i)(\mathsf{c})\\
&\quad = \lambda \mathsf{c}\colon \lfloor\underline{Cont}\rfloor(\mathsf{mv}_i(\mathsf{c}))
\end{aligned}
$$

The following lemma then entails that the two definitions are equivalent.

Lemma 12.2 *For every i:* $\mathsf{c}_i = \mathsf{mv}_i(\mathsf{c})$

Proof: By induction on i:

$$
\begin{aligned}
i = 0\colon\ \mathsf{mv}_0(\mathsf{c}) &= \bot_{Cont} = \mathsf{c}_0\\
i + 1\colon\ \mathsf{mv}_{i+1}(\mathsf{c}) &= {}_c\mathsf{MV'Cond(bv,\ }{}_c\mathsf{MV'Seq(mv,\ mv}_i\mathsf{),\ }{}_c\mathsf{MV'Skip)(c)}\\
&= \underline{\lambda}\mathsf{s}\colon\ \textbf{case}\ \mathsf{deref(s,\ bv(s))}\ \textbf{of}\\
&\qquad\quad \mathsf{b} \in Bool \Rightarrow \textbf{if}\ \mathsf{b}\ \textbf{then}\ {}_c\mathsf{MV'Seq(mv,\ mv}_i\mathsf{)(c,\ s)}\\
&\qquad\qquad\qquad\qquad\qquad\quad \textbf{else}\ {}_c\mathsf{MV'Skip(c,\ s)}\\
&\qquad\quad \textbf{otherwise} \Rightarrow \bot_{State}\\
&= \underline{\lambda}\mathsf{s}\colon\ \textbf{case}\ \mathsf{deref(s,\ bv(s))}\ \textbf{of}\\
&\qquad\quad \mathsf{b} \in Bool \Rightarrow \textbf{if}\ \mathsf{b}\ \textbf{then}\ \mathsf{mv(mv}_i\mathsf{(c),\ s)}\\
&\qquad\qquad\qquad\qquad\qquad\quad \textbf{else}\ \mathsf{c(s)}\\
&\qquad\quad \textbf{otherwise} \Rightarrow \bot_{State}\\
&= \underline{\lambda}\mathsf{s}\colon\ \textbf{case}\ \mathsf{deref(s,\ bv(s))}\ \textbf{of}\\
&\qquad\quad \mathsf{b} \in Bool \Rightarrow \textbf{if}\ \mathsf{b}\ \textbf{then}\ \mathsf{mv(c}_i\mathsf{,\ s)}\\
&\qquad\qquad\qquad\qquad\qquad\quad \textbf{else}\ \mathsf{c(s)}\\
&\qquad\quad \textbf{otherwise} \Rightarrow \bot_{State}\\
&= \mathsf{Cont'Cond(bv,\ mv(c}_i\mathsf{),\ c)}\\
&= \mathsf{c}_{i+1}
\end{aligned}
$$

12.3 Goto's

Many programming languages allow quite unrestricted jumps: not only forward in a program like exits, but also backwards (thus enabling loops) and even – at least in some languages in the Algol family –

into the middle of compound constructs, for instance into branches of conditional imperatives. In this section we show how to specify the semantics of jumps that are disciplined in the sense that we do not allow jumps into the middle of compound constructs like conditional imperatives or while imperatives. But backwards jumps are allowed.

12.3.1 Syntax

Let Jump_1 be the result of extending Proc_0 with the following BNF productions:

$$\langle imp \rangle ::= \ldots \mid \textbf{gtbegin}\ \langle ident \rangle : \langle imp \rangle ; \ldots ; \langle ident \rangle : \langle imp \rangle\ \textbf{gtend} \mid \textbf{goto}\ \langle ident \rangle$$

An imperative **gtbegin** $\mathsf{id}_1 : \mathsf{imp}_1 ; \ldots ; \mathsf{id}_n : \mathsf{imp}_n$ **gtend** is said to be a *label block*, and the identifiers $\mathsf{id}_1, \ldots, \mathsf{id}_n$ are called *labels*.

The informal semantics of the new constructs should be obvious, except possibly for one thing: labels are assumed to be implicitly declared in its enclosing label block. This entails that a label has its label block as its scope, and that jumps into a label block are not allowed (because the label is not visible outside its scope).

An example:

gtbegin Rep: **if** exp **then** imp; **goto** Rep **else skip fi gtend**

We prove below that the effect of this imperative is equivalent to the imperative **while** exp **do** imp **od**.

12.3.2 Semantics

To specify the semantics of **goto**'s and label blocks, we extend the algebra of denotables with continuations, just as we did for Jump_0:

$$D \stackrel{d}{=} \ldots + \mathit{Cont}$$

The semantics of goto's is then simple to specify:

$$\mathcal{M}[\![\textbf{goto}\ \mathsf{label}]\!](\mathsf{env}, \mathsf{c}) = \mathsf{env}(\mathsf{label}).\mathsf{qua\_Cont}$$

This is, of course, identical to how we specified the semantics of exits in section 12.1.

Label blocks are more complex. We would like to specify their semantics as follows:

$$
\begin{aligned}
&\mathcal{M}[\![\textbf{gtbegin}\ \mathsf{lab}_1 : \mathsf{imp}_1; \ldots; \mathsf{lab}_n : \mathsf{imp}_n\ \textbf{gtend}]\!](\mathsf{env}, \mathsf{c})\\
&\quad = \mathsf{c}_1, \text{ where } \mathsf{c}_1 \overset{d}{=} \mathcal{M}[\![\mathsf{imp}_1]\!](\mathsf{env}', \mathsf{c}_2)\\
&\qquad\qquad \text{and } \mathsf{c}_2 \overset{d}{=} \mathcal{M}[\![\mathsf{imp}_2]\!](\mathsf{env}', \mathsf{c}_3)\\
&\qquad\qquad \ldots\\
&\qquad\qquad \text{and } \mathsf{c}_n \overset{d}{=} \mathcal{M}[\![\mathsf{imp}_n]\!](\mathsf{env}', \mathsf{c})\\
&\qquad\qquad \text{and } \mathsf{env}' \overset{d}{=} \mathsf{env}.\mathsf{bind}(\mathsf{lab}_1, \mathsf{D'Cont}(\mathsf{c}_1))\\
&\qquad\qquad\qquad\qquad .\mathsf{bind}(\mathsf{lab}_2, \mathsf{D'Cont}(\mathsf{c}_2))\\
&\qquad\qquad\qquad\qquad \ldots\\
&\qquad\qquad\qquad\qquad .\mathsf{bind}(\mathsf{lab}_n, \mathsf{D'Cont}(\mathsf{c}_n))
\end{aligned}
$$

This is, however, a circular definition: the continuations $\mathsf{c}_1, \ldots, \mathsf{c}_n$ are defined in terms of the environment env', which is defined in terms of the continuations $\mathsf{c}_1, \ldots, \mathsf{c}_n$. We may, however, reduce the circularity to an acceptable level by using fixpoints over $Cont^n$ as follows:

$$
\begin{aligned}
&\mathcal{M}[\![\textbf{gtbegin}\ \mathsf{lab}_1 : \mathsf{imp}_1; \ldots; \mathsf{lab}_n : \mathsf{imp}_n\ \textbf{gtend}]\!](\mathsf{env}, \mathsf{c})\\
&\quad = \mathsf{Y}_{Cont^n}(\lambda\langle \mathsf{c}_1, \ldots, \mathsf{c}_n\rangle : \textbf{let}\ \mathsf{env}' = \mathsf{env}.\mathsf{bind}(\mathsf{lab}_1, \mathsf{D'Cont}(\mathsf{c}_1))\\
&\qquad\qquad\qquad\qquad .\mathsf{bind}(\mathsf{lab}_2, \mathsf{D'Cont}(\mathsf{c}_2))\\
&\qquad\qquad\qquad\qquad \ldots\\
&\qquad\qquad\qquad\qquad .\mathsf{bind}(\mathsf{lab}_n, \mathsf{D'Cont}(\mathsf{c}_n))\\
&\qquad\qquad \textbf{in}\ \langle\ \mathcal{M}[\![\mathsf{imp}_1]\!](\mathsf{env}', \mathsf{c}_2),\\
&\qquad\qquad\quad \mathcal{M}[\![\mathsf{imp}_2]\!](\mathsf{env}', \mathsf{c}_3),\\
&\qquad\qquad\quad \ldots\\
&\qquad\qquad\quad \mathcal{M}[\![\mathsf{imp}_{n-1}]\!](\mathsf{env}', \mathsf{c}_n)\\
&\qquad\qquad\quad \mathcal{M}[\![\mathsf{imp}_n]\!](\mathsf{env}', \mathsf{c})\ \rangle\\
&\qquad)\!\downarrow\! 1
\end{aligned}
$$

12.3.3 A proposition connecting while and goto

The following proposition says that any **while** imperative is equivalent in effect to an imperative without **while**, but with a **goto**. Thus, **while**'s may be emulated by **goto**'s.

Proposition 12.4 *For any Boolean expression* exp, *imperative* imp *and identifier* Rep *where* Rep *occurs in neither* exp *nor* imp*:*

$$
\begin{aligned}
\mathcal{M}[\![\textbf{while}\ \mathsf{exp}\ \textbf{do}\ \mathsf{imp}\ \textbf{od}]\!] = \mathcal{M}[\![&\textbf{gtbegin}\\
&\quad \mathsf{Rep}: \textbf{if}\ \mathsf{exp}\ \textbf{then}\ \mathsf{imp};\ \textbf{goto}\ \mathsf{Rep}\\
&\qquad\qquad \textbf{else skip fi}\\
&\textbf{gtend}]\!]
\end{aligned}
$$

Proof:

$$
\begin{aligned}
&\mathcal{M}[\![\textbf{gtbegin}\ \mathsf{Rep}: \textbf{if} \ldots \textbf{fi}\ \textbf{gtend}]\!](\mathsf{env}, \mathsf{c})\\
&\quad = \mathsf{Y}_{Cont}(\lambda \mathsf{c}_1 : \mathcal{M}[\![\textbf{if} \ldots \textbf{fi}]\!](\mathsf{env}', \mathsf{c}))\\
&\qquad \text{where } \mathsf{env}' = \mathsf{env}.\mathsf{bind}(\mathsf{Rep}, \mathsf{D'Cont}(\mathsf{c}_1))
\end{aligned}
$$

$$\begin{aligned}
&= Y_{Cont}(\lambda c_1{:}\,\text{Cont'Cond}(\mathcal{E}[\![\text{exp}]\!](\text{env}),\\
&\qquad\qquad\qquad\qquad \mathcal{M}[\![\text{imp; }\mathbf{goto}\text{ Rep}]\!](\text{env}', c),\\
&\qquad\qquad\qquad\qquad c))\\
&= Y_{Cont}(\lambda c_1{:}\,\text{Cont'Cond}(\mathcal{E}[\![\text{exp}]\!](\text{env}),\\
&\qquad\qquad\qquad\qquad \mathcal{M}[\![\text{imp}]\!](\text{env}, \mathcal{M}[\![\mathbf{goto}\text{ Rep}]\!](\text{env}', c)),\\
&\qquad\qquad\qquad\qquad c))\\
&= Y_{Cont}(\lambda c_1{:}\,\text{Cont'Cond}(\mathcal{E}[\![\text{exp}]\!](\text{env}),\\
&\qquad\qquad\qquad\qquad \mathcal{M}[\![\text{imp}]\!](\text{env}, c_1),\\
&\qquad\qquad\qquad\qquad c))\\
&= \mathcal{M}[\![\mathbf{while}\text{ exp }\mathbf{do}\text{ imp }\mathbf{od}]\!](\text{env}, c)
\end{aligned}$$

12.4 Expressions that change the state

Many programming languages are such that the evaluation of certain expressions as a side-effect may change the state. If this is the case for a language in which jumps are allowed, we may specify the semantics of the language using so-called *expression continuations* (defined below). In this section we show how this may be done for Jump_0 extended with the following BNF production:

$$\langle expr\rangle ::= \ldots \mid \mathbf{valof}\ \langle imp\rangle\ \mathbf{result}\ \langle expr\rangle$$

The intended effect of evaluating an expression **valof** imp **result** expr is first to execute the imperative imp (thus generally changing the state), and then evaluate the expression exp in the state as it is after imp has been executed.

12.4.1 Expression continuations

An expression continuation is a mathematical object that may be used to represent the rest of a program execution after the evaluation of an expression. It may be looked upon as a function that takes as arguments the value of the expression and the state as it is after the expression has been evaluated, and that has the final state of the program as its value. This means that an expression continuation ec should have the following signature:

$$\text{ec} \in (E \to (State \to State))$$

For technical reasons (namely to be able to prove the continuity of the functions to which the fixpoint operator is applied) we restrict expression continuations to be strict and continuous functions. Remembering that the domain *Cont* consists of the strict and continuous functions mapping states to states, we define expression continuations to be elements of the domain *ECont* defined as follows:

$$ECont \stackrel{d}{=} [E_\perp \to Cont_\perp]^s$$

12.4.2 Semantic mappings

The semantic mapping $\mathcal{E}$ for expressions must be redefined to be able to handle expressions with side-effects. The redefined mapping should have the following signature:

$$\mathcal{E} \in (\mathit{Exp} \to (\mathit{Envir} \to (\mathit{ECont} \to \mathit{Cont}_\perp)))$$

An expression exp is evaluated as follows for an environment env, an expression continuation ec $\in$ *ECont* and a state s: use env to determine the meaning of the identifiers that occur in exp, evaluate exp in s, and give its value e and the state s' as it is after exp has been evaluated to ec (which represents the rest of the program execution). The value of ec(e, s') is the final state produced by the program.

Using the ideas above, we define the new version of $\mathcal{E}$ as follows:

$$\mathcal{E}[\![\mathsf{lit}]\!](\mathsf{env}, \mathsf{ec}) = \mathsf{ec}(\mathsf{E'Int}(\mathcal{A}[\![\mathsf{lit}]\!]))$$

$$\mathcal{E}[\![\mathsf{id}]\!](\mathsf{env}, \mathsf{ec}) = \mathsf{ec}(\mathsf{env}(\mathsf{id}))$$

$$\begin{aligned}&\mathcal{E}[\![\textbf{valof}\ \mathsf{imp}\ \textbf{result}\ \mathsf{exp}]\!](\mathsf{env}, \mathsf{ec})\\ &\qquad = \mathcal{M}[\![\mathsf{imp}]\!](\mathsf{env}, \mathcal{E}[\![\mathsf{exp}]\!](\mathsf{env}, \mathsf{ec}))\end{aligned}$$

$$\begin{aligned}&\mathcal{E}[\![\mathsf{uop}\ \mathsf{exp}]\!](\mathsf{env}, \mathsf{ec})\\ &\qquad = \mathcal{E}[\![\mathsf{exp}]\!](\mathsf{env}, \lambda \mathsf{e} \in E\colon \underline{\lambda}\mathsf{s}\colon \mathsf{ec}(\mathcal{UO}[\![\mathsf{uop}]\!](\mathsf{deref}(\mathsf{s}, \mathsf{e}))))\end{aligned}$$

$$\begin{aligned}&\mathcal{E}[\![\mathsf{exp}_1\ \mathsf{bop}\ \mathsf{exp}_2]\!](\mathsf{env}, \mathsf{ec})\\ &\qquad = \mathcal{E}[\![\mathsf{exp}_1]\!](\mathsf{env}, \lambda \mathsf{e}_1 \in E\colon \mathcal{E}[\![\mathsf{exp}_2]\!](\mathsf{env}, \lambda \mathsf{e}_2 \in E\colon\\ &\qquad\qquad \underline{\lambda}\mathsf{s}\colon \mathsf{ec}(\mathcal{BO}[\![\mathsf{bop}]\!](\mathsf{deref}(\mathsf{s}, \mathsf{e}_1), \mathsf{deref}(\mathsf{s}, \mathsf{e}_2))))))\end{aligned}$$

We must also redefine semantic mappings that use $\mathcal{E}$ in their definitions (only $\mathcal{M}$ in the current language) such that suitable expression continuations are given as arguments to every use of $\mathcal{E}$:

$$\mathcal{M}[\![\textbf{put}\ \mathsf{exp}]\!](\mathsf{env}, \mathsf{c}) = \mathcal{E}[\![\mathsf{exp}]\!](\mathsf{env}, \lambda \mathsf{e} \in E\colon \underline{\lambda}\mathsf{s}\colon \mathsf{c}(\mathsf{s}\,.\,\mathsf{put}(\mathsf{deref}(\mathsf{s}, \mathsf{e}))))$$

$$\mathcal{M}[\![\textbf{get}\ \mathsf{exp}]\!](\mathsf{env}, \mathsf{c}) = \mathcal{E}[\![\mathsf{exp}]\!](\mathsf{env}, \lambda \mathsf{e} \in E\colon \underline{\lambda}\mathsf{s}\colon \mathsf{c}(\mathsf{s}\,.\,\mathsf{get}(\mathsf{ref}(\mathsf{e}))))$$

$$\mathcal{M}[\![\mathsf{imp}_1;\ \mathsf{imp}_2]\!](\mathsf{env}, \mathsf{c}) = \mathcal{M}[\![\mathsf{imp}_1]\!](\mathsf{env}, \mathcal{M}[\![\mathsf{imp}_2]\!](\mathsf{env}, \mathsf{c}))$$

$$\begin{aligned}&\mathcal{M}[\![\mathsf{exp}_1 := \mathsf{exp}_2]\!](\mathsf{env}, \mathsf{c})\\ &\quad = \mathcal{E}[\![\mathsf{exp}_1]\!](\mathsf{env}, \lambda \mathsf{e}_1 \in E\colon \mathcal{E}[\![\mathsf{exp}_2]\!](\mathsf{env},\\ &\qquad\qquad \lambda \mathsf{e}_2 \in E\colon \underline{\lambda}\mathsf{s}\colon \mathsf{c}(\mathsf{s}\,.\,\mathsf{assign}(\mathsf{ref}(\mathsf{e}_1),\\ &\qquad\qquad\qquad \mathsf{deref}(\mathsf{s}, \mathsf{e}_2))))))\end{aligned}$$

$$\begin{aligned}&\mathcal{M}[\![\textbf{if}\ \mathsf{exp}\ \textbf{then}\ \mathsf{imp}_1\ \textbf{else}\ \mathsf{imp}_2\ \textbf{fi}]\!](\mathsf{env}, \mathsf{c})\\ &\quad = \mathcal{E}[\![\mathsf{exp}]\!](\mathsf{env}, \mathsf{ECont'Cond}(\mathcal{M}[\![\mathsf{imp}_1]\!](\mathsf{env}, \mathsf{c}), \mathcal{M}[\![\mathsf{imp}_2]\!](\mathsf{env}, \mathsf{c})))\end{aligned}$$

$$\begin{aligned}&\mathcal{M}[\![\textbf{while}\ \mathsf{exp}\ \textbf{do}\ \mathsf{imp}\ \textbf{od}]\!](\mathsf{env}, \mathsf{c})\\ &\quad = \mathsf{Y}_{\mathit{Cont}}(\lambda \mathsf{c'}\colon \mathcal{E}[\![\mathsf{exp}]\!](\mathsf{env}, \mathsf{ECont'Cond}(\mathcal{M}[\![\mathsf{imp}]\!](\mathsf{env}, \mathsf{c'}), \mathsf{c})))\end{aligned}$$

The function ECont'Cond used above is defined as follows:

$$\begin{aligned}\mathsf{ECont'Cond}(\mathsf{c}_1, \mathsf{c}_2) \stackrel{d}{=} \lambda \mathsf{e} \in E\colon \underline{\lambda}\mathsf{s}\colon &\textbf{case}\ \mathsf{deref}(\mathsf{s}, \mathsf{e})\ \textbf{of}\\ &\mathsf{b} \in \mathit{Bool} \Rightarrow \textbf{if}\ \mathsf{b}\ \textbf{then}\ \mathsf{c}_1(\mathsf{s})\\ &\qquad\qquad\qquad\quad \textbf{else}\ \mathsf{c}_2(\mathsf{s})\\ &\textbf{otherwise} \Rightarrow \perp_{\mathit{State}}\end{aligned}$$

12.4.3 An example

An example to show how expression continuations work: Assume that env is an environment that binds the identifier x to an address a_x, that c_0 is a continuation, and that s_0 is a state such that s_0 . Input . head = 3. The effect of executing the imperative **put(valof get** x **result** x)

$$
\begin{aligned}
&\mathcal{M}[\![\mathbf{put(valof\ get}\ \mathsf{x}\ \mathbf{result}\ \mathsf{x})]\!](\mathsf{env}, \mathsf{c}_0, \mathsf{s}_0)\\
&\quad = \mathcal{E}[\![\mathbf{valof\ get}\ \mathsf{x}\ \mathbf{result}\ \mathsf{x}]\!](\mathsf{env}, \mathsf{ec}_1, \mathsf{s}_0)\\
&\quad\quad \text{where } \mathsf{ec}_1 = \lambda \mathsf{e}_0\!:\!\underline{\lambda}\mathsf{s}'\!:\!\mathsf{c}_0(\mathsf{s}'.\mathsf{put}(\mathsf{deref}(\mathsf{s}', \mathsf{e}_0)))\\
&\quad = \mathcal{M}[\![\mathbf{get}\ \mathsf{x}]\!](\mathsf{env}, \mathsf{c}_1, \mathsf{s}_0)\\
&\quad\quad \text{where } \mathsf{c}_1 = \mathcal{E}[\![\mathsf{x}]\!](\mathsf{env}, \mathsf{ec}_1)\\
&\quad = \mathcal{E}[\![\mathsf{x}]\!](\mathsf{env}, \mathsf{ec}_2, \mathsf{s}_0)\\
&\quad\quad \text{where } \mathsf{ec}_2 = \lambda \mathsf{e}_1\!:\!\underline{\lambda}\mathsf{s}''\!:\!\mathsf{c}_1(\mathsf{s}''.\mathsf{get}(\mathsf{ref}(\mathsf{e}_1)))\\
&\quad = \mathsf{ec}_2(\mathsf{a}_x, \mathsf{s}_0)\\
&\quad = \mathsf{c}_1(\mathsf{s}_1)\\
&\quad\quad \text{where } \mathsf{s}_1 = \mathsf{s}_0.\mathsf{get}(\mathsf{a}_x)\\
&\quad = \mathcal{E}[\![\mathsf{x}]\!](\mathsf{env}, \mathsf{ec}_1, \mathsf{s}_1)\\
&\quad = \mathsf{ec}_1(\mathsf{a}_x, \mathsf{s}_1)\\
&\quad = \mathsf{c}_0(\mathsf{s}_1.\mathsf{put}(\mathsf{deref}(\mathsf{s}_1, \mathsf{a}_x)))\\
&\quad = \mathsf{c}_0(\mathsf{s}_1.\mathsf{put}(3))
\end{aligned}
$$

12.5 Exceptions

Some languages have facilities for catching errors. An example is Java where the following is an imperative that performs a division and handles attempted division by 0 by executing the imperative imp_h:

try {a = b / c} **catch** (ArithmeticException e) {imp_h}

Even Cobol, which was one of the very first programming languages, had constructs that made it possible to catch and handle errors of various kinds. The following is, for instance, a Cobol imperative with the same effect as the Java imperative above (under the assumption that imp_h and imp_c have the same effects):

compute a = b /c **on** ZERODIV **perform** imp_c

In this section we show how to specify the semantics of some versions of exception handling.

Let Jump_2 be the result of extending Jump_0 with the following BNF productions:

$$
\langle imp \rangle ::= \ldots \mid \mathbf{execute}\ \langle imp \rangle\ \mathbf{on}\ \langle ident \rangle\ \mathbf{perform}\ \langle imp \rangle \mid \mathbf{raise}\ \langle ident \rangle
$$

The intended semantics is that the imperative **execute** imp_1 **on** flag **perform** imp_2 is to be executed by executing the imperative imp_1. If the identifier flag is one of a predefined set of special identifiers that name some common error conditions (for instance ZERODIV, that of course names division by zero) and the corresponding error occurs during execution of imp_1, the execution of imp_1 immediately stops and imp_2 is executed instead. The same thing will happen as a result of executing **raise** flag during the execution of imp_1. If neither **raise** flag is executed, nor the error named flag occurs, imp_1 is executed to normal completion, and imp_2 is skipped.

Using continuations, we may specify the semantics of the imperatives for exception handling as follows:

$$\mathcal{M}[\![\textbf{execute } imp_1 \textbf{ on } flag \textbf{ perform } imp_2]\!](env, c)$$
$$\stackrel{d}{=} \mathcal{M}[\![imp_1]\!](env.bind(flag, \mathcal{M}[\![imp_2]\!](env, c)), c)$$
$$\mathcal{M}[\![\textbf{raise } flag]\!](env, c)$$
$$\stackrel{d}{=} env(flag).qua\_Cont$$

The semantics of operators and other constructs in which errors may occur and error-handling exceptions be raised, must be redefined such that suitable error continuations are taken in case errors should occur. Previously, we have specified the denotation of, for instance, a binary operator to be a function that maps a pair of basic values to a basic value. This must now be extended such that the denotation of an operator has access to the environment in which it may find the right error continuation to take should an erroneous computation be attempted. The denotation of an operator should furthermore be given as an argument for an expression continuation (this concept was introduced in section 12.4 above) to which the result of applying the operator should be given when no error occurs. We therefore change the signature of the semantic mapping for binary operators to be as follows:

$$\mathcal{BO} \in (Binop \to (Envir \times ECont \times E \times E \to Cont))$$

The reason we specify that the last two arguments to a binary operator is a pair that may consist of *any* expressible values and not only basic values, i.e., a pair in $E \times E$ and not $B \times B$, is to leave it to the binary operator (or, more precisely, to its denotation) to discover whether or not the values to which it is applied have the right type and to take a suitable error continuation in case not.

It is now not very difficult to define the semantics of the various operators in our language. The division operator may for instance be treated as follows:

$$\mathcal{BO}[\![/]\!](env, ec, e_1, e_2)$$
$$= \underline{\lambda} s\text{: } \textbf{let } b_1 = deref(s, e_1),\ b_2 = deref(s, e_2) \textbf{ in}$$
$$\textbf{if not}(b_1.is\_Int \textbf{ and } b_2.is\_Int)$$
$$\textbf{then } env(\texttt{"typeerror"}).qua\_Cont(s) \textbf{ else}$$

$$\begin{array}{l}\textbf{if } b_2 = 0 \textbf{ then } env(\texttt{"zerodiv"}).qua\_Cont(s)\\ \textbf{else } ec(e_1 / e_2, s)\end{array}$$

We must also redefine the semantics for compound expressions in which operators are used:

$$\begin{array}{l}\mathcal{E}[\![exp_1 \text{ bop } exp_2]\!](env, ec)\\ \quad = \mathcal{E}[\![exp_1]\!](env, \lambda e_1 \in E{:}\ \mathcal{E}[\![exp_2]\!](env, \lambda e_2 \in E{:}\\ \qquad\qquad\qquad \mathcal{BO}[\![bop]\!](env, ec, e_1, e_2)))\end{array}$$

Finally, we redefine the initial environment given to programs:

$$\begin{array}{l}\mathcal{P}[\![imp]\!](inp) = \mathcal{M}[\![imp]\!](\text{ Envir'Default, Cont'Stop, State'Init(inp)}\\ \qquad\qquad\qquad\qquad).\text{Output}\end{array}$$

where the environment Envir'Default is defined as follows:

$$\begin{array}{l}\text{Envir'Default} \stackrel{d}{=} \lambda id{:}\ \textbf{if } id = \texttt{"zerodiv"} \textbf{ then}\\ \qquad\qquad \text{Cont'Error}(\texttt{"Division by zero"}) \textbf{ else}\\ \qquad\quad \textbf{if } id = \texttt{"typeerror"} \textbf{ then}\\ \qquad\qquad \text{Cont'Error}(\texttt{"Wrong type"}) \textbf{ else}\\ \qquad\quad \ldots\end{array}$$

The continuation Cont'Error $\in$ (*String* $\rightarrow$ *Cont*) used above may be defined as follows:

$$\text{Cont'Error(message)} \stackrel{d}{=} \underline{\lambda} s \in State{:}\ s.\text{put(message)}$$

For this to work, we redefine the domain *Output* to accept strings:

$$Output \stackrel{d}{=} (Int \cup String)^*$$

12.6 Exercises

12.6.1 An expression with side-effects

Evaluate

$$\mathcal{M}[\![\textbf{put} \ (\textbf{valof get } x \textbf{ result } x + 1)]\!](env, c_0, s_0)$$

where env, c_0 and s_0 are as specified at the end of section 12.4.

12.6.2 Typed semantics

Specify a typed semantics for Jump_0.

12.6.3 Input in expressions

Introduce a new expression **inint** that may be used to read integers. The intended effect of evaluating the expression **inint** is to input an integer (thus changing the state) whose value becomes the value of the expression.

Chapter 13
Nondeterminism and concurrency

13.1 Introduction

A program is said to be *deterministic* if its execution always produces the same output for the same input, and *nondeterministic* if two executions from the same input may produce different outputs. All programs written in the languages described so far in this book are deterministic.

At first glance it may seem that nondeterministic programs should be considered erroneous and hence to be avoided, and that therefore there is no reason to specify the semantics of nondeterministic programs (as the heading of this chapter undeniably indicates that we will). But for at least two quite different reasons, this is not so:

'Don't care' programs: In many cases the programmer does not care exactly which of possibly many solutions to a problem that is produced as output by a program as long as the output produced really *is* a solution (that is, as long as it satisfies some given specifications), and may consider it an extra and unnecessary burden to have to choose between alternative ways of solving the given problem (or a part of it) even if different solutions may be produced by the alternatives. In such cases, it may be pragmatically and methodologically advantageous to construct a nondeterministic program, which of course must be written in a language that allows nondeterminism. The reader is referred to the book *A Discipline of Programming* by E.W. Dijkstra ([Dijkstra; 76]) for examples of problems for which nondeterministic programs may be suitable and for arguments supporting the claim that nondeterminism in some cases may be methodologically advantageous.

Parallel programs: It frequently is the case that two or more parts of a program may be executed in parallel in order to speed up the execution of the program. An example is the evaluation of a compound expression like $\mathsf{exp}_1 + \mathsf{exp}_2$, which may be evaluated by first evaluating the two subexpressions exp_1 and exp_2 in parallel by different processors, and then adding the two results as soon as both subexpressions have been evaluated. If there are no side-effects when the subexpressions are evaluated, this evaluation strategy is deterministic: the final result does not depend upon whether or not the evaluations of the subexpressions are performed sequentially or in parallel by processors that possibly may operate asynchronously at very different speeds. If, however, the evaluation of one or both of the subexpressions as a side-effect may change the value of variables (or other parts of the state) that are accessed in the evaluation of the other subexpression, the final value of the compound expression may depend upon the relative speed of the processors that evaluate the subexpressions, and the program may hence be nondeterministic.

It is, of course, the case that in most situations we would like to reduce the nondeterminism of parallel programs as much as possible. But as long as we allow asynchronous parallel execution of imperatives (or other constructs) that may interfere by changing a part of the state that is accessible to the executors, we have to be prepared for nondeterminism and accept that some programs are nondeterministic. In order to understand what may happen when nondeterministic programs are executed, and to be able to reason about such programs, it is necessary to give complete and precise specifications of the semantics of nondeterministic constructs of programming languages.

In this chapter we first (in section 13.2) give a formal, denotational specification of a simple programming language that has constructs for nondeterministic choice between different sets of imperatives. In the course of this specification, it will be seen that to be able to specify the semantics of nondeterministic languages we need semantic domains that are mathematically more complex than the semantic domains used to specify the semantics of deterministic languages. In section 13.3 we do the necessary mathematics, and prove that the semantic mappings defined in section 13.2 are well-defined. Finally – in section 13.4 - we specify the semantics of a language that contains some constructs for simple concurrency.

13.2 Nondeterminism

13.2.1 Syntax

In the book referred to in the introduction to this chapter, E.W. Dijkstra introduced a simple programming language that contains constructs that may be used to construct nondeterministic programs. The syntax of this language - which we call Dijk_0 - is determined by the following BNF productions:

$$
\begin{array}{lll}
\langle imp \rangle & ::= & \textbf{skip} \\
 & | & \textbf{abort} \\
 & | & \langle expr \rangle := \langle expr \rangle \\
 & | & \langle imp \rangle ; \langle imp \rangle \\
 & | & \textbf{if } \langle guarded\text{-}imps \rangle \textbf{ fi} \\
 & | & \textbf{do } \langle guarded\text{-}imps \rangle \textbf{ od} \\
\langle guarded\text{-}imps \rangle & ::= & \langle expr \rangle \Rightarrow \langle imp \rangle \\
 & | & \langle guarded\text{-}imps \rangle \, \mathbf{|} \, \langle guarded\text{-}imps \rangle
\end{array}
$$

The set of expressions may be defined as for any of the previous languages described in this book (for instance as for Decl_0). It is, of course, easy to extend this language with declarations and with imperatives for input and output, but in order to reduce the number of details to be described, we refrain from doing this.

13.2.2 Intended, informal semantics

As specified by Dijkstra, the intended effect of **abort** is equivalent to entering an infinite loop.

An **if** imperative

$$\textbf{if } \mathsf{exp}_1 \Rightarrow \mathsf{imp}_1 \,\mathbf{|}\, \ldots \,\mathbf{|}\, \mathsf{exp}_n \Rightarrow \mathsf{imp}_n \textbf{ fi}$$

is to be executed as follows: First evaluate all the so-called *guards*, i.e., the expressions $\mathsf{exp}_1, \ldots, \mathsf{exp}_n$ (in a correctly typed program, these expressions all have type *Bool*). If exactly one of the guards is true, execute the imperative it guards. Should two or more guards be true, choose nondeterministically for execution one of the imperatives whose guard is true. Should none of the guards be true, abort the program, i.e., execute **abort**. An example:

$$\mathsf{ND}_1\text{:}\quad \mathsf{a} := 0; \textbf{ if } \mathsf{a} = 0 \Rightarrow \textbf{skip} \,\mathbf{|}\, \mathsf{a} = 0 \Rightarrow \mathsf{a} := 1 \textbf{ fi}$$

For any initial state s, ND_1 terminates in either s_0 = s.assign(a, 0) or s_1 = s.assign(a, 1). If we, as we habitually do, use $\mathcal{M}[\![imp]\!]$ to denote the denotation of the imperative imp, we express the fact that *either* s_0 *or* s_1 may become the state after the execution of ND_1 by writing

$$\mathcal{M}[\![ND_1]\!](s) = \{s_0, s_1\}$$

Thus, we will in general consider the denotation of a nondeterministic imperative to be a mapping from states to *sets of states*, and let the set $\mathcal{M}[\![imp]\!](s)$ contain all states s' which are such that there exists a terminating execution by imp from s to s'.

A **do** imperative

$$\textbf{do}\ exp_1 \Rightarrow imp_1 \,|\, \ldots \,|\, exp_n \Rightarrow imp_n\ \textbf{od}$$

is to be executed as follows: If one or more of the guards $exp_1, \ldots, exp_n$ are true, choose nondeterministically one of the imperatives whose guard is true, execute this imperative, and restart the **do** imperative when the chosen imperative terminates (if it does terminate). Should none of the guards be true, the **do** imperative terminates. An example:

$$ND_2\text{:}\ \ a := 0;\ \textbf{do}\ a = 0 \Rightarrow \textbf{skip} \,|\, a = 0 \Rightarrow a := 1\ \textbf{od}$$

When started in some initial state s, ND_2 may either terminate in the state s_1 = s.assign(a, 1) or loop indefinitely. Observe that the intended semantics of nondeterminism does not imply that the alternative a := 1 sooner or later must be chosen: there is no implied *fairness* in a nondeterministic choice between alternatives, and imperatives guarded by true guards may be neglected forever. The implementation of the language may in fact be such that the imperative guarded by the first true guard is always chosen for execution. A nondeterministic choice between two or more alternatives is thus not the same as a random or statistical choice between the alternatives.

If we, as before, use $\perp_{State}$ to denote the state which is the 'result' of executing a nonterminating imperative, we may specify the effect of executing ND_2 as follows:

$$\mathcal{M}[\![ND_2]\!](s) = \{\perp_{State}, s_1\}$$

Another example:

$$ND_3\text{:}\ \ a := 0;\ b := 0;\ \textbf{do}\ a = 0 \Rightarrow b := b + 1 \,|\, a = 0 \Rightarrow a := 1\ \textbf{od}$$

For any initial state s, ND_3 may either loop indefinitely – thus requiring that $\perp_{State} \in \mathcal{M}[\![ND_2]\!](s)$ – or terminate after increasing the variable b zero or more times. This means that

$$\mathcal{M}[\![ND_3]\!](s) = \{\perp_{State}, s_0, s_1, s_2, \ldots\}$$

where s_j = s.assign(a, 1).assign(b, j).

An interesting question now arises: Is it possible to construct an imperative imp such that $\mathcal{M}[\![imp]\!](s)$ (where s is some initial state) is infinite but without having $\bot_{State}$ as an element? Such an imperative would be certain to terminate (this is the case because $\bot_{State}$ is not an element in $\mathcal{M}[\![\text{imp}]\!](\text{s})$), and could be used to choose nondeterministically any alternative amongst an infinite number of alternatives. We shall see below (in section 13.3.2) that no such imperative exists: Every imperative that is certain to terminate is only able to choose between a finite number of alternatives. Said somewhat differently: the price of being able to choose any member of a set that has infinitely many members, is that nontermination cannot be excluded. Or - perhaps less scientifically - total and infinite freedom entails the risk of being stuck forever.

13.2.3 Formal, denotational semantics

As described in the examples above, the semantic mapping $\mathcal{M}$ for imperatives of the nondeterministic Dijk_0 language should have signature

$$\mathcal{M} \in (Imp \to (State_\bot \to \mathcal{P}(State_\bot)))$$

where for any set A, $\mathcal{P}(A)$ is the *powerset* of A, i.e., $\mathcal{P}(A) = \{X \mid X \subseteq A\}$. We wish to define $\mathcal{M}$ such that for any imperative imp and any state s

$$\mathcal{M}[\![\text{imp}]\!](\text{s}) = \{\text{s}' \mid \textit{Either: } \text{s}' = \bot_{State} \textit{ and there exists a nonterminating execution by imp from s} \quad \textit{Or: } \text{s}' \neq \bot_{State} \textit{ and there exists an execution by imp from s that terminates in s}'\}$$

Figure 13.1 on page 295 contains equations that define $\mathcal{M}$ for the imperatives of Dijk_0. As seen by these equations, it is not very difficult to define $\mathcal{M}$ for most imperatives such that our wishes for $\mathcal{M}$ are satisfied. But when we get to $\mathcal{M}[\![\textbf{do}\ldots\textbf{od}]\!]$ we encounter problems: As for other imperatives that may loop indefinitely, we specify the denotation of a **do** imperative to be a fixpoint of a certain function - call it mm - that maps the algebra of denotations of imperatives *MV* to itself. But the Fixpoint Theorem (page 90) only guarantees that *continuous* functions mapping a *cpo* to itself have fixpoints. To ensure that the fixpoint specified to be the denotation of a **do** imperative exists and is well-defined, we must therefore 1) define a partial order for *MV* such that *MV* becomes a cpo, and 2) prove that the function mm is continuous relative to the order defined for *MV*. It is not at all obvious how to do this.

It is, of course, not very difficult to order *MV* such that it becomes a cpo. An obvious method that almost suggests itself is based on the fact that $\mathcal{P}(State_\bot)$ is a cpo under the subset order $\subseteq$ (this is observed on page 79 in section 5.3). If we define the algebra *MV* to consist of all functions that map $State_\bot$ to the cpo $\mathcal{P}(State_\bot)$, *MV* is by proposition 5.3 a cpo under the pointwise extension of the subset order of $\mathcal{P}(State_\bot)$, i.e.,

$$(\mathsf{mv}_1 \sqsubseteq \mathsf{mv}_2) \stackrel{d}{\Longleftrightarrow} (\forall\, \mathsf{s} \in \mathit{State}_\perp : \mathsf{mv}_1(\mathsf{s}) \subseteq \mathsf{mv}_2(\mathsf{s}))$$

The function mm is, however, not monotonic, and hence not continuous, given this order of *MV*, and the seemingly so obvious method fails. Any attempt at basing the semantics of nondeterminism on the subset order of $\mathcal{P}(\mathit{State}_\perp)$ is in fact doomed to failure due to the discrepancy between the order of *MV* induced by the subset order of $\mathcal{P}(\mathit{State}_\perp)$ and the intended informal interpretation of $\mathsf{mv}_1 \sqsubseteq_{MV} \mathsf{mv}_2$ for any denotations mv_1, mv_2 of imperatives - which is that mv_2 is at least as well-defined as mv_1: if the imperative denoted by mv_1 terminates for a state s, then the imperative denoted by mv_2 terminates for the same state, and in the same final state. In addition, mv_2 may be defined (i.e., the imperative denoted by mv_2 terminates) for some states for which mv_1 is undefined. By this intended interpretation of $\sqsubseteq_{MV}$ it is obvious that we should have that

$$\mathcal{M}[\![\mathsf{ND}_2]\!] \ \sqsubseteq_{MV}\ \mathcal{M}[\![\mathsf{a} := 1]\!]$$

The reason for this is that the imperative a := 1 is 'at least as well-defined' as ND_2. This is because a := 1 terminates whenever ND_2 does, and in the same state. But for any state s,

$$\begin{array}{rcl} \mathcal{M}[\![\mathsf{ND}_2]\!](\mathsf{s}) & = & \{\mathsf{s.assign(a, 1)}, \perp_{State}\} \\ & \not\subseteq & \{\mathsf{s.assign(a, 1)}\} \\ & = & \mathcal{M}[\![\mathsf{a} := 1]\!](\mathsf{s}) \end{array}$$

which entails that $\mathcal{M}[\![\mathsf{ND}_2]\!]$ is *not* less than or equal to $\mathcal{M}[\![\mathsf{a} := 1]\!]$ in the order induced in *MV* by the subset order of $\mathcal{P}(\mathit{State}_\perp)$.

We will return to these matters in section 13.3 below, where we will show how to define a partial order for *MV* which orders *MV* to a cpo and which is in accordance with the intended interpretation of the partial ordering of denotations of imperatives. We will also prove that under this ordering of *MV*, the function mm *is* continuous. In the same section, we will furthermore see that it is not necessary to define the range of $\mathcal{M}$ to consist of *all* subsets of $\mathit{State}_\perp$, but only of those few (few compared to the uncountably many elements of $\mathcal{P}(\mathit{State}_\perp)$) subsets that in a certain sense may be said to be finitely generated. We will use $\mathcal{P}[\mathit{State}_\perp]$ to denote the algebra that consists of these subsets of $\mathit{State}_\perp$.

Specifications of the semantic mappings for Dijk_0 are given in figure 13.1. In these specifications, we assume the results of section 13.3 where we define a cpo $\mathcal{P}[\mathit{State}_\perp]$ - called the *powerdomain* for $\mathit{State}_\perp$ - that satisfies the following demands:

(1) $\mathcal{P}[\mathit{State}_\perp] \subseteq \mathcal{P}(\mathit{State}_\perp)$

(2) For every $\mathsf{s} \in \mathit{State}$, the *singleton set* $\{\mathsf{s}\} \in \mathcal{P}[\mathit{State}_\perp]$.

(3) $\mathcal{P}[\mathit{State}_\perp]$ is closed under unions:
For every $\mathsf{ps}_1, \mathsf{ps}_2 \in \mathcal{P}[\mathit{State}_\perp]$: $(\mathsf{ps}_1 \cup \mathsf{ps}_2) \in \mathcal{P}[\mathit{State}_\perp]$

$$\mathcal{M} \in (\mathit{Imp} \to \mathit{MV}), \quad \mathit{where}\ \mathit{MV} \overset{d}{=} [\mathit{State}_\perp \to \mathcal{P}[\mathit{State}_\perp]]^s$$

$$\begin{aligned}
\mathcal{M}[\![\textbf{skip}]\!] &= \underline{\lambda}\mathsf{s}\colon \{\mathsf{s}\}\\
\mathcal{M}[\![\textbf{abort}]\!] &= \underline{\lambda}\mathsf{s}\colon \{\perp_{\mathit{State}}\}\\
\mathcal{M}[\![\mathsf{exp}_1 := \mathsf{exp}_2]\!] &= \underline{\lambda}\mathsf{s}\colon \{\mathsf{s}.\mathsf{assign}(\mathsf{ref}(\mathcal{E}[\![\mathsf{exp}_1]\!](\mathsf{s})),\\
&\qquad\qquad \mathsf{deref}(\mathsf{s}, \mathcal{E}[\![\mathsf{exp}_2]\!](\mathsf{s})))\}\\
\mathcal{M}[\![\mathsf{imp}_1;\ \mathsf{imp}_2]\!] &= \underline{\lambda}\mathsf{s}\colon \mathcal{M}[\![\mathsf{imp}_2]\!]^+(\mathcal{M}[\![\mathsf{imp}_1]\!](\mathsf{s}))\\
\mathcal{M}[\![\textbf{if}\ \mathsf{gdimps}\ \textbf{fi}]\!] &= \underline{\lambda}\mathsf{s}\colon \textbf{case}\ \mathcal{G}[\![\mathsf{gdimps}]\!](\mathsf{s})\\
&\qquad \mathsf{Empty} \Rightarrow \{\perp_{\mathit{State}}\}\\
&\qquad \mathsf{ps}\ \textbf{in}\ \mathcal{P}[\mathit{State}_\perp] \Rightarrow \mathsf{ps}\\
\mathcal{M}[\![\textbf{do}\ \mathsf{gdimps}\ \textbf{od}]\!] &= \mathsf{Y}_{\mathit{MV}}(\lambda\mathsf{mv}\colon \underline{\lambda}\mathsf{s}\colon \textbf{case}\ \mathcal{G}[\![\mathsf{gdimps}]\!](\mathsf{s})\ \textbf{of}\\
&\qquad \mathsf{Empty} \Rightarrow \{\mathsf{s}\}\\
&\qquad \mathsf{ps}\ \textbf{in}\ \mathcal{P}[\mathit{State}_\perp] \Rightarrow \mathsf{mv}^+(\mathsf{ps}))
\end{aligned}$$

$$\mathcal{G} \in (\mathit{Guarded\text{-}imps} \to (\mathit{State}_\perp \to (\mathsf{Empty}\colon \mathit{Unit} + \mathcal{P}[\mathit{State}_\perp])))$$

$$\begin{aligned}
\mathcal{G}[\![\mathsf{exp} \Rightarrow \mathsf{imp}]\!] &= \lambda\mathsf{s}\colon \textbf{if}\ \mathsf{deref}(\mathsf{s}, \mathcal{E}[\![\mathsf{exp}]\!](\mathsf{s})).\mathsf{is_true}\\
&\qquad \textbf{then}\ \mathcal{M}[\![\mathsf{imp}]\!](\mathsf{s})\ \textbf{else}\ \mathsf{Empty}\\
\mathcal{G}[\![\mathsf{gdimps}_1 \mathbin{[\!]} \mathsf{gdimps}_2]\!] &= \lambda\mathsf{s}\colon \textbf{case}\ \langle \mathcal{G}[\![\mathsf{gdimps}_1]\!](\mathsf{s}), \mathcal{G}[\![\mathsf{gdimps}_2]\!](\mathsf{s})\rangle\ \textbf{of}\\
&\qquad \langle \mathsf{Empty}, \mathsf{Empty}\rangle \Rightarrow \mathsf{Empty}\\
&\qquad \langle \mathsf{ps}_1, \mathsf{Empty}\rangle \Rightarrow \mathsf{ps}_1\\
&\qquad \langle \mathsf{Empty}, \mathsf{ps}_2\rangle \Rightarrow \mathsf{ps}_2\\
&\qquad \langle \mathsf{ps}_1, \mathsf{ps}_2\rangle \Rightarrow (\mathsf{ps}_1 \cup \mathsf{ps}_2)
\end{aligned}$$

Figure 13.1: Semantic mappings for the nondeterministic programming language Dijk$_0$. The semantic mapping $\mathcal{E}$ may be defined as for Decl$_0$. The *extension* mv^+ of a function mv is defined on page 295

(4) For technical reasons: The empty set $\emptyset$ is *not* an element of $\mathcal{P}[\mathit{State}_\perp]$.

(5) The extension (defined below) of every strict function f that maps $\mathit{State}_\perp$ to $\mathcal{P}[\mathit{State}_\perp]$ is a function f^+ that maps $\mathcal{P}[\mathit{State}_\perp]$ to itself.

For every function $\mathsf{mv} \in (\mathit{State}_\perp \to \mathcal{P}(\mathit{State}_\perp))$, its *extension* mv^+ is a function with signature $(\mathcal{P}(\mathit{State}_\perp) \to \mathcal{P}(\mathit{State}_\perp))$ defined as follows:

$$\begin{aligned}
\mathsf{mv}^+(\mathsf{ps}) &\overset{d}{=} \bigcup\{\mathsf{mv}(\mathsf{s}) \mid \mathsf{s} \in \mathsf{ps}\}\\
&= \{\mathsf{s}' \mid \exists\, \mathsf{s} \in \mathsf{ps}\colon \mathsf{s}' \in \mathsf{mv}(\mathsf{s})\}
\end{aligned}$$

One point in the specifications given in figure 13.1 may need some explanation: We specify the denotation of a **do** imperative to be the least fixpoint of a certain function. The intuitive idea behind the specification is that we wish the denotation of an imperative **do gdimps od** to be an element mv* in *MV* that satisfies the following equation:

$$\begin{array}{l} \mathsf{mv}^* = \underline{\lambda}\mathsf{s}\colon \textbf{case } \mathcal{G}[\![\mathsf{gdimps}]\!](\mathsf{s}) \text{ økw<of>} \\ \qquad\qquad \begin{array}{ll} \mathsf{Empty} & \Rightarrow \{\mathsf{s}\} \\ \mathsf{ps} \textbf{ in } \mathcal{P}[State_\perp] & \Rightarrow (\mathsf{mv}^*)^+(\mathsf{ps}) \end{array} \end{array}$$

13.2.4 Three simple examples

In this section we apply the formal definitions given in figure 13.1 to the three simple programs ND_1, ND_2 and ND_3 presented in section 13.2.2 and see that the formal definitions give the intuitively expected results.

Example 1: ND_1

$$\begin{array}{l} \mathcal{M}[\![\mathsf{a} := 0;\ \textbf{if } \mathsf{a} = 0 \Rightarrow \textbf{skip} \mid \textbf{true} \Rightarrow \mathsf{a} := 1\ \textbf{fi}]\!](\mathsf{s}) \\ \quad = \textbf{let } \mathsf{ps} = \mathcal{G}[\![\textbf{true} \Rightarrow \textbf{skip} \mid \textbf{true} \Rightarrow \mathsf{a} := 1]\!](\mathsf{s}_0) \\ \qquad\qquad = \mathcal{G}[\![\textbf{true} \Rightarrow \textbf{skip}]\!](\mathsf{s}_0) \cup \mathcal{G}[\![\textbf{true} \Rightarrow \mathsf{a} := 1]\!](\mathsf{s}_0) \\ \qquad\qquad = \mathcal{M}[\![\textbf{skip}]\!](\mathsf{s}) \cup \mathcal{M}[\![\mathsf{a} := 1]\!](\mathsf{s}_0) \\ \qquad\qquad = \{\mathsf{s}_0, \mathsf{s}_1\}, \qquad \text{where } \mathsf{s}_i = \mathsf{s}.\mathsf{assign}(\mathsf{a}, i) \\ \qquad \textbf{in if } \mathsf{ps}.\mathsf{is\_Empty} \textbf{ then } \{\perp_{State}\} \textbf{ else } \mathsf{ps} \\ \quad = \{\mathsf{s}_0, \mathsf{s}_1\} \end{array}$$

Example 2: ND_2

$$\begin{array}{l} \mathcal{M}[\![\mathsf{a} := 0;\ \textbf{do } \mathsf{a} = 0 \Rightarrow \textbf{skip} \mid \mathsf{a} = 0 \Rightarrow \mathsf{a} := 1\ \textbf{od}]\!](\mathsf{s}) \\ \quad = \mathsf{Y}_{MV}(\mathsf{mm})(\mathsf{s}_0), \\ \qquad \textit{where } \mathsf{s}_0 = \mathsf{s}.\mathsf{assign}(\mathsf{a}, 0) \\ \qquad \textit{and } \mathsf{mm} = \lambda\mathsf{mv}\colon \underline{\lambda}\mathsf{s}\colon \textbf{case } \mathcal{G}[\![\mathsf{a} = 0 \Rightarrow \textbf{skip} \mid \\ \qquad\qquad\qquad\qquad\qquad\qquad \mathsf{a} = 0 \Rightarrow \mathsf{a} := 1]\!](\mathsf{s}) \textbf{ of} \\ \qquad\qquad\qquad\qquad\qquad \begin{array}{ll} \mathsf{Empty} & \Rightarrow \{\mathsf{s}\} \\ \mathsf{ps} \textbf{ in } \mathcal{P}[State_\perp] & \Rightarrow \mathsf{mv}^+(\mathsf{ps}) \end{array} \\ \quad = (\bigsqcup_{MV} \mathsf{mm}^i(\perp_{MV}))(\mathsf{s}_0) \\ \quad = (\bigsqcup_{MV} \mathsf{mv}_i)(\mathsf{s}_0) \\ \qquad \textit{where } \mathsf{mv}_i = \mathsf{mm}^i(\perp_{MV}) \\ \qquad \textit{i.e., } \quad \mathsf{mv}_0 = \perp_{MV} \\ \qquad\qquad\quad \mathsf{mv}_{i+1} = \mathsf{mm}(\mathsf{mv}_i) \\ \qquad\qquad\qquad\quad = \underline{\lambda}\mathsf{s}\colon \textbf{if } \mathsf{s}.\mathsf{access}(\mathsf{a}) \neq 0 \textbf{ then } \{\mathsf{s}\} \\ \qquad\qquad\qquad\qquad\quad \textbf{else } \mathsf{mv}_i^+(\{\mathsf{s}, \mathsf{s}.\mathsf{assign}(\mathsf{a}, 1)\}) \\ \qquad\qquad\qquad\quad = \underline{\lambda}\mathsf{s}\colon \textbf{if } \mathsf{s}.\mathsf{access}(\mathsf{a}) \neq 0 \textbf{ then } \{\mathsf{s}\} \\ \qquad\qquad\qquad\qquad\quad \textbf{else } \mathsf{mv}_i(\mathsf{s}) \cup \mathsf{mv}_i(\mathsf{s}.\mathsf{assign}(\mathsf{a}, 1)) \end{array}$$

$= \lfloor \mathcal{P}[State_\perp] \rfloor mv_i(s_0)$

By induction on i it is easy to prove that for every $i \geq 0$

$$mv_{i+2}(s_0) = \{ \perp_{State}, s_0 . assign(a, 1)\}$$

and it follows that

$$\mathcal{M}[\![a := 0; \textbf{do } a = 0 \Rightarrow \textbf{skip} \mid a = 0 \Rightarrow a := 1 \textbf{ od}]\!](s) = \{ \perp_{State}, s . assign(a, 1)\}$$

which is in accordance with the intended semantics of ND_2 as described in section 13.2.2.

Example 3: ND_3

$$\mathcal{M}[\![a := 0; b := 0; \textbf{do } a = 0 \Rightarrow b := b + 1 \mid a = 0 \Rightarrow a := 1 \textbf{ od}]\!](s)$$

$$\begin{aligned}
&= \lfloor \mathcal{P}[State_\perp] \rfloor mv_i(s_{0,0}) \\
&\quad \textit{where } s_{i,j} = s . assign(a, i) . assign(b, j) \\
&\quad \textit{and } mv_0 = \perp_{MV} \\
&\qquad\qquad = \underline{\lambda} s: \{\perp_{State}\} \\
&\quad mv_{i+1} = \underline{\lambda} s: \textbf{let } ps = \mathcal{G}[\![a = 0 \Rightarrow \ldots \mid \ldots a := 1]\!](s) \\
&\qquad\qquad\quad \textbf{in if } ps . is_Empty \textbf{ then } \{s\} \textbf{ else } mv_i^+(ps) \\
&\qquad\qquad = \underline{\lambda} s: \textbf{if } s . access(a) \neq 0 \textbf{ then } \{s\} \\
&\qquad\qquad\quad \textbf{else } mv_i(s . assign(b, s . access(y) + 1)) \cup \\
&\qquad\qquad\qquad mv_i(s . assign(a, 1))
\end{aligned}$$

By induction on i it is easy to prove that for every $i \geq 0$:

$$mv_{i+2}(s_{0,j}) = \{\perp_{State}, s_{1,j}, s_{1,j+1}, \ldots, s_{1,j+i}\}$$

Applying this to $j = 0$ we get that

$$\begin{aligned}
&\lfloor \mathcal{P}[State_\perp] \rfloor mv_i(s_{0,0}) \\
&\quad = \lfloor \mathcal{P}[State_\perp] \rfloor \{\perp_{State}, s_{1,0}, s_{1,1}, \ldots, s_{1,i}\} \\
&\quad = \{\perp_{State}, s_{1,0}, s_{1,1}, \ldots, s_{1,i}, \ldots\}
\end{aligned}$$

- which is in agreement with the intended semantics of ND_3.

13.3 Powerdomains

13.3.1 The ordering of powerdomains

We have decided that the denotation of an imperative of the non-deterministic language $Dijk_0$ should be a function in the algebra *MV*, which in this chapter is a function algebra containing functions that map states to sets of states, i.e., the algebra $(State_\perp \rightarrow \mathcal{P}(State_\perp))$. In order to be able to specify the semantics of possibly nonterminating imperatives, we would like to order this algebra to a cpo. As described in section 5.3.6, the canonic way of ordering a function algebra like $(\mathit{State}_\perp \to \mathcal{P}(\mathit{State}_\perp))$ to a cpo, is first to order the range of the functions - i.e., the algebra $\mathcal{P}(\mathit{State}_\perp)$ - to a cpo; and then to order the functions by pointwise extension of the order of the basis cpo:

$$\mathsf{mv}_1 \sqsubseteq \mathsf{mv}_2 \iff \forall\, \mathsf{s} \in \mathit{State}_\perp : \mathsf{mv}_1(\mathsf{s}) \sqsubseteq_{\mathcal{P}(\mathit{State}_\perp)} \mathsf{mv}_2(\mathsf{s})$$

According to proposition 5.3, $(\mathit{State}_\perp \to \mathcal{P}(\mathit{State}_\perp))$ is ordered to a cpo by this order. It only remains to find a suitable order of the algebra $\mathcal{P}(\mathit{State}_\perp)$. We have seen above that the subset order is useless because the induced order of $(\mathit{State}_\perp \to \mathcal{P}(\mathit{State}_\perp))$ does not have the desired intended interpretation, and also because certain functions fail to be continuous.

In the deterministic case, where $MV = (\mathit{State}_\perp \to \mathit{State}_\perp)$, we ordered the range $\mathit{State}_\perp$ to a flat cpo: $\mathsf{s}_1 \sqsubseteq_{\mathit{State}_\perp} \mathsf{s}_2$ if and only if either $\mathsf{s}_1 = \perp_{\mathit{State}}$ or $\mathsf{s}_1 = \mathsf{s}_2$. The pointwise extension of this order to the domain $(\mathit{State}_\perp \to \mathit{State}_\perp)$ is to let $\mathsf{mv}_1 \sqsubseteq \mathsf{mv}_2$ if and only if for every state s: if $\mathsf{mv}_1(\mathsf{s}) \neq \perp_{\mathit{State}}$ then $\mathsf{mv}_1(\mathsf{s}) = \mathsf{mv}_2(\mathsf{s})$, that is if and only if mv_2 is at least as well-defined as mv_1.

A reasonable generalization - which is in agreement with the intended interpretation - of the simple order defined for the flat algebra $\mathit{State}_\perp$ to an order for subset algebra $\mathcal{P}(\mathit{State}_\perp)$, is for any $\mathsf{X}, \mathsf{Y} \in \mathcal{P}(\mathit{State}_\perp)$ to say that $\mathsf{X} \sqsubseteq_P \mathsf{Y}$ if and only if either $\mathsf{X} = \mathsf{Y}$ or Y is the result of replacing an 'undefined' element $\perp_{\mathit{State}}$ of X by some non-empty set of states. More formally:

$$\begin{aligned} \mathsf{X} \sqsubseteq_P \mathsf{Y} \overset{d}{\iff} \; & (\perp_{\mathit{State}} \notin \mathsf{X} \;\wedge\; \mathsf{X} = \mathsf{Y}) \;\vee \\ & (\perp_{\mathit{State}} \in \mathsf{X} \;\wedge\; (\mathsf{X} - \{\perp_{\mathit{State}}\}) \subseteq \mathsf{Y} \;\wedge\; \mathsf{Y} \neq \emptyset) \end{aligned}$$

The pointwise extension of this order of the subset algebra $\mathcal{P}(\mathit{State}_\perp)$ to the function algebra $(\mathit{State}_\perp \to \mathcal{P}(\mathit{State}_\perp))$ is to let $\mathsf{mv}_1 \sqsubseteq \mathsf{mv}_2$ if and only if for every state s: if $\perp_{\mathit{State}} \notin \mathsf{mv}_1(\mathsf{s})$ then $\mathsf{mv}_1(\mathsf{s}) = \mathsf{mv}_2(\mathsf{s})$, and if $\perp_{\mathit{State}} \in \mathsf{mv}_1(\mathsf{s})$ then every state $\mathsf{s}' \neq \perp_{\mathit{State}}$ which is an element in $\mathsf{mv}_1(\mathsf{s})$ is also an element of $\mathsf{mv}_2(\mathsf{s})$ (which may contain some additional states). It is obvious that the interpretation of this is that 'mv_2 is at least as well-defined as mv_1'.

We have to prove that $\sqsubseteq_P$ orders $\mathcal{P}(\mathit{State}_\perp)$ to a cpo. In the proof of that and in other arguments we will give later (and also as a preparation for the more general treatment to be discussed in section 13.4) it is convenient to use a more general definition of the order of $\mathcal{P}(\mathit{State}_\perp)$:

Definition 13.1 The Egli–Milner order:
For any cpo D, define the binary relation $\sqsubseteq_{EM}$ of the subset algebra $\mathcal{P}(D)$ as follows: For every $\mathsf{X}, \mathsf{Y} \in \mathcal{P}(D)$:

$$\begin{aligned} \mathsf{X} \sqsubseteq_{EM} \mathsf{Y} \overset{d}{\iff} \; & \forall\, \mathsf{x} \in X : \exists\, \mathsf{y} \in Y : \mathsf{x} \sqsubseteq_D \mathsf{y} \;\wedge \\ & \forall\, \mathsf{y} \in Y : \exists\, \mathsf{x} \in X : \mathsf{x} \sqsubseteq_D \mathsf{y} \end{aligned}$$

An example: In the Egli-Milner order for $\mathcal{P}(Nat_\perp)$:

$$\begin{aligned}\{\perp_{Nat}\} &\sqsubseteq_{EM} \{1, \perp_{Nat}\} \\ &\sqsubseteq_{EM} \{1, 3, 5, \perp_{Nat}\} \\ &\sqsubseteq_{EM} \{1, 3, 5\}\end{aligned}$$

Observe that there is no $X \in \mathcal{P}(Nat_\perp)$ such that $\{1, 3, 5\} \sqsubseteq_{EM} X$, except, of course, $\{1, 3, 5\}$ itself. It is for instance not the case that $\{1, 3, 5\} \sqsubseteq_{EM} \{1, 3, 5, 6\}$ because there is no $n \in \{1, 3, 5\}$ such that $n \sqsubseteq_{Nat_\perp} 6$.

Proposition 13.1 *For every cpo D and every* $X, Y \in \mathcal{P}(D)$*:*

$$(1): X \sqsubseteq_P Y \Rightarrow X \sqsubseteq_{EM} Y$$
$$(2): \text{If } D \text{ is flat: } X \sqsubseteq_{EM} Y \Rightarrow X \sqsubseteq_P Y$$

Proof of (1): Assume that $X \sqsubseteq_P Y$. To prove that $X \sqsubseteq_{EM} Y$, assume first that $\perp_D \notin X$. By definition of $\sqsubseteq_P$, we must have $X = Y$, and then $X \sqsubseteq_{EM} Y$ follows because $\sqsubseteq_{EM}$ obviously is reflexive. If $\perp_D \in X$, we must by definition of $\sqsubseteq_P$ have (i) $(X - \{\perp_D\}) \subseteq Y$ and (ii) $Y \neq \emptyset$. Then for every $x \in X$: if $x \neq \perp_D$, we must (by (i)) have $x \in Y$, which entails that there exists $y \in Y$ such that $x \sqsubseteq_D y$ (namely $y = x$); if $x = \perp_D$, we must by (ii) have that there exists $y \in Y$ such that $x \sqsubseteq_D y$. Thus, $\forall x \in X : \exists y \in Y : x \sqsubseteq_D y$ follows. That $\forall y \in Y : \exists x \in X : x \sqsubseteq_D y$ holds is immediate when $\perp_D \in X$.

Proof of (2): Assume that D is flat and that $X \sqsubseteq_{EM} Y$. To prove that $X \sqsubseteq_P Y$, we consider first the case $\perp_D \notin X$ and prove that $X = Y$: For every $x \in X$, we can (by the first clause in the definition of $X \sqsubseteq_{EM} Y$) find $y \in Y$ such that $x \sqsubseteq_D y$. Because D is flat, we must have that $x = y$, which means that $X \subseteq Y$. Similarly, $Y \subseteq X$, and hence $X = Y$. We then consider the case $\perp_D \in X$ and prove (i) $(X - \{\perp_{State}\}) \subseteq Y$ and (ii) $Y \neq \emptyset$: If $x \in X$, $x \neq \perp_D$, there must exist $y \in Y$ such that $x \sqsubseteq_D y$. $x = y$ (because D is flat) and (i) holds. Applying $\forall x \in X : \exists y \in Y : x \sqsubseteq_D y$ to the case $x = \perp_D$, we get that (ii) must hold.

Proposition 13.2 *If D is a flat cpo, then* $(\mathcal{P}(D) - \{\emptyset\})$ *is a cpo under the Egli-Milner order* $\sqsubseteq_{EM}$*, with* $\{\perp_D\}$ *as its least element.*

Proof that $\sqsubseteq_{EM}$ is a partial order: Reflexivity and transitivity are immediate. To prove anti-symmetry, assume (i) $X \sqsubseteq_{EM} Y$ and (ii) $Y \sqsubseteq_{EM} X$. We prove $X = Y$ by proving (iii) $X \subseteq Y$ and (iv) $Y \subseteq X$: To prove (iii), let $x \in X$: If $x \neq \perp_D$ (i) entails that there exists $y \in Y$ such that $x \sqsubseteq_D y$. D is assumed to be flat, and hence $x = y$, which means that $x \in Y$. If $x = \perp_D$, (ii) gives that there exists $y \in Y$ such that $y \sqsubseteq_D \perp_D$. But then $y = x$, and hence $x \in Y$ also in this case. That (iv) holds is proved similarly.

Proof of completeness: To prove that $(\mathcal{P}(D) - \{\emptyset\})$ is complete under the Egli-Milner order, let $\{X\}_{i=0}^{\infty}$ be any $\sqsubseteq_{EM}$ chain in $(\mathcal{P}(D) - \{\emptyset\})$. Assume first that $\perp_D \in X_i$ for every $i \geq 0$. We prove that $X^* \stackrel{d}{=} \bigcup X_i$ is the least upper bound of $\{X\}_{i=0}^{\infty}$: That $X_i \sqsubseteq_{EM} X^*$ holds for every $i \geq 0$ follows because $\perp_D \in X_i$ and $X_i \subseteq X^*$. To prove that X^* is the *least* upper of the chain, assume that Y is such that $X_i \sqsubseteq_{EM} Y$ for every $i \geq 0$: To prove that $X^* \sqsubseteq_{EM} Y$, it suffices to prove that $(X^* - \{\perp_D\}) \subseteq Y$. Let $x \in X^*$, $x \neq \perp_D$. By definition of X^*, there exists $i \geq 0$ such that $x \in X_i$. Because $X_i \sqsubseteq_{EM} Y$ and $\perp_D$ has been assumed to be a member of X_i, we must have that $(X_i - \{\perp_D\}) \subseteq Y$, and hence $x \in Y$.

If there exists $n \geq 0$ such that $\perp_D \notin X_n$, we must have that $X_i = X_n$ for every $i \geq n$, and X_n is the least upper bound of the chain $\{X\}_{i=0}^{\infty}$.

13.3.2 The elements of powerdomains

The full powerset $\mathcal{P}(\mathit{State}_\perp) = \{X \mid X \subseteq \mathit{State}_\perp\}$ contains a large number of sets of states, many more than those that possibly may occur as values of functions that are denotations of nondeterministic imperatives, and hence many more than those that are needed to specify the semantics of nondeterministic imperatives. To serve as ranges of denotations of such imperatives we really do not need more than the members of the following, much smaller, set of sets of states:

$$\mathcal{ND}_{Imp}(\mathit{State}_\perp) \stackrel{d}{=} \{X \mid X \subseteq \mathit{State}_\perp \wedge \exists\, \mathsf{imp},\ \exists\, s \in \mathit{State}\colon X = \mathcal{M}[\![\mathsf{imp}]\!](s)\}$$

This set consists of those subsets of $\mathit{State}_\perp$ that are ranges of functions that are denotations of nondeterministic imperatives in our language, that is those sets of states that in a certain sense may be said to be generatable by such imperatives. This set is, however, mathematically not so easy to handle: on the one hand its definition presumes that the mapping $\mathcal{M}$ has already been defined, on the other hand the definition of $\mathcal{M}$ presumes that the set has been defined. We will therefore in this section define a set of sets of states - to be denoted by $\mathcal{P}[\mathit{State}_\perp]$ - which is somewhere between the intractable $\mathcal{ND}_{Imp}(\mathit{State}_\perp)$ and the superabundant $\mathcal{P}(\mathit{State}_\perp)$.

Consider the set of all states that possibly may be generated during execution of a nondeterministic imperative imp from an initial state s_0. For our current purposes, it may be illuminating to construct a tree - the *execution tree* for imp and s_0, denoted by $\mathcal{T}\mathsf{ree}[\![\mathsf{imp}]\!](s)$ - whose nodes are labelled with states that are members of this set. The tree has a root node which is labelled with the initial state s_0. Each branch of the tree represents a possible execution of the imperative from the initial state. Every arch $(s \rightarrow s')$ in the tree is labelled with the atomic imperative whose execution transforms s to s'. Figure 13.2 shows execution trees for the imperatives ND_1 and ND_2 from section 13.2.2. In

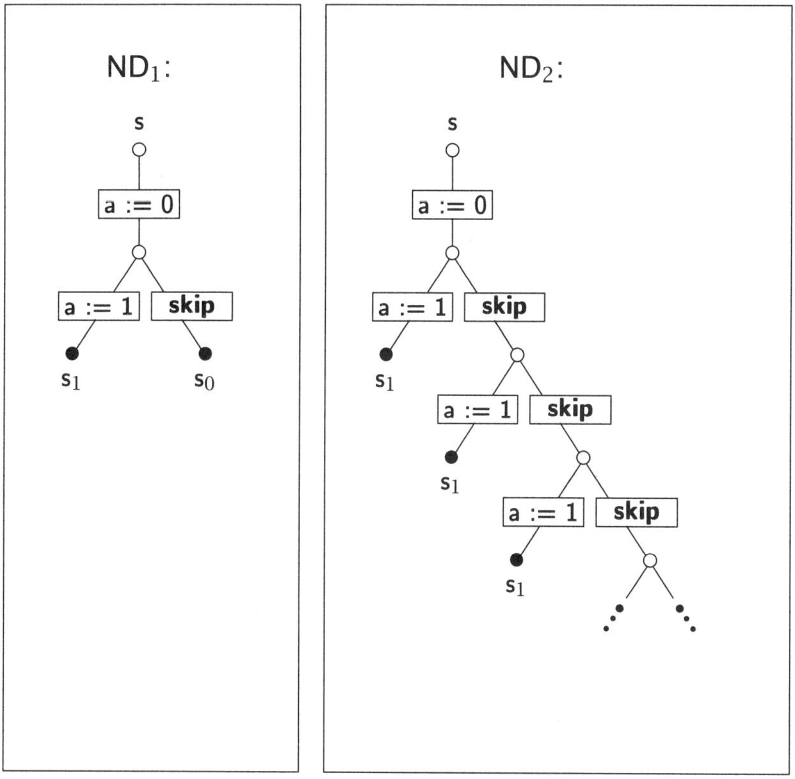

Figure 13.2: Execution trees for the imperatives ND_1 and ND_2 (presented and explained in section 13.2.2) for some given initial state s

order to reduce the amount of formal details the author must describe and the reader absorb, we have only given a rather informal description of execution trees. It is, however, not very difficult to give a formal definition of the execution tree $\mathcal{T}$ree⟦imp⟧(s) for an imperative imp from a given initial state s. The definition is by induction on the syntactic complexity of imp. We leave it as an exercise to give such a definition.

It is obvious that if every execution performed by an imperative imp from a given state s terminates, then every branch of the execution tree $\mathcal{T}$ree⟦imp⟧(s) will be finite, and also that if the execution tree contains an infinitely long branch, then the imperative may – by nondeterministic choice if the tree consists of more than this branch, deterministically otherwise – enter an infinite loop. The leaves at the ends of finite branches of the execution tree are labelled with elements of the set consisting of those states with which the imperative may terminate. This means that

$$\mathcal{M}[\![\mathsf{imp}]\!](\mathsf{s}) = \{\mathsf{s}' \mid \begin{array}{ll} \textit{Either:} & \mathsf{s}' \neq \bot_{\textit{State}} \textit{ and } \mathsf{s}' \textit{ labels a leaf in} \\ & \textit{the execution tree } \mathcal{T}\mathsf{ree}[\![\mathsf{imp}]\!](\mathsf{s}) \\ \textit{Or:} & \mathsf{s}' = \bot_{\textit{State}} \textit{ and } \mathcal{T}\mathsf{ree}[\![\mathsf{imp}]\!](\mathsf{s}) \\ & \textit{contains an infinite branch}\} \end{array}$$

At the end of section 13.2 (on page 293) we raised the question whether or not it is possible to construct an imperative imp and find an initial state s such that $\mathcal{M}[\![\mathsf{imp}]\!](\mathsf{s})$ is infinite but without having $\bot_{\textit{State}}$ as a member. Using execution trees, we may rephrase this question as follows: Is it possible to find an imperative imp and a state s such that the execution tree $\mathcal{T}\mathsf{ree}[\![\mathsf{imp}]\!](\mathsf{s})$ has an infinite number of leaves labelled with distinct states but is without any infinite branches? To answer this question, we observe that the language Dijk_0 (and other nondeterministic languages) at any point in the execution of a program allows only nondeterministic choice amongst a *finite* number of alternatives. This means that every execution tree must be *finitary*: any node in the tree may only be the origin of a finite number of arches. The so-called *König's Lemma* may then be applied. This lemma says that if every branch of a finitary tree is finite, then the whole tree is finite. Applied to our context, this means that if a given imperative imp always terminates when executed from a given state s – no matter what nondeterministic choices are made during the execution of the imperative – then the execution tree $\mathcal{T}\mathsf{ree}[\![\mathsf{imp}]\!](\mathsf{s})$ is finite. König's Lemma therefore answers our question: if an imperative is able to choose nondeterministically any state amongst an infinite number of alternatives, then it may also – nondeterministically – enter an infinite loop. More formally:

$$\mathcal{M}[\![\mathsf{imp}]\!](\mathsf{s}) \textit{ is infinite} \;\Rightarrow\; \bot_{\textit{State}} \in \mathcal{M}[\![\mathsf{imp}]\!](\mathsf{s})$$

This means that if X is a member of $\mathcal{ND}_{\textit{Imp}}(\textit{State}_\bot)$, that is if $\mathsf{X} = \mathcal{M}[\![\mathsf{imp}]\!](\mathsf{s})$ for some imperative imp and some state s, then either X must be finite (but never empty the way $\mathcal{M}$ is defined, see figure 13.1) or $\bot_{\textit{State}} \in \mathsf{X}$. Let us for any cpo D define the set $\mathcal{P}[D]$ to consist of every subset of D that is either finite and nonempty or contains $\bot_D$:

Definition 13.2 $\mathcal{P}[D] \stackrel{d}{=} \{\mathsf{X} \subseteq \mathsf{D} \mid \mathsf{X} \neq \emptyset \wedge (\mathsf{X} \textit{ finite} \vee \bot_D \in \mathsf{X})\}$

The set $\mathcal{P}[D]$ contains all sets in $\mathcal{ND}_{\textit{Imp}}(\textit{State}_\bot)$, and also some (very many in fact) state sets that are not in this set. We will use $\mathcal{P}[D]$ as range for denotations of imperatives in our nondeterministic language, and define the algebra *MV* to consist of all strict and continuous functions that map $\textit{State}_\bot$ to $\mathcal{P}[\textit{State}_\bot]$. It is easy to see that the first four of the five requirements for $\mathcal{P}[\textit{State}_\bot]$ stated in the previous section on page 294 are satisfied when $\mathcal{P}[\textit{State}_\bot]$ is defined as above. That the fifth requirement is satisfied as well, is proved in proposition 13.6 in the next section.

In order for *MV* to become a cpo, and in order to make it meaningful to consider functions that map $\mathcal{P}[State_\perp]$ to itself to be continuous, $\mathcal{P}[State_\perp]$ must be a cpo, which it is by the Egli-Milner order:

Proposition 13.3 *If D is a flat cpo, then the Egli-Milner order* $\sqsubseteq_{EM}$ *orders* $\mathcal{P}[D]$ *to a cpo.*

Proof: By proposition 13.2 it is only necessary to prove completeness, that is that $\bigsqcup X_i \in \mathcal{P}[D]$ for every chain $\{X_i\}_{i=0}^{\infty}$ where each X_i is in $\mathcal{P}[D]$. But this follows immediately by how we in the completeness part of the proof of proposition 13.2 defined the least upper bound of a $\sqsubseteq_{EM}$ chain.

13.3.3 Welldefinedness

In this section we prove that the semantic mapping $\mathcal{M}$ as defined in figure 13.1 is well-defined, strict and continuous. But first we prove a few auxiliary propositions:

Proposition 13.4 *If D is a flat cpo then*

$$f_1 \sqsubseteq f_2 \;\Rightarrow\; f_1{}^+ \sqsubseteq f_2{}^+$$

for all functions $f_1, f_2 \in (D_\perp \to \mathcal{P}[D_\perp])$

Proof: Assume that $f_1 \sqsubseteq f_2$, i.e., that $f_1(d) \sqsubseteq_{EM} f_2(d)$ for every $d \in D$. It suffices to prove that $f_1{}^+(pd) \sqsubseteq_{EM} f_2{}^+(pd)$ for every $pd \in \mathcal{P}[D_\perp]$:

Assume first that $pd \in \mathcal{P}[D_\perp]$ is such that $\perp_D \notin f_1{}^+(pd)$: Then (by definition of $f_1{}^+$) we have (i) for any $d' \in pd$, $\perp_D \notin f_1(d')$. By assumption $f_1(d') \sqsubseteq_{EM} f_2(d')$ for every $d' \in D$. By (i) and the definition of the Egli-Milner order, it follows that $f_1(d') = f_2(d')$ for every $d' \in pd$. But then $f_1{}^+(pd) = f_2{}^+(pd)$, and hence $f_1{}^+(pd) \sqsubseteq_{EM} f_2{}^+(pd)$ because $\sqsubseteq_{EM}$ is reflexive.

Assume then that $pd \in \mathcal{P}[D_\perp]$ is such that $\perp_D \in f_1{}^+(pd)$: In this case, we must prove (i) $(f_1{}^+(pd) - \{\perp_D\}) \subseteq f_2{}^+(pd)$ and (ii) $f_2{}^+(pd) \neq \emptyset$. To prove (i), let d be any member of $(f_1{}^+(pd) - \{\perp_D\})$. We must prove that $d \in f_2{}^+(pd)$. By definition of $f_1{}^+$, there exists $d' \in pd$ such that $d \in f_1(d')$. If $\perp_D \notin f_1(d')$, the assumption $f_1 \sqsubseteq f_2$ gives that $f_1(d') = f_2(d')$, and hence $d \in f_2{}^+(pd)$. If on the other hand d' is such that $\perp_D \in f_1(d')$, then $f_1 \sqsubseteq f_2$ entails that $(f_1(d') - \{\perp_D\}) \subseteq f_2(d')$. But then $d \in f_2(d')$, which entails that $d \in f_2{}^+(pd)$.

To prove (ii) $f_2{}^+(pd) \neq \emptyset$, we observe that because $\perp_D \in f_1{}^+(pd)$, there must exist $d' \in pd$ such that $\perp_D \in f_1(d')$. The assumption $f_1 \sqsubseteq f_2$ gives that $f_1(d') \sqsubseteq_{EM} f_2(d')$, which then entails that $f_2(d') \neq \emptyset$, from which (ii) follows.

Proposition 13.5 *If $D_\perp$ is a flat cpo and $\{f_i\}_{i=0}^{\infty}$ is a chain of continuous functions in $FD = [D_\perp \to \mathcal{P}[D_\perp]]$, then*

$$(\lfloor FD \rfloor f_i)^+ \ = \ \lfloor PD \rfloor (f_i{}^+)$$

where $PD = [\mathcal{P}(D_\perp) \to \mathcal{P}[D_\perp]]$.

Proof: By proposition 13.3 $\mathcal{P}[D_\perp]$ is a cpo, and hence (by proposition 5.6) also FD and PD. By proposition 13.4, $\{f_i{}^+\}_{i=0}^{\infty}$ is a chain, which must have a least upper bound in the cpo PD. Let F be the least upper bound of the chain $\{f_i\}_{i=0}^{\infty}$. We must prove

(i) $\forall i \geq 0$: $f_i{}^+ \sqsubseteq_{PD} F^+$

(ii) For every $G \in PD$: If $\forall i \geq 0$: $f_i{}^+ \sqsubseteq_{PD} G$ then $F^+ \sqsubseteq_{PD} G$

Proposition 13.4 gives that (i) holds. We leave it as an exercise to prove (ii).

Proposition 13.6 *If $D_\perp$ is a flat cpo and f is a strict function that maps $D_\perp$ to $\mathcal{P}[D_\perp]$, then the function f^+ maps $\mathcal{P}[D_\perp]$ to $\mathcal{P}[D_\perp]$. If in addition f is continuous, then f^+ is continuous.*

Proof: We first prove that $f^+(pd) \in \mathcal{P}[D_\perp]$ for every $pd \in \mathcal{P}[D_\perp]$:

If pd does not contain $\perp_D$ as an element, pd must by definition of $\mathcal{P}[D_\perp]$ be finite and non-empty, i.e., $pd = \{d_1, \ldots, d_n\}$, where $n > 0$. Then $f^+(pd) = f(d_1) \cup \ldots \cup f(d_n)$. By assumption, $f(d_i) \in \mathcal{P}[D_\perp]$ for $i = 1, \ldots, n$. If each $f(d_i)$ is finite and non-empty, their union $f^+(pd)$ is the same, and therefore an element of $\mathcal{P}[D_\perp]$. If, on the other hand, $\perp_D$ is an element in $f(d_i)$ for some i, $\perp_D$ is an element in $f^+(pd)$ (because $f(d_i) \subseteq f^+(pd)$), and then $f^+(pd)$ is in $\mathcal{P}[D_\perp]$.

If pd is such that $\perp_D \in pd$, we get - because f is assumed to be strict, i.e., $f(\perp_D) = \{\perp_D\}$ - that $\perp_D \in f^+(pd)$, and $f^+(pd)$ must therefore be an element of $\mathcal{P}[D_\perp]$.

f^+ is monotonic: Assume that $pd_1 \sqsubseteq_{EM} pd_2$. We must prove that $f^+(pd_1) \sqsubseteq_{EM} f^+(pd_2)$. If $\perp_D \notin f^+(pd_1)$, we must (because f is strict) have that $\perp_D \notin pd_1$. Then $pd_1 = pd_2$, and the desired conclusion follows because $\sqsubseteq_{EM}$ is reflexive.

The case $\perp_D \in f^+(pd_1)$ is left as an exercise.

f^+ preserves limits: Assume that $\{X_i\}_{i=0}^{\infty}$ is an $\sqsubseteq_{EM}$ chain in $D_\perp$. The function f^+ has just been proved to be monotonic, such that $\{f^+(X_i)\}_{i=0}^{\infty}$ is a chain in $\mathcal{P}[D_\perp]$. We leave it as an exercise to prove that $\bigsqcup f^+(X_i) = f^+(\bigsqcup X_i)$.

Theorem 13.1 *The denotation $\mathcal{M}[\![imp]\!]$ of any imperative imp - as it is specified in figure 13.1 - is a well-defined, strict and continuous function that maps $State_\perp$ to $\mathcal{P}[State_\perp]$.*

Proof of theorem 13.1: By induction on the syntactic complexity of imp. We only treat a few of the cases here (those that are left out, are similar or simpler):

$\mathsf{exp}_1 := \mathsf{exp}_2$: Let mv_a be the denotation of the imperative $\mathsf{exp}_1 := \mathsf{exp}_2$. As specified in figure 13.1, $\mathsf{mv}_a = \underline{\lambda}\mathsf{s}\colon \{\mathsf{s.assign}(\mathsf{ref}(\mathcal{E}[\![\mathsf{exp}_1]\!](\mathsf{s})), \mathsf{deref}(\mathsf{s}, \mathcal{E}[\![\mathsf{exp}_2]\!](\mathsf{s})))\}$. It is then only necessary to prove that mv_a is continuous, which follows easily by the flatness of $\mathit{State}_\perp$.

$\mathsf{imp}_1; \mathsf{imp}_2$: Let mv_i be the denotation of imp_i for $i = 1, 2$. As induction hypothesis assume that the theorem holds for mv_1 and mv_2. Proposition 13.6 then gives that the function $\underline{\lambda}\mathsf{s}\colon \mathsf{mv}_2{}^+(\mathsf{mv}_1(\mathsf{s}))$ maps $\mathit{State}_\perp$ to $\mathcal{P}[\mathit{State}_\perp]$ and that it is continuous.

do gdimps **od**: The denotation of this imperative is in figure 13.1 specified to be the least fixpoint of the function

$$\begin{aligned}\mathsf{mm} = \lambda\mathsf{mv} \in \mathit{MV}\colon \underline{\lambda}\mathsf{s} \in \mathit{State}_\perp\colon\ & \mathbf{case}\ \mathcal{G}[\![\mathsf{gdimps}]\!](\mathsf{s})\ \mathbf{of} \\ & \mathsf{Empty} \qquad\qquad \Rightarrow \{\mathsf{s}\} \\ & \mathsf{ps}\ \mathbf{in}\ \mathcal{P}[\mathit{State}_\perp] \ \Rightarrow \mathsf{mv}^+(\mathsf{ps})\end{aligned}$$

To prove that the theorem holds for the **do** imperative, it is - by the Fixpoint Theorem - sufficient to prove that mm is a continuous function that maps the cpo $\mathit{MV} = [\mathit{State}_\perp \to \mathcal{P}[\mathit{State}_\perp]]^s$ to itself:

mm *is monotonic*: Assume that $\mathsf{mv}_1 \sqsubseteq_{\mathit{MV}} \mathsf{mv}_2$, and that s is any state. It suffices to prove that (i) $\mathsf{mm}(\mathsf{mv}_1, \mathsf{s}) \sqsubseteq_{\mathit{EM}} \mathsf{mm}(\mathsf{mv}_2, \mathsf{s})$. If s is such that $\mathcal{G}[\![\mathsf{gdimps}]\!](\mathsf{s})$ is empty, (i) follows because $\sqsubseteq_{\mathit{EM}}$ is reflexive. If s is such that $\mathcal{G}[\![\mathsf{gdimps}]\!](\mathsf{s}) = \mathsf{ps}$ where $\mathsf{ps} \in \mathcal{P}[\mathit{State}_\perp]$, (i) follows if we can prove that $\mathsf{mv}_1{}^+(\mathsf{ps}) \sqsubseteq_{\mathit{EM}} \mathsf{mv}_2{}^+(\mathsf{ps})$. But this follows from proposition 13.4 above.

mm *preserves least upper bounds*: We must prove that

$$\mathsf{mm}(\bigsqcup_{\mathit{MV}} \mathsf{mv}_i, \mathsf{s}) = \bigsqcup_{\mathcal{P}[\mathit{State}_\perp]} \mathsf{mm}(\mathsf{mv}_i, \mathsf{s})$$

is true for any MV chain $\{\mathsf{mv}_i\}_{i=0}^{\infty}$ and any state s. That the claim is true if s is such that $\mathcal{G}[\![\mathsf{gdimps}]\!](\mathsf{s})$ is empty, is obvious. Assume therefore that s is such that $\mathcal{G}[\![\mathsf{gdimps}]\!](\mathsf{s}) = \mathsf{ps} \in \mathcal{P}[\mathit{State}_\perp]$. It is then sufficient to prove that

$$(\bigsqcup_{\mathit{MV}} \mathsf{mv}_i)^+(\mathsf{ps}) = \bigsqcup_{\mathcal{P}[\mathit{State}_\perp]} \mathsf{mv}_i{}^+(\mathsf{ps})$$

We leave it as an exercise to prove this.

13.4 Concurrency

A *concurrent* imperative is a compound imperative whose constituent imperatives may be executed at the same time; either on separate processors if such are available, or on a single processor that divides its processing capabilities between several programs in a manner that in results, if not in speed, simulates true parallel execution.

In this section we show how to specify the semantics of a simple programming language that allows concurrent imperatives.

13.4.1 Syntax and informal semantics

The syntax of the programming language which we will use as a vehicle to show how to define the semantics of some simple forms of concurrency is defined by extending and slightly changing the syntax of the **while** language described in chapter 6. The set of imperatives of the new language - which we call Conc_0 - is defined by the following BNF productions:

$$
\begin{array}{rl}
\langle imp \rangle ::= & \textbf{skip} \\
| & \langle expr \rangle := \langle expr \rangle \\
| & \langle imp \rangle ; \langle imp \rangle \\
| & \textbf{if } \langle exp \rangle \textbf{ then } \langle imp \rangle \textbf{ else } \langle imp \rangle \textbf{ fi} \\
| & \textbf{while } \langle exp \rangle \textbf{ do } \langle imp \rangle \textbf{ od} \\
| & \langle imp \rangle \parallel \langle imp \rangle \\
| & \ll \langle imp \rangle \gg
\end{array}
$$

Evaluation of expressions and execution of atomic imperatives (i.e., **skip** and assignments in the current language) and of imperatives on the form $\ll\mathsf{imp}\gg$ - which are said to be *critical regions* - are assumed to be performed *atomically*, i.e., without consuming any time and without anything else happening at precisely the same time. Such imperatives are said to be *noninterruptible*. An imperative $\mathsf{imp}_1 \parallel \mathsf{imp}_2$ is executed either by executing the two imperatives imp_1 and imp_2 in true parallel on two processors (having access to the same state), or - equivalently in effect if not in use of time - by *interleaving* the execution of the constituent noninterruptible imperatives of imp_1 or imp_2 on a single processor. An example: the imperative

$$\ll \mathsf{a} := 3 \parallel \mathsf{a} := 1; \mathsf{a} := \mathsf{a} + 1 \gg$$

may be executed by interleaving the execution of the noninterruptible constituents of $\mathsf{a} := 3$ and $\mathsf{a} := 1; \mathsf{a} := \mathsf{a} + 1$. The interleaving may be done in one of three ways:

$$
\begin{array}{llll}
\textit{Either}: & \mathsf{a} := 3; & \mathsf{a} := 1; & \mathsf{a} := \mathsf{a} + 1 \\
\textit{Or}: & \mathsf{a} := 1; & \mathsf{a} := 3; & \mathsf{a} := \mathsf{a} + 1 \\
\textit{Or}: & \mathsf{a} := 1; & \mathsf{a} := \mathsf{a} + 1; & \mathsf{a} := 3
\end{array}
$$

The result of executing ≪a := 3 || a := 1; a := a + 1≫ is therefore either a = 2, a = 3 or a = 4. The choice between these alternatives is nondeterministically determined.

Generally, the intended operational effect of executing a concurrent imperative imp_1 || imp_2 is found by choosing nondeterministically amongst all possible interleavings of the noninterruptible constituents of imp_1 and imp_2.

13.4.2 Formal semantics

To model the intended semantics of concurrent imperatives, we let the denotation of a given imperative imp that possibly may be executed concurrently with other imperatives with which it may interfere, be a so-called *resumption*. This is a function that maps an initial state s to a set rs whose members may be of two types:

- States s', each of which - there may be more than one if the given imperative imp is nondeterministic - is the result of executing imp to termination. For the set rs to have members of this type, imp must be noninterruptible or at least be a nondeterministic imperative where one of the alternatives is noninterruptible.
- Pairs ⟨res', s'⟩ where s' is the state as it is after executing an initial noninterruptible part of imp and res' is a resumption that represents the rest of the execution of imp.

Two examples: The denotation of the noninterruptible imperative a := 3 is the resumption $\underline{\lambda}$s: { s . assign(a, 3)}. The denotation of a := 1; a := a + 1 is the resumption $\underline{\lambda}$s: {⟨res', s . assign(a, 1)⟩} where res' is the resumption $\underline{\lambda}$s: { s . assign(a, a+1)}.

The point in letting the value of the denotation of an imperative imp for an initial state s contain pairs ⟨res', s'⟩, is to make an opening for the execution of a step of another imperative that is executed concurrently: As the next step to be executed we may choose (nondeterministically) either to take a step in the execution of one of the concurrently executed imperatives or to evaluate res'(s') (thus taking another step in the execution of imp). This models the description given above of how we may find the results of executing a concurrent imperative imp_1 || imp_2 by interleaving the execution of imp_1 and imp_2 in a nondeterministically chosen way.

The semantic algebra *Res* consists of all resumptions. To be in agreement given above of resumptions, *Res* should satisfy the following equation indexres (res)@*Res* (resumptions)

$$Res \stackrel{d}{=} [State_\perp \to \mathcal{P}[RS]]$$

where *RS* is an algebra satisfying the following equation:

$$RS \stackrel{d}{=} State_\perp + (Res \times State_\perp)$$

$$
\begin{aligned}
&\mathcal{M} \in (\mathit{Imp} \to \mathit{Res})\\
&\quad \mathcal{M}[\![\textbf{skip}]\!] = \mathsf{Res'Skip}\\
&\quad \mathcal{M}[\![\mathsf{exp}_1 := \mathsf{exp}_2]\!] = \mathsf{Res'Asg}(\mathcal{E}[\![\mathsf{exp}_1]\!], \mathcal{E}[\![\mathsf{exp}_2]\!])\\
&\quad \mathcal{M}[\![\mathsf{imp}_1;\ \mathsf{imp}_2]\!] = \mathsf{Res'Seq}(\mathcal{M}[\![\mathsf{imp}_1]\!], \mathcal{M}[\![\mathsf{imp}_2]\!])\\
&\quad \mathcal{M}[\![\textbf{if}\ \mathsf{exp}\ \textbf{then}\ \mathsf{imp}_1\ \textbf{else}\ \mathsf{imp}_2\ \textbf{fi}]\!]\\
&\qquad = \mathsf{Res'Cond}(\mathcal{E}[\![\mathsf{exp}]\!], \mathcal{M}[\![\mathsf{imp}_1]\!], \mathcal{M}[\![\mathsf{imp}_2]\!])\\
&\quad \mathcal{M}[\![\textbf{while}\ \mathsf{exp}\ \textbf{do}\ \mathsf{imp}\ \textbf{od}]\!]\\
&\qquad = \mathsf{Y}_{\mathit{Res}}(\lambda \mathsf{res}\colon \mathsf{Res'Cond}(\mathcal{E}[\![\mathsf{exp}]\!],\\
&\qquad\qquad \mathsf{Res'Seq}(\mathcal{M}[\![\mathsf{imp}]\!], \mathsf{res}),\\
&\qquad\qquad \mathsf{Res'Skip}))\\
&\quad \mathcal{M}[\![\mathsf{imp}_1 \parallel \mathsf{imp}_2]\!] = \mathsf{Res'Par}(\mathcal{M}[\![\mathsf{imp}_1]\!], \mathcal{M}[\![\mathsf{imp}_2]\!])\\
&\quad \mathcal{M}[\![\ll\!\mathsf{imp}\!\gg]\!] = \mathsf{Res'Crit}(\mathcal{M}[\![\mathsf{imp}]\!])
\end{aligned}
$$

Figure 13.3: Macro-semantics of imperatives of the concurrent programming language Conc_0

It is very far from trivial to prove that there exist algebras *Res* and *RS* that satisfy these equations. The problems are of two kinds: the first is to define the powerdomain $\mathcal{P}[RS]$ for a cpo *RS* which is *not* flat, the second is to solve the domain equations. In chapter 14 we show how to solve domain equations that are simple in the sense that they do not involve powerdomains. It is, however, outside the scope of this book to prove that domain equations like the ones given here are solvable. The interested reader is referred to [Plotkin; 76], where resumptions were first introduced; [Smyth; 78], where Plotkin's constructions are explained in a comparatively simple manner; or [Gunter, Scott; 90], where a comprehensive treatment of semantic domains is given.

It is convenient to split the specification of the semantics of the imperatives of Conc_0 into layers. The macro-layer is specified in figure 13.3, and the intermediate layer in figure 13.4.

A few points in the specifications of the semantics of Conc_0 as given in figures 13.3 and 13.4 may possibly need some explanation:

Critical regions: The denotation of a critical region ≪imp≫ is defined to be equal to Res'Crit(res) where res is the denotation of imp. The intermediate-level function Res'Crit is a function in (*Res* → *Res*) which is such that for any resumption res the value of Res'Crit(res) is another resumption res_c that may be said to evaluate res to the end: For any state s, the value of $\mathsf{res}_c(\mathsf{s})$ may found by first evaluating res(s), producing a set SC that may contain states and pairs of resumptions and states. The set SC is then transformed: As long as it contains a pair ⟨res', s'⟩, then that pair is replaced

$$
\begin{aligned}
\mathit{Res} &\stackrel{d}{=} [\mathit{State}_\perp \rightarrow \mathcal{P}[\mathit{RS}]] \\
\mathit{RS} &\stackrel{d}{=} \mathit{State}_\perp + (\mathit{Res} \times \mathit{State}_\perp)
\end{aligned}
$$

$$
\begin{array}{ll}
\mathsf{Res'Skip} & = \underline{\lambda}\mathsf{s}\colon \{\,\mathsf{s}\} \\
\mathsf{Res'Asg(lv,\ rv)} & = \underline{\lambda}\mathsf{s}\colon \{\,\mathsf{s\,.\,assign(ref(lv(s)),\ deref(s,\ rv(s)))}\} \\
\mathsf{Res'Cond(bv,\ res_1,\ res_2)} & = \underline{\lambda}\mathsf{s}\colon \textbf{if}\ \mathsf{deref(s,\ bv(s))\,.\,is\_true} \Rightarrow \{\langle \mathsf{res_1,\ s}\rangle\} \\
& \qquad\ \textbf{if}\ \mathsf{deref(s,\ bv(s))\,.\,is\_false} \Rightarrow \{\langle \mathsf{res_2,\ s}\rangle\} \\
& \qquad\ \textbf{else}\ \{\perp_{\mathit{State}}\}
\end{array}
$$

$$
\begin{array}{l}
\mathsf{Res'Crit} = \mathsf{Y}_{\mathit{FR}}(\lambda \mathsf{Crit} \in \mathit{FR}\colon \lambda \mathsf{res}\colon \\
\qquad \textbf{let}\ \mathsf{q} = \underline{\lambda}\mathsf{rs} \in \mathit{RS}\colon \textbf{case}\ \mathsf{rs}\colon \\
\qquad\quad \mathsf{s'}\ \textbf{in}\ \mathsf{State} \qquad\qquad\qquad \Rightarrow \{\,\mathsf{s'}\} \\
\qquad\quad \langle \mathsf{res',\ s'}\rangle\ \textbf{in}\ \mathit{Res} \times \mathit{State}_\perp \ \Rightarrow \mathsf{Crit(res')(s')} \\
\qquad \textbf{in}\ \mathsf{q}^+ \circ \mathsf{res})
\end{array}
$$

$$
\begin{array}{l}
\mathsf{Res'Seq} = \mathsf{Y}_{\mathit{FRR}}(\lambda \mathsf{Seq} \in \mathit{FRR}\colon \lambda\langle \mathsf{res_1,\ res_2}\rangle\colon \\
\qquad \textbf{let}\ \mathsf{q} = \underline{\lambda}\mathsf{rs} \in \mathit{RS}\colon \textbf{case}\ \mathsf{rs}\colon \\
\qquad\quad \mathsf{s'} \qquad\qquad \Rightarrow \{\langle \mathsf{res_2,\ s'}\rangle\} \\
\qquad\quad \langle \mathsf{res',\ s'}\rangle \ \Rightarrow \{\langle \mathsf{Seq(res',\ res_2),\ s'}\rangle\} \\
\qquad \textbf{in}\ \mathsf{q}^+ \circ \mathsf{res_1})
\end{array}
$$

$$
\begin{array}{l}
\mathsf{Res'Par} = \mathsf{Y}_{\mathit{FRR}}(\lambda \mathsf{Par} \in \mathit{FRR}\colon \\
\qquad \textbf{let}\ \mathsf{PS} = \lambda\langle \mathsf{res_1,\ res_2}\rangle\colon \\
\qquad\quad \textbf{let}\ \mathsf{q} = \underline{\lambda}\mathsf{rs} \in \mathit{RS}\colon \textbf{case}\ \mathsf{rs}\colon \\
\qquad\qquad \mathsf{s'} \qquad\qquad \Rightarrow \{\langle \mathsf{res_2,\ s'}\rangle\} \\
\qquad\qquad \langle \mathsf{res',\ s'}\rangle \ \Rightarrow \{\langle \mathsf{Par(res',\ res_2),\ s'}\rangle\} \\
\qquad\quad \textbf{in}\ \mathsf{q}^+ \circ \mathsf{res_1} \\
\qquad \textbf{in}\ \lambda\langle \mathsf{res_1,\ res_2}\rangle\colon \mathsf{PS(res_1,\ res_2)} \cup \\
\qquad\qquad\qquad\qquad\qquad\ \mathsf{PS(res_2,\ res_1))}
\end{array}
$$

$$
\mathit{FR} \stackrel{d}{=} [\mathit{Res} \rightarrow \mathit{Res}], \quad \mathit{FRR} \stackrel{d}{=} [(\mathit{Res} \times \mathit{Res}) \rightarrow \mathit{Res}]
$$

Figure 13.4: Intermediate semantics of imperatives of the concurrent programming language Conc_0

by res'(s'). When SC contains only states and no pairs, it is taken to be the value of $\mathsf{res}_c(\mathsf{s})$.

Res'Crit abides by this operational description if it satisfies the following equation:

$$
\begin{array}{l}
\mathsf{Res'Crit(res)} = \textbf{let}\ \mathsf{q} = \underline{\lambda}\mathsf{rs} \in \mathit{RS}\colon \textbf{case}\ \mathsf{rs}\colon \\
\qquad\qquad\qquad\quad \mathsf{s'}\ \textbf{in}\ \mathsf{State} \qquad\qquad\qquad \Rightarrow \{\,\mathsf{s'}\} \\
\qquad\qquad\qquad\quad \langle \mathsf{res',\ s'}\rangle\ \textbf{in}\ \mathit{Res} \times \mathit{State}_\perp \ \Rightarrow \mathsf{Res'Crit(res')(s')} \\
\qquad\qquad\qquad \textbf{in}\ \underline{\lambda}\mathsf{s} \in \mathit{State}_\perp\colon \mathsf{q}^+\mathsf{(res(s))}
\end{array}
$$

This equation may not be used as an acceptable definition: the definition would be circular. But it is easy to transform the equation such that Res'Crit may be defined to be the least fixpoint of a certain function. The specification of Res'Crit given in figure 13.4 shows how this may be done. (Exercise: Prove that the function of which Res'Crit is defined to be the least fixpoint is continuous.)

Sequences of imperatives: The denotation of an imperative $imp_1; imp_2$ is defined to be equal to $Res'Seq(res_1, res_2)$, where res_i is the denotation of imp_i for $i = 1, 2$. The value of $Res'Seq(res_1, res_2)$ is a new resumption res_s which - in order to be in accordance with the intended semantics - should be evaluated as follows for any state s: First evaluate $res_1(s)$. Assume that SS is the result. SS is then transformed by replacing every state s' by the pair $\langle res_2, s'\rangle$, and replacing every pair $\langle res', s'\rangle$ by a pair $\langle Res'Seq(res', res_2), s'\rangle$. The transformed set is taken to be the value of $res_s(s)$. To be in agreement with this description, Res'Seq should satisfy the following equation:

$$\begin{aligned} Res'Seq(res_1, res_2) = \mathbf{let}\ q = \underline{\lambda} rs \in RS\text{: } \mathbf{case}\ rs\text{:} \\ s' \quad &\Rightarrow \{\langle res_2, s'\rangle\} \\ \langle res', s'\rangle \quad &\Rightarrow \{\langle Res'Seq(res', res_2), s'\rangle\} \\ \mathbf{in}\ \underline{\lambda} s \in State_\perp\text{: } q^+(res_1(s)) \end{aligned}$$

The definition given in figure 13.4 is the result of transforming this circular definition into an acceptable (i.e., noncircular) form using fixpoints.

Concurrent imperatives: The denotation of a concurrent imperative $imp_1 \| imp_2$ is defined to be equal to $Res'Par(res_1, res_2)$, where res_i is the denotation of imp_i for $i = 1, 2$. $Res'Par(res_1, res_2)$ is defined to be equal to the union of $PS(res_1, res_2)$ and $PS(res_2, res_1)$, where PS is an auxiliary function whose value for two resumptions res_1 and res_2 is a new resumption res_p. For the formal semantics of a concurrent imperative to agree with informal intentions, the resumption res_p should be evaluated as follows for any initial state s: First evaluate $res_1(s)$. Assume that SP is the result. This set is then transformed by replacing every state s' by $\langle res_2, s'\rangle$ and every pair $\langle res', s'\rangle$ by a pair $\langle Res'Par(res', res_2), s'\rangle$. The transformed set is taken to be the value of $res_p(s)$. The function PS is as desired if it satisfies the following equation:

$$\begin{aligned} PS(res_1, res_2) = \mathbf{let}\ q = \underline{\lambda} rs \in RS\text{: } \mathbf{case}\ rs\text{:} \\ s' \quad &\Rightarrow \{\langle res_2, s'\rangle\} \\ \langle res', s'\rangle \quad &\Rightarrow \{\langle Res'Par(res', res_2), s'\rangle\} \\ \mathbf{in}\ \underline{\lambda} s \in State_\perp\text{: } q^+(res_1(s)) \end{aligned}$$

In figure 13.4 we define Res'Par to be the least fixpoint of a certain function that has a definition which is based on the equation for PS given here.

13.5 Exercises

13.5.1 An execution tree

Construct an execution tree for the imperative ND_3 (which is defined in section 13.2.2).

13.5.2 Define execution trees

Give a formal definition of the execution tree $\mathcal{T}[\![\mathsf{imp}]\!](\mathsf{s})$ for any imperative imp and state s. Use induction on the syntactic complexity of imp.

13.5.3 A simple concurrent program

Evaluate

$$\mathcal{M}[\![\mathsf{x} := 3 \parallel \mathsf{x} := 1; \mathsf{x} := \mathsf{x} + 1]\!](\mathsf{s})$$

and

$$\mathcal{M}[\![\ll \mathsf{x} := 3 \parallel \mathsf{x} := 1; \mathsf{x} := \mathsf{x} + 1 \gg]\!](\mathsf{s})$$

using the formal definitions given in figures 13.3 and 13.4.

13.5.4 Concurrent expressions

Define the semantics of concurrent expressions. Let the denotation of an expression be a so-called *expression resumption*, which is an element in the semantic domain

$$\mathsf{E\_Res} = [State_\perp \to \mathcal{P}[(E_\perp \times State_\perp) + (E\_Res \times State_\perp)]]$$

Assume that the evaluation of an expression is interruptible and as a side-effect may change the state.

Chapter 14
Reflexive domains

14.1 Domain equations

Domains that are specified to be solutions of domain equations are used to define the semantics of various features of some programming languages. An example: In most languages of the **Algol** family it is legal to declare procedures that take procedures, even themselves, as parameters. On page 236 in section 10.2.3 we specified that the domain P of parameter values should satisfy the following equation:

$$P = AA + PP$$

where AA is a previously defined domain and PP, which is the domain of denotations of procedures, should satisfy the following equation:

$$PP = [P \to MV]$$

This means that P should be a solution of the following domain equation:

$$P = AA + [P \to MV]$$

On page 237 we observed that it is not at all obvious that a domain equation like this is solvable, and promised that we would go deeper into these matters at some later time. The time has now come to fulfil our promise: In this chapter we describe a method, originally introduced by D.S. Scott (first in [Scott; 70], more comprehensively in [Scott; 76]), that may be used to solve domain equations of the form

$$X = \mathcal{F}(X)$$

where $\mathcal{F}(X)$ denotes a domain expression that is constructed from previously defined domains and the unknown domain X, using only the domain operators $(. \times .)$ (Cartesian product), $(. + .)$ (disjoint sums) and $[. \to .]$ (used to construct domains of continuous functions).

We will describe the method the way most mathematics habitually is described – often quite elegantly and economically, but not always very pedagogically – namely *bottom-up*: Instead of starting with a given problem (in this case: how to solve domain equations) and trying to see how the problem may be broken down into subproblems that are smaller and hopefully more easily solved, it is common to start an exposition of a mathematical theory by defining some concepts and proving some propositions about these concepts. Usually when mathematics is presented in this manner, there does not seem to be any connection between these first concepts and propositions and the given problem. Based on the first and primitive concepts, we construct other and more compound concepts, and prove propositions about these, still often without seeing much connection with the original problem. Finally, after having constructed a mathematical structure which may be large and complex, and frequently after having made some detours via concepts and results that seem mathematically interesting, we suddenly 'surface' and show how the given problem may be solved if anybody should still be interested[1]. The reason we will employ a bottom-up way of presenting Scott's method for solving domain equations, is that we see no viable alternative: It is simply necessary to develop a rather large set of mathematical tools before we can tackle domain equations.

We start our exposition of Scott's method for solving domain equations by defining an algebra $\mathcal{P}\omega$ that consists of all sets of integers and defining certain producers and observers of this algebra (no obvious connection to equation solving at this stage). We also define a coding system which is such that the elements of $\mathcal{P}\omega$ may be said to code continuous functions mapping $\mathcal{P}\omega$ to itself. We then define a simple language called **Lambda**, which will be used solely to define various elements of $\mathcal{P}\omega$, some of them rather complex. It is then shown how the **Lambda** language may be employed to construct certain so-called

[1] In a footnote, it may be worth mentioning that even if mathematics is often presented bottom up as described in the slight parody given above, it is hardly ever invented that way: Mathematical results and methods are usually discovered *top-down* but often presented *bottom-up*.

retracts (which are $\mathcal{P}\omega$ elements that satisfy certain conditions). After having stated (but not proved) a few propositions about these retracts (still no visible connection to equation solving!), we finally 'surface' and show how retracts may be used to solve domain equations (if anybody should be interested). Scott's original description of his method contains quite a lot of interesting mathematical detours, which we choose not to follow in our exposition of his ideas. In order to reduce the size of this chapter, we have also chosen not to prove any of the mathematical claims we make.

14.2 Sets of non-negative integers

In this chapter we use ω to denote the set of non-negative integers and $\mathcal{P}\omega$ to denote the set of all subsets of ω:

$$\omega \stackrel{d}{=} \{0, 1, 2, \dots\}$$
$$\mathcal{P}\omega \stackrel{d}{=} \{X \mid X \subseteq \omega\}$$

As observed on page 79, $\mathcal{P}\omega$ is ordered to a cpo by the subset order with the empty set $\varnothing$ as least element::

- $\subseteq$ partially orders $\mathcal{P}\omega$
- For every $X \in \mathcal{P}\omega$: $\varnothing \subseteq X$
- Any $\subseteq$ chain $\{X_i\}_{i=0}^{\infty}$ in $\mathcal{P}\omega$ has $\bigcup X_i$ as its least upper bound.

Observe that $\mathcal{P}\omega$ contains a *greatest* element, namely ω: every $X \in \mathcal{P}\omega$ satisfies $X \subseteq \omega$.

A function we need in the ensuing constructions, is the pair function. This function is used to enumerate all pairs of non-negative integers, and is defined by the following formula:

$$\mathsf{pair}(n, m) = \tfrac{1}{2}(n + m) * (n + m + 1) + m$$

A table of the values of $\mathsf{pair}(n, m)$ for small n and m is given in figure 14.1. Observe that pair is an injective function (it is in fact a bijection between $\omega \times \omega$ and ω), such that for every $p \in \omega$ there exists a uniquely determined pair (n, m) such that $\mathsf{pair}(n, m) = p$.

14.2.1 Finite sets of integers

For reasons shortly to be seen, we are particularly interested in the finite subsets of ω, i.e., those $X \in \mathcal{P}\omega$ that contains only a finite number of integers. It is possible to enumerate these finite subsets: For every integer $n \geq 0$, define a finite set fin_n of integers as follows:

(1) Find distinct integers $a_1, \dots, a_m$ such that $n = 2^{a_1} + \dots + 2^{a_m}$. Observe that these integers are uniquely determined by n.

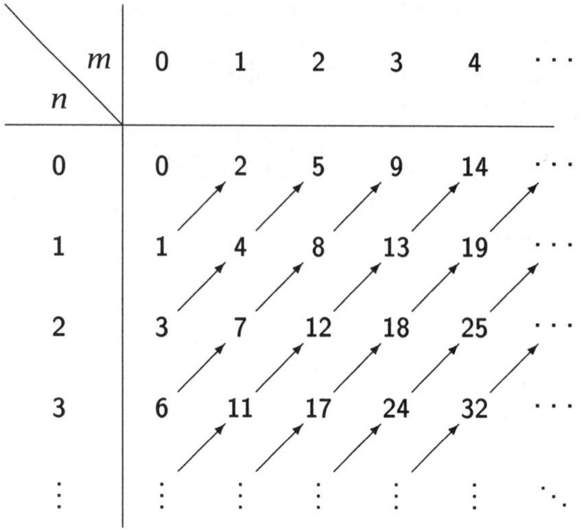

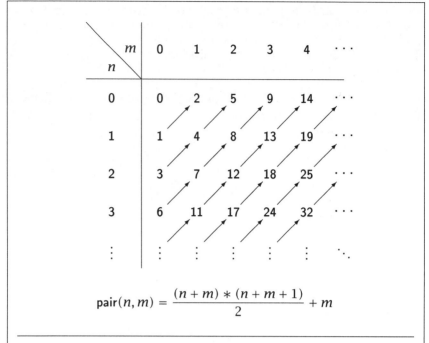

$$\mathsf{pair}(n, m) = \frac{(n+m) * (n+m+1)}{2} + m$$

Figure 14.1: The enumeration of pairs of non-negative integers by the pair function

(2) Let $\mathsf{fin}_n = \{\mathsf{a}_1, \ldots, \mathsf{a}_m\}$.

It is easy to see that $\mathsf{fin}_0, \mathsf{fin}_1, \mathsf{fin}_2, \ldots$ is an enumeration of all finite members of $\mathcal{P}\omega$:

$$\begin{array}{lll} \text{fin}_0 = \varnothing, & \text{fin}_1 = \{0\}, & \text{fin}_2 = \{1\}, \\ \text{fin}_3 = \{0, 1\}, & \text{fin}_4 = \{2\}, & \text{fin}_5 = \{0, 2\}, \\ \text{fin}_6 = \{1, 2\}, & \text{fin}_7 = \{0, 1, 2\}, & \text{fin}_8 = \{3\}, \\ \ldots & & \end{array}$$

14.2.2 Continuous functions

A function f that maps the cpo $\mathcal{P}\omega$ to itself is by definition continuous if and only if

1: For every $\mathsf{X}, \mathsf{Y} \in \mathcal{P}\omega$: $(\mathsf{X} \subseteq \mathsf{Y}) \Rightarrow (\mathsf{f}(\mathsf{X}) \subseteq \mathsf{f}(\mathsf{Y}))$

2: For every $\mathcal{P}\omega$ chain $\{\mathsf{X}_i\}_{i=0}^{\infty}$: $\mathsf{f}(\bigcup \mathsf{X}_i) = \bigcup \mathsf{f}(\mathsf{X}_i)$

A characterization of continuity which frequently is more illuminating than the one given by the definition, is that a function is continuous if and only if for every argument X it is the case that every finite piece of information in the result f(X) is determined by a finite part of the argument X. Translated to functions that map $\mathcal{P}\omega$ to $\mathcal{P}\omega$, this means that a function $\mathsf{f} \in (\mathcal{P}\omega \to \mathcal{P}\omega)$ is continuous if and only if for every $\mathsf{X} \in \mathcal{P}\omega$ and every integer $\mathsf{a} \in \omega$:

$$\mathsf{a} \in \mathsf{f}(\mathsf{X}) \iff \mathsf{a} \in \mathsf{f}(\mathsf{Y}) \text{ for some finite } \mathsf{Y} \subseteq \mathsf{X}$$

We express this characterization - which of course has to be proved, even if we refrain from doing this here - as a proposition:

Proposition 14.1 *A function* $\mathsf{f} \in (\mathcal{P}\omega \to \mathcal{P}\omega)$ *is continuous if and only if for every element* X *of* $\mathcal{P}\omega$:

$$\mathsf{f}(\mathsf{X}) = \bigcup\{\mathsf{f}(\mathsf{fin}_n) \mid \mathsf{fin}_n \subseteq \mathsf{X}\}$$

A very important idea behind Scott's construction is that every continuous function f that maps $\mathcal{P}\omega$ to $\mathcal{P}\omega$ may be *coded* by an element - which we denote by $\mathsf{graph}_\mathsf{f}$ - of $\mathcal{P}\omega$, i.e., by a set of integers; and conversely that every a of $\mathcal{P}\omega$ may be considered to code a continuous function - denoted by func_a - mapping $\mathcal{P}\omega$ to itself. The details in the coding scheme are as follows:

Assume that f is a continuous function in $(\mathcal{P}\omega \to \mathcal{P}\omega)$, and define an element of $\mathcal{P}\omega$ denoted by $\mathsf{graph}_\mathsf{f}$ as follows:

$$\mathsf{graph}_\mathsf{f} \stackrel{d}{=} \{\mathsf{pair}(n,m) \mid m \in \mathsf{f}(\mathsf{fin}_n)\}$$

Knowledge of $\mathsf{graph}_\mathsf{f}$ is sufficient to determine the value of f(X) for any argument $\mathsf{X} \in \mathcal{P}\omega$:

$$\begin{aligned} \mathsf{f}(\mathsf{X}) &= \{m \mid \exists n\colon \mathsf{fin}_n \subseteq \mathsf{X} \wedge m \in \mathsf{f}(\mathsf{fin}_n)\} && \text{(By prop. 14.1)} \\ &= \{m \mid \exists n\colon \mathsf{fin}_n \subseteq \mathsf{X} \wedge \mathsf{pair}(n,m) \in \mathsf{graph}_\mathsf{f}\} && \text{(By def. of } \mathsf{graph}_\mathsf{f}) \end{aligned}$$

We are therefore justified in saying that the $\mathcal{P}\omega$ element $\mathsf{graph}_\mathsf{f}$ codes the function f.

The same method that is used to evaluate a function from the set of integers that codes it, may be used for *any* element of $\mathcal{P}\omega$: If $\mathsf{a} \in \mathcal{P}\omega$, define a function func_a mapping $\mathcal{P}\omega$ to itself as follows:

$$\mathsf{func}_\mathsf{a} \stackrel{d}{=} \lambda \mathsf{X} \in \mathcal{P}\omega\colon \{m \mid \exists\, n\colon \mathsf{fin}_n \subseteq \mathsf{X} \wedge \mathsf{pair}(n,m) \in \mathsf{a}\}$$

A trivial example: If we let $\mathsf{a} = \{8\}$, then for any $\mathsf{X} \in \mathcal{P}\omega$:

$$\mathsf{func}_\mathsf{a}(\mathsf{X}) = \{m \mid \exists n\colon \mathsf{fin}_n \subseteq \mathsf{X} \wedge \mathsf{pair}(n,m) = 8\}$$

The function pair is injective, and only for $n = 1$ and $m = 2$ is $\mathsf{pair}(n,m) = 8$. The condition $\mathsf{fin}_n \subseteq \mathsf{X}$ is equivalent to $0 \in \mathsf{X}$ when $n = 1$ (because $\mathsf{fin}_1 = \{0\}$). We therefore get

$$\mathsf{func}_{\{8\}} = \lambda \mathsf{X} \in \mathcal{P}\omega : \begin{cases} \{2\} & \text{if } 0 \in \mathsf{X} \\ \varnothing & \text{otherwise} \end{cases}$$

It is obvious that if we for any continuous function f let $g = \mathsf{graph}_f$ be the code for f, then the function coded by g, i.e., func_g, is equal to f. More interesting is the fact that every function coded by an element of $\mathcal{P}\omega$ is continuous:

Proposition 14.2 *For any* $a \in \mathcal{P}\omega$*: the function* func_a *is continuous.*

When no reasonable misunderstanding is possible, we will often write a(x) instead of $\mathsf{func}_a(x)$ for $a, x \in \mathcal{P}\omega$, and hence wilfully introduce ambiguity. But ambiguity is not always bad, even in mathematics. On the contrary: as long as one is aware of the fact that certain constructions may have several quite different meanings, and knows how such constructions may be disambiguated, ambiguity may be beneficial. This is partly because it may reduce the amount of typographical frills with which we have to embellish our constructions, and partly because it is often an aid to comprehension to read the same construction with different but related meanings. To live with ambiguity is in fact quite common, easily performed even by small children when they have learnt to distinguish between words and their denotations.

Precisely which functions are coded by various members of $\mathcal{P}\omega$ and precisely by which elements of $\mathcal{P}\omega$ various functions are coded, are details of little or no interest. The two important facts to be used in the following about the coding are first that every continuous function is coded by a member of $\mathcal{P}\omega$ and second that every element of $\mathcal{P}\omega$ codes a continuous function. We may therefore say that $\mathcal{P}\omega$ in a certain sense is isomorphic to $[\mathcal{P}\omega \to \mathcal{P}\omega]$, i.e., that $\mathcal{P}\omega$ satisfies the following condition:

$$\mathcal{P}\omega \;\cong\; [\mathcal{P}\omega \to \mathcal{P}\omega]$$

Thus, suddenly, we see a connection to domain equations!

14.3 The Lambda language

We need to define various elements of $\mathcal{P}\omega$ that satisfy certain conditions, in particular elements that code functions whose ranges are of a certain nature; and introduce a language called **Lambda** to be used to define these elements.

The syntax of the **Lambda** language is determined by the BNF productions given in figure 14.2.

The denotation of an L-term is a function that may be used to evaluate an element in $\mathcal{P}\omega$ given an assignment of $\mathcal{P}\omega$ elements to variables that occur free in the term (i.e., not bound by a λ). The semantic mapping for L-terms is denoted by $\mathcal{L}$ and has the following signature:

$$\mathcal{L} \in (\textit{L-term} \to (\textit{Varval} \to \mathcal{P}\omega))$$

where *Varval* is a semantic domain defined as follows:

$$
\begin{aligned}
\langle \textit{L-term} \rangle \;::=\;& \langle \textit{variable} \rangle \\
&|\; \mathbf{0} \\
&|\; \langle \textit{L-term} \rangle + \mathbf{1} \\
&|\; \langle \textit{L-term} \rangle - \mathbf{1} \\
&|\; \mathbf{if}(\langle \textit{L-term} \rangle, \langle \textit{L-term} \rangle, \langle \textit{L-term} \rangle) \\
&|\; \langle \textit{L-term} \rangle(\langle \textit{L-term} \rangle) \\
&|\; \lambda \langle \textit{variable} \rangle . \langle \textit{L-term} \rangle \\
\langle \textit{variable} \rangle \;::=\;& \langle \textit{ident} \rangle
\end{aligned}
$$

Figure 14.2: The syntax of the **Lambda** language

$$\mathcal{L} \in (\textit{L-term} \to (\textit{Varval} \to \mathcal{P}\omega)), \quad \textit{where Varval} \stackrel{d}{=} (\textit{Ident} \to \mathcal{P}\omega)$$

$$
\begin{aligned}
\mathcal{L}[\![\mathsf{var}]\!](\mathsf{vv}) &= \mathsf{vv}(\mathsf{var}) \\
\mathcal{L}[\![\mathbf{0}]\!](\mathsf{vv}) &= \{0\} \\
\mathcal{L}[\![\mathsf{e} + \mathbf{1}]\!](\mathsf{vv}) &= \{\mathsf{n} + 1 \mid \mathsf{n} \in \mathcal{L}[\![\mathsf{e}]\!](\mathsf{vv})\} \\
\mathcal{L}[\![\mathsf{e} - \mathbf{1}]\!](\mathsf{vv}) &= \{\mathsf{n} \mid (\mathsf{n} + 1) \in \mathcal{L}[\![\mathsf{e}]\!](\mathsf{vv})\} \\
\mathcal{L}[\![\mathbf{if}(\mathsf{e}_1, \mathsf{e}_2, \mathsf{e}_3)]\!](\mathsf{vv}) &= \{n \mid n \in \mathcal{L}[\![\mathsf{e}_2]\!](\mathsf{vv}) \wedge 0 \in \mathcal{L}[\![\mathsf{e}_1]\!](\mathsf{vv})\} \cup \\
&\quad\; \{n \mid n \in \mathcal{L}[\![\mathsf{e}_3]\!](\mathsf{vv}) \wedge \\
&\quad\quad (\exists m \colon (\mathsf{m}+1) \in \mathcal{L}[\![\mathsf{e}_1]\!](\mathsf{vv}))\} \\
\mathcal{L}[\![\mathsf{e}_1(\mathsf{e}_2)]\!](\mathsf{vv}) &= \{m \mid \exists n \colon \mathsf{fin}_n \subseteq \mathcal{L}[\![\mathsf{e}_2]\!](\mathsf{vv}) \wedge \\
&\quad\quad \mathsf{pair}(\mathsf{n}, \mathsf{m}) \in \mathcal{L}[\![\mathsf{e}_1]\!](\mathsf{vv})\} \\
\mathcal{L}[\![\lambda \mathsf{var} . \mathsf{e}]\!](\mathsf{vv}) &= \{\mathsf{pair}(n, m) \mid m \in \mathcal{L}[\![\mathsf{e}]\!](\mathsf{vv}.\mathsf{bind}(\mathsf{var}, \mathsf{fin}_n))\}
\end{aligned}
$$

Figure 14.3: The semantics of the **Lambda** language

$$\textit{Varval} \stackrel{d}{=} (\textit{Ident} \to \mathcal{P}\omega)$$

$\mathcal{L}$ is defined (by induction on the syntactic complexity of L-terms) in figure 14.3. The intuitive ideas behind the definitions given in this figure should (hopefully) be clear at the end of this chapter.

A term without free variables is said to be a *ground* term. Any ground L-term e defines an element val_e of $\mathcal{P}\omega$ defined as follows:

$$\mathsf{val}_\mathsf{e} \stackrel{d}{=} \mathcal{L}[\![\mathsf{e}]\!](\mathsf{vv}) \qquad \text{(where vv is any element of } \textit{Varval}\text{)}$$

We say that val_e is the *value* of e. When no misunderstanding should be possible, we will often write e instead of val_e.

An important fact which we frequently will use in the sequel is that any ground L-term e implicitly defines a function mapping $\mathcal{P}\omega$ to $\mathcal{P}\omega$, namely the function that is coded by the value of the term, i.e., func_v where $\mathsf{v} = \mathsf{val}_\mathsf{e}$, and that this function by proposition 14.2 is continuous. We will often simply write $\mathsf{e}(\mathsf{X})$ instead of $\mathsf{func}_{\mathsf{val}_\mathsf{e}}(\mathsf{X})$ (another case of willed ambiguity).

The *range* of a ground L-term e is the range of the function implicitly defined by e:

$$\mathsf{range}(\mathsf{e}) \stackrel{d}{=} \{\mathsf{Y} \in \mathcal{P}\omega \mid \exists \mathsf{X}\colon \mathsf{Y} = \mathsf{func}_{\mathsf{val}_\mathsf{e}}(\mathsf{X})\}$$

Two L-terms e_1 and e_2 are said to be *semantically equal* if and only if $\mathcal{L}[\![\mathsf{e}_1]\!](\mathsf{vv}) = \mathcal{L}[\![\mathsf{e}_2]\!](\mathsf{vv})$ for every $\mathsf{vv} \in$ *Varval*. We write $\mathsf{e}_1 = \mathsf{e}_2$ to express that e_1 and e_2 are semantically equal.

Proposition 14.3 *For all L-terms* e, e' *and all variables* v, v_1, v_2:

$$\alpha\colon \lambda \mathsf{v}_1 . \mathsf{e} = \lambda \mathsf{v}_2 . \mathsf{e}[\mathsf{v}_1 := \mathsf{v}_2]$$
$$\beta\colon (\lambda \mathsf{v}.\mathsf{e})(\mathsf{e'}) = \mathsf{e}[\mathsf{v} := \mathsf{e'}]$$

For β it is assumed that no free occurrence of v *in* e *is inside the scope of a bound variable which is free in* e'.

(The expression $\mathsf{e}[\mathsf{e'} := \mathsf{v}]$ denotes the L-term that is the result of substituting e' for every free occurrence of the variable v in e.)

14.4 Using Lambda

In this section we use the Lambda language to define a number of $\mathcal{P}\omega$ elements and $\mathcal{P}\omega$ functions.

The fixpoint operator The *fixpoint operator* is a special function that maps $\mathcal{P}\omega$ to $\mathcal{P}\omega$. It is defined by the L-term Y which is defined as follows:

$$\mathsf{Y} \stackrel{d}{=} \lambda \mathsf{f}.\lambda \mathsf{x}.\mathsf{f}(\mathsf{x}(\mathsf{x}))(\lambda \mathsf{x}.\mathsf{f}(\mathsf{x}(\mathsf{x})))$$

More precisely and less ambiguously, we may say that the fixpoint operator is the function that is coded by the value in $\mathcal{P}\omega$ of the ground L-term Y.

Proposition 14.4 *The fixpoint proposition for $\mathcal{P}\omega$:*

$$\mathsf{Y}_1\colon \mathsf{Y}(\mathsf{u}) = \mathsf{u}(\mathsf{Y}(\mathsf{u})) \qquad \textit{for every } \mathsf{u} \in \mathcal{P}\omega$$
$$\mathsf{Y}_2\colon (\mathsf{u}(\mathsf{a}) = \mathsf{a}) \Rightarrow (\mathsf{Y}(\mathsf{u}) \subseteq \mathsf{a}) \qquad \textit{for every } \mathsf{u}, \mathsf{a} \in \mathcal{P}\omega$$
$$\mathsf{Y}_3\colon \mathsf{Y}(\mathsf{u}) = \bigcup \mathsf{u}^i(\emptyset) \qquad \textit{for every } \mathsf{u} \in \mathcal{P}\omega$$

where $\mathsf{u}^0(\mathsf{x}) = \mathsf{x}$ *and* $\mathsf{u}^{i+1}(\mathsf{x}) = \mathsf{u}(\mathsf{u}^i(\mathsf{x}))$ *for* $\mathsf{x} \in \mathcal{P}\omega$ *and* $i \geq 0$.

Y_1 says that $\mathsf{Y}(\mathsf{u})$ denotes a fixpoint of the continuous function coded by u, Y_2 that $\mathsf{Y}(\mathsf{u})$ is the least fixpoint of u, and Y_3 shows how to evaluate the least fixpoint $\mathsf{Y}(\mathsf{u})$ for any $\mathsf{u} \in \mathcal{P}\omega$.

Bottom The L-term $\perp$ is defined as follows:

$$\perp \stackrel{d}{=} \mathbf{0} - \mathbf{1}$$

It is easy to see that the value of $\perp$ in $\mathcal{P}\omega$ is equal to $\emptyset$, and that therefore $\perp \subseteq \mathsf{X}$ for every $\mathsf{X} \in \mathcal{P}\omega$.

Union We define the *union* of two L-terms x, y to be the L-term $\mathsf{x} \cup \mathsf{y}$ defined as follows:

$$\mathsf{x} \cup \mathsf{y} \stackrel{d}{=} \mathbf{if}(\lambda\,\mathsf{v}\,.\,\mathbf{0},\ \mathsf{x},\ \mathsf{y})$$

The value of the ground L-term $\lambda\,\mathsf{v}\,.\,\mathbf{0}$ is easy to determine:

$$\begin{aligned}\lambda\,\mathsf{v}\,.\,\mathbf{0} &= \{\mathsf{pair}(n, m) \mid m \in \{0\},\ n \in \omega\}\\ &= \{\tfrac{1}{2}(n+0) * (n+0+1) + 0 \mid n \in \omega\}\\ &= \{0, 1, 3, 6, \ldots\}\end{aligned}$$

Thus, the value of $\lambda\,\mathsf{v}\,.\,\mathbf{0}$ is an element of $\mathcal{P}\omega$ that contains both 0 and some integer greater than 0 (the term $\lambda\,\mathsf{v}\,.\,\mathbf{0}$ is in fact chosen for use in the definition of the union term precisely for this reason; any L-term that satisfies this requirement could have been used instead), and therefore (by the definition of the semantics of **if** terms):

$$(m \in \mathsf{x} \cup \mathsf{y}) \iff (m \in \mathsf{x}) \vee (m \in \mathsf{y})$$

for all L-terms x, y and ω elements m.

Top The L-term $\top$ is defined as follows:

$$\top \stackrel{d}{=} \mathsf{Y}(\lambda\,\mathsf{x}\,.\,(\mathbf{0} \cup (\mathsf{x} + \mathbf{1})))$$

By Y_1 of the fixpoint proposition for $\mathcal{P}\omega$, we get that $\top = (\mathbf{0} \cup (\top + \mathbf{1}))$. By the description given of $\cup$, this implies 1) $0 \in \perp$, and 2) if $m \in \top$ then $m + 1 \in \top$. But then every non-negative integer must be in $\top$, such that $\top = \omega$, and hence $\mathsf{X} \subseteq \top$ for every $\mathsf{X} \in \mathcal{P}\omega$. $\top$ is therefore a *top* element of the cpo $\mathcal{P}\omega$, just as $\perp$ is its bottom element.

A stronger conditional For any L-terms x, y, z define the L-term **if***(x, y, z) as follows:

$$\mathbf{if}^*(\mathsf{x}, \mathsf{y}, \mathsf{z}) \stackrel{d}{=} \mathbf{if}(\mathsf{x},\ \mathbf{if}(\mathsf{x}, \mathsf{y}, \top),\ \mathbf{if}(\mathsf{x}, \top, \mathsf{z}))$$

It is not very difficult to see that the following holds for any x, y, z:

$$\begin{aligned}\mathbf{if}^*(\perp, \mathsf{y}, \mathsf{z}) &= \perp\\ \mathbf{if}^*(\mathbf{0}, \mathsf{y}, \mathsf{z}) &= \mathsf{y}\\ \mathbf{if}^*(\mathsf{x}, \mathsf{y}, \mathsf{z}) &= \mathsf{z} \quad \text{if } 0 \notin \mathsf{x} \text{ and } \mathsf{x} \neq \perp\\ \mathbf{if}^*(\mathsf{x}, \mathsf{y}, \mathsf{z}) &= \top \quad \text{otherwise}\end{aligned}$$

The integers For every non-negative integer $n \in \omega$, define the ground L-term $\underline{n}$ by induction on n as follows:

$$\underline{0} \overset{d}{=} \mathbf{0}$$
$$\underline{n+1} \overset{d}{=} \underline{n} \mathbf{+ 1}$$

It is easy to prove (by induction on n) that the value of $\underline{n}$ is the $\mathcal{P}\omega$ element $\{n\}$ for every $n \in \omega$.

Tuples For every finite sequence $\langle x_0, \ldots, x_n \rangle$ of L-terms, define the L-term $<x_0, \ldots, x_n>$ as follows by induction on $n \geq 0$:

$$<x_0> \overset{d}{=} \lambda z.\mathbf{if^*}(z, x_0, \bot)$$
$$<x_0, \ldots, x_{n+1}> \overset{d}{=} \lambda z.\mathbf{if^*}(z, x_0, <x_1, \ldots, x_{n+1}>(z - \mathbf{1}))$$

For every L-term u and every non-negative integer $k \in \omega$, we define the L-term $u{\downarrow}k$ as follows:

$$u{\downarrow}k \overset{d}{=} u(\underline{k})$$

It is not difficult to verify that the following equation holds for every sequence $\langle x_0, \ldots, x_n \rangle$ and every integer $k \in \omega$:

$$< x_0, \ldots, x_n > {\downarrow}k = \begin{cases} x_k & \text{if } 0 \leq k \leq n \\ \bot & \text{otherwise} \end{cases}$$

bool We define the L-term bool as follows:

$$\text{bool} \overset{d}{=} \lambda x.\mathbf{if^*}(x, \underline{0}, \underline{1})$$

Let us apply bool (or rather, the function coded by the value of bool) to various arguments in $\mathcal{P}\omega$:

$$\begin{array}{lll} \text{bool}(\bot) & = \bot & \\ \text{bool}(\underline{0}) & = \underline{0} & \\ \text{bool}(\underline{x}) & = \underline{1} & \text{if } 0 \notin x \text{ and } x \neq \bot \\ \text{bool}(x) & = \top & \text{if } 0 \in x \text{ and } x \neq \{0\} \end{array}$$

We therefore see that the range of bool is equal to $\{\bot, \underline{0}, \underline{1}, \top\}$. This set is ordered to a cpo (with a top element) by the subset order. The structure of this cpo is visualized in figure 14.4. It is obvious that bool is isomorphic to the cpo *Bool* extended with a top element $\top_{Bool}$, i.e., to a cpo with universe $\{\bot_{Bool}$, **true, false,** $\top_{Bool}\}$ (ordered in the obvious manner).

Observe also that bool(x) = x for every $x \in$ range(bool), and that therefore bool(bool(x)) = bool(x) for every $x \in \mathcal{P}\omega$.

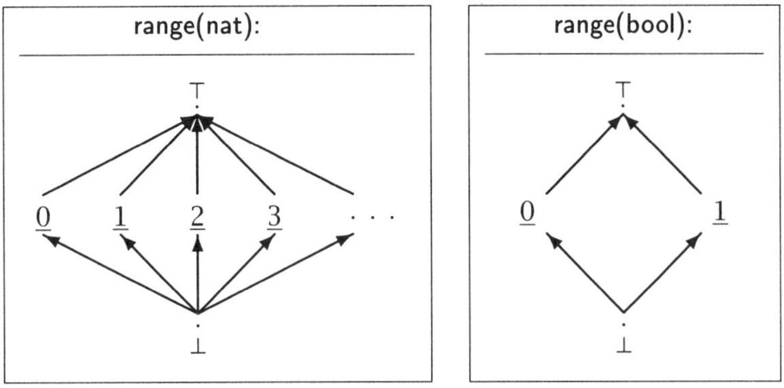

Figure 14.4: The ranges of nat and bool, ordered by the subset relation

nat We define the L-term nat as follows:

$$\mathsf{nat} \stackrel{d}{=} \mathsf{Y}(\lambda \mathsf{n}.\lambda \mathsf{x}.\mathbf{if^*}(\mathsf{x}, \underline{0}, \mathbf{if^*}(\mathsf{n}(\mathsf{x}-\mathbf{1}), \mathsf{x}, \mathsf{x})))$$

By Y_1 and β of proposition 14.3 it follows that for every $\mathsf{x} \in \mathcal{P}\omega$:

$$\mathsf{nat}(\mathsf{x}) = \mathbf{if^*}(\mathsf{x}, \underline{0}, \mathbf{if^*}(\mathsf{nat}(\mathsf{x}-\mathbf{1}), \mathsf{x}, \mathsf{x}))$$

Applying this equation to various arguments x, we get that

$$\begin{aligned} \mathsf{nat}(\bot) &= \bot \\ \mathsf{nat}(\top) &= \top \\ \mathsf{nat}(\underline{n}) &= \underline{n} \text{ for every } n \in \omega \\ \mathsf{nat}(\mathsf{x}) &= \top \text{ if } \mathsf{x} \notin \{\bot, \underline{0}, \underline{1}, \underline{2}, \ldots\} \end{aligned}$$

Hence

$$\mathsf{range}(\mathsf{nat}) = \{\top, \bot, \underline{0}, \underline{1}, \underline{2}, \ldots\}$$

The structure of this set, ordered to a cpo by the subset order, is visualized in figure 14.4. It is obvious that this cpo is isomorphic to the cpo *Nat* extended with a top element $\top_{Nat}$.

It is easy to see that $\mathsf{nat}(\mathsf{x}) = \mathsf{x}$ for every $\mathsf{x} \in \mathsf{range}(\mathsf{nat})$, and therefore $\mathsf{nat}(\mathsf{nat}(\mathsf{x})) = \mathsf{nat}(\mathsf{x})$ for every $\mathsf{x} \in \mathcal{P}\omega$.

Composition of functions For any L-terms x, y we define their *composition* to be the L-term

$$\mathsf{x} \circ \mathsf{y} \stackrel{d}{=} \lambda \mathsf{v}.\mathsf{x}(\mathsf{y}(\mathsf{v}))$$

It is not difficult to verify that the value of $x \circ y$ is an element in $\mathcal{P}\omega$ that codes the composition of the functions coded by the values of x and y.

14.5 Retracts

A ground L-term r, and also its value in $\mathcal{P}\omega$ and the function it defines, is said to be a *retract* if and only if it satisfies the following equation:

$$r \circ r = r$$

Using the definition of bool given above, it is quite easy to see that $\text{bool}(x) = x$ for every $x \in \text{range(bool)} = \{\bot, \underline{0}, \underline{1}, \top\}$. But then $\text{bool}(\text{bool}(x)) = \text{bool}(x)$ for every $x \in \mathcal{P}\omega$, and bool must hence be a retract. Similarly it may be shown that nat is a retract.

We have seen above that the range of bool is isomorphic to the semantic domain *Bool*, and that range(nat) is isomorphic to *Nat*. In the rest of this chapter we will show that every semantic domain that is needed when we give denotational definitions of the semantics of programming languages (except possibly the so-called powerdomains that are needed to specify the semantics of nondeterministic languages, see chapter 13), may be found as the range of some retract (or rather as the isomorphic image of the range of some retract).

Before we show how to construct retracts for the many semantic domains that are needed to specify the semantics of programming languages, we introduce some notation:

- When r is a retract and x an element of $\mathcal{P}\omega$ we use x: r to express that x is in the range of r, i.e., that $x \in \text{range}(r)$. Two examples: $\bot$: bool and $\underline{2}$: nat. It is easy to prove that

  $$x{:}\,r \iff x = r(x)$$

  for any retract r and $x \in \mathcal{P}\omega$.

- If P is a statement, possibly with x as a free variable, and r is a retract, we use $\forall x{:}\,r.P$ to express that P holds for every x in the range of r. It is not difficult to prove that

  $$\forall x{:}\,r.P \iff \forall x.P[r(x){:=}x]$$

- If r is a retract and e is an L-term, possibly with x as a free variable, we use the expression $\lambda x{:}\,r.e$ as shorthand for $\lambda x.e[r(x){:=}x]$. The value of the L-term $\lambda x{:}\,r.e$ is then an element in $\mathcal{P}\omega$ that codes a function that maps range(r) to $\mathcal{P}\omega$.

Definition 14.1 Three retract operators:
For any L-terms a, b *define the three L-terms* $a \otimes b$, $a \oplus b$ *and* $a \ominus\!\!\rightarrow b$ *as follows:*

$$
\begin{aligned}
a \otimes b &\stackrel{d}{=} \lambda x.\langle a(x{\downarrow}0),\ b(x{\downarrow}1)\rangle \\
a \oplus b &\stackrel{d}{=} \lambda x.\mathbf{if}^*(x{\downarrow}0,\ \langle \underline{0},\ a(x{\downarrow}1)\rangle,\ \langle \underline{1},\ b(x{\downarrow}1)\rangle) \\
a \ominus\!\!\rightarrow b &\stackrel{d}{=} \lambda x.b \circ x \circ a
\end{aligned}
$$

Proposition 14.5 *If* a *and* b *are retracts, then so are* $a \otimes b$, $a \oplus b$ *and* $a \ominus\!\!\rightarrow b$. *Furthermore, for every* $x \in \mathcal{P}\omega$:

$$
\begin{aligned}
&\alpha\text{: } x\text{: }(a \otimes b) \iff x = \langle x{\downarrow}0,\ x{\downarrow}1\rangle \wedge x{\downarrow}0\text{: } a \wedge x{\downarrow}1\text{: } b \\
&\beta\text{: } x\text{: }(a \oplus b) \iff x = \langle x{\downarrow}0,\ x{\downarrow}1\rangle \wedge ((x{\downarrow}0 = \underline{0} \wedge x{\downarrow}1\text{: } a) \vee \\
&\qquad\qquad\qquad\qquad\qquad\qquad\qquad\quad (x{\downarrow}0 = \underline{1} \wedge x{\downarrow}1\text{: } b)) \\
&\gamma\text{: } x\text{: }(a \ominus\!\!\rightarrow b) \iff x = \lambda y\text{: } a.x(y) \wedge \forall y\text{: } a.(x(y)\text{: } b)
\end{aligned}
$$

This proposition has two corollaries:

Corollary 14.1 *If* a *and* b *are two retracts then*

$$
\begin{aligned}
\text{range}(a \otimes b) &\cong \mathit{range}(a) \times \mathit{range}(b) \\
\text{range}(a \oplus b) &\cong \mathit{range}(a) + \mathit{range}(b) \\
\text{range}(a \ominus\!\!\rightarrow b) &\cong [\mathit{range}(a) \rightarrow \mathit{range}(b)]
\end{aligned}
$$

Corollary 14.2 *If the ranges of the two retracts* a *and* b *are isomorphic to two semantic domains A and B, i.e., such that* $\text{range}(a) \cong A$ *and* $\text{range}(b) \cong B$, *then*

$$
\begin{aligned}
\text{range}(a \otimes b) &\cong A \times B \\
\text{range}(a \oplus b) &\cong A + B \\
\text{range}(a \ominus\!\!\rightarrow b) &\cong [A \rightarrow B]
\end{aligned}
$$

A final proposition before we 'surface' with the ability to solve domain equations:

Proposition 14.6 *For every L-term* u: *If* u(a) *is a retract for every retract* a, *then* Y(u) *is a retract.*

14.6 How to solve domain equations

Theorem 14.1 *For every semantic algebra A that is needed to define the semantics of the programming languages of this book, with the exception of the nondeterministic languages, there exists a retract* a *such that* $A \cong \text{range}(a)$.

Proof: By induction on the complexity of A:

$A = Bool$ or $A = Nat$:
We have shown above that $Bool \cong \mathsf{range(bool)}$ and $Nat \cong \mathsf{range(nat)}$.

$A = Unit$:
Let $\mathsf{unit} \stackrel{d}{=} \lambda\mathsf{x}.\bot$. It is easy to see that unit is a retract and that range(unit) consists of a single element (namely $\bot$), and that hence $\mathsf{range(unit)} \cong Unit$.

$A = B \times C$ or $A = B + C$ or $A = [B \to C]$
By the second corollary to proposition 14.5.

A is specified to be a solution of a domain equation:
Consider as a generalizable example the equation for the domain P of parameter values:

$$P = AA + [P \to MV]$$

As induction hypothesis, we may assume that there exists retracts raa and rmv such that

$$\begin{aligned}\mathsf{range(raa)} &\cong \mathsf{AA}\\ \mathsf{range(rmv)} &\cong \mathsf{MV}\end{aligned}$$

Define the L-terms s and rp as follows:

$$\begin{aligned}\mathsf{s} &\stackrel{d}{=} \lambda\mathsf{x}.(\mathsf{raa} \oplus (\mathsf{x} \ominus\!\!\rightarrow \mathsf{rmv}))\\ \mathsf{rp} &\stackrel{d}{=} \mathsf{Y(s)}\end{aligned}$$

By β of proposition 14.3 and proposition 14.5, s(x) is a retract whenever x is a retract. Then proposition 14.6 gives that rp is a retract.

Y_1 of proposition 14.4 (the fixpoint proposition) gives that

$$\mathsf{rp} = \mathsf{s(rp)}$$

By β of proposition 14.3 and the definition of s, it then follows that

$$\mathsf{rp} = \mathsf{raa} \oplus (\mathsf{rp} \ominus\!\!\rightarrow \mathsf{rmv})$$

Then the first corollary to proposition 14.5 gives that

$$\mathsf{range(rp)} \cong \mathsf{range(raa)} \times [\mathsf{range(rp)} \to \mathsf{range(rmv)}]$$

We define P as follows:

$$P \stackrel{d}{=} \mathsf{range(rp)}$$

and get

$$P \cong AA + [P \to MV]$$

Our equation is therefore solved: we have constructed a domain P that is isomorphically equal to the domain $AA + [P \to MV]$.

It should be obvious that the method used for solving the equation used as an example here is general and applicable to any equation

$$X = \mathcal{F}(X)$$

where $\mathcal{F}(X)$ is an expression constructed from previously defined domains and the domain variable X using the domain constructors $(. \times .)$ (Cartesian product), $(. + .)$ (disjoint sums) and $[. \to .]$ (domains of continuous functions).

The reader may perhaps wonder: What about sequence domains? They are easy to define: If A is a given semantic domain, then the sequence domain A^* should satisfy the following equation:

$$A^* = Unit + (A \times A^*)$$

We may therefore proceed as we did above: Find a retract ra such that $\mathsf{range(ra)} \cong A$, and let the retract ras be defined as follows:

$$\mathsf{ras} \stackrel{d}{=} \mathsf{Y}(\lambda \mathsf{x}.(\mathsf{unit} \oplus (\mathsf{ra} \otimes \mathsf{x})))$$

If we then define

$$A^* \stackrel{d}{=} \mathsf{range(ras)}$$

we get that

$$A^* \cong Unit + (A \times A^*)$$

as desired.

References

[Algol60] P. Naur (ed). *Revised Report on the Algorithmic Language Algol 60.* International Federation of Information Processing, 1960.

[de Bakker; 80] J. de Bakker. *Mathematical Theory of Program Correctness,* Prentice-Hall, 1980.

[Cousot; 90] P. Cousot. *Methods and Logics for Proving Programs.* In *Handbook of Theoretical Computer Science,* Vol. B, Elsevier, 1990.

[Dahl; 70] O.J. Dahl, K. Nygaard and B. Myhrhaug. *Simula 67 Common Base Language.* S-22, Norwegian Computer Centre, Oslo, 1970.

[Dahl; 92] O.J. Dahl. *Verifiable Programming.* Prentice-Hall, 1992.

[Dijkstra; 76] E.W. Dijkstra. *A Discipline of Programming.* Prentice-Hall, 1976.

[Gödel; 31] K. Gödel. *Über Formal Unentscheidbare Sätze der* Principia Mathematica *und Verwandter Systeme,* In *Monatshefte für Mathematik und Physik,* 38 (1931).

[Gödel; 62] K. Gödel. *On Formally Undecidable Propositions.* English translation of [Gödel; 31]. Basic Books, 1962.

[Gordon; 79] M. Gordon. *The Denotational Description of Programming Languages,* Springer-Verlag, 1979.

[Gunter, Scott; 90] C.A. Gunther and D.S. Scott. *Semantic Domains.* In *Handbook of Theoretical Computer Science,* Vol. B, Elsevier, 1990.

[Guttag; 78] J. Guttag, J.J. and Horning: *The Algebraic Specification of Abstract Data Types*, Acta Informatica, 10, 1978.

[Hoare; 69] C.A.R. Hoare. *An Axiomatic Basis for Computer Programming.* Comm. of the ACM, Vol. 12, no. 10, Oct. 1969.

[Kahn; 87] G. Kahn. *Natural Semantics*, in *Fourth Annual Symposium in Theoretical Aspects of Computer Science*, Lecture Notes in Computer Science 247, Springer-Verlag, 1987.

[Kamin, Reddy; 94] Samuel N. Kamin and Uday S. Reddy. *Two Semantic Models of Object-Oriented Languages*, pp. 463-495 in *Theoretical Aspects of Object-Oriented Programming*, ed: C.A. Gunter and J. C. Mitchell, MIT Press, 1994.

[Kirkerud; 82] B. Kirkerud. *Completeness of Hoare-Calculi Revisited*, BIT 22, 1982.

[Lee; 89] P. Lee. *Realistic Compiler Generation*, MIT Press, 1989.

[Mendelson; 79] E. Mendelson. *Introduction to Mathematical Logic*, Van Nostrand Company, 1979.

[Milne, Strachey; 76] R.E. Milne and C. Strachey. *A Theory of Programming Language Semantics*, Chapman and Hall, 1976.

[Mosses; 90] P.D. Mosses. *Denotational Semantics.* In *Handbook of Theoretical Computer Science*, Vol. B, Elsevier, 1990.

[Nielson; 92] H.R. Nielson and F. Nielson. *Semantics with Applications.* Cambridge University Press, 1992.

[Paulson; 91] L. Paulson. *ML for the Working Programmer*, Cambridge University Press, 1991.

[Plotkin; 76] G.D. Plotkin. *A Powerdomain Construction*, SIAM J. Computing 5(3) (1976).

[Plotkin; 81] G.D. Plotkin. *A Structural Approach to Operational Semantics.* Technical Report DAIMI FN-19, Computer Science Department, Aarhus University, Denmark, 1981.

[Schmidt; 86] David A. Schmidt. *Denotational Semantics: A Methodology for Language Development*, Allyn and Bacon, 1986.

[Scott; 70] D.S. Scott. *Outline of a Mathematical Theory of Computation.* Proc. 4th Ann. Princeton Conf. on Information Sciences and Systems, 1970.

[Scott; 76] D.S. Scott. *Data Types as Lattices.* SIAM J. Computing, (1976), pp. 522–587.

[Shoenfield; 67] J.R. Shoenfield. *Mathematical Logic.* Addison-Wesley, 1967.

[Smyth; 78] M.B. Smyth. *Power Domains,* J. Comput. System. Sci. 16 (1978).

[Stoy; 77] J.E. Stoy. *Denotational Semantics: The Scott-Strachey Approach to Programming Language Theory,* MIT Press, 1977.

[Strachey; 66] C. Strachey. *Towards a Formal Semantics,* in *Formal Language Description Languages,* ed: T.B. Steele, North-Holland, 1966.

[Tennent; 91] R.D. Tennent. *Semantics of Programming Languages,* Prentice-Hall, 1991.

[Winskel; 93] G. Winskel. *The Formal Semantics of Programming Languages. An Introduction.* MIT Press, 1993.

Index